ALL THE POWER
IN THE WORLD

ALL THE POWER
IN THE WORLD

Peter Unger

OXFORD
UNIVERSITY PRESS

2006

OXFORD

UNIVERSITY PRESS

Oxford University Press, Inc., publishes works that further
Oxford University's objective of excellence
in research, scholarship, and education.

Oxford   New York
Auckland   Cape Town   Dar es Salaam   Hong Kong   Karachi
Kuala Lumpur   Madrid   Melbourne   Mexico City   Nairobi
New Delhi   Shanghai   Taipei   Toronto

With offices in
Argentina   Austria   Brazil   Chile   Czech Republic   France   Greece
Guatemala   Hungary   Italy   Japan   Poland   Portugal   Singapore
South Korea   Switzerland   Thailand   Turkey   Ukraine   Vietnam

Copyright © 2006 by Peter Unger

Published by Oxford University Press, Inc.
198 Madison Avenue, New York, New York 10016

www.oup.com

Oxford is a registered trademark of Oxford University Press

Library of Congress Cataloging-in-Publication Data
Unger, Peter K.
All the power in the world / Peter Unger.
p.   cm.
Includes bibliographical references and index.
ISBN-13 978-0-19-515561-7
ISBN 0-19-515561-0
1. Metaphysics.   2. Reality.   3. Physics—Philosophy.   I. Title.
BD111.U54 2005
110—dc22   2005047274

2   4   6   8   9   7   5   3   1

Printed in the United States of America
on acid-free paper

For my wife, Susan
Our son, Andrew

And for two dear friends,

Jonathan Adler,
In lasting friendship

David Lewis,
In loving memory

PREFACE

My big book's Preface will begin with rehearsing just the very first paragraph of the Preface to another big book, that one written by a philosopher with far more knowledge than I'll ever have, and with far more intellectual power, too:

> The following pages are addressed not only or primarily to professional philosophers but to that much larger public which is interested in philosophical questions without being willing or able to devote more than a limited amount of time to considering them. Descartes, Leibniz, Locke, Berkeley, and Hume wrote for a public of this sort, and I think that it is unfortunate that during the last hundred and sixty years or so or philosophy has come to be regarded as almost as technical as mathematics. Logic, it must be admitted, is technical in the same way as mathematics is, but, logic, I maintain, is not part of philosophy. Philosophy proper deals with matters of interest to the general educated public, and loses much of its value if only a few professionals can understand what is said.

There it is, folks. That's the start of Bertrand Russell's Preface to his last sustained, serious and systematic philosophical work, *Human Knowledge: Its Scope and Limits*, published right here, in my native New York, by Simon and Schuster, way back in 1948. Heck, that was just half a dozen years after I arrived here, fresh from my mother's womb.

Right off the bat, I'll say this about Russell's prime paragraph. With almost all of it, I couldn't agree more—and with none do I disagree. (There's one bit on which I must suspend judgment: Is logic not part of philosophy proper? The suggestion seems a tad extravagant. But, then, what do I know? I'm no Bertrand Russell.) Anyway, with the *general sense* of Russell's paragraph, well, I couldn't agree more.

As I blush to confess, I think much the same good thoughts apply to this present work, about as well as they did to Russell's own book. Well, sort of. Look, I realize that my prospects for reaching anything like as large a public as Russell did are, roughly and triply speaking, slim, dim, and none. But, still, I'm certainly *interested* in addressing the general educated public, and not just some few professional philosophers. Accordingly, I've tried hard, mighty hard, I'll tell you, to make this big book a pretty pleasantly accessible work—especially pleasant, I think, for those willing to follow a little *Public Readers' Guide* that I'll right here provide.

Many people find big books daunting, especially when the tomes are works in first philosophy, or substantive metaphysics, as this one certainly aims to be. I know I do. But, if you follow my Public Readers' Guide, that shouldn't bother you much, as you'll only be reading about half the book, and maybe even less than that. What's more, you'll be reading all the parts you're likely to find a most enjoyable read.

So, for almost anyone who's not a professor of philosophy, and for many philosophy professors, too, I strongly recommend you follow this:

Public Readers' Guide

(1) Read the book's first three Chapters, though you needn't bother about the notes. (In fact, you needn't bother about the notes to *any* of the book's Chapters.) As my experience with undergraduates indicates, most will enjoy over three-fourths of this stuff. And, heck, you can do a *bit* of work toward clearly grasping, and greatly enjoying, the truly juicy meat that's yet to come.

(2) Skip Chapter 4 and Chapter 5, proceeding directly to Chapter 6.

(3) Do read Chapter 6—it's on Real Choice; it's on Free Will—and you'll enjoy a lot of it.

(4) Read some of, but only some of, Chapter 7. Though it's all supporting the exciting idea that you're an immaterial soul, I recommend that you read only about half this long Chapter. Besides skipping its many notes and its appendix, folks innocent of recent philosophy should skip, as well, all these listed sections: 2, 5, 7, 9, 10, 11, 14, 17, 18, 20, and 23.

(5) Read Chapter 8; it's fun. It's got stuff on how, very possibly, we may someday become disembodied souls, outlasting our bodies for billions of years. It's got stuff on the main questions about God. Heck; it's even got stuff about reincarnation!

(6) Read just a bit of Chapter 9. In fact, read only its sections 3 and 4, skipping the rest.

(7) Read Chapter 10, the book's last Chapter. Sure, it's long. But, it's packed with all sorts of interesting speculations, none of them, I think, very terribly implausible. Far beyond just encountering new ideas about space and time, you'll find Hypotheses about *additional* Dimensional Aspects of Concrete Reality. Most fun of all—I'll bet you a nickel—there you'll find my most favored form of Substantial Dualism, *Quasi-Platonic Substantial Dualism*. On this surprisingly palatable metaphysic, not only will you outlast your body for billions of years, but, what's much more, you'll also precede it by billions of years.

There it is folks, your handy reader's guide, all up front and, so, all in one place.

And, that's not all. For those of you who, like me, usually forget what you read in a Preface, if you bother to read a book's Preface, at all, do not worry. Separately, and serially, all this good guiding advice will be provided yet again, in the body of the book itself. Rather than all in one piece, each part of this Guide will be provided just right where, or just right before, it will be most useful—to those most wanting to use it. For example, the advice just listed as piece number 2—about skipping over Chapters 4 and 5—that will be provided right near the end of Chapter 3, right before it's most needed. And, the advice just listed as piece number 4—about skipping all those sections in Chapter 7—that will appear quite near the beginning of that very Chapter, well before you've already plunged into any skippable section of Chapter 7. Don't worry, I'll take good care of you on this score. Very well, do I know what it's like to read page after page of humdrum boring philosophy.

Even much more than Russell did, leastways much more than he did in *Human Knowledge*, I avoid extensive use of any highly technical terminology. And, well I should do. For, if anything, in the sixty or so years since Russell wrote the displayed words, matters have become even worse—well, even more extreme, anyway—than they were in the previous hundred and sixty years. At all events, what technical terms I do introduce are happily chosen and colorfully presented. So, they're easily grasped, and they're readily remembered, as I've found with very many beginning undergraduates, and not just the brightest beginning students. Believe me: If you follow my Reader's Guide, everything you read will be pretty easy to understand.

(And, even if you *don't* follow the guide, most of what you'll read—most, by far—will be pretty easy. It's just that, unless you're inclined toward enjoying philosophy, much of it won't strike you as very *interesting* material. Some will; but much won't. Most of it, you'll understand it, all right; of that I'm sure. It's just that your reaction often may be more like "So What" than "Holy Cow.")

To show the Public Reader how serious I am about treating her well, and about treating her to an enjoyable philosophic reading experience, I'll provide some helpful advice right here and now, very useful for most folks, who certainly aren't philosophy professors.

DON'T READ ANY MORE OF THIS PREFACE. GO DIRECTLY TO THE START OF CHAPTER 1, AND PICK THINGS UP RIGHT FROM THERE.

All right, with that done, I'll now offer more words, in the rest of this Preface, for folks who aren't very innocent of much recent philosophy. Though much of it might not be very new, nor very interesting, either, still, a lot of it should be said, I think, in the Preface to a book like this one. (And, I'd rather produce some unnecessary words than leave out something even moderately important for me to say here.) So, even if there should be a shaggy dog story or two, mixed in with the right stuff, I'll press on with what remains to be said.

Almost all contemporary philosophers, leastways almost all with any aspiration toward clear thinking and writing, well, they're almost all greatly influenced by many other contemporary professors of philosophy, both by reading the writing of many others and by conversing orally with quite a few of their philosophical contemporaries. Everybody knows this, of course, leastways anyone who's anybody in mainstream academic philosophy. But, still, it's useful, I think, for it to be articulated, and even for it to be expressed saliently, in published print. Well, so there it is now, plain as day for all the world to see—well, anyway, almost all the tiny world of mainstream academic philosophy. (As I well realize, it's very unlikely that more than a few thousand people will ever read more than ten sentences of this book.) In these little learned circles, what's a central consequence of this well-known social fact? Well, as everyone also knows, that is, everyone who's in the circles, but as also bears articulation and public printing, a singularly salient upshot is nothing less sadly boring than this: Especially in substantial matters of first philosophy, or on ground-level philosophical issues, there's almost no diversity among contemporary philosophers or, at the very least, there's almost none evidenced in the philosophical publications that, over the last three or so decades, have been emanating from these academic thinkers.

(When I speak of contemporary philosophers, I confine my remarks, leastways almost entirely, to philosophical academics in the English-speaking world. About what's considered philosophy in most European continental circles, I really haven't a clue. And, similarly, with what may be, in various Asian circles, considered profoundly philosophical thinking. Heck, for all I know, there may be a multitude of South Americans—way down there, down below the equator—who're all absolute masters of deeply intriguing substantive metaphysical speculation. Keep hope alive! But, right here and now, that's neither here nor there. Realistically, for anyone likely to have read this far in my Preface, no such self-consciously ignorant cockeyed optimism really matters. So, all too soberly, perhaps, I return to discuss the folks, and their works, in our relevant reference class.)

For just one saliently stultifying example of the almost perfect uniformity to which I've alluded—and with which I've so long been bored beyond belief—I'll offer this obvious observation: During the last thirty-some years—or, by now, maybe even yet more years—almost everyone who's anyone, in academic philosophical circles, has subscribed to a materialist metaphysic. Or, if not *quite* that, then, among the just fairly few who haven't been materialists, almost all of *them* have subscribed to a view—to one view or another—that's only most marginally different from unadulterated materialism. These *Marginally Different Views*, as I'll call the terribly similar medium-rare positions—which are also, I suspect, just some several similarly half-baked positions—well, they're all so enormously like flat-out physicalism that there's scarcely any difference, between the former and the latter, as concerns almost all philosophically central matters. (As far as I've been able to discern, there's no more difference here, or just precious little more, than there was between, say, flat-out materialism and, on the other side, the epiphenomenalist sort of mind-body dualism that, a century or so ago, wasn't any horribly unfashionable view.)

Of course, that's just one salient example. And, of course, it's hardly the most stultifying example. That label goes, as all our tiny world knows, to the almost universal endorsement, in prestigious philosophical publications, of almost all of commonsense belief—well, almost all of what's been *called* "commonsense belief" by so many of its aforementioned endorsers. It's only a slight exaggeration to say that, right next upcoming, here's the first commandment of, or the first working principle of, contemporary core philosophy: "Thou shalt not contradict the man in the street" or, maybe better, "Thou shalt not contradict the atheist in the street." Well, it's something like that. So, as must then be expected, not only has this philosophy been a terribly uniform enterprise, doctrinally reckoned, but—what may be still worse—it's been just such a self-consciously modest endeavor as will be, in almost every case, quite utterly tame. But, enough about such surpassing stultification. Now, toward presenting a smoothly flowing Preface, I segue back to my just previous point of focus.

Well, for at least the last several decades, as I was saying, this has been the situation in core academic philosophy: Rather than any substantial diversity of worldview, there's been, instead, just so much mutually reinforcing similarity of viewpoint that even the most picayune family squabble may appear, to the properly initiated participants, to concern questions of great philosophic consequence. Or, so it's been among those intellectually ambitious enough to bother about first philosophy, at all, and among those professionally ambitious enough to make available, in their philosophical publications, the favored fruits of their merely marginally different philosophical thinking.

How is it that so very many highly similar thinkers all manage to stay interested in their inordinately similar projects, for much more than a decade or so?

Maybe the answer lies in this happy state of affairs: Like so many of those in so many of the real sciences, they are greatly excited by, and quite rightly excited by, their taking part in the discovery of, or the production of, an ever-increasing body of knowledge. Or, if it's not quite that, well, then, maybe it's something very like that. Unfortunately, there's not even a snowball's chance in heck that such a suggestion is even roughly right. At least tacitly, anyone who's not innocent of philosophy knows this full well, even unto their heart of hearts. And, upon any even halfway serious reflection, almost all contemporary philosophers consciously realize it, if only for some fleeting moments. So, as everyone who's anyone knows, and knows full well, that's not the answer.

Why is there so much uniformity, then, among contemporary philosophical academics, leastways among those who work mostly on questions central to the subject's time-honored core? Is there, perhaps, something of a mystery here? Is there, perhaps, an actual miracle here, the almost inscrutable upshot, perhaps, of a Divine Presence at work in the world?

Now, it all might seem quite miraculous, I suppose, but for the utterly obvious fact, easily recalled by anyone who's awake, that people often find great enjoyment in the discernment of tiny differences, almost any old tiny differences, in objects of their mutual interest. For an example of this—I admit, it may be a rather extreme case—think of all the many rich folks, most of them quite as smart as they're rich, who delight in the little differences they discern among the gold coins they collect. So, really, there's scarcely any mystery found when what's confronted is just so much enthusiastic conformity among human beings, whether the object of their extremely similar thinking, and their highly uniform interest, and their almost identical thoughtful behavior—well, whether it's this thing, or whether it's that one, or, yet again, whether it's some yet different thing, quite entirely.

As you'll recall, if only because I'll simply repeat it, I just lately said this: Almost all contemporary philosophers, leastways almost all with any aspiration toward clear thinking, and even toward intelligible argumentation, well, they're greatly influenced by other contemporary professors of philosophy, both by reading the writing of the others and by conversing orally with their philosophical contemporaries. Well, almost all isn't quite all. And, as I'm sure you've already guessed—those of you who don't know me—I'm one of the few exceptions. (Few, certainly; unique, certainly not.) Just so, with only a few exceptions, I've been far more influenced, in my working on this book, by material I've read written by Rene Descartes, and by George Berkeley, and by David Hume, and, maybe, by Bertrand Russell, too—far more than I've been influenced by the writing of almost all latish twentieth century authors, or by any writing still more recently. And, with only a very few exceptions, I've been influenced hardly at all by conversations with contemporary philosophers, leastways not by discourse with those already old enough to have established themselves in the circles of academic philosophy. But, then, of course, almost all isn't the same as all. Just so, there are the few exceptions.

In a plainly positive fashion, I've been greatly influenced, in writing much that you'll find in this book, by very many phone-conversations with C. B. "Charlie" Martin, initiated by Charlie, to my great benefit, from his home in western Canada. Unfortunately for most folks, Charlie is, on the whole, a very unclear writer of philosophical prose, as was also his great hero, John Locke. Fortunately for me, as turgid as Charlie is in his philosophical writing, so marvelously lucid is he, hardly always but plenty often enough, in his philosophical talking. Well, wending my way through quite a bit of his writing, some of it lucid, but much of it turgid, I was helped, by this reading, to prompt Charlie into ever more philosophical talking. Most of this conversation was very enlightening philosophically, at least to me, who had previously learned relatively little from my (painfully tedious) reading of Locke. While I've now learned a lot from Charlie—much accepted, and much ultimately left behind—I haven't any idea how much of this is actually just so much updated Locke and how much is mostly the product of Charlie's own distinctive thinking. (At least from time to time, Charlie has said that a very great deal of it is right there in Locke. But, being no historical scholar, what do I know?) Anyhow, whatever the exact proportions, a lot of this book was positively influenced by just Charlie Martin himself, I believe, and, through Charlie, a lot was positively influenced, too, by John Locke.

Next to Charlie Martin, and maybe running a pretty close second, the greatest plainly positive influence on this work, among contemporary philosophers, is the late Roderick M. Chisholm. Oftentimes, Chisholm's writing is technically dense and, to the likes of me, it's nearly unreadable. But, oftentimes, too, he writes just some fine straightforward English prose, full of stimulating philosophy. This may occur side by side, even, in the course of a single work, as certainly happens in his important metaphysical book, *Person and Object*. At any rate, there's no question but that, through his most available passages, which are as numerous as they are widely scattered, Chisholm has greatly influenced my thinking, in this work, and often in a very positive way.

While these two contemporary thinkers, Martin and Chisholm, greatly influenced me in a plainly positive manner, just one contemporary of mine influenced me, perhaps quite equally, in a most useful negative way. On almost every substantive issue I address in this book, I offer a position that's diametrically opposed to the view of my Swarthmore College classmate, and my nearly lifelong friend, the late David Lewis. In fact, it's only a slight exaggeration to say that, as concerns all the main matters of first philosophy, the only one where I tend to accept the same view as does David is the one issue on which he holds his most famously distinctive view, perhaps the only issue on which almost all other contemporary philosophers disagree with David. Just so, I'm very friendly to the idea, which is really his idea, of an infinite plurality of mutually quite isolated concrete worlds—each isolated from all the others spatially, and temporally, and causally, and so on. (Well, I'm not so sure about the temporal isolation business—but, no matter.) In this present work, I don't try to argue in support of that view, as there's so very much else that I do take on here—almost all of which will be, no doubt, quite as unpopular as David's view of infinitely many mutually isolated concrete worlds, and much of which is, as well, about as robustly speculative as David's visionary meta-physical proposal.

That said, this should be more firmly born in mind: As all the world knows, the great mentalistic philosopher, David Hume, has been an enormously great challenging influence on so many who temporally followed him, almost all of whom have tried to oppose so much of what he offered, even including many who've agreed with much else that he said. No surprise, I'm one of those many temporal followers of Hume, opposing very much of what he offered, while also agreeing with a (different) fair lot of it, too. Much as my Humean inspired opposition to Hume has been one of the great influences on this book, so my Lewisean inspired opposition to the later David has been another great influence.

Unlike with David Hume, whom I never met, of course, David Lewis was also a great personal influence on me, and on my intellectual work. His passion for clarity has influenced me greatly, of course, as it has so many of our contemporaries. Even more important, in my case, is his inspired, and his inspiring, development of his Multi-Worldly Metaphysical Vision, one of the terribly few truly visionary philosophic ideas—so far as I can tell—in all of twentieth century philosophy. While possessing only a modest fraction of David's inordinate intellectual power, I still take him as a model, in that absolutely central regard. So, it is that, with what lesser power I myself can muster, I do try, in these pages, to offer some very unusual metaphysical ideas, most of them bound to be quite unpopular, while always caring far more about what intellectual elegance a speculative thought may have, and about how clearly we humans can grasp the conjecture, than about—well, than about how palatable, or how unpalatable, it may seem to most of my philosophical contemporaries. For just one salient example, so it is with the Quasi-Platonic Dualism that I offer in the book's last Chapter, as noted in this Preface's compact Public Readers' Guide.

Though it's not only to him that I dedicate this book, I do dedicate this work, in loving memory, to the greatest philosopher whom I've ever actually met, my dearly departed friend, David Lewis.

Both as concerns the historically great figures, from Descartes through Russell, and as concerns rather more contemporary figures, I've now mentioned all the philosophers who, as far as I can tell, have most greatly influenced this book, whether in one way or whether in another.

Through their philosophical writing, some several others have also significantly influenced my long labor on this book, over the course of some eight very full years, to quite a considerable degree, even if not as greatly as those I've already mentioned as influences. For the most part, that should be pretty plain from mentions made in the book itself. Anyway, I won't try to make it any plainer right here, in this Preface, as I'd be much more likely to just make a mess of things than to do some deserving folks some decent justice.

That said, it's now time to mention quite a few folks, right here in this Preface, all of whom have been very helpful to me, in my progress toward producing this big exploratory philosophical story—a story that, as I hope for it to be, might be a roughly true story. (That's just a hope, of course, nothing nearly so affirmative as a belief. Look, on almost all the most central philosophic matters, pretty much all of my greatest philosophic predecessors each contradicted many of the others. With that obvious overarching truth, how can any seriously systematic thinker, at this quite late date, offer his own distinctive main ideas with more than just a hope for their truth, or even for their being so much as just roughly correct. Much more than that will be, I think, a sort of philosophic lunacy that's owing, in no small measure, to a sort of philosophic myopia.)

A few of my NYU Philosophy colleagues, past, present and partial, showed some interest in this work, leastways after my badgering each a bit, and, once interested in reading some of the material, they offered helpful suggestions for improvements. Especially concerning what I was up to in very early stages of the work, among my past colleagues John Carroll and Keith DeRose were more than helpful enough to deserve mention. Though they'd already left NYU when this book was started, they continued to take an interest in some of my thoughts, and continued to offer helpful suggestions as to how I might improve the ideas.

Concerning pretty early work, and work at medium stages, too, Gordon Belot was much more than helpful enough. Way back when, Gordon read each of what were, way back then, the six chapters of an early draft, making helpful typed comments on all six. Among many other helpful things he did for me, he told me where to make a few alterations—and how each should be made—so that everything I then said would comport, plenty well enough, with anything really established in, or by, contemporary physics and, more generally, recent science. (Well, as that was some several years ago, and the present text is more than twice the length of what Gordon read, right now I can only hope that, at least for the most part, there's still quite enough of that sort of comportment. But, if not, I'm still quite open to making several more changes, in most parts of this work, at least in my own mind—and, even in print, should there ever be a second edition of this book.)

Among my present colleagues, Kit Fine read early versions of a couple of the book's Chapters and, with his famously laser-like mind, made penetrating corrective suggestions, all of which I assiduously tried to follow. As I believe, I pretty well succeeded in doing that.

At a very much later stage, about five years later, Elizabeth Harman read, and persistently raised questions about, the material of three presently important Chapters: 1, 3 and 7. At least one section of Chapter 7 was written in response to Liz's persistent questioning. And, for her persistent treatment of Chapter 1, that Chapter is now far clearer, and rather better, too, I think, than before it encountered her. Imperfect as these three Chapters remain, they have been improved—pretty substantially, I think—by my being spurred to respond to Liz's questions, corrections and suggestions.

During the last year and a half, Don Garrett read, in one version or another, all ten of this big book's Chapters. With most of the Chapters, I made some improvements in response to questions, corrections and suggestions proposed by Don. With some I was prompted to, and even encouraged to, write entire new sections. And, much as Gordon Belot vetted an early draft, to see that I shouldn't badly misrepresent contemporary physical science, or run badly afoul of it, so, Don Garrett vetted a much later draft, to see that I shouldn't badly misrepresent the thoughts of the historically great philosophers that, on my work in this book, have all been such an important influence. (Since I can scarcely stop adding more to a work, at almost any time right up to the moment I actually submit it—so as to meet my contractual obligations—not everything's been vetted, on both of these matters and, of course, on other matters, too. But, as we all know, nobody's perfect.) As with Liz Harman, at least one (other) of Chapter 7's sections was written in response to persistent questioning from Don Garrett.

Among my partial colleagues—that is, among NYU's four (or five) Regular Visiting Professors, one merits mention here. Sydney Shoemaker read pretty recent versions of at least five of this book's ten Chapters—1, 2, 3, 4 and 7—and made very useful comments about, at the least, the longest of these, Chapter 7, now the longest in the whole book. A couple of that Chapter's sections comprise my responses to points raised by Sydney.

Well that's it for the help from NYU philosophy professors, past, present, and partial. Next, I'll mention some other helpful philosophy professors, leastways those I remember to have been helpful here and, after that, I'll mention some of my helpful students, whether past or present.

When acknowledging help from other contemporary philosophers, perhaps I should first mention John Heil, Charlie Martin's great friend, for Heil is often as lucid a philosophical writer as Charlie himself is often opaque. Especially from their jointly authored papers, but also from some of Heil's solo Neo-Lockean writing—if that's what it is—I've been much influenced, and greatly helped, in producing my own metaphysical work. In addition to everything else, John read drafts of several of this book's Chapters, and made helpful comments on them.

Dean Zimmerman was a source of judicious council and criticism throughout, and also a source of great encouragement, particularly when I most needed it. Dean read drafts of at least three Chapters, 3, 6 and 7, and he made very many helpful comments on that material. As well, he read thoughtfully, and he critiqued wisely, an early ancestor of what's now Chapter 10, the book's last Chapter.

Through many timely emails, David Chalmers gave me many helpful comments on, at the least, Chapters 3, 4, 6, and 7. In response to his sharp and stimulating comments, I wrote extra sections for Chapters 3, 4 and 7. His helpful impact on this book greatly exceeded the number of words I'm using to thank him.

Over the last summer that I worked on this book, the summer of 2004, David Robb read email drafts of Chapters 1 through 5, and he sent me helpful commentary on all those five Chapters. In quite a few cases, my responses to his comments meant more material for the book you now hold in your hands, almost all of it beneficial, I like to imagine.

My dear friend Jonathan Adler read the book's first three Chapters, at various stages of their development. And, near the book's completion, he read its last three Chapters. As always, his helpful comments made me make my writing clearer, and more clearly pertinent to the questions I mean to address. For what's now more than a quarter-century of his wonderful friendship—and with hopes for more than another quarter-century, as well—Jon is the only living philosopher to whom I dedicate this book. (Long though this book may be, it is, I trust, only a small tribute to our long and lengthening friendship.)

I exposed a draft of Chapter 6 to three able authors on questions of free will: Richard Double, John Martin Fischer, and Carl Ginet. Their email replies convinced me that I have something worth saying on that perplexing subject. I am happy to thank them.

Many are the students who've I've enjoyed teaching, over these past eight years, here at NYU. Curiously, the one who's impacted this work most greatly, Neil Williams, was never enrolled at New York University, but, rather, was enrolled uptown, for a Ph.D., at Columbia. This fact becomes much less surprising, I imagine, when it's observed that, as an undergraduate in Canada, some several years ago, Neil was a student of Charlie Martin. Twice over, Neil participated in a graduate seminar I gave that was organized around this book's typescript—one year for credit, another year just as an auditor. Chapter 5 of this book owes a very great deal to Neil's thinking.

Some six students enrolled in our own Ph.D. program, here at NYU, had an outstandingly beneficial impact on the book's development.

Alexander "Alex" Guerrero made helpful comments on almost all the book's Chapters. His criticisms of an early version of Chapter 4, led to my revising considerably, and to my expanding substantially, that Chapter, as will be obvious to any who read it.

Yuval Avnur also made useful comments on a great deal of the book. In connection with an early draft of the book's last Chapter, he devised some strikingly original ideas. Adapted somewhat, to better fit my own metaphysical inclinations, Yuval's thoughts led to a significant revision of, and to a substantial expansion of, that Chapter, as will be obvious to any who read it.

Matthew Kotzen read most of a draft of the book—neither a very early draft nor a very late one—and made more than a few comments that were truly penetrating. Among his intellectual offspring are the Yellow-Attractors, introduced in Chapter 3, but observed in many Chapters. The fairly few mentions of Matt in my notes don't begin to do justice to the many benefits he bestowed.

Michael "Mike" Raven read, by my rough estimate, all of one draft of the book and, in addition, about half of the penultimate draft. Mike made trenchant comments on many Chapters, only partially reflected in notes to the book. With Chapter 7, his comments were truly special. At least one section of Chapter 7 was written in response to trenchant questioning from Mike Raven.

Two other NYU Ph.D. students were also very helpful to me in their persistent questioning, and in a variety of positive suggestions, too, but not in ways that can be as specifically identified. Anyhow, both Peter "Pete" Graham and Jonathan "Jon" Simon also deserve my thanks, and here they get that.

Especially over the last three years, I have greatly enjoyed teaching metaphysics to some very responsive NYU undergraduate philosophy majors. Collectively, they have been enormously helpful in getting me to write this book in the way that Bertrand Russell intended his last great work to be written. In other words, they made sure that this wouldn't be any work, nor even remotely like any work, written so technically that "only a few professionals can understand what is said." In this very important connection—very important to me, anyhow—I'd like to thank Marcello Antosh, Lyndsey Butler, Erin Byram, Ellen Parks, and Arthur Schipper.

At least nine-tenths of what's in this book, by my reckoning, hasn't been published anywhere before. But nearly a tenth, I figure, has been. So, some thanks for permissions to reprint are in order.

A fair bit of Chapter 1, as well as just a tad of Chapter 3, originally appeared as part of my paper "The Mystery of the Physical and the Matter of Qualities," *Midwest Studies in Philosophy* 22, 1999, pp. 75–99. According to my letter from Howard Wettstein, who edits that fine series, "Authors who publish articles in Midwest Studies automatically have permission to use materials from their papers in their own subsequent publications." But, I thank Howie, anyway, as well as the publisher of the series, Blackwell Publishing.

Almost half of Chapter 6, I reckon, originally appeared in another previously published paper of mine, "Free Will and Scientificalism," *Philosophy and Phenomenological Research* 65, 2002, pp. 1–25. For permission to reprint that material, I thank the editor of that journal, Ernest "Ernie" Sosa, and its managing editor, Suzanne Bertrand, as well as its publishing home, Brown University.

Finally, a fair swatch of Chapter 7 first appeared in a third published paper, "The Mental Problems of the Many," in Dean W. Zimmerman, ed., *Oxford Studies in Metaphysics*, vol. 1, Oxford: Clarendon Press, 2004, pp. 195–222. For permission to reprint from there, I thank that volume's editor, Dean Zimmerman—already thanked for much else, right above. And, even if it may be quite gratuitous, I thank the volume's publisher, the Oxford University Press, the very same outfit that's publishing this present book, the one you hold in your hands.

Along with some fourteen published papers I refer to rather later in this book—and along with a few other previously published essays—these three aforementioned essays will appear, in their original versions, in a collection of my selected published papers that, like the present volume itself, will come forth from the Oxford University Press. By my best reckoning, this should be most happily convenient for quite a few of those who'll read *All the Power in the World*, or who'll read any goodly part of this big book. As I'm making every effort to ensure, this two-volume collection of my *Philosophical Papers* will come forth simultaneously with the initial appearance of *All the Power in the World*. And, as I'm also trying hard to ensure, not only will each of my *Philosophical Papers'* two beautiful volumes visually match the other quite perfectly, but, just as well, each will also be a visually perfect match for this present work, that is, for a massive but beautifully produced *All the Power in the World*.

New York   P. K. U.
January 2005

CONTENTS

ALL THE POWER
IN THE WORLD

1

THE MYSTERY
OF THE PHYSICAL

For over fifty years, nearly all work by mainstream philosophers made no serious attempt to explore the *nature of physical reality*, even though most mainstream philosophers now take this to be all of reality, or nearly all. Or, at least, so it's been with us who speak English. While we've worried much about the nature of our own experiences and thoughts and words, we've worried little about the nature of the vast physical world that, as we ourselves believe, has them all as only a small part.

In this respect, we've been very different from Bertrand Russell, possibly the twentieth century's greatest philosopher. While Russell thought hard about the things that have preoccupied us, he also thought hard about the nature of physical reality. Why the great disparity?

By contrast with Russell, most contemporary workers, in core philosophic areas, just assume that, largely as a legacy from the physical sciences, we have been granted a happily adequate conception of physical reality. When in this frame of mind, we philosophers aren't moved to think hard about the nature of physical reality, even if we believe it to be all of reality. Rather, we're much more moved by thoughts like this: "Let's leave such terribly large matters to so many successful scientists, and to the few philosophers of science, so concerned to interpret the work of the many."

Just so, when we trouble ourselves about what's what with things grossly physical, or with physical reality that's extralinguistic, and extramental, and so on, our concerns are with quite superficial matters. For example, we may reflect on the apparent fact that, if an ordinary rock should be split down the middle, with the two resulting "halves" never even coming close to being rejoined, the rock that was split ceases to exist, whilst two substantially smaller rocks then begin to exist. And, then, we may reflect on the apparent fact that, when a rock that's as famous as Plymouth Rock is similarly bisected, there's still that rock that's then in two salient pieces, whether or not there are also two smaller rocks then coming into existence. On the basis of these two reflections, we may aspire to a complex theory that, "capturing intuitions" about both cases, will serve to illuminate the "persistence conditions" for rocks in general, both the famous and also the obscure. But, won't such a theory reflect our own interests more than it will tell us about the nature of physical reality? At all events, it won't deliver anything very deep, or very illuminating, about physical reality.

Even while knowing all that very well, we still don't trouble ourselves to be more searching. Rather, we're still affected by thoughts like "Let's leave such terribly large matters to so many successful scientists, and our few colleagues who know their science." Especially in this fearfully complacent philosophical day and age, we do well to remember what Russell counseled: About the rest of concrete reality, we don't know anything nearly so intimately, nor nearly so fully, as we know our own experiencing, or the phenomena we apprehend in experiencing. (This remains true, of course, even if what we know most fully, and intimately, might be known less fully, and less intimately, than it can often appear.) And, we do well to recall that Russell did not exaggerate much, if at all, when, in a generally robust epistemological spirit, he said, "as regards the world in general, both physical and mental, everything that we know of its intrinsic character is derived from the mental side."[1] Nor did he exaggerate very much when, in a specifically Materialistic spirit, he said, "we know nothing about the intrinsic quality of physical events except when these are mental events that we directly experience."[2]

---

1. Bertrand Russell, *The Analysis of Matter*, Kegan Paul, 1927. My own copy of the work is a reprint, Dover Publications, New York, 1954. In that, see page 402. Anyway, the quoted words are from the book's penultimate sentence.

2. Bertrand Russell, "Mind and Matter," in *Portraits from Memory*, Spokesman, 1956, p. 153. Until recently, truths like those just quoted were, for centuries, influential with serious philosophers. For a seminal example, "the father of modern philosophy" advances some in Descartes's *Principles of Philosophy*, Part I, Paragraph 11, "How Our Mind Is Better Known Than Our Body," in *The Philosophical Writings of Descartes*, trans. J. Cottingham, R. Stoothoff, and D. Murdoch, Volume I, Cambridge University Press, 1985.

If there's to be appropriately ambitious work done any time soon, by more than a very few academic philosophers, then we'd best pay heed to such Russellian reminders. And, though our philosophical efforts might diverge from his in many respects, they should be guided by the same realization that so greatly moved Russell: Except for what little of the physical world we might apprehend in conscious experience, which is available if Materialism should be true, *the physical is mysterious to us.*

So, we should wonder: To what extent, if any at all, do we have a philosophically adequate conception of physical reality? However any of our conceptions may have originated, do we have a conception well enough related to the human mind for it to ground a metaphysic in terms of which physical reality can be understood, at all well, by us very limited human thinkers?

Now, my second question, just above, began with the words "However any of our conceptions may have originated." In employing those words, what was my main intention? It was just this. Unlike many of my most illustrious predecessors, including René Descartes, John Locke, George Berkeley and David Hume, I'm not exploring, in this present work, any questions concerning the origin of, or the etiology of, any of our conceptions, or ideas. It's not that such questions aren't interesting issues; to the contrary, many of them are very interesting. It's just that, recognizing my own very real limitations, and my quite daunting ignorance, I realize that, for me to explore any topics at all well, I must be severely selective. So, even as I leave those interesting issues to others, more ready, willing, and able to explore them, I'll be expending my own efforts elsewhere.[3] To be sure, and as I've already indicated, I'll spend great energy on questions concerning *the adequacy of* certain philosophically central ideas and, if I may say so, certain humanly central conceptions. But, quite as this book's developments should make clear, this well may be a very different matter. And, as

---

3. For one very recent exploration, you may do well to notice Jesse J. Prinz's *Furnishing the Mind*, MIT Press, 2002. As it says on the MIT Press website, this is "[a] new empiricist theory of concepts that draws on research from philosophy, neuroscience, and psychology." Why do I single out this contribution? I don't know; maybe it's because Jesse was one of my favorite undergraduate students; and, maybe it's because he drew the sole illustration (or picture) in my ethics book, *Living High and Letting Die*, Oxford University Press, 1996. Well, it doesn't matter.

Of course, it's not only the old Empiricists who have their contemporary champions. Just so, the old Rationalists have done very well for themselves, so far as influencing current thinkers on questions relating to our ideas' origins. Among those favoring Descartes's ilk, Noam Chomsky and Jerry Fodor may be counted among the most prominent, and the most prolific, recent writers.

So, even without my addressing any issues of etiology, these interesting issues will, I'm sure, continue to get plenty of attention.

should also develop, in these pages, we might make very substantial progress with this very different matter, without even barely broaching any questions about the origin of our conceptions, or our ideas.

So, just as I said just before, I'll again ask us to consider these quite central questions: To what extent, if any at all, do we have a philosophically adequate conception of physical reality? However any of our conceptions may have originated, do we have a conception well enough related to the human mind for it to ground a metaphysic in terms of which physical reality can be understood, at all well, by us very limited human thinkers?

Inspired by Russell and many others, including Descartes, Locke, Berkeley and Hume, I'll wrestle hard with these daunting questions. In the course of the effort, I'll aim to raise stimulating new questions or, at least, give old ones newly stimulating presentations.

1. A Brief Exposition of the Scientiphical Metaphysic

As a first step in this effort, I'll briefly sketch the metaphysical worldview that, for many years now, and with no letup anywhere in sight, has been the dominant metaphysic of academic philosophy. It will be useful to have a memorable name for this dominant worldview. Introducing a word with no more of a root in "scientific" than in "philosophical," I'll coin the naming phrase "The Scientiphical Metaphysic," and the equivalent single word *Scientiphicalism*.

Though various modifications of it appear to be required by certain twentieth century scientific developments, notably, by quantum mechanics and relativity theory, the heart of our Scientiphical Metaphysic is, apparently, essentially the same as before the advent of that century. So, even if folks versed in contemporary physics would rightly prefer esoteric analogues of the ordinary terms I feel most comfortable using, for my philosophical purposes the following few paragraphs serve to express our dominant worldview.

First, differently distributed in space at different times, there is physical stuff or *matter*. Placing aside the thought that this matter may have been, very long ago, created by some Extraordinarily Powerful Mind (or Minds), and placing aside thoughts of how such a SuperMind might, even nowadays, occasionally affect matter, this matter is *independent of minds*: To exist, the matter needn't be sensed by, or perceived by, any sentient beings. So, while our Scientiphicalism may be properly embraced by many sorts of theists, as much as by atheists, the Metaphysic does contravene an Idealist philosophy.

Second, and again placing to the side all such "theological" ideas—henceforth I'll generally do that just implicitly—Scientiphicalism says this: Insofar as it's determined by anything at all, and it isn't merely random, the distribution of the world's matter at any given time is determined by, even if maybe only probabilistically determined by, the distribution of the matter at earlier times, all of it proceeding in line with the world's basic natural laws, which are all physical laws.

Third, owing to the variety in these material distributions, at certain times some of the world's matter, or possibly much of the matter, is configured so as to compose various complex material structures and systems, ranging from the slightly complex through the fairly complex to the highly complex. So, here we may have stars, and planets, and rocks, and rivers. Among the more complex of even these highly complex material structures and systems are living entities, or those serving to constitute living entities. And, here we may have plants and animals, including human animals.

Fourth, among the more complex of even these living material entities, and possibly even among some (very distant) nonliving material complexes, there are those that are thinking, feeling, experiencing physical entities. Or, at least, that's how it goes on the Materialist, or Physicalist, version of Scientiphicalism, by far the most influential version of this dominant view. As I'm using the label, there's also an *Epiphenomenalist* version of Scientiphicalism. On this version, the highly complex physical structures will subserve sentient beings, or minds, which *aren't* physical entities. But, even on this Epiphenomenalist version, and certainly on a Materialist version, *all the power in the world is some sort of physical power.* (Myself, I'm not sure that Epiphenomenalism is a fully coherent view; but, in this inquiry, I'm willing to suppose the best for Epiphenomenalism, as that can't make things easier for the inquiry.) At all events, while our Scientiphicalism might possibly allow for certain sorts of Dualism, as with Epiphenomenalism, they must all be weak, unambitious sorts of Dualism. They must be far less ambitious than Dualistic Interactionism, the metaphysic upheld by Descartes, not only the most important Dualistic metaphysician, but the seminal figure for most discussions of mind and matter. So, against Descartes and others, Scientiphicalism says that, insofar as any actual sentient being *lacks physical* potency, the being will be an *entirely powerless* entity, however richly endowed with experiential quality it might be.

Fifth, and now getting more personal, I myself am one of these fully physical complex thinking beings, and so are you. Or, at least that's how it goes on the Physicalist version of Scientiphicalism. On the Epiphenomenalist version, my living body, that subserves me, will be just a certain physical complex and, though I may suffer or enjoy a qualitatively rich experiential stream, I will be absolutely devoid of any nonphysical power or propensity, and so will you.

Sixth, at least if we place aside complications that might arise with Epiphenomenalism, Scientiphicalism says that every (concrete) entity in our world is a wholly physical entity; either it's a basic (nonmental) physical thing—for possible examples, think of an elementary particle or, perhaps, even an infinitely vast insensate physical field—or else it's a physical complex *wholly constituted* of things that are themselves all *wholly physical* entities, with these complexes all being *ultimately* wholly composed of *basic physical* constituents—perfectly elementary particles, or the vast field. So it is that, while a car may be wholly constituted of its engine, and its chassis, and so on, the engine, and the chassis, and so on, are themselves all wholly physical entities. And, like the car itself, its engine and its chassis, and its other complex parts, are ultimately wholly composed of basic physical things. And, quite as it is with the car, so it is also with you, too: Even while your heart and your brain are among your constituents, so your heart and your brain, and you, too, are each a wholly physical complex entity, each wholly constituted of just some quite basic physical things. (On a Nonstandard Version of Scientiphicalism there aren't any absolutely basic entities; rather, there's an infinite sequence of "more and more basic physical constituents." By contrast with a powerful field, that may be incoherent. Anyhow, for most of our essay's discussions, it won't matter which version we have in mind. So, for simplicity of exposition and ease of comprehension, I'll usually just assume the (more clearly coherent) Standard Version of the Scientiphical worldview.[4])

Seventh, Scientiphicalism holds that the powers, or the propensities, of any complex physical thing—like your car and its engine, like your body and your brain—are all physically derivative dispositions. Probabilistic or not, they all *physically derive*, quite wholly and fully, from the far simpler properties of the complex's far simpler physical constituents, saliently including their far simpler powers, and, of course, from the (sufficiently basic) physical relations among these far simpler components. And, this will hold, too, for beings that aren't so clearly physical, as with me and you. On the Standard Version of Scientiphicalism, the powers of any physical complex will thus physically derive, quite wholly and fully, from the *naturally basic* properties of the

---

4. There'll be a discussion of this Nonstandard Version in Chapter 6, "Is Free Will Compatible with Scientiphicalism?," particularly in its Section 11, "Can an 'Infinitely Deep Sequence' of Physical Powers Help Us Have Real Choice?"

complex's basic physical constituents (modulo the case of a single heterogenous physical field that does all the constituting) and, of course, from the (sufficiently basic) physical relations among these far simpler components. So it is, in particular, that all your powers and propensities, including even all your most refined mental abilities, are *physically derivative* propensities or powers. And, in keeping with that, there's this: All your behavior, including even all your most refined and private mental activity, *wholly derives from* that of your simple physical parts and, of course, the physical relations among these parts (along with, perhaps, what similarly obtains with some other nonmental things, also physically simple, that "are in your environment"). Now, in the just previous paragraph, concerning questions of physical constitution, I had to employ certain key terms, like "wholly composed," in a way that's very vague and rather artful. Well, it may be that, in this present paragraph, with my use of certain further terms, like "physically derive," I do that to an even greater extent or degree. Still and all, most readers will find it easy, I think, to understand this usage as serving to express, rather broadly but nicely enough, a view long accepted by many they know, quite likely including themselves.

Eighth, and finally in this brief presentation of the reigning worldview, I should say something about the *naturally basic* properties of matter, the same both for matter that's involved in composing a highly complex material system and, equally, for matter that's never so interestingly involved. To date, it's mainly been the work of physics to discover what actually are these properties. Just so, it might be, for example, that having unit negative electric charge is one of these properties. By contrast, having measles certainly isn't a naturally important property of matter. (In all fairness, this doesn't commit Scientiphicalists to any objectionable Realism about Properties. Rather, I've just compendiously stated some of the Scientiphical View, about how it is with physical reality.)

2. Three Kinds of Basic Property and the Denial of Qualities

For a discussion that may be as profitable as it's protracted, I'll move deliberately toward displaying a doctrine, or a pair of doctrines, assumed true by most embracing the Scientiphical Metaphysic, whether or not any such statement's actually implied by the dominant worldview.

This will be done in two steps. First, I'll try to present, as succinctly and clearly as I can, a popular proposition that I'll call the *Denial of*

Qualities, First Formulation. This effort comprises most of the Section's work. Second, I'll present a related doctrine, or a related Formulation of the same doctrine, the *Denial of Qualities, Second Formulation*.

Toward succinctly presenting this Denial, it will be useful to notice *three categories of basic natural property* of whatever entities, or entity, might constitute physical reality. Just putting main matters in such very convenient terms, I'm not thereby endorsing any Realism about Properties. (Quite to the contrary: Though I won't do very much to explore any such ontological view as that one, my own inclination is, first, to take *all concrete reality* to be *just all the concrete individuals*, perhaps variously propertied and related, and, second, to take *all reality* to be *just concrete reality*. As I see it, my main questions are much more substantial, or philosophically more important, than, say, the question whether there are properties as well as individuals or whether, really, there are just the individuals, variously propertied. Of course, you'll have to decide, for yourself, which philosophical questions are most worth a philosopher's greatest efforts.) Even so, even without my ever endorsing any Realism about Properties, I'll notice, if only as a nice convenience, this point of terminology. In my usage of "property," it will be *redundant* to speak of an entity's *monadic* properties, or of its *intrinsic* properties. The same point phrased alternatively: On my usage, it will be *incoherent* to speak of an entity's *relational* properties, or of an object's *extrinsic* properties. (When tempted by such potentially misleading verbiage, I suggest that, as a first approximation, we speak instead of the relations in which the object partakes, rather than of any alleged relational properties. And, more perspicuous still, we should speak of how the object in question is related to other individuals, never so much as reifying even any supposed relations, much less any nicely avoided "relational property." But, in what follows, it's only pretty rarely that I'll insist on these terminological niceties. In my book, as in many, there's little virtue in pedantry.)

First, I'll note what might be called the *purely Spatial properties* or, for short, the *Spatials*. Central to this group are just the first two of what Descartes considered "the primary or real properties of matter... shape, size, position, duration, movability, divisibility and number."[5] (Absolutely obviously, number is not any Spatial property. And, almost as obviously, neither is movability or divisibility, as both of them are, rather, Propensity properties, which I'll discuss right after I notice the

---

5. The quote is from David Armstrong, *Perception and the Physical World*, Routledge and Kegan Paul, 1961. For Descartes's list, Armstrong refers us to "the second paragraph in the Fifth Meditation, and elsewhere."

Spatials. What's more, duration isn't anything Spatial either, as it is, by contrast, a Temporal feature [maybe, a feature of anything lasting longer than just an absolute instant]. Finally, for this overly long list, position isn't, on my usage of "property" any Spatial property, either. After all, if position should be a property of any sort, it would be a relational property, rather than any monadic, or intrinsic, property. And, as you'll recall, my nice usage excludes any so-called relational properties. Safely placing aside "the problem of incongruous counter-parts," which is quite irrelevant to all my upcoming lengthy discussion, we may take it that, at least nearly enough, the only Spatial properties are Shape properties and Size properties.) Of course, such determin-ables as Descartes's shape, and his size, are just starting points. More fully to the point are such absolutely specific determinate properties as, say, *being perfectly spherical* and as, for another instance, *being exactly one cubic millimeter*.

On my understanding of the Spatials, it may be easy to think that even certain absolutely empty regions of space, or certain absolutely empty spaces, will have some Spatial properties, although they're ut-terly devoid of any other basic properties. And, as with much of our loose and popular speech, it may be useful for us to say, at times, that a certain otherwise perfectly solid cube, for example, has an entirely interior cylindrical hole, deeply inside it. Or, much the same, and quite as loose-lipped, we might say that this considered material individual has an absolutely empty cylindrical cavity wholly contained within it.

Just as we may speak ever so loosely about how voids are shaped, often enough to useful effect, so we may similarly speak about the size, or the volume, or the sheer spatial extent, of absolutely empty spaces, or perfectly vacuous regions, or other only apparently extended perfect nonentities. Using the same example employed just above, it might sometimes be useful for us to say, further, that the wholly contained cy-lindrical void has about one-fourth the volume of the containing con-cretum, the empty cavity being about a quarter as extensive as, or about a quarter as voluminous as, the real spatial individual that completely surrounds the thus notably empty spatial nonentity.

When speaking in a stricter and philosophically more perspicuous way, however, I should say that it's only the cavitied concrete particular that has any real shape here, or, for that matter, any real spatial extent, or volume, or size. So, in this little example of ours, when it's all described most strictly and truly, there's really *nothing* that's shaped cylindrically. Rather, the only entity that's really shaped is the cavitied material concretum—an individual for whose shape we have no fa-miliar name, nor any other very available and convenient expression.

Now, in other scenarios or situations, there will be, no doubt, some things that really are shaped cylindrically. But, each of them will be some concrete particular, a cylindrical object that's a physical object, I should think. Now, as I've been urging, between a cylindrical concrete object, on the one hand, and a cylindrical empty space, on the other, there is, then, a world of difference, maybe unimportant for many to notice, but very important, I think, for serious philosophers to observe. This is the difference between an individual concretum that's really cylindrical and, on the other side, really nothing at all. So, while there may well be many concreta each shaped cylindrically, there can't possibly be any such thing as a cylindrical perfectly empty void.

But, let's not get bogged down in this. For, after all, our interest here is in concrete physical objects, and in how it is that *they* might be most basically propertied. And, whatever confusion is sometimes spread by empty talk about mere voids, it's clear that a central part of our more interesting story is just this: One of the basic ways for a basic physical object to be propertied is for the real physical individual to be Spatially propertied.[6]

In line with this sensible idea—that we should focus on what's philosophically most central—and with a properly humane regard for my very human readers, myself included, in most of this book I'll aim to write prose that's eminently readable and, as I hope, even somewhat enjoyable. To that end, I'll be talking about empty space, from time to time, and absolute voids, and perfectly empty places, or regions, or spaces, and so on. And, from time to time, as well, I'll be talking about the shapes of some of these absolute voids, and the sizes of these perfectly empty regions, as well as saying all sorts of relevantly similar things that, in an ontologically most pristine philosophical text, would never be mentioned. But, except to provide a far better exposition of the work, none of this will much matter. At least so far as I'm aware, none of this loose talk is crucial to advancing any of this book's many central points, and precious few, if any, will be important for advancing any of its very many somewhat secondary statements. In a nutshell: Not much pedantry in these pages!

Now, as I'm painfully aware, the Scientiphical Metaphysic *might not* help provide us with any understanding of concrete reality that's even modestly adequate. But, if it does profit us in that large regard, then we must think of very much of this reality, even if not absolutely all of it, as having spatial properties. Indeed, though I'm far less confident of it, I

---

6. In offering these remarks on (what I call) the Spatials, I've been helped by Neil Williams.

suggest that we should accept even this much more ambitious proposition: For the Scientiphical Metaphysic to do much *for our understanding* of concrete reality, there must be *some* truth in the thought that much of this reality is both temporal and also spatial, in very much the way suggested to us by (what's apparently) our conscious perception of physical reality. Now, it may be that this perception provides us with only a *very partial perspective* on physical reality, and only a *quite superficial* perspective. Still and all, unless there's *something about physical reality* in virtue of which it has familiar spatial properties, or parts of it have these familiar properties, the Scientiphical Metaphysic may do far more toward providing intellectual illusion than toward giving us even a very modestly adequate understanding of reality. Though I'm inclined to believe as much as all that, here I'll rely on less ambitious ideas. At all events, so much for my first category of basic natural properties, the Spatials.

Second, I'll notice what, for want of a better expression, I'll call the *Propensity properties* or, more briefly, the *Propensities*. Often, these properties, or some of them, have been called "powers"; but, inappropriate for us, that term connotes positive force. Others have called the properties "dispositions"; but, despite the valiant efforts of C. B. Martin and others, that term has been so badly abused that it will arouse, in the minds of too many, undue confusion.[7] Anyhow, there is nothing the least bit conditional, or "iffy," about Propensities or, as Locke would have preferred, powers. For example, the Propensity of a Newtonian particle to attract other such particles is as fully real, as completely categorical, and as irreducibly basic, as is the spherical shape of the gravitationally powerful material sphere. As many metaphysicians should like to say, a given Particle's gravitational Propensity is *intrinsic* to that very Particle itself, just as much as the Particle's Shape is intrinsic to just that little concretum. Just so, the Particle's being gravitationally Propensitied, quite as it is, doesn't require there ever to be any other (gravitationally Propensitied) Particles, just as its being spherically Shaped doesn't require there to be any other (spherically Shaped) Particles.

As I mean to understand the Propensities, they're absolutely distinct from the Spatials. Consider a spherical object that may be taken to be an electron, where our supposed electron is well suited to making

7. Though some of Martin's writings on this subject are very hard to understand, others are helpfully clear. For work that helps clarify the fact that *dispositions are as categorical as anything*, see C. B. Martin, "Dispositions and Conditionals," *Philosophical Quarterly*, 1994, and Martin's contributions to *Dispositions: A Debate*, D. M. Armstrong, C. B. Martin, U. T. Place, ed. Tim Crane, Routledge, 1996.

true an early theory of such supposedly simple physical things. Then, that considered physical concretum will be something that has, in addition to its spatial properties, *unit negative electric charge*. Its having *that* property, we may suppose, isn't any Spatial feature of the particle; rather, and by contrast with that, it is the electronish individual's having a certain complex Propensity or, perhaps the same, its having a cluster of simpler Propensities. The complex Propensity of our electron will include, for salient examples, its Propensity to repel any other electron, with a certain force and in a certain direction, and its Propensity to attract any proton, with such-and-such a force and in so-and-so a direction. As with any entity's having any Propensity, the electron's having this one is not dependent, not even in the minutest degree, on there ever actually being any protons—or, on there ever actually being any such things as are fit to be attracted by it. And, it doesn't depend on there actually being any other electrons—or, on there ever actually being any such other things as are fit to be repelled by it. No; not at all. To think otherwise would be to risk conflating a Propensity, or a (Categorical) Disposition, or a Power, with something that's relational, such as an Interaction (among things). And, on pain of giving up any chance for making much progress toward any truly substantive philosophy, that's a conflation we must certainly avoid, no matter what intellectual price must be paid, in terms of however many other conceptions.

Let us be perfectly clear, then, about at least as much as just this: In marked contradistinction to there being any *chance for* the noted Propensities of our electron to be *manifested*, which does require there to be additional concrete things, external to it, the electron's *just having* the indicated Propensity doesn't depend on there ever being *any* such additional concreta.

To avoid confusion, it's also important to avoid conflating our conception of a Propensity with what may be some notions of *possibility*. What do I have in mind? Well, suppose that, replete with its various Propensities, our imagined electron *is spherical* right now. Does this mean, or require, that the object has, among its Propensities, a *Propensity to be spherical* right now? No; it does not. In fact, there *isn't* any Propensity just like that; there's *never* an object Propensitied in *that* way. Rather, whatever may be a present Propensity is something that concerns just how things *will be*, in the *future*. So, supposing that our electron existed just a moment ago, we *may coherently* suppose that its *present shape* is a manifestation of a Propensity it *then* had, even if *just a moment ago*, to be spherical right now, that is, to be spherically shaped *just so soon in the future*. Look; nothing can ever have a Propensity *to have been* spherical; not, anyhow, *as I'm understanding* Propensities, and powers, and dispositions. And, just as nothing can *now* have a Propensity, or a power, or a disposition, to *have been* spherical, so, also, nothing can *now* have a Propensity, or a power, or a disposition, to *now* be spherical. At least as I'm understanding these terms, a way that I take to be perfectly nontechnical and wholly natural, none of that makes any real sense.

(Let's be careful here. Look, I do not say that if what's now an ovoid just before was a sphere, then the sphere must have had a Propensity to become an ovoid. No; not at all. While I certainly do agree that it must have been possible for the sphere to become an ovoid, that may have happened in either of at least two ways. On one hand, of course, the sphere may have had a Propensity to become ovoidal, which disposition will now have been manifested. With that, there's a certain intelligibility as to why there's now that ovoid there. But, the matter needn't be even the least bit intelligible. Just so, and on another hand, it may be entirely accidental, a perfectly unintelligible mere happenstance, that the erstwhile sphere became an ovoid, an instance of real possibility, all right, but with no correlative Propensity at all.[8])

Well, as I hope, I may have helped avoid some stultifying confusions. Anyway, at this juncture, that's enough about Propensities, my second category of basic natural properties.

---

8. While we should be very careful, we shouldn't be stupefied, or intellectually paralyzed. Why that remark? Well, in many of their discussions, various philosophers talk of what's *now possible*, for this or that object—perhaps regarding (what is its) shape, for instance and, then, as they say, it's what's now possible for just how the object's shaped right *now*. Some may say, for example, that, since it's *required* of what's *now* a globe that the object *now be spherical* (which is, I trust, quite unobjectionable)—well, then, it's certainly *now possible for* a globe to be, even just right now, a spherically shaped entity. What can they mean by this last bit, by "it's (certainly) now *possible for* a globe to be, just right now, a spherically shaped entity"? Well, about part of their intent, anyway, I think I may be quite clear: It's *not* anything (merely) epistemological they're after here. It's *not* anything about what's known, or what's not known, about the object in question; and it's *not* anything about what's certain, or what's not certain, concerning, the object; and it's *not* anything else in that philosophical neighborhood. But, of course, to grasp just that much about what they aim to mean—this negative little bit—is to grasp precious little as to what they may be trying to express. And, try as *I* might, I just can't ever get very much further than that with any peculiar and prevalent philosophical verbiage. So, I'm very skeptical about a lot of recent talk as to "what's possible for things" (even while being, at the same time, somewhat uncertain that I should be so skeptical). But, happily, there's something I can say here, with real confidence, that's most pertinent to our present concerns. *Whatever* may be going on with *all that* talk, purporting to concern just so many (putative) *possibilities*, well, it must be very different from my remarks, here in this text, about *Propensities*, and about *powers*, and about *dispositions*.

Third, and last, I'll notice what I call the *Qualities*, a group of properties whose most accessible members are, to a first approximation, just certain of those that quite a few philosophers have called *phenomenal* properties. They will be just those phenomenal properties that, in any very direct way, have *least* to do with the Spatials. So, for a first approximation, think of phenomenal blue, or maybe also phenomenal transparency. By contrast, don't think of phenomenal sphericity, or phenomenal angularity. But, that's only a first approximation. (A little signal: As the book progresses, I mean to avoid using the word "phenomenal" very much, preferring some expressions that may be less confusing and more helpful. In due course, you'll see reasons for such a shift.)

Anyway, your experiencing may come to be as of a transparent blue sphere. This may happen when you perceive a quite uniform blue glass paperweight, or when you vividly imagine the blue glass object shortly after, or when, still later, you have a vivid dream. Or, it may happen when, in the first place, you simply hallucinate as of a transparent blue sphere. Anyway, in none of these cases need you yourself come to be transparent, or come to be blue, no more than you must come to be a spherical experiencer. Indeed, it's most unlikely that you become spherical, or transparent, or blue. And, similarly, when a perfectly specific sort of taste of sweet chocolate is the taste that I saliently experience, it needn't be that I myself am so sweet. It's hard to articulate how Qualities are instantiated. Still, our own conscious qualitative character helps us grasp certain properties of this third main sort and, with that, the kind of properties, the Qualities, that includes them.

As I understand this third kind of basic property, it should be stressed, there may be very many Qualities that completely transcend both anything available in our experience and even anything directly suggested in our experiencing: Beyond any properties suggested in the experiencing of any of the world's finite minds, there may be Qualities that are *deeply analogous to* some of the Qualities discussed already. Through certain *extrapolative analogical thinking*, perhaps we might get some grasp as to the nature of some of these further-fetched properties, even if, perhaps, never a grasp that's very rich, firm, or clear.

So, on the one hand, consider those Qualities apparently best suited to filling space, or pervading space. Here, there will be a perfectly specific sort of translucent blue. And, as well, there'll be an equally specific "colorless transparency," maybe quite as suggested by your experiencing (as of) a very fine windowpane. And, there'll also be an absolutely specific "silveriness," as with what's experienced in, say, my seeing a uniformly shiny fine silver cube. Since they're apparently so well suited to filling space, we'll call these *(Spatially) Extensible Qualities*. Well, that's on the one hand. Now, on the other hand, consider some Qualities apparently *unsuited* to filling space. Here, there's a certain perfectly specific taste (as) of sweet chocolate, which you might call Sweet Chocolate. And, there's a perfectly specific sort of (phenomenal) pleasant sound, *Belltone*, as we might label this other unsuited Quality; and so on. Since they're apparently so *unsuited* to filling space, we'll call them *(Spatially) Nonextensible Qualities*. Now, we can have a conception, it appears, of properties that, though they're *not* available in experience to the world's finite minds, are very much *more like each* indicated Extensible Quality than they're like *any* indicated Nonextensible Quality. The Qualities we're analogically contemplating are very much more like our indicated Extensibles than our indicated Nonextensibles, especially as regards whatever it is that has our Extensibles seem so very much more suited to filling space.

By way of such extrapolative analogical thinking, I'm suggesting, we may have a significant conception of a World featuring many instantiations of Extensible Qualities that can't, at least as a matter of natural fact, be experienced by any of the World's finite minds. In parallel, we can also conceive of properties that, though they're likewise unavailable to experience, are much more like each of our indicated *Nonextensible* Qualities than they're like any of our indicated Extensible Qualities. Here, too, there may be basic properties that are among a World's further-fetched Qualities (though they might not be basic *physical* properties).

In later Chapters, we'll explore how various things may be Qualitied in various ways. But, already we may understand the Qualities pretty usefully. Anyway, at least for now, that's all for this last sort of basic natural property.

As should be clear, on my understanding of the basic natural properties, they needn't be at all mental. Nor must entities that have these properties be mental, in any respect or regard. This should seem obviously so with the Spatials, and with the Propensities, and, now, also with the (Spatially) Extensible Qualities. It's also true, I suggest, with the (Spatially) Nonextensible Qualities.

As should also be clear, a specific basic property belonging to any one of the three basic categories can't, on this understanding, belong to any of the other two. So, imagine a Small Blue Sphere with a Propensity to attract anything basic (there might be) that's a Cube, and another basic physical entity (suppose, or pretend) that's a Large Red Cube with a Propensity to attract anything basic (there might be) that's a Sphere. Now, as we're using our terms for basic properties, the first of these entities has, in our (possibly just partial) specification, just two Spatials, with its being Small and its being Spherical, and just one Propensity, with its being disposed to attract anything basic that's Cubical, and just one (Spatially Extensible) Quality, with its being Blue. Well, then, I'll observe this: Neither of its Spatials is its sole Propensity; nor is either its sole Quality. And, just as its single Propensity isn't either of its Spatials, neither is its Propensity to attract Cubes the selfsame as its Blue Quality. And, finally, its Quality isn't either of its purely Spatial properties. (As I prefer to think of reality as all being just some propertied and related concrete individuals, I don't take this paragraph's sentences to express any serious sort of "identity statement," about reality, nor any serious denial of any such statement. Let's see. Well, here's a more serious candidate, for an identity statement about reality: "This green tube is the same tube as that red tube; there's a variation in the tube's Quality, or its quality—from green to red, or from red to green—where the tube is occluded by a cubical yellow box." And, here's a candidate for a pretty serious *denial* of identity: "No; the green tube *isn't* the red one; rather, it's one of the other tubes that's partially occluded by the box." Even this last sentence may be only a somewhat serious candidate, for expressing a "denial of an identity statement" about reality. Yet, as I allow, it's less objectionable than the denial sentences I lately offered, about a certain *property* not being identical with a certain *property*. But, here, none of that matters. For, with my denial sentences, you'll grasp my main points—roughly, points about how concrete individuals may be differently, and may be similarly, propertied and related.) Well, maybe this paragraph's main points are mostly terminological. Still, terminology can be very useful.

Please don't confuse my terms with terms enormously more famous: In the history of philosophy, it's Locke's name, I imagine, that's most regularly associated with the term "quality." In our philosophical education, few of us fail to encounter Locke's discussion of his so-called *primary qualities*—as with size, shape and solidity—and, by contrast, his so-called *secondary qualities*. Generally, the secondaries are to be certain powers of objects to produce, in the likes of us, certain sorts of experience. But, of course, Locke isn't very consistent here, in what he takes his secondary qualities to be, sometimes having them not be any powers, but, rather, as pertaining more directly to our experience itself. (No doubt, my essay will also be riddled with inconsistencies; when attempting work that's philosophically ambitious, that's one price that each of us mere humans must pay.) Anyway, it should be absolutely clear that my use of "quality," whether in lower case or whether capitalized, is utterly different from Locke's use. For me, Locke's primary qualities are, almost all of them, Spatial properties, with the few exceptions, like solidity, being Propensity properties. *None* are what *I* call qualities, or Qualities. And, for me, his secondary qualities are, at least rather generally, just certain Propensity properties—generally such merely physically derivative powers as are possessed by certain physical complexes, though they're lacking, presumably, in the basic constituents of any complexes. Once again, *none* are what *I* call Qualities. So, my usage is enormously different from Locke's. Though that's all merely terminological, it may be important to remember. For, to the extent that the reader forgets this, and he reverts to his early philosophical education, he's liable to be greatly confused as to what I'm here aiming to offer.

With this threefold classification, I briefly present a doctrine that's assumed, at least implicitly, I think, by most who hold with the Scientiphical Metaphysic, even if it's not actually implied by the dominant worldview:

> *The Denial of Qualities, First Formulation.* Unlike the Spatial properties and the Propensities, which are so widely instantiated in what's physical, there are not (any instantiations of) any of the Qualities anywhere in physical reality. Nor are there, anywhere in physical reality, any mental qualities readily confused with Qualities, with the possible exception, at any given time, of such a small part of physical reality as may then subserve the minds of sentient beings.

With that much clear enough for most, I'll hope and I'll trust, I'll move to present, briefly, *the Denial of Qualities, Second Formulation*.

To begin, we may say that, on the Scientiphical Metaphysic, all the world's sentient beings, all the minds, are each *promoted by* some of the world's matter, whether its promoting matter constitutes the sentient being, as with Materialism, or whether it only subserves the being, as with Epiphenomenalism. At all events, just where there are some suitable physical complexes, as with your active brain now, there are minds promoted. And, we may also say that, on Scientiphicalism, each (humanly) perceptible physical thing, my brown desk, for example, is *promoted by* some of the world's matter, the stuff that constitutes it.

Now, consider a philosopher who holds, as some apparently do, that the (only instances of) colors are found not in the experience of sentient beings, but in certain perceptible objects. Just perhaps, this thinker may go on to hold, more positively, that Qualities are instanced in physical reality, all right, but then only insofar as, or only where, there are perceptible physical complexes promoted by physical reality. Or, better, she'll go on to hold that, only in the case of such complexes,

will there be (instanced) anything (even) readily confused with Qualities. With the Denial of Qualities, in its First Formulation, do we address the concerns of this sort of philosopher? I'm somewhat unsure.
But, in any event, we may nicely address her concerns, I trust, along
with the worries of thinkers already addressed, by saying that, at least
implicitly, they all assume:

> *The Denial of Qualities, Second Formulation*. Unlike the Spatial prop-
> erties and the Propensities, which are so widely instantiated in what's
> physical, there are not (any instantiations of) any of the Qualities
> anywhere in physical reality. Nor are there, anywhere in physical
> reality, any mental qualities readily confused with Qualities, with the
> possible exception, at any given time, of such a small part of physical
> reality as may then promote the minds of sentient beings. Nor are
> there, anywhere in physical reality, any Propensity properties readily
> confused with Qualities, with the possible exception, at any given
> time, of such a small part of physical reality as may then promote
> such complexes as are (humanly) perceptible physical complexes.

According to this Denial, as so Secondly Formulated, very much of the
world's matter has no (Spatially Extensible) Qualities, nor anything
readily confused with any Qualities, whatever might be its Spatial
properties and its Propensities. And, on this Denial, there have been
very long periods, ever so long ago, throughout which *none* of the
world's matter had any (Spatially Extensible) Qualities, nor any (other)
properties readily confused with Qualities.[9]

3. The Denial of Qualities, Particles in Space
and Spaces in a Plenum

For the Scientiphical Metaphysic to provide us with a reasonably adequate view of a World, do its bare bones need such Qualitative flesh as
can be had only when we reject the Denial of Qualities, whatever its
Formulation? I think so.

Toward motivating this thought, I'll suppose that the Denial holds
and, in terms of the Scientiphical Metaphysic as thus Denied, or
Limited, or maybe even Impoverished, I'll begin two *extremely simple*

9. Toward writing this Section as clearly as I've managed to do, quite imperfect
though it certainly still remains, I've been greatly helped by comments from many
people. Most helpful of all, it seems to me, have been persistent questions from Elizabeth
Harman, and from Michael Raven.

attempts to characterize a World. (Toward the Denial's being clearly in force, I'll stipulate that both attempts are aimed at characterizing the World well before the advent of [finite] minds.)

First, and familiarly, I'll begin an attempt to characterize physical reality in generally Newtonian terms: Moving about in what's otherwise uniformly empty space, there are many material Particles, whose motion is governed by physical laws. In that we're supposing the Denial to hold, we must suppose that, in this *Particulate World*, none of the Particles is Qualitied.

Second, and unusually, I begin this attempt to characterize physical reality: In what's otherwise a continuous material Plenum, or a continuous field of matter, there are little perfectly empty spaces, or absolute vacua, or *Bubbles*: As regards both shape and size, each Bubble is precisely similar to a certain Particle, its *counterpart* Particle, in the Particulate World. And, wherever there's a Particle in our Particulate World, there's a counterpart place with a counterpart Bubble in this *Plenumate World*. So, if there are eight Spherical Particles arrayed in a quite cubical pattern in a certain region of our Particulate World, then in the counterpart region of our Plenumate World there'll be eight such Bubbles arrayed in just such a pattern.

Even as various Particles may instance certain physical properties that will have them be suited for governance by certain physical laws, so various regions of a physical Plenum may have certain correlative physical properties that will have them be correlatively suited for governance by apt parallels of, or nice inversions of, the Particle-governing laws. So, in a nice parallel with the law-governed behavior of the Particles in our Particulate World, this Plenumate World features laws governing the distribution of its Plenum, evolving in its time. And, since its Bubbles always *are* at just the places in the World where there *isn't* any Plenum, this World's laws also serve to determine the distribution of all its *Bubbles* over time. So, our Plenumate World's Bubbles will move through its material field along trajectories that, over time, relevantly parallel the trajectories of the Particulate World's Particles through its empty space.

Now, it should seem perfectly evident to you that, in the ordinary run of things, I'll be very successful in attempts like these, just as each of them will proceed, evidently, along a main line that's opposite the other's. (But, of course, in the ordinary run of things, I don't let myself be troubled by any proposition like the Denial. Rather, I allow myself to accept that even an utterly basic physical thing may be well endowed with Quality, however implicit, or automatic, this acceptance may be.) For instance, I'll do fine if, with the first World, I'd conceive the Particles as each being a certain specific Color, say, Light Grey, and, maybe, I'll conceive a nicely contrasting Colored background for them, a nicely color-contrasting empty space, so to say, as with my having that be, say, all Dark Grey. Indeed, in such a Qualitatively Rich event as that, so to say, it will be easy as pie for me to be completely successful. And, it should also seem perfectly clear that I *should* be able, quite easily, to succeed in these attempts, nicely characterizing each World, or each sort of World, in a way that clearly distinguishes it from the other World, of the quite dif- ferent sort. All right? Sure, it's all OK. But, then, what's the thrust of that *should*? Well, at least for the most part, it's this: With the Denial's being in force, I'm unable, apparently, to succeed with these simple endeavors. And this appearance of failure, it seems, is a quite recalcitrant intellectual phenomenon. So, as all this suggests, I *should reject* the Denial. And, in its stead, I should embrace only a very much more positive proposition, far more friendly to the idea of there being physical Quality, even unto what's physically just so terribly basic. (But, of course, this isn't anything just about me. Quite to the contrary, it should apply in your case, dear reader, just as much as in mine. Well, now, I'm on the verge of getting ahead of myself. So, back to our main line let's go: With the Denial in force, we're allowing me only very poor resources, it appears, for suc- ceeding at conceptual attempts that *should* be—there's that "should" again—just as easy as pie, or just a piece of cake.)

Well now, even with our always supposing the Denial holds, it may well appear to you that I've made two extremely simple attempts, and maybe even two successful attempts, at starting to characterize our world, or a World. Before concluding the Section, it may be useful to comment on what may be the two most salient respects in which my attempts were so simple.

First, there's the point that my attempts were conducted in the general framework of classical physics, with its quite intuitive concep- tions of space and of time, rather than the framework of more recent physics, with its quite *unintuitive* conceptions, like the notion of *space- time*. One reason for this, I blush to confess, is that I know precious little about contemporary physical science. A more important reason is that I'm engaged in an endeavor that's meant to transcend the dif- ferences between classical physics and more recent scientific develop- ments. And, it's perfectly possible, it appears, for there to be an endeavor that succeeds in being that comprehensive: Since recent scientific developments make no Completely Revolutionary Break with earlier science, what's new in the recent scientific conceptions doesn't affect the question of how we might, with the Denial in force, have a worldview that's an adequate specification of the Scientiphical Meta- physic or, maybe more likely, never have any such happy worldview.

Apparently with complete sincerity, that's what I've been told by philosophers knowledgeable about contemporary physics. So, apparently, my employing the framework of classical physics means no loss of generality for these philosophical exercises.[10]

Second, there's the point that, in trying to characterize a Particulate World, and also a Plenumate World, I forswore saying anything about complex material structures, or systems, much less anything about any minds that any material complexes might subserve. That was done for several reasons, the most important being that such a simplification would be helpful toward having the Denial be clearly in force. Even if it might be unnecessary, I'll again implore my readers: When trying to think of a Particulate World, *don't do anything even remotely like*, say, thinking of *light gray* Spheres moving through a *dark gray* space or field; and, when attempting thoughts of a Plenumate World, don't do anything even remotely like thinking of dark gray Spheres moving through a light gray space or field!

For holding to this supposition, it will be useful to discuss some relations regarding the Scientiphical Metaphysic, the instantiation of Qualities, and "the place of mind in the world order," or, maybe, just what appear to be some such relations. Well, even while they try to have the Denial be in force, some may have these following thoughts regarding the Scientiphical Metaphysic. As our dominant metaphysic seems fully to allow, where and when a World features creatures with conscious minds, there and then there'll be someplace in the World for Qualities to be instantiated. So, if we should endeavor to characterize, say, a Particulate World, at greater length, then, as we may make specifications for complex living material creatures, and so consciously experiencing creatures, we may thus characterize a part of the World in which Qualities will be instanced, even whilst supposing the Denial to hold. So, if we just go further in our attempts to characterized Worlds, won't we do quite a lot toward characterizing a distinctively Particulate World, and also a distinctively Plenumate World, even while always supposing the Denial?

No; we won't. And, that may be seen in two main ways.

Here's one way: If our physical conceptions are anywhere near as significant as we take them to be, they must sustain a distinction that serves to distinguish between very simple Particulate Worlds and very simple Plenumate Worlds, where there *aren't any interesting* material complexes. Think of a Particulate World, for instance, with just three Spherical Particles, subserving nothing much at all, and also an equally

---

10. Among the scientifically knowledgeable philosophers who've helped me in this matter, Gordon Belot has been most exceptionally helpful.

boring Plenumate World with just three Spherical Bubbles. Of course, in what we believe to be the actual course of nature, for billions of years our actual world was a boringly mindless World and, apparently, quite bereft of perceptible complexes, whatever might best be said, more positively, as to its physical structure and nature.

Here's another way to see the futility of any attempt to gain Qualities for physical reality by adverting to such interesting physical complexes as may serve to promote qualitatively rich minds: Whenever there's something that seems to characterize an experiencing creature as constituted of many Particles, then, in correlative Plenumate terms, there'll be something that, with just as much propriety, affords us a sentient creature that's not so constituted. Let me explain.

In an attempt to characterize an experiencing creature that features a body as well as a mind, with *Particulate* terms we may say this: Ever so many material Particles, perhaps billions and billions, serve to *constitute* the material creature with a mind. Or, at the very least, they all serve to constitute the body of the creature. And, because so many of this body's Particles are going through an appropriately complex sequence of arrangements, this body, it may then be said, subserves the creature's mind. When the duly constituted creature has experiences, then, through or in the creature's experiencing mind, Qualities are instanced in the Particulate World.

But, using *Plenumate* terms, we can say *this* about any materially realized experiencing creature: Ever so many Bubbles in the Plenum, perhaps billions and billions, serve to *institute* the physical creature with a mind, to coin a euphonious Plenumate term. Or, at least they serve to institute the body of the creature, which body subserves the creature with a mind. When the duly instituted creature experiences, then, through or in the creature's experiencing mind, Qualities are instanced in the Plenumate World.

Do we grasp a significant difference here, at all well conceived? I don't see that.

Well, we've raised questions concerning any attempt to contemplate physical reality within the confines of the Denial. Just so, it may have initially appeared that each of my attempts to characterize physical reality, one with Particulate wording and one with Plenumate terms, clearly contrasted with the other. But, mightn't it be that I actually made just one extremely insubstantial start twice over, first using one mutually connected group of terms, the "Particulate terms," and then using another, the "Plenumate terms"? As long as an attempt to conceive a World is limited by the Denial, it may be so extremely insubstantial, I'll suggest, as to be quite futile.

4. When Limited by the Denial, How to Conceive a Particle's Propensities?

In my two attempts at characterizing Worlds, I tried to attribute Spatial properties to the objects of the Worlds. For example, I said that, in one sort of World, there are Spherical Particles and, in the other, there are Spherical Bubbles—or, in ontologically cleaner terms, in that other there's a Plenum that's Spherically Bubbled. Anyway, and in contrast with that, I did little, or nothing, as regards the other basic natural properties of the intended objects, the Propensities and the Qualities. Of course, as the Denial was fully in force, it was forbidden to attribute any Quality to a Particle, or to a Plenum. But, what about Propensities?

On this, we can hardly do better, I should think, than to consider what, historically, appears the Propensity most saliently proposed for philosophical consideration, the supposed *solidity* of material objects. And, on that, we can hardly do better than to begin with Book II, Chapter IV, of John Locke's great *Essay*, which is "Of Solidity," where he aims to present an "Idea" that serves to distinguish material Bodies from the mere Space they may occupy:

> That which thus hinders the approach of two Bodies, when they are moving one towards another, I call *Solidity* . . . but if any one think it better to call it *Impenetrability*, he has my Consent. . . . This of all other, seems the *Idea* most intimately connected with, and essential to Body, so as no where else to be found or imagin'd, but only in matter: . . . the Mind, . . . considers it, as well as Figure, in the minutest Particle of Matter, that can exist; and finds it inseparably inherent in Body, where-ever, or however modified. This is the *Idea*, belongs to Body, whereby we conceive it *to fill space*.[11]

As with other passages, we should understand Locke here as assuming, if not affirming, that the Denial holds. Even as Newton's physics ignores Qualities, Locke excludes them from the world's vast material realm, restricting them to our Minds.[12]

For Locke, solidity is impenetrability. But, with the Denial in force, what can such solidity do for our conception of a Particle? Inspiring remarks on this occur in John Foster's terribly difficult book, but at

---

11. In P. H. Nidditch's edition of John Locke's work *An Essay concerning Human Understanding*, Oxford University Press, 1975, the quoted words can be found on page 123. When referring to this standard text, I use the abbreviated title *Essay*.

12. Locke, *Essay*, pp. 136–137.

least occasionally brilliant work, *The Case for Idealism*.[13] According to Foster:

> Locke...thought that the nature of solidity is revealed in tactual experience....But in this Locke was clearly mistaken....The tactual experience of solidity is no more nor less than the experience of voluminous resistance, and, in so far as our concept of solidity is acquired through tactual experience, the specification of matter as solid is opaque. All it adds to the specification of matter as a voluminous substance is that there is *something* in its intrinsic nature (it does not say *what*) which makes material objects mutually obstructive.[14]

Now, I do not know that Foster is right in his suggestion that Locke thought that solidity was not a Power of material objects. More likely, it seems to me, in "Of Solidity" Locke was involved in muddles: How could *Impenetrability*, which Locke says is the very same as Solidity, *not* be a Power of resistance on the part of Impenetrable Bodies? But, philosophically, there's no more to be gained from Locke here than what Foster contends, nothing much at all. Indeed, insofar as Foster's reading of Locke may be mistaken, his error will be, apparently, *undue charity* toward the old philosopher.

To take full advantage of them, we should conjoin our doubts about Locke, on impenetrability and materiality, with some complementary challenges from a marvelous Section of David Hume's great *Treatise*, "Of the modern philosophy":

> The idea of solidity is that of two objects, which being impell'd by the utmost force, cannot penetrate each other; but still maintain a separate and distinct existence. Solidity, therefore, is perfectly incomprehensible alone, and without the conception of some bodies, which are solid, and maintain this separate and distinct existence. Now what idea have we of these bodies? The ideas of colours, sounds, and other secondary qualities are excluded. The idea of motion depends on that of extension, and the idea of extension on that of solidity. 'Tis impossible, therefore, that the idea of solidity can depend on either of them. For that wou'd be to run in a circle, and make

---

13. John Foster, *The Case for Idealism*, Routledge & Kegan Paul, London, 1982. By contrast with the passages from it that I'll cite, much of the book is written in a difficult technical style. From what I've managed to understand, I'm convinced that the work deserves serious study. A few of its last words convey the thrust of the courageous book: "I hope one day to ... make the case for mentalism irresistible. But until then, I must be content with a Defence of idealism in its anti-realist and phenomenalist forms." With his paper, "The Succinct Case for Idealism," in H. Robinson (ed.), *Objections to Physicalism*, Oxford University Press, 1993, Foster gives an overview of the book.

14. Foster, *The Case for Idealism*, page 63.

one idea depend on another, while at the same time the latter depends on the former. Our modern philosophy, therefore, leaves us no just nor satisfactory idea of solidity; nor consequently of matter.

Add to this, that, properly speaking, solidity or impenetrability is nothing, but an impossibility of annihilation, ... An impossibility of being annihilated cannot exist, and can never be conceived to exist, by itself; but necessarily requires some object or real existence, to which it may belong. Now the difficulty still remains, how to form an idea of this object or existence, without having recourse to the secondary and sensible qualities.[15]

Like Locke before him, we should now understand Hume as assuming the Denial to hold. And, as these passages then serve to show, in fixing on solidity, or on *what's left of that notion when the Denial has been supposed*, Locke found nothing to distinguish adequately between Particles of Matter and Bubbles in a material Plenum. And, for his part, Hume was well aware of this predicament. Indeed, right before the quote just displayed, his *Treatise* features these sentences:

The idea of extension is a compound idea; but as it is not compounded of an infinite number of parts or inferior ideas, it must at last resolve itself into such as are perfectly simple and indivisible. Those simple and indivisible parts, not being ideas of extension, must be non-entities, unless conceiv'd as colour'd or solid. Color is excluded from any real existence. The reality, therefore, of our idea of extension depends upon the reality of that of solidity, nor can the former be just while the latter is chimerical. Let us, then, lend our attention to the examination of the idea of solidity.[16]

As Hume's here suggesting, without phenomenal colors available, or any similarly helpful Qualities, we'll lack the resources for an adequate conception of something's being physically solid or impenetrable. As Hume also seems rightly to suggest, the same pertains to any other alleged physical Propensity. (Except that Locke fixed on solidity as his favorite, there's nothing very special about that candidate, as the passages from Foster can be seen to show.)

In light of what this Section's presented, we may make useful comments concerning the main question that, in the just previous

---

15. David Hume, *A Treatise of Human Nature*, Book I, Part IV, Section IV. My copy of the *Treatise* is the P. H. Nidditch edition, based on L. A. Selby-Bigge's earlier edition, from the Oxford University Press, 1978. In this edition, the quoted words are on pp. 228–29. Generally, when referring to this standard text, I use the abbreviated title *Treatise*.

16. Hume, *Treatise*, page 228.

Section, arose for my attempts to characterize a Particulate World, and also a Plenumate World. That question was this: Though it may have appeared that each attempt clearly contrasted with the other, mightn't it be that I actually made just one extremely insubstantial start twice over, first using one mutually connected group of terms and then using another? As it now certainly seems, neither attempt accomplished very much at all. Indeed, by now this may be so very plain that the whole matter's no longer interesting.

What may still be interesting, I think, is to notice these further points: With both attempts, even my *very talk of particles* may have been badly misleading, as was my *talk of a plenum*. As I'm suggesting, it may be that something's *being a particle* isn't ever a completely Nonqualitative matter. And, similarly, the question of whether there's a plenum, or a field, might not be wholly Nonqualitative. With the *Denial in place*, it may be that we're unable to think of a World as containing any *Particles*. When supposing the Denial to hold, and trying to think of a "Particulate World," perhaps the most we can do is to think, very abstractly and barely, about a physical World where "Quality-purged correlates of true Particles" are to play a certain role in the history of the World. And, with the Denial in place while trying to think of a "Plenumate World," perhaps the most we can do is think, just as abstractly, about a World where a "Quality-purged correlate of a true Plenum" is to play a perfectly parallel role or part, or maybe even the very same part, in the history of the World. With thoughts so abstract and bare, perhaps there's no significant difference between what we're barely thinking with the one attempt and what we're barely thinking with the other.

Now, while it might be wholly unnecessary for many readers, for some it may be very helpful to do this little exercise: Go back and reread the previous paragraph, or two, but, this time make absolutely sure you *don't do anything even remotely like* what, a few pages before, I took pains to *implore* you not to do: "When trying to think of a Particulate World, *don't do anything even remotely like*, say, thinking of *light gray* Spheres moving through a *dark gray* space or field; and, when attempting thoughts of a Plenumate World, don't do anything even remotely like thinking of dark gray Spheres moving through a light gray space or field!" Myself, I get very frustrated when trying to do anything much along any such severely restricted lines, becoming filled with nothing so much as the idea that, with the Denial in force, I'm never attaining any decently clear conception.

Maybe I should soften all this just a bit. Maybe there *is some* conception of spatially extended entities, even very well endowed with various reciprocal Propensities for various sorts of mutual interaction, but all of them spatial things that have no spatially Extensible Qualities. But, *if there is* some such conception, it's a notion that's only very barely available, and very partially available, to us quite limited human thinkers. In terms of a wholly Nonqualitative notion of concrete spatial things, if any such there be, we human thinkers can contemplate only terribly abstractly, and very partially and poorly indeed, whatever might be our world's spatial concrete things. By contrast with notions that allow us no more than such very poor thinking as that, I seek to articulate a conception of physical things that, should we employ it successfully, will allow us humans some fairly rich ideas, and some tolerably clear ideas, as to spatially extended concreta. And, as our exploration suggests, even just that much may be no easy job for a merely human philosopher.

5. Can Particles Rotate, but Not Plenumate Bubbles?

As it seems, a perfectly homogeneous and simple Particle, whether Spherical or another Shape, may rotate around an axis through its center, whether or not it moves translationally through space. Indeed, it seems that many such material spheres may all rotate quite differently. For one thing, even with their rotating axes all perfectly aligned, or all in parallel, different Spheres may revolve at different rotational speeds. For another, some may rotate in a clockwise direction (from a certain perspective) while others may rotate in the counterclockwise direction (from that very same perspective). And, of course, the axes of various Spheres might *not* be aligned in parallel; for example, the rotational axis of one Sphere may be perpendicular to the axes of some others, all having centers in the same plane, while at an irregular angle to the axes of still other rotating Spheres, centered in the same plane. When all three factors are combined, there will be great variety in the rotation of concrete Spheres, even among Particles all perfectly congruent.

By contrast, we don't have a similarly clear idea of a Spherical Bubble rotating about an axis, as Robert Fogelin pointed out to me. And, with that thought in mind, it may often seem that, while material bodies can rotate in empty space, empty Bubbles can't rotate in an (ocean-like) Plenum that may be said to include, or contain, the empty spatial regions. Is this a difference that's adequate for our clearly distinguishing between Particles in empty space and, on the other side, allegedly correlative empty regions within a Plenum? Is it a difference that shows our physical conceptions to have all the significance we've taken them to have?

Taking the second question first, we may note that, even if there's really a very intelligible difference just suggested, it's not enough to underwrite all the content we suppose for physical conceptions, which we take to be quite general notions. For we take these conceptions to be adequate for distinguishing between not just Particulate and Plenumate Worlds with supposed rotational motion, but, quite as well, Worlds where Particles move along *nonrotational* trajectories and, on the other side, Worlds where empty Bubbles move, or "move." So, however things may be for the allegedly very intelligible difference, it's at most only a relatively special conception that it may serve to have us grasp, not as general as our conception of the physical is supposed to be.

And, for the allegedly notable difference, matters quickly get much murkier, as with Particles, and with congruent Bubbles, that *aren't* shaped Spherically. Just as we seem to have a clear conception of an Ovoid Particle rotating in empty space, so we seem to have a clear conception, too, of a (congruent) Ovoid Bubble rotating, or "rotating," in an ocean-like Plenum. So, if the allegedly very intelligible difference allows us a clear distinction between correlative Plenumate and Particulate Worlds, it will be only a narrow range of pairs of such Worlds for which it allows us this presumed clarity.

(This point may be pressed. Now, rather than just thinking of perfectly round Spheres, let's think of nearly-spherical Particles each with a tiny bump on one side and, correlatively, we'll think of nearly-spherical Bubbles each similarly shaped. Or, for those who like symmetry, let's think of somewhat-spherical Particles with spikes that protrude symmetrically from the objects' centers, as with certain ornamental stars; and, correlatively, we'll think of Bubbles each similarly shaped. Either way, there seems no problem for thinking of the Bubbles as rotating, or "rotating."

Let's suppose that, whether they be shaped symmetrically or whether asymmetrically, our presumably rotating Particulate near-spheres have their little protrusions all become progressively smaller until, at the end of the alteration, they vanish entirely, yielding perfectly Spherical Particles. And, let's also suppose that, even so, they'll all continue to have just the suitably simple Propensity profiles that we've been supposing for the Particles. Now, we may ask: Will these Particulate objects also continue to rotate, even once they become Spheres; or, now that they're Spheres, will they first cease to rotate? And, we may answer, of course, that they'll continue to rotate.

Now, let's suppose our Bubbly nearly-spherical regions progressively become more spherical, even as they all rotate, until, at last, the result is just so many perfectly Spherical Bubbles. When it's first true that there are just these empty Spheres, will there then cease to be rotation of

Bubbles? Here, it's not so clear, as with the Particles, what's right to say. But, so far as I can see, this apparent difference, in just this very special situation, won't do much for any allegedly intelligible general distinction between Particulate Worlds and correlative Plenumate Worlds.)

Here's another perspective on these matters. As I think, it may cut deeper. Look, suppose that there really are certain (semantic) restrictions on our proper use of Plenumate terms, so that we can't properly say that an empty Spherical Bubble rotates, or even "rotates." How can any such (semantic) *restrictions* on "empty Spherical Bubble," apparently all to such a very negative effect, yield us a positively adequate grasp of a Plenumate World with Empty Bubbles, allowing us to distinguish, even in the face of holding onto the apparently impoverishing Denial, between Plenumate Worlds and Particulate Worlds? With the Denial fully in force, I can't see that it can do anything much at all. After all, a mere restriction on some terms can't, more positively, yield much about what it is to which we *can* properly apply the terms. So, just knowing that "rotating Bubble" is slightly more restricted than "rotating Particle," that can't be of much help in our clearly grasping how there may be a World with Particles, or how there may be a quite different correlative World with Bubbles, and with no Particles at all. To have more success in this quite fundamental conceptual task, what we may need, I'll suggest, is for a term to be properly employed only when it purports to denote, or to otherwise signify, something that's Spatially Extensibly Qualitied (whether it be a single Extensibly Qualitied Plenum that's so signified, replete with many Bubbles, or whether it be a Plenum with no empty interior space, or whether it be just so many spatially separated Particles that are each replete with Spatially Extensible Quality.) But, of course, so long as we suppose the Denial to hold true, we won't allow ourselves to see much success in any of this.[17]

6. Simple Attempts at Clear Conception
May Highlight Our Mystery

As we noted just a few paragraphs back, we take our physical conceptions to be pretty powerfully discriminative notions. By deploying them,

17. For raising the points that prompted this Section, I'm indebted to Robert Fogelin. For help with responding to the points, I'm indebted to discussion with Dean Zimmerman, both directly and through his referring me to the work of his student, Marc Scala. At the time I first wrote this Section, Scala's stimulating paper, "Homogeneous Simples," was unpublished. The published version is now in *Philosophy and Phenomenological Research*, 2002, pp. 393–397.

we take it, we may adequately discriminate not only among a wide variety of quite complex kinds of Worlds, but also, and quite equally, among various quite *simple* sorts of physical Worlds. So, for example, these conceptions should distinguish not only among various Worlds with both rotational and nonrotational motion, but also, and quite equally, among various Worlds with *only* nonrotational motion. Now, we may observe that, along the same general line, much more may be said.

In the attempts we've so far endeavored, at conceiving physical Worlds, we've aimed at conceiving some pretty simple (sorts of) Worlds. But, in some respects, the (sorts of) Worlds we aimed to conceive weren't so simple. So, rather than aiming to conceive a (sort of) World whose only (basic) physical objects are just two perfectly congruent Spherical Particles, in what then must be only an extremely simple array, we endeavored to conceive a (sort of) World with very many congruent Particles, all of them arranged in what was, no doubt, a very complex pattern, or distribution, or array. And, rather than aiming to conceive any (sort of) World where very few Spheres each move in a very simple (translational) trajectory, or maybe two quite different simple (sorts of) Worlds, a Particulate sort and a Plenumate sort, we tried to conceive Worlds, I presume, with many denizens moving in a very complex pattern of trajectories. To be sure, even with all that complexity in our endeavored conceiving, we had precious little success in our attempts at adequate conceiving. For, whatever we did with presumed Particles, we then did something correlative with presumed Bubbles, quite enough of a parallel to call the whole exercise into question.

The very same sort of perplexity and, perhaps, the very same sort of inadequacy, attends our attempts to conceive much simpler physical Worlds. So, for one thing, we may attempt to conceive a World with just two Particles always moving away from each other, along a perfectly straight line, always further and further apart, with no acceleration or deceleration. But, of course, we may equally imagine there to be a Plenum, whose only two Bubbles are "moving" away from each other in just such a simple manner. Now, just as more complex attempts are frustrated by such apparent parallels, so these simpler attempts are also frustrated from fastening on any simple Particulate World, or on any Plenumate World.

And, perhaps most simply of all, we may imagine two perfectly congruent Spherical Particles always perfectly at rest, neither moving together nor apart (nor, of course, rotating in any way.) But, how is it, now, that we have truly supposed there to be two Spherical Particles here, and not two perfectly empty Spherical Bubbles, in an otherwise perfectly homogenous Plenum? With our Denial still in force, I can't see us to have any success, with the presumed supposition.

In a philosophically famous thought experiment, Max Black asked his readers to suppose there to be a World whose sole objects, or inhabitants, are two precisely similar Spheres:

> Isn't it logically possible that the universe should have contained nothing but two exactly similar spheres? We might suppose that each was made of chemically pure iron, had a diameter of one mile, that they had the same temperature, colour, and so on, and that nothing else ever existed. Then every quality and relational characteristic of the one would also be a property of the other. Now if what if I am describing is logically possible, it is not impossible for two things to have all their properties in common.[18]

So that Black's passage may serve to clarify our issues, let's pass over questions concerning there being, in addition to the spheres, the iron atoms that compose the spheres, and any other such distractions. (And, certainly, let's pass over questions concerning any "mereological sum" of the spheres, or of any of their parts.) Better yet, to avoid all such questions, let's suppose our universe to contain nothing but two exactly similar basic material Spheres, in short two precisely similar (or congruent) Spherical Particles. But, even making things happily simple for ourselves, we won't really have made matters even the least bit happy—unless, of course, we no longer allow the Denial to be in force. For, without Particles that have Quality, how is it that we've supposed, really, that there's a World here with two physical Spheres in it, rather than supposing that there's a World with just one material entity, a vast Plenum perhaps, with two perfectly empty Spherical Bubbles? Maybe we haven't adequately made the former supposition, no more than we've made, doubtless unwittingly, an adequate supposition of a Plenum with just two congruent Bubbles.

With the Denial of Qualities still in force, we have no real success, I'll suggest, in making the sort of very contentful supposition Black intends. To my mind, this helps highlight our Mystery of the Physical.

7. Rejecting the Denial, but Postponing a Resolution of Our Mystery

Unless we reject the Denial of Qualities, in its First Formulation, we'll never be able to form anything like an adequate conception of physical

18. Max Black, "The Identity of Indiscernibles," *Mind*, 1952, page 156.

reality. For, we'll be denying ourselves any chance for our power to experience, and our related mental powers, to help inform us with a conception that's rich enough to be at all adequate to such a mind-independent reality or realm.

And, pretty obviously, we must also reject the Denial of Qualities, in its Second Formulation. If we *don't* have any adequate conception of *what's physically promoting* my perceptible brown desk *before* pondering the presumed quality of this complex physical thing, *we won't have any afterward either.* For this presumed brown quality, maybe the surface reflectance of the desk, is only a *physically derivative feature*, properly pertaining only to material complexes, and not to the matter that promotes such physically derivative complexes. To get anywhere with the Mystery of the Physical, we need to think about what qualities pertain to, and may be instanced in, the constituting matter itself, the physical reality that's presumably promoting.

What seems needed for any good start with this Mystery is, again, a chance for our power to experience, and our related mental powers, to help inform us with a conception that's rich enough to be at all adequate to such a mind-independent reality. And, it seems that, to make progress with this, we should explore how it is with *us*, in our own experiencing.

As I imagine, all this must be exceedingly difficult. As with anything central in philosophy, part of the reason for that is, of course, that we human beings are so limited in our thinking and our understanding. But, in the present instance, there's another large reason, more peculiar to recent work in mainstream philosophy. In doing this philosophy, almost always we're quite complacent about our Scientiphical Metaphysic. And, with this complacency, we can't help but suppose, time and time again, that the physical is really quite well conceived by us all.

Difficult as it may be for us to do it, we must break out of this habitual complacent thinking. We must do this, it's clear, if we're to make much headway with the Mystery of the Physical.

In the Chapter that's upcoming, I'll make a very great effort to avoid this habitual complacency. Rather radically, I'll do that by disallowing myself, in almost every passage, from thinking of myself as being much like the Scientiphical Metaphysic has me be, and by making the pretense, however implicitly, that there might not be any physical reality at all—even if there might be much mind-independent concrete reality, perhaps of some sort that we've never yet so much as even just tried to clearly conceive. That may serve to accomplish some pretty useful things.

First, and as is one of my aims, it may help us see how very much of what we believe most confidently, and that's of the first philosophical importance, may be appreciated, and sustained, even if it may be quite divorced from any presumed knowledge of physical reality.

Second, and another aim, it may help us move toward where we can reasonably deny some of our dominant Scientiphical Metaphysic, perhaps its most stultifying aspects, even while we may retain quite a lot of what it upholds or affirms.

And, third, it may help prepare us to see, at least somewhat well, how our power to experience may contribute to our having a conception of things physical that's rich enough to be at all adequate to physical reality.

To see how we might ever have such a conception, much more must be done. With the next Chapter's inquiry, we may be off to a good start.

2

A HUMANLY REALISTIC PHILOSOPHY

We human beings are quite limited, it's painfully plain, in our experiencing, our thinking and our understanding. Yet, even when mindful of our human limitations, perhaps we may aspire to a humanly intelligible philosophy of the world that, nonetheless, is a fairly substantial philosophy.

What might we expect of such a satisfying philosophy? In what follows, I provide some quite simple and obvious observations. And, I then attempt to articulate some instructive implications of my observations. The implications also may be features of a *Humanly Realistic Philosophy*.

1. I Am a Real Thinking Being and You Are Another

One thing we should want, in our humanly intelligible philosophy of the world, is an idea as to *what are the real entities of the world*, maybe far from comprehensive, but at least pretty accurate so far as it goes.

Though we should expect to add various further things to our idea of what's real, I should start by observing that *I am a real entity*. And, not only is it plain to me that I'm a real entity, as plain as is possible with any substantive matter, it's just as obvious that *I think and I experience*. All in a package, I'll say that, as is quite obvious to me, *I'm a real thinking experiencer* or, in more traditional terms that here will mean the same, I'm a real *thinking being*.[1]

In this I closely follow "the father of modern philosophy," René Descartes. For what I here mean by "experience" is, unless otherwise noted, just *conscious experience*. (So, as I typically use "experience," it's redundant to say, even if it's often also emphatic to say, that we experience consciously.) And, though he's only a human being, and so quite limited in his thinking and understanding, I continue to follow Descartes, quite closely, in thinking that, in *some* philosophically important sense, it's *more obvious to me that I* exist, and I think, and I experience, than it is that *you* do. And, in such a sense, it's also *more* obvious to me that I think and I experience than it is that, at least from

---

1. Though I'm never dogmatic about the issue, and maybe I shouldn't ever claim absolute certainty in the matter, I proceed on the idea that any philosophy that denies my existence, or that doesn't have me be a real being, is, I think, a philosophy that should be rejected by me, and by you too, I think.

Indeed, the only considerations I've ever found to threaten this proposition pretty persuasively, and maybe even that's putting the point too strongly, are challenges to the effect that there's never really been, for human beings at least, any coherent concept of human beings, and any real natural languages. At least for the most part, these are the familiar challenges stemming from such ancient sources as the paradox of the liar and the sorites paradox. For some sorites-style thoughts to some such dismal effects, if you've lots of time, you might look at one of these three old papers of mine: "There Are No Ordinary Things," *Synthese*, 1979, "I Do Not Exist," in G. F. MacDonald, ed., *Perception and Identity*, Macmillan, 1979, and, the one I believe to be most ambitious, and—maybe, the most insightful—"Why There Are No People," *Midwest Studies in Philosophy*, 1979. As will make things convenient for many readers, these papers all are reprinted in a new collection of my (selected) published essays, *Philosophical Papers, Volume 2*, Oxford University Press, 2006.

(Here's a quasi-historical aside: For those few interested in tracking my published thoughts through the years, later I took a more positive stance on these matters, most saliently in my book *Identity, Consciousness and Value*, Oxford University Press, 1990. In that work, see pages 191–210 and, especially, pages 219–223. As I now suspect, it was in the earlier, more "nihilistic" writing that I was more nearly correct. But, as the rest of this note makes clear, for the present work, none of that need concern us much. Now, it's back to the note's main thrust.)

Now, if some such paradoxes really are as effectively challenging as they sometimes strangely seem, then, at this point, it might not be not possible for me to advance any substantive philosophy, as even the very formulation of any substantive view, however partial and sketchy, might await adequate conceptual invention (and, I suppose, adequate linguistic invention). But, in these pages, my whole purpose is to advance a substantive view, indeed, a reasonably ambitious philosophy of reality. So, here, it's clearly most appropriate to say, at the least, that any acceptable philosophy must recognize a plurality of distinct real beings, you and I among them.

About apparently threatening sorites arguments, and about what I call "vague discriminative terms," interested readers may look, rather briefly, I hope, at the appendix I've appended to Chapter 7 of this book. But, please do make that brief. If you don't do it directly, I hope that it's in only a few minutes that you'll return to the body of this present Chapter, just up above.

time to time, I *choose what to do from among actual alternatives* for my own thoughtful activity, at least for my own thinking.

In advancing a Humanly Realistic Philosophy, however, I'll hardly ever make much of any such differences in plainness, obviousness, or certainty. For as I've argued many times over, and at very considerable length, I suspect that anything remotely like that may be impossible for us ever to attain.[2] In this way, then, I *don't* follow Descartes closely, as I

---

2. Very blatantly I first did this, publicly and for the permanent record, in my paper "A Defense of Skepticism," *Philosophical Review*, 1971, now conveniently reprinted in the new collection of my (selected) published *Philosophical Papers, Volume 1*. A little later, I did it in a related paper, where the focus was more on the normative aspect of knowledge: "An Argument for Skepticism," *Philosophic Exchange*, 1974, now also reprinted in my *Philosophical Papers*. Just slightly later still, and perhaps most prominently, I provided a very sustained effort, to such a very skeptical effect, in my first book, *Ignorance: A Case for Scepticism*, Clarendon Press, 1975, reprinted by the Oxford University Press in 2002. With at least a bit of force, in *Ignorance* I argued, against Descartes, that none of us ever knows—not for certain, anyhow—that he or she currently thinks, or that he or she currently exists. Some several years later still, I offered substantially more forceful argumentation to the same skeptical (anti-Cartesian effect) in my "Skepticism and Nihilism," *Nous*, 1980, reprinted in my *Philosophical Papers*.

Finally for now, so far as my early publications are concerned, here's something I noticed only in retrospect, though the first retrospective insight occurred decades ago: In my very old paper "An Analysis of Factual Knowledge," *Journal of Philosophy*, 1968, also reprinted in my *Philosophical Papers*, I argued for the striking claim that someone knows something to be so if, but only if, it is *not at all* accidental that the person is right about that thing's being so. Now, on lenient uses of "it's not at all accidental," no headway will be made from there to skepticism. But, on a strict use of the term, which really may be the only quite correct and literal usage, a very great deal of headway might be made.

(This will be true, I suspect, despite all sorts of currently modish *contextualist* shenanigans—all started by me and my old partner in crime—dear old David Lewis, of course. Though David was, apparently, always steadfast about this slippery stuff, I've been mighty suspicious of it all, for at least some several years now. On the start of the suspected shenanigans, first see David's stimulating old paper "Scorekeeping in a Language Game," *Journal of Philosophical Logic*, 1979, reprinted in David Lewis, *Philosophical Papers*, vol. 1, Oxford University Press, 1983. And, then, see my quasi-anarchistic old book *Philosophical Relativity*, University of Minnesota Press and Blackwell, 1984; reprint, Oxford University Press, 2002.)

At all events, throughout this present book, I never seek to advance any claim about our (allegedly) knowing this thing, that thing or the other. Nor am I concerned, in these pages, about whether such concepts as that of a reason for believing (or for wanting, or for acting) are coherent notions. As far as I'm concerned, right now, it makes no difference whether anyone ever has any *reason* to believe anything at all. What I am concerned to observe, by contrast, are items of just this simpler sort: I do believe that, in addition to myself, there are other sentient beings. And, then, I take things from there, so to say, arriving at some other things I may well believe. Or, as may happen on other occasions, I'll be arriving at certain hopeful hypotheses that, in some weak sense of "accept," perhaps, I accept into my Philosophy. Or, as may happen at still other times, I'll arrive at only something that, for the first time in a long time, I'll take seriously.

As far as anything seriously normative goes, or anything that's heavily epistemological, this book's project is a quite neutral effort or, at least, that's how it's intended.

never seek any real certainty, or any absolute knowledge, or any complete lack of doubtfulness.

At all events, and quite unlike Descartes, I start by also observing that not only am I right now a real thinking experiencer, but, as is also plenty obvious enough, for quite a substantial time, *I've been* a real thinking experiencer, thinking and experiencing varyingly. Indeed, as compared with all the thinking I've already done, the bit I'm involved in right now is, just by itself, extremely paltry and quite narrowly limited. And, compared with all the experiencing I've already been through, the little I'm just now enjoying is almost monotonous. For example, right now I seem to smell nothing at all, while at certain earlier times I've enjoyed happily impressive smells, as with the smell of roses. So, *over quite a substantial period of time, I've thought, and I've experienced, pretty widely and rather variously.*

I also observe that, now as before, I am hardly the only real thinking being; it's also plenty obvious enough, at least to me, that *there are now, and there long have been, many other thinking experiencers.* And, in particular, it's plenty plain that *you are a real thinking being,* whom I now address in writing, and whom, as you're my student, colleague, or friend (please suppose) I've earlier addressed in speaking. And, it's also quite obvious, of course, that, much as have many other thinking experiencers, over quite a substantial period of time, *you've* thought, and *you've* experienced, pretty widely and rather variously.

Here's something else that's rather obvious, even if not so very obvious as most of the points already observed: When I express my thoughts to you, often I successfully communicate with you. And, similarly, you effectively communicate with me, too. As is quite obvious enough to me, we've successfully communicated with each other as to even our innermost thoughts and experiences.

I trust that a little imaginative exercise can make the point more vivid: Closing our eyes for a few moments, each of us is to imagine a solid figure, a cylinder, for example, that, transparently through and through, is a single spectral color, for instance, orange. You'll choose yours and, independently, I'll choose mine. And, then, each of us is to divulge to the other what he chose to imagine. Well, we each do our chosen little bit of imagining. Then, most sincerely and truly, I tell you that I imagined a blue sphere, maybe by saying the words "I just imagined a blue sphere." And, just as truly and sincerely, you tell me that you imagined a red cube, saying the words "Me, I imagined a red cube." As is plenty plain enough, by the end of this exercise I'll have quite a good idea, really, as to how it was with you experientially when you imagined as you just did. And, as is also plenty sure, you'll know, rather well, actually, how it was with me when I imagined my blue sphere. But, of course, there was nothing notably new or unusual in this imaginative exercise. So, now what I said was obvious to me should be vividly clear to you: *We've successfully communicated with each other as to what are even our innermost thoughts and experiences.*

About as obvious to me as the fact that we often communicate with each other successfully, even as regards our innermost thought and experience, is the fact that, at least from time to time, I choose what to do from among real alternatives for my own thoughtful activity. To make this vivid, recall our little imaginative exercise. As it happened, I chose to imagine a blue sphere. But, this was not my only real alternative. It was also open to me to imagine a red cube, or, for that matter, an orange cylinder. Indeed, it was perfectly possible for me not to have exercised my visually imaginative powers at all. To me, this is just about as obvious as your communicating to me, so successfully, how it was for you experientially, with the red cube you imagined. So, in attempting a Humanly Realistic Philosophy, I also start with this pretty plain observation: *At least from time to time, I choose what to do from among real alternatives for my own thoughtful activity.*

Having made even just these simple observations, I've taken on board far more than Descartes allowed himself at the start. But, of course, even as my main purpose is very different from his, my way of proceeding should be quite different.

In the rest of this Chapter, I'll seek to articulate some philosophically important implications of my rather simple and obvious observations.

2. We Are Differentially Responsive Individuals

How is it that, sometimes when there's thinking, it's *me* who is thinking; and how is it that, quite distinct from any of that, sometimes it's *you* who's thinking, not me at all? And, how is it that there's *some* experience that's *your* experience, and there's *some other* experience that's *mine*?

Each of us has a *power to think*, and a power to experience. Or, if, in apparent rebellion against Lockean tradition, you take "power" to be an overly grandiose term, then say that there's my capacity to think, or my disposition toward thinking, or my *Propensity* to think, and, equally but separately, there's *your* Propensity to think. When *my* power to think is exercised, or *my* Propensity is manifested, then *I actually do think*. And, conversely, *unless* there's the exercise of *this mental power of mine*, or unless there is the manifestation of *my Propensity* toward thinking, *I really do not* think. Similarly, unless there is the manifestation of *your disposition* to experience visually, it *won't be you* that experiences visually, however much visual experiencing may be going on. As each of us is a numerically distinct being who actually does think, each of us is a distinct *mentally Propensitied* individual.

Now, having suspended our discussion of the Mystery of the Physical, I've temporarily disallowed myself thoughts as to any physical reality and, in the bargain, as to any spatial relations among any concreta. So, I don't look to grasp, here and now, how things may be with distinct concrete beings that, at every moment of their existence, are always precisely similar and, perhaps for good measure, are always perfectly symmetric, in all their "external relations." Towards the end of the book, I'll address this interesting topic. But, not here and now.

In this limited Chapter, with so very much disallowed, it's worth noting, I imagine, several salient (intrinsic) differences among all actual people currently here on earth. In fact, no two of us are precisely alike; indeed, it's not even a close call. In fact, when considering just our preferences, one of the many respects in which we differ, we notice considerable variation between people, along with undoubted commonality: while there are many things—including many precise sorts of experience—that the both of us like equally, there are many others about which we greatly differ. There are some that you like enormously and I don't like at all, and there are others where the reverse holds true. In all ordinary situations, these differences between us are quite enough to make plain, even to the most distant outsider, that each of us is a numerically distinct concrete individual. Will most readers find the previous few sentences more helpful than confusing? I hope so. Anyhow, I return to the Chapter's main business.

Well, my power to think is a *differentially responsive mental Propensity*: the specific (way of) thinking that I actually manifest, at any given time, is but one of many that, even at that very time, I have a Propensity to manifest. Just so, my power to think may be manifested, in some situations, in my thinking that someone has just told me something true. And, in some *other* situations, where it's quite different considerations that engage with me, this selfsame mental power may be manifested in my thinking someone's just told me something *untrue*. And, in *still* other situations, where what I encounter is very different still, my power to think may be manifested in my thinking that recently nobody's told me *anything at all*, true, untrue or neither. So, to a large degree, how my power to think is actually manifested, at any given time, will depend on what's my situation at the time, including what considerations I'm then confronting, or considering.

Those general remarks seem quite right. But, we want a better grasp of what they entail.

As a start toward that, we'll suppose that I have labored hard to draw a certain metaphysical distinction, say, that between my Propensity to feel emotions variously and, on the other side, my feeling happy on a particular occasion. I may then consider the question of whether, in my own immediate experiencing, this mental power's *current manifestation*, my currently feeling quite happy, will be more fully available to me experientially than is the whole Propensity toward feeling emotions. In response to considering this yes-or-no question, I emphatically think "Yes!"

Now, let's suppose that, contrary to fact, I considered the converse question, whether, in my own immediate experiencing, this *whole Propensity toward feeling* will be more fully available to me than is the power's current manifestation, again, my currently feeling happy. And, let's suppose that, in response to considering this quite *opposite* question, I should *also* emphatically think "Yes!"

Much more extravagantly still, we may suppose this much: At the time in question, *no matter what* I should (be supposed to) consider— whether I like to drink paint, whether green is more like red than it's like blue, I'll then respond with the same old emphatic mental "Yes!"

Though we've hardly covered every base in the complex field of human psychology, by this point we're getting fairly close to where there's precious little substance in the proposal that, at the time in question, I have the power to think about "yes-or-no questions." And, if it were supposed that "I" then have *no* differentially responsive mental Propensity at all, then there wouldn't be supposed a real thinking being. Instead, there'd be supposed, at the most, just such a *nondifferentially* responsive entity as would enjoy something like a certain subvocal experiential modification, perhaps labeled aptly with our inscriptions of "Yes!" At all events, the supposed entity would lack the power to think and, so, it won't ever think at all.

As I imagine, we've just made some progress toward understanding how it is that the power to think must be a differentially responsive mental Propensity, toward grasping how it is that a real thinker must respond differentially to different considerations, or to some of them at least, that the thinker may consider. Still, it may be useful to offer clarifying illustrations.

So, let's consider an analogous case that's far simpler, an example that features nothing so impressive as real mentality. We'll consider a pocket calculator or, if you like, a very simple really old-fashioned adding machine. Now, if you push the 7-button on your machine, and then the plus-button, and then the 5-button, and then the equals-button, the machine will display [12]. As we should take it, this machine "added" 5 to 7 and arrived at 12 as their sum. Next, consider a look-alike object that, upon having just such buttons just so sequentially pressed, also displays [12]. But, *unlike* your machine, this lookalike device displays [12], and only [12], *no matter which sequence* of (four or more) buttons are pressed. This machine *doesn't* add 7 and 5 to yield 12, nor does it ever add at all. (Nor can the lookalike, just as it is, be used by thoughtful beings really to add 7 and 5.) That's because, unlike your machine, this lookalike *isn't differentially Propensitied*, at least not in any way relevant to being a calculator.

A far more impressive object than the monotonous lookalike, your machine *is* differentially Propensitied in relevant ways. When you press its 7-button, and then its plus-button, and then its *4-button*, then (unless it's broken, or things are otherwise amiss), it *won't* display [12]. (Presumably, it will display [11]. And, if it doesn't now display [11], then your supposed calculator is blatantly limited or, more likely, it's poorly made or badly broken.)

Placing aside the useless "one-track" lookalike object, let's continue to consider your differentially Propensitied device. At any time, its *power to add*, if I may so verbally dignify the Propensity in focus, is, at best, only very partially available in your experience: At the time in question, or during that brief episode of its use, there's *just the one manifestation* of its additive Propensity, which we may loosely label as 7, +, 5, =, [12]. At that time, there *isn't* available in your experience, not even quite indirectly, any manifestation that we may well label as 7, +, 4, =, [11], *nor* any we should label as 5, +, 7, =, [12], and so on. At *that* time, there *are no other* manifestations at all. And, so, beyond the actual manifestation noted, there's *nothing for you to* experience at all. Nonetheless, you know well enough that, at the very time in question, your machine has the power "to add." Not all objects are as monotonous as that useless lookalike. And, as you well enough know, your differentially Propensitied calculator is among them.

Much as it is with the lookalike object that displays [12] no matter what sequence of its buttons are pressed, so it also is with the supposed "thinker" that suffers a subvocal "Yes!" no matter what "considerations" just previously occur to, or in, it. And, on the positive side of our analogy, much as it is with the crude instance of your calculator's manifesting its power to add when it manifests 7, +, 5, =, [12], so it is with you manifesting your power to think when you answer "Yes!" to our supposed metaphysical "yes-or-no" question.

Indeed, in at least two respects, the case is clearer with your real thinking than with your effective calculator: First, even as the Propensities of an effective calculator are pretty impressively differentially responsive, the mental Propensities required for you really to think about anything, much less about matters metaphysical, must be *far more richly* differentially responsive. These mental Propensities must be, indeed, richly differentially responsive in ways whose details we mere humans can hardly hope to imagine. And, second, of course, when you yourself are thinking, you know full well, or as well as anyone ever knows anything substantive, that *you're really thinking*.

There are, of course, many other substantial differences between what goes on with your thinking and what occurs with a mere calculator's "adding." But, for highlighting the points central to our subject, a specification of them is a detrimental distraction.

Now, in articulating what's involved in your power to think, even just so far as I've just managed, I described various scenarios only one of which could possibly be, at any given time, your actual situation. So, in describing more than one, I resorted to employing conditional sentences. But this should *not* lead us to think that your power is something you have only conditionally, or, indeed, that there's anything more conditional with your power than there is with, say, an episode of your thinking. Not at all. The fact that, at a certain time, you have the *power* to think is no more conditional than the fact that, at the time, you imagine a blue sphere. To be sure, I may very usefully employ conditional sentences in making clearer many ideas about you and your thinking. For example, I may say that if it's your power to think that's manifested in the imagining of a blue sphere, then it's you who'll be thinking in the course of that imagining. But, there's nothing of any great philosophical depth, nor of any metaphysical moment at all, in any of these clarifying comments.

Of course, it's a perfectly general point that there's nothing fundamentally conditional about powers, or dispositions, or Propensities. As C. B. Martin has often emphasized, the point applies whether what's in focus is the electrical power of an insensate electron, supposing there are such basic enough physical entities, or whether it be your power to think, or my power to experience.[3]

Any philosophy that denies the reality of my thinking, or its distinctness from your real thinking, is a philosophy, I think, that we should reject. If the fact of your thinking requires you to have your very

3. As in, among other writings, his contributions to D. M. Armstrong, C. B. Martin and U. T. Place, *Dispositions: A Debate* (ed. Tim Crane), Routledge, 1996.

own richly differentially responsive mental powers, as surely it does, then our philosophy must have it that you do indeed have your very own richly differentially responsive mental powers. Of course, that's firmly affirmed in the Humanly Realistic Philosophy we're advancing.

From focusing on our thinking, I turn to focus on our experiencing. Now, just maybe the concept of experience is extremely lenient and, unlike with thinking, experiencing doesn't require a differentially responsive mental Propensity on the part of an entity that's engaged in it. Just maybe there could be some mutant clams, say, that always sense perfectly monotonously. While I suspect that's not really a coherent suggestion, I don't really know. But, for assessing the claims to be made in our Humanly Realistic Philosophy, we needn't know about that. For, it's plenty obvious that *our own* experiencing, or at least much of it, *is differentially responsive experiencing*. Here's one example of what that means: Should my immediate experience be as of my wife's enjoying success in her pursuits, then, typically, I respond by experiencing happiness, or by feeling happy. And, here's another: Should my experience be, instead, as of her being embroiled only in trouble and failure, then, typically, I will respond by experiencing unhappiness, or by feeling unhappy.

Again I've used conditional sentences, now using the "should" form of locution. But, of course, my power to experience isn't riddled with conditionality, whatever that might mean. I'll try to put the point with jargon that's helpful: My power to experience is *categorical*, or *nonconditional*; it's as categorical an aspect of *me*, right now, as is my *feeling happy*, the power's present *manifestation*.

Even when properly taking powers to be perfectly real, we should accept nothing less than this: Any philosophy that denies that we are richly differentially responsive Propensitied experiencers is a philosophy to be denied. But, of course, our Humanly Realistic Philosophy affirms that each of us has quite rich powers of experiencing, insisting even that, at any moment, each of us manifests only an extremely minute aspect of, or extraordinarily tiny fraction of, her full experiential power.

3. Against Descartes, We Are Intermittently Conscious Individuals

Descartes famously held that, at every moment of his existence, he was, and must be, conscious. This profoundly philosophical thought is decidedly contrary to our commonsense belief. And, though I'm hardly the greatest friend of common sense, I think that here Descartes is in error.

Descartes also held that his existence wasn't ever temporally intermittent, or interrupted. By contrast with his belief that he always was conscious, this philosophical thought accords fairly well, I think, with commonsense thinking. And, as I think it's at least roughly right, I won't contest this second proposition.

Because he held (incorrectly) that he must always be conscious, along with holding (correctly) that he existed quite continuously, Descartes held, against common sense (and incorrectly) that there never were any periods of his sleep, in any night or day, when he wasn't conscious; it *only appeared that way*. What really happened in his deepest sleep, he held, is that he completely forgot a conscious thought, or that he just failed to remember it, immediately after, quite consciously, he did think the thought.[4]

A Humanly Realistic Philosophy wants a more plausible view of the matter: When you come to be completely unconscious, as may well happen in deepest sleep, or with a powerful anaesthetic, it may come to be that your power to experience isn't manifested even while you still exist, complete with that mental power then unmanifested.

For just a moment, I'll go out on a limb, just a tiny little bit, to offer an "instructive speculation" that's radically opposed to Descartes's position. In addition to having a Propensity toward experience, quite certainly manifested in certain conditions, you may also have a real Propensity toward *unconsciousness*. So, even as your Propensity to experience will be manifested in *just certain* conditions, this opposite Propensity may be manifested in many *other* conditions. Generally, when you're well rested and going about your business, your Propensity *to* experience is manifested. But, when you're extremely tired, or when you pass out from drinking lots of alcohol, then, not only will *it*

---

4. See Descartes's *Author's Replies to the Fifth Set of Objections*, as available in *The Philosophical Writings of Descartes*, vol. II, translated by J. Cottingham, et. al., Cambridge University Press, 1984. The most pertinent paragraph is, in this volume, on pages 246–247:

> You say you want to stop and ask whether I think the soul always thinks. But why should it not always think, since it is a thinking substance? It is no surprise that we do not remember the thoughts that the soul had when in the womb or in a deep sleep, since there are many other thoughts that we equally do not remember, although we know we had them when grown up, healthy and wide-awake. So long as the mind is joined to the body, then in order for it to remember thoughts which it had in the past, it is necessary for some traces of them to be imprinted on the brain; it is by turning to these, or applying itself to them, that the mind remembers. So is it really surprising if the brain of an infant, or a man in deep sleep, is unsuited to receive these traces?

No stranger to all this, I discuss Descartes's views, on this and related matters to be explored here shortly, in my *Identity, Consciousness and Value*, especially on pages 45–47.

cease being manifested, but, there *will be manifested*, instead, your diametrically *opposite Propensity*, your Propensity *not to* experience.

Think about it for a minute. Do you think that, when you've passed out, for example, and you aren't experiencing, it's just mere happenstance that, right then, you're not experiencing? No; not at all. Far from it's being the least bit coincidental that, shortly after having downed a liter of high-proof whiskey, you weren't experiencing at all, it was, rather, that the situation was like this. With your brain then quite differently configured, or with some other suitable shift in you, or in your immediate interaction partners, there's then (satisfied the conditions for) the manifestation of your Propensity *not to* experience.

Well, so much for my not-very-speculative little "speculation." Now, some much less ambitious words of opposition: Whether or not you have a Propensity for unconsciousness, there's no question but that, when you're unconscious, you still have your power to experience. It's just that this power of yours isn't manifested. And, even as you still have this power, so do you still exist. Let me elaborate on this sensible, unambitious point.

Sometimes, in deep sleep people think intelligently, but unconsciously. Sometimes, they awaken to find they have the solution to a hard problem that they lacked the day before. When in sound sleep, their power to think intelligently is, apparently, still being exercised, though their Propensity to think consciously is not. When this happens, their power to think may be exercised greatly while their power to experience might be manifested not at all.

At other times, say, when stunned by some shocking experience, many people can't think intelligently, even though they remain quite awake. When in such stunned stupid awareness, a person's power to think consciously is, evidently, still manifested. Not so with her power to think intelligently. As seems clear, that power's then "blocked by" what's so shocking. Or, maybe better, in consequence of her being so shocked, there isn't, at that time, (the satisfaction of conditions conducive to) the manifestation of the person's power to think intelligently.

But, of course, that's not all. Or, do you think that, right upon the shock, it was just quite happenstantial that the stunned person, though he was still thinking consciously, didn't think intelligently? Of course, you don't. Rather, a more credible fullish description of what happened runs much more like this. The suddenly stunned person *then didn't* think intelligently *because her Propensity not to* think intelligently was then manifested (as there *then* obtained conditions so conducive to *its* manifestation).

Even as all that is, doubtless, quite true, at least this much is pretty certainly true. Just as you may exist while your power to think intelligently isn't manifested, so you may exist, quite equally, while your power to think consciously isn't manifested. Indeed, you may exist, quite certainly, while neither power is manifested, or exercised, or activated, at all.

4. Our Realistic Response to Descartes Raises a Problem of Our Unconscious Quality

When I'm conscious, there's no mystery, to me, about what's my *qualitative character*. Sometimes it involves my experiencing visually and not auditorally, sometimes the converse holds, and sometimes my character has, at once, both a visual and an auditory aspect.

Now, though I'm no expert on philosophy's history, so far as I can tell, in consultation with experts, Descartes did not think much about, nor did he care much about, questions of qualitative character. For him, apparently, you might *consciously* think that you exist, for example, while having, even right then, no qualitative character at all. But, if you're *consciously* thinking something, you're then *not just* thinking, but you're *also experiencing*. And, in that you're experiencing, you must have some qualitative character; indeed, specifically, you then must have some *experiential quality*. This may be a deficiency, in Descartes's philosophy. But, no matter; for it's very easy to remedy. For a Cartesian position that's quite fully intelligible, we may enrich Descartes's severe view, with apt ideas as to qualitative character. Already, we've done enough of that to proceed productively, with our discussion of imagining a red cube, or imagining a blue sphere, and with our points about feeling happy, and feeling unhappy. (In the course of the book, I'll be doing this more, and more, and more.) So, let's proceed with what are, for me here, the central questions.

Well, then, when I'm *wholly unconscious, how is it with me qualitatively?* Suppose that, following Descartes, we hold that we're nonphysical mental beings, entirely lacking in spatiality. Then, even if an insensate physical thing each has qualitative character, whatever that might be, still, it won't be enough for any of us, when unconscious, to have any quality. Anyhow, what are we to think about ourselves here? When we're wholly unconscious, do we then have *only* powers, or Propensities, and *no quality* at all? The suggestion seems perfectly empty. So, as it seems to me, there's a problem here for a Dualist Metaphysic, the Problem of our Unconscious Quality, which Descartes can handle only quite heroically. And, he does this, in effect, by heroically holding that we never are unconscious.

Now, this Problem also needs a treatment from Materialist philosophers and, indeed, from all those holding with our Scientiphical Metaphysic. And, preferably, the treatment shouldn't be heroic. Whether such a nice treatment's ever available will depend, I imagine, on whether there's a nice resolution of a difficulty that, for all Scientiphicalists, may be a larger problem. I refer, of course, to the Mystery of the Physical, a Problem whose treatment is postponed until the next Chapter.

For serious Substantial Dualists, at all events, the Problem of Our Unconscious Quality looks to be a rather serious difficulty. Near the end of the book, I'll try to offer a Dualistic treatment of this Problem that's not an overly heroic response. But, that's then, and this is now. Right now, let's notice some further features of a Humanly Realistic Philosophy.

5. Against Hume's Restriction, Human Understanding Transcends Human Experience

Among us mere human beings, it's hard to do better than David Hume's *Treatise* for deeply thoughtful and challenging work in philosophy. But, if we follow Hume more than just a very little, we'll have no chance, of course, to advance a philosophy that's even very modestly ambitious. This is not to say that an acceptable philosophy must avoid all substantial Humean influence, or every Humean aspect. But, it does mean that, in reasonably ambitious attempts at a Humanly Realistic Philosophy, we should employ conceptions Hume would have us avoid. Indeed, even with the few thoughts this Chapter's already considered, we've seen enough to make this compelling and clear.

I don't pretend to advances in Hume scholarship, no more than I take myself to make scholarly contributions to Cartesian studies. Rather, I want only to have us explore a certain aspect of Hume's enormous appeal. In that way, perhaps we may earn a sensible liberation from Hume's most constraining requirements.

As a check on what he took to be our rather empty philosophical pretensions, sometimes with much justice, Hume suggested we adhere to quite strict demands of experience. Briefly but usefully, we may render his injunction like this: (At least if you're to be fully justified in what you believe, including even those beliefs of yours most deeply and directly involved in your philosophically most ambitious endeavors) you should believe to be real entities only such things as are *fully available* to you in your own *direct experience*; about these available entities, you should believe *only so much as* is fully available to you in your direct experience.

Here are some examples to help with what that means: A certain feeling of heat may count as an entity fully available to you in your direct experience. But, as it's conceived by Locke and, I daresay, by us, too, not so with a hot sticky-bun. Quite as it's so fully available in your direct experience, the feeling of heat, or the felt heat, is presumed free of anything so suspect, and so unavailable, as a real Propensity or power. By contrast, the hot sweet bun itself will be, we presume, replete with powers and, so, it won't be fully available. For example, as it's a hot individual, the bun should have the Propensity to transfer heat to colder Propensitied particulars or individuals. And, as it's presumably sweet, it should have the power to affect you, a typical human taster, in certain experiential ways, under certain familiar conditions. And, while these conditions might be fulfilled, it also might be that, in fact, they are never fulfilled. Now, all this business about such a variably and elusively powerful particular won't be anything like fully available in your direct experience. So, here's Hume: As you should reject pretentious thought, you should accept only the feeling to be a real entity, and maybe the felt quality, but not any such supposedly powerful particular as the bun itself is supposed to be.

As Hume allows, you may feel felt heat. But, what is this *experiencer*, you yourself, of course, *that feels* this felt quality? Are you something that, in your direct experience, is fully available to yourself? Well, you are a differentially responsive Propensitied particular. Indeed, during almost any pretty short period of your life—anything that, when being most properly metaphysical you'll take to be *the present time*, there'll be, in actual fact, only some very few manifestations of what are, at that very time, your richly differentially responsive mental Propensities, or powers. So, right now, as I imagine, you're not hearing sounds characteristic of songbirds, though you have the mental Propensity to have auditory experience like that. Anyhow, your actual auditory experiencing is only a tiny sample, so to say, of all the auditory experiencing of which you're now capable. And, you're not having visual experience as of gold, or silver, I'll imagine, though you're fully able, right now, to enjoy just such visual experiencing. And, until I'm just mentioning it now, you weren't thinking about mighty mountains, though you had the capacity, then as now, to think about majestic peaks. Because you're a highly differentially responsive Propensitied particular, *extremely little* of your impressively powerful nature will ever be, in your direct experience, fully available to you.

What's more, the vast majority of what are, for you, your real experiential possibilities, you'll never manifest, or actualize. You'll never even come anywhere close to doing that, not even throughout your whole existence, or lifetime. Just think about it: There are many strange songbirds whose songs you'll never hear, if only because you'll never be close enough to them to have such auditory experiences. Nor will you ever have any auditory experience, not even in a dream, that's qualitatively very like those experiences. And, there are many strange sights that, though you're visually well enough endowed to enjoy such experiences, you'll never experience the likes of. And, though you'll enjoy the experiences that come your way when reading certain narratives, there are many other such experiences, engendered by perusing other stories and novels, that you'll never happen to suffer or enjoy. All this is quite obvious. Though your power to experience is certainly limited, your actual experiencing, even over your whole lifetime, is far more limited.

Similarly, though my power to think is notably limited, all my actual thinking will be much more limited still. For instance, since I engage in a very great deal of thinking about metaphysics, I don't engage in so much thinking of other sorts, on other subjects. Though I have the power to think in various of these other ways, I don't do so very much, I suppose, by way of manifesting my power in these other modes or directions.

Not with any great constancy, it seems to me, but, still, and as a rather general rule, Hume allowed that you have available in your direct experience, apparently quite fully enough, whatever is so experientially available to you throughout your whole existence. He did not require, nor did he even regularly suggest, that you should believe to be real entities only such things as are *fully available* to you in your own direct *momentary* experience; nor did he require that, about such perfectly present entities, you should believe *only so much as* is fully available to you in your perfectly present and direct momentary experience. For several reasons, it was only natural that he not require so *very* much as *that*. Yet, it pays to explore this terribly severe requirement.

At any experiential moment, we've already agreed, I have no great variety of impressions. Sometimes I feel heat, but usually not. And, as well, only sometimes do I feel cold. Very rarely do I feel both at once. And, right now, I can assure you, isn't any such very rare time as that. And, so it is with love and hatred, and pain and pleasure. Since you're a very human being, quite like me, I suppose, the same is true of you. So, if you were restricted to what your *present moment* experience makes fully available to you, you'd have available a very poor corpus of

(Humean) *impressions* indeed. With just that as your working basis, you'd never get far at all in trying to do any substantial philosophy or, for that matter, anything else of intellectual interest.

After all, we can't have serviceable (Humean) *ideas*, of course, except insofar as we've impressions that service them. But, all this is blatantly obvious. So, it's also obvious that if he imposed a temporal restriction on us that's so extraordinarily severe as what we're discussing, there'd be little we could learn from Hume. But, of course, he didn't do that.[5]

Hume's directive, that you accept only what's so very available in your own direct experience, is enormously more appealing than the blatantly stultifying directive that you accept only what's so available in your own momentary, perfectly present direct experience. But, at the end of the day, as I've been arguing, Hume's directive really isn't any more tenable. In your own direct (very human) experience, over the course of your whole (very human) existence, not even your own mental powers can be fully available to you, much less any of my quite distinct powers. Yet, even in your most theoretical frame of mind, you should accept the idea that, right now, you have a terribly rich power to think, manifested only very partially, indeed, in how it is that you're now actually thinking. And, right now, you have the Propensity to experience very differently from just how it is that, right now, you're actually experiencing.

5. For my main purposes, it's best to leave this matter just with that. So, in the text, I do. For some other fine philosophic purposes, however, it may be well to make further remarks. So, here I do.

Especially for Hume's own writing on the subject, but quite intuitively for us, too, there's a problem about how it might be that, not in memory, but in actual experience itself, you can apprehend temporal change, even when it's you yourself that's changing, from being in more pain to being in much less. Without benefit of imported memory, and for Hume any such importing must be vigorously disallowed, each present perception must be, it seems, too restricted to comprehend more than just one side, or one end, or the supposed change. Of course, it's just the presently available side or end. You can *experience* the pain that's less, as *it's* the pain that's *now*. But, can you *experience it as being less*? Not with a suitably strict understanding of "experience," you can't.

There may be a *succession of impressions* or perceptions here, as Hume has us notice. But, especially for Hume, how can there be any *impression of succession*? Apparently, there can't be. So, you have no impression of temporal change. And without just such an impression to secure, for you, an acceptable idea of temporal change, you'll have no decent idea of change. So, you'll have no decent idea of what it is for you to change from experiencing very painfully to experiencing far less painfully.

If you accept only what's fully available in your own direct *momentary experience*, even if it be only in your most theoretical endeavors, then, at least in those most deeply philosophical endeavors, you'll have to rely on a terribly poor corpus of ideas. So, again, and as I said in the text, you should accept very much more.

For a Humanly Realistic Philosophy that's even modestly ambitious, we must accept a view that has each of us be, as we doubtlessly each are, an individual whose mental powers greatly outrun what's fully available in her direct experience. Perhaps all the clearest or fullest human understanding must be somehow informed by our limited power to experience, even if often very indirectly. Still, as against Hume, human understanding greatly transcends human experience.

6. We Are Experientially Varying Individuals

When writing philosophically about himself, sometimes Hume is so extreme as to claim he can't really have any idea of himself:

> If any impression gives rise to the idea of self, that impression must continue invariably the same, thro' the whole course of our lives: since self is suppos'd to exist after that manner. But there is no impression constant and invariable. Pain and pleasure, grief and joy, passions and sensations succeed each other, and never all exist at the same time. It cannot, therefore, be from any of these impressions, or from any other, that the idea of self is deriv'd; and consequently there is no such idea.[6]

Avoiding cheap shots at Hume's extremities, we may learn more by supposing that, contrary to evident fact, I do have an impression constant and invariable.

Suppose that I always hear a certain tone, *belltone*, with a certain pitch, loudness and timbre, *constant and invariable*. Maybe I won't then notice the constant tone. But, so what? And, along a line I'll now suggest, maybe I'd sometimes notice belltone: Sometimes I hear other tones that accord well with it; and, so, I hear a pleasant chord. Bemused, I might then think that my variable experience was harmonizing well with me, or with my constant and invariable nature. Other times, I hear tones that accord very poorly with belltone; then, I hear a "belltone-based" cacophonous sound. Aggravated, I might then think my variable experience was grating for me, conflicting with my constant and invariable nature.

Of course, what I've just suggested is rather silly: Why should my experiencing this *constant belltone* be my experiencing *myself*? Or, maybe better, why should my experiencing *constantly in any* specific

---

6. Hume, *Treatise*, 1739, –pages 251–52. I use what's now the standard edition of Hume's *Treatise*, first edited by L. A. Selby-Bigge, in 1888, and with the current second edition revised by P. H. Nidditch for the Oxford University Press in 1978.

respect be a case of my experiencing *myself*, whereas my experiencing *variably*, in any such respect, *not* be my experiencing myself?

It's only if I think that I must have a constant qualitative character, fully available to me in my own direct experience, that I'd entertain, at all seriously, any such strange notion. But, as against this, I've been arguing that, quite as we should expect, we're powerfully variable persisting particulars, sometimes manifesting our power to experience in a certain sort of qualitatively rich experiencing, other times in very different sorts. And, as I've also urged, sometimes we won't manifest this mental power at all, as may happen in deepest sleep, between dreams.

It was on purpose, of course, that, in making these pretty plain points, I chose such an obviously weak candidate as an impression of belltone. For, who would ever, ever think that in experiencing belltone, then, *but only then*, he was experiencing himself? But, of course, once you've so easily seen these main points I've just made, using that obviously weak candidate, you'll realize that the same points hold, just as well, with less obviously weak candidates. So, we might contemplate a certain (possible) metaphysician who always felt very depressed, to just such a certain severe extent, and in just such a certain psychically painful way. Though he's certainly worse off, on the whole, than most other philosophers, is there a certain way in which he is better off than them? Is he more fortunate than they are, at least in this one respect: While each of them lacks any adequate idea of herself, for lacking an impression that's quite constant and invariable, he has just such a nice idea of himself, just for always feeling so depressed, just so utterly constantly and terribly invariably? Not at all. Though it might possibly have some bad side effects on this constantly depressed thinker, it certainly won't be that, should his regularly taking Prozac often stop him from feeling so depressed, *that* will put him at *any philosophical disadvantage*.

Realistically, when will it be that I should experience constantly, or invariably? Well, maybe something strange will be going on with me, as with my having a glitch that's completely stultifying my differentially responsive powers. Or, it may be, suppose, that I should always be similarly interacting with things that, owing to their perfect monotony, always appear to me exactly the same. Or, something else strangely monotonous might come to pass. But, nothing like that is going on with me, as my varying experience evidently attests. As I'm happy to say, I'm an individual with a highly differentially responsive Propensity to experience, at certain times experiencing in certain qualitatively rich ways, at other times in others.

Maybe some of the simplest of our supposed mutant clams, simply sensing and never really thinking, will have, throughout a sleepless existence, an impression constant and invariable. Or, maybe not. However that may be, we are far more complex, in our real mental powers, than are even any real clams. So, in a lifetime of variable experiencing, why should I expect to have an impression that's constant and invariable? Quite as nothing useful should be served by such constancy, there's not the slightest reason, of course, to expect myself to experience so very invariably as all that.

7. We Are Not Bundles of Experiences, Thoughts or Perceptions

With just the first two of the following three sentences, Hume provides one of the most famous passages in all modern philosophy:

> For my part, when I enter most intimately into what I call *myself*, I always stumble on some particular perception or other, of heat or cold, light or shade, love or hatred, pain or pleasure. I never can catch *myself* at any time without a perception, and never can observe anything but the perception. When my perceptions are remov'd for any time, as by sound sleep; so long am I insensible of *myself*; and may truly be said not to exist.[7]

But, on the face of it, it's the third of these sentences, apparently not so much attended, that shows Hume most blatantly contradicting our commonsense thought about ourselves. Why is this striking sentence less attended? For one thing, and as we've already observed, Descartes had already upheld the idea that, should you not be consciously experiencing or thinking, then you should not exist at all. So, we see nothing both basic and new in Hume with "When my perceptions are remov'd for any time, as by sound sleep; so long am I insensible of *myself*; and may truly be said not to exist."

But, while there is nothing peculiarly Humean in our passage's last sentence, it's important for us to notice the great difference between Descartes and Hume as regards your existence and your conscious states: Descartes, as we've observed, held that, as *our existence isn't ever temporally intermittent*, there never are any periods of utterly unconscious sleep; with periods of deepest sleep, we undergo conscious episodes, all right, but we just completely forget them, or we fail to

---

7. Hume, *Treatise*, page 252. The first two sentences are quoted, quite alone, in many recent works, I must imagine. For salient instances, see page 39 of Roderick M. Chisholm's *Person and Object*, Allen & Unwin, 1976, and page 213 of John Foster's *The Immaterial Self*, Routledge, 1991.

remember them, directly as they occur, or directly after they occur. Hume, by contrast, holds that *our existence can be, and actually is, temporally intermittent*. You exist *before* dreamless sleep, and *also after* perfectly unconscious sleep, but *not during* the intermediate period, when *you're supposedly* sleeping (and, so, existing) without consciousness.

Common sense differs from both these great thinkers, of course, as concerns their very general point of agreement; as it says, we needn't be conscious at every moment of our existence. Should you not be conscious during sound sleep, or when under a powerful anaesthetic, as it appears does happen, you nevertheless exist at that time. And, as I've been arguing, during your periods of unconsciousness, you continue to be a particular with the power to think, and to experience, even while your persisting mental powers aren't manifested in conscious episodes. Offering a more Humanly Realistic Philosophy than either, there is this large difference between the present work and, on the other side, both Hume and Descartes.

Hume's idea that we have temporally intermittent existence comports well with his view that each of us is, though *not* nothing whatever, "nothing but a bundle or collection of different perceptions." (This is less extreme than the view Hume seems to take in the passage quoted at the start of the previous Section, where he says that he has no idea of himself whatever.) In an ostensible expression of openness toward the possibility of great differences in human experience, as between himself and, perhaps, someone who might always hear belltone, Hume soon sarcastically segues into offering us his famous "bundle theory" of himself, and of you and me, too:

> If any one upon serious and unprejudic'd reflexion, thinks he has a different notion of *himself*, I must confess I can reason no longer with him. All I can allow him is, that he may be in the right as well as I, and that we are essentially different in this particular. He may, perhaps, perceive something simple and continu'd, which he calls himself; tho' I am certain there is no such principle in me.
>
> But setting aside some metaphysicians of this kind, I may venture to affirm of the rest of mankind, that they are nothing but a bundle or collection of different perceptions, which succeed each other with an inconceivable rapidity, ...[8]

Now, as I've already argued, a metaphysician who always experiences belltone, for example, would really be no better placed than I am, or than you are, to experience or perceive himself. But, now setting aside

8. Hume, *Treatise*, page 252.

all that, we do well to note how nice is the fit between Hume's idea that we are each a "bundle or collection of different perceptions, which succeed each other," and his thought that we have intermittent existence. With plenty of logical room to do so, he need only add this specification: Some perceptions in my bundle, or in the bundle that's me, call them "Earlier Perceptions," may precede some others, call them "Later Perceptions," with times *between* the Earlier and the Later when there occur *no perceptions in my bundle*, or, more colloquially, none that are *my* perceptions.

Hume's bundle theory of ourselves may be seen, I think, to be perfectly absurd. Indeed, to my mind, the simplest consideration against the view is perfectly decisive: We must acknowledge the possibility of just a single thinking, or a solitary perceiving, or a lonely experiencing. As such a lonely experience is so perfectly solitary, it can't be part of any bundle or collection of perceptions. On a bundle theory, then, it must be an experiencing of no experiencer at all, which is obviously absurd. Nor will we be helped in avoiding absurdity, it's evident, by a clever logical dodge, as with defining a "minimal bundle" comprising just one single experiencing, which may somehow serve to comprise, or to compose, a being whose experiencing it is. For, it's also obviously absurd to think that an experiencing may be its own subject, or to think that there may be no difference at all between an experiencer, however small and impoverished, and, on the other side, the experiencing that this subject enjoys.

Please don't misunderstand me here. I'll allow that it's perfectly possible for there to be a person who only ever engages in extremely little experiencing. Just so, it's perfectly possible, I'll at least allow, for there to be someone who exists for only a tiny fraction of a single second, experiencing only just then, and then only in just a certain absolutely specific way, perhaps as simple as just experiencing bell-tonely, for instance. As I'll happily allow, this "terribly fleeting" being won't ever enjoy, or he won't ever suffer, any more experiencing than just that, during his single existential moment. What I'm *not* prepared to allow, by contrast, is that there's ever any experiencing, or any (so-called) experience, that somehow *constitutes an experiencer*; no more than there's any experience, or any experiencing, really, that's *not the experience of an experiencer*. Rather, in every possible case, it's the *experiencer that's quite basic*, with the experiencing, or the (so-called) experience, only ontologically parasitical (on the sentient being). It may be helpful, I think, to put the point this graphically: An Almighty God, if Such there be, could make an experiencer who never enjoys any experience; maybe, during his very brief existence, he's always in absolutely deep sleep, say, and, for that reason, he's never experiencing. But, not even an Almighty God could make there be some experiencing (or, what's colloquially called some experience) that wasn't the experiencing (or the so-called experience) of an experiencer, who's ontologically more basic than the experiencing.

On views very different from bundle theories, as with Descartes's idea of substantial individual souls, there's no place for such absurd thoughts as that of an experiencing, or an experience, without any experiencer. (Nor is there any place for such an absurd idea as that of an experiencer who's identical with his experiencing.) Rather than an experience that's floating free of all souls, we should have each experience be an experience of a properly powerful individual, maybe a *manifestation of* the individual's *power to* experience. Though we may disagree with Descartes on many other matters, on this critical point, he is, apparently, right on the money. By contrast, Hume's bundle theory is wrong.

8. We Substantial Individuals Are More Basic Than Our Thoughts and Experiences

The key difference here, favoring not Hume but Descartes, can be helpfully marked, I think, with some useful technical terms. You are a *substantial individual*; by contrast, your particular perceptions, thoughts and experiences are *ontologically parasitical* on you. Here are some thoughts that should help us with the distinction just marked.

It's perfectly possible for you to exist always having quite different specific experiences and thoughts from those you actually do have, different in many respects even if, perhaps, not in absolutely all. But, if there's never a being that's you, then there never could have been any of your particular thoughts and experiences.

Because we habitually take uses of nouns and pronouns to designate entities, there are certain dangers for us. In particular, there's the danger of our failing to note that what we apparently designate with some uses are ontologically parasitical on more basic things, designated with other uses. So, it may be more perspicuous, for metaphysical purposes, to speak of *you* thinking, and *you* experiencing, rather than of *your thoughts* and *your experiences*. (There's some heuristic point, therefore, in speaking, somewhat barbarously, of your experiencings, rather than talking, more colloquially, of your experiences.)

Ordinarily, we may think of you now as having several different experiences, as with one that's visual and another that's auditory. We might then suppose that there are then these three entities: you, your visual experience, and your auditory experience. And, we may wonder about the relations among the entities: Are you in a special "having relation" with respect to your visual experience? Is this the very same relation that you're in with respect to your auditory experience; or is it, rather, a suitably similar relation; or what? I don't think these are philosophically important questions. More likely, I think, they're the reflection of philosophical confusions. To forestall falling into any such confusion, we may avail ourselves of descriptions that are relevantly more perspicuous. Here's a pretty good start with that: You are experiencing in a visual way and, at the same time, you're experiencing in a nonvisual auditory way. Few would want to reify ways; fewer still would have you be a bundle or collection of ways.

But, some might. Following Roderick Chisholm, we may clarify matters still more for them. Just so, here's a description that's relevantly still more perspicuous: You are experiencing visually and, at the same time, you're experiencing auditorally.[9]

Consider a troubled woman: First, she has a headache; and then, for a little while, she's not bothered by any headache; and then, right after that, she has just such a bothersome headache once again. There seems a small problem here: Is the headache at the end the selfsame headache once again, or is it a second headache she then suffers that's just so like the first? As I'll suggest, this small problem should now seem even smaller: As compared with the individuals on whom any headache is ontologically parasitical, headaches are *ontologically superficial items*. So, as far as our very small problem goes, we may do well to say something like this: First, the woman experiences headachely, and then she doesn't, and then again she experiences headachely. For certain purposes, such strange talk may be detrimental; but, for present metaphysical purposes, it may be helpful.

---

9. As many will recognize, in these metaphysical, as with some other main metaphysical matters, I'm greatly influenced by Chisholm, as in his *Person and Object*, pages 48–52. Though there's much that we agree on here, there are also great areas of disagreement. For the most part, I won't note the differences, or the similarities, as that would do more to distract than advance.

In any case, however, I want to be very clear about this: My use of adverbial expressions, like "experience auditorally," is meant to be only a helpful heuristic. I don't offer anything that might be labeled, even if somewhat misleadingly, an "adverbial theory of experiencing." What's adverbial is, of course, something that's linguistic. And, experiencing is, at most, only rarely linguistic. More generally, it's my belief that, whether from considerations of common parlance, or from more-or-less useful paraphrase, we shouldn't expect much substantive philosophy.

For a Humanly Realistic Philosophy, we might do best, even, to deny that such apparent parasites, like headaches, are real things at all. But, adequately defending this severe stance would take, I think, far more effort than the issue here warrants. Anyhow, whether we deny the reality of headaches entirely, or whether we allow them as real but ontologically superficial items, we may be clear about the philosophic status of the issue just discussed. Problems concerning the individuation of such presumptive things as headaches are philosophically superficial issues. It's a philosophically superficial issue whether, during a certain brief period, a certain experiencer has a single headache, which headache exists only intermittently, or whether the experiencer then has a sequence of several headaches, none existing just intermittently, and all of them qualitatively much the same.

These considerations are hardly peculiar, it should be noted, to mental modifications, to the likes of headaches and experiences. Consider *your fist*, as we say, or *your lap*. When you're seated, you are so configured (or maybe it's just your body that's so configured) that you have a lap. And, when you stand up tall, or you lie down straight, you don't have a lap; then, there's nothing that's your lap. When you sit, and then stand up, and then sit down again, is it the same lap that you have, both before and after the interim of standing? Or, do you first have one lap and, after the interim, you have another lap that's so similar to the first? Well, I'm inclined to say it's the same lap. But, for serious philosophy, that's no important question. And, for much the same reason, our question about individuating a woman's headaches isn't very important, either.

Let's think some more about things apparently quite different from ourselves and our mental affections. So, let's suppose a perfectly solid object that's almost perfectly spherical. To get a tolerably clear conception of this supposed physical individual, imagine that it's transparent pink, through and through, with its pink matter being so perfectly homogeneous that the little solid has no substantial parts. Now, suppose that a searching look at the sphere's scratched surface, as with a magnifying glass, reveals nine separated scratches, each of them quite continuous, that are so nicely arranged like this: MADE BY GOD (As we suppose, that's the *end* of this issue, no *matter how much* magnification.) Now, there may ensue a discussion as to whether there are only THESE nine here, or whether, in addition to them, there's also a larger discontinuous scratch, comprising all nine of the smaller scratches (and more directly serving to reveal the scratched object's origin).

Is there really such a larger discontinuous indentation, comprising the nine continuous scratches? This isn't a question of much substance.

Not so concerned with such ontologically superficial parasites as scratches, or indentations, a serious philosophy will be enormously more concerned with more substantial individuals, in this case, with the very nearly spherical pink object. Without wishing to suggest that there exist any such things as ways, we may say, quite simply, that our pretty spherical object is indented in a certain way, just like so: MADE BY GOD And, then, we may speculate as to whether its being *so indented* may serve to reveal the object's origin.[10]

Now, let's think about both you yourself, as modified variously, and also a simple nonmental individual, which presumed particulars may be modified very simply and straightforwardly. I'll start with you. Well, you may experience visually, all at once, as of a Dark Grey Square, as "in the upper left of your visual field," and a Light Grey Square, in the upper right, and a Dark Grey Circle, in the lower left, and a Light Grey Circle, in the lower right, each spatially separate from the others. Let's grant or suppose that, as Frank Jackson has argued, we can't use *our adverbial expressions* to say, adequately, how it is that you're then experientially modified.[11] Indeed, let's grant or suppose that, using ordinary English locutions, we can't express adequately how things will be with us experientially, unless we use expressions that, at least to all appearances, will have us suggesting, at least, the existence of entities other than substantial individuals. Can *that* mean any serious problem for the thought that it's we experiencers that are substantial, with our experiences just ontologically parasitical on us? No; it can't. Why should we think, after all, that this language of ours should be well suited for any adequately perspicuous presentation of anything like a basic metaphysics?

Indeed, as it might well be, even should some metaphysically better language somehow be made available to us, as with a gift from a

---

10. I borrow this marvelously entertaining example from John Leslie, *Universes*, London: Routledge, 1989. Leslie has us look at matter under very powerful microscopes, and he has us find little inscriptions of MADE BY GOD on every bit of observed matter. Well, isn't this very suggestive evidence in favor of the hypothesis that a powerful agent created the observable universe? In this work, I pass on that large question. For my much less momentous purpose, one imagined object is sufficient. And, of course, my point here is that, when we're thinking about whether ontologically parasitical items are real entities, we're *not* involved in any very momentous question.

11. As Frank Jackson has urged, in his *Perception*, Cambridge University Press, 1977, there are problems with using our adverbial constructions to report the variety in what I take to be our experiential modification.

In Jackson's wake, there has ensued a long discussion of the matter. For a recent contribution to the discussion, see Michael Tye, *Ten Problems of Consciousness*, MIT Press, 1996, pages 74–77.

beneficent God, matters metaphysical still would elude our systematic codification. For, though some mentally powerful beings might be up to employing that theoretically fine language to good philosophical effect, we merely human beings might not, by contrast, possess the requisite mental powers. But, what of it? In basic metaphysics, I believe, the last thing we should do is conclude anything much about which (concrete) entities exist, from anything about our own mental Propensities, or our limitations and lacks thereof. Better for me simply to think that, say, I'll never be very good at saying how it is with me experientially, or visually, and that's that, rather than my thinking that there exists, in addition to just me myself, something that's my visual field, for instance, as well as something that's the real relation between me and this visual field of mine, maybe something that's a certain real "having relation." Unless we may take it that they're just some ontological parasites on unproblematic substantial individuals, it's truer to deny, and so it's better to deny, I think, that there really are any such metaphysically peculiar particulars as, say, visual fields, our denial being a nice expression, I think, of an aptly robust sense of reality.

For good measure, we consider a relevantly related *nonmental* example. Well, a cubical object may have impressed upon it, all at one square face, several shallow *indentations*, a Rough-bottomed (or Dark) Square indentation, and a Smooth-bottomed (or Light) Square indentation, and a Rough-bottomed Circle (or circular) indentation, and a Smooth-bottomed Circle (or circular) indentation. A power press may do that to a pretty perfect cube, thus turning it into a less than perfect cube. For a philosophically perspicuous description of the situation, I might well say that this near-cube is *indentationally configured* in a certain complex way. And, now, let's grant or suppose that we can't use *our adverbial expressions* to say, adequately, how it is that this near-cube is shaped, or how it's been impressively modified. Can *this* be a serious problem for the thought that cubical concreta are more basic particulars, with their *literally* superficial indentings ontologically parasitical on them? Again, no.

As Bertrand Russell noted, sometimes there won't be a nice parallel between an experiential case and the presumably grosser material case.[12] Putting it crudely, that's due to "experiential orientation." In one subject's visual field, so to say, there is a Dark Grey Square (color patch) to the *left* of a Light Grey Circle (color patch), and that's *it*. In another's, there's just a Dark Grey Square to the *right* of a Light Grey

12. Bertrand Russell, *Human Knowledge: Its Scope and Limits*, Simon and Schuster, 1948, 198–199.

Circle, and *that's* it. Now, grant or suppose that we can't use our adverbial expressions to say, adequately, how it is that these experiential subjects are experientially modified, thus adequately expressing both the experiential difference between them and also the similarity. And, with Russell, suppose that *here there is no relevant parallel* with physically geometrical cases. Can *this* mean a serious problem for the thought that we experiencers are more basic entities, while our visual fields, and our experiences, are ontologically parasitical on us? No, once again.

As I've been suggesting, you and I are each substantial individuals. By comparison with us, who are said to "have" the supposed mental items, all our thoughts, experiences, and *perceptions*, finally to use Hume's favored term, are *ontologically superficial* items, each *parasitical on* the being said to "have" it. For that reason alone, nobody is "a bundle or collection of different perceptions."

Right now, I'll do just a bit more toward articulating my developing distinction between substantial individuals and, on the other side, ontological parasites. A bundle of solid physical cones and spheres is ontologically parasitical on individual cones and spheres. At least if they themselves *aren't bundles* or collections, each cone, by contrast, and each sphere, may be a substantial individual. Again, a group of people is not any substantial individual, but is ontologically parasitical upon the people in the group. Each person, by contrast, may be a substantial individual.

So, we see a second reason why no substantial individual can be "a bundle or collection of different perceptions." Apparently, we couldn't be a mere bundle or collection of *anything*. As it appears, then, Hume *compounded* ontological errors. First, even if it should be supposed that you're a bundle of somethings, it won't be mere perceptions, or perceivings, that can compose the wonderful bundle. For, it's you that's the ontologically more basic entity here, with your perceptions parasitical on you. And, second, even if you should be somehow composed of constituent parts, it's not any mere bundle, or collection, that your parts should then serve to compose. On the issues we've been so far discussing, the first error is more influential and, so, it's been more in focus.

9. As We Communicate with Each Other, We Are Reciprocal Interaction Partners

Though I can't get you to read my mind, or to be most directly affected by my mental modification, yet, by expressing my thoughts to you, often I successfully communicate with you about many things. I succeed in communicating to you, indirectly, how it is that my thinking is progressing, and how it is with me experientially. And, in a similarly indirect manner, you sometimes effectively communicate with me, too. Any philosophy that denies this should, I think, itself be denied.

To make this clear, recall the little imaginative exercise where we imagined colorful solid figures: Closing our eyes, each of us imagined a regular solid that, transparently through and through, was a single spectral color. You chose yours and I chose mine; and, each divulged to the other what she imagined. Most sincerely and truly, I told you I imagined a blue sphere, by saying the words "I just imagined a blue sphere." And, you told me you imagined a red cube, saying the words "Me, I imagined a red cube." As is plenty certain enough, by the end of this exercise I knew, rather well, how it was with you experientially when you imagined as you just did. And, you knew how it was with me when I imagined my blue sphere.

Inasmuch as I can communicate with you, I have the mental power *to affect you*. And, just as necessary for there to be any communicating between us, *you* have the mental Propensity, or the Lockean "passive" power, *to be affected by me*. So, at least to some extent, you and I are *reciprocal disposition partners*, as C. B. Martin aptly characterizes the relation between us.[13] I'll amplify on Martin's message.[14]

Whether you (still) exist or not, and whether or not you're "within the reach of my communicative attempts," I am categorically disposed to affect the thinking of any existent that's precisely like you actually are. And, correlatively or reciprocally, you are Propensitied to be so affected by someone just like me. As you're now listening to these sentences of mine—please pretend—expressed by me for you in our seminar room, you're now within the reach of my communicative attempts, whatever that may precisely involve. And, so, these reciprocal dispositions now are actually manifested, by me and by you: I actually

13. A fairly full-dress expression of these ideas is in Martin's contribution to D. M. Armstrong, C.B. Martin and U. T. Place, *Dispositions: A Debate*, Tim Crane (ed.), Routledge, 1996. But, to my mind at least, much of that is hard to understand well. A much more accessible presentation, with what may be a few improvements, is C. B. Martin and John Heil's paper "The Ontological Turn," *Midwest Studies in Philosophy*, 1999.

14. In continuing fairness even to those long dead, I should report that, as regards his general lines of thought Martin takes himself to follow the lead of John Locke in these matters, though there are substantial differences, of course, between Martin and Locke. As I'm here following Martin, I suppose that, in turn, I also follow Locke's lead. So, while in some large respects I'm following Descartes, and in others Berkeley, and, of course, Hume, in still others it's Locke whom I'm following. As will transpire over the course of this essay, a very big follower am I.

do modify you mentally, at least somewhat, and, correlatively, you're mentally affected by me.

As we discuss these metaphysical questions together, not only do I communicate with you, which even the dead Descartes may do, but you also communicate with me, which you don't do with Descartes. Even as I communicate so as to affect you, so, correlatively, you have the mental power, or the mental Propensity, to affect me. And, on my part, there's my categorical disposition to be affected mentally by your communicative attempts. So, in that we quite fully communicate *with each other*, it's very fully that we're reciprocal disposition partners.

Here, we have a reciprocal disposition partnership that isn't always dormant, as may be a somewhat similar partnership between me and, say, some philosophy student somewhere in Saskatoon, soon to leave the field. In some sense or way, I suppose, she and I can communicate with each other, if only the conditions for our doing so were far more favorable. But, for better or worse, they never will be. So, though we may be reciprocal disposition partners, we aren't, she and I, what may be called *reciprocal interaction partners*. By contrast, as you and I actually do communicate with each other, we *are* reciprocal interaction partners.

When we converse about matters metaphysical, as we often do, generally I affect you as regards both your experiencing and your thinking, and also as regards how you're Propensitied.

First, when you hear my voice, then, obviously, I affect you as to how it is with you *experientially* in auditory ways. Just so, I have the power, or the Propensity, *to affect you like that*, and, reciprocally, you're Propensitied *to be experientially affected by me*. This may be a power of mine that I exercise only rather *indirectly*; more directly, I affect, for instance, some medium through which we communicate. But, this does not change the main point.

Second, with your hearing these meaningful sounds I've made, there's a new exercise of your power to understand English sentences; truly enough, this is an exercise of (part of) your very complex, highly cultivated power to think. This episodic understanding affects, in turn, your Propensity to think, particularly, to think about metaphysical matters. For example, it might consciously occur to you to disagree with me in a certain way. Wholly novel, at least wholly new with you, this disagreeable thinking is, no doubt, a manifestation of your newly increased Propensity to think about philosophy, at least very slightly more complex than just previously was this mental power of yours. In orally communicating my metaphysical thoughts to you, I affect you as regards your mental Propensity, too, not just your experiential character and your occurrent thinking. So, though the interactions here are quite indirect indeed, I do have the Propensity to affect your mental power, while you have the reciprocal Propensity to be so affected by me.

Our metaphysical conversation is, of course, a two-way street. So, as often happens, you will express your disagreement to me, which it is also well within your power to do. And, then, correlatively with how things went just before, you will affect me, and *I will be affected by you*, as regards both *my* experiencing and *my* thinking. Just as you certainly do have the power to affect me so, and this is so successfully exercised, I have the Propensity, or the passive power, to be so modified by you. Nor does your success end here. With respect to me, at least, you are powerfully effective. And, as is required for that to be so, I am very receptive with respect to you. And, as is also required, the conditions for our philosophical interaction are, no doubt, quite favorable. So, you modify my philosophical Propensity. When some of my newly modified philosophical power is manifested, as often happens very soon, then there may occur to *me* a novel conscious thought, new for me at least.

As we are such successful interaction partners, communicating with each other so very consequentially, all of this really does obtain. A philosophy that denies it should itself be denied.

10. There Is Perplexity Concerning How We Commonly Communicate

Often you effectively communicate with me, though I can't ever read your mind, nor can I do anything of the kind. As I must believe, there are more things involved in our reciprocal interaction partnership than just you and me. In addition to the two of us, there is a mediating entity, or some mediating entities, *through which* you communicate to me how it is with you. It is by your more directly interacting with these "third parties" that, less directly, you interact with me and, thereby, you affect me aptly, both experientially and otherwise. And, correlatively, it is by my being directly affected by them that, less directly, I'm so affected by you.

Let me try to put a bit of concrete meat on these rather abstract bare bones.

The most commonly effective way for us to communicate much occurs with oral conversation. What happens here? Well, it's said that you give oral expression to your thinking. And, at least in the many cases where your innermost thinking precedes, and results in, its oral expression, when you're conversing with me, I'm more directly affected by the oral expression than by the innermost thinking itself. At first blush, none of this seems very perplexing. But, perplexity does befall us when we look into the details of how it might actually have been accomplished.

When you express your thoughts to me by speaking some happily expressive words, and this occurs in effective communication, then, I should *perceive an audible expression* of your thinking. But, what is the perceptible expression that I here perceive? Well, we may say that it's an *audible utterance*, you've produced. But, then, what real entity can *that* be?

Maybe, it's a certain disturbance in some of the air in the room. But, even the air in the room is a pretty bad candidate, it would seem, for being any genuine individual, much less a perceptible entity. (Indeed, the room itself is little better than a mere *region* of a certain building.) And, a mere *disturbance in* what's merely *some of* this "air in the room"? I'm already quite perplexed.

When you audibly communicate with me, what perceptible entity, pray tell, is a really relevant mediator between you, who's indirectly affecting me, and, on the other side, me, who's being so affected by you? Between the two of us, there's little more to pick on than a certain disturbance in some of the air in the room, the sad candidate we've lately noted. Is *this disturbance of air in the room* your audible utterance? To me, at least, it *doesn't seem* that I *hear any* disturbance of the air, nor do I seem to perceive air disturbances in any other way. So, what's going on?

To be sure, not only do we say that I hear your utterances, but, as well, we say that I hear *you*. But, noting *this* can't help. Even if you think common parlance is often a fount of deep truth, you shouldn't think it does anything here. For, it's a *mediating* entity we're here seeking, or several presumably perceptible mediators, *between you* and me. And, *you* can't be *that*.

Even if we should be Substantial Dualists, your body won't be a very relevant mediator. For, I didn't hear your body, as you were just sitting and talking, not crashing into a chair. And, though I see your body, and even your moving mouth, I'm no lip reader, nor anything else so interesting. Rather, this case is just so commonplace, though it remains very perplexing.[15]

---

15. The most usual case of communication is, of course and by far, where we converse auditorally. Far less common, and much more peripheral, is the case where we communicate visually. Now, in the visual case, perplexity isn't anywhere near as blatant as in the auditory case. Let's see. I've written laser-printing on circulated pages:

THE RELATIONS BETWEEN COMMUNICATION AND PERCEPTIBLE PARTICULARS ARE PUZZLING.

Here, there seems a quite *visible expression* of my puzzled thinking.

Still, we observe some perplexity attaching even to this visual case, though it's not especially blatant. To foster this observation, we ask: When I just communicated with you via this visual expression of my thinking, what was the (or even an) entity that, while it expressed my thinking, you were perceiving?

In a world far more marvelous than what's actual, there might be, as with supposed mental telepathy, quite direct communication between you and me. In such a world, perhaps, we'd have no need of mediating partners, whether unproblematic perceptible particulars or whether most-mysterious whatnots. As we're well-habituated to this actual world, that may seem magically mysterious. But, from a philosophical perspective, it may be *less* perplexing than what's supposed to go on in the actual world, in the most common cases of human communication.

The commonest cases of communication between us, where we come to grasp each other's thoughts quite effectively, are very far from receiving any philosophically adequate human understanding. Still, any philosophy that denies that you communicate your thoughts to me, or that I communicate mine to you, is a philosophy to be denied.

11. Much of the World Interacts with Us, but Doesn't Communicate with Us

It's plenty obvious that I experience variously as my life progresses. This is, no doubt, a manifestation of my complex power to experience. Obviously enough, this complex power is manifested by my interacting variously with things *external* to me, or, just possibly, a single *external* thing. Apparently, this holds true even with the straightforward spatial sense of "external" in force, but, at the least, it holds true in *some* sense of this traditionally useful philosophic term. Just so, there's a very

---

Following a certain philosophical tradition, we may say that it's a visible *inscription*, right there on this piece of paper, on this very page. But, even as compared with the visually perceptible piece of paper, which itself might harbor a host of deep problems, the supposed inscription is a very problematic object. Passing over however many problems, perhaps we might say that, at best, the inscription is a somewhat scattered row of slightly raised, "letterly" shaped mounds of inky stuff, each separated from the next by some moundless space on the paper, with each such mound protruding outwards from one of the two main surfaces of the piece of paper. But, first, are mounds real entities? I'm not so sure. Even Mount Everest is, after all, just a protuberance of the earth's crust. Maybe the earth itself is a substantial individual, or near enough so to merit a pretense to such an effect, or to be a fair candidate for a perceptible entity. But, a mere protuberance? And, as if that's not enough to engender some perplexity, what about a *scattered row of* protuberances?

But, anyhow, these puzzling rows are the *comparatively good* candidates for real entities helpfully perceived. As compared with the common case, which is the auditory conversations case, here we have things that apparently approximate, at least, to being perceptible particulars, to being plausible third partners that might mediate, unmysteriously enough, between communicating individuals. So, far more blatantly than in any quite marginal visual case, it's the enormously common case of our very many oral conversations that's got me perplexed, flummoxed, and bamboozled.

considerable external reality that's my continually affective interaction partner, whether this external reality be just one vast heterogenous entity or whether it might comprise, in fact, many quite distinct external entities.

By contrast with the likes of you, let's consider my more direct disposition partner or, maybe, many such more direct partners. As appears plain enough, it's nothing like that which ever *communicates* with me, certainly not in the most straightforward sense of the term. Certainly, there's no communication to me, from most of external reality, as to *any mental* processes or activities on its part. Nor does it communicate any such thing to any of the beings with whom I do communicate, as with you, for example. So, even while you are external to me, and I to you, our communication, about our mental processes is a pretty exceptional occurrence. For the most part, my interactions with external reality involve no such communication, and neither do yours.[16]

The *noncommunicative* external reality that interacts with me affects how it is with me in various regards. Most saliently, it affects how it is with me as regards my experiencing. Thus, even as I am disposed to be experientially affected by this external reality, so, reciprocally, *external reality is disposed to affect how it is that I experience*. Now, this same external reality is rather similarly disposed, I feel sure, to affect how it is that *you* experience. And, if I may presume that (not being blind, or deaf, and so on) your senses function quite as well as do mine, as I certainly hope I may, then, reciprocally, you're disposed, very much like I'm Propensitied, to be experientially affected by this selfsame external reality. After all, both of us are reasonably ordinary human beings, quite devoid of supernatural powers. In very general terms, that's why it is that,

---

16. The expression "disposition partner," which I find quite useful, was first introduced, as far as I can tell, by C. B. "Charlie" Martin. But, apparently, my use of the term is very different from his. So, for me, it's always substantial individuals that are disposition partners, as with two (minimally) massive Newtonian Particles, each gravitationally disposed to attract (the likes of) the other. For Martin, who believes in so-called tropes (or so-called abstract particulars) it's always such particularized properties, apparently, that are (to be considered as the) disposition partners. So, with a certain couple of Newtonian Particles, the mass-trope of one of these Particles is a disposition partner with the mass-trope of the other Particle and, of course, vice versa. Now, I'm not perfectly sure that, with this gloss of Martin's use, I've correctly characterized his preferred employment of the term. But, in this present exposition, which is, of course, my own attempt to articulate a certain Humanly Realistic Philosophy, that's not very important. What is important, of course, is that we be clear about, and that I be consistent with, my own use of "disposition partner." So, on my part, I'll try hard to be consistent in my usage of this expression. And, I hope that, on your part, you'll try to be clear about what I mean, in this present work, by the expression.

in many respects and overall, your experiencing is, even unto its innermost aspect, rather like my experiencing.

I'll illustrate. As it might well be, *part of* this external reality is what I'll call, properly enough, *my computer*, which comprises my CPU, my monitor, my keyboard, and so on. And, *another part of* the external reality, distinct from my computer, though very similar, is what we'll call *your computer*. Then, I'm experientially modified by external reality, we might say, *by being so affected by my computer;* this computer is disposed to affect me experientially and, reciprocally, I'm so disposed to be so modified by it. And, by being similarly modified by your similar computer, you're experientially modified similarly by external reality. So, first, that similar part of external reality is similarly Propensitied to affect you experientially. And, reciprocally, you're so disposed to be so affected by it.

At least from time to time, I affect this external reality, the selfsame external reality that, from time to time at least, you also affect. So, I'm disposed to affect, or modify, the external reality that often affects us experientially.

Again, I'll illustrate. Sometimes I may affect this external reality in affecting the part of it that's *my computer*. So, I'm *disposed to* affect this part of reality; and, presumably, under similar conditions, I'm similarly disposed to affect anything relevantly much like it, as with similar computers. And, reciprocally, my computer is disposed to be affected by me (and, by things much like me, such as a similarly skilled computer user.) Now, suppose *your computer* is much like my device. Well, then I'm similarly disposed to similarly affect your computer, that other part of external reality, and your computer, for its part, is reciprocally disposed to be affected by me.

In an awkward and roundabout way, I've just sketched something of my philosophical approach to ordinary tables and chairs, rocks and trees, and so on, as well as to our own bodies and what does most to sustain them. Why so roundabout? Perhaps owing mainly to my philosophical confusions, I feel that a great deal of caution is appropriate here.

As one facet of this desired caution, I want to leave open many ontological questions that, on more straightforward formulations, would at least seem to be closed, or settled in advance. For example, I want to leave it open whether my effective interaction partner might be a single vast heterogeneous field—and, if so, whether there then will be, most really and truly, just one single entity, perhaps, comprising all "noncommunicative" external reality. On this open option, all alleged rocks might be, really and truly, not any entities in their own right, and, just possibly, no real entities at all. As well, I want to leave open whether my noncommunicative partnering might comprise very many quite distinct, but also quite fundamental, particles or, if that's not the best term, many distinct external items each entirely lacking any substantial parts. On this other open option, I want to leave it open, further, whether there might then be, most really and truly, just these very many distinct basic particles, perhaps, together comprising all noncommunicative external reality, whilst all alleged rocks might be, again, no real entities at all.

What goes on when I'm perceiving some of external reality, as when I perceive you, or your body, or your *nose*, which I can hardly discriminate, of course, from all the rest of your body? (Of course, it's supposed to be no more problematic for me to see your nose than it is for me to see your body. But, then, maybe both are very problematic. But, we'll let this pass.) First, when I'm perceiving your body, as we say, then there's *something* going on that involves me, on one hand, interacting with our external reality, on the other, but not all of external reality. (For your body isn't all of external reality and, as I'm not seeing your kidneys, I'm not really perceiving, even, all of your body.) And, no doubt, this interaction has *something* to do with my being mentally altered in *some such way* that, in circumstances typical or normal for me, I'm then set to be more likely successful in my upcoming transactions with some of external reality. But, much more than that is hard to say. Well, I'll just leave it at that.

Though in most of the book I'll suppose them all settled, and all settled in a most common and boring manner or way, for another few moments I'll leave open several large metaphysical issues. For example, I leave it open whether our external world might be a single vast basic noncommunicative external entity that thinks, or experiences. And, I leave open whether there might possibly be many distinct basic noncommunicative external entities, each of them thinking but never communicating that to us. So, in this Chapter I'm leaving it open whether some sort of panpsychism, or idealism, might be true. Of course, even in this Chapter I reject any Absolute Idealism that denies I'm one potent particular and you're another. And, so, too, with any phenomenalism that has you be a bundle of parasites. But, there are also other views, not so obviously to be rejected.

12. We Often Choose What to Think About, and Even What to Communicate

From time to time, at least, I *choose what to do from among actually available alternatives* for my own thoughtful activity. In particular, I choose what I'll think about from among actually available options for me. As sometimes happens, I choose to think about metaphysics, even while there are other alternatives available for my thoughtful activity, including an option to think about soul music. Now, knowing my very limited self as I do, I know that typically, and at a certain short time that's upcoming, I can't do more than one of these things, all at once. Yet, I also know that each is a real alternative for me. And, when I choose to think about metaphysics, from among my real alternatives, often *I do that because I choose to do it*.

To make the point usefully vivid, again return to consider the little imaginative exercise used, in the first instance, to illustrate how very effectively we communicate with each other, even as concerns our innermost thoughts and experiences. As it happened, you'll recall, I chose to imagine a blue sphere, whereas you chose to imagine a red cube. But, as is obvious enough, at least to me, imagining a blue sphere wasn't my only real alternative. It was also then open to me to imagine a red cube, or, for that matter, to imagine an orange cylinder. Indeed, it was perfectly open to me then not to have exercised my visually imaginative powers at all, and to let you do all the envisioning and divulging. To me, this is just as obvious as was your successfully communicating to me, in our supposed exercise, that it was a red cube that you imagined.

In fact, just a few *minutes ago*, I chose again. This time I chose to imagine a red cube, not a blue sphere. But, as I'm quite sure, my imagining a blue sphere was, this second time, just as much a real alternative for me as first it was, when I actually imagined a blue sphere, and did so just because I chose to do so.

When I choose to think about something, then, as I feel sure, this is a *nonderivative* choice of mine. Now, a committee may make choices, from among the alternatives available to it, and these will be only derivative choices. They'll be derivative because the committee will make choices only when, in a more central and unqualified sense, some of its members, some thoughtful individuals, each makes nonderivative choices. But, when I choose to think about metaphysics, it's nothing even remotely like what happens when such a committee chooses. Rather, it's very much like what happens, of course, when a thoughtful member chooses.

It is not quite so obvious to me that I ever really choose, I hasten to admit, as it is that I sometimes experience, or that I sometimes think. But, nor is it so perfectly obvious to me that you effectively communicate to me what you're thinking, or experiencing. But, for progress toward a Humanly Realistic Philosophy, all that's plenty obvious enough to me, and, I think, to you, too.

Any philosophy that denies that each of us really chooses, from actual options for his own thoughtful activity, is, I think, a philosophy that we should deny. Indeed, any acceptable philosophy must have it that sometimes I effectively communicate to you my innermost thinking *because I choose* to do so, and sometimes I'm affected mentally by you *because you choose* to communicate just certain of your own innermost thoughts to me.

Do you remember Scientiphicalism, the dominant worldview sketched in the previous Chapter? On that view, I'll remind you, all your powers are physically derivative Propensities, all deriving from the far simpler physical properties of your simple physical constituents, saliently including their simple Propensities, and the (sufficiently basic) physical relations among those simple components. Can your power to choose, quite evident enough to you, possibly be any such physically derivative power? I suspect not. And, I find this suspicion so enormously intriguing that I can hardly wait to investigate the matter.

But, wait we must. For, though we've made some progress, I think, in advancing a Humanly Realistic Philosophy, we've done it without employing any very intelligible idea of *physical reality*. But, of course, questions concerning Scientiphicalism *are* questions concerning physical reality. So, to make some progress with those questions, we must return to address the Mystery of the Physical. And, that's what we'll now do.

3

DEMYSTIFYING
THE PHYSICAL

Even without employing any notion of physical reality, we've made some progress in advancing a Humanly Realistic Philosophy. But, at some point, we should become involved in trying to conceive the physical. For one thing, when we communicate with each other, this is done through our each interacting with an *external reality*, quite distinct from me and also from you. Nowadays, we take it that this possibly mysterious external reality, through which we communicate, is physical reality. But, what can any of this really amount to? As it seems, we're on the verge of confronting, all over again, our Mystery of the Physical. So, I'll proceed to address it.

1. We Recall the Denial of Quality and the Mystery of the Physical

Toward presenting the Mystery of the Physical, you'll recall, we presented, in two Formulations, a doctrine concerning the Denial of Quality. In its fuller Formulation, that doctrine was this:

> *The Denial of Qualities, Second Formulation.* Unlike the Spatial properties and the Propensities, which are so widely instantiated in what's physical, there are not (any instantiations of) any Qualities

anywhere in physical reality. Nor are there, anywhere in physical reality, any mental qualities readily confused with Qualities, with the possible exception, at any given time, of such a small part of physical reality as may then promote the minds of sentient beings. Nor are there, anywhere in physical reality, any propensity properties readily confused with Qualities, with the possible exception, at any given time, of such a small part of physical reality as may then promote such complexes as are (humanly) perceptible physical complexes.

According to this Denial, accepted by most Scientiphicalists, all the world's matter lacks (Spatially Extensible) Qualities, even as a lot lacks anything even easily confused with (such) Qualities, however well matter may fare with the other two sorts of basic properties for physical things, the Spatials and the Propensities. So, while an elementary particle may have spatial extent and shape, and while it may have many Propensities, it can't have, by contrast, any basic property that's remotely like any phenomenal color, or that's readily confused with, say, phenomenal red.

Earlier, I argued that, should we mere human thinkers be restricted from thinking of physical reality as having Spatially Extensible Quality, we'll have no conception of the physical that's even moderately adequate to such a supposedly fundamental realm. Rather, we'll have our Mystery of the Physical.

Let's recall the thrust of the argument. First, we attempt to conceive a physical reality in Qualityless Newtonian terms: Moving in what's otherwise empty space, there are many physical particles, our previously presumed Particles, whose motion is governed by physical laws. These laws concern no Qualities, of course, but only the likes of such Nonqualitative properties as may be supposed for our Particles. Second, we attempt to conceive a physical reality to be, at least as it seems, very different indeed. In what's otherwise a continuous material plenum, or field of matter, there are little perfectly empty spaces, or Bubbles: As regards shape, size, and so on, each Bubble is precisely congruent with a certain Particle, its *counterpart* Particle, in the Particulate World. As with congruence, so with arrangement: Wherever there's a Particle in that Newtonian World, in a counterpart place there's a Bubble in this Plenumate World. What's more, in a perfect parallel with the law-governed behavior of the Particles in our first World, and as simultaneously as you may please, our Plenumate World's laws govern the distribution of its Plenum. Since its Bubbles always *are* just where there *isn't* any Plenum, this World's laws also serve to determine the distribution of all its *Bubbles* over time. So, this second World's Bubbles move through its matter on trajectories that perfectly parallel the trajectories of the first World's Particles through its empty space.

In those attempts at conception, there may be dizzying failure. Indeed, if our thinking never concerns any Spatially Extensible Quality, there might be no significant divergence, as opposed to a merely notational difference, between our attempting to think of a World that's Particulate and our attempting to think of a World that's Plenumate, with no Particles at all.

Without our having made much progress with our Mystery of the Physical, so it is that matters still stand. In this dizzying state, we're as devoid of adequate conception as Hume saw Locke to be, when Locke didn't allow that basic physical reality should have any Qualitative Color, or any Spatially Extensible Quality whatever—or even anything readily confused with Quality. (From now on, I'll write more simply, not requiring more talk about what might be readily confused with Spatially Extensible Quality.)

To make significant progress beyond where Locke left us, we should liberate ourselves from the Denial, as stultifying as it's unnecessary. Instead of an impoverished conception of the physical, we may think of physical objects pervaded with Spatially Extensible Quality.

2. Spatially Extensible Qualities and Intelligible Propensities

With Qualities having "real existence" in the physical realm, we may have a systematically rich variety of physical conceptions, perhaps far beyond anything imagined by Locke or Hume. In this Section, I'll begin to articulate that thought.

For us contemporary philosophers, it's hard to *believe* that any matter is a certain Qualitative Color, say, a certain Absolutely Specific shade of something like what many philosophers called "phenomenal red." Yet, it certainly seems that we can *conceive* there being matter, even perfectly insensate matter, that's entirely just one Qualitative Color, and that has no other Absolutely Specific Spatially Extensible Quality. As I'll say, we can contemplate matter that is *Red*.

It's also helpful to have our considered stuff be, through and through, *pretty highly transparent* (and, just maybe, *just somewhat translucent*). As with any Spatially Extensible Quality our matter may have, its (degree of) transparency must be Absolutely Specific. So, it's Red

Transp-Taso matter that you're to conceive. For easy exposition, we'll call this matter just by its first name, Red.

This Absolutely Specific Color Quality, this Red you've conceived to pervade some matter, most likely isn't any experiential Quality. Rather, it's just a Spatially Extensible Quality, a Quality that's fit for pervading space, as with all the space of a particular Sphere, even if the Sphere is perfectly insensate, with no mentality at all. *When you're most clearly and fully conceiving an imagined Spatially Extensible Red Sphere, then you yourself will exemplify what might be called "experiential red."* To put the point in what may be metaphysically more perspicuous terms, we might say that, when you're engaged in this humanly fullest conceiving of a spatially extended concretum, that is, of a *spatial body*, then you yourself will be *experiencing redly*. Anyhow, your being *experiential red* is something that's very different, of course, from *anything's* being *Extensible Red*. (Well, there may be some interesting relations between these two, an issue I'll explore in the next Chapter. But, that's another matter.) So, even if you're a spatially extended being, when you're most fully conceiving a Sphere that's Red through and through, it's most unlikely that you'll then be Red through and through. There's no more chance of that, I imagine, than that you should be spherical in shape when clearly conceiving such a spherical particular. At all events, in demystifying the physical, what we're to bear in mind is how it may be Qualitatively with the space of some conceivable material things, space that may be, perhaps, Qualitied Extensibly.

Though it might not be very believable, it's perfectly conceivable, I think, that all of a World's matter be Red. In particular, it's conceivable that all of a World's matter be distributed so as to comprise eight Red congruent material Spheres, each separated from the others by Qualityless empty space. In such a humanly conceivable World, nothing beyond these Spheres has any Qualities. And, where there's a Sphere, the only Spatially Extensible Quality (instanced) is Red, just that Absolutely Specific Spatially Extensible Color Quality.

What's more, we may think of very many Red Spheres, I suppose even an infinite number, each of which is absolutely impenetrable to every other, with the matter of these Spheres comprising all the matter of the World in which there are the Spheres. When two such Spheres (apparently) collide, each directly recedes from the other—maybe even right before there's any true contact between the Spheres; anyhow, neither Sphere intrudes into the other. Here, we have a very clear idea, indeed, of solid spatial individuals; each Red Spherical particular is impenetrable to all the World's other perfectly basic material individuals.

(What's now presented in parentheses may be something of a long-ish digression. But, as I think, it may be a usefully stimulating digression. Anyhow, here goes.

By contrast with that quite clear notion of material impenetrability, various other ideas of such solidity aren't nearly so clear, leastways not for any of us merely human conceivers. For example, we might think to explore an idea according to which there may be Spheres, whether only one or whether very many, each of which is impenetrable to *some of* the material concreta external to it, but *not to all of* these other material individuals.

For this exploration, we may contemplate a World that contains, in addition to all our Red Spheres, an infinity of Extensible *Blue* Spheres. Let's contemplate all these Spheres like so: Just as each Red Sphere is completely impenetrable to all other Red Spheres, each Blue Sphere is impenetrable to all other Blue Spheres. More interestingly, but perhaps also not so clearly, each *Red* Sphere might be *perfectly penetrable* by any *Blue* Sphere, and vice versa. So, without even the least resistance or temporal delay, Red Spheres and Blue Spheres will pass through each other. Or, so we might try to suppose. But, how may we do this quite successfully?

To conceive such a "perfect passing" most vividly, perhaps we might think of a region where a Blue and a Red Sphere supposedly overlap in this way. The region of supposed overlap is suffused with a certain Absolutely Specific Transparent Purple; it's *Purple*, to give what's now considered a usefully short name. Very well; but how helpful, really, will any of that be?

It takes no great philosophical sensitivity to feel difficulty with what may be, at first, presumed a quite clearly enough supposed state of affairs. Once the matter of a Red Sphere and a Blue presumably intrude into each other, it's unclear, to us quite limited humans, whether we still have our original individuals or not. Are our Spheres still existent? Or, with the purple region of mutual intrusion, have they merged so as to form just a single "three-dimensional figure eight"? Or, are there then *three* only *relatively solid* entities in the situation; each of the two original Spheres, still existing whilst passing through each other and, maybe only quite temporarily as compared with them, also a single morphing "figure eight" that the first two, together, then serve to form? Or, is the real situation a *still different* state of affairs? At least for us merely human thinkers, disturbing difficulties attend our conceptions of *relative impenetrability*, so to put such a baffling idea.

For present purposes, however, none of that really matters. For, however baffled we may be by various esoteric ideas of solidity, or of near-solidity, we will still have, at the least, at least one very clear conception of material impenetrability. This is, of course, the old Lockean conception, on which each basic material thing, or each Particle, is perfectly impenetrable with respect to every other basic physical individual. With a firm hold on that happy fact, it's back to the main track. And, so, I'll now close with a matching parenthesis.)

In our attempts at conceiving physical Worlds, we'll contemplate Worlds in which, wherever there's space occupied by matter, there'll be space pervaded with Spatially Extensible Quality. And, as we'll be conceiving things, it's *only where* there's matter, or only where there's physical reality, that there'll be space pervaded with Spatially Extensible Quality. In those serviceable terms, we may express, in the next three paragraphs, three quite intelligibly different possibilities.

In a Particulate World, there'll be Spatially Extensible Quality where, and only where, there are Particles, these being relatively small bounded regions of materially filled space. Each suffused with Spatially Extensible Quality, every particle is surrounded by an empty region that, even as it's completely devoid of Extensible Quality, will also lack physical Propensity.

In a Perfectly Plenumate Physical World, Spatially Extensible Quality is instanced everywhere, and always, in the whole space of the World. And, this Qualitied space will be pervaded with physical Propensities. Accordingly, such a World is entirely filled with matter.

In a Plenumate World with Bubbles, finally, such well-Qualitied materially filled space won't exhaust the space of the World. Rather, with each of them separated from the others by well-Qualitied matter, there'll be many regions without Spatially Extensible Quality, and without anything of physical reality.

(None of this should be taken, I trust you'll know, as implying that "empty space" denotes anything real, or that, among the real entities, there are empty spaces, or that mere regions are any genuine existents, and so on. Just thought I'd offer a little reminder here.)

With those three characterizations, we may express our fairly clear, and pretty full, conceptions of some simple physical Worlds, each World conceived as clearly different from each of the others.

Now, in clearly conceiving the first of these Worlds, our familiar Particulate World, and also the third, a correlative Plenumate World, we conceived Worlds with empty space. But, then, in our clear conceptions, which have a visual experiential aspect, how do we conceive the empty space of a World? We can't really conceive it, not at all well, as being pervaded with Spatially Extensible Quality. Yet, at the same time, as our best concrete spatial conceiving does have a visual experiential aspect, any spatial region we conceive clearly seems conceived as having, or as being pervaded by, some Extensible Color. In my own case, usually it seems that I'm conceiving an empty region as having its space be Black, to name a certain dark achromatic Extensible Color. What is going on here?

Well, inasmuch as I best conceive even these Worlds visually, or with a visual aspect to my conceiving, I conceive their empty space visually. So, for example, I may conceive the Particulate World as being Black everywhere that it's not Transparent Red, that is, everywhere in the world where there isn't any physical entity at all. But, along with having an experiential aspect, my conception has an intellectual aspect. And, in having the intellectual aspect that it does, my conceiving discounts the Extensible Black that, in its experiential aspect is advanced in this very conception. There's an evident difference, I take it, between my conceiving a World with Red Particles in an (ocean-like) Black Plenum, where there's *no* such intellectual discounting and, on the other side, my conceiving a World with Red Particles in empty space, where there *is* precisely that. Let me take some steps toward some clarification.

After conceiving a World with Red Particles in empty space, where my conceiving's visual aspect "has the Particles surrounded with Extensible Black," I may then conceive precisely the same (sort of) Newtonian World once again, but this time with my conceiving's visual aspect "having the Particles surrounded with Extensible Sky Blue." In both cases, my conceiving's intellectual aspect *discounts* any thought to the effect that, in this very conceiving, the empty space is pervaded with an Extensible Color. And, owing to that, these are just two very different conceivings of precisely the same (sort of) World. By contrast with all that, I may follow up my conceiving a World with Red Particles in an (ocean-like) Plenum that's Black, by my conceiving a World with Red Particles in an (ocean-like) Plenum that's Sky Blue. This time, in the intellectual aspect of each conceiving, there's *no* discounting. Rather, there may be, with a given conceiving's intellectual aspect, the *taking* of what's experientially (presented as) the Colored surrounding Plenum *as being* a Plenum with just the Extensible Color—in one case Black, in the other Sky Blue—that's presented with that conceiving's experiential aspect. Well, that's not very perspicuous ontologically, as we shouldn't reify any of our conceiving, let alone any of its so-called aspects. Still, these comments make matters clear enough, I trust, to proceed on the thought that, while my best efforts at conceiving empty space all have a visual aspect, I needn't take empty space to have Spatially Extensible Quality.

To be sure, when I'm involved in intellectual discounting, I won't be as directly conceiving anything, whether real concreta or whether empty space, as when I'm not so involved. So, I'll never conceive any empty space as directly as I'll sometimes conceive spatial bodies. And, indeed, the disparity here may be very substantial. But, that's all right. For along with a great disparity in directness, there may be only a small disparity in clearness, and in fullness. So, as I'll suggest, we may conceive how it is Shapewise with a Red Bubbly Plenum very nearly as clearly, and very nearly as fully, as we may conceive how it is Qualitatively with just so many Spherical Red Particles.

To corroborate that suggestion, I offer this exercise. For this, I'll provide you with these instructions: Imaginatively conceive Spherical Red Particles as Yellow, and conceive the empty space, surrounding the Particles, as Purple. That's not hard to do. And, with just that, you've conceived a World with Spherical Red Particles moving about in (Colorless) empty space. Though rather indirect, isn't it quite clearly, and fairly fully, that you've conceived this Particulate World?[1]

Please don't think that, philosophically, there's very much going on here. Rather, what's salient is only something about the psychological abilities of us sighted normal human conceivers (who, I suspect, may have a fuller idea of how it is with Spatial objects, especially regarding how they may be Qualitied, than do otherwise normal congenitally sightless human thinkers). Anyway, for us normally sighted humans, at least for folks whose conceptual powers are anything much like mine, we can't think of any spatial region, whether absolutely empty or whether fully material, without thinking of it as Colored somehow or other. In contemplating the "empty space" separating two spatially separate Red Spherical Particles, which "empty space" may also surround each of the two Particles, we might think of it as mainly Pink with thin Yellow tubular stripes, or we may think of it as crosshatched Beige and Grey. But, though we may have lots of choice as to what Colorful background we'll be providing for our two Red spatial concreta, even while we're so nicely conceiving them, each as spatially distant from the other, we still must, as a matter of psychological fact, think of our spatially separate Red Particles as surrounded with Color, or with Colors, somehow or other. Or, at the very least, that's how it is with this very limited human thinker.

Look, there's nothing here that's very deep, or very contentious, or very special. It's the same point that applies to our conception of a piece of Swiss cheese. With our best conceptions of such cheesy slices, we have the most material part of the slice, where the cheese is, be a certain color,

---

1. In Chapter 4, there's another discussion of intellectual discounting. As is my aim, each of the two discussions will help clarify the other.

typically, pale yellow. And, where there are just the holes in the cheese, our conceiving of the slice may have there be, typically, Extensible Black, well, some black, anyway. In this conceiving, we're *not* thinking that, where there's no cheese, there are regions of something that's Black. Rather, as our successful intended conception goes, the empty spatial regions *aren't any* Color. In such an ordinary case, too, our conceiving's intellectual aspect discounts a salient feature of its experiential aspect. Quite as with our best conceptions of *ordinary* physical things, I've suggested, so it is, too, with our best conceptions of *basic* physical things.

3. Spatially Extensible Qualities Are Perfectly Pervasive Properties

Quite clearly, I think, we may conceive a spatially extended object, as with a Particle, to be *perfectly pervaded* with a *single Absolutely Specific* Spatially Extensible Quality, say, with our Red. For us mere human beings, this is the clearest case of a spatial entity Extensibly Qualitied. With this very clear case, every region of the Red entity, however small, will itself be Red, quite as perfectly pervaded by this Spatially Extensible Quality as is the whole extended object, of which it's but a small spatial part. Let me amplify, perhaps so as to clarify.

Consider a basic spatial physical object that's both perfectly Spherical and all perfectly (Transparent) Red. Now, as this physical body is basic, there's no physical object that's a substantial part of the basic spatial concretum. But, quite clearly, we can conceive indefinitely many spatial regions of the Particle, saliently including many that are wholly internal to the considered Sphere itself. Let's now consider how things stand, in several basic respects, with various of these internal regions and, on the other side, with the Monochromatic Red Spherical entity itself.

My main point, in this Section, concerns how it is that this Red Sphere is Extensibly Colored. To express this main point, I'll say that the Sphere's (Transparent) Red *perfectly pervades* the basic spatial body. But, what does this mean?

For a helpful explication of my intended meaning, I'll need to use phrases that suggest the existence of dubious entities: at least the likes of *regions*, and maybe lots more. But, as you already know how very limited I am, we needn't think that this is important.

Anyway, we're considering how it is, Qualitatively, with our supposed Monochromatic (Transparent) Red of our Particle. Well, using some punchy language, here's something to say: It's positively *required of* each internal region of the Sphere (no matter how small) that, like the whole Sphere itself, the region be Red. So, as each of the Particle's regions are Red, Extensible Red is, with respect to the Particle, a *perfectly pervasive property*.

Parallel points hold for other cases of basic physical particulars. For a most salient contrast, we consider an infinitely vast shapeless physical field, or Plenum, that's all (Transparent) Red. And, we consider various regions of this field, some shaped one way, say Spherically, others shaped differently, say, Cubically. As to how they're shaped, all these regions will differ from the field itself, which isn't shaped at all. And, so far as size goes, they'll also differ from the field, a vaster object that wholly includes all the regions. But, there's not any difference as concerns Spatially Extensible Quality. To the contrary, even as our originally conceived field is (Transparent) Red, so every region of it is also (Transparent) Red, the finite Cubical regions, the finite Spherical regions, and so on.

When saying that our Red Particle's Quality is a perfectly pervasive property of the thing, I dramatically contrasted the matter with how things stand as regards the Particle's Size, and the Sizes of its internal regions. Not wanting to reify regions any more than properties, nor wanting to reify empty spaces, either, still I may hope to expound on these matters in some such terms as with these next few sentences, which I think almost any happy reader will quite readily grasp.

All right, then, let's now consider our Particle's Size, or its sheer spatial volume. Well, each of the Particle's internal regions will be smaller in Size, or will have a lesser volume, than the volume of the (whole) Spherical Particle. And, so, each region will have a Size *different from* the whole Particulate Sphere, say, Size S, a certain larger Size. To mark this point vividly, we may say this: Having Size S is a property that, with respect to the Sphere, is *precluded for* every last one of its regions; having Size S, or being Size S, is a *perfectly precluded property*.

Next, let's consider our Particle's Shape. Well, many of our Sphere's internal regions won't be shaped Spherically; for example, many will be shaped Cubically. So, many regions will have a Shape that's *different from* the Shape of the (whole) Spherical Particle. But, as well, many of our Particle's internal regions *will* be shaped Spherically. So, as well, many regions will have a Shape that's *the same as* the Shape of the (whole) Particle. So, on the one hand, and unlike the property of being Size S, the property of being Spherical *won't* be, with respect to the regions of our Sphere, a *perfectly precluded* property. At the same time, and on the other hand, being shaped Spherically *isn't* a property that, for the Sphere's internal regions, is perfectly pervasive.

At all events, we may see a clear contrast between the salient Spatial properties of a Monochromatic Plenum, which aren't perfectly pervasive, and the Plenum's Spatially Extensible Quality, which is a perfectly pervasive basic natural property of the Plenum, or the Material Field.[2]

As I really do hope, the prior paragraphs have been helpful, in getting readers to know what I mean when saying that a spatial concretum's Extensible Color is a perfectly pervasive property of the body in question; well, at least with more than just a few readers, even if not nearly all. At any rate, let's try another tack now, seeking another route to making some progress in the matter.

How things are with very intelligible basic physical objects, each Extensibly Colored so pervasively, differs dramatically from how things are with ordinary colored objects, as with my brown wooden writing desk. First off, most of the *interior* of the desk *obviously isn't* brown. That's quickly revealed in many ways. For instance, when I open a drawer and look at the opened drawer from underneath, I notice the nearly white wood that there was left unstained by the desk's maker. So, most of the desk's wood, and most of the desk, isn't brown. But, that may not be philosophically interesting. Well, even if it's not, this will be pretty interesting: Under apparently revealing magnification, what we take to be the desk's brownest areas, as with regions of its top surface, seem to be not really brown at all! Now, *that* comment may prompt a philosophically useful discussion.

Here, I find helpful some bold suggestions from David Armstrong. In his fearlessly challenging *Perception and the Physical World*, Armstrong presents a pretty disturbing discussion of magnifying glasses and microscopes, including even picture-taking electron microscopes.[3]

---

2. It's obvious that these points all hold if the wholly internal, fully included regions are all finite regions, as with our imagined Spherical and Cubical regions. They also hold, I'll observe, for what we may call a "somewhat included region, that's not finite." Let me explain this observation: Consider an infinitely vast region that's to the left of my central plane of present imaginative focus, but that includes nothing to the right of this plane. Though itself infinitely vast, there's a very definite way in which that region will be far smaller than the originally conceived field as a whole. For the "full-field" will include all the infinitely vast space that the "half-field" pervades, includes, or occupies; and, as well, it will include infinitely more space besides, namely, all that's to the right of the supposed plane. That's it for size. Now, what about shape? Well, as the half-field has a planar surface, whilst the full-field hasn't any surface, the two differ as dramatically in shape as in size. And, finally, what about Extensible Color? Well, just as our whole shapeless field is all (Transparent) Red, so also is the "half-field," the "somewhat included region" we're considering, as is, of course, any of the whole field's regions, whether wholly or only somewhat so.

3. David Armstrong, *Perception and the Physical World*, Routledge, 1961, pages 159–164.

To have matters be still more vivid, I'll modify his discussion: Suppose that, over there on our left, we place a fairly good magnifying glass over my desk's brownest area, so that its pretty flat surface still looks quite brown, but appears bumpy and uneven. And, to the right of that, there's a more powerful magnifier; and to the right of that a still more powerful one, and so on, and so on, and so on. But, to make matters vividly disturbing, there needn't be many of these increasingly powerful magnifiers; even just three will probably do; and four will certainly do just fine. So, let's have the two leftmost (of four) magnifiers each be just a simple glass lense, not a true microscope, but with the lense on the right far more powerful than the just pretty powerful lense on the left. And, to the right of them both, there'll be two true microscopes, with the microscope on the right far more powerful than the one on the left. With these lenses and microscopes, there's provided a well-placed sequence of mirrors, so that, even to see very clearly what each reveals, I don't need an eye placed anywhere very near any of them. Sitting back here, right where I am, and looking straight ahead at the big mirror before me, I can see, all at once, all the images produced by all four magnifiers, as well as, fifth of all, the much larger image, of course, of the desk as unmagnified. Now, with just those five terribly salient things to notice, I can visually apprehend, all at once and quite fully, some very telling appearances of the desk's top surface. Especially as it's so natural for me to read from left to right, I can hardly fail to be very impressed by what I certainly seem to see: Never mind all the mostly whitish unstained wood that mostly composes the desk, even its topmost surface isn't really brown. This appearance may be almost as disturbing as it's compelling. So, we must continue our discussion.

With the ordinary desk, generally taken to be brown, it strikes us as paradoxical, maybe incoherent, to think that *none* of its *very small parts* is actually brown. Indeed, the polar opposite of that seems wanted by our most intuitive, natural and central idea of a colored object: By contrast with an object whose surface is very largely brown, but is dappled with tiny white dots, an object whose surface is (all just plain) brown should be one *all* of whose regions are brown, however small many of these regions may be. Well, I suppose we may allow that what seems to be our most intuitive idea might really be, here, a badly exaggerated notion. Well maybe; I'm not sure. But, then, at the very least, we'll want, as a cautious fallback position, a conception of colored things according to which *some* of our desk's minute parts, or tiny regions, are brown. The idea that *none* of a brown object's tiny regions is actually brown, though the whole big object is truly brown, this idea really clashes very severely, I imagine, with our intuitive, natural and central idea of a colored object. At the least, there's something of a paradox here, at least a small and modest paradox.

This paradox may be dissipated, perhaps, through the service of two complementary ideas.

First, we may think of the brown desk's color as something like a Propensity of that physical complex to participate in promoting certain visual experience, *experiential brown*, on the part of normal human (color) perceivers, on condition that such (color) perceivers be in conditions conducive to their normally perceiving the physical object. Well, something like that. And, as we suppose, the relevant participation may concern, in fact, the brown desk's reflecting, from its topmost surface, certain patterned light. Now, with large regions of the surface, enough of the desk's peripheral constituents are suitably structured for them to reflect light with the requisite patterning. But, with very tiny areas of the desk's surface, there's not so much by way of suitably structured constituents to reflect such happily promoting light as that. And, in line with all that, we may say such very various things as these: First, in a use *appropriate to such* matters, we say the very small topmost regions of the desk *aren't brown*, though much larger top areas *are*. And, in such a use, we also say that the desk is brown. But, this may not be a use of "brown" that's well suited for philosophical discussion. And, more generally, so it may also be with correlative uses of the more general term "colored."

Second, then, we observe that our *most intuitive* idea of colored objects may find its true home in our thought about the pervasion of space, notably the pervasion of a colored object's space, by an Absolutely Specific Spatially Extensible Color. And, as we may then suspect, there can be an easy slide from how it is Qualitatively with a basic physical entity, on the one side, to the more superficial concerns of the everyday case, to how it is qualitatively with the presumably perceptible physical complexes, like my brown desk. Providing we speak of just the basic cases, those that are philosophically most central, we may express and apply, without paradox, our most intuitive idea. And, it's in just this more philosophical use that we may see something useful for resolving the Mystery of the Physical: Insofar as physical reality might be very intelligible to us human thinkers, there will be spatially extended physical objects (or maybe just one vast spatially extended Plenum) perfectly pervaded with, or by, Spatially Extensible Color.

(For this Section's discussion, so concerned with how Spatially Extensible Colors may be perfectly pervasive Qualities, I've focused only on the simplest cases, where a basic body is entirely just one Absolutely Specific Extensible Color. For a simple example, a basic body's only Color is just Transparent Red, throughout all the space it occupies. But, of course, there are also more complex cases. By aptly considering that, we may become clearer about what's been claimed for the simpler Monochromatic cases. Consider a basic Cube that's Colored so as to seem like ten square tiles, all in a perfectly neat stack or, rotating your mind's eye through ninety degrees, all in a perfectly neat row. On the square surface facing you, and for one unit inward, or one unit along the row, the Cube is Extensible Red. Then, also one unit deep, there's a "square tile" that's Extensible Blue; and then another that's Extensible Red, and so on. There are, then, five separate regions of this Cube that are each Extensible Red, and five other separate regions are Extensible Blue. Now, there must be, of course, indefinitely many regions of this conceived Cube that are partly Extensible Red and partly Extensible Blue. With each of *these* regions, of course, we *don't* have anything that's all the same Extensible Color. But, for our point about Extensible Colors being perfectly pervasive, that doesn't matter. What matters is this: Wherever the Cube *is entirely Extensible Red*, and *not* where it's Partly Red and Partly Blue, every wholly included region of the Cube *will also be Extensible Red*.)

4. Intelligible Physical Reality and a Principle of Constrained Contingency

In terms of our three kinds of basic property, the Spatials, the Propensities, and the (Spatially Extensible) Qualities, what's required for there to be a humanly intelligible mind-independent *physical* reality, whether or not it's the World's only realm of reality? Without much detail, I'll try to give the question a serviceable answer.

First, some words about some necessary truths: For a World to feature a *physical* reality that *we humans can conceive*, quite clearly and fully, the World *must* include at least one entity such that (1) it has *some* Spatial Properties—even if it may be, in a quite extreme case, only the property of being, in all directions, infinitely extensive, and (2) it has *some* Spatially Extensible Qualities—even if it may be, in a quite extreme case, only the property of being, everywhere and always, the very same Quality, and also (3) it has *some* Propensities—even if it may be, in a quite extreme case, only the Propensity to exemplify, in each place at each time, exactly the same Spatially Extensible Quality it exemplifies right there at the just previous time. Now, though the parallel between the two isn't perfect, it still seems useful to suggest a close comparison between the necessity proposed and certain more familiar necessary propositions, like this Nonqualitative statement, expressing how Size and Shape should be related: As does any Euclidean geometrical closed solid, a physical entity precisely bounded by such a figure that we humans can conceive, quite clearly and fully, *must* be such that (1) it has *some* shape and also (2) it has *some* size.

Second, some complementary words about some contingent relations: With physical entities generally, there is *no necessary connection* between (1) precisely *which* Spatial Properties the thing has, and (2) exactly *which* Qualities the thing has, and (3) precisely *which* Propensities *comprise all* the Propensities of that physical thing. The *lack* of necessity just stressed, and the *contingency* just indicated, is the same as with this more familiar proposition: As is true of a Euclidean closed solid figure, a physical entity may be a certain given *shape* even while being *any* one of *numerous distinct sizes* and, equally, it *may* be a certain given *size* even while being *any* one of *numerous distinct shapes*. At the same time, I'm not sure exactly how far this analogy extends, between our fully Propertied basic physical bodies and, on the other side, the Euclidean solid figures. So, trusting that it's served us usefully so far, I won't bother to press it further.

What's my main purpose here is to suggest, at any rate, how very much contingency there is, or how much range for real variation, as to how basic physical concreta are Propertied. To advance the suggestion vividly enough, let's consider a Monochromatic Yellow Sphere. Now, among the possible disposition partners for this Sphere, there are Blue Cubes that are Propensitied to attract any object that's a Sphere, even if no such Blue Sphere-Attractor currently exists in our Yellow Sphere's World (or there are none anywhere near enough, or whatever) and, equally, there are Red Spheres just so similarly Propensitied for attracting Spheres, and so on. [Remember, each of many individual electrons may be (electrically) Propensitied to strongly attract any protonish entities, or protons, even if there aren't actually any protons.] There's a vast range of attractive disposition partners, then, for our supposed Yellow Sphere. But, then, of course, our Sphere will be a reciprocally attractive disposition partner for any of them. So, along with being Shaped Spherically, our Sphere will be *Propensitied to be Attracted by any such Sphere-Attractors* as there may be (and as may be situated suitably for just such interactive attracting). As well, our Sphere must also be Propensitied for all sorts of other interactions.

Strikingly, we may consider another sort of Blue Cube, whether or not any of these actually do exist, one that's *not* Propensitied to attract any Spherical individuals, but that's *Propensitied to annihilate,* completely and forever, any Spheres there may be (or, as may be more palatable, any that are within a meter of such an Annihilator, or whatever). Now, with respect to *these* possible Blue Cubes, our Sphere is also a reciprocal disposition partner; so, it's *Propensitied to be annihilated by any such Sphere-Annihilators* as there may be (and as may be situated suitably for just such interactive annihilating). So, when we have a Spherical basic physical body it's required that, in the whole full scheme of things, our concretum is Propensitied in a vast variety of ways. Let me be perfectly clear about that: An object *can't* be a basic Spherical physical body and yet, somehow, *fail to be Propensitied in these ways.* (And, to get the hang of things still better, please also notice this: When a Blue Cube is a Sphere-Annihilator, that will *preclude* the Cube from being Propensitied to attract Spherical Particles, as what's annihilated can't be attracted anywhere.)

As to how our basic physical bodies are Propertied, we should notice, then, both a great range of variation, what we might call a great deal of contingency, and also quite considerable constraints on all the contingent variety. Noticing this, we may say that, with our metaphysic of physical individuals, we uphold a *Principle of Constrained Contingency (concerning How Basic Physical Bodies May Be Propertied).* Always respecting our Principle, let's elaborate a little.[4]

For ease of exposition, we'll focus on Newtonian Particulate Worlds: In these happily manageable Worlds, each of enormously many Particles has the same "mass," the same "amount of matter," and each will attract the others with a force that varies inversely with the square of the distance between the centers of the interacting Particles. Now, we've just said how, even when each World is Monochromatic, there may be great qualitative variation among these nicely manageable Worlds. Now, while that's old hat, we may newly notice this: In a certain *Tutti Frutti* Particulate World, many Particles are Red and many others Blue, with yet many others being Yellow, and also Green, but there may be no Brown, or Grey, or Silvery, or Goldenish Particles. In another Tutti Frutti World, there may also be many Red and Blue Particles, but no Yellow and Green Particles. (Along with such Qualitative variety, in many Tutti Frutti Worlds there's also much Qualitative stability. In these Qualitatively Stable Tutti Frutti Worlds, any Particle that's Red, for instance, will always be Red, and it won't ever have any other Color Quality.)

---

4. On working toward a decently constrained Principle of Constrained Contingency, I got important help from Matthew Kotzen. What deficiencies may remain, well, they reflect my own deficiencies.

Our supposition of Tutti Frutti Worlds is perfectly intelligible. So, even as our Principle of Constrained Contingency is nicely grasped, it may be grasped, quite nicely, how vastly great is all the contingency it allows. Yet, this Principle may appear to raise a serious problem.

5. Extensible Qualities as a Factor in the Development of Physical Reality: A Problem

As often appears, the Qualities of physical things won't ever be an influence in (determining) the development of physical reality; rather, Qualities must be always entirely idle. What are we to make of this appearance? This question poses the *Problem of Influence for Qualities (in Physical Reality)*.

To appreciate the puzzle, we'll compare a Monochromatic New-tonian World and, on the other hand, a Tutti Frutti Newtonian World. Except that the first has no Qualitative variety and the second has a great deal, the two Worlds may be exceedingly similar. So, the be-havior of the Tutti Frutti World's Particles may precisely parallel the behavior of the Particles in the Monochromatic World. And, then, all the Tutti Frutti's Qualitative variety will make no difference to the physical development of the Tutti Frutti World. But, wait a minute! Are there *any* Worlds where Qualitative variety means *much more than that* for the development of the World's physical reality? All too often, it seems there are none. So, our Problem often appears acute.

We've quickly made some progress toward appreciating our Prob-lem of Influence for Qualities. Yet, to appreciate this Problem properly, it's also important *not to overestimate* the predicament. Rather than doing that, we should realize this: To resolve our Problem, we *shouldn't* try to show how it might be that, in *every* World with physical reality, all the Qualities of physical things are significant factors in the physical de-velopment of the World. Nor should we try to show how it may be that, in *every* such World, *at least some* such Qualities are such significant factors. Indeed, it follows from the Principle of Constrained Contin-gency that there's no more chance of doing such a thing than of drawing a perfectly round square. Rather than any of that, our Problem asks us, much more modestly, to show how it might be that, in *some* Worlds with physical reality, at least some Qualities of physical things are significant factors in the development of the Worlds' physical reality.

With even just this much, we'll have, I trust, a tolerably good grasp of our Problem. And, with even just that much attained, it's now best, I think, to attempt a solution to the Problem.

6. The Problem of Influence for Extensible Qualities in Physical Reality: A Solution

At least since Galileo, physics has made great progress by ignoring thoughts as to Qualities. Quite rightly, we're all very impressed with that. But, because we're so very impressed, when we consider physical Propensities, Qualities may never enter our consideration. For progress with the Problem of Influence for Extensible Qualities, however, this must change radically. In suggesting how we might change, I proceed in several steps.

First, we'll contemplate a Monochromatic Particulate World: While all the World's Particles have the very same Spatially Extensible Quality, perhaps *Grey*, these Spherical Particles come in ten different Sizes, with many Particles of each Size. As regards both its volume and its "amount of matter," each of the smallest Particles is one tenth as great as each of the largest Particles; each of the next smallest is two tenths as great, and so on. Now, each Particle has the Propensity to attract each of the others, and to be attracted by each of the others, with a force that varies directly with its Size (and, say, inversely with the square of the distance between its center and the centers of each of the other Particles). It's easy enough to take seriously the thought that a World works this way.

Next, we'll contemplate a *Multichromatic* Particulate World: While all this World's Particles have the very same Size, perhaps the Size of the smallest Particles in the foregoing Monochromatic World, these Spherical Particles come in ten different "Achromatic Colors," with many Particles of each such Color. The lightest Particles are all Snow White. Each has one-tenth "the amount of matter" as the darkest, each of which is Jet Black. Each of the next lightest Particles, all Very Light Grey, is two-tenths as "massive" as the Jet Black, and so on. In this World, each Particle has the Propensity to attract each of the others, and to be attracted by each of the others, with a force that varies directly with its *Qualitative Darkness* (and, say, inversely with the square of the distance). For many of us, it's hard to take seriously the thought that a World works in *this other* way.

To make progress on our Problem, we must take seriously not only the thought that all physical entities have Qualities, but also the thought that, at least in some Worlds, at least some physical objects have Propensities *with respect to Extensible Qualities*. In other words, we must adopt a *more inclusive mode of thinking* than the one that's proved so successful scientifically for Galileo and so many successors. To that end, let's now gain more experience with such thinking.

So, we now contemplate a different contrasting pair of Particulate Worlds, again one a Size-Propensity World and the other a Quality-Propensity World. In both these Worlds, there are four sorts of Spherical Particles: Each exactly the same as the other in Spatially Extensible Quality, there are Large Red Particles and Small Red Particles, the former ten times the Size of the latter. With Spatially Extensible Quality very different from that of our Red Particles, there are Large Blue Particles and Small Blues, with the Large Blues the same size as the Large Reds, and the Small Blues the same as the Small Red Particles.

Now, in the first of our two Worlds, each Particle will have a Propensity to attract any Particle that's *different from it in Size*, and a Propensity to repel any Particle that's *the same Size*. In this World, the Large Reds and the Large Blues will repel each other, as will the Small Reds and the Small Blue Particles. And, the Large Particles, Red and Blue, will attract, and will be attracted by, the Small Particles, Red and Blue. In this World, when Particles attract others, and when Particles repel others, it's *because* they have Propensities *with respect to the very Size* the others possess.

In the second World, no Particle will have any of those Propensities. Rather, each will have a Propensity to attract any Particle that's *different from it in Spatially Extensible Quality*, and a Propensity to repel any Particle that's *the same Spatially Extensible Quality*. In this World, the Red Particles, Large and Small, will attract, and will be attracted by, the Blue Particles, Large and Small. Far from repelling each other, here the Large Red Particles and the Large Blue Particles will *attract* each other. As I'm envisioning this other World, when Particles attract, or repel, other Particles, it's *because* the former have Propensities *with respect to the very Quality* the latter possess.

Toward gaining comfort with the thought that physical entities may have Propensities *with respect to Qualities*, I've considered a couple of relevantly contrasting pairs of Particulate Worlds. But, I see no reason to think that it's only with such contrasting Worlds as those that Spatially Extensible Quality may be a physically relevant factor. Rather, in various Worlds, how it is with physical entities Qualitatively may be highly significant in the development of physical reality.

Perhaps it should go without saying that, in this Section's discussion, I was supposing all the usual truths about reciprocal disposition partners that, by now, are so familiar. Now, of course, and quite as we've been supposing, in an *interaction* between a Large Particle Propensitied to attract one that's Small and a Small Particle, the Small Particle has, *as well as* its Small Size, a *Propensity to be attracted by* Large Particles. And, in a perfect parallel with that, we should suppose, as well, that in an *interaction* between a Red Particle Propensitied to attract one that's Blue and a Blue Particle, the Blue Particle has, *as well as* its Blue Quality, a *Propensity to be attracted by* the Red Particles. In short and in sum: Just as well as it applies to the more familiar Propensities, the general point about interaction partners applies to Propensities with respect to Spatially Extensible Quality.

7. Mutually Isolated Concrete Worlds and Distinct Eons of the Actual World

In much of my exploratory discussion, I've adverted to a variety of possible Worlds. Now, so far as this book's exploration goes, these allusions may be taken as just heuristically helpful performances, all in the service of articulating the variety that may obtain with physical individuals (and, maybe also, with some purely mental nonphysical concrete particulars).

In other books, talk of Worlds has much more substantial import. For the most substantial import it's been given in this Scientiphical era of philosophy, we turn, of course, to the brilliantly bold work of David Lewis, certainly this past century's greatest speculative philosopher and, quite as with Russell well before him, one of the century's greatest philosophical thinkers. From Lewis's philosophically powerful and intellectually courageous masterwork, *On the Plurality of Worlds*, let's listen to some Worldly talk with quite enormous philosophical import:

> Are there other worlds that are other ways? I say there are. I advocate a thesis of plurality of worlds, or *modal realism*, which holds that our world is but one world among many. There are countless other worlds, other very inclusive things. Our world consists of us and all our surroundings, however remote in time and space; just as it is one big thing having lesser things as parts, so likewise do other worlds have lesser other-worldly things as parts. The worlds...are not remote. Neither are they nearby. They are not at any spatial distance whatever from here. They are not far in the past or future, nor for that matter near; they are not at any temporal distance whatever from now. They are isolated: there are no spatiotemporal relations at all between things that belong to different worlds. Nor does anything that happens at one world cause anything to happen at another. Nor do they overlap; they have no parts in common....
>
> The worlds are many and varied. There are enough of them to afford worlds where...there are no people at all, or the physical constants do not permit life, or totally different laws govern the doings of alien particles with alien properties. There are so many worlds,

in fact, that absolutely every way that a world could possibly be is a way that some world *is*. And as with worlds, so it is with parts of worlds....

The worlds are not of our own making.... We make languages and concepts and descriptions and imaginary representations that apply to worlds. We make stipulations that select some worlds rather than others for our attention. Some of us even make assertions to the effect that other worlds exist. But none of these things we make are the worlds themselves.[5]

To be sure, almost all of us lucky enough to have been Lewis's contemporaries think him to be not only an astonishingly fertile and brilliant thinker, but also a philosopher who, on many metaphysical matters, is a very sensible thinker, even often quite commonsensical and conservative. But, regarding his claim as to there being many concrete worlds, all ontologically on a par with this one we call "the actual world," almost all think it's unduly heroic, at best, and most think it's *crazily* philosophical.

Myself, I don't think it's so crazy. And, though I'm not so free and easy with worlds as once I was, I take very seriously the thought that there are very many concrete worlds, each ontologically on a par with our own, and each completely isolated from all others.[6] Much more than I did so long ago, I'd like to see convincing *limits* specified, convincingly, for an (infinite) plethora of such worlds. For instance, I can't believe there's any world that, for billions of years is just like ours, and, then, for billions of years, contains nothing (notable) beyond just so many trillions of parsnips and turnips (and their parts, and the collections containing them, and so on) floating about in otherwise empty space.[7] Or, if you think that

---

5. David Lewis, *On the Plurality of Worlds*, Basil Blackwell, 1986, pages 2–3.

6. See my badly titled paper "Minimizing Arbitrariness: Towards a Metaphysics of Infinitely Many Isolated Concrete Worlds," *Midwest Studies in Philosophy*, 1984, reprinted in the new collection of my essays, *Philosophical Papers, Volume 1*, Oxford University Press, 2006. Better to have had the title's first words be "Localizing Arbitrariness." With a metaphysics that has all specificity be merely local features of "reality entire," not universal features, the *appearance* of arbitrariness is reduced. So, the thought runs, as we can see that there's nothing terribly specific that's also horribly universal, there was only the appearance that "all-reality," or reality entire, prefers that there be, say, precisely two electrons in a first shell around an atomic nucleus. And, on pages 128–133 of *On the Plurality of Worlds*, you should see, I must suppose, Lewis's discussion of, and rejection of, what I erroneously thought would be a little gift to him. But, I reject that discussion, as missing the point of my meager offering. There's many more sorts of successful explaining, as I see things, than all the explaining that's ever anywhere even near the neighborhood of causal explanation.

7. For a most interesting discussing of this, that helps makes more intelligible how there might be such limits, see Derek Parfit, "The Puzzle of Reality: Why Does the Universe Exist?" *Times Literary Supplement*, July 3, 1992, pages 3–5, and, if you can get your hands on them, longer pieces by Parfit, unpublished as far as I know, to similar effect.

"parsnip" can't be true of such free-floating complexes, then let it be a world that, for these billions of years, contains nothing (notable) beyond just so many parsnipy complexes and turnipy complexes (and *their* parts, and the collections containing *them*, and so on). [In *some* sense, I guess, such a strangely shifty situation is *possible*. But, even if that's so, there *isn't*, I think, any concrete world that contains nothing but so many trillions of parsnips and turnips for billions of years.] Through some nicely elegant limits for worlds, there may be precluded any such strangely vegetarian world as that. Denying there'll ever be any such elegant limits or, for that matter, limits not so elegant, Lewis holds there *are* such strangely vegetarian worlds. Yet, though I'm sure my inclinations as to other worlds are less liberal than Lewis's, I'm not so sure that they're less crazy than my old friend's.

In the book you're now holding, I won't dare to speculate seriously regarding existing other worlds, for a very human reason that I'll try to make plain pretty soon. But, before ducking these metaphysically important issues, I'll say a bit about what I take myself to be foregoing.

What sometimes inclines me to think there are many worlds, elegantly enough limited, are these "rationalist" considerations, which I so often itch to explore: Often I can't help but wonder, in ignorance so frustrating as to be somewhat painful, at what are (supposed to be) not just highly specific aspects of our actual world, but features that are as fundamental for our world, and as perfectly universal, as they're peculiarly specific. Here, let's start with this: It's a feature of our world that, in the nearest group of electrons orbiting an atom's nucleus, there can be no more than two electrons; for an atom to have more electrons than two, others must orbit at a greater distance. Why just two there, and not three as the limit? Or, why not just one allowed? An answering derivation may proceed from yet more fundamental physical features. But, for the derivation to yield a limit of *precisely two* in the first ring, these more *basic* features must *themselves* be so highly specific and quirky. Can it really be that, even unto its basic nature, *all* reality is, for *all* eternity, so very *specially specific*, apparently so "specially preferential"?

A variety of answers have been offered. None do I find very satisfactory. What often seems the least bad—I daren't say it's any good—is this: Our entire universe, throughout all its history, is just one concrete world among very many—infinitely many, I should suppose, though maybe not an infinity of an enormously high order. Now, in some of these very many mutually isolated worlds, the fundamental physical features have it that atoms replete with electrons may have just one electron, never as many as two, in the first ring. And, in others—ours is

Multi-vund

one—basic physics will have there be precisely two. In still others, there may be three in that ring; and so on, and so on.

Well, as a rational antidote to my painful wonder at the world's peculiar specificity, all that's not so bad, I sometimes think. And, so, I also sometimes think that, so long as we're not extremely profligate in our hypothesizing worlds, we may see some philosophic sense—and not just philosophic craziness—in thoughts as to many mutually isolated concrete worlds.

But, I'll now sidestep these important issues. In this present work, I'll place to the side, as much as I can, the questions about apparent arbitrariness that, at various other times, engage me in painful wonder. Why do that? Well, even without delving into those deep issues, there'll be far more discussed here than, with my quite limited intellect, I can discuss to any very progressive effect. And, that's not all. As well, in the Humanly Realistic Philosophy I'm here offering, there's already been advanced what, by almost any currently respectable standard, is more than enough philosophical speculation. And, what's still more, in coming Sections, there'll be quite a few more speculations. Not only to conduct this study to progressive effect, then, but also for the work to be at all plausible, or palatable, I won't speculate as to a plurality of isolated real concrete worlds.

Well, then, in this present inquiry, how are we to take my talk of Worlds? As I trust, we can take it to be just a very usefully vivid heuristic. We needn't bother about whether, in addition to all that's ever in the actual world, there's more to concrete reality.

For many, that simple disclaimer will suffice. But, some may want to hear something more literal or realistic. In short order, I'll now do something for them.

Intuitively, we may think of our actual world as temporally limitless. In particular, we may think of this world as having always existed, with an infinity of past eons each featuring some concrete physical reality (whether or not all the past eons do.) Now, where I've been talking about Worlds, we may talk instead about (past) *Eons* of this one actual world. In line with that, I'll now come close to rehearsing a passage above, where I talked about different Worlds; in the near rehearsal, I'll talk, instead, of different Eons.

We may consider a contrasting pair of Particulate Eons, one a Size-Propensity Eon and the other a Quality-Propensity Eon. In both Eons, there are four sorts of Spherical Particles: There are Large Red Particles and Small Red Particles, the former ten times the Size of the latter. And, there are Large Blue Particles and Small Blues.

Now, in the first of our two Eons, each Particle will have a Propensity to attract any Particle that's *different from it in Size*, and a Propensity to repel any Particle that's *the same Size*. In this Eon, for example, the Large Reds and the Large Blues will repel each other, as will the Small Reds and the Small Blue Particles. In this Eon, when Particles attract others, and when Particles repel others, it's *because* they have Propensities *with respect to the very Size* the others possess.

In the second Eon, no Particle will have any of those Propensities. Rather, each will have a Propensity to attract any Particle that's *different from it in Spatially Extensible Quality*, and a Propensity to repel any Particle that's *the same Spatially Extensible Quality*. In this Eon, for instance, the Red Particles, Large and Small, will attract, and will be attracted by, the Blue Particles, Large and Small. Far from repelling each other, here the Large Red Particles and the Large Blue Particles will *attract* each other. As I'm envisioning this other Eon, when Particles attract, or repel, other Particles, it's *because* the former have Propensities *with respect to the very Spatially Extensible Quality* the latter possess.

Why should the actual world ever go through such very different Eons? For advancing our Humanly Realistic Philosophy, it matters little whether this question is answered. Yet, aiming to please readers, I'll present a couple of possible answers. First, it may always be a sheer accident that an Eon ever ends, and that it ends at the time it does, and, as may almost always happen, that it's succeeded by another whose concrete things have different basic features. Well, though it's hardly my favorite answer, that's one possible answer. Here's a quite different answer. Along with the Propensities already noted for them, the first Eon's Particles have other "more special" Propensities. Among these other powers, these Particles may be Propensitied jointly to produce, under certain rare specific conditions, an implosion involving all of what's then current concrete reality. These conditions may obtain when, and only when, the Particles are in a certain perfectly specific array, or when in one of just a few such rare and specific arrays. And, just as those special Propensities and rare conditions will have it, such a momentous implosion may be followed by a momentous explosion, wherein there's a proliferation of Particles with quite different salient basic features, maybe along with quite the same "more special" features. As it might be, after our first exemplary Eon ended in such an implosion, there were explosively proliferated the Particles of our second Eon.

After adverting to a variety of possible Worlds, as I've earlier done, I've just alluded to a variety of temporal Eons, supposed as having actually occurred. But, of course, I really have no idea whether there's actually occurred any such variety, nor whether our actual world ever will be so various physically. But, no matter. Like my talk of the Worlds before, so my talk of the Eons may also be taken, for our present

explorations, as just a heuristically helpful performance, as just another help toward articulating the variety that may obtain with concrete
reality, especially with physical concreta. Following tradition, from now
on I'll revert to talk mainly of Worlds, not Eons. Those for whom the
latter sort of talk is more helpfully vivid may, if they wish, take my
remarks to be vivid temporal speculations. Still others will be dissat-
isfied, no doubt, with both suggested alternatives. They're invited to
construct their own heuristics, and to construe my comments in terms
of their own most comfortable conceptual constructions.

8. Mightn't the Recognized Physical Properties Just Be Spatially Extensible Qualities?

Concerning the Demystification of the Physical here offered, by now
some main things should be quite clear. But, others may yet need more
clarification. Very possibly, that's how it is with our Principle of Constrained Contingency and, equally, with my claim that, even in the
realm of insensate basic physical reality, there may be *enormous variety.*
So, let's discuss the matter.

Against my commodious metaphysical approach, some will say,
more parsimoniously, that we shouldn't think there to be more than
what, in a Galilean frame of mind, we take there to be. So, as my
colleague Gordon Belot observed, some may offer words like these:

> You take your opponents to think that, when a sparse Newtonian
> world contains some particles, then the only properties exemplified
> there are mass density (absolute vacuum gets 0, space occupied by
> particles may get varying amounts) and impenetrability, and position.
> And, as they think, this will yield an adequate, intelligible, account of
> the world.
>
> But, you say: No. The Particle vs. Bubble example, or whatever
> you want to call such a case, shows this is not so. We must also include
> some Qualities, deeply analogous to, but not necessarily identical to,
> phenomenal qualities, to fix the distinction between occupied and
> unoccupied space. For convenience, you may call this Spatially Ex-
> tensible Quality *Blue.* We describe the world by attributing different
> shades of Blue to different parts of space: null to vacuum, different
> shades corresponding to parts filled by particles.
>
> But, then, having done this, we notice that (if the laws are non-
> haecceitistic) we can formulate the dynamics in terms of (the Spatially
> Extensible Quality) Blue, rather than in terms of mass density. So,
> physics is about qualities, or, as you say, Qualities. Well, then, isn't
> "Blue" just another name for mass density? Doesn't it really have all

the same features (varying with degree of occupation of space, etc.)? Indeed, it must; or it wouldn't be possible to write dynamical laws in terms of it! Why shouldn't we directly take mass density to be deeply analogous to phenomenal qualities, and save ourselves the effort of making up the name "Blue," a placeholder for Spatially Extensible Quality we know nothing about except that it plays the same role in dynamics as does mass density?[8]

Now, to be fair, these words may be taken not only in the quite strong sense I suggested for them, where they express a parsimonious stance. They may also be taken in a rather weak sense, where there's no attempt ever made to deny the great variety that, as I've claimed, may possibly obtain in physical reality. Before turning to examine what's expressed with the words in their stronger sense, let's discuss what may be meant with the weaker interpretation.

With only a weak sense for the expressions, someone may use our displayed words without denying any allegedly rich variety for physical reality. Using the words to make only a small point, someone may allow that there may be, in different Eons, Small Blues of very different Propensitive sorts. What he wants to claim is that, even while Small Blue Particles are both Qualitied and also Propensitied, each a very different aspect of how they're basically propertied, the term "Blue" is best taken as just an exotic shorthand for a previously *familiar* term for a *Propensity*, like the term "mass density," rather than taken as a shorthand for, or a name for, anything *unfamiliar*, especially anything so terribly unfamiliar as a Spatially Extensible Quality. Now, since that claim amounts to little, I have little quarrel with it. Indeed, so long as we have enough terms available to discuss all the metaphysically basic aspects of concrete reality, and so long as we can keep our terms straight enough for a reasonably clear discussion of reality, who can care very much which term is used for which metaphysically basic aspect of basic physical individuals? Not me; and, I trust, not you. Of course, as you know from my uses of "Blue" in previous Sections, *I* think it's natural to use the capitalized word as a term for a perfectly pervasive *Spatially Extensible Quality*, and not for a Propensity. But, precious little depends on whether it's my use that's the favored employment for the word or whether, contrarily, it's for labeling some

8. Lightly edited by your author, these words were provided by his erstwhile colleague, Gordon Belot, as but a small part of the very helpful notes that, on an early draft of this work, he penetratingly produced. Needless to say, Belot needn't actually endorse these words, and he certainly needn't bear responsibility for anything that, in (the very final draft of) this book, I'm placing before you.

Propensity that the word's mainly employed. Well, so much for the displayed words' weaker interpretation.

With a much stronger sense for them in force, the words mouthed by Belot's dialectical character will be used to deny, parsimoniously, that there's so very much variety in basic physical reality. Here, they'll be used to deny, of course, propositions like this: *Beyond all* a basic physical object's Propensities, there is the Spatially Extensible Quality of the individual (which *isn't* a Propensity at all.) Now, when they're used to do *that much*, then the words express a view that, as I'll suggest, is a very badly mistaken and stultifying idea.

9. The Identity Theory of Qualities and Dispositions

During much of the last century, many philosophers thought a main business of science was to provide important identifications, as with identifying lightning as being a certain electrical discharge, and as with identifying water as being a substance composed entirely of H_2O molecules. And, these identifications, it was believed, allowed science to deliver important "identity statements," statements on a par with "Paris is the City of Light," though this last, of course, has nothing to do with science. Well, I have very many doubts about all that; but, here and now, let's not mind my multifaceted skepticism. For, here, the main point is just this: Through such identifications, it was supposed, science showed how an apparently terribly various world really wasn't all that wildly variegated; but, in fact, it was reasonably sparse and, so, pretty orderly. At all events, quite as many philosophers like to think of what they do as somehow being rather scientific, this is one reason that, for some decades, even able philosophers offered substantial statements of identity.

It's in this philosophical context that there appears an important paper, "The Ontological Turn," by C. B. Martin and John Heil. In this metaphysically serious essay, these authors express variously, and they advocate vigorously, an *Identity Theory of Qualities and Propensities*. As I believe, here's a fair sample of this, which may also be called an *Identity Theory of Qualities and Dispositions*:

> every property is at once dispositional and categorical or, as we prefer, dispositional and qualitative. Dispositionality and qualitativity are built into each property; indeed, they *are* the property....
>
> What we propose is a surprising identity: the dispositional and the qualitative are identical with one another and with the unitary intrinsic property itself. The suggested identity is surprising only because we

have grown used to distinguishing the dispositional and the qualitative. Once it is recognized that these are simply different ways of
representing the selfsame property, the identity can be seen to resemble countless others.[9]

Separable from most of Martin's fruitful metaphysical thinking,
and from most of Heil's, too, the proposal of this Identity Theory is, I
think, some philosophical heroism that's carried to the point of heroic
stultification. (And, as this view is much like many other philosophical
identity theories, so many of them may also be heroically stultifying,
even if, perhaps, less obviously so.)

From such serious metaphysicians, why such heroics? As I imagine,
several factors figure in an instructive diagnosis. Here are just four.

In the first place, by talking about properties, rather than just an
individual that's propertied, our authors suggest to us all that there are
such things as properties. Though they might not really want an ontology where properties are reified, still, in their writing they're off and
running. So, right off the bat, we may be in the business of asking
whether a certain property, which we may call "Prop," is the very same
thing as, or whether it's really a different thing from, a certain property
that we may call "Erty." Well, some of our authors' opponents may say
Prop *isn't the same* thing as Erty, and I can imagine myself among them.
The authors themselves disagree, saying that Prop and Erty really *are
one and the same* thing.

In the second place, and perhaps most instructively, there's this:
Among the basic properties our authors class as qualities are both what I
class as Qualities and also what I class as Spatials. Now, both these sorts
of basic property are manifest, or are relevantly surveyable, or something of the sort. What do I mean by that? Well, suppose someone said
this to you "That Spherical Red Particle's vivid Color *just is* the Particle's
round Shape," or "The Particle's being Red is the very same thing as the
Particle's being Spherical." This will strike you, manifestly, as sheer
nonsense. But, now, think about this: How it is with a supposed basic
thing Shapely is manifest to your mind (when the shape is fairly simple).
And, how it is Colorly is similarly manifest. But, by contrast, it's *nothing
like manifest* how it is with a Particle *Propensitively.* In relevant ways, this
parallels the point I made before, when noting how very little of your
power to experience will be, at any time, available to you, in your
experiencing. So, by contrast with claims as to the Shape of a thing, and

9. C. B. Martin and John Heil, "The Ontological Turn," *Midwest Studies in Philosophy,*
1999, pages 46–47.

as to the Color of the thing, a claim as to the thing's Propensity has us drawing a blank. And, with what we ponder when we draw such a blank, it may be that any one of numerous different things will seem perfectly compatible or, at least, quite compatible enough. Just so, there may seem no conflict in the thought that the thing's (manifest) Shape *just is* its (nonmanifest blanky) Propensity. And, similarly, though alternatively, there may seem no conflict in the idea that the thing's (manifest) Color *just is* its (nonmanifest blanky) Propensity. And, once something seems perfectly compatible with a nonmanifest blanky whatnot, there may be much appeal, deriving from other considerations, in the idea that the thing's being a certain Color *just is* the thing's having a certain Propensity. Or, equally, there may be appeal in the idea that its being a certain Shape *just is* its having a certain Disposition. (But, though there here may be a door that seems open, there's never really a door that is open. No more should such ideas be appealing than a thought that something's Color *just is*, really, the Shape of that very thing. About these matters, it seems to me, Berkeley was much more correct than so very many twentieth century identifiers.)

In the third place, there's the noted urge to be parsimonious, to reduce reality's apparently wild variety to something far more sparse and orderly. Now, just above, I said once a thing's having a certain manifest property seems perfectly compatible with the thing's having a nonmanifest blanky property, there may be much appeal, deriving from other considerations, in the idea that the thing's having the manifest property *just is* its having the nonmanifest blanky property. Well, whatever's involved, exactly, in our urge to be parsimonious, that's something from which the appeal derives.

In the fourth place, and most closely related to central points of this Chapter, here's another consideration from which there derives the appeal of (what's maybe illicit) identifying: As it may well seem, whatever contribution is made by a (basic) physical object to the evolvement of physical reality concerns just the Propensities of the thing, or, in other words, its Powers, or its Dispositions. But, as it may well seem, a physical thing must have some qualities, in some sense of that term, at least such qualities as Shape (whether or not there's its Extensible Color). Now, if the entity's Shape *isn't* among its Propensities, then, as it appears, the object's Shape *won't* have any influence on how physical reality evolves. Well, we must avoid concluding that the Shape has no influence. So, the entity's Shape is, after all, among the Propensities of the object.

All that, I suggest, may contribute more to stultifying confusion than to philosophic progress. Anyhow, I'll next attempt to show, more directly, the inadequacy of what I've called the Identity Theory of Qualities and Propensities. As I trust, you'll find these remarks pretty persuasive; as I realize, they're not absolutely conclusive.

As this Identity Theory will have it, a Small Blue Particle's being Qualitied Bluely *just is* the Particle's having certain of its Propensities. (If the Particle's Spatial properties are its only other basic "blatantly qualitative properties," then maybe its having those Spatials *just is* its having its other Propensities?) Well, now, for a supposition that's here as good as any, let's suppose that our Small Blue Particle is Propensitied to *repel* any other Small Blues there may be, *and* it's Propensitied to attract any Large Reds. Could our Particle's being Blue just be the Particle's being Propensitied in this complex Qualitatively-directed way? As it seems to me, that can't be quite right.

If we embrace any such Identity Theory, we'll have to deny how great may be the real variety in concrete reality. Toward seeing that clearly, we first notice some fairly simple considerations, though they can be readily confusing considerations. Much as just before, we may start with a Small Blue Particle that's Propensitied to attract Large Red Particles, and that's Propensitied to repel Small Blues, and that's not otherwise saliently Propensitied. Well, perhaps even accidentally, there may occur a change in the Spatially Extensible Quality of this Particle, from Blue to Yellow, even while no other Particle changes in any such Qualitative regard, and even though our target Particle doesn't change Propensitively in any salient respect. Though now Yellow and not Blue, our Particle is still Propensitied to attract Large Reds, and it's still Propensitied to repel Small Blues. So, it appears that, even while our Particle *has* changed as regards its *Spatially Extensible Quality*, it *hasn't* changed as regards its Propensity. And, so, the appearance is, first, that how it is with our Particle Qualitatively *isn't* the same as how it is with our Particle Propensitively, and, second, that any claimed identity, to such an effect, isn't a true identity.[10] But, this is too fast; indeed, there's far more here than first meets the eye.[11]

What's this? Well, how it is Propensitively, with our Particle, comprises not only the Particle's Propensities for interaction with actual partners, but it comprises, as well, Propensities for interacting with

10. Much as Locke did, Martin and Heil use "quality" rather more liberally than I do. So, quite as with Locke, for them an object's shape (and, presumably, its size) is a quality of the object, even when the object is a basic physical entity. But, this isn't important for assessing the Identity Theory of Qualities and Propensities, leastways it won't be important in our discussion of the Theory.

11. As with some other matters discussed in the Chapter, with this point, too, I'm indebted to Matthew Kotzen.

partners (of sorts) not actually instanced. This concerns the Con-straining aspect of our Principle of Constrained Contingency (con-cerning How Basic Physical Bodies May Be Propertied).

When introducing this Principle, you'll recall, we considered a Monochromatic Yellow Sphere. Then, we focused on the Sphere's being Shaped Spherically, and what this meant for its Propensity profile. Now, we'll focus on its being Qualitied Yellow, and what this may mean for that. So, among the possible disposition partners now, for our Sphere that's lately turned Yellow, there are Blue Cubes that are Propensitied to attract any object that's Yellow, even if no such Cubical Yellow-Attractor currently exists in our Yellow Sphere's World (or there are none anywhere near enough, or whatever). And, equally, there are possible Red Spheres just so similarly Propensitied for at-tracting Yellow physical bodies, and so on. [Again, remember that each of many individual electrons may be (electrically) Propensitied to strongly attract any protons, even if there *aren't actually any* protons.] So, there's a vast range of attractive disposition partners, then, for our currently supposed Yellow Particle. But, then, of course, our Yellow object will be a reciprocally attractive disposition partner for any of them. So, along with its now being Yellow, our Sphere is *Propensitied to be Attracted by any such Yellow-Attractors* as there may be (and as may be situated suitably for just such interactive attracting). As well, our Yellow Particle must also be Propensitied for all sorts of other interactions, including annihilating ones. So, somewhat as before, we now consider another sort of Blue Cube, whether or not any of these actually do exist, one that's *not* Propensitied to attract any Yellow individuals, but that's *Propensitied to annihilate*, completely and forever, any Yellow ob-jects there may be (or, as may be more palatable, any that are within a meter of such an Annihilator, or whatever). Now, with respect to *these* possible Blue Cubes, our newly Yellow Sphere is *also* a reciprocal dis-position partner: Though *before the Sphere wasn't* so disposed, now it's *Propensitied to be annihilated by any such Yellow-Annihilators* as there may be (and as may be situated suitably for just such interactive annihilat-ing). So, when our Sphere became Yellow, it first *acquired these Pro-pensities*, and indefinitely many further Propensities. And, so, our considered Sphere did not just change Qualitatively; in the bargain, it also changed Propensitively.

We'll need another argument, then, if we're to expose inadequa-cies in the Identity Theory of Qualities and Propensities. Prompted by our most recent discussion, here's one: Our (newly) Yellow Sphere's Propensity to be attracted by a Yellow-Attractor is one thing; it's Pro-pensity to be Annihilated by a Yellow-Annihilator is something else.

Now, our Sphere's being Yellow is no more the one Propensity than it's the other. Since they're not the same, its being Yellow, or its Yellow Quality, must then be both or neither. While it's not completely crazy to think it's both, it's far more plausible to think it's neither: Rather than so much as *being* these Propensities, the Yellow Quality of our Sphere is *necessarily linked with* these Propensities of the Particle, and with ever so many of its other Propensities (each a Propensity with respect to things that are themselves Propensitied with respect to Yellow individuals). Well, that's a better argument.

Reminiscent of our overly fast argument, here's another better argument: For this, we do well to consider, once again, certain thoughts about Worlds, or thoughts about Eons, that we've found useful in recent Sections: Just so, in a certain Eon, there may well be Small Blues with a Propensity to attract *Large Particles*, and also Large Reds with a Propensity to attract *Small Particles*, and no other basic physical entities at all. And, in a certain other Eon, there may be, just as well, Small Blues with a Propensity to attract *Red Particles*, and Large Reds with a Propensity to attract *Blue Particles*. In both of these Eons, there may be precisely similar behavior on the part of all the Eon's actual basic Particles, even while, Qualitatively, the actual Particles of each Eon are precisely like those of the other. But, as far as the Propensities go, matters are very different in the first Eon from how things are in the second. So, *how it is Qualitatively is precisely the same* in the two Eons, while *how it is Propensitively is very different*. It defies belief, I take it, that the Particles of *one* Eon don't have it that *their* Spatially Extensible Quality *is* their Propensity, while the Particles of the *other* Eon do. Much more believable is this: In *each* Particulate Eon, how it is with its Particles *Qualitatively* is *one* thing, while how it is with the Particles *Propensitively* is something else, however nicely related the two may be.

As it suggests there isn't even a necessary covariance between an object's Propensities and its Qualities, this argument serves to show, quite convincingly I think, that our targeted Identity Theory is an inadequate view of how individuals may be Propertied. For, as you'll remember, it claims that:

> ...every property is at once dispositional and categorical or, as we prefer, dispositional and qualitative. Dispositionality and qualitativity are built into each property; indeed, they *are* the property....

And, very far from that being true, our discussion suggests that a particular's Propensities may outrun the individual's Qualities.

10. A Limited Identity Theory?

At the same time, in the neighborhood of this ambitious Identity Theory, we may spot a far less assertive view, which may also lay claim to the title of the (or an) Identity Theory of Qualities and Dispositions:

> Though some of a particulars' Propensities may not be any of its Qualities, every one of an individual's Qualities is one of the particular's Dispositions.

Against this *Limited Identity Theory*, as we might call it, there won't be any argument that's as upsetting as (a consideration concerning even) a lack of necessary covariance between an object's Propensities and its Qualities.[12] But, then, against this Limited Theory, there's this to be said.

First of all, at least to all appearances, our Limited Theory doesn't have nearly so much independent motivation as what it's advanced to replace. For instance, while it also won't have Qualities and Dispositions as even apparently isolated from each other, which is all to the good, it will have there be, among the Dispositions, a radical bifurcation between those Dispositions that are Qualities and those that aren't Qualities, which isn't all to the good. (In the bargain, whatever advantage there may in disallowing any "purely Dispositional properties," this will be lost with the Limited Identity Theory. And, without recognizing Dispositions with respect to Spatially Extensible Quality, a recognition apparently awaiting our own new inquiry, there may appear to be, in this disallowing, a very considerable advantage for an Identity Theory.) As it appears, then, we come to consider such a Limited Identity Theory, largely just *as a response to* difficulties observed with a more elegant, and more appealing, metaphysical view. Though this *doesn't* mean that the Limited view is *wholly ad hoc*, there does appear *something ad hoc*, anyhow, with the thought of advancing this largely responsive view.

Second, quite relatedly, and more importantly, even this Limited view seems to confuse a necessary covariance with an identity. So, let's again consider the Disposition of a Yellow Sphere to be attracted to a Yellow-Magnet, or to a (merely) possible particular that's Propensitied to attract any Yellow individuals. As our Limited Theory will have it, this Quality of the object *is* a certain one of the particular's Dispositions. But, to my mind, that doesn't seem right. Rather, this will just be a Quality of the individual *with respect to which* anything that's Disposed to attract (or,

12. For help toward spotting this Limited Identity Theory, I am indebted to Dan Cowper.

to repel, or whatnot) Yellow individuals will be (and must be) directed, just because any Yellow-Attractor (or Yellow-Repellors, or whatnots) must be Disposed to attract (or to repel, or whatnot) any Yellow individuals. And, then, so that the two kinds of thing may be suited for mutual interaction, our Yellow Sphere must have, for its part, the Disposition to be attracted by (and maybe, thus, the Disposition to attract) any Yellow-Attractors (that there might possibly be.) This is the real situation, I submit, concerning the necessary covariance between something's having a given Quality and, on the other hand, the thing's being Propensitied with respect to any individuals (there might be) that are themselves Propensitied with respect to (something's having) that very Quality. As I'll submit, then, the Limited Theory fails to recognize what must be the real situation in these matters, conflating a mere necessary covariance with a genuine identity. In this central respect, the Limited Theory is as faulty, I submit, as is the more ambitious Theory it's advanced to replace, a fault that's to be found, I suggest, with any view that's aptly termed an Identity Theory of Qualities and Dispositions.

At this point in our inquiry, that's about as much as we can profit, I think, from a consideration of any such Identity Theory. (In the Fifth Chapter, we'll look to profit some more.[13])

Before proceeding with further inquiry, I'll make a little comment. Look, in most of this essay, I'm not bothering to engage with very much of the contemporary literature. Rather, almost insofar as it's possible, I'm trying to conduct my exploration in some very different ways from what's to be found there. How may I give you a useful idea of what I mean? Well, shortly before introducing their Identity Theory, Martin and Heil try to contrast what they're about to offer with some other views, already placed on offer:

> Philosophers commonly distinguish dispositional and categorical properties. Dispositional properties endow their possessors with particular dispositions or powers; categorical properties endow objects with nondispositional qualities. [As Martin and Heil say a tad later than what's here displayed, they prefer "qualitative" to "categorical," which is all to the good, as the latter term is bound to mislead. Still, it's "categorical," I suppose, that more frequently occurs in the literature to be mentioned.] Some philosophers have denied the existence of categorical properties, arguing that every property is purely dispositional (see,

13. In the book's Fifth Chapter, "A Plenitude of Power," I'll embark on a much more comprehensive exploration of Dispositions. Midway through that Chapter, I'll introduce ideas about Propensity for Monotony and Propensity for Change. Those ideas will reveal further inadequacies, I think, in the Identity Theory and, most important, they may do so in a way that helps illuminate a wide range of philosophical considerations.

for instance, Mellor, 1974; Shoemaker 1980). Others deny dispositional properties (Armstrong 1968, 85–88). Still others have regarded dispositional properties with suspicion, treating them as grounded in or realized by categorical properties (see Prior, Pargetter, and Jackson 1982; and Jackson 1996).[14]

Well, now, our authors have just mentioned some very talented, and deeply serious, philosophers. And, as I'll here trust, the views attributed to them are views they've actually advanced, or at least very much like their actual views. Still and all, if much of what I'm advancing is anywhere even remotely near being right, none of those views can possibly have very much rightly to offer. Well, maybe one of these views does have a lot to offer, whilst everything I uphold is a hopelessly lost cause. Maybe so; but, so what? At all events, what's most useful for me to do here, with our time and our energy, is to develop a philosophical position that's usefully very different from all already extant views, rather than engaging you in detailed discussions of various familiar alternatives.[15]

Far from being employed with just these present issues, I follow this working strategy with almost all the topics that, in this book, I explore. That being so, there are many fine thinkers whose work I don't mention, and very few that I so much as discuss. As I imagine, you've

14. From their references, placed at their essay's end, we observe that these are the works Martin and Heil just mentioned. First, there's Hugh Mellor, "In Defense of Dispositions," *Philosophical Review*, 1974, and also Sydney Shoemaker, "Causality and Properties," in P. van Inwagen, (ed.), *Time and Cause*, Reidel, 1980. Next, and apparently quite oppositely, there's David M. Armstrong, *A Materialist Theory of the Mind*, Routledge and Kegan Paul, 1968. And, for the last putative position, there's E. W. Prior, R. Pargetter, and F. Jackson, "Three Theses about Dispositions," *American Philosophical Quarterly*, 1982, and also Frank Jackson, "Mental Causation," *Mind*, 1996.

15. In the recent philosophical literature, there's certainly no shortage of essays on Dispositions, and how they may compare with other Properties, each of them heavily engaged with just previously written essays on the selfsame subject. Notable among them, in my view, is John Heil's fine, clear, and exceptionally helpful paper, "Properties and Powers," in Dean W. Zimmerman, ed., *Oxford Studies in Metaphysics*, vol. 1, Oxford University Press, 2004. As might be expected, a central concern of this paper is to advance, refine and defend what I've called the Identity Theory of Qualities and Propensities, clearly indicated by the name of the paper's 10th Section, namely, "The Identity Theory." But, equally, nothing less than the titles of earlier Sections clearly indicate substantial discussions of earlier authors on these topics: the 5th Section is Armstrong on Dispositionality; the 6th is Prior, Pargetter and Jackson; the 7th is Humean Contingency; and the 9th is an Argument from Armstrong. Not unlike various other essays in the area, this paper's references list over 60 other works on its topics, with over 50 of them published in just the last few decades.

For most of my readers, whose interest in these topics is less than enormous, I'll try to be helpful by making just two recommendations, one positive and one negative. Do read this helpful paper by Heil. And, please, don't get bogged down in almost all the rest of the recent literature. Of course, just as I believe that you really do choose, I realize that here, as elsewhere, the choice is yours.

been getting that idea. But, still, it's best for me to be explicit on that matter, and this seems a good place for that.

11. Can There Be Spatially Extensible Yellow Entities That Aren't Ever Propensitied?

In considering our Mystery of the Physical, we considered the question of whether there can be Propensitied Spatial entities that aren't ever, and at all, Qualitied. More directly, we considered the question of whether we human thinkers can conceive, at all fully and clearly, any such putative entities. As I've been arguing, of course, we do very poorly, indeed, in any attempt at conceiving Spatial concreta entirely lacking in Quality, however richly Propensitied we may (try to) suppose them to be. And, as I've been openly suspecting, even if maybe not quite suggesting, this may not be owing just to some human lack or deficiency; rather, it may be that, for even the Most Mentally Powerful Being, there's no idea to be had, that's at all clear or full, of a Spatial concretum that's not (Spatially Extensibly) Qualitied.

The reason I rehearse all that now, I hasten to note, is to provide a nice preamble to some very closely related questions: So, paralleling the question of whether there can be Propensitied Spatial entities that aren't ever, and at all, Qualitied, we shall consider the question of whether there can be *Qualitied* Spatial concreta that *aren't ever, and at all, Propensitied*. And, then, of course, paralleling the question concerning what we humans can conceive about the first matter, there's the question concerning whether we humans can conceive, at all fully and clearly, such putative entities as may be alleged not to be Propensitied, however richly Qualitied we may (try to) suppose them to be.

Before the discussion of the last several Sections, I guess, we might have been in a pretty poor position to answer these closely related questions. But, at this present juncture, I think, we may be in a rather good position to do so. Indeed, it may be that, by this point, we may quite clearly conclude that, not only can't we humans conceive of any Qualitied Spatial entities that aren't ever Propensitied, but, what's more, there simply can't be any such concreta as that. Let me amplify.

As it first seems to us, well, to me, anyway, hardly anything is easier to imagine than an utterly Propensityless Extensible Yellow Sphere, or, just as well, an utterly Propensityless Extensible Red Cube. With the supposed Yellow Sphere, for instance, I'll be imagining that, while there may be many and varied other concreta in its World, perhaps even existing quite simultaneously with the conceived Sphere, none of them are Propensitied to attract it, or to rotate it, or to annihilate it, or to interact with it in any other way. Whatever actually happens with this Yellow Sphere, I'm apparently imagining, it will be an absolutely random happening. That's all very peculiar, no doubt; but, nonetheless, it's clearly conceivable; and, presumably, it's all perfectly possible, too.

Well, on a most natural understanding of the previous paragraph, there's nothing seriously amiss with its claims, so far as those sentences go. The trouble is, though, that, for the questions we're now considering, they don't really go all that far. What does that mean?

For any question concerning an utter lack of all Propensity, on the part of any considered concretum, we must consider not only what might transpire in connection with such other individuals as may actually inhabit its World, and may do so simultaneously, but we must also consider such further-fetched concreta as may exist only in other possible Worlds or, not quite so terribly far afield, as may exist only in other Eras, or Eons. So, much as we did just a Section or two ago, we may imagine a variety of Yellow-Attractors, some of them also Spheres, some of them Cubes, and whatnot. Now, when we're imagining a Yellow Sphere, I submit, then we must be imagining, right in the bargain, a Sphere that's Propensitied to be attracted to, or by, any concretum that's a Yellow-Attractor, though we needn't be imagining, of course, that the supposed Yellow Sphere ever gets the chance to be suitably partnered with any Yellow-Attractor, so that there's ever a real attractive interaction involving the imagined Yellow concretum. So, with any supposed Yellow concretum, we must be supposing, in the bargain, a concretum that's Propensitied to be attracted by any concretum that's Propensitied to attract Yellow individuals—and, in the bargain, a concretum that's Propensitied to be rotated by any particular that's Categorically Disposed to rotate Yellow concreta, and so on.

None of this, it should be noted, has anything especially to do with any of this book's emphasis on Spatially Extensible Quality, for humanly well-conceived Spatial concrete particulars. Instead of focusing on our supposed Yellow Sphere's being a Yellow concretum, we may make the same central point, just as well, by focusing on the supposed particular's being a Spherical concretum. Just so, when we're imagining a concrete Sphere, whether it be Yellow or not, we must be supposing, in the bargain, that we're imagining a Spherical concretum that's hardly Propensityless. Rather, in supposing a (Yellow) Sphere, we must be contemplating, right in the bargain, a concretum that's Propensitied to be attracted by any concretum that's Propensitied to attract Spherical individuals, and that's Propensitied to be rotated by any particular that's Categorically Disposed to rotate Spherical concreta, and that's Propensitied to be annihilated by any concrete entity that's Disposed to annihilate concrete Spheres, and so on.

Of course, the points made in the two previous paragraphs are the merest start here. Indefinitely many other points each serve to teach the same lesson: Not only can't we conceive of any Qualitied Spatial entities that aren't ever Propensitied; there simply can't be any such concreta as that.[16]

12. Can an Extensible Blue Body Be Attracted by Concreta That Aren't Blue-Attractors?

At this point in our work, it may be helpful to consider this question: Can a Blue Particle, a basic (spatial and) physical concretum that's Blue, be attracted to (and correlatively attract) a Particle that's a Yellow-Attractor, and that's *not* a Blue-Attractor?

At first blush, the answer may seem to be 'No.' But, once we notice that Particles are quite richly Propertied, or that they're not *just* some Extensibly Qualitied concreta, we'll reject that negative answer. Let me explain.

Just as much as it's a concretum that's Blue, our considered Particle may be a Spherically Shaped concretum. (Indeed, I should think that, if it's a Particle we're here talking about, and so it is, then the considered concretum must have Some Shape (or other)—whether the Particle be Shaped Spherically, or whether Cubically, or whether only in some quite Irregular way, perhaps not any way for which we have a decent name. But, in the present context, I needn't rely on this stronger claim.)

So, for all relevant intents and purposes, our starting question becomes this: Can a Blue Spherical Particle, a basic physical concretum that's Blue and Spherical, be attracted to a Particle that's a Yellow-Attractor, all right, but that's *not* a Blue-Attractor? With just that nice little shift, many will see the propriety of an affirmative answer.

But, some won't. At least for them, it will be helpful to notice that, even if a concretum isn't a Yellow-Attractor, the particular may be, nonetheless, a Sphere-Attractor. The individual may be Propensitied to attract any Spherical concreta, just because they're Spherical, even

16. Even with all I've put into this Section, just completed, I've just been warming up, so to say, compared with any serious attempt at delineating all the major sorts of possible Propensities, or even all the main sorts of what are clearly physical Propensities. For a lot more in this direction, you may want to read the book's Fifth Chapter, "A Plenitude of Power." But, even if so, you'll do best to stay the course here, and plunge more fully, with me, into issues of Propensities when the time for that exploration is really ripe. When will that be? Well, as best I can reckon, it'll be just after you've finished reading the book's Fourth Chapter, "A Cornucopia of Quality," and you're facing the first page of Chapter 5.

though it's not Propensitied to attract, just because it's Yellow, a con-cretum that, in fact, is a Yellow concretum. For instance, a certain Red Cube may be Propensitied just like that, almost no matter how else it might be further Propensitied. Just so, and just because *it's Propensitied to attract Spherical concreta*, this considered Red Cube—which is a Yellow-Attractor, all right, but isn't any Blue-Attractor—may be Propensitied to attract our other considered concretum. This latter, even as it's a Blue Sphere, you'll recall, is a *Spherical* individual. So, right here, as we can easily see, there's a clear case of a Blue Particle that's ever so fit to be attracted to (and correlatively to attract) another individual that's not a Blue-Attractor (even whilst it's a Yellow-Attractor). For, without being a Blue-Attractor, this other individual may be a Sphere-Attractor; and, just as surely as it's a Blue Particle, our Blue Sphere is a concrete Sphere (whatever else it might also be, besides being a Sphere and being a Blue concretum). And, for that reason, this Red Cube may attract our Blue Sphere, even without its ever being Propensitied with respect to how it is that the Blue Sphere is Extensibly Qualitied.

13. Can an Extensible Blue Body Be Perceived to Be Extensible Blue?

In this actual world, and in this present Eon of the world, it seems quite certain, at least to me, that there aren't any sentient beings able to perceive how it is Qualitatively with a Spatially Extensibly Qualitied physical object. (Or, at the very least, it seems certain that there aren't any finite beings ever able to do that, however matters might stand regarding a (putative) Godlike Being. In what follows, I'll omit this quasi-theistic qualification.) For example, even if it should be that, in our World, and in our Eon, every electron is the very same Absolutely Specific Shade of Extensible Color, say, Transparent Blue, there won't be any perceivers, in our World, and in our Eon, who're ever able to perceive any of the electrons to be (Transparent) Blue.

Possibly owing to such considerations, many may think that *it's in principle impossible* for a finite being, whatever its World, or its Eon, to see (or to otherwise perceive) how it is Qualitatively with a (basic) physical individual, as with, say, a basic Particle. Now, insofar as any such thought as that might have much metaphysical import, even anywhere near as much as I reckon it may have, it's a quite badly mistaken idea. In this Section, I'll aim to show how very badly mistaken any such metaphysically significant thought must be. Far from aiming to do that in great detail, I'll aim to advance my main point so that few will miss the general shape of the metaphysical terrain.

Just a very short while ago, you'll recall, we encountered a Section devoted to the question, Can There Be Extensibly Qualitied Spatial Entities That Aren't Ever Propensitied? Though initial appearances suggested an affirmative answer for the question, we concluded, quite clearly, I think, that any perfectly Propensityless entities are, in truth, perfectly impossible. Even while we might at first think we're conceiving a Blue Sphere that's perfectly without Propensity, reflection reveals that, on any philosophically most relevant reckoning, including entities in other Worlds, and certainly including objects in some of this world's 'temporally distant' Eons, there are entities each Propensitied to rotate Blue objects, and others each Propensitied to annihilate Blue objects. Now, our conceived Blue Sphere, initially presumed Propensityless, will be a reciprocal disposition partner for, or with respect to, any of the Blue-Rotators, and to any of the Blue-Annihilators. Well, then, just as *they* are Propensitied to rotate, or to annihilate, the Blue Sphere (because the Sphere is Blue), so the considered Sphere is, for its part, *Propensitied to be rotated by* the Blue-Rotators, and it's *Propensitied to be annihilated by* the Blue-Annihilators.

Well, in an intuitive sense of the terms "affected" and "modified," in these interactions it's only the (initially considered) Blue individual that's *affected*, and that's *modified*, whereas, correlatively, the Blue-Rotator, and the Blue-Annihilator, are *un*modified, and they're *un*affected, in the interaction among, or between, these objects. So, along with an agreeably manifested reciprocity, there will also be a notably intuitive asymmetry, in these interactions between the reciprocal Propensity partners.

In quite this same intuitive sense, or way, much the same happens in (a paradigm) perceptual interaction between a (perceptible) object perceived by a subject (that's not itself the perceived object) and, on the other side, the perceiving subject who's mentally affected by, or so mentally modified by, the (relevantly external) object this subject perceives. Whether it's quite directly, or whether it's only much more indirectly, this perceiving subject and perceived object must, of course, *inter*act with *each other*. Otherwise, of course, there won't be the *perception of one* entity *by quite another* entity—where the perceiver is relevantly *independent of* the perceived object, and where the perceived object, for its part, is relevantly *external to* the subject who's perceiving it. As with any other interactions, with such perceptual interactions, too, the interacting entities must be, at the least, aptly Propensitied reciprocal partners—even if the whole story of their reciprocity will involve, as happens in ordinary visual perception, a reference to intermediary partners, as with the photons of light that pass from what's perceived to the perceiver consequently impacted by them. But, of course, for all that undoubted reciprocity, there must also be, quite as well, this intuitively notable asymmetry in the (typical and paradigmatic) perceptual inter- action: The (unperceiving) perceived object is relevantly quite *unaffected by*, and it's similarly *unmodified by*, the subject who perceives it, whereas, on the other hand, that perceiving individual *is* affected by, and she is modified by, the object she perceives—all of it occurring, of course, in the aforesaid perceptual interaction.

Not to lose the forest for the trees, we'll make some vividly instructive suppositions: First, we'll suppose that there are, in some possible Worlds, at least, and maybe even in some "temporally distant" Eons of this actual world, many *mentally richly Propensitied* Small Transparent Red Spheres. (For these Worlds, or these Eons, Scientiphicalism won't hold, let's agree; but nobody ever thought—well, almost nobody—that Scientiphicalism must hold in absolutely every possible circumstance, or in absolutely every possible sort of concrete reality.) Notable in its Propensity Profile, each supposed Red Sphere has a (richly various) Power to Experience. About that, we may illustratively say this: When a Red Sphere is within ten meters of a Transparent Blue Sphere, the Red Sphere experiences transparently bluely (just insofar as it experiences spherically). How it is that this Sphere's then visually experiencing is very much like how it is that I sometimes visually experience, as when, for instance, I'm most successfully and compellingly observing a wonderfully fine monochro- matic transparent blue glass sphere. When this happens with me, a very rare circumstance, I assure you, then, as it appears to me, I'm encoun- tering a sphere that's even so much as Spatially Extensibly Blue. (Well, maybe I'm then undergoing a perceptual illusion, though none that's ordinarily called any illusion.) Anyhow, it's quite in this same experiential way, I'm supposing, that, in its interaction with the nearby Blue Sphere, the interacting perceptually sensitive Red Sphere is experientially af- fected.[17] (And, as I'll now suggest, it's then *not* undergoing any percep- tual illusion, neither ordinarily so called nor, even, otherwise.)

Some will think that, in this simple little case, things are simply too simple for there to be any real perception. As they might say, I imagine,

17. What we've just described, ever so sketchily, is an extremely simple instance of one entity perceiving how it is Qualitatively with the perceived spatial entity. Not only is this an instance, of course, where the Red Sphere perceives how it is with the Blue just by perceiving the Blue Sphere itself, and not by perceiving something else that's aptly related to the Blue, as with a picture of the Blue Sphere on a TV set, but there isn't any medium of perception either, no information-carrying light-waves, for instance, that's a third party for the salient interaction partners, for the perceived and the perceiver.

anything that's really a (color) perceiver must be differentially responsive, much as anything that's really a thinker must be. (Recall our discussion in the previous Chapter.) And, as their objection may well continue, the supposed Red Sphere isn't differentially responsive enough, in this terribly simple illustrative example, for it to be a truly qualified *perceiver*, that is, for it to be experientially modified bluely by the Blue Sphere.

Maybe so; but, maybe not so. Myself, I kind of doubt it. After all, when our Red Sphere *isn't* within ten meters of a Blue Sphere, then the sensitive Spherical being *doesn't* experience bluely. She experiences bluely, we've agreed, when, but only when, she's at least that close to at least one Blue aptly Propensitied spatial concretum. In most of my philosophical moods, so to speak, that's plenty enough for me, in the way of a candidate (color) perceiver's being selectively responsive. But, look, for our main question, *none of this really matters!* Why? Well, in terms that relevantly parallel those already provided, we can have our Red Sphere be enormously much more differentially responsive.[18]

Whatever complexities may enrich, or may endow, the fullest and clearest cases of a Specially Sensitive Subject perceiving how it is Qualitatively with a Spatially Extensible Transparent Blue Sphere, they'll be much the same, in all sorts of apparent ways, as those that actually enrich, or actually endow, the fullest and clearest cases of an ordinarily sensitive subject, very like you and like me, who's consciously perceiving how it is (colorly) qualitatively with an actual fine glass blue ball. Or, so it certainly seems to me.

Indeed, there's no third party, or third parties, of any sort at all. So, as we may well say, this is a case of *direct perception*, about as direct as perception ever gets, I imagine, when the perceiver is perceiving something that's really quite external to herself. But, for present purposes, this last bit's not very important.

18. When she's within ten meters of a Transparent Green Cube, but only when within ten meters of a Transparent Green Spatial object, our Red Sphere will experience transparently greenly. And, as she's so good at perceiving Yellow Particles, when she's within twenty meters of a Transparent Yellow Particle, she'll be modified by the distal Yellow entity, quite directly, so that she experiences transparently yellowly. But, even with Yellow Particles, she's not all that powerfully "sighted." If nothing Extensible Transparent Yellow is within twenty meters of our Red Sphere, then she won't experience transparently yellowly.

As others may very often be, some of the time, I'm inclined to think that our (color) perceivers must be at least that differentially responsive, and maybe even much more so. And, some of the time, I want further things, as well, to hold true of anything that's to be rightly counted a real (color) perceiver. Not only should she be experientially modified differently, by just so many differently Qualified and Propensitied external disposition partners, but she must be Propensitied, as well, toward forming certain beliefs, maybe as to the Extensible Color of certain nearby spatial objects, which further Propensity is typically triggered, for its part, so that it's also manifested, by certain changes in (or by certain continuities in) how it is with our (candidate color perceiver) experientially, and qualitatively. Or, if not quite that, then something rather like that.

Indeed, that might even greatly understate the matter. For, as I'll unconfidently suggest, with the first sort of case, there might be, perhaps, a far clearer paradigm of a subject who perceives the color (or the Color) of a (transparently monochromatic) presently perceived object, external to the perceiving subject, and with the latter, more ordinary case, there just might be, perhaps, only a middling approximation to the properly preferred paradigm.[19]

(In what I've just been offering, please don't think I've attempted to provide so much as an *analysis* of what should be the perfect paradigm of a subject's consciously visually perceiving (how it is Colorwise) with a spatial concretum (that's relevantly external to the subject). For a variety of reasons, I doubt that anything that grand, or even anything quite nearly so, is attainable. To help you get behind this pessimism, here's a little tidbit: Suppose that, just a meter from our Sensitive Red, but in diametrically opposite directions, there are two precisely similar Transparent Blue Spheres. All right, then; let's agree that, even as the Red Sphere is now mentally modified transparently bluely, that's entirely owing just to its perceptual interaction with precisely these Transparent Blues. But, even granting that, still, how should it be that, in this case, the Sensitive Red perfectly perceives how it is Colorwise with *both* of these Spheres, or with *each* Blue Sphere, rather than its being the case that the Red perfectly perceives "the particularized Color of" *just one* of them, or, yet better, rather than its being the case that the perceptual situation is quite *indeterminate* between the two aforesaid (only?) apparent possibilities? Now, if there may be provided a sufficiently rich story about the Red Sphere's perfectly perceiving how it is Positionally with each Blue Sphere or, maybe, an impressively rich story about the Red's perceiving how it is Perspectivally with each Blue, then, perhaps, that might serve, quite sufficiently well, to settle that question. Though I certainly have my doubts; I really don't know. But, heck, with just that question, we've confronted only one of this area's easier issues. This next one's a bit harder. Suppose that, in the very same direction from our Sensitive Red, there are two Transparent Blues, one right behind the other, so that the further is, from the Red's visual perspective (whatever exactly that may be) quite fully occluded. [This may be

---

19. Among passages on perception produced by presently prominent philosophers, perhaps those most similar to this Section's material, at least in philosophical spirit, are those comprising the helpfully imaginative first section, entitled "Eden," of David Chalmers's paper "Perception and the Fall from Eden," in (T. Gendler and J. Hawthorne, eds.) *Perceptual Experience*, Oxford University Press, forthcoming. As with so many of Chalmers's papers, this one may be retrieved from his website; its specific "address" is: http://consc.net/papers/eden.html.

because the further Transparent Blue is somewhat smaller; but that needn't be so. Equally, it may be because it's sufficiently further away and, thus, eclipsed by the nearer Transparent Blue.] Well, let's again agree that, even as the Red Sphere is now mentally modified transparently bluely, that's entirely owing just to its perceptual interaction with precisely these two Transparent Blues. But, again granting that, how should it be that, in *this* case, the Sensitive Red perfectly perceives how it is Colorwise with *both* of these *Transparent* Blue Spheres, or with *each Transparent* Blue Sphere, rather than its being the case that the Red perfectly perceives "the particularized Color of" *just one* of the *Transparent* Blues, or, yet better, rather than its being the case that the perceptual situation is quite *indeterminate* between the two aforesaid (only?) apparent possibilities? As far as I can tell, here the matter must remain quite hopeless, no matter what rich stories ever will be provided. And, in several ways, philosophy fans, I've just been warming up, with this little lineup of perfectly unmodified Transparent Blue concreta. But, enough is enough; and more than enough is more than that.[20] Anyway, that's all I'll now offer toward getting clearer on why there's an affirmative philosophic answer to this Section's title question, "Can an Extensible Blue Body Be Perceived to Be Extensible Blue?")

Well, despite its leading us to some unsuspected complexity, I trust that, even so, this Section's discussion helped clarify my views on its main topic. Anyhow, it's time to turn to another topic, even if we might not always be afforded much clarity in our consideration of its deeply difficult issues.

14. We Consider an Antinomy of Spatially Extensible Quality

Though I don't think it undermines our attempt to demystify the physical, I'm perplexed by an Antinomy of Spatially Extensible Quality.

20. Though I'm far from certain of it, here's what I've come to think: For a conscious perceiver to inhabit a world in which she may engage in perfectly perceiving external spatial concreta, she must inhabit a world in which, in all (perceptible) intrinsic respects, each concretum she (perfectly) perceives differs from all the other (potentially competing) concreta. So, for instance, if she's to (perfectly) perceive how it is Colorly with each of various concreta, each of the perceptible bodies must be a different Color from any Color that's a Color of any other concretum. Then, as each observable object is uniquely Color-coded, there'll never arise any problems from complexities concerning positioning, or eclipsing, or anything else. Notice: This is just a necessary condition I'm here hypothesizing, though maybe it's a pretty interesting one. For much more than that, many matters might be, perhaps, just impossibly hairy.

And, honesty requires, I believe, that I divulge my perplexity. But, just as honestly, and with a method to this present Section's near madness, I may also say this: With quite a few of this Section's passages, there'll be provided, if only in passing, a background that's useful toward gaining clarity, in some Sections succeeding this present one, as to the import of our developing Humanly Realistic Philosophy. Of course, all that's to happen a little later. Right now, before any of that clarification's offered, we'll experience some puzzlement.

Very sketchily, the Antinomy proceeds as follows: On the one hand, Spatially Extensible Qualities *can't ever* be instantiated at extensionless points. And, on the other hand, there are *perfectly possible* cases in which the Qualities *must* be instantiated *only* at extensionless points.[21] Let's try to put some usefully vivid color into this very sketchy statement.

Consider a spatial region entirely filled with only matter that's Red, the matter having no other Spatially Extensible Quality. Whether or not this matter is physically divisible, we can conceive the Red region to contain indefinitely many decidedly smaller Red volumes, none overlapping any other. These smaller regions may be perfectly adjacent, it seems, and may together exhaustively partition the whole. Along one line of such purely conceptual division, each of two smaller volumes will be a distinct half of the original; along another, each of three will be a distinct third of our whole. At all events, each of the smaller regions will itself be entirely filled with only matter that's Red. Always with such a boring consequence, a sequence of such conceptual divisions may proceed without limit.

Even if it might be only in some suitably refined sense of the terms, we may then say that, within our original volume of Red matter, there's an *infinite sequence of decidedly ever-smaller* regions each fully filled with just Red matter. And, then, in what must be a similarly refined sense, it might be said that, in our original Red region, there's an *infinite* number of *points* where there's Red matter.

---

21. Apparently, this Section's main matters are much discussed in the literature on Hume and Berkeley. For Hume, I'm directed to the *Treatise*, Bk. I, Pt. II, Sections III and IV. In the secondary literature, there's David Raynor's paper "'Minimal Sensibilia' in Berkeley and Hume," *Canadian Journal of Philosophy*, 1980, and Robert Fogelin, "Hume and Berkeley on the Proofs of Infinite Divisibility," *Philosophical Review*, 1988. As well, there's "Flavors, Colors, and God," the last piece in Robert Adams's book of essays *The Virtue of Faith*, Oxford University Press, 1993.

As almost goes without saying, there are certainly some important commonalities between the antinomy considered here and certain antinomies, or paradoxes, due to Zeno, the great Eleatic thinker. But, as I suspect, there also may be certain differences that are at least as important as the shared features. I leave to other times, and perhaps to other writers, the efforts needed to sort out exactly how the present paradox does, and how it does not, relate interestingly to problems posed by my predecessors, quite a few of whom are, evidently, extremely seminal.

But, these points cannot themselves be perfectly extensionless. Even if every so-called point should contain others still smaller, still each must be of some finite volume. In the present context, it may be useful to say that this is true for two different reasons, each quite sufficient for the truth.

Not peculiarly tied to questions of Spatially Extensible Quality, the first reason is perfectly general. In order for a point to contribute toward the spatial composition of, or the spatial exhaustion of, a finite volume, the point must itself be of some finite volume. However many extensionless points should ever be added together, they'll never compose anything spatial that itself is more than extensionless. Insofar as we focus on this first reason, the Antinomy of Spatially Extensible Quality may seem so very like some other problems that few will see much interest in this Antinomy. But, then, they may want to notice the other reason why a point where there's a Spatially Extensible Quality instanced can't be a spatially extensionless point.

The second reason stems, I think, from *the nature of Spatially Extensible Quality*. Not only is such Extensible Quality suited, by its very nature, for filling space, or for spatial pervasion, but, what's more, *the exemplification of an (Absolutely Specific) Spatially Extensible Quality requires that there be some spatial volume, or something with spatial extension, that the (Absolutely Specific) Spatially Extensible Quality spatially pervade.*

Over the course of many years, penetrating philosophers have embraced the idea that real concrete spatial points must have finite extent. Though, in certain respects, he may take a few matters too far, this is Hume's position when he writes:

> I first take the least idea I can form of a part of extension, and being certain that there is nothing more minute than this idea, I conclude, that whatever I discover by its means must be a real quality of extension.... Upon the whole, I conclude that, the idea of an infinite number of parts is individually the same idea with the idea of an infinite extension; that no finite extension is capable of containing an infinite number of parts; and consequently that no finite extension is infinitely divisible.[22]

Mathematically much more sophisticated than Hume, and than me, Russell is also mightily concerned to offer an understanding of points on which they *aren't* extensionless infinitesimals, productive of absurdities.[23]

22. Hume, *Treatise*, pages 29–30.

23. In *The Analysis of Matter*, Dover, 1954, Russell's chapter 27 is "The Construction of Points." comprising pages 290–302 of the book. There he presents an elaborate construction of space-time points out of what he calls "events." These quotation marks are taken right from Russell.

Bringing us forward to contemporary times, I'll note that it's a treatment of points as very small, but as extended, that makes decent sense of David Lewis's approach to the matter:

> Many of the papers, here and in Volume I, seem to me in hindsight to fall into place within a prolonged campaign on behalf of the thesis I call "Humean supervenience." ...
>
> Humean supervenience is named in honor of the greater denier of necessary connections. It is the doctrine that all there is to the world is a vast mosaic of local matters of particular fact, just one little thing and then another. (But it is no part of the thesis that these local matters are mental.) We have geometry: a system of external relations of spatiotemporal distance between points. Maybe points in spacetime itself, maybe point-sized bits of matter or aether or fields, maybe both. And at those points we have local qualities: perfectly natural intrinsic properties which need nothing bigger than a point at which to be instantiated. For short: we have an arrangement of qualities. And that is all. There is no difference without difference in the arrangement of qualities. All else supervenes on that.[24]

On the sensible interpretation of his words, Lewis here is just as concerned as were Russell and Hume to offer an understanding of points on which they *aren't* extensionless infinitesimals. To the contrary, points have a certain *size*; always very small, no doubt, they're still *extensive enough* for point-*sized* bits of matter to be *just that big*.[25]

So, the thought that concrete points must have finite extension, *especially points where Spatially Extensible Quality is exemplified*, falls in line with the treatment given points by penetrating philosophers. But, even

24. David Lewis, *Philosophical Papers*, vol. 2, Oxford University Press, 1986, pages ix–x. Attached to the sentence ending with "instantiated," Lewis places a footnote where he refers the reader to work that endeavors "to explain what makes a property natural and intrinsic." At this juncture in this present paper, it would be too large a digression, I think, to pursue Lewis's suggestions regarding the indicated explanations.

25. As a by-the-way, I should say this: By "qualities" Lewis *doesn't* mean anything even remotely like our (nonmental) *Qualities*. Against Hume himself and also against most of those concerned to follow Hume's lead in Certain Main Metaphysical Matters—like Russell and, I think, like me, too—what Lewis means by "qualities" is, most likely, something like *basic physical properties*. So, roughly, but still tellingly, he means to denote properties in the neighborhood of, say, having such-and-such point-mass, and, say, having unit electric charge.

At all events, Lewis is greatly concerned not to treat basic physical properties in anything like the way that I do. Not for him an approach to propensities that has them be anywhere near the likes of Lockean powers, as irreducible as they're categorical. That's much too unavailable for him, or unsurveyable—quite as, long ago, it was much too unavailable for Hume. Toward being Humean about powers and propensities, Lewis offers analyses of law, causation, and various other notions in the neighborhood of power. In this Chapter's last Section, I'll offer a short discussion of his Humean endeavor.

while this understanding seems completely clear and undeniable, the same fine appearance attends certain thoughts that seem to point in a completely contrary direction.

Nowadays, it's true, almost all physicists hold that, in all its basic physical aspects, reality "comes" in discrete units. And, in harmony with this, they might hold that, as regards the physically allowable possibilities for the instantiation of Spatially Extensible Qualities, matters are just as discrete, just as "quantized," as they are with, say, the possibilities for electrons to occupy orbits around atomic nuclei. But, even if some such Proposition of Discrete Possibilities for (the Instantiations) of the Spatially Extensible Qualities may hold true in our actual World, still, in some possible Worlds (or, maybe, in some long-ago Eons) there may hold true a quite different proposition, a Proposition of Continuous Possibilities for (the Instantiations of) the Spatially Extensible Qualities. In what next follows, we'll follow the relevantly more liberal line of such a Proposition of Continuous Possibilities.

In a relevantly continuous World (or Eon) there may be Spheres that spatially vary continuously as to their Spatially Extensible Quality. At the center of one of these Spheres, the matter is Red. And, at the Sphere's surface, the matter is Blue. And, the Sphere's Extensible Quality may spatially vary continuously, it surely appears, from the Red at its center, to a Purple a fair ways outward, to the Blue at its surface. Intuitively, doesn't this seem perfectly possible?

Well now, let's look very closely, with our mind's eye, at what may really be there, Qualitatively, within our supposed Sphere. So, let's consider a very small region of the Sphere, with just a trillionth of a trillionth of the whole Sphere's Moderate Size, with one "end" of it nearer the center and the other "end" nearer the Sphere's surface. Throughout this tiny region, we must now suppose, there'll also be spatially continuous Qualitative variation. Even as the original Sphere's matter continuously proceeds (or varies spatially) from Red to Blue, so this tiny region's matter continuously proceeds (or varies spatially) from One Color to Another Color. Still, and as we must suppose, the One Color is more like Red than is the Other Color, whilst the Other is, for its part, more like Blue than is the One. Now, in our chosen small region, the Qualitative Difference may be completely unnoticeable by any actual being. But, that may not be telling. For the presumably so slightly different Spatially Extensible Qualities need not be phenomenal qualities. Nor need these supposed Qualities be available, through its imaginative experiencing, to any finite creature, let alone any human being.

As it intuitively seems to me, within this minute region there may yet be an Infinity of Qualitative Difference: However many times we reiterate the procedure just imagined, getting Very Decidedly smaller regions at every step, there will always remain a completely continuous variation, as regards to Spatially Extensible Quality, along the very same Qualitative line as in previous steps.

As the foregoing suggests, in our Qualitatively continuously varying Sphere, there'll never be any region, at all, that's fully filled with any Absolutely Specific Color Quality. Rather, every region, however small, will be fully filled by matter that's all Continuously Varied in respect of Spatially Extensible Quality. So, as then also seems clear, there's no finite (voluminous) spatial region, however small, that instantiates just one single Absolutely Specific Color Quality. Well, on the one hand, and as I've just been suggesting, this thought is quite intuitive to me. But, on the other hand, the thought can be quite strangely disturbing. Let me try to articulate the strange disturbance.

As concerns *Absolutely Specific* Spatially Extensible Qualities, or *Absolutely Specific* Colors, what are we to think about our supposed Sphere? Well, as best as I can tell, we're forced to face this disjunction: Either *no* Absolutely Specific Colors are really exemplified anywhere in our contemplated regions, and anywhere in our whole Sphere, or else, though many are instantiated, each is exemplified only at some *perfectly extensionless* point, or points. Now, with our original supposition, apparently so agreeably intuitive, we rule out the first (and negative) disjunct; as we've originally supposed, our continuously varied Sphere is completely filled with matter that's some (one or another) Absolutely Specific Spatially Extensible Quality. So, given our original supposition, we must embrace the only other disjunct, the only one remaining: Everywhere in our Continuously Qualitatively Varied region, there are Absolutely Specific Colors instantiated *only* at some perfectly extensionless point, or points!

Well, then, we confront a perplexing Antinomy of Spatially Extensible Quality. What are we to do? Though I'm not certain of it, I think something's gone amiss with (what's here presented as) the Antimony's second side, with the supposition that there may be spatially continuously varying Extensible Colors. And, on that score, there are two main options. First, there may be error in the reasoning to show that completely continuously varying Spatially Extensible Quality requires there to be Absolutely Specific Spatially Extensible Quality only at extensionless points. Or, second, there may be incoherence in the thought that there can be a spatial region whose Extensible Quality varies completely continuously. Without resolving it, I leave this Antinomy for others to consider, along with so many other Antinomies, still unresolved, that philosophy's accumulated over millennia.

To proceed most manageably with our inquiry, and to provide a most readable exposition, in discussing basic spatial entities, I'll generally contemplate just some nicely shaped Particles, with each of my considered Particles having just a single Absolutely Specific Spatially Extensible Quality that perfectly pervades all its space, through and through, and with none having any other Spatially Extensible Quality at all. Thus, ever so far from any Sphere that's marvelously marbled Qualitatively, I won't contemplate even a Sphere that, in one of two perfectly hemispheric regions, is all Transparent Red, through and through, and, in the perfectly discrete and adjacent complement region, is Transparent Blue through and through. Of course, this very discretely Qualitied Sphere certainly doesn't exemplify our Antinomy. (While this "discretely two-tone" entity is Qualitatively unproblematic, the Particle's variegated Spatially Extensible Quality provides nothing really needed, I think, for progress with our inquiry.) But, though it avoids our Antinomy, such a two-tone Particle is too snazzy for optimal exposition. At all events, generally I'll be conceiving such discrete basic physical things, or basic Particles, as are Qualitatively homogeneous, each perfectly pervaded by its one Absolutely Specific Extensible Color.

15. The Ontological Parity of Qualities and Propensities: By Contrast with Hume

We've glimpsed an aspect of Lewis's systematic metaphysical vision that, aptly enough, he calls "Humean supervenience." As I think may prove illuminating, we may take the two Davids as going against the contemporary common grain, at least inasmuch as they reject the (commonly assumed) Denial of Qualities. (Well, with Lewis, it's a stretch; but, never mind that.) Even as the many who assume the Denial favor Propensities over Qualities, the Davids, Lewis and Hume, *favor Qualities over Propensities*. Against both the many and the two, of course, I've been upholding, and I'll continue to uphold, an *Ontological Parity of Qualities and Propensities*, favoring neither sort of basic property over the other.

Even as we've spent considerable effort upholding Parity as against those who favor Propensity, it will make for a useful change now, I think, to advance Parity against those who think to move in the opposite direction. So, in this Chapter's last Sections, I'll examine Hume's and Lewis's favoring of Qualities, with an eye toward finding, in them, a highly appealing motivation for their favoritism. In the bargain, I confess, I'll urge resistance to their marvelously high-minded appeal. As I'll advise, we should adopt a much more modest standard, than the Davids do, for what's a clear enough conception, and a full enough conception, of how things may be with concrete reality.

That said, let's again turn to discuss Hume. For our discussion to be most beneficial, I'll start by recalling, from our just previous Chapter, his stringent requirements for our believing: You should believe to be real entities only such things as are *fully available* to you in your own *direct experience;* about these available entities, you should believe *only so much as* is fully available to you in your direct experience. That recalled, I now propose we understand Hume as being very strict, as well, concerning our *conceiving:* You can conceive to be real entities, at all adequately, fully or clearly, only such things as are *fully available* to you in your own *direct experience;* about these available entities, you can conceive, at all adequately, fully or clearly, *only so much as* is fully available in your direct experience. Bearing also that in mind, we turn to Hume's greatest work.

From the *Treatise,* many passages show how very negative is his view of our capacity to conceive anything as being Propensitied or, in older terms, to conceive anything as having any *power.* Here's one that's very short, enormously general, and remarkably stark:

> All ideas are deriv'd from, and represent impressions. We never have any impression, that contains any power or efficacy. We never therefore have any idea of power.[26]

In later writing, Hume appended an argument, right after the last word above, the word "power," in which he says that, if someone thinks the stark remarks might pertain just to bodies, that's shortsighted. We no more have any impression of mental power, really, than any impression of bodily power; so, in particular, we never have any idea of mental power.[27]

Now, just a very little further along in the original text itself, there's a passage that makes vivid how very frustrating is an attempt to conceive things as Propensitied, when all that's allowed us are notions, or ideas, that meet Hume's experientially stringent demands:

> Now, nothing is more evident, than that the human mind cannot form such an idea of two objects, as to conceive any connection be-twixt them, or comprehend distinctly that power or efficacy, by which

26. Hume, *Treatise,* page 161.

27. See the appendix that, in my standard edition of Hume's *Treatise,* is at page 632 and following.

they are united. Such a connexion wou'd amount to a demonstration, and wou'd imply the absolute impossibility for the one object not to follow, or be conceiv'd not to follow upon the other: Which kind of connexion has already been rejected in all cases. If any one is of a contrary opinion, and thinks he has attain'd a notion of power in any particular object, I desire he may point out to me that object. But till I meet with such-a-one, which I despair of, I cannot forbear concluding that since we can never distinctly conceive how any particular power can possibly reside in any particular object, we deceive ourselves in imagining we can form any such general idea.[28]

Indeed, to be very vividly clear as to what's the real heart of this apparently disheartening matter, we can take this Humean line a bit further than its seminal progenitor does in the passage just cited.

For one thing, we can usefully ignore, at this juncture, Hume's allusion to an asymmetry in time, to one object's following upon, or not following upon, another. (It's hard to know why Hume spoke of objects here, rather than events, say, or changes. Maybe, it's because he thought the only real objects were perceptions and their like, each very temporary and fleeting. But, never mind.) Just so, in the case of mutual disposition partners, or interaction partners, there needn't be any temporal asymmetries, or any entities with efficacious priority. Indeed, what's most basic in Hume's worthy worries is to be found, very fully, in the case of Newtonian Particles that (perhaps through even all of an infinite past) have proceeded on their *mutually determined* trajectories. And, it's fully present even where such reciprocally partnered Particles never even so much as come close to colliding, never so much as even tempting us to take anything that transpires as any cause, nor anything as any mere effect. Yet, when we resort only to what's fully available in direct experience, how can we "point out," or conceive at all adequately, any power, or any real Propensity, on the part of any of the moving Particles? How it is that each is Shaped, let's allow, may be experientially available to us, at least in some of our imaginative experiencing; and, so, too, let's allow, with how each is Extensibly Qualitied, or Colored. By contrast, how it is that a Particle's *Propensitied*, well, that *isn't* so terribly available. For conceiving things clearly, there's no more chance of success here than with a case that's "causally asymmetric," or that's "asymmetrically directional," in its temporal aspect or regard.

For another thing, it's not the alleged existence of any necessary connection that's really the most challenging Humean point in this

28. Hume, *Treatise*, page 161.

neighborhood, though Hume often talks as though it is. Rather, the most disturbing thought is, I suggest, a most general idea, with many (alleged) necessary connections as just some of its very many quite diverse instances. To help us see that this is so, I'll note two other sorts of instance.

First, there's this. For many years now, scientists have conceived various physical entities as each having one or another *probabilistic Propensity*, or so it's said by folks who ought to know. Thus, perhaps it may be only with a certain probability, say, a chance of 0.7, that a certain Particle, Alpha, will attract another Particle, Beta, and, reciprocally, it's with that probability, a chance of 0.7, that Beta will be attracted by Alpha. Now, let's suppose that this Propensity is actually manifested, with Beta now moving closer to Alpha, or, maybe less tendentiously, with the two of them moving closer together. Here, there's no necessity about anything that's just happened. But, though it's probabilistic and not necessitating, Alpha's Propensity, and Beta's, will be just as unavailable, so far as what immediate experience ever makes plain, as any necessitating Propensity ever is.

Second, there's a power that, in an entirely different way, is very different from any necessary connection. Here we have, in your person, your power really to choose, from among truly open options for your thoughtful activity. (Hume might not think it's very different; but, if so, he's wrong about that, as I'll argue vigorously, mainly in our Sixth Chapter.) Look, you can continue to think about metaphysics with me or, for just one salient option, you can choose to employ your mind otherwise. Really, it's up to you; it's your choice. Suppose that, somewhat influenced by my nice writing style, you choose to continue to think about qualities and powers. For that, I gratefully thank you: In your exercise of that power of yours, your power to choose, there wasn't anything necessitating what happened. Yet, going by just what direct experience makes plain, it doesn't seem that there's anything for you to "point out," either. Even in a situation where there's just an illusion of real choice, you can have immediate experience that's precisely similar, in qualitative feel and character. This is worth our noting, I trust, though none of us really believe, I'm sure, that in every single case where it seems to you that you choose, it's just an illusion that you do. Rather, as all of us deeply believe, sometimes you really do exercise your power to choose, and sometimes you really do choose from among distinct options actually available to you.

Through the points just noted, I want only for us to recognize this: Should we adopt Hume's very tough demands, for what's to count as a clear enough conception, we'll be left with quite a bit less than Hume allowed in the passages I've lately cited. Just so, in keeping with the deeply demanding spirit of Hume, we should be deeply suspicious of any idea of propensity or power whatever, whether asymmetric or not, whether necessitarian or not, whether probabilistic or not, whether volitional or not—*any* idea of power or propensity.

Well, that's Hume, in his negative, or skeptical, mood. But, of course, sometimes he's in a more positive frame of mind. Then, Hume attempts to provide us with a quite modest idea that's in the neighborhood of our notion of power. This is, of course, a quite modest idea of cause, sometimes called "cause and effect," that comports fairly well with his demand about experiential availability.

Of course, Hume says very many things about cause and effect, in a valiant effort to make some cheerful sense of what he's first made seem such a frustratingly gloomy neighborhood. And, quite a few of them may conflict, it seems to me, with quite a few others. But, for our purposes, that's neither here nor there. What we must consider are only those of his remarks that are most consonant with his demands concerning just what's directly available in our immediate experience. And, happily, most of what's so consonant can be conveyed with just a few sentences from the *Treatise*:

> We may define a CAUSE to be "An object precedent and contiguous to another, and where all the objects resembling the former are plac'd in like relations of precedency and contiguity to those objects, that resemble the latter."... When I examine with the utmost accuracy those objects, which are commonly denominated causes and effects, I find, in considering a single instance, that the one object is precedent and contiguous to the other; and in inlarging my view to consider several instances, I find only, that like objects are constantly plac'd in like relations of succession and contiguity.... However extraordinary these sentiments may appear, I think it fruitless to trouble myself with any farther enquiry or reasoning upon the subject, but shall repose myself on them as on establish'd maxims.[29]

Many have noticed that this statement, about cause and effect, is wanting in several ways all at once. But, especially as regards our present purposes, most miss the main points.

What we should notice, in the above passage, are these two related things. First, while Hume denies himself any ideas as to Propensity, or power, that can't be serviced just by his direct experience, he seeks to employ, perhaps in their place, a complex of ideas that are each nicely

---

29. Hume, *Treatise*, page 170.

serviced experientially. (In this, he does not go all the way toward satisfying his demanding requirements, I think, but he does go a long way.) And, second, such ideas of cause as Hume does allow himself are attained, in large measure, through his "inlarging [his] view to consider several instances." It's via this famous enlargement strategy that Hume thinks there to be enough observable patterns among things, involving their qualitative similarity, their temporal succession and their spatial contiguity, as may promote a pretty useful significance for "cause" and "effect."

What's the main lesson to be learned from this Humean offering? To my mind, it will prove to be this: Though it first seems to promise us some enlightened thinking—about power, Propensity, cause, and the rest—Hume's enlargement strategy really must be more stultifying than illuminating.

To appreciate this, we should consider a World that's very small and quite simple, without much ever happening at all. For, with such a World, there's no room to employ an enlargement strategy.

So, let's consider a World where there are just two basic entities, both of them basic physical Particles, a single electronish entity, Ed, and, fairly near Ed, a single protonish object, Pete.

Most relevant to our consideration, here's how it is that Ed is Propensitied. He's Propensitied to attract any protons there may (near enough) be, maybe just because he's Propensitied to attract any Large Red Particle; as Pete's a (near enough) proton, quite as Red as you please, and quite sufficiently Large, we'll expect that Propensity to be manifested. Less relevantly now, Ed will have certain other Propensities; for instance, he'll be Propensitied to repel any other electrons, maybe just because he's Propensitied to repel any Particle that's Small and Blue. Less relevantly, because, as there aren't ever any other electrons, that Propensity won't ever be manifested. Well, I'll not waste time going on about how Ed may have many other unmanifested powers. Rather, I'll explicitly specify, if only quite crudely, how it is with Ed Spatially, and how it is Qualitatively: Ed's an entity who's Shaped Spherically and Sized Smally; less bizarrely put, Ed is a Small Sphere. And, Ed's Qualitied Bluely; he's a Blue Sphere. Well, that's enough, I think, for you to have a pretty clear conception of Ed; you know how it is with him Spatially, and Qualitatively and, as much as is needed, Propensitively, too.

Next, here's how it is with Pete. First, Pete's a Large Red Sphere; with that, we know how it is with him Spatially and Qualitatively. How is it that Pete's Propensitied? Most relevant to our consideration, he's Propensitied to attract any electrons there may (near enough) be, maybe just because he's Propensitied to attract any Small Blue Particle; as Ed's a (near enough) electron, and as Ed's certainly true Blue, and quite sufficiently Small, we'll expect this (reciprocal) Propensity to be manifested. Also less relevantly now, Pete will have various other Propensities. So much for our World's two characters.

Now, let's have there be some action, or at least some motion. For that, first a sentence of stage-setting. Well, at some time in the near past, Ed and Pete were fairly far apart, though not so far that there'd be no interaction. Then, Ed and Pete moved closer together. For what's here the main matter, that's all the action, or motion, we need consider.

Why did Ed and Pete move closer together? On the Humanly Realistic View I'm advancing, this experientially available enough change came about through a real *inter*action between Pete and Ed. How so? Well, because Ed's *Propensitied to attract Large Reds*, and because Pete *is* a Large Red, Ed did attract Pete. And, because there was this attraction, in these circumstances so conducive to motion, Ed and Pete moved toward each other. (As well, of course, there's a *reciprocal development*—or, here much the same, the development just described may be conceived reciprocally: As we know, *Pete's* Propensitied to attract *Small Blues*, and because *Ed is* a Small Blue, Pete did attract Ed. And, because there was this attraction, Ed and Pete moved toward each other.) At all events, Ed and Pete's moving together was far from any merely accidental happening. On the contrary, it was the manifestation of certain of their reciprocal Propensities—an intrinsic power of Ed's, with respect to (the likes of) Pete, and, reciprocally, an intrinsic power of Pete's, with respect to (the likes of) Ed.

Now, let's consider what, to my mind, is an utterly different simple World, though it's a World that, as regards what's experientially most available, even if available only in our imaginative experiencing, is perfectly similar to the World we've just left off considering. As with the World contemplated just before, this World's only salient objects—or its only decent candidates for being basic Particles—are two perfectly Spherical entities. One is a Small Blue Sphere—we'll call it "Earl," and the other, to be called "Pat," is a Large Red Sphere. But, utterly unlike just before, in this World there's nothing that's "plagued with propensity." Or, at least, for the sake of some instructive reasoning that's what we'll pretend, or presume. So, even in the fullness of its being, Earl is *humanly quite surveyable*, as we may usefully say; there's nothing that's basic to how it is with Earl that's not perfectly manifest to your experientially intellectual imagination. In marked contrast with our nicely surveyable Earl, and for being so "plagued with propensity," our electronish Ed *wasn't* humanly surveyable. And, as with Earl, so it is with Pat, too: By contrast with protonish Pete, who wasn't anything like humanly very surveyable, Pat's about as surveyable as can be. Apparently, Earl and Pat do far better by strict Humean demands than Ed or Pete ever can do.

(Look, for at least two reasons, I'm holding in abeyance for this discussion, or I'm "bracketing," the considerations that yielded a relevantly Negative answer in our Section about the question Can There Be Spatially Extensible Yellow Entities That Aren't Ever Propensitied? First, I'm not so much as really certain that the reasoning there is perfectly sound, though I do believe it to be so. And, second, I want to provide, in the rest of this Chapter, a very readable discussion. Further, and as will become very clear very quickly, whatever Propensities Small Blue Earl may have (and, maybe, Earl must have)—as with a Propensity to be attracted to Blue-Attractors, and a Propensity to be repelled by Blue-Repellors, and a Propensity to be attracted to Small-Sphere-Attractors, and so on—well, they'll all be specified as always unmanifested, in our supposed scenarios. For, as we may happily specify, the only other concretum (other than Earl) that's ever in Earl's World, our happily presumed little Pat, *never is* a Blue-Attractor, or a Blue-Repellor, or a Small-Sphere-Attractor, and so on. Just so, and for one thing, we do well to focus on this thought: For anything relevant for our present discussion, at least, any Propensity that Earl might have, or that Pat might have, won't ever (have any chance to) be at all (operative or) relevant. In particular, and quite unlike how we've supposed things with our Ed and our Pete, we're supposing that Earl and Pat aren't (even anything remotely like) real reciprocal Propensity Partners. All right already; enough with all the nice caution; let's get going.)

In our little exposition, the time is ripe for some action, or at least for some motion: Just as with the World just before, here Earl and Pat are, at a fairly early time, fairly far apart. Then, along a path that perfectly parallels that of Ed and Pete, or along an apt counterpart-path, Earl and Pat move toward each other. So, as concerns what's humanly surveyable, this second World is just like the World supposed just before.

Why did Earl and Pat move closer together? By the very suppositions of the case, there isn't any substantive answer to the question. Of course, this surveyable change wasn't the upshot of any interaction between Pat and Earl, as they lacked all Propensity, including any for mutual interaction. Nor was it the result of anything else, nor anything even remotely like a result, or a culmination, or even a manifestation. Rather, the change in the array of these Colored Spheres simply happened; it was the sheerest happenstance. Now, as I've conceived this World to have lasted longer than the briefest instant, it *had* to be that *something or other* happened in the World. But, it might have been that what happened was that Earl and Pat stayed put, and didn't move anywhere at all. Indeed, it might have happened that they ceased to exist, or one of them did. Had any of *those* things occurred, then, on our suppositions, *that* would have been the sheerest happenstance. But, as we've assumed, none of them did happen. Rather, it just happened that, even as both Earl and Pat continued to exist, they moved closer together.

In his not very skeptical moments, what can Hume say about our two simple Worlds, in order to distinguish the one from the other? Nothing much, it seems to me. Following his enlargement strategy, he'll look to have the denizens of our first World, our Ed and Pete, each be "regularly" related to certain *other* particulars, each as nicely available experientially as are Ed and Pete themselves. Ed, for instance, should be nicely paired with *other Small Blue* Spheres, each of them elsewhere or elsewhen. But, by hypothesis, there *aren't any* such other things for Ed to be paired with. Indeed, other than Ed, Pete's the *only (substantial) concrete thing there is*. So, it's just a certain *Large Red* Sphere (namely, Pete) with which Ed may paired. But, of course, *that* pairing won't help Hume at all. As I warned, there's simply no room to employ any relevant enlargement strategy. So, with nowhere to turn, Hume must now say, I suppose, that there really isn't any difference between our two apparently quite disparate Worlds. But, few will long believe that.

(Though it might be considered just some overkill, still, it might be well worth mentioning, for all I can surely tell, this opposite inadequacy of any regularity view of Propensitive manifestation, including Hume's regularity view: Even while there will be *some* Worlds where each of many Red Spheres and, correlatively, each of many Blue Spheres will, in nicely proper pairings, move toward each other *as a manifestation of their Propensity for, or their Propensities for, attracting* just such (nicely nearby) "Oppositely Colored" individuals, there'll be *other* Worlds (even if they'll be much rarer Worlds) where, also properly pairwise, each of many Reds move towards its correlative (nearby) Blue Particle, and vice versa, *all quite by accident*, so to put it, or *all as a matter of happenstance*, now putting the point just a bit differently. So far as what's humanly most surveyable goes, or so far as what's available to our mind's eye, so to put this point just a bit differently, there'll never be any difference between these two sorts of Worlds. And, on a regularity view of Propensitive manifestation, or of anything like causation, there really won't be, and just can't be, any difference between the two. But, so far as what's really a humanly intelligible metaphysics goes, there really may be just such a difference. Or, so it surely seems to me.)

Look, here's what I think: Never to be denied, there's a glaring difference between how very fully, clearly and directly we can conceive how it is with concrete particulars (Spatially and) Qualitatively and, on the other side, how very much less fully, clearly and directly we can conceive how it is with our individuals Propensitively. Exactly why this is so, I'm not sure. In part, it may concern certain *powers of the human mind*, a (sort of) mind that's quite well endowed, perhaps, for conceiving how it may be with individuals (Spatially and) Qualitatively, at the same time concerning certain *limits of the human mind*, a (sort of) mind that's *not* well endowed, perhaps, for conceiving how it may be with individuals Propensitively. And, in part, it may concern certain differences between Quality and Power themselves: For all I can tell, it might be that *any* mind, even the mind of a God, will more fully (and more clearly) conceive how things are Qualitatively with something, and will less fully (and less clearly) conceive how things are Propensitively with the selfsame concrete particular. Whatever the reason for it, there is, at all events, the great discrepancy we've been emphasizing: We can conceive how it is with things Qualitatively (and Spatially) far better than we can conceive of how it is with them Propensitively. (Perhaps, this may be especially evident with blatantly physical things, though the point's certainly not limited to them, as Hume himself clearly recognized, as in the appended writing we've noted.) Quite generally, then, we do far better at conceiving how it may be with things Qualitatively than at conceiving how it may be Propensitively. And, with the Qualitative aspect, our far greater success is attained far more directly.

All of this is, I think, important to notice. But, none of it entails anything, I feel sure, as to the ontological status of the Qualitative, and certainly not that it's prior to, or it's more basic than, the Propensitive. Rather, there's *Ontological Parity* for, or between, Quality and Propensity. Each being utterly basic and perfectly real, neither can be, in any philosophically significant way, reduced to the other. Well, that's perfectly true in any event. And, it's just this Ontological Parity of Qualities and Propensities that most fully accords with our Principle of Constrained Contingency. This speaks well of the Principle. And, it suggests that, in any metaphysic with a physical World that's even moderately intelligible to us human thinkers, this Principle will be fundamental. That may not be so high a degree of intelligibility as some would like, as with Hume, and, as I'll be urging, with Lewis, too. But, it may be quite high enough to satisfy those who, perhaps quite rightly, don't expect more from human understanding than our limited powers can provide.

16. The Ontological Parity of Qualities and Propensities: By Contrast with Lewis

While David Hume enjoins us never to stray at all far from what our experience directly teaches, David Lewis's philosophy doesn't have us cleave tightly to experiential delivery. But, as I read him, Lewis is just as exercised as Hume by our notion of Propensity, and by all the notions in its neighborhood. Why? Doubtless, there are several reasons. But, I suspect what's most operative is much like what mainly motivates Hume. It's what I've called the *surveyable;* metaphorically, and only very roughly, it's what can be surveyed by the mind's intellectually imaginative eye. So, while geometric arrangements of quality (or Quality) *are* surveyable, the nonqualitative Propensity of a particular *isn't* surveyable, whether the candidate particular is point-sized and perfectly adjacent to many others, or whether it's larger and usually surrounded by perfectly empty space. (And, at least to a pretty considerable degree, changing quality mosaics are surveyable.) So, broadly framed, Lewis's Humean idea may be put like this: We conceive concrete reality as surveyable insofar as, in our imaginative conception of it, we have it be a spatial reality that's pervaded, at least in parts, by quality that's fit for spatial occupancy. And, since our conceiving concrete physical reality as surveyable is our most adequate conception of this reality, we may have it that, so far as what's ontologically basic goes, a mosaic of qualitative spatial "occupants" is all there is to physical reality.

(Apparently, if we can properly conceive a quality mosaic's temporal change on a par with its spatial variegation, we may take its temporal development to be as fully humanly surveyable as its qualitative heterogeneity at just a moment in time. Unlike Lewis, and others before him, I don't think we can properly do that. But, for the meanwhile, I forgo discussing this matter.[30])

In the philosophic ideas he allows as tenable, Lewis is much more liberal than Hume. But, here, that doesn't much matter. Rather, what's central is this: Even as Hume holds that the world is a surveyable (mental) reality, so Lewis holds that the actual world is a surveyable (physical) reality, in a sense of "surveyable" about equally apt for both Davids. And, so, quite as with Hume long before him, Lewis also thinks that, so far as any alleged powers or Propensities are concerned, there's

---

30. I discuss this in several later Sections, notably in Section 7 of Chapter 5, "Temporal Monotony and Temporal Change" and in Section 9 of Chapter 9, "Much More Accommodating Than Space, Time Is No Spacelike Dimension."

nothing ontologically fundamental. In a fashionable technical term that we've seen Lewis saliently employ, any of that just "supervenes" on what's really basic, presumably on a nicely enough surveyable (spatial, or spatiotemporal) array of Extensibly Qualitied point-sized concreta. So, as much as for Hume, for Lewis, too, Propensities will be onto-logically inferior to Qualities, and inferior to Spatial (or spatiotem-poral) features, and to whatever else figures fundamentally in how it is that concrete reality is so suitably surveyable. So, with both of these brilliant Davids, this is my somewhat unconfident and reluctant diag-nosis: As against our idea of Ontological Parity for Qualities and Propensities, they'll have Propensities be ontologically inferior to what's more fully and directly (involved in such concreta as are, quite fully and directly) conceivable by us human thinkers.

Moments ago, we saw how Hume would think about powers when in a pretty positive mood, not any very skeptical frame of mind. Well, now, how does Lewis, who's hardly ever very skeptical, treat such on-tologically superficial items as Propensities, or powers? It's through a complex *enlargement strategy* that he does this, far more sophisticated, of course, than his early predecessor's, but, a strategy that also looks for large regular patterns in, or among, what's really quite surveyable, to serve as something like (what I believe to be real) instances of Pro-pensity-manifestation, or power-exercise, or natural laws, or, in more directly Humean terms, cause-and-effect. So, here's Lewis on laws of nature: "Like any regularity theory, the best-system analysis says that laws hold in virtue of patterns spread over all of space and time."[31] In essence, this is Hume all over again, as on his very next page, Lewis himself says, "The best system analysis is Humean. The arrangement of qualities provides the candidate true systems, and considerations of simplicity and strength and balance do the rest."[32]

For the best-system analysis of laws to do anything much, indeed, for there to be even just an appearance to such an effect, it must be quite complex Worlds that are under consideration. Of course, the actual world is quite complex. So, just as it is with Hume, it's quite under-standable how Lewis should become attached to a regularity theory.

But, for any account to cut much philosophic ice, in these matters, it must do well by very simple Worlds, at least as well as with Worlds much more complex. And, to my mind at least, Lewis does no better here than

31. David Lewis, "Humean Supervenience Debugged," *Mind*, 1994, reprinted in David Lewis, *Papers in Metaphysics and Epistemology*, Cambridge University Press, 1999. In the reprinting, the cited words appear on page 232.

32. Ibid., page 233.

Hume did, not very well at all. To persuade us of this, let's again consider our two apparently quite different, very simple Worldly cases: our World with Propensity-plagued Ed and Pete, and our World with Presumably-Propensityless Earl and Pat. To help us distinguish between these two Worlds, Lewis's best-system proposal has no room to do anything. And, that's no particular fault of Lewis's. For, of course, *by the very simple nature of the cases, no* regularity proposal, and *no* enlargement strategy, has any room to do anything. Well, like Hume well before him, Lewis might say that there's really no difference between our two cases. But, as happened with Hume, few will believe that for long. Or, less "heroically," he may say that he's interested only in the actual world, and wants to remain silent about such sparely simple Worlds.

But, such quietism, I think, won't really do. For, in parallel with what we just said for apparently different Worlds, we may also say, even if quite speculatively, for apparently different Eons: Over very many Eons, we may speculate, the actual world may go through very many vast changes. In certain Eons, even if only a tiny minority of its epochs, our world may contain, and comprise, only a very few concrete particulars. In some Eons, there might be just a couple of basic concreta. Maybe, in each Eon, there are just two *utterly novel* concreta, without any prior existence at all; what's more, each may first exist quite by accident. Yet, happily, they are reciprocal disposition partners, each set to interact with the other (or anything precisely intrinsically like the other) from the first moment of its existence. And, they interact in just such a way that they move closer together. And, as it may be, there may never again be, quite as there never before was, any concretum much like either of these exotic Particles, nothing much like either in Shape, or in Size, or in Color, and so on. In each of these many ways, both of our exotic Particles may be far more different from all other actual Particles than any one, of all the rest, is different from any other one, of all the rest.

(Though it's now likely to be overkill, still, it just might be worth mentioning, even at this point, the opposite inadequacy of any regularity view of Propensitive manifestation, paralleling the point I mentioned just before, in connection with Hume's regularity view: Even while there may be *some* Worlds where many Red Spheres and many correlative Blue Spheres will, properly pairwise, move toward each other *as a manifestation of their Propensity for, or their Propensities for, attracting* just such "Oppositely Colored" individuals, there'll be *other* Worlds (even if they'll be much rarer Worlds) where, properly pairwise, many Reds move towards many correlative Blues, and vice versa, *all quite by accident*, so to put it, or *all as a matter of happenstance*, now putting the point just a bit differently. But, though these two sorts of Worlds differ metaphysically, in this quite fundamental way, the best-system approach won't ever deliver the difference. For, just as we've noted, Lewis does say, "Like any regularity theory, the best-system analysis says that laws hold in virtue of patterns spread over all of space and time." In essence, this is Hume yet once again.)

Though it means some repetition, I'll now make, in connection with Lewis, remarks lately made in connection with Hume. For, they exemplify a philosophic approach that I myself find recurrently appealing, even while I regard it as stultifyingly restrictive: First, and as I agree, there's a glaring difference between how fully, and directly, we conceive how it is with things Qualitatively and, on the other side, how much less fully and directly we conceive of how it is with things Propensitively. Exactly why this is so, I cannot be sure. But, whatever the reason, there certainly is the noted discrepancy. And, though it may be especially evident with blatantly physical things, the disparity is quite general. Just as much as with the physical, we conceive our own experiential qualities far more fully, and somewhat more clearly, than we conceive our mental Propensities, or powers. (This is so whether we be physical beings, as well as mental beings, or whether we be only mental entities, not physical at all.) But, though there's this wide discrepancy in our conceiving, there's not a parallel disparity in the ontological status of our quality, or our Quality, and that of our Propensity. Rather, at least in our own case, there's Ontological Parity for Quality, or for quality, and for Propensity: Each is perfectly real and utterly basic, with neither reducible to the other. And, as it is with us, so it is, too, I say, for basic physical concreta. Or, so it's philosophically best for us to believe.

Best taken as the truth, by us human thinkers, it's just this Ontological Parity of Qualities and Propensities that most fully accords with our Principle of Constrained Contingency, a proposition central to any metaphysic allowing a physical realm that, *to a fairly significant degree*, is conceivable by us humans. To be sure, this may *not be as high a degree of conceivability* as some would like, including our two Davids, Lewis and Hume. But, it's enough to satisfy those of us who, perhaps quite rightly, don't expect a very great deal from our quite human, quite limited powers.

17. What May We Learn from Our Demystification of the Physical?

Against those who've assumed the Denial to hold, I've argued that, without conceiving a concrete reality that's Qualitatively endowed, we humans, at least, can't conceive, at all adequately, any physical reality at all. This was argued, of course, in our book's first Chapter, "The Mystery of the Physical." At the same time, and just as so much of this present (Third) Chapter's argued, once we reject the Denial, we may resolve our Mystery of the Physical.

Conceiving a concrete reality replete with Spatially Extensible Quality, we may have tolerably clear conceptions of those metaphysical views on which there is a physical reality, at least insofar as the views claim that concrete reality, whether all of it or whether only some, has a physical aspect or nature. Among the views that make that claim is, of course, Scientiphicalism, the metaphysic currently dominant with, at the least, mainstream analytic philosophers. So, in resolving our Mystery, one thing we've done is to remove an obstacle to our having a tolerably clear conception of a World that's the way Scientiphicalism claims our actual world to be. So, in at least one important sense, we've performed a service for Scientiphical philosophers.

But, as it is also important to notice, we've also performed such a service, quite equally, for those holding certain alternative views, on which some of concrete reality, though only some, has a physical aspect or nature. Salient among these others will be various Substantial Dualists, perhaps some of whom might be fairly counted as Cartesian thinkers or, at any rate, counted as Quasi-Cartesian. So, while our "demystification of the physical" should be welcomed by Scientiphicalists, it shouldn't increase what seems the already complacent confidence in the Scientiphical View.

That's one large lesson, I think, that may be learned from this Chapter's discussion. What might be some others?[33]

In discussing our attempts to conceive a physical world, with the Denial in force, we concluded, quite rightly, that such Qualitatively impoverished attempts won't yield ideas that are any humanly very intelligible conceptions. Being such terribly poor conceptions of ours, these notions won't have, at least for us, much lasting philosophical interest. Thus, there's no philosophically interesting debate, or choice, really, between what we might call a Qualityless Galilean conception of physical reality and, on the far greater hand, a conception where physical concreta have Spatially Extensible Quality. For us humans, at least, the latter conception is to be preferred.

By contrast with all that, our more recent discussions, concerning the claims of the Humeans, do seem to leave us with a debate, or choice,

---

33. With passages I hope will illuminate just such difficult and dicey issues, in Chapter 5 I'll explore these matters.

that's philosophically more interesting. What is this more interesting debate? Well, we may begin by agreeing that we do have an idea of Propensity, or power, that, at least at first blush, can serve in distinguishing between, say, the Propensity-rich World of Ed and Pete and, on the apparently much lesser hand, the Presumably-Propensityless World of Earl and Pat. But, as it often should seem, the Humeans will go on to say, this may be a distinction without a philosophically important difference. Perhaps, all that's going on here is that there are two different ways for us adequately enough to conceive concrete reality, or at least so much of it as we're wont to call "physical reality." With the Lockeans, or Neo-Lockeans, we may, if we wish, conceive physical reality in a way that involves us in relatively complex notions, maybe even rather baroque ideas, where we employ both very clearly intelligible human conceptions, as with various of our Spatial and Qualitative conceptions, and also some far less clear conceptions of ours, as with our conceptions as to Power, or Propensity. Or, it may be suggested, in what we take to be a Humean spirit, or Neo-Humean approach, we may conceive physical reality in a simpler and sparser way, where the only conceptions ever employed are quite clear, and quite full, human conceptions. Then, we'll again employ conceptions of Spatially Extensible Quality, all right, and our Spatial conceptions, as well; but, we'll avoid such far less clear ideas as are our conceptions as to Propensity, or Power. But, in all of this, there's nothing of much metaphysical moment that's ever at stake. Rather, however we may be thinking of concreta, it's always the very same physical reality that's adequately conceived: Sometimes it's conceived in a way that's quite simple and sparse, whilst other times in a way that's far fancier and, maybe, much more pretentiously and unhappily convoluted.

As it appears, I've just begun to articulate a residual philosophic issue. Apparently, there's a Humean challenge remaining; or, at the least, there's a recalcitrant point that apparently favors the Neo-Humeans over us Neo-Lockeans. To this apparent Humean challenge, what can we reply?

If we confine our attention to such concrete reality as is *obviously* all physical reality, and if we never take pains to focus on any of mental reality, there won't be much for us to say. True enough, we might say that it's implicit in the meaning of "physical object" that things properly so-called be things with Propensity. But, even if that's right (and I think it is), it may mean little more than who gets the rights to the use of some philosophically fashionable words, namely, "physical object," and to kindred expressions. And, while that may count for something, it's no very big deal. So, evidently, we shouldn't confine our attention to what's obviously all physical; instead, we should focus on some of mental reality (whether or not it's, unobviously, also some of physical reality).

Let's attend, then, each one of us, to a most simple *mental* episode. And, with our attention so focused, we should recall some thoughts central to a salient Section of the just previous Chapter, the Section "We Are Not Bundles of Experiences, Thoughts or Perceptions." So, in the first place, we should acknowledge the possibility of a World, an entire World, whose only occurrence is just a single episode of quite simple thinking, or perfectly simple experiencing. As such a lonely simple experience, or experiencing, is so perfectly solitary, it can't be any part of, or any member of, any bundle or collection of perceptions. And, as it is both so solitary and so simple, it also can't be any part of any pattern of experiencing. For there is nothing else experiential with which it can be partnered in any pattern. Nor can it serve toward composing any relevant regularity. For there is nothing else, in all the World, with which it might be regularly grouped (or, for that matter, even conjoined quite irregularly). But, as it is an experiencing, or (more colloquially) it's an experience, it must be the experiencing *of an experiencer*, a real Propensitied individual that's engaged in this solitary experiencing she's just then enjoying. And, far from the experiencer's being composed of her experiencing, or being identical with it, the experiencing is, rather, a manifestation of a certain mental power of this individual, namely, a manifestation of her power to experience.

Such a Neo-Lockean description of our bare experiential episode, or such a Quasi-Cartesian description, is the only sort of description, I submit, that makes any real sense of things. At the least, it makes far more sense than does any Neo-Humean description, replete with reference only to quality, and without ever acknowledging any real Propensity, or power, at all.

As it is with the simplest sort of mental case, so it is, also, with the much more complex case of your own actual mental life. The only way to make any real sense of this is to acknowledge that all of your experiencing is the manifestation of your power to experience, occasionally dormant but often active, just as all of mine is the manifestation of my numerically distinct experiential power. As should be very clear, here there is not any serious debate, or real choice, as to how we should conceive things. Rather, to make any real sense of ourselves, we must conceive ourselves each to have real irreducible mental powers: When it's just *you* who's experiencing in a certain absolutely specific way, then there's a certain manifestation of just *your* power to experience, a manifestation of just such an absolutely specific sort. By contrast, when it's just your perfect *twin* who's experiencing, maybe in just that same absolutely specific way, then there's the perfectly parallel manifestation of *her* perfectly similar power. And, of course, in *that* event, there's no manifestation of *your* experiential power.

In our metaphysical philosophy, we should acknowledge that certain individuals, at least ourselves, you may be sure, do have powers that aren't reducible to any Quality, of course, nor even to any quality at all (or to anything that's not perfectly Propensitive). But, once we've acknowledged that much, should we still always *demand decisive* reason to affirm proper Propensities, also irreducible to what's not Propensitive, for *all other* individuals, or for *all those that aren't mental* beings? To my mind, that seems unduly restrictive. Rather than that, I'll suggest, we may take *basic physical objects* to be just as irreducibly Propensitied as we experiencers take ourselves to be. As against the Humeans, I suggest, we should accept a metaphysic that accords real irreducible Propensities to such basic physical particulars as we've supposed electronish Blue Ed and protonish Red Pete to be. Against the Humeans, we should be content to accept, as in fact we do accept, a metaphysics that finds a real difference between their mutually resultant motion, the result of their real attraction to each other, and, on the other hand, the merely accidental movement, toward each other, of Presumably-Propensityless Colored Spheres, as with our instructively posited Blue Earl and Red Pat.

What I've just offered *isn't* meant as any *refutation* of a Humean approach to what we take to be physical reality. For, as a matter of course, there's no guarantee that there's really very much at all to such a supposedly vast concrete realm, purportedly comprising (so very much of) mind-independent reality. But, in attempting to advance a Humanly Realistic Philosophy, there's never any need for any such guarantee. Nor, then, is there any point in bemoaning the fact that there isn't any. Nor is there any point, either, in bemoaning the fact that, even as we might sometimes conceive, quite fully and directly, how it may be with things qualitatively, or Qualitatively, we can't ever conceive, anywhere nearly so fully or directly, how it is with things Propensitively.

That said, we've concluded articulating the large lessons that may be learned from this Chapter's discussion. Informed by these ideas, we look to advance, considerably further than what's so far been done, a Humanly Realistic Philosophy worth some considerable attention.[34]

34. Look, you've got to take everything I've been saying here in a pretty accommodating spirit. For it's just such a spirit, really, that's most appropriate to grasping the import of the book's main project, as well as most of its secondary themes, too. Just so, none of what I'm saying is meant to go against any sort of philosophical skepticism on main issues of epistemology. That was made clear enough, I should hope, by the very long second note to the Second Chapter.

18. Remarks on What's Been Done and on What's to Come

As I'll remind you, the book's first Section provided a Brief Exposition of the Scientiphical Metaphysic. Now, having very nearly finished three full Chapters, you may be wondering about whether, and if so how, the material so far presented bears on the status of that currently dominant Metaphysic: In what's been presented so far, is there anything that argues in favor of Scientiphicalism, as against all its most salient rivals, including, for instance, a Substantial Dualism much like Descartes's? Or, contrarily, is there anything here, already presented, on this book's preceding pages, that poses a serious challenge to Scientiphicalism? Very briefly, I'll answer these questions.

With the exception of a couple of Sections in Chapter 2, far more tantalizing than they're truly argumentative, I've said nothing, so far in this book, that contravenes the Scientiphical Metaphysic. At the same time, neither have I said anything that truly argues, in some serious and substantial way, against our implicit Scientiphicalism. At least for the most part, then, so far I've said only such things as comport well, or well enough, both with Scientiphicalism itself and with the denial of the currently dominant worldview. For those looking for something substantial as to Scientiphicalism's status, they'll have to look elsewhere, even if the elsewhere may be much later in this book's own pages. So far, I've done nothing, or nothing much, about that interesting issue.

What I have done, I believe, is to show that we should abandon, in any of its Forms, the Denial of Qualities, maybe especially if we're (to

---

When push comes to shove, I'm willing to side with those few hearty souls who, even nowadays, hold that we may know precious little about ourselves and the world, and maybe nothing whatever. And, what's more, I'm quite willing to side with those few, even fewer I imagine, who hold that we may never have any reason for believing anything (or for wanting anything, or for doing anything). On the other hand, I don't feel absolutely committed to those skeptical positions, either.

Anyhow, as I see the matter, what I'm trying to treat, in this big book, are much more substantial philosophical matters than any questions concerning epistemological skepticism, the sorts of issues that may allow us to appreciate , if we are sufficiently receptive to new ideas, the benefits that may attend each of various worldviews. Otherwise, we may be, for several more decades, perennially stuck solely with our dominant Scientiphicalism. Heck, before we made our very recent exploration, that wasn't even any decently articulated View, much less was it any Enlightened Scientiphicalism.

For most folks, this note might be quite redundant and even gratuitous. But, as I imagine, not so for all. So, here it is. Now, with it providing everyone with a clear reminder, I should think that everyone may be on the same page, so to say, without even a single soul barking up the wrong tree.

be) Scientiphicalists, but not only if we're (to be) Scientiphicalists. But, of course, it was never any part of Scientiphicalism, on my offered understanding of the dominant View, that the Denial should ever be accepted.

In actual fact, as I've noted early on, almost all who've implicitly accepted the Scientiphical Metaphysic have also implicitly accepted the Denial of Qualities. As we might usefully say, they've embraced, at least implicitly, a *Qualitatively Impoverished* Scientiphicalism. But, as I've been arguing, there's never been any need for anything like that. Rather, as I've been seeking to show, anyone wishing to hold that concrete reality comprises (or includes) physical individuals, or at least one physical entity, should hold that concrete reality comprises, or it includes, things that are Spatially Extensibly Qualitied. And, as we're quite well able to think that there are just such nicely Qualitied concreta, itself a thought that's perfectly coherent, there's no serious objection to, nor any real obstacle to, our believing there to be concrete particulars each Extensibly Colored. So, if we're to continue to be Scientiphical thinkers, we should accept a *Qualitatively Rich Scientiphicalism*. Or, as I'll also say, even if it may be overly optimistic of me to do so, we should accept an *Enlightened Scientiphical View*.

But, then, and quite equally, this is also true: If we should come to abandon Scientiphicalism, as just possibly we should eventually come to do, we should still accept a *Qualitatively Rich* Metaphysic, at least so long as we believe that concrete reality does comprise, or it does include, some real physical individuals, even if it might *also* comprise, or it might *also* include, some real *nonphysical* individuals, as with, say, some immaterial minds, or souls.

In arguing against the Denial of Qualities, and in providing a positive treatment for our Mystery of the Physical, I've done nothing, really, to argue for Scientiphicalism itself, as against all its main metaphysical rivals. But, equally, I've done nothing, either, to argue against Scientiphicalism, to the benefit of the rivals. To a pretty fair extent, perhaps, I may have done something to defend both Scientiphicalism and Substantial Dualism, quite equally, against certain arguments of a Quasi-Berkeleyan sort. Or, at any rate, I may have provided some resources, for both sorts of View, to defend against certain sorts of consideration that, whether rightly or wrongly, may have been thought to favor, at both of their expense, some Fully Mentalistic Metaphysic, a View absolutely opposing the idea that there are any physical individuals at all.

So, on all the main matters that this Section's addressed, that's the state of play so far. And, at least for the most part, things will be quite the same, in these respects and regards, in the next couple of Chapters, too, that is, in Chapters 4 and 5.

Just so, to find the first real attempt to challenge Scientiphicalism, in this book's pages, we'll have to wait until we come to Chapter 6. And, comporting with that, it won't be until then that we'll find anything to raise serious doubts about a Materialist Metaphysic. Finally, as part of that same bargain, it's only then that we'll first find even just the start of any serious case that, by the case's end, may do anything much to favor (some sorts of) Substantial Dualism. Before that, we may encounter a few tantalizing suggestions to some such effects, alluding to the unfashionable ends I've just mentioned.

As I'm pretty sure, what I've just said, in this short Section, will be very helpful to quite a few readers.

Now, while it may not be quite as helpful as that, it will be useful nonetheless, I think, for me to make, very briefly, this quite different observation: Especially in several very recent Sections, I've argued for a Neo-Lockean View, on which Propensities, and powers, *are ontologically on a par with* Qualities, and qualities. Of course, in doing that, I've argued against a Humean View, or a Neo-Humean Metaphysic, that's absolutely opposed to the Neo-Lockean Approach I've favored. But, by contrast with this, my case for my Neo-Lockean View never involved, at any point, anything that's opposed to Scientiphicalism as such. Nor did it involve, even in the least degree, anything that positively supports the Scientiphical Metaphysic. Now, at least to my way of thinking, that's all just as it should be: Indeed, even as David Hume was, himself, a thoroughly Mentalistic metaphysician, so David Lewis was, by contrast, a thoroughgoing Materialist—and, by implication, this later David was a Scientiphical Metaphysician. Well, I said this would be very brief; and, so, it's all done now.

Now, let me become a little personal with you or, perhaps, just a bit informal: Different readers have different philosophical interests; heck, everyone knows that. For some smart readers, it's almost impossible to become embroiled with too much systematic metaphysics. Most of them, I imagine, will be motivated to read straight through this book, Chapter by Chapter.

With others, also very smart, and likely rather more numerous, their interests will be quite different. To these other readers, I'll suggest that they now skip to Chapter 6, which they're quite likely to enjoy, and then go on, from there, to several further quite widely enjoyable Chapters.

By doing that, I imagine, some may come to be, just possibly, pretty highly motivated to confront, in due course, and after all, the book's intervening material, in its Chapters 4 and 5. Of course, at least as far as I'm concerned, that will be all to the good. And, as I like to think, even as far as they themselves are concerned, it will also be all to the good.

With some readers, I'm sure, even though they're very smart, there won't ever arise a very great deal of quite purely metaphysical motivation. Of course, that's quite all right, too. Why do I say that? Well, partly it's just this: Even without their ever being greatly motivated to explore a lot of issues involved with Qualities, or to think long and hard about Propensities, they may be strongly motivated, nonetheless, to engage with Chapter 6's engaging discussion of real choice, or "free will," as so many philosophers label that humanly central subject. And, they'll also be interested, I think, to engage with Chapter 7's intriguing advancement of a Substantial Dualist View, on which each of us is an immaterial soul.

Of course, I've no way of knowing into which group any given reader will fall. So, each reader should decide the matter for herself: If you can scarcely get enough of the sort of philosophy you've just been confronting, then just go on to the next Chapter, and you'll find more of it there. But, if you've had enough of this pretty impersonal material, then skip ahead to Chapter 6, where you'll confront a challenge to your belief that you really choose, a much more poignantly personal matter.

4

A CORNUCOPIA
OF QUALITY

Though it wasn't without difficulties, we've articulated an idea of physical things as Extensibly Qualitied. This idea is so aptly related to our power to think experientially that it may serve us humans fairly well, when it comes to our clearly conceiving physical individuals. Accordingly, the physical needn't be so opaque to us as it sometimes seemed to many philosophers, myself included.

That's well and good; but it's hardly a sign that we should rest from our exploratory labor. Indeed, several hard questions forcefully arise for us. This Chapter means to explore some.

1. The Qualities Most Available to Me Are My Own When Consciously Experiencing

For a perspicuous Humanly Realistic Philosophy, I should take myself to be a substantial individual, well qualitied and Propensitied, with my experiences ontologically parasitical on me. But, when this realization is upon us, there arises the question as to what are the qualities or, as some prefer, the quality-instances, that are most directly, and most fully, available to me.

A quality will be most available to me only insofar as it's the quality *of a substantial individual that's available to me most directly, and most fully.*

145

Indeed, when we speak of a certain quality exemplified in an individual, the matter is related more perspicuously by saying that the particular is qualitied in a certain way. (More perspicuous still would be a characterization that avoided reifying—or treating as real things—both qualities and ways, as well.)

Which substantial individual is most directly available to me? Even if it's just a matter of (contingent) fact, only one candidate appears plausible: Me. To be sure, even I myself *won't ever be as* fully available to me, or *as directly* available, as many fine philosophers have wished or dreamed. For, right off the bat, and to a very great extent indeed, *my Propensities and powers won't be very available*. But, I'm not just a Propensitied individual, I'm also qualitied. And, insofar as I'm a *qualitied* particular, then, during much of the time that I'm conscious, anyway, I may be very impressively available to myself, even though nothing like completely available.

When I'm exercising *my power to introspect*, more on which later, I pay particular attention to myself, particularly insofar as I'm an experientially qualitied particular. In so doing, I may appreciate how variously I am modified experientially. In less barbarous though less perspicuous terms, I may appreciate various of my experiential qualities.[1]

Well, how may we think most perspicuously about my experiential qualities? Most of our common language is ill suited to the purpose, including our very most common expressions. Most of our language is, by contrast, well suited to refer to what (we suppose) is commonly suffered, or enjoyed, by so many of us rather equally. In traditional philosophical terms, it's suited for "the external world of everyday life."

So, it's straightforward to say that a (spatially extended) ball is blue, and that the ball may be accurately perceived to be blue by me or you. By contrast, it's forced, at best, and it's *likely even false*, to say that, when I'm most accurately perceiving a blue ball, *I am blue*. Except in the most

---

1. In one of his most penetrating periods, I think, Russell held a certain unfashionable view, perhaps poorly expressed by this thinker himself, about our consciously perceiving external particulars—ordinary physical things, like rocks, for instance. When consciously perceiving a rock, on this view, in the first instance, or most directly, each of us senses himself. And, in sensing himself, each of us appreciates, quite directly and rather fully enough, his current qualitative character. See Bertrand Russell, *The Analysis of Matter*, Kegan Paul, 1927, page 320. And, for a recent interpretation of, commentary on, and possible extension of Russell's view, see Michael Lockwood, *Mind, Brain and the Quantum*, Blackwell, 1989, pages 161 and following.

There are certain similarities, I think it plain, between what Russell then held and, on the other side, what I'm now advancing. But, just as plainly, there are also great differences. Rather than distract us with a discussion of the differences and the similarities, I just record Russell's influence.

extraordinary conditions, which I'm quite sure don't actually obtain, *I* am *not* blue. (I'm using "blue," of course, in its central sense.) And, it's also forced, and likely even false, to say that then *my experiencing* is blue, or my *experience* is blue. But, whatever device we may need for the purpose, we should be able to say *something positive about how I'm qualitied* when, quite normally and typically, I consciously perceive a blue ball. What are we to say?

Some small help might be found with this traditional response: When I'm consciously perceiving a blue ball accurately, there's a certain visual quality that *my experience* exemplifies. Equally, my experience will exemplify this visual quality should I have a completely comprehensive hallucination to just such an effect. So, as some have said, in both cases my experience exemplifies *phenomenal* blue. Or, saying the same more simply, that experience of mine *is* phenomenal blue. But, this is, at most, only a small help. Let me explain.

Sometimes little noted, *some* of common parlance *is* rather well suited to report what we commonly call *our experience* (or, to report how it is that we're modified experientially). So, I may sometimes say, quite truthfully enough, that my experience *is very painful*. Similarly, I may say that your experience is extremely pleasant experience.

Now, suppose that it's as true to say that sometimes my experience is phenomenal blue as it is to say that sometimes my experience is painful. Even so, we will have made hardly any progress, if any at all, with our problem of qualitative characterization. Why so? Well, when we correctly say my experience is painful, it's generally *not* true that *I am painful*. Now, if I should make effectively hurtful remarks to many folks, well, maybe then I'm painful. Or, if I poke folks in the eyes with my sharp fingernails, maybe then. But, of course, cruel and callous people may poke painfully without themselves feeling pain, and anyone may feel pain without inflicting any. So, when I'm *just feeling* severe pain, it's inappropriate, even incorrect, to say that *I am painful*. That's no better, really, than saying of me, when I'm normally perceiving a blue ball, that *I am blue*.

When I'm feeling pain, in certain ways, it may be said of me that I'm *pained*. Well, that's both common enough parlance and relevant enough to these issues. But, apparently, it's still not very much help here. For one thing, it hardly does justice to what's going on when I'm suffering agony. And, for another, when you're truly ecstatic, as in the throes of sexual orgasm, it hardly does justice to what's going on to say that you're extremely *pleased*.

To express how it is with us qualitatively, in our conscious experiencing, we want some linguistic invention.

Putting the matter in most colloquial terms, expressions that seem to reify qualities, my task is to give expression to those qualities *of me*, an experiencing substantial individual, that are (sometimes) qualities most available *to me*, the very selfsame experiencing particular. Now, quite a few years ago, some philosophers coined certain expressions, like "phenomenal blue," to characterize their (wrongly reified, but, of course, commonly acknowledged) visual experiences.[2] Not entirely unlike that, now I should coin correlative expressions, philosophically more perspicuous than theirs, as I hope, to characterize *myself*, as I am when I'm consciously experiencing. With these new terms, I should be able to say something, perspicuously enough, as to how it is with me experientially when, for instance, I'm (consciously) visually experiencing a blue ball to be blue. Equally, I suppose, the term should characterize me as I am when I'm vividly *dreaming as of* just such a (perceptual) experiential episode. As I'll suggest, I may usefully do this by saying that, in both experiential cases equally, I'm *experiential blue*. And, correlatively, I'll say that, when I'm suffering pain, I'm *experiential painful*. And, for our imagined metaphysician who always auditorally experiences belltone, "constant and invariable," we'll say he's always *experiential belltone*.

These coined terms may be only very vague indicators, of course, as to how it is with folks experientially. But, for our fairly modest present purpose, that doesn't much matter.

Moving to address what matters more, I'll say something about how it is that I'm most available to myself, sometimes, when I'm an experientially qualitied particular: At least quite typically, when I'm consciously experiencing, I can exercise my power to sense myself, or, maybe more fully, my power to sense myself as consciously experiencing. Sometimes, I suppose, I don't exercise any such power, whether that's because I'm so engrossed in "external affairs," as with throwing a ball, or whether for some other reason. But, sometimes I do exercise, or manifest, this

---

2. Some other philosophers, sometimes debating those just mentioned, used "phenomenal blue" to characterize certain alleged entities, often called "sense data," that they took themselves to be directly experiencing at certain times, those times when, as I'd describe them, they experienced bluely. Among these other philosophers, different thinkers held different views about the nature of these alleged sense data, or sensa. And, since some changed their minds somewhat, certain thinkers held different views at different times. Myself, I don't believe there are any sensa at all; there are no such entities as what were posited by any of these various views. But, then also, as alert readers by now well know, I also don't believe that there are any such entities as experiences, either (even though, in common parlance, many of us often speak in ways suggesting that, among all the world's real entities, there are many experiences each of which is a real entity). At all events, for most of what's important to this Chapter, the points made in this note are rather secondary remarks. That said, let's get back to the text, and to what's of much more central importance.

Propensity for, or toward, "experiential self-consciousness." Adapting traditional terminology to my present purpose, I then exercise *my power to introspect*.[3]

Typically, at least, when I'm consciously experiencing, I'm qualitied in such a way that, should my power to introspect be manifested as fully as possible, I'll appreciate how it is that I'm then experientially qualified. Even if I won't completely appreciate how it is with me experientially, at least I'll appreciate fairly fully how I'm experientially qualitied. Yet, for all I know, some poor human beings may lack a power to introspect altogether, possibly because they never had much cranial development. And, even among those of us who do have this power, there might be, for all I know, many large differences as to its potency, its versatility, and its conditions of exercise. So, at the very least, I want to leave it open whether my being experientially qualitied requires, on my part, any power to attend to myself as experiencing.

These ideas make some progress, I think, even if only a very little progress, to resolve some problems in their neighborhood.

Now, it must be admitted that there are problems in this area for which, at least apparently, our proposed ideas do nothing: Consider how things are with an experiencer, yourself, for example, when *you are extremely painful*. Let's try to express your severe condition in our newly coined terms. Is it *then* possible for you *not* to attend to, and *not to notice*, how it is with you experientially? On the one hand, it seems that (1) the experiencer's *experiencing* severely painfully and (2) the experiencer's *appreciating* how it is with himself experientially, each of them *must* be quite *contingently* related to each other. But, on the other, it seems *impossible* for me *not to notice* how it is with me when I'm in such severe pain. Indeed, it seems impossible for me *not to hate* how it is experientially with me then. Are these the makings of another Antinomy, a problem possibly well-called the *Antinomy of Experiential Quality*? I'm quite uncertain, and I'm very perplexed.

But, at least in this present context, I don't think my perplexity should lead to philosophical paralysis, or intellectual inertia. Rather, as our experience with the Antinomy of Extensible Quality suggests, there may be unresolved philosophic problems attending a metaphysical conception and, even so, that very idea may serve to promote some philosophical progress. As I'll now suggest, the same may prove true with our idea of experiential quality, and with the thought that, in her introspective attention to her own experiencing, someone may have

3. In the next Chapter, where Propensity is the main topic, there's a protracted discussion of a human experiencer's power to introspect.

available to herself, and very directly so, (quite a lot of) her own experiential quality. That is, she may then have available to herself (quite a lot of) how it is with her insofar as she's then experientially qualitied.

2. Our Power to Experience Promotes Our Conceiving Concrete Individuals

Whatever its deficiencies, the restrictive empiricism Hume epitomizes shouldn't be completely abandoned. True enough, our power to experience can't be our only resource for understanding concrete reality. For one thing, it won't deliver understanding of how it is that we'll only ever manifest a tiny fraction of its own ample range for our manifesting; it won't deliver understanding of how it is that there's a wide variety of experiencing that we *often can* enjoy, but that we'll *never actually* enjoy. Still, if it's to come anywhere near our aspirations for it, our comprehension of concrete reality must connect, in some serviceably central way, with our power to experience.

Why should that be?

Well, you and I, we're a couple of temporally enduring mentally Propensitied particulars, each perfectly distinct from the other, however alike, or however dissimilar, in our profile of mental powers. Now, through reflecting on my own immediate experiencing, as with my introspecting on how it is with me experientially, I have a fair grasp of *my own qualitative nature*, as with my sometimes being qualitied visually, sometimes auditorally, sometimes painfully, and sometimes all three ways at once. Well, that's how it is with my own case. Now, while it's never through introspection, and it's never done so fully as in my own case, I also know that, very much as I myself do, you sometimes experience visually, and sometimes auditorally, and sometimes painfully, and sometimes all three ways at once. So, even without introspection figuring in the business, it's quite safely enough that we may agree upon this: In knowing all that I do about you, I have a pretty fair grasp of *your* qualitative character.

For me to have some significant understanding of you, it's not necessary that I have nearly such specific qualitative knowledge of you as that. But, I must have a fair idea of *something* as to how it is with you qualitatively, sometimes, at least, if I'm ever to have any significant understanding of you at all. Let me amplify.

So long as you're involved in some experiencing that's similar to some of mine, as with your experiencing *visually* in *somewhat* the same way I sometimes do, that's enough for me to have a fair grasp, even if perhaps no very great grasp, as to your qualitative character. Now, should you experience a green circle on a red square background when I experience a red circle on a green square background, that might be unsettling. Still, it would certainly suffice, plenty well, for me to understand, well enough, how it is with you experientially, and qualitatively.

Or, perhaps, unlike me, you never enjoy any visual experience, maybe because you've always been completely blind. But, still, you may enjoy some *olfactory* experience. Now, providing that your experience as of odors is even just moderately similar to some of my experience, then *that's* enough for me to have a fair grasp as to your qualitative character. By gloomy contrast, if *all* my experiential quality is *so utterly unlike all* yours as, say, my own visual character is unlike my own olfactory aspect, then I'll have a horribly poor grasp of how it is with you experientially, and qualitatively.

In such a sad circumstance, happily just so wildly hypothetical, I'd have hardly any understanding of *you* at all: With my having no idea at all as to your experiential character, my presumed grasp of your putative mental powers seems quite weak and empty. For, some of your powers, at least, must sometimes be manifested in some qualities. And, I won't grasp any of your mental powers, at all well, unless I grasp, fairly well, some of these "qualitatively manifested" powers. What's more, I won't do *that* unless I grasp, fairly well, some of these powers as being manifested in (some of) *your experiential* qualities. In short: Without my grasping some of your experiential qualities, my thought as to your mental Propensities seems scarcely significant, nothing that can ever amount to, on my part, any substantial understanding of you.

So far in this Chapter, I've said little about *nonmental* concrete reality. And, until quite a bit later, generally I'll continue like that, with hardly any exceptions. But, here's one: Even as I must have some fair grasp as to *your* (experiential) quality, if I'm to have any decent understanding of *you*, so I must have a fair grasp as to the nonmental Quality of a *nonmental* concretum to have a decent grasp of whatever nonmental individual may be in question. Now, unless there's some illuminating connection between *its nonmental Quality* and, on the other hand, *my experiential quality*, however analogical might be the tie, all my attempts at grasping the character of the mindless object must end in only darkness and futility. At the same time, I can grasp an object's Propensities only insofar as I can understand what it is for some of them to be manifested, on occasion, in qualitative change, or in qualitative stability, with respect to the selfsame object's qualitative character. So, very much as it is with my understanding of you, a substantial mental individual, I'll understand a nonmental concretum only when there's a helpful relation between some of my own experiential quality, as with, say, my (being) experiential blue, and, on the further side, some Quality of the insensate individual, say, its (being) Extensible Blue. Without any such illumination whatsoever, well, then, all nonmental concreta will be, for me, more an object of empty gesticulation than a subject of which I have more than only the very poorest understanding.

In this large matter, I suspect that we really should follow Hume, somewhat as Russell often followed him, among ever so many others. Indeed, in our work with the Mystery of the Physical, we've already seen some reason, I imagine, to think that some such broadly Humean approach provides the most fertile field for human philosophical progress. Inspired by those broadly empiricist ideas, I'll offer a novel Hypothesis:

THE HYPOTHESIS OF OUR FULLY CONCEIVING THE PHYSICAL AND OUR EXPERIENCING COLORLY. In our clearest conceiving of a physical entity, we fully conceive it as pervasively Qualitied with Spatially Extensible Color and, accordingly, we ourselves then experience colorly.

Here's an illustrative instance of THE HYPOTHESIS: In your *fully conceiving a physical entity* as being Monochromatic *Spatially Extensible Blue*, *you'll* be (Spatially Nonextensible) *experiential blue*. In some later Sections, we'll explore this HYPOTHESIS.

(Before the next step of inquiry, I'll notice a likely qualification, or addendum. Suppose God were to make a precise duplicate of me, just as I am right now, with all my Propensities, and powers, but with no real experiential past. Just as it is with me right now, this duplicate's present experience will be rather limited. Better yet, let's have God make a duplicate of me *as I am when utterly unconscious*, perhaps as in deepest natural sleep, between dreams, perhaps as when under a most powerful anaesthetic. Now, there's *some* sense of our terms, I suppose, in which, even when I'm so deeply asleep, and not experiencing anything at all, I'll *still* have a pretty fair conception as to how it is Qualitatively with a Blue Sphere. Well, in *such* a sense, even my neverexperiencing duplicate may have a pretty fair conception. But, then, here's something that *won't* be true of my utterly unconscious duplicate, never even so much as dreaming at all, not even the least little bit. He *won't* be clearly conceiving any Blue Sphere. (Indeed, for all I know, in that he's utterly unconscious, it might well be that he's *not actually conceiving* anything at all, even while it may be, as we say, that he has many impressive concepts, as to a great variety of things.) Now, even if it should be the case that, when he's utterly unconscious, he's actually conceiving various things, well, it still won't be true that he'll be very clearly conceiving, and fairly fully conceiving, a Blue Sphere. At the very least, he won't be conceiving a Spatially Extensible Blue concretum as clearly, or as fully, as I'm now consciously conceiving a Spatially Extensible Blue individual.)

3. Our Power to Experience Visually Promotes Our Conceiving Concrete Spatial Things

When I consciously perceive a sphere that's all transparent blue, as with my seeing certain fine blue glass ornaments, then, as I've suggested, we may say that *I am experiential blue*.

Partly because sometimes I so fully and directly grasp how it is with me qualitatively when I'm experiential blue, I can conceive, quite fully and directly, *how it might be Qualitatively with a certain sort of spatially extended object*. Specifically, I can so happily conceive how it may be, Qualitatively, with a Sphere that is, through and through, a certain Absolutely Specific Spatially Extensible Quality, the Quality that I've called *Spatially Extensible (Transparent) Blue*.

At least since Descartes, many able philosophers have felt a conflict, or an apparent conflict, between an entity's (allegedly) engaging in conscious mentation and the selfsame entity's (allegedly) having spatial extent. Well, who knows whether there's any genuine conflict here, or whether it's just an appearance? I can't be sure. But, with rather more confidence, there's still this to be said: In the cases where I *most fully and clearly* conceive an Extensible Blue entity—just the very best that I can ever do—well, then, the object I conceive to *occupy space* is, first, *not conceived as being an experiencing* individual, and, what's more, it even *is conceived not to be* an experiencing individual.

At the same time, it's *not* required, by my most clearly conceiving a Spatially Extensible Blue Sphere, that such a clearly conceived Blue particular should ever be perceived by any sentient being, or anything of the sort.

Now, the foregoing comments on my conceptions, as to real spatial objects, are nothing more than that, just some comments concerning some conceptions. Regarding concrete external reality itself, my remarks have no existential import at all. Bottom line: Nothing involved with my having such clear conceptions entails, or in any way serves to ensure, that there ever actually are any such concrete Spheres as I've just been conceiving, or that there actually are any Spatially Extensible Blue concreta. Indeed, for all I really know, external reality may not really satisfy any human conception that's even just so much as only a quite modestly rich notion. But, though we can't be guaranteed much, in our attempts to understand our external reality, we may reasonably hope for some small success in the matter.

Human experience is quite various, in point of fact, comprising several quite different modes of sensing experientially (as well as still other forms of experiential modification). Visual experiencing is quite different even from tactile-kinesthetic experiencing, another mode that's been said, by historically great philosophers, to promote greatly our spatial conceiving. And, quite obviously, both of them are very different from auditory experiencing, and from olfactory experiencing, and from gustatory experiencing, not to mention some less noted modes of experiencing. How well would we be able to think of spatial things were our experience diminished, by excluding one of these experiential modes, or more than one?

Were I to lack entirely all power to experience visually, including even all my imaginative visual power, I should have no appreciation of any visual experiential quality. And, were I to lack entirely any power to experience tactilely and kinesthetically, I should have no appreciation of any tactile or kinesthetic experiential quality. In such a sad case as this, I should have only the poorest grasp, if any grasp at all, of any spatial concrete particulars. Of course, those thoughts are hardly new with me. Rather, on this point there's great agreement between what I'm advancing and George Berkeley's ideas:

> For my own part, I see evidently that it is not in my power to frame an idea of a body extended and moved, but I must withal give it some colour or other sensible quality which is acknowledged to exist only in the mind. In short, extension, figure, and motion, abstracted from all other qualities are inconceivable. Where therefor the other sensible qualities are, there must these be also, to wit, in the mind and no-where else.[4]

By contrast with Berkeley, I say that the Extensible Quality of the Blue Sphere I've supposed *isn't one of my own qualities*, unless my electrons,

---

4. George Berkeley, *Principles of Human Knowledge*, Pt. I, Section 10, 1710. I used the edition prepared by Howard Robinson, Oxford University Press, 1996, where the quote is on page 28.

say, should be Blue, or unless something similar should be just so extremely lucky. Nor is this imagined Blue a quality of *anyone else*, any *other* sentient being. Nor is there any *other* Quality of my supposed Sphere, or any Nonqualitative Property of that assumed insensate spatial object, that inheres in any of us sentient beings.

(By the way, when I imagine my ordinary brown desk, the *brown of this desk* also *isn't one of my qualities*, of course; nor is it, so far as we can tell, the quality of any other sentient being. In the case of such a presumably common physical complex, its brown color is a certain *Propensity* of the complex object, doubtless just a physically derivative power, and doubtless, too, a power as to the promotion of experiential brown in such humans as might be appropriately related to the desk.)

Despite the fact that Berkeley's work is still widely studied, nowadays his thought isn't taken seriously by more than a very few active philosophers. At any rate, Hume seems to be taken far more seriously now. This is true even when the topic is one on which Berkeley's work is not only historically prior, but where it may well be philosophically superior. So, I note that, in the present issue, I follow not just Berkeley, but also the currently very seriously followed Hume:

> But if the idea of extension really can exist, as we are conscious it does, its parts must also exist; and in order to that, must be cosider'd as colour'd or tangible. We have therefore no idea of space or extension, but when we regard it as an object either of our sight or feeling.[5]

(Later, I'll argue that, in a certain very central respect, colors can do far more for our conception of insensate solid Spheres than can be done by any tactile qualities. On this matter, Berkeley may be the more insightful thinker, whose lead we should more closely follow.)

Thanks to my successful communication with you, the Blue Sphere I've just conceived is, evidently, quite well conceived by the both of us now. (Or, maybe more perspicuously put, you're now conceiving, quite as well as I am, a (generic) Spatially Extensible Blue Sphere.) Conceived to be geometrically fit, as well as richly enough Propensitied, such a nicely Extensibly Qualitied object is fit to be, in some World at least, a physically basic entity. (At a bare minimum, it's fit to be, in at least some World, some sort of physical object, whether basic or not.) Anyhow, inasmuch as our conceived Sphere is a *spatially voluminous object*—a concretum that's Spatially Extensible Blue throughout its entire spatial volume—well, it's quite doubtful, I imagine, that any conceived Sphere such as *that*, should it actually exist, will be something

5. David Hume, *Treatise*, p. 39.

existing only "in the mind," or even largely "in the mind." Leastways, in any ontologically important sense of the expression, none of that will be so. Of course, I may "have in mind," as we say, a Sphere that's Blue through and through. But, such talk signifies nothing of any metaphysical moment. For all the while, the situation may be just this: No more is the Blue of a spatial Sphere in anybody's mind than is the Sphericity of a Sphere in anyone's mind. To be sure, my supposed Blue Sphere isn't anywhere *else*, either. For, in making my supposition, I haven't been thinking of any one particular concrete individual. (When I'm thinking of the blue rubber ball that's on my desk, then the object I have in mind really *is somewhere*: It's on my desk; it's in New York; and, least informatively, it's *somewhere* in space. But, that's a different sort of matter than the one we've been discussing.) Quite so, I've just been imagining one pretty complete way, so to say, though not any absolutely specific way, for a (basic) spatial concrete object to be: It may be Spherical, and also Spatially Extensible Blue, and also well-enough Propensitied.

As against Berkeley's philosophy, I favor a Humanly Realistic Approach. In particular, the realistic approach I favor accords with THE HYPOTHESIS OF OUR FULLY CONCEIVING THE PHYSICAL AND OUR EXPERIENCING COLORLY. Just so, I hold that my appreciation of how it is with me when I'm qualitied visually in a certain way, say, when I'm qualitied transparently experientially bluely, allows me to conceive, pretty fully and clearly, how it may be Qualitatively with some (basic) spatial concrete objects, as with a spatial object that's Qualitied (Spatially) Extensibly Bluely. Though I don't ever mean to reify Qualities, I'll also say, more colloquially and conveniently, that my appreciation of one of my experiential qualities, my experiential blue, allows me to conceive, pretty clearly and fully, a *correlative* Spatially Extensible Quality, Extensible Blue. And, *quite unlike* (my) experiential blue, this (conceived) Extensible Blue *is well suited to pervading (volumes of) space*. Just so, it's this Spatially Extensible Correlative of experiential blue, this Extensible Blue, that I can so clearly conceive to pervade the space of a (possible) nonmental concrete spatial body.

Those are my differences with Berkeley. As should be clear, they're quite substantial. By contrast, a quarrel over how to use the term "sensible qualities" isn't nearly so substantial.

My agreement with Berkeley is just as notable. Right here and now, I'll express one of his ideas with which I agree: Without conceiving *quality* for "a body extended," paradigmatically a quality like "colour," we can form *only a very poor* conception of a *spatial* concrete particular, maybe nothing worthy of the term "concrete particular." Whatever we may try to conceive for a putative body, just by way of spatial features and presumed Propensities or powers, but without ever conceiving some Quality for our candidate, we'll end up with only a miserably empty failure.

4. Might Our Idea of Spatially Extensible Color Be Our Most Central Concept of Color?

In these Scientiphical times, at least for mainstream academic philosophy, it will be hard, for very many of my readers, to keep in mind, quite clearly and constantly, this following thought, clearly important for grasping the import of our current exploration: When I talk about colors, or Colors, I'll be talking about the Spatially Extensible Colors. (Or, more perspicuously for serious metaphysics, I'll be talking of how it is that Spatial Entities should be Spatially Extensibly Colored.) Most unfortunately, I suppose, they'll often revert to thinking about what *they'd like* to refer to by "color" or "Color," and by more determinate color expressions, like "blue," and "Blue."

With most, I'm afraid, they'll revert to thinking about some (supposedly) ordinary property of (supposedly) ordinarily visible physical entities, generally, no doubt, some (supposed) macroscopic (not terribly tiny) complex physical entity (each presumably constituted by ever so many quite colorless little physical objects, as with, perhaps, just ever so many colorless quarks and colorless electrons). But, in fact, and of course, anything much like that has only a most peripheral place in any of this present discussion.

With most of the rest, I fear, they'll revert to thinking about some (supposedly) ordinary property of (supposedly) ordinarily enjoyed visual experiences (or visual sensations, or whatever.) But, in fact, and of course, anything much like that also has only a most peripheral place in any of the current discussion of color, and Color.

To help all these recidivists keep their eyes on the relevant balls, as with our Spatially Extensibly Blue Spheres, for instance, I must do something, probably something pretty substantial, to help them resist their proclivities to revert to their quite habitual thinking, about the Colors, and about what's Colored, whatever might be the favored form of the currently counterproductive reversion. With that clearly in mind, I'll now make a quite bold conceptual claim—probably a far bolder claim than any that's needed, really, for this Chapter's central philosophic contentions. A bit roughly, I'm sure, but, still quite well enough, I think, that bold claim may be put like this: It's just the (clearly conceived)

Spatially Extensible Colors that *best* answer to our *most central conception of color*, better than do any Lockean dispositions of perceptible complexes, to promote visual experience, and better than do any intrinsic features of any visual experience. (Related to the three ideas we've been discussing, there are, of course, various further conceptions as to color. For instance, there's the notion of blue that's expressed with typical uses of "When they're in *blue* light, white objects don't look white to us." But, these further notions are less central to what are, in this discussion, at least, the philosophically most central issues.)

Now, quite apart from its great psychological utility, for many of my readers, it will be very interesting, I think, to notice several considerations that indicate that our conception of the Spatially Extensible Colors is, indeed, our most central conception of color. While they aren't completely conclusive, I'll admit, these interesting considerations will be, at least, quite strongly suggestive.

Apparently, here's one key feature of our most central conception of color, a feature quite familiar from the philosophic literature: *Anything that's colored is (spatially) extended.* So-called points of color there may be. But, then, these will be points of finite spatial extension, not extensionless quasi-abstracta. (And, in the clearest instance of something colored, what's colored will be a *spatially voluminous concretum*.) Now, my brown desk is a spatially extended voluminous object, even if it might be a "spatially scattered" entity, present in precisely those places (suppose) that its constituent Particles occupy. In that all this may be so, it may just be that my brown desk meets *this* condition (for the proper application) of our most central conception of color. That said, I'll postpone, for a moment, discussion of the brown of my brown desk.

Right now, let's consider my experience as of brown, which I may often enjoy in visually perceiving my brown desk. By contrast with my complex brown desk itself, and by contrast with a basic Brown Particle, my visual experience *isn't anything that's spatially extended*. (Quite certainly, the experience isn't a voluminous concrete entity.) Indeed, my experience may best be viewed as just a logical upshot of *me experiencing*, this last being metaphysically more fundamental. Anyway, my experience of brown doesn't satisfy the requirement that what's colored is extended.

We return to discuss the ordinary color of my brown desk, which might possibly satisfy that requirement. But, we should now notice another apparent requirement, also implicit in, and imposed by, our most central conception of color: Colors are *perfectly pervasive* properties. Let me remind you what this means. Well, if something spatially extended is a certain Absolutely Specific Color, say, it's Transparent

Brown, then every region of *that* spatial thing, however small, is *itself* that same Absolutely Specific Color, in the present instance, Transparent Brown.

Everyone knows, of course, that this is perfectly intuitive. But, as I'm quite certain, there'll be some who'll say this alleged requirement really must be too strong a claim. So, at least for them, we may (pretend to) replace our perfectly intuitive requirement with this much weaker proposition: Colors are *weakly pervasive* properties. What does this mean? Well, it's a thought to this effect: If something (extended) is a certain absolutely specific color, or Color, then, at the *very* least, *some* of its much smaller regions, *however small they may be*, must be that very same absolutely specific color, or Color. Though I don't think it's certainly true, this is, I think, eminently plausible.

Return to consider my so-called brown desk. Well, as it certainly seems, *none* of its *very* small parts is brown, as a powerful magnifier so suggestively reveals. So, like my visual experience of brown, my brown desk also fails to meet an apparent requirement, at least one apparent requirement, of our most central conception of color. Of our three conspicuous candidates, then, it may be that the Spatially Extensible Colors best satisfy our most central conception of color.

For now, that's enough to give us a decent *prima facie* case for our bold conceptual claim about the Colors. It's no conclusive case, of course; but, neither is it any pushover, either. And, that's just a warm-up, at least with respect to these more vigorous activities: First, what's been done, in this Section, should do plenty toward stopping habitually academic readers, and academically habitual readers, from reverting to thinking about (only) such colors as may *not* answer our notion of Spatially Extensible Color, but may answer (only) *other* conceptions of color—notions more widely employed than this central idea, perhaps, but, also, perhaps, each a far less deeply used conception. Second, there's this to say: Near the Chapter's end, when I'm in a better position to do it, I'll strengthen the case for the claim that our most central conception of color is our notion of Spatially Extensible Color. But, that will be then; just as this is now.

5. Our Power to Experience Auditorally Can't Promote Such Full Spatial Conceiving

Trying to make some progress, I'll urge us onward with this gentle little comment: At least to my mind, it seems that none of my *experiential* qualities really pervades space, not even my experiential color qualities.

Of course, as with so many other appearances, this one, too, might be illusory. But, since we've no reason to think there's an illusion here, we reasonably side with the appearance. So, though it's not done very confidently, I'll adopt the suggestion that my experiential blue, for example, never really pervades space at all. At the same time, of course, I continue to recognize that my Propensity to be qualitied experiential blue sustains in me the power to conceive concrete spatial particulars as Qualitied Spatially Extensible Blue.

At all events, it's a good idea for us to compare the experiential colors with nonvisual experiential qualities, especially in regard to the question of space-pervasion by whatever Qualities might be their Extensible Correlatives, much as the Spatially Extensible Colors are the Extensible Correlatives of the experiential colors. In this Section, I'll explicitly consider just the *experiential sounds*; the lessons learned with them may be extended, we'll soon see, to (almost all) other experiential qualities that aren't visual. Anyway, with the experiential sounds, a central point appears to be this: These auditory experiential qualities *have no* Spatially Extensible Correlatives. Though I certainly won't be the first to do it, I'll observe how this suggestion might profit us.

It's no accident that both Berkeley and Hume consistently omit *any sort of sound* quality as among those fit to be features of spatially extended objects. And, more explicitly, Peter Strawson states that pure sounds, by contrast with such physical phenomena as vibrations in vocal chords and waves in air, are intrinsically unsuited to be features of spatial entities:

> Sounds of course have temporal relations to each other, and may vary in character in certain ways: in loudness, pitch and timbre. But they have no intrinsic spatial characteristics: ... Let me briefly contrast hearing in this respect with sight and touch. Evidently the visual field is necessarily extended [at] any moment, and its parts must exhibit spatial relations to each other. ... Of a purely visual, or a purely tactual-kinaesthetic, concept of space, one might feel that it was impoverished compared with our own, but not that it was an impossibility. A purely auditory concept of space, on the other hand, is an impossibility.[6]

Maybe this much may be said, as well, for our auditory experiential qualities.

When a certain church bell rings, you may consciously hear a certain sound, with a certain loudness, pitch and timbre. Recalling our earlier discussions, I'll suppose that the heard sound is *belltone*.

---

6. Peter F. Strawson, *Individuals*, Routledge, 1959, pp. 65–66.

Following common parlance, for whatever that's worth, it might be said that this sound you hear, this belltone, is *the sound of the bell*. But, what can that amount to?

Well, when you're experiencing belltone, you're experientially qualitied in a certain auditory way. And, when you're so qualitied, *you are experiential belltone*. As seems quite certain, a spatially extended entity, like a physical ball, simply can't (have its space) be qualitied in just *this* way. What's more, experiential belltone apparently has *no* Spatially Extensible Correlative: Though there seems perfect sense in the notion of a Sphere pervaded with an Extensible Quality that's an apt Correlative of experiential blue, there's simply no sense, it seems, in the notion of a Sphere pervaded with Extensible Quality that's a similarly apt Correlative of experiential belltone. At the very least, there's little sense that we, with our quite limited human minds, can make of such a notion.[7]

At this juncture, I'll note that the claim I've just made is far more modest than the apparently parallel claim made by Strawson, and more modest than what we find with Berkeley and Hume. So, I do not say, as Strawson does, that "A purely auditory concept of space, on the other hand, is an impossibility." Nor do I say, as Hume does, that we have "no idea of space or extension, but when we regard it as an object either of our sight or feeling." About anything much like that I remain quite agnostic. For all I can tell, there may be an aspect of pure sounds themselves that may serve to provide those who hear them with an idea of where the sounds are, in relation to the apparently hearing subject, or to each other, or to both at once. Indeed, my own auditory experience, on many an occasion, at least faintly suggests that to be a real possibility. And, if that's so, then we may doubt the statement from Strawson, and also from Hume. Nor am I prepared to say that we humans can't ever conceive space in purely auditory terms. No, my point is far more modest than any of that.

---

7. In anticipation of some far-fetched work I intend to undertake rather later, it may interest some folks, even now, to toy with this speculative suggestion: Even if experiential belltone can't have a *spatially* Extensible Correlative Quality, which the intrinsic nature of the sonic may necessarily preclude, yet mightn't there be something "on a par with space" call it *sone*, that a *Nonspatially* Extensible Correlative of experiential belltone, may be wholly suited to pervade? Mightn't there then be, correlative with experiential belltone, *sonally* Extensible Belltone?

What I've just suggested is, at best, a just barely intelligible metaphysical speculation. To grasp its import, even the least bit well, requires us to engage in extremely extrapolative analogical thinking. To my mind, it might be just such a very far-fetched idea, both analogically extreme but also experientially informed, that may light the brightest philosophical fire.

My auditory experience may occasionally suggest spatial location; or, so I'll allow. Still, it will never do anything to suggest, not even faintly, (a conception of) spatial objects each *pervaded with auditory quality, or Auditory Quality*. But, it's only this latter suggestion, a far more modest point, that's important for of our inquiry. So, while I remain agnostic about the more ambitious ideas that exercised my illustrious predecessors, I'll stress my concern to advance what's only a much more modest proposal: Though there seems perfect sense in the notion of a Sphere pervaded with a Spatially Extensible Quality that's an apt Correlative of experiential blue, there's simply no sense, it seems, in the notion of a Sphere pervaded with Spatially Extensible Quality that's a similarly apt Correlative of experiential belltone.

Now, what does this modest proposal really mean? Well, it means at least this much: When I'm experiential blue, that lets me conceive, as fully as ever I can do, how spatial individuals might be pervaded with Spatially Extensible Quality. By contrast, when I'm experiential belltone, that *doesn't* let me conceive, quite fully, how spatial individuals might be pervaded with any Spatially Extensible Quality at all. Nor does my being experientially qualitied in any other auditory way ever help me, or let me, fully conceive any such thing.

In this Section, we've found some support for THE HYPOTHESIS OF OUR FULLY CONCEIVING THE PHYSICAL AND OUR EXPERIENCING COLORLY. Well, even while I'm happy enough at this turn of events, I'll move to discuss some rather different matters. As I expect, my divergent discussion will, eventually, lead us to a point where there'll be still more favorable light cast on this HYPOTHESIS.

6. Might an Extensible Red Object Be Qualitatively Like an Experiential Red Subject?

When ordinarily favorable conditions prevail, which often happens with us humans, our experiencing visually helps us conceive, quite fully, how basic bodies may be pervaded with Spatially Extensible Color. When I conceive bodies in this way, and I reflect on my conscious conceiving, I can apparently appreciate that an experiential red conceiver, or a subject that's experiencing redly, is qualitatively quite like an Extensible Red spatial concretum. Just so, I apparently appreciate that there's an *intrinsic similarity* between myself, when I'm experiential red, and an insensate spatial object that's all Spatially Extensible Red. But, this idea can seem very puzzling: How can there be an intrinsic similarity between things so *radically disparate*?

Well, as I believe that anything real is one or another concrete particular, and I don't really believe there are any such things as properties, or ways, or respects, I'm not sure that there's much for me to say here. So, even while I'm contravening my better judgment in making the attempt, I'll endeavor, nonetheless, to be explanatorily helpful in this metaphysical matter.

In what I hope may be a pretty innocuous utterance, I'll say that, in a *certain* way, or in a certain respect, my experiential red, it seems, is very *unlike* the Spatially Extensible Red of an insensate spatial body. In this respect, or in this way, my experiential red is far more like my experiential blue, for instance, than it's like the Spatially Extensible Color of a Red Sphere, or a Red Cube. Indeed, in this respect, my experiential red is more like *any* of my experiential qualities, or any of *your* experiential qualities, than it's like any spatial object's Spatially Extensible Red. For instance, in this respect, my experiential red is more like my experiential belltone than it's like any Spatially Extensible Red. How should this be so? Well, each of my experiential qualities concerns just how it is with a certain sentient entity experientially, with me myself, of course. At least in that regard, each of my experiential qualities is like each of the others. At the same time, none of any insensate body's Extensible Qualities concerns anything experiential. So, at least in this regard, none of those Extensible Qualities, even including Extensible Red, is like any of my experiential qualities, even including my experiential red.

At the same time, I'll propose, there may be another way in which my experiential red is terribly like a Red body's Spatially Extensible Red. In this other way, I'm proposing, my experiential red is far more like the body's Extensible Red than it's like my experiential blue. What does this mean? Well, it means something like this: When I'm experiencing redly, then, *just insofar as that's* going on, there's *a respect* in which *I'm more like a body that's Extensible Red* than I'm like how *I myself* was when, at another time, *all* my (visual) experiencing was just my experiencing *bluely*. And, as it seems, this idea may be usefully extended. So, in this other way, my experiential red is *rather more like* an Orange body's Spatially Extensible Orange than it's like my experiential blue. If only for expository purposes, perhaps we may usefully call this *the Respect of Pure Quality*.

In this Respect of Pure Quality, the experiential colors and the Spatially Extensible Colors resemble each other much more than any of them resembles any Sound Quality or, for that matter, any Quality that's no color at all. As this suggests, and as I'll propose, there are *Families of Qualities*, membership in which *transcends* the distinction between the experiential and the nonexperiential, and that between the mental and the nonmental, and that between the spatial and the nonspatial, and so on. Thus, however variously they fare with those familiar distinctions, the experiential colors and the Spatially Extensible Colors all belong to a certain single Family of Color Qualities. As I'll be proposing, this Family is just one among many Families of Qualities.

My absolutely specific experiential red may be, in Respect of Pure Quality, even *precisely* similar to a certain (possible) spatial body's Spatially Extensible Red. But, as we've agreed, there's also *another respect*, quite different from the Respect of Pure Quality, in which my experiential red *differs drastically* from any Extensible Quality. What should we say about that? While it may contravene our basic dictum, that anything real is one or another concrete particular, it might still be helpful to elaborate the point like this: *In respect of the (way or) mode in which a quality is exemplified in concrete reality*, my experiential red differs drastically from the Red of a basic spatial body. Anyway, even as we may sometimes mostly attend to the Respect of Pure Quality, at other times we may mostly attend to this other respect, which I'll call *the Respect of Exemplifying Mode*.

To a certain degree, we may employ this new terminology along with metaphysically more perspicuous terms. Insofar as that's feasible, maybe we needn't be greatly misled by using the new locutions. So, perhaps we may usefully say this: When I'm experiencing just redly, and not greenly, then, just insofar as my experiencing goes, in Respect of Pure Quality, *I'm* far more like a Spatially Extensible Red body than I'm like how I myself was, experientially, when I was experiencing just greenly, and not redly. And, extending these lines, we may then similarly say this: When I'm experiencing just redly, and not greenly, then, just insofar as my experiencing goes, in Respect of Pure Quality *I'm rather more like* a Spatially Extensible *Orange* body than I'm like how I myself was, experientially, when I was experiencing just greenly. And finally, for now, perhaps we may correlatively say this contrasting thing: Even when I'm experiencing just redly, and not greenly, then, also just insofar as my experiencing goes, but, in Respect of Exemplifying Mode, *I'm* much more like how I was when I was experiencing just greenly, and not redly, than I'm ever like any perfectly insensate Red Particle.

While I've just tried to make some helpful proposals, I wish to remain neutral on matters whose exploration those proposals may appear to invite. In particular, I don't advocate, nor do I deny, any position on whether we should think that experiential red, and similarly

Spatially Extensible Red, is really "a complex property" or whether, alternatively, we should take it to be "a simple property."

No doubt, some will find my proposals to be ways of promoting the idea that experiential red, and also Extensible Red, is a complex property, or a complex feature, comprising a purely qualitative simple feature—a pristine red feature—and, in addition, a feature concerning how it is, in concrete reality, that the purely qualitative feature is exemplified. On this idea, in being experiential red, a subject will enjoy this purely qualitative simple feature—this pristine red feature—and, in being Extensible Red, a spatial object will also enjoy this very same feature. So, there may be, on this idea, an apparently satisfying *explanation of the intrinsic similarity between* the Extensible Red object and the experiential red subject. At the same time, of course, in being experiential red, the experiencing subject won't have its color quality exemplified in a Spatially Extensible way, but will have it instanced only in an experiential Nonextensible way. And, by contrast, of course, in being Extensible Red, the insensate Colored body will have its quality—maybe also the same pristine red feature—exemplified only in a Spatially Extensible way, not in any Nonextensible experiential way. So, on this idea, there may also be an apparently satisfying *explanation of the drastic difference between* the Extensible Red object and the experiential red subject. For all I can tell, this idea, or an idea rather like it, may be correct.[8]

As should be noticed, these ideas, or ideas much like them, find roots in longstanding discussion. Here's an example of that. First, and as so many have observed, in respect of color, orange things are more like red things than they're like blue things. Second, and with so many observing that, quite a few have endeavored to explain it. Third, in promoting a certain explanation of this target, some have held that being orange, at least, is a complex property, as may well also be true of red, and also blue. On this idea of complexity, it may then be said that *there's something that's present*, even to a rather substantial degree, in the orange of an orange thing, and, also to quite a great degree, that's present in the red of a red thing, too. At the same time, it may be said, somewhat similarly, that *there's nothing present*, leastways not to any such great degree, in the blue of a blue thing, that's also present in the orange of an orange thing. As it appears then, on this treatment of colors as complex properties, there may be a satisfying explanation of

---

8. For my thoughtful contemplation, something somewhat like this—maybe only very roughly like it—was proposed to me, in informal discussion of this Section's material, by David Chalmers.

the intrinsic similarity, in respect of color, between the orange object and the red object, that greatly transcends any similarity, in respect of color, between the orange object and the blue object. At all events, that's what some philosophers will hold.[9]

Others will resist any such approach to the great similarity, in respect of color, between orange things and red things, and the far slighter similarity, in respect of color, between orange things and blue things. When in a mood to allow for the existence of properties, these others will take orange to be a simple property, anyway a property that's not complex, and they'll then take red to be another simple property, and blue still another. And, correlatively, they'll resist the analogous approach to the great similarity, in Respect of Pure Quality, between Extensible Red insensate bodies and experiential red sentient thinkers, and the far slighter similarity, in Respect of Pure Quality, between experiential red thinkers and experiential blue thinkers. When in a mood to allow for the existence of properties, these others will take Extensible Red to be a simple property, anyway a property that's not complex, and they'll then take experiential red to be another simple property, and experiential blue still another.

Insofar as I can take seriously the existence of properties, which isn't, really, very much at all, well, I'm more inclined to side with those who favor treating all our (absolutely specific) candidates as being (absolutely specific) simple properties. Extensible Red, experiential red, and experiential blue are, each of them, an absolutely specific simple property. But, as far as I can see, none of the points I'm most concerned to make, in advancing a Human Realistic Philosophy, require my favoring either side here.

While they may not amount to a very great deal, perhaps we can agree on these two propositions: First, an experiential red subject, just insofar as she's so experiencing, may be very like, in a certain way, an Extensible Red object, just insofar as it's a Colored concretum; in this way, the experiential red subject will be far more like the Red object than she's like an experiential green subject, who's not experiential red. Second, the experiential red subject, even just insofar as she's experiencing, will be very unlike, in another way, an Extensible Red object, even just insofar as it's a Colored concretum; in this other way,

9. In his *Perception and the Physical World*, on pp. 174–176, David Armstrong holds, against Hume, that the secondary qualities, and in particular the color qualities, are complex properties. The view Armstrong endorses is somewhat like, though not precisely like, what I've just sketched in the text. Against anything much like that, I'm inclined to prefer Hume's view. But, as nothing central to my inquiry depends on choosing sides here, I'm not actually endorsing, nor am I denying, any of these positions.

the experiential red subject will be far more like an experiential green subject, who's not experiential red.

Well, that's enough of anything much like that. Now, let's explore some further matters.

7. The Great Range of Color for Spatially Extended Concreta

In most of this book, my understanding of the term "color" is very broad. So, even as I take Light Grey to be one Extensible Color, I take Silver to be quite a different Extensible Color. And, I take Silvery Grey to be still another Absolutely Specific Extensible Color Quality. Likewise, even as Transparent Red is one Color and Transparent Maroon is quite another, very different from both of them is, on my view, yet another Transparent Color, one that I'll call (Almost?) *Perfectly Transparent Hueless Clearglass*. Or, for short, it's just *Clearglass*. While it's no more Transparent than the first two Transparent Colors just mentioned, this Clearglass is entirely lacking in what might be called "chromatic hue." Yet, it's still a Color. And, on my understanding of Color, in addition to this hueless Clearglass, there's another hueless Transparent Color that's *Fairly Transparent* Hueless Clearglass, and still another, a bit less Transparent, that's *Fairly Translucent* Clearglass. And, what's yet still more, there may be many other Absolutely Specific Colors that aren't, and whose experiential correlatives aren't, experientially at all available to us human thinkers.

That said, I want to explore some very general Qualitative matters, notably my suggestion concerning Families of Qualities. Here, our paradigms will be, as must needs be, those Families whose members— or, at least, some of whose members—are among our own experiential qualities. This includes the Colors, of course, but also the Sounds, the Odors, and a few more quite familiar Families. From these paradigms, we may extrapolate to the idea of there being further Families, all of whose members will always be, for us humans, experientially unavailable. First off, it seems likely that there are *some* sentient beings whose experiencing is, in Respect of Pure Quality, *deeply* different from ours. Now, consider just one type of such exotic experiencers, who all experience in a certain exotic modality for experiencing that's as unlike sight, and hearing, and smell, as each of them is unlike the others. Well, in Respect of Pure Quality, their terribly exotic experiences may greatly resemble each other, while they all differ drastically from all other experiential qualities. In such a circumstance, I'll submit, all these exotic experiential qualities may belong to a single distinct Family of Qualities (whether or not any of them have Extensible Correlative Qualities, that is, whether or not this Family has any Extensible members). At least for the meanwhile, that's enough about such qualitative exotica.

We return to consider some quite familiar Families of Qualities. Now, more obviously than does any other Quality Family, it's the Family of Colors that has, in addition to experiential members, members that are Extensible Qualities. What's more, it seems that some of these Extensible Colors may be *Spatially* Extensible Qualities, intrinsically suited, apparently, to pervade spatial concreta. So, reasonably enough, we may then hypothesize to this optimistic effect: In this actual world, some Spatially Extensible Colors are exemplified in spatial concreta, perhaps in basic physical entities, or perhaps, even, in the sole (vast and Qualitatively heterogeneous) physical entity. Much as I've been saying for quite a while now, for our hypothesis to be reasonable enough, and not just a wildly optimistic speculation, we must allow that all the Extensible Colors actually pervading spatial things may have *no experiential* correlative that's ever exemplified in any experiencing human—and, very possibly, in any actual (finite) sentient being.

Supposing that our hypothesis is right, what will that mean? Well, in quite concrete terms, it will mean pretty much what I've been saying for quite a while: First, it's likely that actual physical things *won't* be Spatially Extensibly Colored in any of the Absolutely Specific Ways that, quite directly and clearly, *we can conceive them to be Colored*. Most likely, things *won't* be so nice as with a Particle that's conceived to be Spatially Qualitied *Bluely*, nor as with a vast field that's conceived to be Spatially Qualitied Redly except where it's Qualitied Greenly. But, still, the basic concreta, in our actual world, will be Extensibly Spatially Colored concreta. Their space will be pervaded by less available Absolutely Specific Color Qualities. These Colors may never be, in human experiencing, any available qualities, leastways not at all specifically, or fully, available. Let's call one of them *Col*, and another *Lor*. So, though it may be that no real spatial concreta are Qualitied Redly, many may be Qualitied *Lorly*.

Well now, both Col and Lor are intrinsically somewhat like our Red and our Blue, far more so, at least, than either is like Belltone (if there should be any Extensible Correlative of (experiential) belltone). And, except in Respect of Pure Quality, both Col and Lor pervade spatial regions in just the way that Red does. But, of course, that's just how it is with Blue, too: Except in Respect of Pure Quality, Blue also pervades spatial regions in just the way that Red does. But, then, of course, in Respect of Exemplifying Mode, a concretum that's Qualitied Lorly is just the same as—it's precisely similar to—a concretum that's Qualitied Redly, or Bluely. And, even in Respect of Pure Quality, a spatial object's being Qualitied Lorly *isn't all that different* from its being Qualitied Redly. As even this very paragraph's starting sentence rightly implies, that difference is much less than the difference between how it is with me right now, when I'm experiencing visually but not auditorally, and how it was with me yesterday, when I was experiencing just auditorally. In Respect of Pure Quality, then, the difference between Red and Lor, for instance, is much less than the difference between experiential red and experiential belltone.

8. Contrasting Quality Families and a Sketchy Speculation

This is a good place, I think, for me to explore some ideas about how the Family of Colors may contrast with other Quality Families, in particular, with the Family of (Pure) Sounds. Now, as it appears, even while there are certain members of the Color Family that are exemplified Nonextensively, as with experiential blue, there are others, Extensible Correlatives of those members, that are exemplified Extensively, as with Extensible Blue. By contrast, with the Sound Family, it *appears* that there are *only* such members as may be exemplified *Non*extensively, as with our experiential belltone. At least as it *seems*, while experiential blue has a Correlative Extensible Quality, namely, Extensible Blue, experiential belltone has none. What's more, it *seems* that, with this difference, there's a large metaphysical asymmetry.

But, mightn't this appearance be illusory? Indeed, even for philosophically interesting reasons, it might be that there's really only a small asymmetry in the neighborhood, and maybe no real asymmetry at all. Let's explore the matter.

We may start with this very intuitive idea: It's impossible for a (Pure) Sound to pervade a spatial body or, for that matter, any spatial region at all. Why do I think this? Well, as seems certain, I can quite clearly conceive a cubical spatial region to be pervaded by Blue, an Extensible correlative of experiential blue. But, and by contrast, I can't even begin to conceive how it might be that a spatial Cube should be pervaded by anything that, in Respect of Pure Quality, is very like, say, experiential belltone. Indeed, any suggestion to such an effect strikes me as absurd. Impressed by the absurdity of such apparent nonsense, I'll suggest this: The nature of the Colors and the nature of Space accord perfectly with each other; just so, Extensible Color is intrinsically fit to pervade what's spatial, and what's spatial is intrinsically fit for pervasion by Extensible Color. By contrast, the nature of the Sounds and the nature of space conflict completely with each other; just so, any member of the Sound Family is *intrinsically unfit to pervade what's spatial*, and what's *spatial is intrinsically unfit for pervasion by any member of the Sound Family*. Though this thought's dauntingly metaphysical, it's also, I think, quite nicely intuitive.

But, even while we humans may have a good idea as to which Quality Families have members suited to pervading *space*, and which not, we may have scarcely any idea as to what the true situation may be as to *absolutely all (nontemporal, dimensional) extension*. So, while it may be that, by their very nature, all the Sounds are precluded from pervading anything that's (strictly speaking) spatial, and we can have a good a priori idea as to that, it also may be, for all we can tell, that the Sounds *aren't* precluded from pervading some (nontemporal) *nonspatial* dimension, or aspect, of concrete reality. This encourages some metaphysical speculation.

In this event, I'll venture to speculate that there may actually *be* some such "merely spacelike" aspects of concrete reality, each ontologically on a par with space itself. Ontologically on a par with space, there are *spacelike* dimensions—at least one such—fit for occupation by *nonspatially extended concrete entities*. Further, it then might be that some members of the Sound Family—some *Nonspatially* Extensible members—comport completely with such a merely spacelike dimensional aspect. To give a nice expression to that very specific speculation, I'll call the hypothesized spacelike aspect *sone*. Occupying this sone—some would say, even, serving to constitute it—there may be (nonspatially) *sonally extended* concrete entities. As I'll speculate, something like this might be true: Just as my experiential blue has a correlative Spatially Extensible Quality that may pervade basic spatial entities, namely, Extensible Blue, so my experiential belltone has a correlative *Sonally Extensible Quality that may pervade basic sonal entities*, namely, Extensible Belltone. (These speculations leave it open whether—some, many, all—basic spatial entities are also sonal entities, and vice versa. Near the book's end, I'll speculate, further, that all spatial concreta are distinct from all sonal concreta.)

This speculation, I'll suggest, or one much like it, might allow for a huge philosophical payday. It might allow us, or enable us, to have a decently clear conception of concreta considered quite central, in much traditional metaphysical philosophy. In line with that, consider this quite specific suggestion: Just perhaps, nonspatial immaterial souls might be sonal entities, sonally related to each other much as, or at least somewhat as, spatial bodies are spatially related to other spatial bodies. Indeed, while a soul will lack *spatial* extension, of course, each immaterial soul might be, then, a *sonally extended* concretum. But, of course, right now, all this can be little more than a tantalizing signal of what's yet to come, in the book's later Chapters. There, I'll argue for, and I'll try to develop, some plausible sorts of Substantial Dualism. But that's then, not now. So, without getting very far ahead of myself, I'll get back on this Chapter's main track or, at least, to this Section's main theme.

If this Section's speculation is at least roughly right, then, where there first seemed a large metaphysical asymmetry, between the Colors and the Sounds, there actually will be only a quite small asymmetry. Maybe, it will be too small to qualify as a metaphysical asymmetry.

As I've been signaling right along, I'm very unconfident about this speculative offering, and, as I suspect, I must always remain very doubtful. Nor do I have much confidence, even, in what's just meant to form the basis for the speculation. So, to be fair, and to be sensible, I'll note an alternative approach to these issues, enormously more cautious than the one I've taken.

Maybe there really isn't any philosophically interesting connection, or relation, between my being qualitied experiential blue, on the one hand, and, on the other, a spatial object's being any Spatially Extensible Quality. Maybe all that ever goes on is this: There's a causal connection, or a quasi-causal connection, between certain of our powers to experience and, on the other hand, certain powers to conceive. Nothing, in any of this, requires there to be anything that's metaphysically revealing.

Myself, I prefer to be more optimistic about the possibilities for philosophy. Near the end of the book, when there's more motivation to do it, I'll employ metaphysical speculations much like what I've just adumbrated. In this Chapter, by contrast, I won't offer any more such speculative ideas, much less attempt to employ any. Instead, I'll now offer only some far less provocative material.

9. Transparently Colored Bodies and Opaquely Colored Bodies: A Neglected Distinction

Just for the moment, please think about an ordinary red billiard ball. Starting with that thought, you can come to conceive, fairly well, a basic Spherical body that's Opaque Red, that's pervasively Qualitied with just *that* Absolutely Specific Spatially Extensible Color. Now, when a spatial body is Opaque, as with this Red Sphere you're conceiving, then, it's not optimally or maximally clear, in your conception of the body, just how it is Qualitatively with the spatial object. For, you can't very directly grasp, nor so very clearly grasp, how it is that *pervasively*, or *through and through*, a spatial object is a particular Opaque Color, for instance, Opaque Red.

In parallel with our ordinary opaque billiard ball, you can conceive a transparent red spherical ornament, or paperweight. Except as regards the "color dimension" of perfect transparency through translucency to utter opaqueness, the transparent solid red object you're now imagining is precisely the same in color as the opaque red ball you imagined just before—it's the same as regards hue, and as regards "brightness," and as regards "saturation," and so on.

With this parallel thought, you can come clearly to conceive a Spherical body that's Transparent Red, that's pervasively Qualitied with just *this other* Absolutely Specific Spatially Extensible Color.

There's an interesting disparity here: By contrast with how we conceive an Opaque Red Spherical basic object, with a Transparent Red Sphere we *quite directly* grasp, and we *rather more clearly* grasp, how it is that the spatial thing is pervaded with *its Extensible Quality*. Though this is, I think, an interesting difference, it's been a neglected difference. Let's remedy the situation.

Now, in the case of our Opaque Red Sphere, to us human conceivers it must always be *somewhat opaque*, at least, how it is with the Particle's being so perfectly pervaded with, or by, its Spatially Extensible Quality. Still and all, we should realize, it's to quite an impressive degree that we can conceive, somewhat indirectly, a pervasively Qualitied Opaque object. For instance, we can do rather well at conceiving there to be any one of myriad "imaginative cuts" performed on our Opaque Red basic object, pretty much anywhere and anyway we care to choose. Now, these merely imaginative cuts through our (supposed) basic Opaque Red Object are purely conceptual partitions, not physically real divisions. With that in mind, it may be very easy, indeed, to see how we may conceive each of these merely imaginative cuts as not altering the Particle's Color one whit, with each imagined division conceived as merely exposing some of the object's previously unexposed, or "obscured," Opaque Red Quality. Just so, we can conceive that, in consequence of any such arbitrarily chosen division of our basic body, it's an Opaque Red surface that's exposed, or revealed, one that's perfectly similar, as regards Color, to the Opaque Red conceived, at the start, for the whole body's Spherical surface.

With Opaque objects, we must engage in conceiving that's less than fully direct. By contrast, in conceiving a Transparent Red Sphere, there's no need for any imagined cuts, divisions or exposures. Rather, everything about how the body's Extensible Quality pervades its shaped space is quite directly available to us human conceivers. Not just metaphorically, but even quite literally, here it's *transparent to us* how it is Qualitatively with the perfectly pervaded Red Particle.

Interestingly, there's not a great gap here. To the contrary, two "spectra of color" vary nicely together. We have the spectrum of Hue, which varies from Red all the way to Yellow, for instance, with very many intermediate shades of Reddish Orange, and Orangey Red, and so on. As well, we have the spectrum that varies from Perfectly Transparent, through Imperfectly Transparent, through (various "degrees" of) Translucent, all the way to Completely Opaque. So, just as we can conceive a Transparent Red region as "spectrally changing to" an Opaque Red region, we can similarly conceive a Transparent Red region as "spectrally changing to" Transparent Yellow, and even as "spectrally changing to" Opaque Yellow. So, we can quite clearly grasp how it is that, just as a Red Color is on a relevant spectrum with a Color that's Yellow, so it is also that an Opaque Color is on a spectrum with a Color that's Transparent.

It's also interesting that *almost all our everyday* visual experience as of colored objects is experience of (or as of) *opaque* colored objects; very *little* is experience as of *transparent* colored things. Even with our dreaming, almost all our experiencing is of, or is as of, opaque bodies, with their interiors entirely obscured by their surface colors. Just so, it's only a very small fraction of our visual color experiencing that's most closely related to our clearest Qualitative conceptions of basic spatial bodies, which are conceptions of Transparently Colored bodies. Our far more common visual experiencing is closely tied to only much less direct, and somewhat less full, conceptions of how it may be Qualitatively with a basic physical entity. In sum, and in brief: More directly than does any other power to experience visually, our power to experience as of *transparently colored* things sustains our power clearly to conceive basic physical objects.

10. Is This Neglected Distinction Philosophically Significant?

We've been arguing that our best conceptions of how it is Qualitatively with spatial bodies are conceptions of bodies as Transparently Colored, not Opaquely Colored. Is this really true? Alex Guerrero has doubts about this idea, or challenges to it. To gain more confidence in the thought, and to see some of its implications, it's worth exploring these interesting challenges.

Following Guerrero, we may conceive a Transparently Qualitied Sphere that's Transparent Red only at, and very near to, its surface. The Sphere has a Spherically Thin Hollowish Red Region, whose thickness is, say, only one thousandth of the diameter of the whole Sphere. All the rest of the Sphere, all that's "right below" its Transparent Red Outer Region, is (Hueless) Transparent Clearglass. But, then, how does our conception of *just such a nicely variegated* Sphere differ from our *apparently simpler* conception of a *pervasively Qualitied Transparent Red* Sphere? As viewed with the mind's eye from the outside, so to say, with both Spheres things appear the same, to us human conceivers. So, there's an aspect of both these conceptions, let's say, their *experiential aspect*, in which each conception of a Sphere is just like the other.

To distinguish the one conceived Sphere from the other Sphere we've conceived, we must consider, in each case, the Extensible Quality that should be revealed when the Sphere is suitably sliced, or partitioned. So, for example, a happy bisection of the two-tone Sphere reveals, in a "frontal" facet, a circular section of Clearglass surrounded by a thin Transparent Red Ring. And, a similarly happy bisection of the Monochromatic Sphere reveals, in a similarly frontal facet, just a Monochromatic Transparent Red circular section. Well then, by contrast with our two conceptions' experiential aspects, which are precisely alike, the two conceptions may differ, evidently, in another aspect. We may usefully call this, I'll suggest, the *intellectual aspect* of the conceptions. Then, since each conception is so different in its intellectual aspect, we can conceive matters quite differently as to how it is Qualitatively with the Monochromatic (Red) Transparent Sphere and, on the other side, how it is Qualitatively with the Variegated (Red and Clearglass) Transparent Sphere.

But, isn't there a perfect parallel between what we've just described and, on this parallel's other side, with our best conceptions of Opaque Spheres? Let's explore this challenging suggestion.

Well, first, we may conceive a Sphere that's *Opaque* Red only at, and very near to, its surface—as with a Spherically Thin Hollowish Red Region, whose thickness is, say, just one thousandth of the diameter of the whole Opaque Sphere. All the rest of this conceived Sphere, all that's "right below" its Opaque Red Outer Region, is Opaque White. (Or, just as before, what's right below may be Transparent Clearglass; that doesn't matter.) And, then, we may simply conceive a pervasively Qualitied *Opaque* Red Sphere. Now, as "viewed with the mind's eye from outside," with *both these Opaque conceptions*, there's precisely the same "visual appearance." Both Spheres appear to be, simply, Opaque Red. As far as the experiential aspects of *these two* conceptions go, they are precisely alike.

Quite as it was with our two Transparent Spheres, conceived just before, so it is now, with our two Opaque Spheres: To distinguish the one conceived Sphere from the other, we must conceive, in each case, what Extensible Quality will be revealed when the Sphere is suitably sliced. So, a happy bisection of the two-tone Sphere reveals, in a "frontal" facet or aspect, a circular section of Opaque White (or of Transparent Clearglass) that's surrounded with a thin Opaque Red Ring. And, a similarly happy bisection of the Monochromatic Sphere reveals, in a similarly frontal facet, just an Opaque Red circular section. As in the Transparent case, the two ideas don't differ in their experiential aspects. But, since these conceptions are quite different in their intellectual aspect, we conceive matters quite differently with regards to how it is Qualitatively with the Opaque Red Sphere and, on the other side, how it is Qualitatively with the Opaque Sphere that's partly Opaque Red and largely Opaque White. That's also just as in the Transparent case.

So, as it seems, matters are all quite the same with our conceiving concrete Spheres that are (as regards their exterior surfaces) Transparently Qualitied and, on the other side, with our conceiving Spherical concreta that are (in their exterior surfaces) Opaquely Qualitied. In order to achieve the fullest ideas we can attain, and the most direct conceptions we can manage, in *both* cases we must engage in conceiving that's imbued with both experiential aspect *and also with intellectual aspect*. So, as it appears, there's no philosophically important difference between our conceiving bodies as Opaquely Qualitied and our conceiving bodies as Qualitied Transparently. Fleshed out in my own terms, that's Guerrero's Challenge. How should we reply to this Challenge?

Well, when I most fully, clearly and directly conceive a Transparent Red Sphere, then, in my very conceiving of the concrete thing, it *imaginatively appears to me*, most fully, clearly and directly, that the concretum conceived is pervasively Transparent and, quite equally, it's pervasively Red.

But, when I conceive a Sphere that's Transparent Red just on its surface—or just some of the ways inward—and that's Transparent Clearglass inside, then, in my very conceiving of the concrete thing, it *doesn't* imaginatively seem that the concretum conceived is Transparent Red just on its surface—or just some of the ways inward—and that it's Clearglass inside. Rather, it *also appears* to me to be Transparent Red, quite plainly and simply, all through and through.

With both conceptions, equally, there's the "visual appearance" that what's conceived is a *Transparent Red* Sphere, plain and simple. And, with both conceptions, also, there's *no* such "visual appearance" that what's conceived is *Qualitatively Variegated*.

As concerns their experiential aspect, then, there's an evident asymmetry between these two acts of conceiving. And, what's more, this asymmetry favors the first and simpler conception over the second, more complicated idea. With *both* attempts to conceive Transparent concreta, we attain a conception that, in its experiential aspect, is simply the idea of a Monochromatic Transparent Red Sphere, perfectly pervaded just with Transparent Red Color Quality. So, in its experiential aspect, our attempt to conceive a Transparent Red Sphere is enormously well suited, for us to conceive precisely the sort of pervasively Qualitied concretum we then aim to conceive. Not so with our attempt to conceive a Sphere that's Transparent Red only on its outside, while another Color within.

Now, observe our best efforts at conceiving concreta Colored Opaquely: When I conceive a Monochromatic *Opaque* Red Sphere, quite as fully, clearly and directly as ever I can, it *doesn't imaginatively appear* to me that the concretum conceived is *pervasively* Opaque. *Nor does anything opposite* imaginatively appear to me. Rather, as regards the *experiential aspect* of my idea of an Opaquely Colored Sphere, there's *nothing* that's apparent to me, as to how it is Qualitatively with the object, *anywhere excepting its (frontal) Opaque Red exterior*.

Both with my conceptions of Opaquely Colored concreta and with my notions of concreta Colored Transparently, in their intellectual aspects the ideas involve me in a certain *Expectancy*. Indeed, with concreta conceived as Qualitied Opaquely, this may comprise about all I'll ever attain. With a well-conceived Opaque Red Sphere, for instance, maybe all I'll attain is an Expectant thought to the effect that, wherever I should imaginatively slice the conceived thing, there'll be exposed things that are also Opaque Red (and even quite apparently so, as regards their Frontal Surfaces). Now, we *also find that* with our conceptions of *Transparently* Colored spatial objects. But with concreta conceived as Qualitied Transparently, this *doesn't* comprise *all* I'll attain. Far beyond just that, with my conception of what's *Transparent* Red, there's the *imaginative appearance* that, throughout the whole of the spatial object, it's just this Transparent Red that's the Sphere's Spatially Extensible Color. With the Transparent Red Sphere, what's exposed with a conceived slicing *seems already conceived imaginatively in the whole Sphere*. With the Opaque Red Sphere, that's not so. In its *experiential aspect*, then, my conceiving an Opaque Red Sphere yields a *less full* conception, and an idea that's *much less direct*, than does my conceiving a Transparent Red Sphere. And, in its *intellectual aspect*, there's *no advantage* for my conceiving an Opaque Red Sphere. Indeed, as it appears, there's no advantage, at all, for my conception of an Opaque Object. So, overall, my idea of a Spherical concretum that's Transparent Red is a far more direct conception of a Red spatial object; and, it's a somewhat fuller conception. So, Transparent Color Quality is the Spatially Extensible Quality most fit for the fullest human conceptions of basic spatial bodies.

11. Conscious Perceiving as an Aid to Fuller Conceiving

For many human thinkers, myself included, external visual aids may help promote the fullest conceptions of spatial concreta we ever actually enjoy. How does that work?

For our discussion, we should explore how visual aids may help us attain quite full conceptions of physical things as *Extensibly Qualitied*. Eventually, that should be this Section's focus. But, first, let's ask how external aids can help us conceive how it is Shapewise with some spatial concreta.

Toward helping myself here, I bought some plastic objects, each rather simply and regularly shaped. Unfortunately for me, all the plastic supply stores I shopped had quite limited inventory. And, almost everything sold was cheap and junky. But, as I'll explain, that didn't entirely defeat me.

Here's something about what I bought: Among my purchases were quite a few rectangular solids. Some were cubical, but most were oblong. The oblong boxes I purchased came in many different sizes. Color? Well, many of my purchases are composed of opaquely colored plastic. Of these, almost all are opaque black or else opaque white; the exceptions are a few small cubical things, some opaque red and others opaque blue. By contrast, many more of my boxes are made with plastic that, as it appears to me, is very imperfectly transparent. These came in a wide variety of imperfectly transparent colors—transparent red, transparent yellow, transparent green, transparent blue, transparent clearglass, and more. Anyhow, I did the best I could; and it wasn't all that bad.

Right now, I'm *consciously thoughtfully perceiving* two oblong solids, one of them opaque white and the other imperfect clearglass. When thus perceiving these two oblongs, I can conceive, at least fairly well, *how it is with the Shape* of such oblongs.

These two conceptions may differ instructively. So, I ask: How does my conception of the Shape of a Transparent Clearglass Oblong compare with my conception of the Shape of an Opaque White Oblong? Now, there's a *certain respect*, I think, in which the two conceptions may be equally full and clear. But, at least as surely, there's *another respect* in which my (perceptually aided) conception of the Shape of the Transparent Oblong is clearer, and it's certainly fuller, than my (perceptually aided) conception of the Shape of the Opaque Oblong. By employing terms coined earlier, we may express both contrasting points: As regards its *intellectual* aspect, my (aided) conception of how it is with the Transparent Oblong's Shape is *no fuller* than my (aided) conception of how it is Shapewise with the Opaque Oblong or, at the most, it's scarcely any fuller. But, in its *experiential* aspect, my (aided) conception of how it is with the Transparent Oblong's Shape is *far fuller than* (and it's also *clearer than*) my (aided) idea of the Opaque Oblong.

(None of this is to say that, with the Opaque Oblong, my best conceiving as to its being so Oblong delivers only what's always a quite poor idea, always a distantly abstract and terribly bare conception. Perceptually aided nicely, my best conception of an Opaque Oblong's shape is, overall, a pretty clear conception and, by any humanly realistic standard, it's a fairly full conception. Indeed, by any relevant standard, this conception of mine is a better idea, overall, than, *however* nicely aided, I ever attain when trying to conceive the Shape of a basic solid with six hundred sides, or sixty sides, even when optimally perceiving an object that seems to be Optimally Transparent.)

What I've said about some visually aided conceiving holds true, in my own case, for much unaided conceiving. To begin, I'll note that, much less vividly, I engage in much the same sorts of concrete conceiving without perception of shaped external objects. Away from my boxes, and with my eyes closed tight in my bedroom at night, I try to conceive, as fully as I can do on my own, how it is that a Transparent Clearglass Oblong is Shaped. And, just a bit later, I similarly aim to conceive how it is Shapewise with an Opaque White Oblong. Now, in their *intellectual* aspects, there's no notable difference in *these two perceptually unaided* conceptual endeavors. But, as regards their *experiential* aspect, my (unaided) conception of how it is Shapewise with a Transparent Oblong is at least *somewhat fuller than* my (unaided) idea of how it is Shapewise with an Opaque Oblong.

Now, let's return to consider my consciously perceiving the two little oblong solids I bought, one of them opaque white and the other imperfectly transparent clearglass. And, let's explore my two visually aided conceptions: first, my aided conception of how it is Qualitywise, or Qualitatively, with a basic *Transparent* Clearglass Oblong and, second, my aided idea of how it is, Qualitatively, with an *Opaque* White Oblong. Much as we found with Spatial Shape, we now find with Extensible Color: As regards its *intellectual* aspect, my (perceptually aided) conceiving as to the Color of the Transparent Oblong is scarcely fuller than my (perceptually aided) conceiving as to the Color of the Opaque Oblong, and maybe not fuller at all. But, as regards its *experiential* aspect, my (aided) conception of how it is with the Transparent Oblong's Quality *is far* fuller than, and it's notably clearer than, my (aided) idea of how the Opaque Oblong's Qualitied. And, there's the parallel disparity with my *unaided* conceiving of the two Colorly Qualitied Objects.

My cheap plastic boxes are, as I said, quite imperfect products. So, when looking at one of my transparent red boxes, it visually appears to me that there's an object, right before me, that's *mostly* transparent red, all right, but that features, along with its predominant red, many little whitish flecks, all in a quite irregular pattern. That being so, I *don't* experience the box as being *perfectly pervasively red*. And so, my perceptual experience *isn't an enormously* helpful aid, nor is it a *terribly direct* aid, to my conceiving a basic concretum as being Monochromatic Transparent Red. (It's a much more direct aid to my conceiving a basic concretum as being Mostly Transparent Red, while flecked, irregularly, with Opaque White.) But, I can *intellectually discount* the experienced Opaque White Flecks, and, in so doing, I may attain, somewhat indirectly, a fairly clear (aided) conception of how it is Qualitatively with a Monochromatic Transparent Red Oblong, even if it's not an optimal conception. Then, my conceiving a Monochromatic Transparent Red concretum has a very substantial intellectual aspect. So, even when I'm aided by perceiving just a box that's so imperfect, my conscious perceiving can be a quite helpful visual aid, for my clearly, and my fully, conceiving how it is Qualitatively with a Monochromatic Transparent Red concretum. True, I'd do better, in my conceiving, were I to be perceiving a very fine plastic box, that should visually appear perfectly pervasively Transparent Red. But, not all that much better.

12. Full Conceiving of Concreta Is both Experiential and Intellectual

As I've been suggesting, and as I'll continue to argue, when we humans adequately conceive a concretum, there must be an experiential aspect of our conceptual thinking (and that must be sufficiently suitable for the sort of concretum that we might then adequately conceive). As should be clear, my reliance on this fact is a central feature of this book's whole approach. Just for one thing, my treatment of the Mystery of the Physical required a recognition of this proposition or, at the least, it involved an application of its implications. In these pages, then, it now comes as no news that we most fully conceive a concrete object only when we engage in some thinking that's experiential thinking, whatever other aspect, or aspects, our thoughtful conceiving may also feature.

While we shouldn't lose sight of this point, we mustn't let it obscure the fact that any conceiving worth the name must be some intellectual thinking, too, utterly different from any mentation that's only sensational (even if there should be, as I suspect, much mentation that's wholly sensational). Especially as concerns our fullest conceiving of concreta, what is my main point here?

Well, let's see. All too often, you're likely to say, I've had you conceive a Blue Sphere, for instance, or a Red Cube, or some other Monochromatic Nicely Shaped Solid Object. And, as I'm sure, with each of these boringly numerous requests that I made, you complied very well indeed. Even putting to the side anything Propensitive, as with a Solid Blue Sphere's being relevantly impenetrable, how was it that you succeeded so well at conceiving, say, a Blue Spatially Extensive Spherical Concretum? Was this all just a matter of your experiencing a certain way, whether it be real perceptual experiencing, or so-called imaginative experiencing? Not by a long shot.

Once again imagine, in your mind's eye, a Monochromatic Transparent Blue Sphere. No doubt, once again you're quite successful. But, let me play devil's advocate: How do you know that what you just conceived was really a Sphere, rather than an object whose Shape very closely approximated the shape of a Sphere? And, how do you know that all of your presumed Sphere's space was precisely the same Extensible Color, the Extensible Shade that, naturally enough, I'm calling "Blue"? Those may seem to be quite baffling questions. How shall we handle them?

The devil's advocate continues: Have another go at conceiving a Monochromatic Transparent Blue Sphere, only this time make damn sure that what you're conceiving really is perfectly Spherical, and make sure that it's really all Monochromatic. How should you do that, you ask? Well, just make sure that, when you're doing your conceiving, you're experientially modified in the right way. Get that mental image really right and tight! No laxity, or sloppiness, this time, or I'll have to give you an Incomplete!

While we feel a certain appeal here, this appeal is to be resisted. Actually, we may do very well in conceiving a Blue Sphere, without producing any extraordinarily complete, or precise, mental images. Or, much the same point, now expressed in terms that are, I think, ontologically more perspicuous: To do well in conceiving a Blue Sphere, we needn't get ourselves to be modified experientially in any way that's exceptionally complete, or that's inordinately precise, or, even, that's unusually vivid. No, not at all. Rather, even with an experientially casual first attempt, we are so very successful. Why? Well, even in such an attempt, our conceiving isn't *only* experiential; it's *also* *intellectual*. And, when you conceived your Monochromatic Transparent Blue Sphere, your conceiving's intellectual aspect *appropriately complemented* your conceiving's experiential aspect, whatever may be involved, exactly, in such an appropriate complementation. (The relation we want here is, I think, a symmetric relation. So, at the same time, your conceiving's experiential aspect appropriately complemented its intellectual aspect.) Here's the same point expressed in terms that are, I hope, ontologically much more perspicuous: When you conceived your Sphere so well, how it was with you experientially appropriately complemented how it was with you intellectually (and, so, how it was with you intellectually thus complemented how it was with you experientially).

In a way, all that I've said in this short Section is so perfectly obvious that it scarcely needs saying. In another way, all that I've said is so terribly vague that it can't amount to very much, and it's barely worth saying. Because these two points appropriately complement each other—in quite a different way, of course, from what I've just been indicating—well, they together suggest that I end their Section. Following the suggestion, I'll do that right now.

13. Extrapolating from the Highly Experiential in Conceiving Spatial Individuals

Far from being recognition machines, we human beings are thinking experiencers or, equally, experiencing thinkers. Any conception of ours that's suited, at all well, to our having some grasp of concrete reality must either itself have a suitable experiential aspect or else, and at the least, it must be suitably related to conceptions with suitable experiential aspect.

Sometimes, my conceptions themselves are suitably experiential: I may imaginatively conceive how it is Shapewise with a Transparent

Red object that has exactly five sides. Here, I may imagine a Red Triangular Tile-Shaped object, with a relatively broad flat front face, and a congruent back face, along with three narrower faces, perpendicular to the two first mentioned. And, I can also imaginatively conceive how it is with a Transparent Red spatial concretum that has exactly *six* sides. For, as well, I may imagine a Red Rectangular Tile-Shaped object, with a relatively broad flat front face, and a congruent back face, along with *four* narrower faces.

Now, extrapolating from those conceptions, I can also conceive, though not nearly as fully, or clearly, spatial concreta with very many more sides than six. Using my more intellectual conceptual powers more heavily, I may conceive Red Tile-Shaped objects with any number of sides: As the need for it may occur, I can stipulate discursively, at least for myself, that I conceive a Tile-Shaped Red concretum with five thousand six hundred twenty-three sides. And, later, I can stipulate that I be conceiving a Tile-Shaped Red concretum with four thousand nine hundred forty-seven sides. Now, in their experiential aspects, these two conceptions of mine don't differ at all. But, in their intellectual aspects, they differ greatly, and quite systematically. Owing to that, we can see, quite clearly, that the first of my two conceptions concerns a spatial object with many more sides than that which my second conception concerns—over six hundred more sides.

For clear conceptions of many-sided spatial objects, it may be required that there be a certain flexibility in, and a certain variety in, our highly experiential conceptions of spatial concreta with only a few sides. Now, it just might be that, if all we can do is imagine our Tiles, we won't ever have that. But, we can do more.

Here's another way for me to have highly experiential conceptions as to the Shapes of concreta: First, returning to my conception of a Red Triangular Tile, I may realize that, with just one Red Triangular face as a base, not two, I can conceive a Red concretum with just four sides. Opposite its Triangular base, a Red *Pyramid* will come to a point. Now, with this point kept constant, I can conceive the base opposite to have *four* sides. Just so, I'll clearly conceive, quite highly experientially, a five-sided Red concretum that's suitably Pyramidal, and that's *not* a Tile-Shaped concretum. Of course, by clearly conceiving a five-sided base, a base that's pentagonal, I can, pretty similarly, conceive a *six*-sided Pyramidal Red solid, with fully five triangular sides meeting at a point that's opposite its base. So, much as I did with many-sided Red Tile-Shaped concreta, now I can stipulate, discursively, for Pyramidal objects with however many sides. With conceiving that's much more heavily intellectual than it's experiential, I can thus conceive, pretty clearly, a Pyramidal Red concretum with five thousand six hundred twenty-three sides, and also a Red Pyramid with four thousand nine hundred forty-seven sides. As with my correlative conceptions concerning many-sided Tile-Shaped solids, in their experiential aspects these two ideas don't differ. But, in their intellectual aspects, they differ greatly, and very systematically. So, again, we can tell, quite clearly indeed, that the first conception concerns a concretum with many more sides than what the second conception concerns—over six hundred more sides. (Also, there are these "opposite" points: Each of my heavily intellectual ideas of many-sided Tile-Shaped concreta is, in its *experiential* aspect, extremely like the other. At the same time, each is very *unlike*, in this experiential aspect, both of my heavily intellectual conceptions of many-sided *Pyramidal* objects. Of course, each of the latter conceptions is, in *its* experiential aspect, extremely like the other conception of a many-sided Pyramid.)

Since there's a certain flexibility in, and a certain variety in, our highly experiential conceptions of spatial concreta, we can extrapolate, from these conceptions, to fairly clear ideas of many-sided solids with Shapes far beyond anything we can ever conceive very experientially. By itself, this extrapolation will be of quite limited philosophical interest. But, as we should notice, our extrapolation to ideas of experientially unavailable Shape finds a parallel in our extrapolation to experientially unavailable Quality. Without engaging in extremely analogical thinking, we humans are quite limited in our conceptions of spatial objects as Spatially Extensibly Qualitied. Or, so it seems to me. As it seems, just as there are many experiential colors all quite unavailable to us, so there are many Spatially Extensible Colors whose existence we can grasp only extrapolatively, each of them being the Extensible Correlative of such a far-fetched experiential quality. Very possibly, many of these unavailable Colors differ very, very greatly from all those that are experientially more available, maybe more than any of the fairly available Transparent Colors differs from any of the available Opaque Colors. Now, let's suppose that there are many spatial concreta that are each of those far-fetched Extensible Colors. Well, we'll never have any very *full* conception as to how it is, Qualitatively, with any of *those* concreta. Yet, worth a lot more than nothing, we may have an extrapolative conception of how it is with those peculiarly Qualitied entities, a conception that's very great in intellectual aspect, and very slight in experiential aspect. In this way, I'll unconfidently suggest, we really might have a tolerably clear conception as to how it is, Qualitatively, with some actual basic spatial concreta, even if it can never be a very full idea.

14. Conceiving Concreta All Qualitied Uniformly, but Propensitied Quite Variously

Before engaging in further attempts at making much philosophical progress, it may be instructively stimulating for me to present you with a certain singularly imaginative set of philosophical exercises. Indeed, beyond those I'll provide for you, it may be yet more stimulating, in somewhat the same way, for you to develop, for yourself, some complementary exercises, thereby enriching, and customizing, your set of instructive exercises. But, of course, that's all entirely optional. Anyhow, it's certainly me, your hard-working author, who should provide the first exercises in any such potentially instructive group of conceptual activities.

To set the stage for our exercises, I'll recall from our previous Chapter, and from our very first Chapter, what we can, in fact, clearly conceive to be two very different (sorts of) Worlds.

In our First (sort of) World, there are ever so many spatially separate Particles. (Well, maybe we needn't forbid contact among them, but, heck, let's do that anyway, so that we'll be very happily helped, indeed, with our clearly conceiving each as distinct from all the others.) All these Particles move around, and about, at least relative to each other, in what we may call, well enough, the World's vast empty space. We'll also suppose, as before, that these Particles are all of the World's real concreta; certainly, they'll be all the World's basic physical individuals. For simplicity's sake, each of these Particles is precisely like all the others, as regards all its intrinsic features, as we metaphysicians like to say. In my tripartite terminology, hopefully happily helpful, they're all precisely alike, and completely congruent, as regards all their (intrinsic) Spatials, and all their (intrinsic) Qualities, and all their (intrinsic) Propensities. So, for instance, each Particle may be a Small Blue Sphere, with "Small" signifying how each Particle is Similarly Sized, and with "Blue" signifying how each is Similarly Qualitied, with "Sphere" signifying how each is Similarly Shaped. Propensitively, as I've said, each Particle is just like all the others. Just so, each Sphere is solid, with respect to all the others, and each is Propensitied gravitationally, to just a certain specific degree, for attracting any other such Particle. What's more, we'll say that, with each Particle, its gravitationally attractive Propensity is directed at, or it's with respect to, anything and everything (else) that's Spherical, just because the (other) objects are Spherical; by contrast, it's not directed at any and every (other) object that's Blue (just because any such object is Blue). Of course, it's through the mutual manifestation of their gravitational Power, or Powers, that the Spheres' trajectories are thus fully determined, from time to time, to still later time. All right, that's enough about this First (sort of) World, this Blue-Particles-in-an-(Otherwise)-Empty-Space World.

Our Second (sort of) World, I'll remind you, is a perfectly nice converse of the First. So, this is a Plenumate World that's *almost* everywhere (Spatially Extensible Monochromatic Transparent) Blue or, for short, (just plain) Blue. That is, this World itself is, or its infinitely extensive Blue Plenum is, almost everywhere Blue, that is, everywhere *except where* there are the Plenum's Empty Bubbles, as we might colloquially say. Or, as we might also vulgarly say, it's everyplace but where there's one of the many Small Spherical Holes in the Plenum. How many Absolutely Empty Bubbles? Just precisely as many as there are Spherical Particles in the First (sort of) World, in the Blue-Particles-in-Empty-Space World. Why's that? Well, in our suppositions, we're taking care to ensure that, as we may quite colloquially say, each Bubble, in the Second World, is perfectly paired with a Particle, in the first, so that, precisely for this suppositional pairing, each Spherical Bubble has its very own counterpart Particle and, conversely, each Small Sphere has its very own counterpart Bubble. Now, as you may recall, not only is each Bubble the same Shape and Size as is its very own counterpart Small Sphere, but, what's more, each Bubble's trajectory perfectly parallels the trajectory of its counterpart Particle, completely and forever. Why is that? Well, as I'll recall, we suppose our Blue Plenum to be Propensitied in precisely such a way that, as a manifestation of its being Propensitied just so, the Plenum *pulsates* in a certain nicely accommodating way or, if you prefer, it accommodatingly *evolves*. Anyway, and as I'll continue to recall, the Propensitively determined pulsation, or evolvement, is of just such a sort that, as its epiphenomenal upshot, there are, for all of the Plenum's ontologically parasitical Bubbles, just such (parasitical) trajectories as guarantee that each one of the First World's Particles has just one, and only one, "dynamically duplicating" counterpart Bubble. And, in the bargain, of course, it will be guaranteed, as well, that each Bubble have one, and only one, counterpart Particle. Boring though this may be, it's soon coming to a close; at least for the meanwhile, no more about this Second (sort of) World, this Empty-Bubbles-in-an-(Otherwise)-Blue-Plenum World.

Of course, all that's old hat. But, in rehearsing it, we've been setting the stage for presenting our (newly) instructive conceptual exercises. In each of these exercises, we'll seek to suppose some new (sorts of) World (or Worlds). Each of these will be a blatantly fuller World, materially speaking, than is the Blue-Particles-in-an-(Otherwise)-Empty-Space World. And, also quite obviously, each will be materially fuller than is even the Empty-Bubbles-in-an-(Otherwise)-Blue-Plenum World. But, at the same time, each newly supposed (sort of) World will be an obviously salient variant on both those old (sorts of) obviously emptier worlds.

In a Third (sort of) World, there's always Blue matter everywhere. But, though this world may always be Uniformly Colored, or always Qualitatively Unvariegated, it features a certain notable *Propensitive Variegation*. How's that? Well, the World's *concrete individuals* are precisely these material entities: First, there's a vast Blue Plenum. Not a Plenum that's everywhere, instead it's spatially just like the Plenum of our Empty-Bubbles-in-an-(Otherwise)-Blue-Plenum World. Second, wherever there isn't the Bubbled Plenum, and there's one of its holes, as we say, well, there's also, or there's quite really present, a Small Blue Sphere, completely and perfectly filling the hole, or the space, that's without any of the Blue Plenum itself. So, there are no spatial vacancies in this Third (sort of) World. Most of the World's matter is the Blue Plenum's Blue matter. And, the rest is, collectively, the Blue matter of the many perfectly ensconced Blue Spheres.

Well, with just that much said, we've made a nice *start*, I think, though it's no more than a start, toward characterizing our Third World's *Propensitive* Variegation. Now, let's get on with the job.

This will be a piece of cake. Indeed, we may now be confronted with an embarrassment of riches; at the least, we have many salient options for nice specification. Here and now, I'll opt for this one: Each of these Small Blue Spheres has all the Propensities we've specified for the Small Blues in our first World. And, as well, they're Propensitied to penetrate quite perfectly the vast Blue Plenum that will, without the slightest surcease, always surround them, wherever they go, and wherever they are. Just so, and because they're gravitationally Propensitied with respect to each other, the Blue Spheres each will be, in effect, Propensitied to move right through its continuously ensconcing Plenum—without the slightest resistance, without any slowing at all. Indeed, each Sphere and its Plenum are reciprocally Propensitied so that the Plenum never has any influence, so far as any change is concerned, on the Sphere's trajectory. So, for its part, this World's Bubbly Blue Plenum is Propensitied, of course, to be perfectly penetrable by, and to be perfectly without any resistance to, the Small Blue Spheres, moving around, and about, within it.

What's the upshot of all this? Well, in our Third World, as we're supposing it to be, the Spherical Particles (always) move in trajectories that perfectly parallel those of our first World's perfectly similar Small Blue Spheres, paths perfectly paralleling those of the parallel Particles, or counterpart Particles, in our Blue-Particles-in-an-(Otherwise)-Empty-Space World. And, what's more, the determination of their trajectories is, in relevant respects, very like the determination of those counterpart Spheres, in the first World. In both (sorts of) Worlds, it's all owing to the gravitational attractions of the Spheres that the Spherical Attractors (always) travel as they do; by contrast, nothing surrounding the Spheres, in either World, contributes anything to any of that. With that said, I'm finished characterizing this Third (sort of) World, this Dynamically-Propensitied-Blue-Particles-Ensconced-in-a-Penetrably-Propensitied-Bubbly-Blue-Plenum World.

As an old Polish saying goes, where there's a Third World, there's also a Fourth. Anyhow, and against the background of what's just been provided, I'll now describe this Fourth (sort of) World. In ever so many respects, and especially Qualitatively, this World will be just like our Third World, our Dynamically-Propensitied-Blue-Particles-Ensconced-in-a-Penetrably-Propensitied-Bubbly-Blue-Plenum World. So, everywhere there's matter, and all the matter is Transparent Blue matter. Again, most of it is the Blue matter of the ensconcing Blue Bubbly Plenum, and the rest is the Blue matter that is, collectively, the matter of the many Small Blue Spheres, each ensconced, quite fully and perfectly, and so on. But, Propensitively, it's a very different story now; Propensitively, the concreta of this Fourth World will be very different from the Third World's basic physical individuals. With a nice turn of phrase, I hope, we may say that, in this Fourth World, the Spherical Particles will be like (perfectly passive) submerged blue cork balls, always moving about, around, and through, a powerfully turbulent (exactly similarly colored) blue sea. (But, of course, just as this sea is supposed as infinitely vast, in all directions, it no more has any top than it has any bottom.) Or, to get in a friendly kick at Hume, we may liken our Blue Spheres to (perfectly passive) submerged blue billiard balls, never so much as in any true contact, of course, but, rather, always moving around just for their all being so nicely ensconced, each one of them, in an (exactly similarly colored) blue sea that's mightily Propensitied. Not only is this sea quite powerfully turbulent, in its manifesting pulsation, or evolvement, but, quite as well, it's perfectly impervious to, and absolutely impenetrable by, every last one of the blue balls, all moving around within it.

More literally, of course, the Fourth World's Propensitively like this: As we may again allow, each physically basic Sphere may be solid with respect to, or it may be impenetrable with regard to, any other

Spherical Particle. But, in this World, that Propensity won't ever get any chance to be manifested. For, as each ball will always be fully ensconced in, and surrounded by, the Plenum, none of the balls will ever make any true contact with any other ball. How's that? Well, much as with our metaphorical blue sea, each Sphere will be impenetrable with respect to its ensconcing Plenum and so, of course, the ensconcing Plenum will be impenetrable by any of the Spheres it's so perfectly surrounding. And, on top of all that, for very good measure we'll also have this: No Sphere will have any Propensity to attract anything that's Spherical, nor any other Power that's even remotely like any gravitational Propensity. For that matter, no Sphere will be Propensitied to attract, or to repel, any other concretum at all, neither for any one reason, nor for any other reason, nor, even, quite beyond any such reasonable considerations. So, especially insofar as their Propensities go, it's only in an extremely indirect sense, or way, that any Sphere will have any influence on the trajectory of any other Spherical Particle.

At the same time, still and all, each Sphere will have, regarding its own trajectory, a certain indirect influence or, maybe better, an indirect quasi-influence. How so? Well, first of all, this World's *Plenum is Propensitied* quite dynamically. Indeed, just like the plenum of the Second World, the Empty-Bubbles-in-an-(Otherwise)-Blue-Plenum World, its Plenum is Propensitied to pulsate in a certain amazingly beguiling manner: Through its continual pulsating, which is this Propensity's manifestation, this present Plenum is having its ensconced Spheres move in trajectories that perfectly parallel those in the Third World, the Dynamically-Propensitied-Blue-Particles-Ensconced-in-a-Penetrably-Propensitied-Bubbly-Blue-Plenum World (and, what's here the same, all those in the First World, the Blue-Particles-in-an-(Otherwise)-Empty-Space World). But, how's the pulsating Plenum to do that, really? It needs apt reciprocation from its ensconced Propensitied Spheres. Or, to put the question the other way round, how is an ensconced Sphere to take advantage of its Plenum's pulsating activity, so to speak, so that it may go along for a very nice trajectorial ride? Well, when you think about it, the answer is obvious: Since a Sphere will always be solid with respect to its ensconcing Plenum, and vice versa, whatever pulsating the Plenum ever does, well, it will provide for each sphere, just as an upshot, a very nice trajectorial ride.

Punily passive and barely noticeable that mentioned solidity well may be. But, still and all, with the manifestation of that apparently passive Power, each Sphere makes a real Propensitive contribution toward determining how it moves. Well, that's it, you weary philosophy fans; I'm all done with describing the Fourth (sort of) World, the

Impenetrably-Propensitied-Blue-Particles-Ensconced-in-a-Dynamically-
Propensitied-Bubbly-Blue-Plenum World.

And, with that, I'm taking a break from describing any newly far-
fetched Worlds.

What have we learned from our two little exercises, from our two
latest attempts at conceiving wholly physical Worlds, all of whose salient concreta are—fortunately for the conceiving likes of us human
thinkers—Spatially Extensibly Colored basic physical individuals?

With both new (sorts of) Worlds, we aim to conceive a World that's
Qualitatively Unvariegated, or Colored Uniformly. Nonetheless, we
certainly don't aim to conceive a World that's (supposed to be) entirely
bereft of Quality, or entirely bereft of Qualitied individuals (though,
supposedly, inhabited by, or containing, some basic physical things, all
the same). So, with our two new exercises, I'll strongly suggest, we don't
confront our Mystery of the Physical. Nor do we encounter, I'll also
suggest, any other philosophically serious Mystery, or Problem.

With both our Third World and also our Fourth World, our conceptions of them are, I think, fairly full and clear. Of course, with both
these, we don't conceive its ensconced Particles to be Qualitied any
differently from its perfectly ensconcing Bubbly Plenum. So, in helping
ourselves to distinguish the ensconced from the ensconcer, what do we
do? Well, I can't read your mind, of course, but I suspect that, being
about as normally visually Propensitied as I am, you do much as I do.
And, I sure know what I do: I have the ensconced Particles all be one
Extensible Color and, at the same time, I have the ensconcing Bubbly
Plenum be, all of it, a *different* Extensible Color. For instance, I might
have all the Spheres be *Light Blue* Small Spheres while, at the same time,
I have them ensconced in a Monochromatic *Dark Blue* Bubbly Plenum.

So, in terms I've been trying to make familiar, how does this very
human conceiving of mine proceed, this conceiving that, with both
these new Worlds, may be fairly full and clear? Well, for one thing, I
have my conceiving's experiential (visual) aspect be nicely variegated,
or differential, or discriminating. Thus, insofar as I'm conceiving the
ensconced Spheres, as with the illustrative case just above, I'm experiencing light-bluely or, what's here the same, I'm experientially thinking light-bluely. And, insofar as I'm conceiving the ensconcing Bubbly
Plenum, I'm experientially thinking dark-bluely. Hardly any big surprise, that's one thing I do. But, of course, I don't just let matters rest
with that. For, as I know full well, the ensconced Spheres I'm conceiving are to be, quite as I've specified, (Spatially Extensibly) Qualitied *precisely just like how it is* that the ensconcing Plenum's (Spatially
Extensibly) Qualitied. Look, I might not be any great intellectual; fair

enough. But, heck, I'm no dope, either. So, now highlighting, for you, dear reader, my conceiving's intellectual aspect, I directly discount, lickety-split, just such qualitative variety as modifies or, heck, as simply qualifies, this very conceiving's experiential aspect. Or, much the same, I take it that, in its experiential aspect, my conceiving's character just helps me grasp how it is with the spatial distribution of the materially full World's basic physical individuals. I take it that it helps me with this, all right, but without its having the least bit of relevance, none at all, to any question concerning whether (some of, or most of, or all of) those conceived individuals are quite alike, or whether they're really dissimilar, as regards how they're (Spatially Extensibly) Qualitied. And, almost needless to say, with each of our two new Worlds, it's just the intellectual aspect of my conceiving that has me grasp, quite clearly and fairly fully, I imagine, how it is Propensitively with the World's individuals—with the ensconced concreta and also, of course, with the ensconcing concretum.

Well, now, in something of a nutshell, that's how it is that, fairly fully and quite clearly, I conceive our Third World, the Dynamically-Propensitied-Blue-Particles-Ensconced-in-a-Penetrably-Propensitied-Bubbly-Blue-Plenum World. And, also at least for the most part, it's how I conceive, just as fully and quite as clearly, our Fourth World, the Impenetrably-Propensitied-Blue-Particles-Ensconced-in-a-Dynamically-Propensitied-Bubbly-Blue-Plenum World. And, adding just a tad more, it's how I conceive, quite clearly and fairly fully, just what Propensitive difference there is between the Third (sort of) World and the Fourth (sort of) World. Or, put in ontologically more perspicuous terms, that's how I conceive just how it is that the Third World and the Fourth World really do differ, Propensitively, each from the other.

By this point in this book's exploration, almost all my readers should feel well satisfied with what, in the previous paragraph, I've just said. Well, pretty well satisfied anyhow; seeing as how I may have seemed a mite boastful there, about how well I did with my new little exercises. But, some stubborn souls, I'm afraid, will have found precious little satisfaction. What can I say to you, you stubborn souls, you?

Look, you'll agree, won't you, that I do quite well, at this rather latish hour, in conceiving each of the two Worlds that, in this latish Section, I described just by way of doing some stage-setting. All right, then. So, it was fairly fully and quite clearly, you'll agree, that I conceived the First (sort of) World, the Blue-Particles-in-an-(Otherwise)-Empty-Space World. And, with our Mystery of the Physical well behind us, it was also quite clearly and fairly fully, you'll agree, that I conceived the Second (sort of) World, the Empty-Bubbles-in-an-(Otherwise)-Blue-Plenum

World. And, even without adding so much as just a tad more, you may be sure that, in that whole beginning bargain, I conceived, at least decently clearly, and at least modestly fully, just how it is that the First (sort of) World and the Second (sort of) World really do differ, each from the other. Well, for goodness sakes, you stubborn souls, how in the heck do you think I managed all that?

In all the essentials, was my conceiving, back there, with those two stage-setting Worlds, relevantly different, really, from my conceiving, closer to here, with our two newer Worlds? I certainly can't see any substantial difference. Both with the stage-setting and also with the new exercises, I had the experiential aspect of my conceiving be distinctly richer than anything so much as just suggested in the suppositional specifications themselves. And, quite as with the new exercises, with the stage-setting conceiving, too, I had my conceiving's intellectual aspect directly discount, most appropriately, any such experiential richness, or variegation, as went beyond what was warranted, pretty specifically, by the wording of the specifications themselves. And, so it goes, in a rightly relevant parallel, right to the ends of these relevantly similar suppositional stories.

A nice little surprise all that; wasn't it? And, quite happily, it didn't take any great shock, just a nice little surprise, to have even all you laggards cease with your stubbornness.

Anyhow, many of you may wish, on your own free time, to conjure up, for yourselves, some additional instructive exercises, in much the same mode, more or less, as those that this Section's actually featured. It's fun. And, it's good for you, too. But, of course, it's in no way obligatory.

As for the time we'll next spend together, beginning in just a moment, I'll aim to have us head off in another direction, one that I hope you'll find a quite refreshing direction.

15. Are Felt Bodily Qualities Well Suited to Conceiving Nonmental Individuals?

In helping us have clear and full ideas of spatial individuals, how does your power to experience visually compare with your power to experience *your body kinesthetically*? For most cases, I'll suggest, it's only your power to experience visually that does much. Let me explain.

By contrast with questions concerning tactile qualities, such as felt hardness, philosophers have largely neglected this Section's starting question. Before turning to address the tactile qualities, the task of the next Section, I'll now try to remedy the situation.

Especially when I'm lying still in silence and darkness, I may, pretty often, vividly experience my body as filling space. At these times, as it appears, I apprehend *Qualities felt as suffusing space*. Or, maybe more perspicuously, I'm sensing a certain substantial individual, myself, of course, as being Spatially Extensibly Qualitied Kinesthetically. At all events, and quite naturally enough, I'll call these apparently Extensible Qualities the *Felt Bodily Qualities*.

Now, with these apparent Extensible Correlatives, these seemingly Spatially Extensible Qualities, I can clearly conceive, at the very most, *only* such instances as are, themselves, *experienced*. Indeed, with *these* Qualities, I can conceive, at all clearly, only such instances as are *experienced as pervading space occupied by (at least some of) the very being that experiences the Felt Bodily Quality instances*. This is quite true, I'll submit, whether or not the apparently experienced Quality really does pervade any such space. Maybe more perspicuously put, it's true whether or not the experiencing individual really is, in just the apparently experienced way, Spatially Extensibly Qualitied.

By contrast with the Felt Bodily Qualities, I can conceive there being instances of *Color* Qualities that *aren't* ever experienced; indeed, I can do that about as well, it appears, as I can conceive instances that *are* experienced. (Of course, this may well go against Berkeley. But, of course, the Humanly Realistic Philosophy I aim to articulate isn't any Idealist Philosophy.)

Suppose all that's all right. Then, the experiential colors may have Extensible Correlatives that are, even as we humans can clearly conceive, fully applicable to nonmental, insensate spatial individuals. Not so with the Felt Bodily Qualities.

First of all, and pretty quickly dismissed, there are the purely experiential felt bodily qualities. No more than does any experiential color quality, they don't really pervade any space, however much we may sometimes feel as though they do. (Not really necessary to mention, but, still quite a helpful illustration to notice here, we do well to think of the stock example, for philosophers, of an unfortunate person's experiences as of her phantom limb.)

Second of all, and not quite so easily dismissed, there's this thought: Even as there are Spatially Extensible Correlatives of the experiential colors, so there may be, as well, Spatially Extensible Correlatives of *these* experiential qualities. For the sake of instructive reasoning, let's suppose that the suggestion is correct. Well, then, while these Kinesthetic Correlatives may be Spatially Extensible Qualities, as we're supposing, even so, we humans, at least, can't conceive them as pervading space that's *not* occupied by a being who has bodily feelings or, in other words, a being with kinesthetic experiential qualities. And, at least as it seems, this isn't owing to any conceptual limitation of ours. On the contrary, the appearance is that (the instancing of) any member of *this* Family of Qualities, even any (alleged) Spatially Extensible member, requires there to be (an instancing of) kinesthetic *experiential quality* or, in still other words, *experiential bodily* quality. This is very different, indeed, from how things are with the Family of Colors.

At least as it appears, then, we might have tolerably clear conceptions of two quite different sorts of Spatially Extensible Quality. Represented well by the Spatially Extensible Colors, there's one that may pervade any sort of spatial thing, both insensate concrete particulars and, as we're continuing to grant, also experiencing spatial individuals (if any such there ever should be). And, represented by the Felt Bodily Qualities, there's another that's fit for pervading only such spatial entities as are experiencing individuals (if any such there ever should be).[10]

[But, what if there aren't, really, any spatially extended experiencers, as many Substantial Dualists hold, and not just so many Idealists? Well, then the situation may be this: Any appearance as of there being a real instance of a Felt Bodily Quality will be just an illusory appearance.]

Regarding some of the bolder ideas this Section's offered, I'm rather uncertain. At the same time, the ideas most pertinent to this Chapter's main themes aren't very bold ideas. And, about those more relevant claims, I'm not so uncertain. That said, let's turn to a different topic, an issue that, in my view, has often been conflated, quite unfortunately, with that of the Section that's closing.

16. How Well Do We Conceive Insensate Bodies as Pervaded with Tactile Qualities?

In everyday life, sometimes the deliverance of sight conflicts with the deliverance of touch. Then, we generally go with what touch

---

10. As best I can tell, this point may be worth noting: Though it may require some significant intellectual discounting, there seems little difficulty, nonetheless, in conceiving a spatial body as being all just a certain specific Extensible Color Quality, say, Transparent Red, or even Opaque Red. It's pretty easy, I think, to conceive a basic body to be a Monochromatic Extensibly Qualitied body. By contrast, there seems great difficulty in conceiving a spatial body as being all just a certain specific Extensible Kinesthetic Quality. Quite as my experiencing as of my own sensible qualities seems to be experiencing that's very variegated qualitatively, with different sorts of tingles in different of my body's parts, or places, so it seems enormously difficult for me, and maybe quite impossible for me, to conceive a spatial body to be a Mono-Felt-Quality Extensibly Qualitied body.

delivers, writing off the visual deliverance as a mere optical illusion. For philosophers, a stock example concerns a straight stick that looks bent when, at a certain angle, it's partly immersed in water. Feeling the stick to be straight, we take the visual appearance to be illusory. In these rare everyday matters, our tactile experiencing generally dominates our visual experiencing, a point often noted by philosophers.

In the matters we're now exploring, however, the situation is reversed. For even as we can clearly conceive a basic body as being perfectly pervaded with Spatially Extensible Color, thanks to our visual imagination, we can't similarly conceive, not nearly so well, a basic body to be pervaded with any Spatially Extensible Tactile Quality.

Certain properties sometimes suggested through touch, as with certain shapes, or shape properties, don't even come up for consideration here, as they're the familiar Spatials. As we've usefully been using "quality," and "Quality," the spatial properties aren't Qualities of any sort, neither experiential, nor Spatially Extensible, nor otherwise. At any rate, the Spatials *aren't* perfectly pervasive properties; though all the regions of a Blue Sphere are Blue, it's *not* true that they're all Spherical. What's more, there's nothing about the Spatials that's peculiarly tactile, or tangible; those properties may be suggested, for our conceiving, as much by our visual experiencing as by our tactile experiencing.

For one or more of the reasons just suggested, certain candidate Qualities are, it seems to me, obviously poor candidates for being Spatially Extensible Tactile Qualities. That's how things appear with whatever may be an Extensible Correlative of experiential roughness, and with any Extensible Correlative of experiential smoothness. Let's imaginatively divide a smoothly surfaced Sphere. Is there anything to the idea that the surfaces then exposed must themselves be smooth, and not rough? No; not at all. Rather, it all depends on what sort of imaginative cut we make. With some, there may be surfaces exposed that are as smooth as they're flat, maybe quite perfectly so. But, with others, there'll be exposed surfaces as rough as they're bumpily jagged. Of course, things are no better here with roughness. With some other tactile quality, how might we do better?

Let's use "Hardness" to denote a sort of tactile Quality, by contrast with any Propensity property. And, now, let's assume that, among the Spatially Extensible Qualities, there's an Absolutely Specific Extensible Hardness, Hardness H. We ask: Without conceiving it as pervaded by any Color, how well can we conceive an insensate body, say, a Spherical Particle, as perfectly pervaded by H?

When trying to conceive a body to be perfectly pervaded with Hardness H, we *don't* do as well as when, without any thought of that at all, we aim to conceive a body to be perfectly pervaded by an Absolutely Specific Spatially Extensible Color. That's true even when the Extensible Color is an Absolutely Specific Opaque Color, as with, say, our Opaque Red. And, there's a world of obvious difference, when the Extensible Color is a Transparent Color, as with our Transparent Red.

Here's an indication of that. Even with Opaque Colors, we have a clear conception as to how there may be a body that's, Monochromatically, that Absolutely Specific Color, say, Opaque Red. We have an intuitive conception as to how it simply *must be* that every *region* of the body is pervaded with *just that* Extensible Color, with Opaque Red. This is our idea of perfect pervasion. To be sure, we can imagine exposing the exterior of a body conceived to be pervaded with Opaque Red and, then, having the exposed surfaces be Opaque Orange, not Red. But, how do we think of that? We imagine the circumstance as being more complex than any where there is, from start to finish, a single body pervaded with a single Extensible Color. For instance, the offered circumstance may be one where there's first just such a single body, but, upon its splitting, so much of its former interior *became* Orange. By contrast, we don't have parallel intuitions about a body that's assumed to be pervaded with Hardness H. In that case, it seems our conception involves little more than a discursive stipulation, quite removed from the conception's experiential aspect. So, we conceive a body's Quality more fully, and more clearly, when conceiving it to be Opaque Red than when conceiving a body to be Hardness H.

At the same time, there's an instructive difficulty, or limitation, attending both those attempts, even the attempt to conceive an Opaque Red Particle. This limitation *doesn't* similarly attend an attempt to conceive a *Transparent* Red Particle. And, that may explain, or partly explain, why our conception of an Opaque Red body is fuller than, and it's clearer than, an idea of a Hardness H body.

Here's what I have in mind: The Colors vary along several dimensions, including these two: There is the spectrum of Hue, along which there is gradual variation from Red to Yellow, for example, with ever so many intermediate shades of Reddish Orange, and Orangey Red, and so on. And, most important to note now, there's a spectrum of Transparency-Opacity—for short, a spectrum of Transparency. Along this spectrum, the Colors vary gradually from Perfectly Transparent, through Imperfectly Transparent, through Somewhat Translucent, say, all the way to Completely Opaque.

We can conceive a Transparent Red Sphere to become *progressively less* transparent. So, we can have our imagined Sphere first become Translucent, and then, eventually, become Completely Opaque. Though it changes as regards Transparency, it suffers no other changes as regards its Color. Just so, and in particular, it doesn't change as regards its Hue. Thus, we may conceive, quite clearly, how an Opaque Red Sphere is, in a certain respect, Qualitatively so similar to a Transparent Red spatial object. As we can have that clear conception, we can conceive, pretty clearly, how even an Opaque Red object should be Spatially Qualitied perfectly pervasively.

By contrast, there's nothing remotely like a transparency for hardness, or for Hardness H. So, there's nothing that allows us to clearly conceive how it may be that, in a certain respect, an H Sphere is Qualitatively so similar to a spatial object whose pervasion, by its Spatially Extensible Quality, is quite clearly conceived by us, and is so very directly conceived, and, as well, is so impressively fully conceived. So, for at least that reason, we don't have any terribly clear conception as to how an H Sphere may be perfectly pervaded with just that Absolutely Specific Hardness Quality. We have a considerably clearer conception with an Opaque Red Sphere, a much clearer conception with a Transparent Red Sphere.

17. Extensible Qualities, Experiential Qualities and Powers to Affect Experientially

The Spatially Extensible Colors, which I've been so much discussing, are nothing at all like what we take to be the colors of visible physical complexes, like the color of my grey computer keyboard, and the color of your tan body. What are we to make of these *ordinary colors*, as I'll call them? Well, they're *not* properties that perfectly pervade a spatial object. What's more, they're *not* properties of anything that's physically basic, or even remotely close to that: We're not talking about grey electrons here, or tan hydrogen atoms, or even blue water molecules; it's my grey computer we're contemplating, and the tan color of your handsome body. Just so, the grey of my keyboard is a certain power, or a certain Propensity, not very unlike the visibility of my keyboard. Should my keyboard somehow become *invisible*, then it's hard to see how, in any straightforward sense of "grey," it should still be grey. (An historical note: When it's just the grey of your computer, and not, say, the Solidity of a Newtonian Particle, then we've left behind what's as basic as Locke's Primary Qualities and we've moved to, or quite close to, what are his merely Secondary Qualities.[11])

Following Locke, maybe not very closely, we may take the ordinary colors to be certain physically derivative Propensities of colored physical complexes. Since we can perceive these common physical complexes, each of them is a reciprocal disposition partner with each of us, though the partnership requires, of course, intermediary partners as well, as with the light that my keyboard reflects to my eyes. (Strictly speaking, this crude characterization of ordinary colors might not be quite true. But, at least so far as basic metaphysics goes, it's in the right ballpark.)

As far as basic metaphysics goes, my keyboard's color is on a par with the keyboard's rigidity. In saying that, I mean this: Both the keyboard's rigidity and its ordinary color are *physically derivative* Propensities of a *physically derivative* entity. Neither is anything like the Extensible Color Quality of (suppose) the keyboard's physically basic Blue electrons, which is not a Propensity at all. Nor is either like the Extensible Color of the keyboard, supposing the complex to be Extensibly Colored, as with its being Blue just where its electrons are and, say, Red just where its protons are. In those cases, it's really a Quality

---

11. This will be true even though, in one evident sense, both basic Solidity, on the one hand, and our ordinary tan and grey, on the other, naturally together get classed as Propensities, or Powers, or Dispositions.

To be sure, the so-called colors of physical complexes are what we usually mean to designate in our everyday talk as to color. But, for metaphysics, common parlance may here be more a hindrance than a guide. By contrast, Locke's *Essay* may serve us better philosophically. With a tad of editing, here is Locke introducing his Primaries and, right on the heels of that, his Secondaries:

9. Qualities thus considered, in Bodies are, First, such as are utterly inseparable from the Body, in what estate soever it be; such as in all the alterations and changes it suffers, ... and the Mind finds inseparable from every particle of Matter, though less than to make it self singly be perceived by our Senses. *v. g.* Take a grain of Wheat, divide it into two parts, each part has still *Solidity, Extension, Figure,* and *Mobility*; divide it again, and it retains still the same qualities; and so divide it on, till the parts become insensible, they must retain still each of them all those qualities.... These I call *original* or *primary Qualities* of Body, which I think we may observe to produce simple *Ideas* in us, *viz.,* Solidity, Extension, Figure, Motion, or Rest, and Number.

10. *2dly,* Such *Qualities,* which in truth are nothing in the Objects themselves, but Powers to produce various Sensations in us by their *primary Qualities,* ... of their insensible parts, as Colours, Sounds, Tastes, *etc.* These I call *secondary Qualities....* For the power in Fire to produce a new Colour, or consistency in Wax or Clay by its primary Qualities, is as much a quality in Fire, as the power it has to produce in me a new Idea or Sensation of warmth or burning, which I felt not before, by the same primary Qualities, ... of its insensible parts.

The cited passage is from John Locke, *An Essay concerning Human Understanding,* ed. P. H. Nidditch, Oxford University Press, 1975, pages 134–35.

that's predicated. With the keyboard's ordinary grey, by contrast, it's a Propensity that's predicated, quite as obtains with the keyboard's rigidity. What's more, there's also this to observe: Just as with the keyboard's rigidity, the keyboard's grey color isn't all that much like the electrical Propensity of the selfsame keyboard's Blue electrons, here supposed as basic constituents of the keyboard. The electron's electrical Propensity is a physically *nonderivative* property, in no wise reducible to anything metaphysically more fundamental. By contrast, the keyboard's grey color, and also its rigidity, are just some physically *derivative* properties—supposing that such there be. Supposing that, they'll be properties of a physically complex entity that itself is a physically derivative individual—supposing that *such* there be.

Among a cornucopia of Quality and, as well, a plenitude of Propensity, there are these "properties of particulars," we do well to suppose, that are very important to distinguish, each from the two others.

First, there are the experiential color qualities, exemplified in sentient beings insofar as they're experiencing visually.

Second, and relatedly, there are the Spatially Extensible Color Qualities, featured in physical reality as perfectly pervading the space of any real physical entity (at least if any such physical concretum will be decently conceivable by us quite limited human thinkers). Note, I just said "relatedly." What relation did I have in mind? Well, quite as I've hypothesized, for us this relation may be quite central: In *our fullest conceiving* of a physical entity, we'll be quite *clearly* conceiving an object as being Extensibly Colored, in some Absolutely Specific Way, say, as being Spatially Extensible Blue. And, in our doing all that, we ourselves will be some absolutely specific experiential color, say, experiential blue. (What I've just said may be only a rough statement of what's strictly so. But, for the main aims, and claims, of this metaphysical endeavor, the niceties won't matter.)

Third, there are certain categorical dispositions that, as I imagine, are much like those Locke persistently pondered. Very saliently, these Propensities include what we may like to call the *colors of ordinary perceptible physical objects*. For example, there's the Propensity of my solid *brown* desk to promote, in the likes of you and me, experiential brown, as a mental modification on your part, or on mine. Paradigmatically, this experiential brown will be promoted, in the normal likes of us, in cases where we're most normally experientially perceiving my brown piece of furniture. Now, the very *perceptibility* of such a (physically derivative) object is just a physically derivative Propensity, not any basic property, at all. And, similarly, the brown color of the (physically derivative) desk is also a physically derivative Propensity. (Here, what I've just said is, quite certainly, only a very rough statement of what's strictly so. For one thing, as things actually are, when the two of us are consciously perceiving the same brown desk, it's likely that I won't be experientially modified colorly precisely like how you're experientially modified colorly. But, for the main aims, and claims, of this metaphysical endeavor, this also won't matter.)

18. Why Our Idea of Spatially Extensible Color May Be Our Most Central Idea of Color

To help many academic philosophers focus fully on points central to our discussion of Spatially Extensible Colors, pretty early in the Chapter, as early as just its Fourth Section, I had us consider that Section's titular question, Might Our Idea of Spatially Extensible Color Be Our Most Central Concept of Color? And, quite boldly, I gave this question nothing less than a perfectly positive answer, while arguing—much more suggestively than conclusively, as I admitted—for this perfectly positive answer. As that Section came to a close, you'll recall, I said this: Near the whole Chapter's end, I'd present a stronger case for the claim that our most central idea of color is our idea of Spatially Extensible Color. It's time, now, to make good on what I said then.

First, I'll rehearse, very briefly, that Section's quick case for the claim. To begin the rehearsal, I'll recall this key feature of our most central conception of color, familiar from the philosophic literature: *Anything that's colored is (spatially) extended*. So, your wonderfully fine transparent red spherical paperweight is a spatially extended voluminous object, even if it might be a "spatially scattered" entity, present in precisely those places (suppose) that its constituent Particles occupy. In that all this may be so, it may just be that your transparent red paperweight meets *this* condition (for the proper application) of our most central conception of color. That said, I'll postpone, for a moment, further comment on the red of your red paperweight, moving to discuss matters less directly concerned with that expensive physical complex.

Just so, I'll now consider your experience as of transparent red, which you may enjoy in visually perceiving your transparent red sphere. By contrast with your complex red paperweight itself, and by contrast with a basic Transparent Red Particle, your visual experience *isn't anything that's spatially extended*. (Quite certainly, the experience isn't a voluminous concrete entity.) Indeed, your experience may best be viewed as just a logical upshot of *you experiencing*, which is, I'll remind you, metaphysically much more fundamental. Anyway, your experience of transparent red doesn't satisfy the requirement that what's colored is extended.

We return to discuss the ordinary color of your red sphere, which, inasmuch as it's a spatially extended entity, might satisfy that requirement. But, we now notice another requirement that's to be satisfied by anything that's up to satisfying our central conception of color: Colors are *perfectly pervasive* properties: If a spatially extended thing is a certain Absolutely Specific Color, say, it's Transparent Red, then every region of that spatial thing, however small, is itself that very same Absolutely Specific Color, here, Transparent Red. Or, at the *very* least, at least *some* of these included regions must be that very Color, this Transparent Red, however small the included regions might be. But, with your so-called red paperweight, it seems that *none* of its *very* small parts is red, as a very powerful magnifier so strongly suggests. So, just as much as does your visual experience of transparent red, even if, perhaps, for rather different reasons, your transparent red sphere fails to meet this requirement of our most central conception of color.

Of our three conspicuous candidates, as we nicely concluded, the Spatially Extensible Colors best satisfy our most central conception of color.

Now, it's time for us to advance another thought that favors our claim. Here it is: Let's consider a most perfect case of an experiential subject perceiving how it is colorly with an external colored object. Can we do this, at all well? I think so. We're in pretty good shape to do this now, largely thanks to work we did in the previous Chapter, when we obtained a perfectly positive answer to the "in principle" titular question of its Section 13, Can an Extensible Blue Body Be Perceived to Be Extensible Blue? In a nutshell, the heart of the wanted consideration is this: When someone *perfectly perceives* how it is colorly with a Red external object—say, when a Blue Cubical Someone perfectly perceives how it is colorly with a somewhat distant Red Sphere—then the perceiver is experientially modified, in a certain mental manner, by her (direct interaction) with the external object perceived. What is this mental manner? What is this experiential way in which the perceiving subject is thus modified? Well, just as the perceived object is Red, so, in the course of her perfectly perceiving the Red object, the perceiver experiences redly. Or, quite the same, even as the object she sees is Spatially Extensible Red, so the perceiving subject herself is experiential red (even if, as it may often be, that's only because she now comes to be experiential red).

Well, I don't know about you, but, with my own most intuitive conception of color perception, there's a certain definite hierarchy among, or between, the salient relata in the relation between the perceiving concretum and the perceived. As my intuitive conception has it, in a perfect case of color perception, at least, the item that's most perfectly colored, or that's in the first place quite clearly colored, is the colored extended object that's perfectly perceived. In the first place, it's not the perceiving subject that must be, so clearly and so centrally, a colored concretum.[12] No matter how perfectly she may perceive a Red object, it will always be the Red object itself, and not this perceiver of it, that does best to satisfy our most central conception of color. Well, as I suspect, that's also your intuition.

Is this intuition a splendidly isolated idea? Or, alternatively, may we find ties between it and, on the other hand, points we've already observed, as to what's most central about (our ideas) of colors, and about (our ideas) of what's colored? Right now, I'll aim to disclose a connection.

Return to consider our perfectly perceiving subject, our Blue Cubical Someone who's perfectly perceiving how it is colorly with a somewhat distant Red Sphere. In a certain respect, we should certainly agree, in her perfect visual perceiving of the distant Red object, the experiencing subject should (come to) perfectly resemble, so far as color is concerned, the object that, visually, she perfectly perceives. Well, what respect is this?

Listen, doesn't that ring a bell? Earlier in the Chapter, didn't we hear something like this before? Of course, we did, especially when we provided a very positive answer, as we certainly did do, in the Section whose title question was, Might an Extensible Red Object be Qualitatively Like an Experiential Red Subject?[13] Now, from our remembrance of that Section, we know what's the respect that's now in question: It's in Respect of Pure Quality, we recall, that the experiential red subject exactly resembles, or is precisely like, the Extensible Red Object (the Red object that, in our present case, she so perfectly perceives). But, then, this is quite as it should be. Why? Well, as I'll submit, for our most intuitive, most central notion of color perception to be fully satisfied, this is one thing that should occur, or should obtain: It should be that there's a central respect concerning color such that, in *this* central respect, the visually perfectly perceiving subject perfectly

12. Here, I'm placing to the side, of course, any idea to the effect that the perceiver may be, herself, a suitable object for someone's perfect perceiving. For with such an idea in the midst of our discussion, we might be diverted from our discussion's central questions.

13. For, just as it must be, such qualitative likeness is all a perfectly symmetric matter: When an Extensible Red object is qualitatively just like an experiential red subject—whether it's in this respect, or in that one—well, that's exactly when the experiential red subject is qualitatively just like the Extensible Red Object—whether *it's* in this respect, or in that one.

resembles colorly the Colored object that she's so perfectly perceiving (if she didn't already, in this central respect, perfectly resemble the perceived object colorly, then she'll now come to do so).

But, that's not all; no, not by a long shot.

At the same time, and as I also submit, there's also a very different side to this same perceptual story: Even in a most perfect case of external color perception, it should be that there's *also a central* respect concerning color such that, in *this other* central respect, the visually perfectly perceiving subject usually *doesn't* perfectly resemble the Colored object that she's so perfectly perceiving, leastways not because she's perceiving that Colored thing. Indeed, *in this other respect*, that's *also just so central*, the perfectly perceiving subject *needn't ever* resemble, even at all, the object she's so perfectly perceiving. What is such a *very different* respect? Well, once again taking a cue from the aforementioned Section, we also know what that one is. It's in Respect of Mode of Exemplification that the experiential red subject needn't resemble, at all, the Extensible Red Object (that, as in our present case, she visually so perfectly perceives).

In the foregoing discussion of (perfect visual) color perception, we've seen additional reason to think that, at least as compared with our ideas of experiential colors, our notion of Spatially Extensible Color is our more central notion of color. But, what about the other leading candidate, in our traditional trio of color conceptions; what about the idea that, first and foremost, colors are certain Propensities of colored (spatial concrete) objects to promote, in the likes of (roughly) visually normal human perceivers, certain characteristic color experiences? The same question, but focused more specifically: What about the idea that, first and foremost, the transparent red of your wonderful round paperweight is (just roughly, now) the Propensity of that fine transparent red sphere to promote, in the likes of visually normal human perceivers, experiencing transparently-redly or, in reifying words, transparent-red experience? Well, while our earlier argumentation certainly gave this candidate some notably severe demerits, there's nothing in our current discussion of perception that did anything very severe. Why? Well, nothing in this discussion said very much, really, about this Propensitive notion of color or, for that matter, about any idea on which colors are, first and foremost, any sorts of Propensities, Dispositions or Powers.

That said, I'd now like to provide you with a discussion, I hope one that's blessedly brief, that will really bear on the issue of whether colors are, first and foremost, certain Propensities, or anything of that ilk. To do this, here and now, I hardly need reinvent the wheel. For, as I'll remind you, most of what we now want I've already provided. I did that, it's my belief, when arguing, in the previous Chapter, against (what I there called) The Limited Identity Theory of Qualities and Dispositions. Anyhow, from that nicely familiar spot, I'll recall, word for word, some passages that, for our current discussion, present some highly relevant material. (Now, as it may be, I'll now be employing a new literary device. Or, I may be inaugurating use of the device in philosophical works that are ontologically serious and intellectually ambitious essays.) All right, here goes:

> So, let's again consider the Disposition of a Yellow Sphere to be attracted to a Yellow-Magnet, or to a (merely) possible particular that's Propensitied to attract any Yellow individuals. As our Limited Theory will have it, this Quality of the object *is* a certain one of the particular's Dispositions. But, to my mind, that doesn't seem right. Rather, this will just be a Quality of the individual *with respect to which* anything that's Disposed to attract (or, to repel, or whatnot) Yellow individuals will be (and must be) directed, just because any Yellow-Attractor (or Yellow-Repellors, or whatnots) must be Disposed to attract (or to repel, or whatnot) any Yellow individuals. And, then, so that the two kinds of thing may be suited for mutual interaction, our Yellow Sphere must have, for its part, the Disposition to be attracted by (and maybe, thus, the Disposition to attract) any Yellow-Attractors (that there might possibly be). This is the real situation, I submit, concerning the necessary covariance between something's having a given Quality and, on the other hand, the thing's being Propensitied with respect to any individuals (there might be) that are themselves Propensitied with respect to (something's having) that very Quality. As I'll submit, then, the Limited Theory fails to recognize what must be the real situation in these matters, conflating a mere necessary covariance with a genuine identity.[14]

Well, holy cow, all you philosophy fans, and, if you're still with me, all you sports fans, too! Right off the *bat*, we can't help but see that on our *most central* idea of color, or, indeed, any color conception that's a *highly intuitive* notion, it just *won't be allowed* that a Color (or, really, any sort of Quality at all) is ever any Disposition at all, or any sort of Power, or Propensity. No; it won't; not even for a minute, not even if the Color (Quality) should be ever so closely connected, even tightly tied conceptually, with very many Dispositions, and Propensities, and Powers. Well, then, what should we think of an idea, any idea, that our most central conception of colors is an idea of a Propensity, or an idea of some Propensities? Heck, right of the bat, we know that *any such idea* must be far more embroiled with conflation than with illumination.

---

14. See Chapter 3, Section 10.

Quite obviously, in offering the foregoing considerations, pretty conclusive thoughts, I think you'll agree, I didn't present any ideas peculiar to the topic of perception, much less any ideas specially concerned with the conscious visual perception of a colored concretum. Allowing myself only very limited resources here, I was quite able, even so, to seal the deal. For my money, all the necessary ball games are over. Clearly beating to pieces both our conception of experiential color and our conception of Propensitive color, our idea of Spatially Extensible Color is, by a long shot, our most central conception.

Not that I want to gloat about any of this, but, before closing this Chapter, it may yet be useful to provide a discussion of perception that, as we now must expect, will prove a discussion to quite the same effect. In that way, we may see some more connections among certain ideas advanced in this Chapter and, on the other side, certain thoughts from the preceding Chapter. Best of all, we may do that while, at the same time, we prepare for what's soon upcoming, in the succeeding Chapter.

Much as with the argumentation concluded just above, for this present argument, too, or for this current discussion, most of what we want is something already provided. It was provided, I think, when arguing, in the previous Chapter, for the idea that, at least "in principle," an Extensible Blue Body can be Perceived to be Extensible Blue. Now, from that happily remembered place, I'll informally rehearse its presently most relevant material:

> In [a quite] intuitive sense, or way, [here's what] happens in (a paradigm) perceptual interaction between a (perceptible) object perceived by a subject (that's not itself the perceived object) and, on the other side, the perceiving subject who's mentally affected by, or so modified by, the (relevantly external) object this subject perceives. Whether it's quite directly, or whether it's only much more indirectly, they, too, will *inter*act with *each other*, of course; otherwise there won't be the *perception of one* entity *by quite another* entity, where the perceived object is relevantly external to the perceiver and where the perceiver, for her part, is correlatively independent of what's there for her to perceive. As with any other interactions, with such perceptual interactions, too, the interacting entities must be, at the least, aptly Propensitied reciprocal partners—even if the whole story of their reciprocity will involve, as happens in ordinary visual perception, a reference to intermediary partners, as with the photons of light that pass from what's perceived to its impacted perceiver. But, of course, for all that undoubted reciprocity, there must also be, quite as well, this intuitively notable asymmetry in the (typical and paradigmatic) perceptual interaction: The (unperceiving) perceived object is relevantly unaffected by, and it's just so unmodified by, (the perceiving subject in) the perceptual interaction,

whereas that perceiving particular *is* affected by, and it is modified by, (the perceived object in) the selfsame perceptual interaction.

Not to lose the forest for the trees, we'll now suppose, as well we may do, that there exist, in some possible Worlds, and maybe even in some "temporally distant" Eons of this actual world, *Mentally Richly Propensitied* Small Transparent Red Spheres.... Notable in its Propensity Profile, each Red Sphere has a (richly various) Power to Experience. About that, we may illustratively say this: When a Red Sphere is within a meter of a Transparent Blue Sphere, the Red sphere experiences transparently bluely (just insofar as it experiences spherically).[15]

Anyhow, to advance our present discussion, we should extend these useful passages along some such line as this: In order that it be perceived by a Mentally Richly Propensitied Small Transparent Red Sphere, our Transparent Blue Sphere must itself be aptly Propensitied. How's that to be? What Propensity will be, here, a most apt Disposition? Well, as you'll expect, we'll now take note of quite an eyeful, but, of course, a familiar enough sort of eyeful: Our Blue Sphere must have a Propensity to modify, in a certain experiential way, any entity that is itself (reciprocally) Propensitied to be modified, in that selfsame experiential way, by an entity that has the aforementioned experientially modificational (reciprocal) Propensity. Now, anything that's Spatially Extensible Blue must have, of course, just that aptly experientially modifying Propensity. And, for its having that Propensity, it will be a quite perceptible object, even as to how it's Extensibly Colored. (Not that it will be perceptible to, or by, just any old object—this twig, or that quark—or by just anyone at all—this Dick, or that Jane. But, it will be perceptible and, even, it will be perceptible as a Blue external entity, by the most appropriate perceivers. Who will they be? Well, they'll be those experiencers, of course, that are aptly Propensitied, themselves, to perceptually interact with our aptly perceptible Blue Sphere, that is, of course, to do that in an appropriately modificational manner.)

Now, though there's a necessary covariance between the two, still and all, our Perceptible Sphere's being Blue is one thing and its having the noted (convolutedly expressed) Propensity is something else. (Well, I don't really believe we're talking of distinct entities here or, even, any real individual at all. Just so, there'll be no Property Realism for this philosopher. But, of course, you knew that, all you philosophy fans.) And, there's a certain conceptual order here, quite obvious enough, I think, between these two necessarily covariant Properties. Just so, what's true is something like this: The Sphere has the noted (convolutedly

15. See Chapter 3, Section 13.

expressed) Propensity—well, it's sort of the Propensity to promote experiential blue in any real Blue-perceiver there may be—and it has this Propensity precisely *because it's Blue*. To my mind at least, that's as intuitive as all get out. And, equally intuitive, what's *not* true, then, is anything like this: The Sphere is Blue *because it has the Propensity to promote experiential blue in any real Blue-perceivers*. Quite to the contrary, and quite unlike its opposite number, this last sentence simply gets things back-to-front.

What's the force of the "because" that's so saliently occurring in the foregoing paragraph's salient sentences? It doesn't express any causal force, of course. Rather, it expresses a certain conceptual force or, maybe better, a certain conceptual ordering: As far as anything about its being colored goes, what's most central about our Sphere is that it's Spatially Extensible Blue. What's relatively secondary, by contrast, is something about a certain Propensity that the Sphere has—something like its Propensity to promote experiential blue in any real Blue-perceivers.

Well, I don't know about you, dearest reader, but, as far as I'm concerned, all that just knocks the socks right out of the box: Our central idea of color is our idea of Spatially Extensible Color.

19. We Focus on Substantive Metaphysics, Not Natural Languages or Conceptual Relations

While I do think that what I've just argued is largely correct, I'm fully aware that I'm a very fallible fellow, quite like my fellow human thinkers. So, I'd now like to explore with you, if only just briefly, what we should think, about this philosophical neighborhood's material, in the event that, in the just previous Section, I should be quite wrong in most of its central contentions.

Let's suppose, then, that something quite like this is really true: Far more than just within the bounds of small repairs, I'm incorrect in saying that our central conception of color is our idea of Spatially Extensible Color. Why? Well, maybe it's because *another* color conception of ours is the most central one. Or, maybe it's because our color conceptions are all such a mishmash that *none* really earns the title, "the most central conception." Or, maybe it's for some *still further* reason. The specific reason, if there is one, needn't much matter. And, far more importantly, even the very fact of my being so wrong, if there is one, won't much matter, either, leastways not for this Chapter's most central questions. Indeed, it won't ever mean much for anything of much metaphysical moment at all, whether or not it was discussed here.

Look, for any truly central philosophic issue, or any very substantive philosophic endeavor, what can it matter, really, which conceptions of color (or of almost anything else, for that matter) we may come to have most naturally, or most readily, or most centrally, or anything even just remotely like any of that? It's of no great importance, it should be crystal clear, which conceptions are our most central ideas *before* we make much of an attempt to develop a serious metaphysical philosophy, or even when we *first begin* to attempt a decently adequate and articulated worldview. All that matters here, really, are things like this: First, we should make a pretty wide variety of decently plausible attempts here—heck, even just some several truly diverse halfway plausible efforts will mean *something*. In doing this, some may take the lead in giving a certain worldview a decent run for the philosophical money, maybe some halfway plausible form of idealism, or panpsychism, while others may take the lead in giving other sorts of worldview a decent run. (In much of this book's first four or five Chapters, I endeavor to do this for our implicitly accepted Scientiphical Metaphysic. And, less directly, perhaps, I also attempt, at that same time, to do it for some pretty serious forms of materialism, maybe each of them only a halfway plausible view, perhaps, but, on the more positive side, each a sort of materialism that's decently intelligible to human philosophers.) With quite a few different philosophical flowers encouraged to bloom, we may begin to observe, eventually, that certain conceptions may be doing far more than others in affording some central propositions for some of the very most plausible and appealing of these seriously ambitious worldviews. So, when engaging in serious philosophical discourse, we may do well to say that, philosophically, it's just these conceptions that are among our most central ideas.

Taken in such a philosophically serious context, my claim about various conceptions as to colors might be, both most charitably but also most relevantly, *reinterpreted as* something like this: In developing and articulating a most decently adequate worldview, the conception of Spatially Extensible Color will play a more central role than will any other conception of color that's been championed, or even that's just been placed on offer, by any past or present human philosopher. Or, here much the same, my claim may be *replaced by* this reasonably optimistic statement, that our philosophically central idea of color is our idea of Spatially Extensible Color.

Be very clear here, all you philosophy fans. If we're to make any serious progress in most of our subject, which is, presumably, an intellectually deep discipline, and an extraordinarily comprehensive enterprise, we can't be very much exercised by questions concerning the meaning of those words we happen to have, in our natural languages, or by anything that's even quite largely a semantic issue, let alone mainly or merely a semantical matter. That way lies only comparatively narrow and shallow inquiry, far too narrow and shallow to count as anything remotely like first philosophy. Quite obviously, for anyone mostly concerned with exploring genuinely substantive metaphysical issues— like Descartes, Spinoza and Leibniz, like Locke, Berkeley and Hume, and like the mature Bertrand Russell, the mature David Lewis, and even the lesser likes of the (somewhat mature) Peter Unger, it won't much matter, not very much at all, what conception of experiencing does most justice to the meaning of the English "experiencing," or what conception of choosing does best by what the English word "choosing" means, or how best to match the main meanings of the English words "spatial" and "temporal," and so on, and so forth. And, so it is, too, with any issue about which available conception, if any, does most justice to the central meaning of the English word "color." Philosophically, none of it's any very big deal. Heck, none of it's even close to being a moderately big deal.

So, whether it's color you think you're interested in, or it's life, or it's matter, or it's mind, don't waste much of your time, or your energy, in thinking about what we mean when, having done very little painfully serious philosophy, we're in no position to mean anything of much philosophic significance at all.

And, insofar as you're interested in trying to develop a view as to what's what with concrete reality, and you're resolved to be most fundamentally concerned about just what's (likely to be) most fundamental as concerns all our concreta, then don't waste much of your time, or much of your energy, with *logic*, whether it be what's currently called *mathematical logic* or, alternatively, whether it be what's lately been labeled *philosophical logic*. In their own right, fine fields they are, the both of them—just as may also be said for several sorts of *semantical* studies, and for a couple of kinds of *linguistics*, too. But, none of that is any first philosophy, surely, nor even anything remotely similar.

All right, first philosophy fans, it's time to wrap up this Chapter. I'd like to do that in a way that may be happily nostalgic for us, already, while also driving home several of the Chapter's central points, most of them duly substantive, a few more methodic than substantive.

Well, as you'll surely recall, near this book's beginning, I related to you some sentences from Bertrand Russell, wisely taken, I thought and

I think, to be both true propositions, leastways pretty nearly true, and, as well, pretty nice offers of excellent philosophical advice. Here's me, again, remarking on that fearlessly great philosopher, while relating some of his excellent sentences:

> Especially in this fearfully complacent philosophical day and age, we do well to remember what Russell counseled: About the rest of concrete reality, we don't know anything nearly so intimately, nor nearly so fully, as we know our own experiencing, or the phenomena we apprehend in experiencing. (This remains true, of course, even if what we know most fully, and intimately, might be known less fully, and less intimately, than it can often appear.) And, we do well to recall that Russell did not exaggerate much, if at all, when, in a generally robust epistemological spirit, he said, "as regards the world in general, both physical and mental, everything that we know of its intrinsic character is derived from the mental side." Nor did he exaggerate very much when, in a specifically Materialistic spirit, he said, "we know nothing about the intrinsic quality of physical events except when these are mental events that we directly experience."[16]

Well, now, by employing our idea of Spatially Extensible Quality and, more specifically, our notion of Spatially Extensible Color, we may attain a conception of physical reality that may be, in all its essentials, decently adequate to concrete reality's "physical side," to use Russell's phrase. And, with the extrapolative conceiving we've been doing, in terms of this *philosophically central* Color conception, we may have come to possess, in a happily general way, a decently adequate conception of the *intrinsic character* of reality's physical side. And, equally, of course, we may possess just such a nice notion of the *intrinsic quality* of what's physical.[17]

16. See Chapter 1, note 2, for citation of quotations from Russell.

17. All this may be so, quite as I've been suggesting, even if it should (also) be that, at least in the first instance, it's (basic) *physical individuals*—about whose intrinsic quality, and about whose intrinsic character, we may have such a nice notion. Though Russell prefers to talk first of *physical events*, any such events that I can understand are, at best, somewhat ontologically parasitical, all of them being "grounded in," or "dependent on," some basic physical individuals or, perhaps, one vast basic physical individual. But, anyway, in the present context, this may well be just a tangential issue.

Well, to be a very responsible writer, that's one difference between Russell and me that, even if it's in only a mere note, I should notice. And, here's just one more: Quite unlike Russell, I don't think that anything in the neighborhood will amount to any real *knowledge* on our part, as to how it is, qualitatively, with physical reality, or with concrete reality's "physical side." And, while it may be a somewhat unfortunate thing, I suppose, all this will still be true, I think, even if we should possess much real knowledge of other

On a nicely nostalgic note, this little rehearsal happily sums up this present Chapter's central themes, all of them primarily concerned, as well they all should be, with substantive metaphysical questions, quite heavily involved in philosophically central matters.

---

things, including (at least each in our own case) quite a lot of knowledge of mental reality, or concrete reality's "mental side." But, then, as I've been arguing at some length in this work, quite as much against Russell, I suppose, as also against Hume, our actual situation has always been just this one: Nothing so much as real knowledge, concerning the character of physical reality, should ever have been expected, leastways not for the very limited likes of us merely human thinkers.

5

A PLENITUDE OF POWER

Having discussed how it is Qualitatively, with substantial individuals, we turn to explore how it may be that they're Powered, or Propensitied. Centrally, we'll discuss the Propensity of basic physical entities. But, we'll also explore the Propensity of other possible concreta, including immaterial minds.

To enter gently into this discussion, I'll first ask whether all the Propensities, of any possible individual, can be taken, well enough, to *concern only something about how it is Qualitatively with (Propensitied) individuals*. As I'll suggest, there's initial appeal in such an approach. But, pretty soon, I'll also suggest, its prospects may look bleak. Eventually, its worst failures will move me to articulate an idea of *Individualistically directed Propensities* or, for short, *Individualistic Powers*.

(Later in the book, this notion may be needed. For, it may be just such a conception that's needed by a Substantial Dualism about mind and body. Or, at the least, to make much sense of such a time-honored view, we may need just such a notion. But, I'm getting ahead of myself. Now, let's gently enter our discussion.)

1. The Idea That All Propensities Concern Something as to Quality

In the Chapter on the Demystification of the Physical, we encountered the Problem of Influence for Qualities (in Physical Reality), and we

211

offered a solution to this neglected Problem. Toward offering the solution, we found it useful to distinguish between Size-directed Propensities, or Size-directed Powers, and Quality-directed Propensities,
or Powers. And, for the solution itself, we thought to focus on Quality-
directed Propensities, or Propensities with respect to Qualities. Now,
we'll explore some related ideas.

As we saw fit to hypothesize, there'll be *some* Worlds in which each
of the World's physical objects has Propensities with respect to the *Sizes*
of other physical things, with which it's *thus* set to interact. And, quite
equally, we hypothesized that, in some *other* Worlds, each physical
object has Propensities with respect to the *Qualities* of its physical disposition partners. This marks a certain contrast among the Propensities, or the Powers. Might there be a more perspicuous way to put the
marked contrast?

Instead of taking a physical object to have a Propensity with respect
to just the *Sizes* of its physical disposition partners, perhaps we might
conceive the matter more fully, and more clearly, by taking the object
to have a Propensity with respect to *the degree to which the partners'
Qualities are spatially extended in them*. So, for example, with a partner
whose Size is greater than another's, it's to a *greater degree that the
Quality of the first is spatially extended in that particular*. To my mind, that's
a pretty appealing suggestion.

That said for Size, what might be said for Shape? What might we
say, quite perspicuously, about a physical object that has a Propensity
with respect to the *Shapes* of its physical disposition partners? For
specificity, we might have our considered object be set to attract
Spheres, and set to repel Discs (no matter the Size of, or the Quality of,
the Discs and the Spheres).

Instead of taking our physical object to have a Propensity with respect to just the *Shapes* of its physical disposition partners, perhaps we
might conceive the matter more fully, and more clearly, by taking the
object to have a Propensity with respect to *how it is configurationally that
the partners' Qualities are spatially extended in them*. When a partner is a
Sphere, then, configurationally, the partner is Qualitied *Spherically*.
Because *that's* how, configurationally, the concretum is Qualitied, its
Propensitied partner is set to *attract* it. When a partner is a Disc, by
contrast, then, configurationally, the partner is Qualitied *Discally*. And,
because that's how, configurationally, *this* concretum is Qualitied, its
partner is, on the hypothesis, set to *repel* it. To me, that's also appealing.

Well, now, why shouldn't we go this "highly Qualitative route" not
only with Size, and with Shape, but, just as well, with any basic property
of a basic concretum? For, as it appears, it's across a very wide range

that we may take a physical object's Propensities to *concern only something as to the Quality* of disposition partners.

With Particles, easy to think of in terms of their Shape and Size, matters will generally proceed pretty much as just indicated. (In special cases, as with a Particle that "spontaneously" probabilistically annihilates, perhaps its Propensity to do that may be a Propensity with respect to *how it is with that very Particle, itself, Qualitatively.*)

With a Plenum, perhaps infinitely spatially extensive in all directions, it may be that, in a more interesting way, the Single Basic Entity's Propensities, or its Powers, are all with respect to its own (Variegated) Quality. Presumably, at least some of our Plenum's Propensities will be manifested. And, presumably, that will involve change concerning only something as to the Spatially Extensible Quality of that selfsame vast Field.

2. Power-directed Powers (Propensities with Respect to Propensities)

The previous Section's discussion suggests a philosophical hypothesis that's now quite appealing:

> *The Hypothesis that All Physical Propensities concern only Something as to Quality.* Whenever a physical entity has a Propensity with regard to physical reality, the power *always* concerns, or it's always with respect to, *only something as to the Quality of some physical things* (either it concerns only something as to the Quality of its disposition partners or, in a more special case, it concerns only something as to the Quality of the physical entity itself).

As will become clear, this Hypothesis isn't meant to hold just in, or just of, our own actual world. Rather, it's meant to hold in, of, and for, any other possible Worlds with physical realms. Just so, it's even meant to be a *conceptual truth*, in a sense that may be most useful for first philosophy.

Taking the offered Hypothesis in that grand manner, we may still treat quite variously the phrase "concerning only something as to Quality." Now, if we treat this phrase awfully liberally, the Hypothesis may be taken to express nothing more than the idea that, in "Demystifying the Physical," we endeavored to advance: For any Propensitied physical concretum to be conceived by us, at all clearly and fully, we must conceive the thing to be Extensibly Qualitied, just as much as it's conceived to be Propensitied and Spatially Extended. But, then, the Hypothesis won't be saying anything particularly relevant to the just previous Section's discussion.

So, we should take "concerning only something as to Quality" more strictly. On one stricter interpretation, the Hypothesis might be advocated by a certain extreme proponent of Lewis's noted Humean supervenience. Not Lewis himself, mind you, but, rather, someone who takes such supervenience to hold (at least for any wholly physical realm) as a conceptual truth. Now, when the Hypothesis is understood in such a much more ambitious manner, then it will be undermined, I suspect, by what we may call *Propensities with respect to Propensities* or, with fewer letters used, Propensity-directed Propensities, or, with fewer still, *Power-directed Powers*. Let me explain, if only very partially, this suspicion.

Consider a World that has, in addition to many Small Blue Spheres and Large Red Spheres, many Particles of many other sorts, too. There are Small Yellow Ovoid Particles, and Medium-Sized Blue Ovoids, and Small Green Spheres, and so on. Not just a Tutti Frutti World, this is a *Whoopi Tutti Frutti World* or, for short, a *Whoopi World*.

In our supposed Whoopi World, we'll further assume, there are some Particles that are each disposed to attract others of Any Different Size (from its own Size) no matter what Shape, or what Color, might be the other Particles. We'll call them *Different-Size-Attractors*. And, there are Particles each set to attract others of Any Different Shape, no matter what Size or Color. We'll call them *Different-Shape-Attractors*. And, there are Particles each disposed to attract others of Any Different Color, no matter what Shape or Size. You can guess what they'll be called.

In this Whoopi World, it's plain, there are Small Blue Spheres that are Different-Size-Attractors, each set to attract any Particle (or, any that's near enough, or whatnot) *except those that are Small*. And, there are Medium Yellow Ovoids that also are Different-Size-Attractors; but, of course, with these Ovoids, it's *all except Medium* Particles that they're set to attract.

Now, it's time to hear about some very different Particles, still, which I'll call *Selective Spinners*. With a Different-Size-Attractor, a *Size-Divergent* Selective Spinner will have it that the Different-Size-Attractor starts to spin—or, if it's already rotating, that its speed of spinning will increase.

What's going on with these various Selective Spinners, and with the various Spinnee Particles that are, in the ways just remarked, their reciprocal disposition partners?

Each of our Selective Spinners has a certain Power-directed Power. Each has a Propensity *with respect to a certain Propensity*, that may be found in, or with, some other possible Particles. Just so, each Spinner is selectively Propensitied for a certain sort of (spinning) interaction with just such possible Particles as are *Propensitied*, in a certain complexly selective way, for a different sort of (attracting) interaction with still other possible Particles. Except for a potential Spinee's *Propensity*, the Spinners are entirely indifferent. And, as we've been supposing, this "targeted" Propensity, itself, is only quite barely related to anything as to Quality. Now, given all that, is it right to say that a Selective Spinner's noted power, so clearly directed at just the Propensities of some possible Particles, is a Propensity concerning *only* something as to *Quality?*

Though I could be wrong, I can't see much point in giving this question an affirmative answer. Rather, I think it better to answer negatively: No; our Selective Spinners' noted power *isn't* a Propensity "concerning only something as to Quality." So, if we take the Hypothesis to be a fairly ambitious statement, ambitious enough to be philosophically interesting, I think we should reject the Hypothesis that All Physical Propensities concern only Something as to Quality.

In what's just been presented, I've offered you a pretty long and slow story. After hearing this story from me, Neil Williams noted that, to quite the same desired effect, there can be told a far shorter and faster story. From as early as Chapter 3, recall our Yellow-Attractors. Though they're present only in just certain Worlds, it's true, and, maybe, in certain Eons, each of these Particles has the power to attract any concretum that's Yellow. Now, in having this power, it's true, these Yellow-Attractors have a Propensity directed at, or with respect to, just a certain Quality; and, of course, that Quality is none other than Spatially Extensible Yellow. With that, we've been just warming up.

To make real progress vividly, let's now suppose a World with both Yellow-Attractor Particles and, to boot, Yellow Particles. Indeed, we may suppose that all these Particles are so nicely situated that each Yellow-Attractor interacts with at least one Yellow concretum in just such a way that, in this very interaction, each Attractor does attract the interacting Yellow, or Yellows. But, of course, for such interactions to occur, it must be that, in each case, an attracted Yellow entity has a Propensity that's the apt reciprocal of the Quality-directed Power of a Yellow-Attractor that's attracting the Propensitied Yellow entity. And, what Propensity will *that* be? None other than this, of course: It's a paradigmatic Propensity to be attracted by just such entities (the Yellow-Attractors) as each have a certain *Propensity*, whether these entities (the Yellow-Attractors) be Qualitied Red or Blue, whether they be Sized Large or Small, and so on. None of that matters; all that matters is that, with each of them, they have the noted Propensity, the Power to attract Yellow things, toward which the Yellows' reciprocal power is itself so relevantly directed. This is a Power-directed Power. End of story.

Well, quite as I said, that's certainly short and fast. As some might think, it's so very short, and so very fast, that it must be "too good to be true," so to say, not really anything sound, or properly convincing.

But, if that's what you think, please return to our much slower and longer accounting, offered just before. Neither fast nor short, at all, it's certainly not "too good to be true." Is it, rather, too long, slow and complex to be really reliable, or sound, or convincing?

Come on, now; that's just desperately silly. Putting silliness and desperation to the side, I now repeat, just a little more confidently, this perfectly serious suggestion: If we take the Hypothesis to be a fairly ambitious statement, or any newly interesting philosophic proposition, then we should reject the Hypothesis that All Physical Propensities concern only Something as to Quality.

3. Power-directed Powers May Distinctively Distinguish among Other Powers

Maybe, quite like me, you also think that Power-directed Powers undermine the Hypothesis that All Physical Propensities concern only Something as to Quality. Or, maybe, unlike me, you disagree. Rather surprisingly, I think, and for two very different reasons, it may be that this disagreement, between us, doesn't matter very much. How's that?

Well, for one thing, and beginning only a few Sections from now, I'll offer a very different consideration against that Hypothesis. What's more, not only will this be perfectly decisive against the noted conjecture, but, it will also be so decisive against any proposition that's even remotely similar to the Hypothesis that All Physical Propensities concern only Something as to Quality. So, that's one thing. Or; it soon will be.

And, for another thing, very different from the first, we may employ the notion of Power-directed Powers toward achieving, very successfully, I think, a variety of other important philosophic ends. Some of them are quite worthwhile, I think, and none of the goals has anything to do with (undermining) our noted Hypothesis, nor with (undermining) any even remotely similar conjecture.

I want to consider these two points, or two reasons, in the reverse order, not so much as even broaching the one just mentioned first, about decisively undermining our noted Hypothesis, until a couple of more Sections have elapsed. Just so, during the rest of this Section, and then some, I'll try to help us recognize how our idea of Power-directed Powers is a notion that, in its own right, should enjoy a pretty central place in our developing Humanly Realistic Philosophy (or, for that matter, in any philosophy that, in the further future, may prove to be its eventual superior).

Toward this large end, I'll begin by observing that, intuitively, we may distinguish these following five different (sorts of) Worlds.

In all five, there are many Large Red Spheres and many Small Blue Spheres, with none of the Large Red Spheres spinning, but with many of the Small Blue Spheres spinning, exactly all those many Small Blues that are each less than a meter from at least one Large Red. What's more, every concrete entity that's ever been in any of these Worlds is either a Large Red Sphere, and it stays that way, or else it's a Small Blue Sphere, and *it* stays *that* way. (Or, at the least, those are all the basic spatial entities in each World, whatever may be said about a World's complexes, or mereological sums, or quasi-abstracta, or any other such dubious and irrelevant falderal. Now, back to the main specificational track, where there's this awaiting.) What's yet more, in *four* of these five Worlds, all the Large Red Spheres are Propensitied to spin all the Small Blue Spheres, with the condition for manifestation being that the interacting partners should be less than a meter apart. (After specifying these first four Worlds, I'll mention the Fifth, which serves as sort of a "control group of one.")

For each of these (first) four Worlds, we may ask: Why are all those Small Blue Spheres spinning, all those, of course, within a meter of at least one of the World's Large Red Spheres?

Now, intuitively, at least, it seems that, with giving these following four answers, we're specifying four very different (sorts of) Worlds, with each differing from the others by, at the very least, a difference as to how the (sort of) World's Large Red Spheres are Propensitied.

In the First World, the Large Reds are all *Terribly Fastidious* Spinners: These Large Reds are Propensitied to spin anything that's *both Blue and also Small*—with the condition of manifestation being that a candidate Spinee should be less than a meter from any such successful Spinner—but they're *Propensitied not to spin anything else*, anything that's *not both Blue and Small*.

In the Second World, the Large Reds are all a *certain type of Fairly* Fastidious Spinners: These Large Reds are Propensitied to spin anything that's *Blue* (whether it's Small or whether not)—with a correlative condition of manifestation—and *they're* Propensitied not to spin anything that's *not Blue*. As we may well say, they're all *Type B* (*B* for Blue) Fairly Fastidious Spinners.

In the Third World, the Large Reds are all *another type of Fairly* Fastidious Spinners: These Large Reds are Propensitied to spin anything that's *Small* (whether it's Blue or whether not)—with a correlative condition of manifestation—and *they're* Propensitied not to spin anything that's *not Small*. As we may well now say, they're all *Type S* (*S* for Small) Fairly Fastidious Spinners.

In the Fourth World, the Large Reds are all *Barely* Fastidious Spinners, as I'll rhymingly say: These Large Reds are Propensitied to spin anything that's *either Blue or Small (or both)*—with a correlative condition of manifestation—but they're *Propensitied not to spin anything else*, anything that's *neither Blue nor Small*.

Well, as to the experiential aspect of our conceiving, or to "the mind's experiential eye," to put it more poetically, in all four Worlds, everything will seem the same. And, that will also be true of our "minimal control group," our Fifth (sort of) World.

In this Fifth World, which I'll dub our *Incredibly Well-Behaved Happenstantial World*, the Large Reds aren't dynamically Propensitied with respect to the Small Blues, nor vice versa. (Nor is it the case, let's add, for good measure, that the Large Reds are Propensitied *not* to spin anything that's here under consideration.) In fact, the situation is simply this: It's always just utterly happenstantial that, whenever a Small Blue is within a meter of a Large Red, the Small Blue is spinning and, with any Small Blue that's never been that close to any Large Red, it's not spinning. (This echoes, or mirrors, Worlds we've considered before, as with our Third Chapter's World containing [not protonish Pete and electronish Ed, but, rather, just] Earl and Pat, those fondly remembered utterly happenstantial little movers.)

Suppose, now, that someone suspects that, in saying all that we just did, we didn't really specify five different sorts of Worlds. Maybe, quite rightly and strongly impressed with our Third Chapter, she'll go for two sorts of Worlds here—one with Propensitied Large Reds and the other (what I called) our Fifth World, or our Incredibly Well-Behaved Happenstantial World. That's something, she'll say, and I shouldn't be so Humean as to deny it. But, that's all you've done, no more than that; I shouldn't be so *un-Humean* as to think you did anything more. Words, words, words, and more words, she'll say, but, with all the words you used in "specifying your first four (sorts of) Worlds," you really didn't specify any World, not even the least bit adequately. Just so, you specified nothing, really, that serves to distinguish any of these so-called Propensitive Worlds from any of the alleged other three so-called Propensitive Worlds, each with Large Reds well Propensitied for spinning the World's (nearby) Small Blues.

What are we to say to such a suspicious person? Well, the first thing to say, even while saying it most gently and kindly is, really, I think, something quite like this: Just maybe, just possibly, these suspicions aren't very well warranted; just maybe, just possibly, they may stem more from philosophic confusion than from any alleged Humean illumination.

But, as I'll suggest, even though all that's quite true, it should be only the first thing. After all, our suspicious friend may think the world of us and, for much that reason, she may say something like this: In these suspicions of mine, I'm probably quite wrong, and very confused, just as you so kindly suggest. But, please, don't just make that suggestion. Please say something more, to help me see things more clearly, so that I may get beyond my stultifying confusion.

Well, to be helpful to our friend, there are, I think, two main sorts of things to say. Much the more obvious aiding device, the first sort of thing may be more readily helpful and, perhaps, more easily useful. But, the second, which involves Power-directed Powers, may be, in the end, rather more widely helpful. And, even right from the start, it may be the more deeply useful thing to say. But, of course, I must elaborate. In doing so, I'll first discuss the device I just mentioned second, the one that requires me, quite happily, to continue my discussion of Power-directed Powers.

Here's how we may use our idea of just that, our notion of Propensities with respect to Propensities, to aid our admittedly befuddled friend.

Consider five Worlds very much like the five we specified just before, but with just this very clear difference: Each World will first come to have, at a certain latish time in its history, five Large Gold Spheres, with each of the five very differently Propensitied toward, or with respect to, differently Propensitied Large Red Spheres.

A First (sort of) Gold Sphere, present in all five (sorts of) Worlds, is Propensitied dynamically with respect to just such Large Red Spheres as are Terribly Fastidious Spinners. (With respect to any *other* concreta, including any other Large Red Spheres, it's Propensitied *Not to interact dynamically*—with respect to any of them, it's *Propensitied just for Static Interaction*, a phrase suggested by the work of (my thoughtful student) Neil Williams.[1] With respect to the other four (sorts of) Gold Spheres, there'll be *correlative* Propensities for Stasis; so, throughout, where there's *no* Propensity for Dynamics, there *is* a Propensity for *Stasis*, or for *Monotony*. That's all just specified.) But, you ask, as well you should,

---

1. See Neil Williams, "Static and Dynamic Dispositions," *Synthese*, forthcoming.

for what sort of dynamical interaction, with just such Large Reds, is this First (sort of) Gold Sphere Propensitied? Well, it's Propensitied for *Rotating*, or for spinning, just such Large Reds as are Terribly Fastidious Spinners. (This Propensity will be manifested, I specify, provided only that such a Large Gold and just such a Large Red are within a trillion light years of each other, a condition that, I specify, always obtains, just so long as there exist Spheres of these sorts, Large Golds and Large Reds. And, instead of bothering to be explicit about it for each case, paragraph after paragraph, I'll now specify, in one fell swoop, precisely this: With all our (sorts of) Gold Spheres, the Propensities I'll be specifying are Propensities that *will be manifested*.) So, each of our five (sorts of) World has, or it will have, right soon, a (Gold) Terribly-Fastidious-Spinner Rotator, as well as four other (sorts of) Large Gold Spheres.

A Second (sort of) Gold Sphere, also present in all five (sorts of) Worlds, is Propensitied dynamically with respect to just such Large Red Spheres as are *Type B* (*B* for Blue) Fairly Fastidious Spinners. And, as you ask, *for what sort* of dynamical interaction, with just *such* Large Reds, is this Second (sort of) Gold Sphere Propensitied? Well, it's Propensitied for *Attracting* just such Large Reds as are *Type B* (*B* for Blue) Fairly Fastidious Spinners—for having them move towards the Large Gold, along a line passing through the reciprocally partnered Sphere's centers. So, each of our five (sorts of) Worlds will have, right soon, a (Gold) Type-B-Fairly-Fastidious-Spinner Attractor, as well as four other (sorts of) Large Golds.

A Third (sort of) Gold Sphere, also present in all five (sorts of) Worlds, is Propensitied dynamically with just such Large Reds as are *Type S* (*S* for Small) Fairly Fastidious Spinners. Now, *for what sort* of dynamical interaction is this Third (sort of) Gold Sphere Propensitied, with just *such other* Large Reds? Well, it's Propensitied for *Repelling* just such Large Reds as are Type S Fairly Fastidious Spinners—for having them move away from the partnered Large Gold, along a line passing through the reciprocally partnered Sphere's centers. So, each of our five (sorts of) Worlds will have, right soon, a (Gold) Type-S-Fairly-Fastidious-Spinner Repellor, as well as four other (sorts of) Large Golds.

A Fourth (sort of) Gold Sphere, yet also present in all five (sorts of) Worlds, is Propensitied dynamically with just such Large reds as are *Barely* Fastidious Spinners. Now, *for what sort* of dynamical interaction, with just *such yet other* Large Reds, is this Fourth (sort of) Gold Propensitied? Well, it's Propensitied for *Color-Changing* just such Large Reds as are Barely Fastidious Spinners—for having them Change from Extensible Red to Extensible *White*. So, each of our five (sorts of)

Worlds will have, right soon, a (Gold) Barely-Fastidious-Spinner Color-Changer, as well as four other (sorts of) Large Gold Spheres.

Finally, a Fifth (sort of) Large Gold Sphere, also answering any relevant Worldly roll call, is Propensitied dynamically with just such Large Reds as aren't Propensitied for Spinning (or for not Spinning) anything that's Small or anything that's Blue. Anyway, with respect to these *Relevantly Random* Large Reds, as I'll call them, for what sort of dynamical interaction are these Fifth (sort of) Large Golds Propensitied? Oh, let's say that they'll *Change the Shape* of any Relevantly Random Large Red Spheres, for having them Change from being Spherical to being *Cubical*. So, each of our five (sorts of) Worlds will have, right soon, a (Gold) Relevantly-Random-Sphere Shape-Changer, as well as four other (sorts of) Large Gold Spheres.

Well, now, throughout their histories so far, and even from time immemorial, each of our five (sorts of) Worlds has been, just so far as just our conceiving's experiential aspect is concerned, precisely like all the others. All the same, each World has been, Propensitively, very unlike each of the others. In just a minute, each World will acquire five Large Gold Spheres, one of each of our five Propensitive sorts. And, then, just insofar as any Gold sphere finds a suitably matched Propensity partner, there will be manifested that (sort of) Large Gold's peculiarly telltale specified reciprocal Propensity, mutually manifested, of course, with all the Large Reds, right there in its World, for which the happily matched Large Gold is dynamically Propensitied.

Now, the minute's up, and, into each of these Worlds, there come our five (sorts of) Large Gold Spheres and, right in each World's bargain, there's the manifestation of just all the crucial Propensities, each so nicely indicative of what Propensitive sort of Large Reds do find, all of them in just that World, a suitably matched Large Gold interaction partner.

So, in our First World, a Large Gold Terribly-Fastidious-Spinner Rotator rapidly Rotates all the World's many Large Red Spheres, with no Large Red being Attracted toward a Large Gold, or Repelled by a Large Gold, or Changing its Color, or Changing its Shape. For, in this World, it's only the First (sort of) Large Gold that finds any Large Red Propensity partners; it's only *this* (sort of) Gold that's endowed with an aptly *matching Power-directed Power*, apt for matching the Power of just (any Large Red) Terribly Fastidious Spinners.

At the same time, in our Second World, a Large Gold Type-B-Fairly-Fastidious-Spinner-Attractor is the only Gold Sphere with an apt Power-directed Power. As it's only this Gold Sphere that here finds Propensity partners, so, in this Second (sort of) World, all the World's

Large Reds are Attracted towards a certain Large Gold Sphere; of course, it's this aforesaid Sphere. No Large Red is ever Rotated, or ever Repelled, or ever Changes Color, or ever Changes Shape.

Also at the same time, in our Third World, a Large Gold Type-S-Fairly-Fastidious-Spinner-Repellor moves all the World's Large Reds further, and further, and further, away from itself. For, in this World, it's only *this* (sort of) Gold Sphere that's ever partnered properly, with any Large Red Spheres, for any (telltale) dynamical interaction. And, so, all the World's Large Reds partake of just its distinctive sort of interaction, all of them being Repelled away, and away, and away, from a Large Gold Sphere. Of course, that's not just any old Large Gold Sphere; rather, it's just the one that's so nicely in question.

What's more, of course, in our Fourth World, what happens, at this same time, is just an interaction between our Fourth (sort) of Gold Sphere and this World's Large Reds. This is a Gold Sphere, you'll recall, with a Power that's directed at just such individuals as are Pro-pensitied to spin anything that's Small, and also anything that's Blue (and, so, of course, anything that's both Small and Blue). Just so, here all the Large Reds *Change Color*, from Red to *White*, without under-going any other intrinsic Change, and without undergoing, either, any Change as concerns any motion, or any spatial position, location, or orientation.

Finally, in our Fifth (sort of) World, the only Gold Sphere to find propensity partners, particularly among the World's Large Reds, is the World's only (Gold) Relevantly-Random-Sphere Shape-Changer, with none of its other four Golds finding any apt Large Red partner at all. So, in this World, filled, as it is, with just so many *quite Accidentally* Spinning Small Blues—so to put matters—all the Large Red Spheres Change in Shape. Quite suddenly, the World's Large Red Spheres all become *Cubical* concreta, even while they *don't* undergo any *other* (sort of) notably relevant change.

With what we've just been through, we may have provided our quasi-Humean friend—she who was just so lately quite badly confused—with some very helpful philosophic instruction. This instructive exer-cise will prove nicely to complement, I think, the more obvious sort of instruction that's to be next provided. Why? Well, somewhat as that subsequent instruction will also do, what we've just done provides her with, for each distinctive World, aptly different Propensitive manifes-tations, each quite fit to satisfy, very differently, *the experiential aspect of* our conceiving. Or, much the same, there were just provided five *hu-manly surveyable* Propensitive manifestations, each so manifestly dif-ferent from the others, so much so as will satisfy, surely, almost any confused quasi-Humean who hungers for instruction. (To be sure, for these manifestations to occur, each of the manifesting (Large Red) *individuals* must be matched with an apt Propensity partner. And, in each case, the matching (Large Gold) partner must be, for its part, an aptly reciprocal object. And, indeed, it must be just so apt for just this signally central reason: It's Propensitied with respect to how it is that *its reciprocal concreta*, its now-manifesting Large Reds, *are themselves Propensitied* (with respect to Small Blue Spheres.) As we made sure to specify, these "targeted Propensities" are *directed at some still other (sorts of) individuals*, most saliently including, most certainly, Propensitively various Small Blue Spheres. And, as we further made sure, it wasn't just willy-nilly that, in each case, a given Large Gold "targeted" just those Large Reds that were (to be) its interaction partners. To the contrary, each Large Gold "targeted" just those Large Reds it matched because, and only because, the Large Reds had certain Powers, or Propensities, just those that, in each case, we specified for the Propensitively distinctive Large Reds in question.)

With this aid we've just provided, we've seen some real philosophical utility in our notion of Power-directed Powers. And, quite as it seems to be, what's here been helpful may be a perfectly distinctive sort of intellectual resource.

Now, I'll present the other sort of aid I mentioned, rather more obvious than the assistance we've just lately observed. Unlike with the aid we've just observed, this won't be at all novel. Quite to the contrary, and as those embroiled with recent philosophy can't help but notice, what I'll now offer, and even my presentation of it, will be much the same as might be done by ever so many other philosophical writers—a pretty homogeneous throng that includes both many very recent writers and, as well, many writers from about fifty years ago. (I'll now pretend, of course, that the folks in the throng took the trouble to accept anything like Spatially Extensible Colors, along with making some other apparently generous pretenses.)

Here's how so many of us, all in the throng, might start to provide some rather obvious aid: If the first World were to contain various other sorts of basic physical concreta as well, in addition to just so many Large Red Spheres and Small Blue Spherical Particles, and if many of them were within a meter of the nicely Propensitied Large Reds, then, even pretty nicely available for our conceiving's experiential aspect, there'd be various spinning differences among the four (sorts of) Worlds' additional Particles. To make this all usefully specific and helpfully vivid, we'll suppose that, in addition to the Large Reds and the Small Blues, there are, in each of our four (sorts of) Worlds, these other (sorts of) Particles as well: There are Small Yellow Spheres; and there are Large Blue Spheres; and, for good measure, there are Large Green Cones. And, while many of each sort may be far from any Large Reds, even so, many will be very near at least one Large Red Sphere.

Well, then, in the First of our four Worlds, whose Large Reds are such Terribly Fastidious Spinners, it will still be that the only Particles ever spinning are the World's Small Blues. Why? Well none of the additional particles, just so happily supposed, is both Small and also Blue. And, in this World, as I specified, it's only something that's both Small and Blue that a Large Red's ever Propensitied to Spin, while, quite oppositely, Large Reds are Propensitied *not* to spin anything that's not both Small and Blue.[2] So, this bit of aiding concludes, none of the newly supposed Particles will be spinning, not even those well within a meter of Large Red Spheres.

(But, even passing over the point lately made in our note, is that conclusion really right? Mightn't some of the other Particles start to spin *anyway*, even if it's *not* the manifestation of *any* Propensitive interaction? Mightn't they start spinning just as the sheerest happenstance? At least to my mind, that certainly seems a very real possibility. So, even after we've been quite generous with it, as with neglecting our note's point, it sure doesn't look so hot, this more common and obvious putative philosophical assistance. With that observed, let's see what our hopefully helpful instructors might next say.)

By contrast with what will go on in our First World, in the Second World, whose Large Reds are all *Type B* (*B* for Blue) Fairly Fastidious Spinners, there'll be spinning not only so many nearby Small Blues but also all the many similarly nearby Large Blue Spheres. But, there won't be spinning any of the other newly supposed Particles. Why? Well, this World's Particles are Propensitied to Spin anything that's Blue, you'll recall, and, just as much as the Small Blue Spheres are Blue (basic entities), so, also, the Large Blue Spheres are truly Blue Particles. But, none of the other newly supposed Particles are Blue concreta; so, none of them will ever be spinning. So, this next bit of aiding concludes, even while the nearby Small Blue Spheres will be spinning, of course, and now also the nearby Large Blue Spheres, none of the other newly

2. Well, of course, there's *quite a leap* here. For, it was never specified, one way or the other, whether anything *else should be Propensitied to Spin something that's not Small and Blue*, anything that's not a Large Red Sphere [or, maybe, too, anything that's not a Small Blue Sphere]. I never said, one way or the other, whether Large Green Cones, for example, should be Propensitied to spin Large Blue Spheres, or any other sorts of extant concreta. But, what the heck, let's pass over that now. All right, then, letting that pass, let's get back to the text.

supposed Particles will be spinning, not even those well within a meter of Large Red Spheres.

(Well, that conclusion can't really be right, either, and for just the same deep reason, just previously related parenthetically: Quite as just before, so, in this Second World, too, some of the nearby Large Green Cones, say, may start to spin. Indeed, they *all* might do so. Why? Well, quite as before, for no reason, really. Rather, it may all just happen, as the sheerest happenstance. At least to my mind, this also certainly seems a very real possibility. So, even after we've been generous with this putatively more obvious help, this allegedly easy aid looks like anything but hot stuff. With this now also observed, let's see what our hopefully helpful instructors might *next* say.)

By contrast with all that's above, concerning both our First World and also our Second, in the Third World, whose Large Reds are all *Type S* (*S* for Small) Fairly Fastidious Spinners, there'll be spinning not only so many nearby Small Blue Spheres, but also all the many similarly nearby Small Yellow Spheres. But, there won't be spinning any of the other newly supposed Particles. Why? Well, this World's Particles are Propensitied to Spin anything that's Small, you'll recall; and, just as much as the Small Blue Spheres are, so, also, the Small Yellow Spheres are Small Individuals. But, none of the other newly supposed Particles are Small concreta; so, none of them will ever be spinning.[3]

(Except, of course, it's perfectly possible for all the (nicely nearby) Large Green Cones to start spinning, if only as the sheerest happenstance, coincidence, accident or random event. Indeed, it's perfectly possible for them all to start to spin and never stop spinning. Indeed, one thing that's possible for these Cones is to keep spinning just as long each is quite near a Large Red Sphere, which might be forever and ever. Indeed, *another thing possible*, for them, is (for them) to keep on spinning, maybe forever and ever, *whether or not* they remain near any Large Red Sphere. Not so? Heck, it sure seems so to me.)

---

3. Now, even having passed over the points we've already parenthetically granted, just above, it's *quite a skip-and-a-jump*, I'll suggest, to say all that. For one thing, it should have been specified that there's nothing around to hinder, or to obstruct, or to prevent, the Large Red's Spinning-Propensity from being manifested, maybe especially in respect of the "would-be spun" Small Yellow Spheres, so to say. Just so, we certainly shouldn't have there be *Large Green Cones*, say, that are each *Propensitied to prevent just such Large Reds from spinning anything that's Yellow*, no matter how nicely Small the Yellow thing may be, even while, of course, they're *not Disposed to prevent* Large Reds from spinning Small *Blue* (Spherical) concreta. But, what the heck, let's pass over this, too, right now. So, letting all this also pass, in an ever more sweeping protracted act of charity, let's listen, even once yet again, to our hopefully helpful throng of philosophy instructors.

Contrasting with the three Worlds already observed, in our Fourth World there'll be spinning all the noted (sorts of) Particles *except for* the Large Green Cones. With its Barely Fastidious Spinners, not only will the Small Blue Spheres be spinning, of course, but the Large Blue Spheres will be spinning, too—because, of course, they're Blue concreta—and, just as truly, the Small Yellow Spheres will also spin—because, of course, they're Small concreta.

(Except, of course, the Large Green Cones needn't really be any exception. As soon as anything else starts spinning, as the manifestation of its Propensity to be spun, just that soon the Large Green Cones may start spinning, but not as the manifestation of any Propensity at all. By now, of course, this is old hat. But, it sure looks like it's a good old hat. In contrast, the quite common and obvious putative philosophical assistance doesn't look nearly so good.)

All right, then; that's it. And, with that, we've provided our previously befuddled friend, maybe by now just a former quasi-Humean, with two contrasting, and complementary, sorts of helpful assistance, maybe one of them really much more truly helpful than the other.

Now, as you'll recall, I said that the first sort of aid, the instruction in terms of *Power-directed Powers*, was more deeply useful, and it was more widely useful, philosophical, assistance. Especially in the parenthetical remarks with which I've peppered this Section—and, also, with points made in notes provided for the Section—I've already given you some substantial reason, I submit, for you to think that to be a correct assessment.

And, that's not all; not by a long shot. Just a Section or two down the pike, you should look for yet more reason to agree with this rather unorthodox assessment or, maybe better, with this happily heterodox approach to Powers, Propensities, Dispositions, and all their cousins.

4. Propensity, Possibility, Accident and Probability

When first introducing our idea of Propensity, pretty early in our First Chapter, I noticed that there are certain differences between the Possibilities for an object—or what's possible for it—and, on the other side, the Propensities of the object. For one thing, there are certain temporal differences: Propensities must be for future happenings, while Possibilities can concern the present, and the past, as much as the future. With that point in mind, let's now notice some related conceptions.

I don't know about you, but, myself, I think that chance phenomena are metaphysically possible. And, so, I don't think that this strong conditional proposition is any metaphysically necessary truth: If an entity is *not* Propensitied *to* do so-and-so (or to be such-and-such), then, as must needs be, the entity *is* Propensitied *not to* do so-and-so (or to be such-and-such). Rather, there might occur, for example, the movement of a Green Sphere toward a Yellow Cube, even while the Green Sphere has *no Propensity, at all, to* move toward a Yellow Cube, and even while, just as well, the Green Sphere has *no Propensity, either, not* to move toward a Yellow Cube. The moving of this Green Sphere, toward this Yellow Cube, will be, then, a *random happening*. And, likewise, there might occur *no* movement of a Green Sphere toward a Red Cone, even while the Green Sphere has *no Propensity, at all, not to* move toward the Red Cone, nor any Propensity, either, and of course, to move toward the Red Cone. This lack of movement, this relative rest, if you like, will also be a mere matter of sheer chance.

With just that much said about sheer accident, I'll now move to notice something about another sort of chance, so to say, now becoming concerned with some matters of objective probability: So, as much in order now as they'll ever be, here are some words about Probabilistic Propensities. As sometimes seems forced on us, by certain things physical scientists say nowadays, certain physical entities have Probabilistic Propensities for interaction with others.

So, in certain Worlds, it may be that a Blue Sphere, any old Blue Sphere, is Probabilistically Propensitied, to the degree 0.9, to attract any Red Spheres, or maybe just such Red Spheres as are each within a light-year of the Blue Sphere in question. At the same time, it may be that each Blue Sphere is Probabilistically Propensitied, to the degree 0.1, *not to* attract the (aforesaid) Red Spheres. Well, then, whether or not a given Blue Sphere attracts a certain Red Sphere (less than a light-year apart), either way that *won't be a purely chance* phenomenon. Rather, either way, there will be the manifestation of the Blue Sphere's Propensity with respect to attracting Red Spheres, and its correlative Propensity not to attract. And, there'll be manifested, in this same way, the reciprocal Probabilistic Propensity (of Red Spheres and, in particular, the Red Sphere in question).

(With reciprocal Probabilistic Propensities, the Probabilities must, of course, mathematically match. So, with a Blue Sphere Propensitied to attract Reds to that degree, the degree 0.9, the Reds must be Probabilistically Propensitied to be attracted by a Blue Sphere to just that same degree, the degree 0.9. And, correlatively, the Red Sphere must Probabilistically match the Blue, on the other side of the same story. That is, the Reds will have a mathematically matching Probabilistic Propensity *not* to attract, and not to be attracted by, the Blue Spheres. In our example, and as was specified for it, this will be a Probabilistic Propensity to just the degree (1-0.9), that is, to just the degree 0.1.[4])

Anyhow, if our Blue Sphere attracts our Red Sphere here, in this little example, there will be the *more likely* manifestation of the Blue Sphere's whole Propensity in the matter, and, correlatively, also the more likely manifestation of the Red Sphere's relevant Propensity. And, if there *isn't* any such attraction, there'll be the *less likely* mutually Probabilistic manifestations. But, in *either* event, there'll be the manifestation of Probabilistic Propensities. And so, there *won't* be, in such an event, any *purely random* happening.

Similarly, a certain Green Sphere may be Propensitied, to the degree 0.3, to attract a nearby White Sphere, which is itself Propensitied, to just that degree, to be attracted by the Green Sphere. If there is the attraction, or there's the coming together, then there'll be the unlikely manifestation of these things' mutual Probabilistic Propensities. If not, then there'll be the likely manifestation. But, of course, there'll also here be, in any event, the manifestation of Probabilistic Propensities. Even if it's the unlikely manifestation that occurs, there *won't* be an *utterly random* happening.

Probabilistic Propensity must make as much sense in a single instance, and in the simplest sort of case, as it will ever make in any case. And, since I can't make much sense of it when things are so suitably simple, I can't really make much sense of this notion at all. But, no very central point of this essay, from its first Section through its last Section, depends on Probabilistic Propensity, even if some secondary points may do. So, at least for the sake of a nicely ecumenical discussion, I go along with these baffling alleged Propensities. Anyway, what's now important to note is just this, which I'll again repeat: When *they're* fully involved, these Probabilistic Propensities, then we *don't* have a *purely random* happening.

As I'm quite prepared to admit, it may be owing only to a lack in me, a being who's intellectually wanting in many ways, that I find these (single-case) objective probabilities so baffling. Or, at the least, it may be partly owing just to my own intellectual inadequacy. Anyhow, quite far from bemoaning any of this, I'll try to turn it to some advantage. To be sure, this attempt must be a terribly unconfident endeavor. Still and

---

4. What I mean here is, of course, that 0.1 is the total probability of the reciprocal Propensities (both) being mutually manifested. Do not interpret me as saying, absurdly, that there are independent probabilities here, or any quite independent events in the offing, say that there should obtain a total probability of (0.1×0.1), a probability of 0.01. Not that I expect you to do that; but, still, it's nice to be explicit.

all, it may be very well worth the undertaking, if only because it might provide another thinker, relevantly far more able than I, with a way to uncover some fruitful new conceptions, quite beyond what I'm ever able to discern, contrive, imagine, or uncover.

With all that in mind, I now turn to describe another employment of our idea of Power-directed Power, related to those we've already observed.

5. Power-directed Powers and Probabilistic Propensities of Very Low Degree

The Section before the one just previous, that is, the Section on how Power-Directed Powers May Distinctively Distinguish Among Other Powers, was quite a long Section, providing, I think, a very clear, detailed and quite thorough discussion. Because it did all that, we may now hope to provide, in a rather short Section, a perfectly adequate discussion of how our notion of Power-directed Powers may be a very powerful notion, relevantly far more powerful than any more directly "surveyable notions," or any ideas that may afford just some *more commonly* accessible instruction or explication.

Once again, we'll consider five Worlds, each with Large Red Spheres and Small Blues. And, in each, when a Small Blue is nearby a Large Red, the Small Sphere spins. As before, in four of these Worlds, the Small Blue's spinning isn't a random matter. Rather, in each case, it's the manifestation of a Power, possessed by a nearby Large Red, for spinning certain nearby things. But, this time things will be notably different, and in just the following sorts of ways (here indicated only through a representative example, rather than through anything like exhaustive specification).

So, for example, in the Second (sort of) World, before, a Large Red was, quite simply, Propensitied for spinning any (nearby) concretum that's Blue (and, as well, it was, quite simply, Propensitied for *not* spinning any *other sort* of concretum). By contrast with what's quite simple Propensitively, in the current Second (sort of) World, a Large Red is, maybe not so simply, *Probabilistically Propensitied* for just such effects. And, what's more, it's only a "Very Weak" Probabilistic Propensity that these Large Reds possess, say, it's a Probabilistic Propensity, only to degree 0.1, for spinning a (nearby) Blue concretum. Accordingly, and in the same bargain, these Large Reds each also has a "Very Strong" Probabilistic Propensity, precisely to degree 0.9, *for not* spinning (even a nearby) Blue Concretum. And, so it goes: Wherever there

was, before, a certain Propensity for spinning, there is, with our currently considered Worlds, only a Very Weak Probabilistic Propensity
for such spinning, along with, correlatively, a Very Strong Probabilistic
Propensity for *not* spinning. Still, in all our current Worlds—except, of
course, for the "minimal control group," our Fifth (sort of) World—
well, in all these (first four sorts of) Worlds, with all their Large Reds
and their many nearby spinning Small Blues, this remains true: The
spinning of the Small Blues, and it is actually going on quite ram-
pantly, well that just *isn't any random happenstance*. Rather it's the (unlikely) manifestation of the Large Red's (Very Weak) Probabilistic
Propensities for spinning certain concreta. And, in each (of these first
four sorts of) World, it's a different Very Weak Probabilistic Propensity
for spinning that's manifested—each precisely as Weak as the probability 0.1 is Low. Of course, the differences run along precisely the lines
that, in such a thorough way, we delineated for our previously considered group of such "lookalike" Worlds.

With these present Worlds, it should be clear, we can't give anything
like the easy explications that, just a couple of Sections ago, we were so
readily able to provide—quite sketchily, to be sure, but quite happily
enough even so. Why? With a Large Red that's so Very Weakly Probabilistically Propensitied to spin Blue Individuals, just to the degree 0.1,
what are we to expect from any Large Blue Sphere as may be instructively
introduced? We certainly won't have it that such a Large Blue Sphere will
be spinning. No; not even should it be ever so near each of four Large
Reds, all at once, will we have anything like that. Rather, even as any such
Large Blue *will itself be only Very Weakly Probabilistically* Propensitied *to be
spun*, so it will be so Propensitied *just to degree 0.1*. And, so, it's quite
unlikely, in the case of any of the Large Blue Spheres, that it will be a
spinning individual. This will be quite unlikely even if it should be placed
very near a (Very Low Probability) Type B Fairly Selective Spinner, the
best it can hope for, so far as specified spinning goes, in the Second (sort
of) currently considered World. Just so, now all we'll have, with a hopefully instructive conditional (sentence) is something like this: If a Large
Blue Sphere were to be near one of *these* (Very Low Probability) Large
Red Spheres, then, or even then, *it probably wouldn't spin*, or it *probably
won't* spin. (Similarly, if a Large Blue Sphere *were to have been* near one of
these Large Reds, then, or even then, it *probably wouldn't have* spun.) Just as
I've been suggesting, what worked so handily before or, maybe better,
may have only seemed to do so, now *won't even appear* to work, not even in
the least bit, it won't, not even at all.

But, in a perfect parallel with what we did before, here, too, we can
provide our other sort of instructive exercise, where what we centrally

employ are apt notions of Power-directed Powers. This time around, in giving each sort of specification for a different Large Gold Sphere's apt Power-directed Power, we'll just have to use a few more words than before. Just so, for our Second (sort of) Gold Sphere, which we'll continue to have as our nice Worldly Representative for the whole group of (sorts of) Worlds, we'll now specify matters, just enough to be most helpfully instructive.

A Second (sort of) Gold Sphere, also present in all five (sorts of) Worlds, is Propensitied dynamically with respect to just such Large Red Spheres as are *any sort at all of Type B* (*B* for Blue) Fairly Fastidious Spinners, even should they be only Very Low Probability Type B Spinners. And, quite as with our previously considered Second (sort of) Worlds, so, now too, the Second Gold Spheres will be Propensitied for Attracting just certain Large Reds. But, of course, now they'll be Propensitied to Attract *any sort at all of Type B* (*B* for Blue) Fairly Fastidious Spinners, even those with only a Very Weak Probabilistic Type B Propensity. So, even each of our currently considered five (sorts of) Worlds will have (right soon) a Gold Type-B-Fairly-Fastidious-Spinner-Attractor (even as, each will also have, quite as well, four other (sorts of) Correlatively Propensitied Large Golds).

It's quite easy, as you can see, to specify, correlatively, Properly Powerful Large Golds of the other (currently wanted) four sorts. So, even with Very Low Probabilistic Propensities, it's easy for us to repeat, with much the same solid upshot we obtained previously, a quite deeply instructive sort of instructional exercise. Let's do it.

We'll begin with this little passage, pretty largely repetitive: Though it's now such a terribly unlikely thing, still, quite as with our Five Worlds before, throughout their histories so far, and from time immemorial, each of our five currently considered (sorts of) Worlds has been, for our conceiving's experiential aspect, precisely like all the others. All the same, each World has been, (Probabilistically) Propensitively, very unlike each of the others. In just a minute, each World will acquire five Large Gold Spheres, one of each of our newly, and very highly, specified five Propensitive types. And, just when as any Gold sphere finds a suitably matched Propensity partner, just then will its own peculiarly telltale Propensity be manifested, straightaway and lickety-split, with all the Large Reds for which it's dynamically Propensitied.

Using our same representative example, our (Probabilistic) Second (sort of) World, we'll now obtain, of course, the *very same full-blooded upshot* that we obtained before, when considering a relevantly *Nonprobabilistic* Second (sort of) World. To refresh your mind, I'll rehearse this full-blooded upshot, with a just few apt changes of wording: In our Second (sort of) Probabilistic World, a Large Gold Type-B-Fairly-Fastidious-Spinner Attractor is the only Gold Sphere with an apt Power-directed Power. As it's only this Gold Sphere that here finds Propensity partners, here in this Second (sort of Probabilistic) World, all this Probabilistic World's Large Reds are Attracted, quite simply and surely, towards just this Large Gold Sphere, without any Large Red being Rotated, or any being Repelled, or any Changing Color, or any Changing Shape.

It's an awfully nice result that we've obtained, so distinctively, by employing our distinctively useful notion of Power-directed Powers. For doing serious metaphysics, I'll suggest, this notion may be a centrally important conception.

Look here, now: I don't want to spend almost all of our Fifth Chapter going on about this business. But, it may be well worth our while, I'll suggest, to spend one more Section mainly focused on how we may be philosophically benefited, in a fashion that's quite distinctive to the conception, by this philosophically central idea, this notion of Power-directed Powers.

6. Powers Are Nonconditional, Including Powers to Acquire and Lose (Other) Powers

Thank goodness, many philosophers have, by now, quite given up on any search for "a conditional analysis of dispositions"—a hopelessly misguided task, if ever there was one.[5] But, it's still true, I'm afraid, that many think there's something interestingly conditional, or inherently conditional, about Propensities. But, whatever it might mean for something to be interestingly conditional, or inherently conditional, that's all just so much philosophically superficial hogwash.

For just a few moments, think about this little story: Tom is a triangular tile, with two big flat faces, top and bottom, and also with three skinny "more edgy" faces, its three mere sides, as we say. Tom sat alone in a certain drawer, a drawer named Dave, until Tom was

5. The *locus classicus* of work against "conditional analyses of dispositions" is C. B. Martin, "Dispositions and Conditionals," *Philosophical Quarterly*, 1994. Also, though on the wrong side of the issue, see David Lewis, "Finkish Dispositions," *Philosophical Quarterly*, 1997. Finally for now, and on the right side of this issue, see, first, George Molnar's paper "Are Dispositions Reducible?" *Philosophical Quarterly*, 1999; and see, next and especially, his fine and stimulating book, the posthumously published *Powers*, Oxford University Press, 2003, focusing on pages 83–94.

pulverized, or maybe even utterly annihilated. All right, so Tilewise Tom was triangular—even as, more fully, or more perspicuously, Tom was a five-sided voluminous concretum. Then, of course, we'll have this conditional holding true: *If there had been* placed in Dave, and right next to Tom, a square tile—that is, a tile with big flat faces, top and bottom, and *four* skinny "more edgy" faces—and this occurred without inducing any intrinsic Change in any concretum, not in Tom, not in Dave, and so on, well, *then there would have been* placed, right there in Dave, and right next to Tom, a tile with one more side than Tom had. Or, at the least, something very like is true. So what? Should we conclude from this, or from anything much like it, that there's something interestingly conditional about how it is that an individual is *Shaped?* I sure don't think so.

Why, then, have so many philosophers thought that there's something very interestingly conditional about how it is that an individual's Propensitied, or Disposed? Well, no doubt, there are various reasons here. But, what's been most forcefully operative on (most of) these benighted thinkers? Here's my partial diagnosis: Not only with the highly alert likes of a David Lewis, but also, and maybe more so, with ever so many quite pedestrian practitioners, there's been prevalent, for many decades, a Quasi-Humean craving for human "surveyability," as I've been calling it. In any event, this craving is a philosophically ill condition. Get over it.

Those who persist in such a nutty idea will, I'm sure, become embroiled with a lot of confused philosophy. And, what may be worse, they're apt to miss out on quite a bit of pretty decent philosophy. In a discussion that's entertaining enough to be engaging, I'll try to make that clear.

In the Eleventh Section of Chapter Three, we addressed the question, Can There Be Spatially Extensible Yellow Entities That Aren't Ever Propensitied? Quite rightly, I think, we provided the question with a negative answer. As you may recall, we arrived at this answer through considering certain nicely Propensitied concreta that we aptly labeled Yellow-Attractors (and also by considering certain others that might be labeled, just as aptly, Yellow-Annihilators, and, then, Sphere-Attractors, and Sphere-Annihilators, and so on). Probably, you remember that. Heck, rather than take any chances here, I'll just rehearse, verbatim, this paragraph from that Section:

> For any question concerning an utter lack of all Propensity, on the
> part of any considered concretum, we must consider not only what
> might transpire in connection with such other individuals as may

actually inhabit its World, and may do so simultaneously, but we must also consider such further-fetched concreta as may exist only in other possible Worlds or, not quite so terribly far afield, as may exist only in other Eras, or Eons. So, much as we did just a Section or two ago, we may imagine a variety of Yellow-Attractors, some of them also Spheres, some of them Cubes, and whatnot. Now, when we're imagining a Yellow Sphere, I submit, then we must be imagining, right in the bargain, a Sphere that's Propensitied to be attracted to, or by, any concretum that's a Yellow-Attractor, though we needn't be imagining, of course, that the supposed Yellow Sphere ever gets the chance to be suitably partnered with any Yellow-Attractor, so that there's ever a real attractive interaction involving the imagined Yellow concretum. So, with any supposed Yellow concretum, we must be supposing, in the bargain, a concretum that's Propensitied to be attracted by any concretum that's Propensitied to attract Yellow individuals—and, in the bargain, a concretum that's Propensitied to be rotated by any particular that's Categorically Disposed to rotate Yellow concreta, and so on.[6]

All right, so now I can be sure you're right with me on this.

Now, in reply to our fine argument, for the truth that all Spatially Extensible Yellow concreta must be Propensitied individuals, someone might object, in some such beguiling terms as these: Who can say whatever may be going on with all this Propensitive business you're mongering? Look, instead of how you want to have things be, it seems that, just as well, things might be quite a different way, supposing that there are any real differences in all this Propensitive falderal. Instead of its really being that the so-called Yellow-Attractors are ever attracting Yellow concreta, what may happen is something rather more complicated, but with just the same apparent upshot. For example, just consider a World that, while it has several Maroon Spheres, has no Yellow concreta at all. But, just as soon as a so-called Yellow-Attractor comes into being—or, if it already exists, then, just as soon as it comes to be near enough, or whatever—the Maroon Spheres all acquire, just as *they're* Propensitied *then* to do, the Propensity to be attracted by, and to, the Yellow-Attractor. Well, then, *they'll then be* attracted to the so-called Yellow-Attractor, just as much as would any (originally) Yellow concretum. So, what the heck is going on here? Can there be any genuine Propensitive difference, really, between these Propensitively active Maroon objects and the supposedly not so Propensitively active originally Yellow individuals? To my mind, it seems not. So, as far as I

---

6. The quoted passage is from Section 11 of Chapter 3 above.

can tell, all this Propensity business is just a lot of senseless hocus-pocus. Let's give up on all that stuff, and return to what may be more nicely Humean ways or, at least, to what may be less peculiarly metaphysical.

All right, all right; let's calm down a bit. If we're patient about all this, perhaps we may see that, rather than any confusion attending our offered Propensitive thinking, and our argument against there being any Propensityless Yellow entities, it's this objector's thoughts that are all in a fog.

Look, right off the bat, we must say this about our presumed originally Maroon Spheres. It wasn't just sheer happenstance that they became Propensitied for attraction by a Yellow-Attractor, by a concretum that's Propensitied to attract anything that's Yellow. Rather, their becoming just so Propensitied was, in our objector's scenario, the manifestation of *another* Propensity. And, quite clearly, this *other* Propensity is, or it was, a Disposition *they already had*. So, right off the bat, one thing we know is that these presumed Maroons certainly weren't ever any Propensityless concreta. Whatever else might be said of them, or might not, they certainly aren't any counterexample to the claim that all Spatially Extensibly Qualitied concreta must be Propensitied individuals. Heck, they're at least as Propensitied as anything's ever been. And, metaphysics fans, we're just warming up.

What's more, we can say quite a lot about what Propensity it was that, right from the get-go, was possessed by the presumed Maroons. Right from the start, they had a certain Propensity to acquire another Propensity, to wit, the Propensity to be attracted by Yellow-Attractors. Nor are we wholly ignorant about the nature of this acquisitive Propensity, right there in all our Maroons, right from the get-go. Just for one thing, we know a lot about its conditions of manifestation. It will be manifested when (and, just maybe, only when, but maybe not) there exist some Yellow-Attractors. (Or, on our other version of the example, they'll be manifested when existing Yellow-Attractors are within a certain distance of the richly Propensitied Maroons.) And, philosophy aficionados, we're still just warming up.

In the obviously intended version of this scenario, when the Maroons acquire their Propensity to be attracted, by the likes of a Yellow-Attractor, they change so that this is quite fully ensured. They undergo *just such* a change that, once it's taken place in them, *they'll be* attracted, and that's that. It's certainly *not* that, as it just coincidentally happened, a presumed Yellow-Attractor was *also a Cube-Attractor* and, it was *for this* reason that the presumed Maroons became, for the (Yellow-Attractor) Cube-Attractor, some suitably attractive Propensity partners. Heck no;

that would be to change the whole darned subject! So, sticking to the subject, the point is that the Maroons became *Propensitied to be attracted by just such concreta as are Yellow-Attractors* (whatever else those concreta also might be.) Well, jeepers creepers, folks, it's pretty obvious, when you think about it, what sort of individuals those are, the ones that, as *must needs be*, are of *just such* a sort as will be *attracted* by any and all *Yellow-Attractors*. They're *Yellow* individuals, of course. So, in acquiring their presumably new Propensity, our presumed original Maroon Spheres *became Yellow* Spheres. [Of course, it's not that their (having their) newly acquired Propensity *is* (their being) Yellow. Nor is it, of course, that any Propensity of theirs, ever possessed by them, at any time, is any Quality, at all. No; as we've seen several times over, nothing like that can ever be in the cards.]

Just so, the Maroons acquired just that Propensity that's necessarily coextensive, everywhere and everywhen, with being Spatially Extensibly Qualitied exactly as just all the Yellow things are. But, of course, and quite as I've already said, this can obtain only if the Maroons became Yellow individuals. And, so, in acquiring their (proposed) new Propensity, *that's exactly what* the Maroons became. No longer being any Maroon concreta, *they all became Yellow individuals*.

Now, as should be plain, there's all the difference in the world between *being Yellow*, all along, and, on the other hand, (changing from being Maroon, or from being White, for that matter and) *becoming Yellow*. And, as we can now so plainly see, there's just as much difference between *being Propensitied*, all along, to be attracted by Yellow-Attractors and, on the other hand, (changing from not being so Propensitied and) *becoming so Propensitied*. So, as is now perfectly plain, there's all the difference in the world between *being Propensitied*, all along, to be attracted by Yellow-Attractors and, on the other hand, *becoming so Propensitied*.

As I indicated, there's nothing here that's special to questions about Qualities. And, quite equally, the lessons just learned aren't confined to questions of acquiring Propensities, as against, for instance, losing Dispositions.

To drive home all this Section's central points, in all their full generality, it will be enough to consider just this one more example. So, let's contemplate some 22-sided solid concreta, where "solid" means 3-D, as in the phrase "solid geometry." Now, to put things quite dramatically, they're all "in danger of" being Rotated by some impending 22-sider-Rotators. But, very easily, we may greatly decrease the drama, and the so-called danger. For, very easily, we may also suppose this further Propensity for the 22-siders that we're contemplating: They are

Propensitied to become 24-sided, whenever they should encounter any 22-sider-Rotator. Well, then, because they'll no longer be 22-sided, *they won't* be Rotated by any 22-sider-Rotators, even if ever these 22-siders should ever encounter such Propensitied concreta. For, the very encounter that will *have them be partnered* will, in the bargain, have them *become unsuitable* interaction partners, so far as induced Rotating goes, for the 22-sider Rotators.

The difference between just plain having a certain Propensity and, on the other side, gaining that same Propensity, well, that's just a perfectly real, categorical, and nonconditional difference. And, equally, so is the difference between having a certain Disposition and losing that same Propensity. It's quite as nonconditional, really, as the difference between being 22-sided and, on the other hand, being 24-sided. In other words, it's perfectly nonconditional, not the least bit conditional at all. And, possibly excepting some rare and tricky exceptions, so it is with all Propensities. They are absolutely nonconditional features of concreta, just as are Shapes, and Qualities, and anything else you might care correctly to name.[7]

As it strikes me, it's quite interesting, really, to see how our idea of Power-Directed Powers comports so nicely with this Section's central themes. Twice over, this can be done quickly, and clearly, and quite decisively, too.

First, consider a World that has both Yellow Spheres, already Propensitied to be Attracted by Yellow-Attractors, and also Maroon Spheres, so far just set to acquire that Propensity, upon the presence of Yellow-Attractors. Into this World, there may first appear, just a little later, two Large Silver Spheres, each Propensitively very different from each other. One of the Silver Spheres *attracts*, towards itself, anything that's Propensitied to be attracted by a Yellow-Attractor; but, with (respect to) anything that lacks that very Propensity, it's Propensitied *not to interact dynamically*. By contrast, the other Silver Sphere repels, away from *itself*, anything that, even while it lacks the aforesaid Propensity originally (or it lacks it at the relevantly ripe time) is Propensitied to acquire that Propensity on condition that there be (or there near enough be) Yellow-Attractors; as regards *any other concreta*, it's Propensitied *not* to repel them. Then, whether or not there ever actually are any Yellow-Attractors, in the same World with our considered Yellows and Maroons, or in the same Eon, there will be, between our Yellows

7. As with many of this Chapter's other Sections, my thinking about this was greatly influenced by C. B. "Charlie" Martin and, more recently, by his student, and also my student, Neil Williams.

and our Maroons, *this manifested* Propensitive difference. The Yellows will all move *toward a certain* Silver Sphere and, in very marked contrast with that, the Maroons will all move *away from a certain other* Silver Sphere. (If our two Silver Spheres are always close together, then all the Yellows will move toward their little area and all the Maroons will move away from that tiny neighborhood.) To my mind, at least, that's both forcefully instructive and instructively forceful.

Next, consider a World with both *Blue 22-sided solids*, currently "in danger of" being Rotated by (not necessarily yet present) 22-sider-Rotators, and also *Blue 24-sided solids*, already "safe from" being Rotated by 22-sider-Rotators. Of course, our 22-siders also have *this following* Disposition: They're Disposed to *lose their Propensity* to be Rotated by any 22-sider-Rotators, and they're Disposed to *gain the Propensity not* to be Rotated by any such objects, which Disposition(s) will be manifested providing only that there exist (or that there be near enough, or whatever else you may most like here) some 22-sider Ro-tators. Now, as we may further suppose, quite specifically, should *this* Disposition of these 22-siders be manifested, then, in that very same event, they'll all *become 24-siders*. Anyhow, into this supposed World, there may first appear, just a little later, two Large Bronze Spheres, each Propensitively very different from each other. One of the Bronze Spheres suddenly turns *White* any concretum that's Propensitied to be Rotated by 22-sider-Rotators. And, with (respect to) what lacks that very Propensity, it's Propensitied *not to interact dynamically* at all. Just so, it's Propensitied *not* to induce Change of Color in any 22-sider (and also, of course, in any 24-sider) that's not Propensitied to be Rotated by 22-sider-Rotators. By contrast, the other Bronze Sphere turns *Red* just those concreta that, all along, *lack* the Propensity to be Spun by 22-sider-Rotators. So, whether or not there ever actually are any 22-sider Rotators—in a relevantly chosen World, or in an aptly selected Eon—there will be, between our original 22-siders and our original 24-siders, *this manifested* Propensitive difference. The 22-siders will all suddenly change Color, from Blue to *White*, while the 24-siders, by contrast, will all Change from Blue to *Red*.

While the main point made by this example is the same as the prime point of the case just before, the one featuring the Yellows and the Maroons, we get a nice bonus with this second case that, I think, wasn't provided with our first example. Briefly, I'll try to explain my meaning here.

Now, at least without the help of some terrifically effective visual aids, I simply can't attain any very clear conception, or any very full idea, of any 22-sided solids; and, likewise, for 24-sided solids. And, insofar as I have any success here at all, and do attain some just decently clear and full ideas, that's very heavily due to the intellectual aspect of my conceiving. As far as just my conceiving's experiential aspect goes, and without the use of terrific aids, I'm not up to conceiving 22-siders any differently from how it is that I conceive 24-siders. So, in very salient experiential regards, I'm much less successful here than I am with my conceiving of Yellow Spheres, and also Maroon Spheres. So, in a certain salient respect, I find the present exercise even more forcefully instructive, and more instructively forceful, than was the just previous helpful activity. Indeed, toward seeing the philosophic utility of Power-directed Powers, who could ask for anything more?

Even before this Section's involvement with Power-directed Powers, we saw strong reason, I submit, for thinking that a concretum's Propensity is just as nonconditional a matter as the concretum's Shape; each is *perfectly nonconditional*. Or, to use a positive (sounding) term, how it is with something Propensitively is a perfectly *categorical* matter. So, in the Section's second half, we certainly didn't *discover* that. Still, for those who like clarity in systematic metaphysics, it was very nice to observe, I'll suggest, how well our Section's first half comports with its second, where, quite rightly, I'll also suggest, our focus was trained on Power-directed Powers.

For the nonce, I'll stop discussing Power-directed Powers, returning to employ this notion only quite a bit later in the Chapter. In the bargain, I'll return to what is, or to what first was, our Chapter's main line of discussion. So once again, I return to consider the Hypothesis that All Physical Propensities concern only Something as to Quality. And, well beyond that, I'll also discuss a much less beleaguered proposition, a statement that's in very much the same philosophical spirit.

7. Standard Scientific Thinking and Generalistically-directed Propensities

As I've already argued, we should reject the Hypothesis that All Physical Propensities concern Something as to Qualities, however appealing that philosophic conjecture may initially appear. And, as I've been saying, I mean to offer, in this Chapter, quite decisive points against any such claim. Now's the time to make good on that offer or, at the least, to make a solid start in that direction.

To begin, we may want a very worthy target now, at which to aim those points that, at least as against the beleaguered Hypothesis, we may take to be perfectly decisive. For, toward gaining philosophical understanding, we should aim for just such decisive points as may have quite general application, not points that are, or that even seem to be, tailor-made for undermining just the Hypothesis that All Physical Propensities concern Something as to Qualities.

Rather than anything much like that, we should want to target an Hypothesis that, even while it's in something of the same spirit as the already-rejected conjecture, is a much more general proposition. And, what's more, it should generalize in just such ways as will have it be, at least apparently, an intuitively plausible hypothesis and, as well, a metaphysically important proposition. For those reasons, and maybe more, too, I'll suggest that we should now consider some such statement as:

> *The Hypothesis that All Physical Propensities concern only General Features of Entities.* Whenever a physical entity has a Propensity with regard to physical reality, the power always concerns *only some general feature, or features, of some physical things* (either some general features of such entities as are its disposition partners or, in a more special case, some general features of the physical entity itself).

As I understand this Hypothesis, which is logically less ambitious than its rejected predecessor, it guides all ongoing scientific attempts to understand physical reality, or almost all.

If this Hypothesis provides any real guidelines, there must be some "possibilities" it will have us to ignore. What might they be?

Return to consider, for a moment, our familiarly electronish Small Blues. With each Small Blue perfectly similar to any other, each is set to repel *any other* Small Blue there may be, if only the other should be suitably situated in relation to the Propensitied-Repellor, as with being spatially near enough. And, each Small Blue is set to attract any protonish Large Red there may be, if only the Large Red should be suitably situated in relation to the Propensitied-Attractor. With any Blue electron, then, it's *not* true that there's just a *certain* Red proton that it's disposed to attract. It's *not* that the Blue electron's quite inert, with respect to attracting, all the other protonish Red Particles, no matter how favorably situated. That "possibility," our Hypothesis counsels, should be ignored. Nor is any electron set just to favor a *certain seven* protons, or just a certain seven trillion, being inert, with respect to attracting, any other Red Particles, beyond them. Such a "possibility," our Hypothesis counsels, also should be ignored. Just so, each Small Blue is Propensitied with respect to only *general features* of

Large Red Particles; and each is Propensitied with respect to just *general features* of other Small Blues; and so on.

Now, let's turn to physically *complex* entities (still continuing to suppose, of course, that there really are such physically derivative individuals). On our *standard scientific thinking*, reflected in our familiar Scientiphicalism, all the powers of these complexes will be, of course, physically derivative Propensities, or Powers, derivative from the basic physical properties, saliently the basic Propensities, of their fundamental physical constituents and, equally important, from the (sufficiently basic) physical relations among those basic components.

As a nice instance of that, let's consider a pretty complex device of my modestly imaginative devising, a *Videotaping Security Box*. This is a sturdy lock-box that includes, as a central part, a video-camera taping system. Now, when an ordinary complex object is placed in the Box, as with my paperback copy of Hume's *Treatise*, the camera will make a taped record of that very copy. Then, there will be a videotape of *just my* copy of the book, not the (suppose) precisely similar copy that belongs to my colleague. But, though there is thus a (videotape) impression of *just my copy*, that's owing to Propensities of the interacting complexes *with respect to general features of physical things*. (In the physical realm, there are various physical patterns produced in such a way that, quite aptly, we may call them "impressions." So it is with the photographic pattern of my book on the considered videotape.) Now, had it been my colleague's precisely similar copy that was in the Security Box, at the time we've just been supposing, then, instead of interacting with my copy, the Box would have interacted with *that other* copy of the *Treatise*. And, it would have done that in just precisely the way that, as we've supposed, it did interact with my copy. Supposing everything to be precisely similar in the two cases, in all general features or respects, there would then have been produced on the videotape, in such a numerically different circumstance, just an impression of *only that other* copy of the *Treatise*, precisely similar to the impression of my copy that, on our suppositions, was the impression actually produced.

Whenever there's produced a physical impression of a physical object, we Scientiphicalists suppose, the identity of the physical object impressed—*which* object it *is*—will be determined by which physical object is in the place at which (the relevant part of) the impressing system is appropriately directed, at the time of the impressing. This is true whether the system is inanimate or whether, as with your conscious perception of visible material things, it involves you. But, of course, there needn't be anything mysterious here, or suspiciously nonphysical. For, much as we believe, it's only certain *Generalistically-directed* Propensities, or, for short, it's just certain *Generalistic Powers*, that are manifested in the processes producing physical impressions. Just so, when there's a physical impression produced *of just a certain physical particular*, and not any other physical individual, no matter how like the impressed object, then, characteristically, it's because a camera, for instance, or an observer, is "confronting" the object photographed, or observed. Of course, that's a terribly sketchy verbal gesture, as the scare-quotes highlight. But, the gesture's point is pretty clear: Which physical object a camera photographs, and which is the one you sense, will depend on which individuals are in which particular places, at the particular times in question, as well as upon certain *Generalistically-directed* Powers of the objects involved. Just so, any particularity in such a situation will derive, quite completely, from facts about which particular things are in which particular places, and from other systematically related spatial (or other dimensional?) considerations. They will not derive, by contrast, from the very character of the Propensities being manifested, as these are all just Generalistically-directed Propensities. Or, so says our Scientiphicalism. And, a bit more explicitly, so says the Hypothesis that All Physical Propensities concern only General Features of Entities.

By this point, you should have a pretty fair idea, I imagine, of the Hypothesis that All Physical Propensities concern only General Features of Entities. In the next Section, I'll try to notice a possibility that contravenes this Hypothesis and, as I'll suggest, that does so quite decisively.

8. Individualistically-directed Propensities

In a certain possible World, there may be a certain single Small Blue Particle that strongly attracts, and that's strongly attracted by, only a *certain single* Large Red Particle. This particular Small Blue, that we're so singularly imagining, *won't* strongly attract *any other entity at all*, other than the aforementioned Large Red, no matter how Large, or how Red, or however nicely situated, any such other individual ever might be. And, for its part, this selfsame Large Red Particle may be strongly attracted by (and it may strongly attract) only this one Small Blue Particle, and not any other individual thing, no matter how like this Blue Sphere, in all *its Generalistic* features, any other concretum may be, and no matter how nicely situated may be any other (such terribly similar Small Blue) concrete particular.

Let's imagine, now, that our original Large Red is suddenly whisked far away, even into a galaxy that's many light-years distant. And, as we're imagining, in what was that Large Red's place just a moment ago, there's now *another* Large Red, precisely like the first in all Generalistic respects—it's precisely as Large, and it's precisely as Red, and so on. Will our selected Small Blue strongly attract, or be strongly attracted by, this precisely similar Johnny-come-lately? No, it *won't*; not in a World just as the one I've just specified. To be sure, our Scientiphicalism urges otherwise. And, more explicitly, so does our noted Hypothesis. But, those may be just the dictates of some apparently quite optional propositions.

How shall we characterize how it is Propensitively with these peculiarly finicky particulars? By contrast with concrete particulars that are all just Generalistically Propensitied, we may say they're *Individualistically Propensitied* Individuals or, for short, concreta with *Individualistic Powers*.

By contrast with concreta for which our usual Propensitive thinking suffices, which I've called our standard scientific thinking, to treat finicky particulars adequately, we must think in a more unusual manner. Because it's so unusual, I'll take pains to clarify how it proceeds.

Suppose that, several light-years apart from each other, there are two Blue Spheres that may each be physically divided, Blue Boy First Mentioned and Blue Boy Next Mentioned. Suppose further that, at the same time, each Sphere divides in just such a way that what was one hundredth of its matter, before the division, comes to form a Very Small Sphere, and, what was ninety-nine hundredths forms a Fairly Large Sphere. So, the matter of Blue Boy First Mentioned thus comes to form Very Small Sphere Number One and Fairly Large Sphere Number One; and, the matter of Blue Boy Next Mentioned forms two other Spheres, correlatively featured and correlatively named. Now, in all Generalistic respects, each Fairly Large Sphere is precisely similar to the other, we may suppose, and each Very Small Sphere also is, in those respects, precisely similar to the other. But, even as not all Propensities are Generalistic Powers, so there may be this diversity concerning how the newly arrived Spheres are mutually Propensitied: Providing only that they're within a light-year of each other, Fairly Large Sphere Number One will spin *only* Very Small Sphere Number One. And, providing only that *they're* no more than a light-year apart, Fairly Large Sphere Number *Two* will spin *just* Very Small Sphere Number *Two*. In any other event than what's just been specified, each Very Small Sphere won't spin. Well, near the beginning of our contemplated scenario, as we may imagine, the first Fairly Large Sphere *is* so close to the first Very Small Sphere, and the second *is* so close to the second. So, during this early interval, both Very Small Spheres are spinning. Then, the first Very Small Sphere changes places with the second Very Small Sphere (maybe owing to the sudden act of an Almighty God). Anyway, just as soon as that happens, both Very Small Spheres stop spinning. And, unless a Very Small Sphere once again comes to be suitably close to "*its own* Fairly Large origination partner," that Very Small Sphere won't ever spin again.

This is very different, I imagine, from how it is that, in almost all our thinking, we suppose matters to proceed in any physical realm, or reality. As our usual thinking goes, whatever particularity may be involved in the interaction among physical concreta, that will be determined by which particular places are the locations of which physical individuals, at which particular times, along with Generalistic features of the concreta in question, including their Generalistic Powers. Or, at the least, something to a similar effect will be in effect. Accordingly, the notion of Individualistically-directed Powers doesn't figure greatly in our usual thinking, including our standard scientific thinking, at least not insofar as such thinking concerns only physical concreta. But, perhaps this is just a needlessly restrictive feature of this apparently optional thinking.

Let's be very clear here; these certainly are real Propensities, not anything relational. Just so, nothing less than all this must surely be so: Consider, for a few moments, the Propensity of a certain Very Small Sphere to be spun by just its originating Fairly Large Sphere, a Disposition I'm calling an Individualistically-directed Propensity of this Very Small individual. Is this Propensity a *relational* property of this particular Very Small concretum, and *not an intrinsic* feature of this Very Small individual? No; the Propensity in question isn't anything relational. And, yes; it is an intrinsic feature of this Very Small thing. What does this mean? Well, suppose that, a bit later, the aforementioned Fairly Large Sphere is utterly annihilated, so that it ceases to exist, completely and forever, whereas the correlative Very Small Sphere continues to exist. Now, even though its originating Fairly Large Sphere doesn't exist any more, this bereft Very Small Sphere *still has the Individualistically-directed Propensity*, the Disposition to be spun by just that erstwhile (and presently nonexistent) individual. It's just that, from now on, there *won't ever again be any manifestation of* that Individualistically-directed Propensity of the bereft individual.

So, while there are important differences between the two, there are these parallels between Individualistic Dispositions and, on the other side, Generalistic Powers: In *both* cases, the Propensity in question is intrinsic to the entity whose Propensity it is; the entity's having the propensity doesn't require, in either case, the existence of any other concreta. And, also in *both* cases, there's something *else*, in the *neighborhood* of the Propensity, that *does* require there to be an appropriate external entity, or entities. This is, of course, the *manifestation* of the Propensity in question, a manifestation that must involve, by hypothesis, the *interaction between* (or the *interaction among*) reciprocally Propensitied partners. And, of course, such an interaction must be, in both cases alike, a perfectly relational occurrence, wherein a certain particular (or just some certain specific particulars) is conducively related to a certain other individual (or to just some certain other particular individuals). But, that's not required for simply *being Propensitied for* such interaction. Not even when a particular's Propensity is Individualistically-directed, then, will the concretum's *just having* the Propensity be anything that's relational, or extrinsic, or external.

Among Individualistically-directed Propensities, or Individualistic Powers, we may note that some may be *Strong(ly)* Individualistically-directed Powers. They'll have all the apparently peculiar features of those that aren't so strong, along with some others, too: Suppose that a certain particular Fairly Large Red, let's call it "Len" is Propensitied to attract, and Len's Propensitied to be attracted by, a certain single Very Small Blue, that's called "Sergei." And, suppose that Len may radically change, even in all sorts of intrinsic respects, even while Len still continues to exist. Even while still continuing to exist, we're supposing, Len may become Small, and Len may become Blue, and so on. Now, since Len and Sergei are each *Strongly* Individualistically-directed, for attracting each other, we're supposing that, even with all of this alteration, Len and Sergei will still be Propensitied for just such reciprocal interaction. And, for its part, a very changeable Sergei also will continue to be, throughout ever so many large Generalistic changes, in ever so many Generalistic respects, just so Individualistically Propensitied, for attracting Len. Due to Sergei's Propensity to retain that very Propensity, and a correlative Propensity on Len's part, all this will be so, just so long as Sergei exists, and Len also exists.[8]

---

8. Consider a parent's love for her particular child. That love may be quite unconditional love; even if the child suffers great brain damage, and his mind is greatly diminished, still his mother may so strongly love the child. And, this love may not transfer to, or not transfer very much to, a precise duplicate of the original child, known by the mother to have replaced her brain-damaged child—or yet more dramatically, her utterly annihilated child—as with a perfect duplicate of her originally normally healthy child, the duplicate instantly arriving from a distant galaxy, perhaps, owing to the replacement activity of a misguided wizard.

Analogies are, of course, just analogies. And, quite generally, wherever there's a mere analogy, not an identity, there's also a disanalogy. Still, often an analogy can be helpful. As is my hope, the one just offered may be, for quite a few readers, pretty helpful right now.

For most of our discussion, maybe we needn't be much involved with these Strong (Individualistically-directed) Propensities, these Strong Individualistic Powers. So, maybe you needn't bother to keep in mind this technical use of "Strong." Anyway, if we do encounter them, I'll give you a helpful reminder. What should seem important now, at all events, is that we should realize that we might develop, very fully and variously, our ideas of Individualistically-directed Propensities.

To folks gripped by our standard scientific thinking, myself so often included, any idea of Individualistically-directed Propensities may seem utterly incredible. Indeed, any such idea may seem so bizarre as to be worth no serious consideration. Of course, for readers of this book, that won't be any very novel experience. Already, we've had a somewhat similar experience with our idea of Spatially Extensible Quality, and then also with our idea of Propensity with Respect to Quality. Heaping one unsettling idea upon another, am I about to lose your interest, dear reader? My hope is that you'll continue to give my work your thoughtful attention. And, with the next Section's material, I'll aim to sustain this interest of yours, and maybe even increase it.

9. Individualistically-directed Propensities and Cartesian Dualism

In what I hope may be a happily coherent Cartesian frame of mind, I look to appreciate some thoughts at the heart of much modern philosophy. To this end, we'll look to extend our notion of Individualistically-directed Propensities. Specifically, we'll look to extend this idea to some nonphysical individuals, perhaps including, even, some immaterial minds, or truly nonspatial souls.

With a feint toward a little realism, suppose that, some seven months after "your conception," your body first promoted, or it first causally gave rise to, an immaterial mind. This presumed soul will be, of course, just *your* immaterial mind, which your body continues, we'll suppose, to (causally) sustain. As we may also suppose, your body and, more specifically, your brain, interacts with your nonphysical mind in a great variety of ways. You ask, "How can it be that my body interacts with just *my* immaterial mind, and not also with (or even only with) the always very similar soul of My Duplicate, always so similar in all Generalistic respects, whose Generally (or Generalistically) so similar body is many galaxies removed from my body?" (It can't be that my immaterial mind is closer to my body, of course, since this nonspatial soul hasn't any spatial location at all.) Well, the answer lies in our idea of

Individualistically-directed Propensities. Among all the World's many immaterial minds, your body is Propensitied with respect to only the one mind that's your mind, and not with respect to your Duplicate's mind; whereas your Duplicate's body is Propensitied with respect to only *his* mind, and not with regard to yours. And, for its part, of course, your mind is Propensitied with respect to just your body, not any body but yours, while your Duplicate's mind is Propensitied for interaction with just his body. That being so, this will also be so: When your body is stuck with a pin, it's just with *you*, or it's just with *your* immaterial mind, that there's a manifestation of an Individualistically-directed Propensity to feel pain, whereas (suppose) your currently pin-free Duplicate will be, at this time, pain-free, as well. Now, when *you want* to assuage this pain, this (Propensitive) desire of yours will serve to influence just your own body, and not your duplicate's body. For, this other Propensity of yours also will be, of course, aptly Individualistically-directed.

As the previous paragraph makes pretty clear, what we are wont to call "My Duplicate," even in Cartesian scenarios, won't be precisely like me in absolutely all intrinsic respects, including Individualistically-directed respects. And, what we are wont to call "My Duplicate's body" won't really be precisely like my body, either, for it's lacking (on our Cartesian suppositions) the Individualistically-directed Propensities that, in all the physical realm, will be peculiar to just my body. But, then, typical philosophical talk of My Duplicate, or My Duplicate's body, will be as contentious as are any of the propositions that this talk presupposes. And, as I've been suggesting, these will be propositions quite as optional as is the Hypothesis that All Physical Propensities concern only General Features of Entities.

At any rate, I should now notice that, in recent years, many philosophers have sought to show Descartes's Substantial Dualism to be an incoherent metaphysic or, at the least, to be a philosophy not very intelligible to us human beings. Almost all these attempts seem so superficial, to my mind, that I can't imagine how they should merit the effort of serious scrutiny. Not so, however, for those that rely, however implicitly, on the appealing Hypothesis that All Physical Propensities concern only General Features of Entities, or a natural extension of that Hypothesis.[9] Yet, as we now can see, even these not-so-superficial

9. Ernest Sosa is, I believe, one able philosopher who holds that, for having just such a deficiency, it's doubtful that traditional Dualism is coherent. As I understand it, this is a main theme of his essay "Mind-Body Interaction and Supervenient Causation," *Midwest Studies in Philosophy*, 1984.

attempts don't succeed. For, the idea of Individualistically-directed powers, which is a perfectly coherent notion, allows Descartes's Dualism, famously an Interactionist Substantial Dualism, to be a perfectly coherent stance on the issue of how there may be appropriately interacting minds and bodies. (As is apparent from earlier Chapters, I disagree with Descartes on many matters metaphysical. Still and all, I see no serious error in the *Dualistic aspect* of the Worldview he offers.) In later Chapters, this will be important for us.

Our antipathy to Individualistically-directed Propensities, which I myself find hard to overcome, shows how strongly we're gripped by the Hypothesis that All Physical Propensities concern only General Features of Entities. Though it's implicitly accepted by us all, that substantive Hypothesis clearly isn't any purely *conceptual* truth. Indeed, it may be only with something like a *Scientiphical Faith*, I imagine, that we take our actual world to be a world for which the Hypothesis holds true.[10] Rather than always being so Faithful, I'll suggest, it may be more fruitful to take a more truly exploratory attitude toward central questions of first philosophy.

10. Individualistic Propensities and the Intellectual Aspect of Our Conceiving

Before we try to make much more philosophical progress, it may be instructively stimulating, I think, to present a certain singularly imaginative set of philosophical exercises. Of course, quite beyond those that I'll provide, you may develop, for yourself, some complementary exercises, thereby learning still more about the matters they'll all concern, maybe more than I myself now know. Anyhow, much as I did before, in Chapter 4's (Fourteenth) Section on Conceiving Concreta All Qualitied Uniformly, but Propensitied Quite Variously, I'll now provide you with four further intellectual exercises that, as I hope, may be an equally helpful set of conceptual activities.

Quite as we did in that happily imaginative Section, so here, too, we'll contemplate four (sorts of) Worlds. But, of course, in various ways,

10. At least in recent decades, hardly any philosophers have been concerned with thoughts even remotely like our idea of Individualistically-directed Propensities. But, there's at least one who has, John Foster. And, in his book *The Immaterial Self: A Defence of the Cartesian Dualist Conception of the Mind*, Routledge, 1991, Foster employs similar ideas to argue for the coherence of Cartesian Dualism, in the face of what he aptly calls the Problem of Causal Pairings. For Foster's treatment of this Problem, see pages 163–172 of the book.

these will be newly different (sorts of) Worlds, or at least most of them will be. At all events, my exposition will proceed here, most clearly and quickly, if I first specify what's common to our current four (sorts of) clearly conceivable Worlds, and if, a bit later, I go on to describe salient ways in which the Worlds differ.

Especially useful in bringing together several of this book's main points, or themes, it may be best for me to make a start on all this by doing a bit of nicely reminiscent stage-setting.

Well, as many will recall, toward the end of Chapter 3, I presented two Worlds (or two sorts of Worlds). One of the these Worlds was inhabited only by an Electronish Ed, a Small Blue Sphere, and by a Protonish Pete, a Large Red Sphere, each Propensitied to attract the (Generalistic) likes of the other. And, for the manifestation of their reciprocal Propensities, so it was that Ed and Pete moved together, or each moved toward the other. A nice bit of nostalgia that, don't you think? Well, just as nicely nostalgic, I'm sure, you'll recall the Qualitatively similar World inhabited by only Small Blue Spherical Earl and Large Red Spherical Pat, neither of them *Propensitied for* any impressive dynamical interaction with the other and, as well, neither *Propensitied against* any such impressive interaction. Still and all, Earl and Pat also moved closer together, in trajectories perfectly paralleling Ed's and Pete's. So, just insofar as the experiential aspect of our conceiving goes, there was, as I said, no difference between the two Worlds—Ed and Pete's and, on the other hand, Earl and Pat's. But, very unlike what happened with Ed and Pete, when Earl and Pat moved toward each other, that was sheer happenstance. So, as far as the intellectual aspect of our conceiving goes, which is a lot further here, we could grasp quite clearly, and fairly fully, the difference between these two Worlds. And, in the bargain, we grasped, quite clearly and fully, how very different (Propensitively) Ed was from Earl (and, so, Earl from Ed) and, equally, of course, how very different Pete and Pat always were.

Well, in each of our four new Worlds, there will be just four (basic) individuals. And, each of them will be precisely like all the others, insofar as that's possible, or, at the least, each will be perfectly symmetric with all the others. Just so, each of these four Worlds will be inhabited by, or it will contain, exactly four Large Green Spheres, each Qualitatively exactly like the others, and each Spatially precisely congruent with, or exactly similar to, all the others. And, in every case, in each of the Worlds, not only is each Sphere spatially separate from all the others, but, at every moment, it will be the same distance from each of two others, and a certain larger distance from the third, quite as all four always will be in a "square's-corners-pattern." This will be so, even though, at different times, they'll be differently distanced—quite as the corners of a larger square are differently distanced from those of a smaller square and, of course, vice versa. Just so, and as we'll be supposing, throughout the entire history of each of these Worlds, which may be of infinite duration, both pastward and futureward, each of a World's four Spheres is positioned, in its World, just as a certain Green Sphere, one of its three counterparts, is positioned in *its* World. In sum: In all four Worlds, there's always precisely the same patterning of Green Spheres.

For each of the Worlds, the Spheres always move in a very simple trajectory: Sometimes each Sphere is just a meter away from the two that are its nearest Spheres, quite as with three of the four corners of a square that's one meter on each side. Then, they all move away from each other, at precisely similar speeds, until each is two meters away from its two nearest Spheres, much as with the corners of a square that's two meters on each side. And, when once they're that far apart, they directly change direction, moving together, at those same similar speeds, until each is, again, just a meter away from its two nearest spheres. And, so it goes, one oscillation after another, ad infinitum.

For the experiential aspect of our conceptions, as I've indicated, each of the four (sorts of) Worlds is precisely like each of the three others; or, at the very least, that's how things always appear.

But, Propensitively, things are very different in each of our four Worlds.

In the First (sort of) World, each Large Green Sphere is Propensitied to interact dynamically with anything else that's Green (maybe just when other Greens are pretty nearby, or maybe even when anywhere in its shared spatial framework). Dynamically, in what way is each Large Green Sphere Propensitied? Well, of course, it's in just such a way that, for the mutual interaction of just four such Green concreta, there's always just the trajectories, and the patterning, that we've described, and we've clearly conceived. (Or, each Large Green Sphere may be so Propensitied to interact with anything else that's Spherical. Or, alternatively, it may be so Propensitied with respect to anything else that's both Green and Spherical, and so on. In the present context, it doesn't matter which of these, or which further candidates, gets specified as to how it is that the Spheres should be Generalistically Propensitied. All that matters, is that they *are* Generalistically Propensitied, and that *these Propensities be* reciprocal Powers *for just the nicely conceived trajectorial manifestations.*) Hence, in this World, so far is it from really being an accident that the four Spheres move as they do that, to the contrary, their mutual movement is the mutual manifestation of the Generalistically-directed Propensities of the Spheres, each an apt Generalistic Disposition partner for each of the others.

In our Second (sort of) World, none of the Spheres has any Propensity that's relevant, whether positively or negatively, for any dynamical interaction with any of the other Spheres. So, far from being the manifestation of anything at all Propensitive, in this World it's a sheer accident that, even forever and ever, the Spheres move as (nicely as) they do. Of course, that may be hard to *believe*. But, *it's not at all hard to (just) conceive*, and even to (just) conceive quite clearly.

Now, it's time for a brief intermission, in our set of exercises, during which we'll take stock.

What we've so far observed doesn't go any further, in any philosophically important way, than what, in Chapter 3, we observed with our World with Ed and Pete, nicely paralleling the First of the Worlds just lately offered, and, on the other side, our World with Earl and Pat, nicely paralleling the Second of the Worlds offered just lately. So, if we stopped right now, with our set of exercises, there's little that we'd learn from them or, at least, little that's both truly new and philosophically important. To be sure, we'd have observed another way, but maybe just a slightly different way, to make some central points against the Humeans. And, we'd have seen another way, but maybe also just slightly different, to observe how it is that the intellectual aspect of our conceiving may transcend our conceiving's experiential aspect. And, I guess, maybe we'd have seen, rather similarly, some other old things, in a somewhat new light. Well, all that's worth something, I suppose. But, philosophically, it's not worth very much. So, to see something, in our current set of exercises, that's worth a lot philosophically, we should end our intermission, and engage in some further exercises.

In our Third (sort of) World, quite as much as in our Second, none of the Spheres has any *Generalistic* Propensity that's relevant, whether positively or negatively, for any dynamical interaction with any of the other Spheres. But, as the italicized term hints, in this World that's hardly the end of the hefty Propensitive story. For, in our Third World, each of the four Spheres is Individualistically Propensitied with respect to each of the other three Spheres. And, of course, at least in vague and general terms, it's quite obvious how I should proceed to notice the Individualistic Propensity that each of these four Spheres possesses, each Sphere's Power directed at precisely each of the three others. With respect to precisely each of the others, each Sphere is Propensitied for mutual interaction of just such a sort as will have that Sphere manifest its noted trajectory, and as will have each of the other Spheres, too, move in just such a similar, and a similarly noted, trajectorial way. So, there's no Generalistic Propensity that's here manifested, leastways none that's relevant to the dynamical patterning of the Spheres. Yet, in this Third World, unlike what happened in our Second World, it's no accident that the Spheres move as (nicely as) they do. Rather, here the four Spheres move as they do for a clear Propensitive reason: Their mutual movement is the mutual manifestation of an extremely relevant Propensity of the Spheres. This certainly isn't any Generalistically-directed Propensity. But, rather, it's an Individualistic Propensity of the Spheres that's manifested, with each Sphere being, in this other way, an entirely apt disposition partner for each of the others.

With just this one new exercise, we're now able to observe further things each philosophically quite worthwhile. First, who would have thought that our Humeans have espoused a metaphysics that, as we only now observe, is just so very terribly impoverished, quite unable, as it is, to distinguish among what are, as it surely appears, some several sorts of Worlds that are, each of them, so terribly different from each of the others? And, who would have thought that, in what's apparently a newly extreme way, the intellectual aspect of our conceiving transcends our conceiving's experiential aspect? Not me, for one; leastways, not in the (or my) old, dark days. But, with even just a little illumination provided, I sure think it now.

What's more, all that we've done so far, in this Section, may be taken as just a big warm-up, for a grand finale, which is the fourth exercise, and the last exercise, in the set comprising our current quartet. Ready or not—well, heck, by now, I'm sure you're very ready—here it comes.

Our Fourth (sort of) World features all the Propensitive Power that our First World featured and, in addition to that, all that was featured in our Third World. To use our Chapter's naming phrase, in the Fourth World there's this Plenitude of Power: First, and just as in our First World, each of this World's four Large Green Spheres are Generalistically Propensitied, each precisely like each of the others, for the noted oscillatory interaction with any of, and with all of, the World's other Large Green Spheres. (To repeat a point from up above, this may be so whether it's because, as we may specify, each is so Propensitied with respect to anything (else) that's Green, or with respect to anything (else) that's Spherical, or with respect to anything (else) that's Large, or with respect to anything (else) that's both Green and Spherical, and so on. Right here and now, it doesn't matter what's the precise nature of the Generalistic Propensities involved.) Second, and just as in our Third World, each of this World's four (Large Green Spherical) entities is Individualistically-directed at, or with respect to, each of the World's three other basic spatial concreta, the World's only other (basic) inhabitants. In the case of any of these Spherical Individuals, that may have nothing to do with any of the others being Large, or with any of them being Green, or with any of them being a Sphere, or with any combination of those. Of course, it may have nothing to do with *any General* feature of its three Individualistically-directed interaction partners. Nor need it have anything to do, either, with the fact that, in this World, those are the only other entities ever to exist, occur or obtain. No; not at all. What we have here is, after all, just this: We have entities that *are Generalistically matched*, each with all the others, for oscillatory interaction, and, quite equally, these very entities *are also Individualistically matched*, for precisely that selfsame trajectorial manifestation.

It's very important to be clear about all this. Just so, we should be very clear about both of these complementary metaphysical conceptions. First off, and as we've been agreeing for several Sections, there's *nothing* about an entity's being Generalistically Propensitied, whether in one way or in any other, that entails that the entity *has any Individualistic* Propensities (leastways not any that are directed at any other entity, at any entity other than itself). But, second off, and equally, there's also *nothing* about an entity's being Generalistically Propensitied, whether in one way or in any other, that entails the entity *hasn't any Individualistic* Propensities (even including just such as are directed only at, or with respect to, other entities, entities other than itself). Now, since all that's clear, it's clearly possible for there to be a World whose concreta are Propensitied just like those of our Fourth World.

Let's hammer home, very hard, the lessons learned from this Section's exercises: The philosophically important points we observed so recently, when confronting just our Third World, we may now observe once again and, maybe, this time yet still more vividly: First, who would have *thunk* that our Humeans espoused a metaphysics that, as we may now observe, is just so quite *inordinately impoverished*, quite unable to distinguish among what are, as it surely appears, who *knows how many* very different sorts of Worlds that are, each of them, just so extremely different from each of the others? And, who would *ever have thunk* that, to what's a perfectly extreme degree, the intellectual aspect of our conceiving transcends our conceiving's experiential aspect? Not me, for one, as I'll now repeat; Certainly not in the (or my) old, dark days. But, with even just this one Section's illumination, how could I, while in my right mind, possibly fail to think it right now?

11. Self-directed Propensities: A Special Case of Individualistically-directed Propensities

In our discussion of Individualistically-directed Propensities, so far we've focused only on the cases where the entity *with* the Propensity is distinct from the individual (with respect) *to which* the possessed Propensity is directed. But, there may be, of course, Individualistically-directed Propensities *without* that numerical difference. Just so, an individual may be Propensitied Individualistically with respect to *itself*.

Imagine, if you will, a Small Blue Particle, but, this time, you may be imagining a simple physical object that *won't always* be Small, and *won't always* be Blue. After just a second, the Particle's Color is Red. Then, a second after that happens, the Particle is Large. A while later, the Particle is Blue, once again. And, then, a second after that happens, the Particle becomes Small.

Now, in a certain sort of situation, the changes in the Particle's *Color* may be the manifestation of a certain Individualistically-directed Propensity of the Particle *with respect to a certain other entity*, say, a certain Yellow Particle that's all wholly external to our notably Propensitied Particle itself. For example, it may have the Propensity to change Color, whether from Blue to Red or from Red to Blue, whenever it's within a certain distance of the aforesaid Yellow Particle. By contrast with that, it may be interesting to observe (the possibility of) this: The changes in the Particle's *Size*, whether from Small to Large or from Large to Small, may be the manifestation of a certain Individualistically-directed Propensity of our very same Particle *with respect only to itself*. As a manifestation of this Propensity, when the Particle is Large, it soon becomes Small, and, when Small, it becomes Large.

Now, there are other ways for it to happen that a Particle should go from being Small and Blue, to being Large and Red, and then to being Small and Blue again. For one thing, it might all happen just as a random occurrence, without there being a manifestation of any real Propensity at all. But, right now, I'm not very interested in that. Rather, I'd like to draw attention to a way for this to happen that, while it's certainly not random, still concerns no object but the very Particle itself. Just so, our Particle may be Propensitied to become both Large and Red whenever *it* is, or *it* has just been, Small and Blue, and also Propensitied to become both Small and Blue whenever *it* is, or *it's* just been, Large and Red. Not random, these changes are manifestations of the Particle's Self-directed Propensities.

As I'm a very human being, there are other Self-directed Propensities that are, to me, far more interesting than any such (happily supposed) blatantly physical Self-directed Propensities. Very saliently, these are certain of my *mental* Self-directed Propensities (which, as I'll here allow, might also be physical, even if not blatantly, or obviously, so). Well, among the very most interesting of these mental Propensities, to me, are my own Propensities with respect to my own experiencing. No doubt, they're very like *your* Propensities with respect to *your* experiencing. To these interesting Propensities of ours, I next direct our attention.

12. A Human's Self-directed Propensities with Respect to Her Own Experiencing

Until only about half a century ago—oh, maybe a bit longer—there was scarcely any distinction drawn, by leading philosophers, between experience and belief. Like experiencing, believing also was taken to be always a conscious phenomenon. As all the world knows, of course, Descartes held that all mentality is conscious, belief, or believing, along with all the rest. And, just as famously, Hume is just as extreme. In the *Treatise*, he writes "the *belief* or *assent*, which always attends the memory and sense, is nothing but the vivacity of those perceptions they present; and this alone distinguishes them from the imagination."[11]

I don't know how much of it was due to Freud's enormously widespread impact, but, at all events, in the middle of the twentieth century, all this took a turn for the better, as all seasoned philosophers well know. Rather than conscious occurrences with vivacious experiential quality, our beliefs were taken to be certain of our mental dispositions, or mental Propensities. So, in combination with others of your mental Propensities, one of your typical beliefs might be, under conducive conditions, manifested in your behavior, or activity, or the like. At a most covert extreme, your belief that you're depressed might be manifested, quite completely and entirely, by your mentally producing, with a feeling of conviction that it's true, a conscious mental tokening of "I'm depressed." But, equally, and much more overtly, that belief might be manifested, instead, by your producing an audible overt utterance of "I'm depressed." This is all rough and crude, of course. Even as just a first approximation, it's only barely adequate, at best, to consider a belief to be a Propensity, or a desire to be a mental disposition. Still and

11. Hume, *Treatise*, page 86.

all, the central point is fair enough: Far from being (very like) ways that you're experientially qualitied, your beliefs are much more like ways that you're mentally Propensitied.

Indeed, the change for the better was enormous, affecting even our philosophic view of our beliefs about our own current conscious experiencing. No more do we think that, whenever you're experiencing as of a maroon color patch, *you must be aware that* you're then experiencing maroonly, or as of maroon. Nor do we, even, hold that, whenever you're experiencing maroonly, you *won't* believe that you're *not* experiencing maroonly. For one thing, we may note occasions where, looking at a vast and dense color chart, you may be experiencing, all at once, hundreds of different colors, maroon among them. Especially if you're then focusing mostly on bright oranges and yellows, it may well be that, first, you haven't even the least belief to the effect that you're experiencing maroon and, second, for being under the strong impression that all the colors present have bright warm hues, you may think that you're not experiencing any maroon. Much nearer the truth of the matter, I imagine, our contemporary view is very different, indeed, from that of many pioneering predecessors.

Once it's recognized that our believing as to our experiencing is distinct from any of our experiencing itself, we may learn something from a potentially instructive exercise: Consider a precise physical Duplicate of you (perhaps instantaneously brought here from his parallel position in a distant precisely similar galaxy). Until now, the two of you have led lives that, both mentally and physically, have been precisely similar. But, right now, the two of you will be provided with notably different stimulation: Over *your* two open eyes, we place the two halves of a translucent *maroon* ping-pong ball. (Right then, you'll know there's a sudden great change in someone's experiencing—indeed, in your own experiencing, though he won't know anything of the kind.) Maybe a second later, and maybe even sooner than that, over *his* two open eyes, we place the two hemispheres of a ball that's *violet*. (Right *then, he'll* know there's a sudden great change in someone's experiencing—indeed, in *his* own experiencing, though, this time, *you won't* know anything of the kind.) [To make other points be most salient, we may employ a version of the case where it's quite simultaneously that the two of you are so differently "ping-pong balled."] Anyhow, once all that's done, the two of you are [perhaps for the very first time] quite *differently* experientially modified *visually* (even while it's [still] the case, as we may suppose, that you're both *similarly* experientially modified *nonvisually*).

Now, let us ask what may be some suitably stimulating questions: How does it happen, as no doubt it will, that it's *just you* who comes to believe (and even to know) that you're currently experiencing uniformly maroonly, or as of just maroon—or, *even, (just) that someone's* now experiencing so completely maroonly? And, pointedly, why *doesn't* it happen that you come to believe that you're experiencing (uniformly) *violetly*, or as of (just) *violet*—or, *at the very least, (just) that someone's* now experiencing so completely violetly? And, just as pointedly, why doesn't it happen that, quite as much as with you, *your duplicate also* comes to believe that *he's* experiencing (uniformly) maroonly, or (just) as of maroon—or, *at the very least, (just) that someone's* now experiencing so completely maroonly?

Maybe I need to be more dramatic. Well, for that, I'll use familiar metaphorical talk of "streams of conscious experience." In these terms, you have a stream replete with experiential maroon, but quite barren of experiential violet. And, your duplicate has a stream replete with violet, but barren of maroon. Now, why is it that *you'll* now have a belief (doubtless quite correct) as to the character of *just your* experiential stream, and you *won't have any* beliefy disposition at all (neither correct nor incorrect) as to the character of your *duplicate's* stream? Yet more dramatically still: Why is it that you're so enormously able to "read *your own* mind," thereby (correctly) registering the quality of *your* experiential stream; indeed, why is it that, at least typically, *you can't help but* (correctly) exercise this enormous mind-reading ability? And, on the other side of our imaginary mental wall, why is it that you're so completely *unable* "to read *your Duplicate's* mind"; why is it that, at least typically, you haven't even the least inclination to form *any* belief as to *his* color experience?

To profit most from our little exercise, we want to provide answers that are neutral between major metaphysical positions, as with materialism, and dualism, and even subjective idealism. This may be just such a usefully neutral answer: Each of us human thinkers has certain Propensities with respect to herself, certain Self-directed Propensities, that *aren't paralleled by* Propensities she has with respect to any *other* sentient beings. How's that? Well, *I* have a Propensity, for instance, to *quite directly* form beliefs as to *my (immediate) experiencing*. Whatever my metaphysical status—whether I should be a complex physical being, or whether a nonphysical nonspatial Cartesian being, or whether an entity of a still different metaphysical sort—I do have this Self-directed Propensity, this Propensity with respect myself, in regards to my own (at least very nearly current) experiential modification. What's more, this Propensity is often manifested. So, should I be experiencing

maroonly, there'll obtain, typically and usually, conditions quite conducive for it's apt manifestation. And so, typically and usually, I'll then
believe myself to experience as of maroon. (And, should I experience
just *belltonely*, I'll similarly believe myself to be experiencing in just that
auditory way.)

By contrast, I have *no* Propensity to *quite directly* form beliefs as to
anyone *else's* experiencing. Not being able to read other people's
minds, nor able to do anything even remotely like that, the *only* experiencer with respect to whom I have any notable Individualistically-
directed Propensity, at least as concerns these experiential matters, is
just me, myself. In other words, the only notable Individualistically-
directed Propensity I have with respect to anyone's experiencing is my
Self-directed Propensity regarding my own experiencing.

Sometimes happening just so willy-nilly, but, other times, just
through my own intentional effort, I *do successfully attend* to how it is
with me experientially. And, at least at those times, often I directly
come to have many firm beliefs as to how I'm qualitied experientially.
Because I often introspect successfully, and because I sometimes experience maroonly, for instance, sometimes I'm *rightly confident* that
I'm experiencing as of maroon.

On a materialistic metaphysic, and on a Scientiphical Worldview,
everything that's particular to just me will be understood as deriving
from the particular locations of my basic physical constituents, at
particular times—along with General features of these constituents, of
course, and (largely in virtue of the aforementioned spatial locations
and temporal periods) along with the evolving physical arrangements
of my basic physical components. On a Substantial Dualistic view, by
contrast, that won't be available, as I won't ever be spatially located at
all. And, on a Subjective Idealist view, like Berkeley's position, that
won't be available, either, for quite the same reason. But, on these
more unfashionable views, there'll still be all the noted, and all the
needed, particularity. It will just be that, rather than deriving from
anything about particular spatial locations, on these views I'll have
certain Propensities that are Individualistically-directed Powers, all of
them being Propensities with respect to just myself alone, and none of
them being any merely derivative Propensities, or Powers, at all.

What I've just provided is, of course, the merest sketch of how
things might be with us human thinkers, in regard to a central feature
of our experiencing and our correlative believing, on a couple of saliently traditional metaphysical positions. It is perfectly compatible
with this crude sketch, I want to stress, that it's only quite rarely that we
human thinkers actually *attend to* our experiencing. Indeed, most of

your experiencing is enjoyed, no doubt, in your conscious perception of a world that's external to you, with your attention going, quite directly, to various features of this world that, as we almost automatically assume, our conscious perception allows us to know. No doubt, it's these beliefs of yours, beliefs about "external things," that are most forcefully operative with you.

Yet, at the same time, what next follows may also be true: It may be that, along with your most usefully operative doxastic Propensities, dispositions to form beliefs crucial for your very survival, you also often form, in typical conscious perception, beliefs concerning the character of the (perceptual) experiencing you're then enjoying. My own inclination is to think that, fairly often, this happens in, or with, our conscious perceiving of our external world. So, as I'm inclined to think, it's fairly often that, along with your forming powerfully operative beliefs concerning external objects, you also acquire beliefs about how it is with you, right then, experientially. But, as I emphasize, that thought isn't required by the Section's main ideas.

13. Can There Be Any Concrete Entities That Aren't Ever Propensitied?

In our Third Chapter, you'll likely recall, we gave a Negative answer to the question, Can There Be Spatially Extensible Yellow Entities That Aren't Ever Propensitied? For, as we there observed, any Extensible Yellow entity must be Propensitied to be attracted by (any suitably situated) *Yellow-Attractors*, even if there never should be any Yellow-Attractors in its World, or in its Eon.

With what we've just recently observed, in this present Chapter, we may give an equally Negative answer, I think, to this saliently correlative question: Can There Be *Experiential* Yellow Entities that Aren't Ever Propensitied?

To begin the answering business nicely and gently, I'll rehearse the words with which we first broached the first of our two correlative questions:

> As it first seems to us, well, to me, anyway, hardly anything is easier to imagine than an utterly Propensityless Extensible Yellow Sphere, or, just as well, an utterly Propensityless Extensible Red Cube. With the supposed Yellow Sphere, for instance, I'll be imagining that, while there may be many and varied other concreta in its World, perhaps even existing quite simultaneously with the conceived Sphere, none of them are Propensitied to attract it, or to rotate it, or to annihilate it, or

to interact with it in any other way. Whatever actually happens with this Yellow Sphere, I'm apparently imagining, it will be an absolutely random happening. That's all very peculiar, no doubt; but, nonetheless, it's clearly conceivable; and, presumably, it's all perfectly possible, too.[12]

Well, I'm sure you remember what that bit of musing soon led us to, even way back when (since I've just so lately reminded you about the likes of Yellow-Attractors).

Along a relevantly parallel line, I'll now try to show that a concretum that's experiential yellow must be Generalistically Propensitied. Now, to do this really well, we should show that, *even* for the *very most stupidly unresponsive* concretum ever experiencing yellowly, it must be a Propensitied individual. But, you might ask, what can I possibly have in mind here? Let me explain.

Like you, I'm *not* among the very most stupidly unresponsive individuals, not even when I'm experiential yellow. Just so, often while I'm experiencing as of yellow or, as I like to say, when I'm experiencing yellowly, then I know I'm experiencing yellowly or, as many like to say, I know I'm experiencing as of yellow. Or, at the very least, when a most vividly dominant aspect of my total current experiencing is my currently experiencing yellowly, then, quite often, I believe that I'm experiencing yellowly. This is the manifestation of a certain Self-directed Power of mine, of course, a Propensity with respect to how it is with *me* experientially. For short, we might call this Self-directed Power *my power to introspect* (myself experiencing).

By contrast with me, the *very most stupidly unresponsive* experiencing concreta are, each of them, entities that utterly lack any such a power as that. All right, so that's a bit of useful explaining.

At all events, and as you'll no doubt recall, earlier in the Chapter we instructively discussed these matters, in the Section about a Human's Self-directed Propensities with respect to Her Own Experiencing. To provide some useful stage-setting for what's soon upcoming, I'll recall, from that Section, a passage concerning certain evident limits on my mental powers, or mental Propensities:

> By contrast, I have *no* Propensity to *quite directly* form beliefs as to anyone *else's* experiencing. Not being able to read other people's minds, nor able to do anything even remotely like that, the *only* experiencer with respect to whom I have any notable Individualistically-directed Propensity, at least as concerns these experiential matters, is

12. The quoted passage is from Section 11 of Chapter 3.

me myself. In other words, the only notable Individualistically-directed Propensity I have with respect to anyone's experiencing is my Self-directed Propensity regarding my own experiencing.[13]

As I'll now add to that, not only is there never any other experiencer—other than me, of course—with respect to whom I have an Individualistically-directed Propensity, for directly gaining beliefs as to the character of her experiencing, but I don't have any Propensity that's even just a little like that. So, not only do I utterly lack any such Power that's Individualistically-directed, but, just as surely as that, I utterly lack, as well, any Generalistically-directed Power that, in one way or another, manages to be serviceable, for me, in experiential matters where, in fact, it's not me who's experiencing. Just so, I can scarcely hope to do much, at all, in even the most mildly widespread sort of mind-reading business. And, in this respect, I may very well be quite like all other human beings, now living on this earth, including some charlatans, perhaps performing on fancy stages in Las Vegas.

But, hey; that's just how it is in some Worlds, and some Eons. In others, matters may be, I'll suggest, very different in these regards.

Here's one way for that to happen—maybe in some Eon billions of years from now: When she'll be near enough to somebody, or to somebody's body, or to somebody's brain, which might be, say, ten meters, a (supposed) lady whom I'll call "Distant Futurewoman" will form, quite directly, many accurate beliefs as to how it is, experientially, with her futuristic neighborly experiencer. So, when a being (whose body will be) just five meters in front of her (body) should experience yellowly, then, through manifesting her power of *extrospection*, as we might call the Propensity, she'll directly come to believe that there's someone, or there's something, that's then experiencing yellowly. Even if the nearby experiencing being is a *most stupidly unresponsive* concretum, she'll come to believe this. That is, even if the experiencing being itself never believes that something's experiencing yellowly, still, Distant Futurewoman will come to believe this, even quite straightaway and lickety-split. But, then, even such a most stupidly unresponsive experiential yellow concretum must be a Propensitied individual. For, it must then have, at the very least, a Propensity for certain interaction with the likes of Distant Futurewoman, indeed, just such interaction as will have her acquiring, quite directly, correct beliefs as to its current experiential character. So, somewhat similarly to how it is that a Yellow-Spinner and a Yellow individual are reciprocal disposition partners, so

13. The quoted passage is from Section 12 above.

Futurewoman and her experiential yellow "neighbor" are reciprocally Propensitied.

In this little example, the yellowly experiencing neighbor isn't himself (further) mentally modified, in the manifestation of his nicely needed power of *extrojection*, so to label his reciprocal power, even as Futurewoman doesn't mentally modify her neighbor, in the manifestation of her (reciprocal) power of extrospection. Anyhow, any experientially qualitied Cartesian Soul, that's interacting with its properly Propensitied body, will be nicely read, in this specified sense, or way, by Futurewoman, just so long as her own body, interacting with just her own Soul, is within ten meters of the aforementioned interacting body.

Here's another way for that to happen—and maybe it happened billions of years ago. There are a few mind-readers, each of them extremely sensitive, even while there may be many whose minds they read. Now, so long as anyone at all experiences in a certain way, say, transparently silverly, each of the few mind-readers will believe, licketysplit, that someone, at least, is experiential transparent silver. Well, strange as this seems, I'm sure you get the hang of it all.

This Section's main point, it's clear, amounts to this idea: With *even the very most stupidly unresponsive* concretum ever experiencing yellowly, or ever experiencing silverly, it must be a Propensitied individual. Through a slightly more detailed story, hopefully so detailed as to be an engaging little tale, we may see, I think, that this idea simply must be correct.

Look, as we may very well suppose, there may be some terribly stupid and simple souls, maybe the soul of a shrimp and a crab, perhaps, that sometimes experience yellowly, but that have no responsive Propensity whatever with respect to their experiential quality; they aren't Propensitied to form beliefs as to their experiencing, nor are they Propensitied to feel happy, or sad, in consequence, nor are they otherwise responsively Propensitied with respect to their own experiential quality.

But, by contrast with this shrimp and this crab, *Futurewoman is* responsively Propensitied with respect to their experiential quality. So, if she's within ten feet of (them or) their bodies, say, she'll believe, straightaway, that some beings, at least, are, right now, experiential yellow. Even though our shrimp and our crab can't read their own minds, our Futurewoman can do better.

As these examples show, any individual that's experiential yellow will have, and must have, certain powers, or Propensities, just because she's experiential yellow. And, as you might easily imagine, these

Propensities must be numerous and various, much as an Extensible Yellow object's correlative powers, or Propensities, must be numerous and various.

It's high time, you're thinking, to wrap up this Section. And, so it is. Let us agree, then, to unconfidently accept this summation: Any qualitied concretum, which may well be any concretum at all, is a Propensitied individual. Whether it be Spatially Extensibly Qualitied, or whether it be experientially qualitied, or whether it be qualitied only in some still other way (if there is any such other) a concrete individual is, as must needs be, a Propensitied concrete particular.

14. Scientiphicalism, Self-directed Propensity and Experiential Awareness

In fairly short order, I'll move to discuss some very general questions concerning Propensity, in no wise confined to us human experiencers or, indeed, to any thinking or experiencing beings. But, for just this one Section, I'll continue to explore, both directly and indirectly, some issues concerning mental Propensity. And, quite specifically, I'll try to see how a sensible approach toward them might affect how we feel about Scientiphicalism.

Now, according to the Scientiphical Metaphysic, all your powers are physically derivative physical Propensities, of course, all deriving from the nonderivative physical Properties of your (sufficiently much more) basic physical constituents, and the (sufficiently basic) physical relations among these basic components. In particular, your Propensity to experience variously, and your Power to introspect your experiencing, are just such physically derivative powers. Can we human thinkers make much sense of how that might be so? Maybe so; and maybe not. Even if it must be done quite tentatively and unconfidently, we'll discuss the matter.

We'll consider a case that, at least at first glance, looks like it might help us make some sense of our notably complex situation. Fortunately, even with just a very little addition to it, our case of the Videotaping Security Box looks promising. The little addition is this: Inside the big box there's a spinning Lazy Susan, a wheel with many pie-wedge-shaped, open-top compartments. In each compartment, there's a different small physical object: In one there's an ordinarily blue steel ball; in another there's a brown wooden rectangular block, and so on. Slowly turning clockwise, the big wheel spins. In that way, the various objects may each come, in turn, to be centrally available to the video camera's lense. So, in turn, each of the Box's various "internal objects" may make, and may leave, a (physical) impression on the Box's videotape.

Now, we may consider *all of that* to comprise a single complex physical entity, I'll call it the *Secure System*, this complex System including even the System's steel ball, in a sector of the System's slowly spinning wheel, videotaped with the System's camera, and registered on the System's videotape. As we may then say, one of the System's powers is its power to videotape certain of its parts, parts like the steel ball, that we've taken to be, fairly enough, the System's internal objects. Well, then, each of the videotapeable (almost introspectable?) internal objects will be a part of the very System that successfully videotapes (almost introspects?), and thus registers, that very part of the selfsame (almost introspecting?) System. However much the System's video-taping activity may be like someone's introspecting her visual images, or however little, we may take the System's videotaping power to be, at any rate, a Propensity *with respect to itself*, a *Self-directed Propensity of the System*. (To be sure, this may not be a power with respect to *all of* the complex entity; but, maybe hardly *any* Self-directed Power is so completely comprehensive.)

To help us make Scientiphical sense of our power to introspect, our case of the Secure System seems to do something. But, how much? Is the System's power to register its internal objects relevantly quite like, or helpfully quite parallel to, your power to introspect your visual experiencing?

To my mind, there's a great disparity between the Secure System's Self-directed Power, so clearly a physically derivative Propensity, and your commonplace power to introspect your experiencing. Why the great disparity? First, there seems something artificial in taking our specified System to be a *single entity in its own right*. And, second, even if we allow that, there's *still* something strained in taking the System's specified Propensity, its power to videotape some of its innards, to be a *Self-directed* power, in any strong sense of that term. And, maybe this isn't peculiar to the Systematic case I've supplied. As I suggest, there's always something strained, and even quite false, with *anything* said to have *Self-directed powers* when its Propensities are *all physically derivative* Propensities.

Look, for ease of exposition, I've been using "Self-directed Propensity of X" as an easy-to-say stand-in for "Propensity of X with respect to itself." By contrast, in ordinary talk of an individual directing himself, there's something much richer that's implied. A bit badly, lately I've equivocated between my expository use, plainly anemic, and our more ordinary use, with much richer implications. Now, using

"Self-directed" in just my anemic sense, there really isn't anything strained, of course, in saying that a thoughtless thing, like our Secure System, has Self-directed Propensities. In effect, that's just saying the thing is Propensitied with respect to itself, as even certain basic Particles may be, without any thought, will, or experience. This doesn't imply there's an entity that's directing something, whether directing itself or anything else, nor anything even remotely like that. It's only with our ordinary use of "directing," with its much richer implications, that talk of Self-direction will often seem strained, as when this richer talk is trained on physically derivative complexes. From now on, enough of such seductive confusions.

Still and all, there does seem to be a great difference between your introspecting your experience and our Secure Systems' registering its internal objects. To be sure, my anemic sense for "Self-directed Propensity" applies to both cases equally. But, the more ordinary sense for such a term isn't so equally applicable. With that richer sense, there's great strain in using the term for our System's power to videotape its innards. But, when we use it for your power to attend to your experiencing, there's nary a hitch in our employment. Now, that's a much better way to express a real worry.

Still, the expression of a real worry needn't be the indication of any deep distinction. And, of course, nothing I've lately said shows any insuperable difficulty with the thought that all your powers may well all be physically derivative physical Propensities. But, it might be a fair start, I imagine, toward being more open to certain unfashionable Anti-Scientiphical ideas, some of them to be presented in the very next Chapter. Just so, I'll close the Section with a bit more toward that effect.

When you choose to attend to your experience in a certain way—say, when you choose to attend to how it is with you now auditorally—then, typically and usually, you introspect quite in the way you chose to do. And, in consequence of your introspecting like that, you become, typically and usually, at least pretty well aware of how it is auditorally with yourself now, as regards your current experiencing. Well, as I'll suggest, it's in just such common cases as this, where you choose, for yourself, your own thoughtful activity, that it's *most appropriate* to consider the power you've exercised to be one of your *Self-directed Powers*. By contrast, with the very great deal of your introspecting that you never chose to do—introspecting that you engaged in quite unintentionally, much of it almost automatically—it's *far less* fitting to think of your introspecting as being Self-directed. But, it's just when you exercise your power to *choose* your very own thoughtful activity, whether the activity be introspective or whether it be other otherwise, well, it's just then, of course, that it's hardest to take all your powers to be just so many physically derivative Propensities.

For the meanwhile, that's enough that's specially about sentient beings, or about any specifically mental Propensities. Now, it's back to more general metaphysical issues.

15. Temporal Monotony and Temporal Change

Throughout, we've been accepting certain propositions that are needed for us humans to make sense of any concrete reality featuring any Propensity. Central among them are certain statements concerning real concrete change and, by contrast, certain statements concerning the contrasting situation, where concrete reality doesn't really change.

About all that, I should be a bit more specific. So, consider a basic Small Blue Sphere, Steve, that's at rest with respect to a basic Large Red Sphere, Lou. In a quite clearly conceivable World, these may be the only two basic concrete things, both of them lacking any substantial parts, and there being no question, either, as to their together composing any third thing. Or, so we'll suppose. And, as we'll also be supposing, it may be that, for ever so long a time, there is, in this little World, *no change at all*. That certainly sounds very restful, and boring. But, seeking at least a little specificity, what should we take our restful supposition to entail?

For one thing, as we should now understand things, in this unchanging little World, there are, for ever so long a time, just the same number of concrete individuals: There are exactly two. So, the World is temporally unchanging *as regards the number* of its basic inhabitants. Or, to express the point with a memorable term, the World is *temporally Monotonous* as regards the number of its basic inhabitants. In this little World, why is that so? Well, it's because this World is temporally *Monotonous as regards the identity* of its basic inhabitants, that is, as regards which are the basic entities of the World.

What's more, for ever so long, Steve is always Small, while Lou is always Large. So, we may also say this: Even though the World is (always) *spatially Variegated as regards the Sizes* of its basic things, the World is, fully in the face of all that, *temporally Monotonous as regards the Sizes* of its basic inhabitants. Not only is there never any change in the *difference between* their Sizes, but there's no change, either, in what seems the more fundamental situation, in virtue of which that's true: Steve is always a certain (lesser) specific Size and Lou is always another (greater) specific Size. Or, not reifying Sizes: Steve is always Sized so-and-so; and Lou is always Sized (more greatly than so-and-so, being Sized, as he is, just so much as) such-and-such.

Further still, Steve is always Spherical and Lou is also always Spherical. So, even as the World is *spatially Unvariegated as regards the Shapes* of its basic objects, so, quite as really, and truly, our World is *temporally Monotonous as regards the Shapes* of its basic inhabitants. Not only is there never any *difference in* their Shapes, but there's also no change, either, in what seems the more fundamental situation, in virtue of which that's true: Steve is always a certain specific Shape and Lou is always the precisely same specific Shape. Or, not reifying Shapes: Steve is always Shaped perfectly spherically, and Lou is also always Shaped perfectly spherically.

What's yet more, Steve is always Spatially Extensible Transparent Blue, while Lou is always Spatially Extensible Transparent Red. So, even though the World is *spatially Variegated as regards the Qualities* of its basic things, the World is *temporally Monotonous as regards the Qualities* of its basic inhabitants. Not only is there never any change in the *difference between* their Quality, but there's no change, either, in what seems the more fundamental situation, in virtue of which that's true: Steve is always a certain specific Color and Lou is always another specific Color. Or, not reifying Qualities, and Colors: Steve is always Qualitied Bluely, never Redly; and, never Qualitied Bluely, Lou is always Qualitied Redly.

Though we've remarked on Spatial properties, as regards Monotony and Change, and also on Qualities, we've said nothing yet about our third sort of basic property, Propensities. Well, we'll take that up in the next Section, for which our present discussion hasn't yet finished fully preparing us. With that made explicit, let's further proceed with this preparatory discussion.

Well, with Propensities placed aside, we may suppose that, in the simple physical World we're now considering, we've now remarked on all the intrinsic (basic) properties of its basic spatial particulars. So, Propensities aside, there's never any temporal Change as regards the intrinsic properties of any of our World's (basic) concrete particulars. Avoiding reification of properties, we may say that Steve is always intrinsically propertied Transparently Bluely, and it's always intrinsically propertied Spherically, and so on; while Lou is always intrinsically propertied Transparently Redly, and it's intrinsically propertied Spherically, and so on. Or, more compendiously, we may say that, with each of our little World's two basic objects, how it is intrinsically is temporally Monotonous.

Finally for now, we may suppose that there is also no temporal Change in the *external relations* of our World's basic concrete individuals. Now, if only for the sake of instruction, we'll suppose these are just the *spatial relations* among, or between, the two concrete entities. So, in particular, the distance between Steve and Lou is always the same. And, insofar as there is any definite sense to the idea, the direction from Lou to Steve is also always the same, as is the (opposite) direction from Steve to from Lou. All in all, this is a terribly restful World we're considering: Not only is this terribly restful World temporally Monotonous intrinsically, it's also temporally Monotonous extrinsically.[14]

This Section's now presented, I believe, the most salient sorts of temporal Monotony, and temporal Change, that attend our simplest conceptions, and our clearest conceptions, of (spatial and temporal) concrete reality. But, of course, any reality that qualifies as physical will have some entities, at least, endowed with Propensity. And, so will any that features even so much as just one thoughtful individual.

So, now, we must ask this: With regard to an entity's Propensities, what are we properly to take as *Propensities for* temporal Monotony and, by contrast, what are we to take as *Propensities for* temporal Change?

16. Propensity for Monotony and Propensity for Change

Consider a basic Small Blue *Sphere* that's resting on the (horizontal top) surface of a basic Large Red Cube. And, suppose that the Cube rotates, and tilts, so that the Sphere no longer remains at rest. Now, on the *most natural further* suppositions, so to say—something about how unsupported things are supposed to go downward, or whatever—the *Sphere will roll* down the tilted surface of the Large Cube—perhaps eventually rolling off the Large Cube into "outer space."

Next, consider a basic Small Blue *Cube* that's resting on the (horizontal top) surface of a basic Large Red Cube. And, suppose that the Large Cube rotates, and tilts, so that the Small Cube no longer remains

---

14. Some will say that what's here taken to be Monotony, and what's taken to be temporal Change, is really so interwoven with our language, or with our discursive thinking, as to be hopelessly insubstantial. Various ingenious arguments can, of course, be employed to some such apparent effect. We may think of Nelson Goodman's riddles about whatever properties may be expressed by his predicates "grue" and "bleen." And, we may think of Peter Geach's discussions of so-called "Cambridge change." But, of course, our Humanly Realistic Inquiry won't be halted by any such puzzles, no matter how ingenious or appealing.

at rest. This time, on the most natural further suppositions, so to still say, the *Small Cube will slide* down the surface of the Large Cube, and *not roll* down it—perhaps eventually sliding off into "outer space."

Why are there such different interactions here? Or, much the same, why are there, here, such different manifestations, as different as sliding is from rolling? Is it *all just a matter of Spatial* properties, of the difference in Shape between the (Small Blue) *Sphere* and the (Small Blue) *Cube* that's responsible for the difference? Well, in certain contexts, we may say it's just that simple. But, then, I ask you this: Is that simplifying talk philosophically harmless?

Myself, I don't think so. Indeed, I suspect that, even inasmuch as we're inclined to take it quite seriously, we're inclined, as well, to feel friendly toward badly conceived metaphysical views, like the one I've called the *Identity Theory of Qualities and Dispositions*. (As you'll likely recall, when discussing this conception in Chapter 3, we found ample reason to reject any such stultifyingly false philosophical position.) In a way that may help us make progress with some rather large issues, I'll try to elaborate instructively.

All right, I've allowed that, in certain contexts, we may say that what explains manifestations as different as sliding is from rolling, with our (Small Blue) Sphere, on one hand, and with our (Small Blue) Cube, on the other, well, that's *all just a matter of Spatial* properties: It's just the difference in *Shape* between the *Sphere* and the *Cube* that's responsible for (the different interactions, and) the different manifestations. But, to speak more fully, and to explain more deeply, we must say much more. Why's that? Don't worry; I'll explain.

Agreeably, I ask you: When the Large Cube tilted, why didn't the Small Sphere *turn into a Small Cube*—and then *slide* down the tilted surface? And, I also ask: When the (other) Large Cube tilted, why didn't *that* induce the Small Cube to *become Spherical*—and *have it roll* down the tilted surface?

In even a modestly ambitious explanation of the (original) Sphere's rolling, we must *say a great deal more* than just that, at the *start of our time period*, that Small Particle *is Spherical*. Beyond that, and at a bare minimum, we must say at least this much more: Throughout that period, our Small Blue Sphere had the *Propensity to retain its Shape* and, *throughout the time of its interaction with* the Large Cube, *this Propensity was manifested*. So it was that, *throughout that time*, the Small Sphere *remained*, and it *then always was*, a Spherical solid object. And, on the other side of this interactive partnership, the Large Cube had a *Propensity to retain its own Shape (and continued to have the Propensity) throughout* the time of its interaction with the Small Sphere. And, what's more, of course, *this*

Cube's (Continuing) Propensity for Shape Monotony was manifested. So, it's not just a matter of Shape, as it may be at any moment, that explains our (first) Small object's rolling down the side of our Large object. Rather, there must also be, at the very least, the manifestation of their (Continuing) Propensities for Shapewise Monotony, to explain why the (object that began as a) Sphere rolled down the tilted side of the (object that began as a) Cube.

At each moment of our interactive period, the Small Sphere, in particular, had a *Propensity for Monotony* with respect to *(its own) Propensity for Monotony with respect to (its own) Shape*. And, throughout (enough of) our interactive period, *this Propensity also was manifested*. Of course, even with that said, there's *still a lot left to be said*, for anything like a satisfyingly complete explanation, maybe even an indefinitely great deal more.

(Look, just as those who've learned their Hume know full well, a lot of what's left has nothing to do with (anything that's even remotely like) whatever's available in direct experience, or available to our conceiving's most experiential aspect, and so on. For that matter, it has nothing to do with the how anything's Shaped, among our putative Propensity Partners, nor how any of them may be (or may not be) Propensitied with respect to (its own) Shape. So, just for one thing, the Small Sphere must be Propensitied to stay on, or with, (the surface of) the Large Cube, when the latter begins to rotate (and for the saliently ensuing period) *rather than being*, for example, *Propensitied to "fly off" into outer space*, maybe quite straight up from the Large Cube, at a perfectly right angle, like a proverbial "rocket to the moon." Indeed, for the Sphere to roll here at all, it had better not have any Propensity to fly off the Sphere, at any angle, or speed of departure, and so forth, leastways none that's (to be) manifested here and now, simultaneously with the Large Cube's beginning to rotate. And, of course, it's in contrast with ever so much else, too, that our hopefully rolling Sphere should have the noted Propensity, to stay on, or stay with, the Large Cube (if the Sphere's rolling is to be explained by, or has anything worldly to do with, its (even apparently) rolling down the Cube's suddenly slanting surface.) Saliently, it *shouldn't* be that our Sphere has *no Propensity at all*, neither one way or the other, concerning whether it's to stay on, or with, our Large Cube. For, in such a (bad) case, it will be only sheer happenstance, or just a perfectly random matter, what happens with our Small Sphere, upon the Large Cube's beginning to rotate. Unless that Small Sphere is Propensitied to stay with, or on, that Large Cube, as the latter starts rotating, it will be sheer happenstance should the Sphere stay on the Cube, and not, say, fly right up from, or right up off, the newly rotating Large Cube, like a rocket to the moon or, to use another phrase, like a bat out of hell.

Listen, I'll be the first to agree that those who've learned little from Locke, whether directly or only indirectly, have learned little that's philosophically central. But, just as well, those learning little from Hume, directly or indirectly, also still have much to learn, before they'll have learnt much that's philosophically important. But, enough of this pretty pedantic scolding. For, as I'm now happy to trust, there's already plenty enough on your metaphysical plate, quite sufficient for you to grasp, very well, all the central points here. So, it's back to the discussion's currently main line.)

In other circumstances, there will be Spherical Particles, all of them ever so richly Propensitied, that, during long periods of time, don't engage in any notable interactions. Still and all, it may be that these Particles remain Spherical. And, what's more, it may be that their remaining so is far from being any merely random matter. Rather, it may be that, as with the rolling Sphere just considered, with each of these objects, there's the manifestation of its Propensity for Monotony as regards Shape.

Whether a Monotonously Shaped Sphere is notably interactive, or whether its behavior is notable at all, its Propensity for Monotonous Shape is, in any case, a Propensity *with respect to itself*. The Sphere is so Propensitied that (in the conducive conditions obtaining) *it* will remain Spherical. In our anemic sense of "Self-directed," where no choice or agency is implied, we may say that this Propensity for Monotony is a Self-directed Propensity of the basic Spherical Particle.

By contrast with this Self-directed Propensity, we can notice, just as well, a Propensity for Monotonous Shape *with respect to other* Individuals, a Propensity that may be a Generalistically-directed Power. So, consider a "superbly gelatinous" Sphere (maybe, even, a Sphere with no Propensity, at all, to Solidify, or to Rigidify, and so on) that's just on the verge of becoming Non-spherical. Now, right before that happens, the imminently wobbly object is somehow placed inside a Large Rigid Near-Cube, a Solid object with a Spherical hollow at, or near, its center. This is a Near-Cube that, as we're supposing, is very well suited to serve as a so-called *Sphere-Retainer* (so-called, of course, by me). Because the gelatinous thing's nicely ensconced in this Retainer, it remains Spherical. That's not due, of course, to any (Self-directed) Propensity the object then has to remain the same in Shape, for the gelatinous object *doesn't have any* such Propensity for Shapewise stasis. Rather, the gelatinous concretum's remaining Spherical is due to a certain Propensity that the *Retainer* has, for interaction with such "Shapely impressionable" entities as may be snugly confined by it. So, in addition to a Self-directed Propensity, *to retain its own* Shape, that we're supposing for our supposed Sphere-Retainer, this interacting object has, as well, a (Generalistically-directed) Propensity to *retain* the Spherical Shape of, or for, various *other* Spatially propertied individuals. While the first Propensity is Self-directed, not so the second. Indeed, as the second Propensity isn't any sort of Individualistically-directed Power at all; it can't possibly be, then, the special sort of Individualistic Power that's properly reckoned a Self-directed Propensity.

Look, gelatinous though it be, and not the least bit rigid or solid, the merely retained Sphere may be, for all that, a genuinely Spherical object. What can I usefully mean by those words? Listen up, and I'll tell you a thing or two.

Here's a first thing, for you to hear: There may be certain Particles that will continue to exist when, but only when, they're more than a meter from the nearest Sphere. When one of these Sphere-vulnerable Particles comes close to an empty retainer, it continues to exist. (As you'll recall from this book's first pages, empty regions aren't any real Spherical entities, or any real entities at all.) Not containing any object at all, a truly empty retainer won't, in particular, feature any internal Sphere; just so, it won't feature anything that's up to annihilating any of our Sphere-vulnerable Particles. But, when one of these Particles comes within a meter of a Retainer filled with gelatinous substance, then, lickety-split, it's out of business, quite directly ceasing to exist, completely and forever. Now, suppose that another Sphere-vulnerable Particle comes within a meter of a Solid Sphere, also perfectly rigid, and what-all. That vulnerable object will, of course, also be annihilated; and, that will happen just as fully, and just as quickly, as with the aforementioned obliterated Sphere-vulnerable individual. But, at the same time, it won't happen any more quickly, or any more fully, either. A Sphere, after all, is a sphere, whether very gelatinous and wobbly, or whether solid and rigid.

Well, that's one thing, and, secondly, here's thing number two: There may be *Sphere-Color-Imitators*, Particles that when within an inch of any Sphere, whether it be solid, or rigid, or neither, will come to be the same in Extensible Color as the nearby Sphere (if not already that Color). When a Blue Sphere-Color-Imitator Cone approaches an empty retainer, or when it approaches a solid Ovoid, nothing happens Colorwise, at least so far as that Cone is concerned. But, when it approaches an Interiorly Spherical Container, filled with *Yellow* gelatinous matter, then, lickety-split, the Cone becomes a *Yellow* Conical Particle, quite directly Changing as to its Spatially Extensible Quality.

It changes Colorwise just as fully, and just as quickly, as when, on a previous day, perhaps, it similarly approached a perfectly Solid Sphere, as rigid an object as you please. A Sphere, after all, is a sphere, whether very gelatinous and wobbly, or whether solid and rigid.

Well, with what's just been done, I trust, you've a fairly full grasp, at least, of the point I'm aiming to help you comprehend.

Toward that same end, it will now be useful to consider a much further-fetched case (more wildly hypothetical, no doubt) where the continuation of an object's shape depends on its being appropriately partnered with another object, or some other objects. So, please imagine a World that has very many Spherical Particles, and just a few Cubical Particles, and no other objects occupying any of its vast space. Now, so very many are the Spheres that, even in the vastness of the space, it's very hard for any Cube ever to be at all far from at least one Sphere, even as much as just an inch; and it's only very rarely that any such thing ever happens. Now, as we're also supposing, each Sphere is Propensitied to retain its Spherical Shape, and each is also Propensitied to preserve the Shape of any Cube that's within a certain distance from it, a distance that's fully five inches. And, correlatively, each Cube is Propensitied so as to have its Shape preserved by any pretty nearby Sphere, or Spheres. Anyhow, quite as the Spheres remain Spherical, and quite as, almost always, each Cube is within five inches of a Sphere, there will be, in this World, much Monotony with respect to its Particles' Shapes. And, far from being an accident, or any coincidence, this Monotony will be the manifestation of the Propensities just mentioned.[15]

___

15. But, very infrequently, a Cube moves to a point that's *more than* five inches from even the nearest Sphere. As concerns its Shape, what becomes of such a wayward object, originally Cubical? Given just our *explicit* suppositions so far, and nothing more, there's simply no saying. Here's what I'm getting at, a point that's important: First, and on one sort of further suppositional specification, a Cube *is Propensitied to Change Shapewise*, from Cubical to Non-Cubical, upon being even so much as an inch from the nearest Sphere. With *this* further supposition in place, we *can* say what will become of a wayward Cubical object (at least when allowing ourselves the most natural still further suppositional specifications). Maybe we can't say very much, but we can say this much: The object will become Shaped *Non-Cubically*. (Look, I haven't done very much in way of articulating the first sort of further specification.)

Right off the bat, I've left it open *what* (sort of) Non-Cubical Shape, the too-distant particular will come to have: I didn't, say for example, that the Cubes were Propensitied to Change in Shape, in such a circumstance, so as to become Ovoidal. So, with just the specification of Non-Cubical, it may be entirely accidental what will be the Shape of the wayward individual: It might (accidentally) become Ovoidal; it might (accidentally) become Cylindrical; it might (accidentally) become Spherical; and so on. All right; that's enough about our first sort of further suppositional specification.) Second, and on a quite different sort of further supposition, a Cube *isn't Propensitied to Change Shapewise*, upon

Well, then, with that scenario, there's this to say about all the many Cubes that always do stay near at least one Sphere. First, they remain Cubical; and, second, that's no random matter. Rather, and third, it's the manifestation of certain Generalistically-directed Propensities, both some dispositions on the part of the Cubes themselves and, as well, some Propensities on the part of the Spheres, the Cubes' reciprocal disposition partners. Fourth, and since all that's so, any one of these Cube's remaining Cubical *isn't* the manifestation of a *Self-directed* Propensity of the Cube in question. Indeed, not only *isn't* it a disposition directed at that very individual itself; it isn't any Individualistic Power of any sort, Individualistically-direct at, or with respect to, any of the World's concrete entities.

Except for a supposedly gelatinous Sphere partnered with a Shapely Monotonous Sphere-Retainer, and except for a few wayward Cubes noted just lately, so far it's been things Propensitied to be Monotonously Shaped that have been our central focus. But, for a while, let's turn to focus on objects that are *Propensitied not to* retain their Shape. Indeed, they'll be objects *Propensitied to Change* in respect of Shape.

With complex physical objects, replete with physically derivative dispositions, this isn't uncommon. In the spring, a tree grows leaves; so, in the summer, it's Shaped quite differently from how, quite leafless, it was Shaped in the winter. A button is impressed, a motor operates, and the top of a convertible car goes down; by the end of this process, the overall Shape of the car is quite different from the car's Shape at the start. But, of course, with these common complexes the Changes of Shape are themselves physically derivative, just as are the Propensities in question. At least for the most part, what goes on with a common complex's Change of Shape is quite exhausted by the spatial rearrangement of its tiny constituents, which themselves may never

---

becoming too distant from Spheres. With this *different* further supposition in place, we *can't* say anything about what will become of a wayward Cubical object so far as its Shape is concerned. (Not even when allowing ourselves the most natural still further suppositional specifications.) For, we've now supposed that, when a Cube's so far from all Spheres, it isn't Propensitied for Monotony in respect of Shape and it isn't Propensitied for Change, either. Supposing that it will have *some* shape then, we've now left it entirely open what shape that will be: The object might (accidentally) remain Cubical; and, it might (accidentally) become Ovoidal, or else Spherical, or else some other Non-Cubical Shape. So, on our second sort of further supposition, what will become of wayward Cubes Shapewise is left open and, as such, may best be considered *purely random* matter. Anyway, with all this I may be getting ahead of myself. So, now, it's back to the body of text, with this note's issues to be dealt with, a bit more fully, just a little later in that textual body.

Change in Shape, and by the accretion of such constituents, and by the loss of such constituents, and so on. But, even if all that Shapewise Change is a quite derivative phenomenon, and it isn't anything fundamental, there may be *other* Changes in respect of Shape that *are* quite fundamental Changes. Ignorant as I am, for all I know this may happen with certain actual physically basic entities.

So it may be that a basic Blue Sphere is Propensitied to Change its Shape, under certain conditions, and become an Ovoid. These conditions may include those where the Blue Sphere is within a meter of at least one basic Red Sphere. Let's suppose that, while it's long been further than that from any Red Sphere, now our Blue Sphere is within that distance of a Red Sphere. Well, now the Blue Sphere's Propensity for Shapewise Change will be manifested and, in consequence, it will become Ovoidal. (By contrast, the nearby Red Sphere remains Spherical, a manifestation of *its* Propensity to *retain its* Spherical Shape.) So, just as there are Propensities for *Monotony* in respect of Shape, which may be enjoyed even by quite basic spatial objects, so also there may be Propensities for *Change* in respect of Shape, which also may be enjoyed even by basic physical concreta.

As already observed, when a Propensity for Monotony of Shape is manifested, then, not only will a concretum remain the same Shape, but its doing that won't be a mere matter of chance. And, as we now note, when a *Propensity for Change* of Shape is manifested, then, not only *will* a concretum *Change* in Shape, but, quite equally, its doing *that* won't be merely a random matter.

The interplay between the Quality properties of basic entities and their Propensity properties might never be, perhaps, as intimate as the interplay between certain of their Spatial properties and some closely correlative Propensities. (Or, perhaps, they might be, even if I can't see, either very clearly or very fully, how that should be so.) In any event, the most central points just offered find parallels with the interplay between Qualities and Propensities: So, very much as before, we again consider a World where Small Blue Particles attract Large Reds, and vice versa. And, also quite as supposed before, the Blues repel other Blues, just as they're Propensitied to do, and, correlatively, the Reds repel other Reds. This is so, we're supposing, *because* the Blue entities have the relevant *Propensities with respect to the Quality* of basic things, as is similarly the case with how the Reds are Propensitied.

Now, consider a case in which a certain Blue Sphere and a certain Red Sphere are continually attracting each other. For the distance between the two Spheres continually to decrease substantially, and for this to be a similarly necessitated manifestation, the interaction must go on for some time, much more than a single absolute instant. Well, as far as Qualitative Monotony and Change go, what must happen, during this time, in order that the noted interaction should continue for the period in question? Well, one thing to be said is this: The Sphere that's Blue *must continue to be Blue*, and the one that's Red must *continue to be Red*. Magic and accident placed aside, how will *that* happen?

Here's a pretty decent short answer: First, the Blue Sphere is *Propensitied to remain Blue*. And, correlatively, the Red Sphere has the *Propensity to remain Red*. It is *because* the Blue Sphere is Propensitied to remain Blue, and (conditions are such that) this Propensity *is manifested*, that the Sphere *does* remain Blue. And, it's *because* there's the correlative manifestation of the Red Sphere's Propensity for Qualitative Monotony that *this other* Sphere *remains Red*. So, owing to the manifestation of their Propensities for Qualitative Monotony, the one will always be Blue, throughout the considered period of attraction, and, correlatively, the other will be Red. And, it's because of this that each Sphere will continue to be an apt disposition partner for the other, with each well suited to the other's Quality-directed Propensity for attraction. And, owing to all *that* (and, of course, owing to very much more, quite as well) the Spheres will move toward each other for more than just a moment: At the start of this protracted interaction, they'll attract each other for at least a moment and, so, they'll move together, at least a little bit; and then, a moment or so later, they'll still attract each other, for at least another moment and, so, they'll move further together, at least another little bit; and so on, for however long there obtains this attractive interaction.

Shamelessly, I'll now focus the discussion on myself. Whether I'm physical or whether not, and whether I'm a basic being or whether not, it's quite clear that *I myself* am Propensitied for *Monotony*, and also that *I myself* am Propensitied for *Change*. Serving conciseness more than ontological clarity, we may well enough say that, with the manifestation of some of my Propensities for Change, there are Changes in my experiencing. And, we may also say that, with the manifestation of some others, there are Changes in my thinking, in my moods, in my convictions, and so on. Having offered those words regarding Change, here are words concerning Monotony: With the manifestation of one of my Monotony Propensities, there's my continuing interest in philosophy, day after day, year after year, decade after decade. With the manifestation of another, there is my continuing love for my son. (For metaphysical purposes, this last Propensity will be more perspicuously indicated, as will be any of my Propensities, without any reference to any entity quite distinct from me, as my son most certainly is.) Anyway, all this should certainly be acknowledged in any Humanly Realistic

Metaphysic: Whether or not I'm spatially complex, I'm *very complex Propensitively*. In this present work, I've aimed, time and time again, to acknowledge this Propensitive complexity.

17. Possibility, Accident, Probability and Self-directed Propensity

At the very beginning of this Chapter's Fourth Section, concerned with Propensity, Possibility, Accident and Probability, I presented some sentences that expressed some ideas that, to my mind, are of the first importance for a comprehensive metaphysic of concrete reality. As these ideas are utterly central for our inquiry, I'll rehearse the sentences expressing them:

> When first introducing our idea of Propensity, pretty early in our First Chapter, I noticed that there are certain differences between the Possibilities for an object—or what's possible for it—and, on the other side, the Propensities of the object. For one thing, there are certain temporal differences: Propensities must be for future happenings, while Possibilities can concern the present, and the past, as much as the future. With that point in mind, let's now notice some related conceptions.
>
> I don't know about you, but, myself, I think that chance phenomena are metaphysically possible. And, so, I don't think that this strong conditional proposition is any metaphysically necessary truth: If an entity is *not* Propensitied *to* do so-and-so (or to be such-and-such), then, as must needs be, the entity *is* Propensitied *not to* do so-and-so (or to be such-and-such).[16]

In our discussion of these ideas, in the Fourth Section, we considered only some cases of concreta that changed as to how they were spatially related to each other, as with movement, and, on the other hand, some cases where concreta *didn't* change as to how they were spatially related. But, of course, that was before we became explicitly involved with Individualistically-directed Propensities. And, so, in particular, it was before our explicit involvement with Self-directed Propensities, a special case of Individualistic Powers.

For quite a while since then, by contrast, we've been up to our ears with these central ideas and, in particular, we're becoming ever more wholly embroiled, quite happily, with Self-Directed Dispositions,

16. The quoted passage is from the beginning of Section 4 above.

Propensities and Powers. So, at this point, I'll extend Section Four's discussion, very explicitly, to these utterly central conceptions.

Well, even as concerns its own intrinsic features, an individual may undergo change, just *quite by chance*, or it may *not* undergo change, *also* quite by chance. Then, rather than its owing to any of the object's Propensities, there might occur, for example, a Shapewise Change in an entity that has *no Propensity whatever to Change* in Shape, and also *no Propensity whatever not to Change* in Shape. Its Change of Shape will be a perfectly random happening. Likewise, or quite the same thing, really, there might occur no Shapewise Change in an entity that has no Propensity whatever to remain the same in Shape, and also none whatever not to remain the same. Its Continuity of Shape will be, then, a perfectly random happening.

With just that much said about sheer accident, I'll now move to notice something about another sort of chance, so to say, now becoming concerned with some matters of objective probability. So, as much in order now as they'll ever be, here are some words about Probabilistic Propensities: As sometimes seems forced on us, by certain things physical scientists say nowadays, certain physical entities have Probabilistic Propensities for interaction with others. And, some may have Probabilistic Propensities with respect to themselves. So, some Blue Sphere may be Probabilistically Propensitied, to the degree 0.9, to become Red in the next second, while being Probabilistically Propensitied, to the degree 0.1, to remain Blue. Whether this Sphere actually becomes Red, or whether it remains Blue, either way that *won't be a purely chance* phenomenon. Rather, either way, there will be the manifestation of the Sphere's Propensity with respect to Color. If it becomes Red, there will be the more likely manifestation of the Sphere's whole Propensity in the matter. And, if it remains Blue, there'll be the less likely manifestation. But, in any event, there'll be, right here, the manifestation of a Probabilistic Propensity. And, so, there *won't* be, right here, any *purely random* happening.

With enough said about Probabilistic Propensity, especially in connection with Self-directed Propensity, I return to the heart of our discussion.

18. Basic Concreta, Propensity for Annihilation and Propensity for Continuation

Though you've had hardly any respite from exposure to bizarrely novel conceptions, I'm about to confront you with still more. As I'm hoping, you'll enjoy the confrontation.

Well, as I've been told from time to time, there are certain elementary particles that go out of existence. Or, less dramatically, they
cease to exist. Whether or not that's actually so, we may certainly suppose, at least, that some such particles cease to exist. Indeed, we may
coherently conceive basic Particles that come to be *completely annihilated*.
When one of them ceases to exist, there's simply *nothing left of* the
erstwhile concretum. In particular, none of its matter exists any more.
Though it *was* a physical concretum, absolutely *nothing* of it *remains*.

Certain cases of such complete annihilation provide fertile ground
for philosophical progress. In seeking such progress, we may first
imagine a case where the absolute annihilation of a basic concretum is
sheer happenstance, a perfectly random occurrence. But, then, we must
diametrically reverse our supposition, maybe the sooner the better. So,
now we'll suppose some basic Particles whose *utter annihilations* aren't
the *least bit* random.

How so? Well, in these perfectly *nonaccidental* cases, what explains
the entity's ending may be just this: First, the Particle *is Propensitied to
Annihilate*, that is, it's *Propensitied to cease to exist*. Perhaps, it's just in certain conditions that this Propensity will be manifested. But, of course,
that's no problem. For, we may suppose, quite easily, that those conditions come to obtain. Well, then, quite as its Propensity for Annihilation is manifested, so, quite nonaccidentally indeed, our happily
considered Particle ceases to be, maybe even completely and forever.

With the 'Annihilating Propensity' of a basic concretum, often the
conditions for manifestation—for the concretum's utter annihilation—
involve the concretum's external relations to other things, most saliently its
spatial relations to other basic concreta. But, in other cases, the condition
may be entirely internal, sometimes even entirely Qualitative, as well.

Here's one way for that to be so. In some "Annihilational Worlds,"
there'll be Spherical Particles that, until very recently, have always been
Red Spheres. (For the longest time, they'll all have been Red Spheres,
whether this initial "Red period" be just some few billions of years or
whether it be a temporally infinite past period.) In some of these
Worlds, our Red Spheres will be Propensitied for Change as regards
their Extensible Color Quality. When manifesting this Propensity,
some of the Spheres may undergo a gradual Change of Color, with a
Red Sphere becoming Purplish Red, and then Reddish Purple, and
then Purple, and then Purplish Blue, and then Blue. What's more, such
a Sphere may be Propensitied, so far as annihilation (or continued
existence) goes, with respect to its own Color. In the manifestation of
this Self-directed "Color-sensitive" Propensity, there may be such an
annihilational occurrence as this: Within a second of the Sphere's

becoming Blue, the Spherical concretum ceases to exist, completely and forever. Far from being accidental, that cessation is the manifestation of the Particle's Propensity for Annihilation. Well, that's one way for a basic concretum to have a Self-directed Propensity for Annihilation, and to manifest that Propensity.

Whether the conditions for the Annihilational Propensity's manifestation are all internal to the object, as in the case just considered, or whether they're external to the entity, an object's Propensity for Annihilation is an *extremely radical Propensity (of that entity) for Change*. This is a far more radical Propensity for Change, it's clear, than any Propensity for Change we've already considered, as with a concretum's Propensity for Change with respect to Shape. For with just this Propensity, we're involved with nothing less than something's existence itself and (a bit later) with the thing's (subsequent) nonexistence.

Taken all by themselves, those words may sound impossibly highfalutin, almost entirely empty of any real sense or meaning. But, in just a minute or two, we may provide them a usefully instructive context: Consider a Blue Sphere with these two conditional Propensities. First, it's Propensitied for Annihilation, or for Change as regards Existence, providing only that it comes within a meter of a Green Cone. Second, it's Propensitied for Change as regards Color (say, so as to become Red) providing only that it comes with a meter of a Yellow Cube. Now, throughout some billions of years, this Blue Sphere hasn't come within a country mile of either a Green Cone or a Yellow Cube. But, now, all of a sudden, and quite simultaneously, it comes well within a meter of both. What will happen? Which Propensity for Change will be manifested? Well, on my understanding of all the most relevant terms employed here, the Blue Sphere will simply cease to exist, completely and forever, without ever being any Color other than Blue. As must needs be, the Sphere's Propensity for Annihilation (which is it's Propensity for Change as regards (its own) Existence) necessarily trumps any other Propensity that the individual may have, including, of course, its Propensity to Change as regards (its own) Quality, or Color. This very same understanding may be expressed, of course, in many different ways. So, equally well, we might say that the concretum's Propensity for Annihilation must have priority over any other Disposition the individual might have. Or, the manifestation of the concretum's Propensity for Annihilation must override, or it must undermine, the manifesting of any other Propensity of the selfsame individual, the manifestation of which will be precluded by the imminent cessation of the individual. That, as I say, is my understanding of how these term relate to each other, and how their possible referents must be related.

Now, did that surprise you? Were you surprised at which under-standing was my understanding, so that my little accounting seemed rather more eccentric than normal or natural? Not for a minute were you surprised! So, what I'll do now is say to you that, throughout the whole of this book, my understanding, just so normal and so natural, is to be taken as our common understanding, yours just as well as mine. (If need be, I'll simply stipulate to just that effect. But, as I reckon, that's not really necessary; rather, right off the bat, we're all quite alike here.)

Though the Propensity for Annihilation is extremely radical, as we've just observed, still, in certain supposed Worlds, it won't be at all unusual. With some of these Worlds, the history of concrete reality will be ex-tremely short. Consider, for instance, Worlds with just one (basic) con-cretum. (We may take a World's only concretum to be an infinitely vast, Qualitatively heterogenous, Spatially extensive Field. Or, we may take it to be a Monochromatic Red Spherical Particle. That doesn't matter.) With some of these Worlds, the sole (basic) concretum is Propensitied to Annihilate just shortly after it first exists, under any compossible condi-tions. Now, in some of *these* Worlds, no concretum will ever (again) come to exist quite by accident, nor as any random happening, nor anything of the like. Well, then, just as this Propensity is manifested in very short order, even in Worlds of this last specified sort, it's quick curtains for concrete reality in all the Worlds just like those, just so recently specified.

In the actual World, it's plain enough, things stay around for a goodly while. If there's absolute annihilation here, it's much more the exception than the rule. I've been around a goodly while already, it's safe enough to say, and so have you. And, so, it is, too, with our physical bodies, even though these human bodies are, no doubt, mere physical complexes, whose Propensities are all just physically derivative Propen-sities. Presumably, that's how it is, too, with (most of) our bodies' most basic physical constituents, as with (most of) your current quarks, or most of my electrons, or whatever. Just so, with ever so many of our World's concrete individuals, including just so many quite basic concreta, there's great continuity of existence. Or, at the least, so we do well to believe.

What's more, with most concreta, (their) *continued existence isn't a random* matter. Recall our Sphere that Changed Color, from Red to Blue, and, within a second of its becoming Blue, the Spherical concretum *ceased to exist*, completely and forever. Far from being accidental, *its ceasing to exist* was the manifestation of a certain Propensity of the Par-ticle: the Particle's *Propensity for (its) not* continuing to *exist*, or, in fewer words, its Propensity *for (its) not existing*. As we were supposing, that Self-directed Propensity of the Particle, for (its) not existing, was with respect to, or was directed at, how it was with the selfsame Particle Qualitatively.

Now, consider the Red Sphere during all the long time that it was Red. During all that long time, of course, the Red Particle *continued to exist*. And, as we were supposing, at least implicitly, *its continuing to exist* was the manifestation of a quite opposite Propensity of the Particle, or a quite correlative Propensity of the individual. It was, of course, the manifestation of the selfsame Sphere's *Propensity for (its) continuing to exist*, or, in fewer words, its Propensity *for (its) existing*.

Perhaps owing to our philosophical education, it may often seem, unfortunately, that it's a quite empty remark, or maybe it's a quite tautologous comment, to say that an object's continued existence is explained, either wholly or even just partly, by its having a Propensity for (its) Continued Existence. Well, when you find yourself in that stultifying mindset, please do recall this Section's discussion. Myself, I've found it to be quite helpful, in getting me to avoid, if only for an hour or two, that stultifying mindset. (But, still, often this is hard to do. So, in some of the Section's later paragraphs, I'll try to provide further help, in an attempt at making it less hard to do.)

With a great variety of *actual concrete individuals*, (their) *continued existence is*, at least almost always, *a manifestation of their Propensity for (their) continued existence*, rather than its being any random, or coincidental, or accidental matter. That's what I believe about *my own continued existence*, and about yours, too. And, indeed, it's my view about the continued existence of (whatever may be most of) the actual world's most basic physical things. Their continued existence, from one moment to the next, *isn't just* some chance phenomenon, *unrelated to* all their Propensities. But, then, *why does* a basic concretum continue to exist?

In my philosophical education, as I've so lately indicated, I somehow got the idea that, benign deities and their ilk placed aside, the continued existence of a quite simple individual, as with a Democritean atom, just never does have any real explanation. Unlike what may be said for continuing *complexes*, as with a persisting ship always composed of many wood planks, there's simply nothing to be said as to how it is, or why it is, that a partless atom continues to exist. And, as I suspect, you've learned that, too. But, even if there's *not very much* to say about such a matter, why think there's *never anything at all to be said*? As I suspect, that may be an unwarranted dogma. And, far from its being philosophically harmless, an attachment to this dogma may hinder metaphysical understanding. So, I'll try to lessen our attachment to such a suspect and stultifying statement.

First, we consider a World with (at least) one vast physical particular, perhaps a vast heterogeneous physical Field that's richly Propensitied, though it never has any Propensity to Annihilate. And, as we'll suppose, much of our Field's Propensity comprises its Propensity for Change with respect to Quality. Over much time, this Propensity is variously manifested. Consequently, and for that very reason, the Field's Variegated Qualitative panoply Changes (in the distribution of its Spatially Extensible Quality) from time, to later time, to later time still. Just so, the World's Qualitative temporal Changes *aren't* random happenings. Rather, they're the manifestations of the World's, or of the Field's, Propensity for Change as regards Quality.

Now, second, let's suppose, alternatively, another World, whose sole concretum is also a vast physical Field, but whose Field *never undergoes* Qualitative temporal Change.

Our Field might be supposed as heterogeneous in the spatial distribution of its Quality. In other words, we may suppose that the Field is Qualitatively Variegated, in a certain absolutely specific way. To make that easy to conceive, think of a certain recurring 3-D Qualitative patterning, as with a 3-D analogue of a certain tartan, or of a certain simply patterned sort of wallpaper. Well, Qualitatively, the considered Field will always be Variegated *just like that*.

Alternatively, we may suppose our Field to be Qualitatively absolutely homogeneous, or completely Unvariegated. For instance, we may suppose our Field to be everywhere just Extensible Red. So, equally, it may be *just like this other way* that we should suppose our Field always to be, namely, Qualitatively everywhere just Extensible Red.

Either way, whether Variegated or Unvariegated, we do well to make a further supposition. Now, just as we're already supposing that (in every last one of its regions) the Field never Changes Qualitatively, so we'll do well to suppose, further, that *this isn't any random matter*. Rather, as we'll be supposing, and ever so differently from that, the Field's always being the same, Qualitatively, is *the manifestation of the Field's Propensity for Monotony as to (its) Quality*. It's *for just this very reason that*, with this World's Field, there's *no Change in (its) Quality*, from time, to later time, to later time still.

Well, just as a vast Field can be Propensitied for Monotony as to Quality, so it also may be Propensitied for Monotony as to Existence.[17] Then, rather than any mere accident, it may be owing to *this Propensity's manifestation* that, in the case of the Field, there's *no Change as regards Existence*. In other words, it's for just *this* reason that the Field *doesn't*

---

17. Well, as I've been Capitalizing "Quality" and "Propensity" and "Change" and "Monotony," I'll also capitalize "Existence." But, please don't think I have any very grand view about what it is for something to exist. Please don't think, for instance, that I hold Existence to be a Perfection, or that things that exist are more perfect than things that don't exist. No; I just like to Capitalize.

cease to exist, but *it continues to exist*, from time, to later time, to later time still.

As I'll emphasize, another Field may be Propensitied in a way that's *radically different* from the Field we've just been imagining, that's even *diametrically* different. Such a Field will be Propensitied for *Change* as to Existence. Then, should this Propensitively opposite Field cease to exist, *that* won't be any accident, either. To the contrary, its cessation will be the manifestation of the Field's Propensity for *Change as regards (its) Existence*.

Now, symmetrically with such a Self-annihilating Field, I submit, or in an ontologically relevant parallel with it, our Self-persisting Field may *not* Annihilate—and it may, instead, *Continue to Exist*—as the manifestation of *its* Propensity for *Monotony* as regards (its) Existence. All right, then—at least for the meanwhile, that's enough about Fields.

With other basic physical particulars, as with Particles, must things be very different? No; not at all. All the main points hold, just as well, for basic physical Particles.

A little while ago, we imagined a basic Blue Sphere Propensitied to Change its Shape, under certain conditions, so as to become an Ovoid. Salient among the conditions was this: The Blue Sphere might (come to) be within a meter of at least one basic Red Sphere. As you'll recall, we supposed that, though for a long time it was further than a meter from any Red Sphere, eventually our Blue Sphere came within that distance of a Red Sphere. And, then, the Blue Sphere's Propensity for Shapewise Change was manifested. So, the Blue individual became Ovoidal, no longer Spherical.

What did that help us see? Well, just as there are Propensities for *Monotony* in respect of Shape, which may be enjoyed even by quite basic spatial objects, so also there are Propensities for *Change* in respect of Shape, which also may be enjoyed even by basic physical concreta. And, of course, the Propensity that was helpful here, in getting us to see that, *wasn't any Self-directed Propensity* (of the Blue Sphere). Rather, the instructively helpful Power was, of course, a Propensity of the Blue Sphere for a Shapewisely Changeful Interaction with Red Spheres, an obviously Generalistic Propensity.

Now, let's do a nicely altered version of that little example, aiming for a case that's comparably helpful with our current clarifying aims. So, first, let's suppose this: A White Sphere has a Propensity for Annihilation, or for Change as to (its) Existence, that's directed at, or that's with respect to, Black Spheres. Should a White Sphere (come to) be within a meter of a Black Sphere, the White Sphere will cease to exist, completely and forever. And, this will be no accident. Rather, it will be the manifestation of a certain Propensity of the White Sphere for Change as to (its) Existence. But, of course, this won't be any Self-directed Disposition of the White

Particle that's here manifested. To the contrary, what's at work is, or it will be, the manifestation of a certain reciprocal Propensity of our White Sphere, a Propensity that it has (not with respect to itself, but, rather) with respect to any (nearby) *Black* Sphere. So, as clearly different as White is from Black, it's one thing for an individual to have a Propensity for Change as to (its) Existence, and it's quite another for a particular to have a Self-directed Propensity (and, it's still quite another thing, of course, for an individual to be Propensitied with respect to disposition *partners*, each of them being some other entity).

We want to get just as clear, I trust, that there's a huge difference between something's being Propensitied with respect to itself, or its having a Self-directed Propensity, and its having a Propensity for Monotony as to (its) Existence. Well, we may consider a Yellow Cube that's Propensitied to continue to Exist, with this Propensity directed at, or with respect to, any Purple Sphere that's within a mile of it. For the longest time, the Yellow Cube has been well within a mile of many Purple Spheres. But, finally, it comes to be more than a mile from any and, straightaway, it ceases to exist. Why did that happen? Well, without further specifications, this can be only very partially explained. But, by way of explanation, there's already this to be said: It came to be that the Cube was no longer in conditions where there would be manifested its Propensity for Monotony as to (its) Existence; it came to be that it was no longer within a mile of even just one Purple Sphere. So, if the Yellow Cube continues to exist anyway, that's a sheer accident, a random happening. And, as we've been supposing it *not to have a Propensity for Change* as to (its) Existence, if the Cube should cease to exist, when first it's far from any Purple Sphere, well, that's also a sheer accident.

But, of course, the main point here concerns what happened with our Cube *before* it got so dangerously distant from Purple Spheres. For all *that* time, it *continued to exist*. And, it's temporally protracted persistence, we may suppose, *wasn't any sheer accident*. Rather, it was the *manifestation of the Cube's Propensity for Monotony as to (its) Existence*. And, as we said when first contriving this case, that's *no Self-directed* Propensity of the Cube. Rather, this Propensity for Monotony as to (its) Existence is directed at, or it's with respect to, suitably sustaining disposition *partners*, none of them the Yellow Cube itself, of course, as any of them is, instead, a Purple Sphere.

Well, I don't know about you; but, for me, that does it. I'm now about as clear as I can be that there's a huge difference between something's being Propensitied with respect to itself, or its having a Self-directed Propensity, and its having a Propensity for Monotony as to (its) Existence.

But, of course, even as an object's Propensity for Monotony as regards (its) Existence *needn't* be a Self-directed Propensity, still, it *may* be a Self-directed Disposition. And, it's just that possibility that I'm urging us to acknowledge. If I've been at all successful in this attempt, then, by this point, a certain central thought won't seem very bizarre at all, and certainly not too bizarre for us to take it quite seriously. This is the idea, of course, that a basic concretum may continue to exist as the manifestation of just that object's Self-directed Propensity for Monotony as regards (its) Existence. Presumably, I should think, this idea is very commonly instanced, far more commonly, I should think, than any *utterly happenstantial* continuations of the careers of basic concreta.

Just so, in certain Worlds, many of the basic concreta will be Small Blue Spheres, little round concreta that, in these Worlds, have each always existed. And, in many of these Worlds, each of the *Blueternalons*, as I'll call them, will have a Perfectly Unconditional Self-directed Propensity for (its) Continued Existence—even while, in these Worlds, there's never anything else, quite distinct from the Perfectly Propensitied Blueternalons, that ever bears on questions as to the (present or future) existence of any of these Small Blue Spheres. Now consider a certain one of these Blueternalons, one *Blueto*, to give him a name. Is there anything that will (help) explain why Blueto currently exists? Yes; there is. And, for the most part, it goes a lot like this: Blueto just did exist, nicely Propensitied for Continued Existence. And, with nothing to prevent that Power from being manifested, it *just was* manifested. What was this manifestation? Of course, it's nothing more than, but also nothing less than, Blueto's currently existing. Or, in still plainer terms, it's Blueto himself, existing right now.

19. Self-directed Propensities with Respect to Propensities: The Basis of Stable Monotony

As early in the Chapter as just its Second Section, we became familiar with ideas about Propensities with respect to Propensities, that is, about Power-directed Powers. Now, much later in the Chapter, we'll let these ideas show what terribly central philosophic work they're so very well suited to do.

Consider a Blue Sphere that's Propensitied to remain Blue, and that's Propensitied to remain Spherical. How long will this entity remain Blue, or stay Spherical; will it be for more than just a mere moment? Well, if longer than that, and if all that's not the least bit happenstantial, then the Sphere's staying that Shape, and its remaining that Color, will be the manifestation of some Propensity, or Propensities, to just such effects. Now, in simple Worlds, and, just maybe, even in the actual world's most suitably simple situations, the reason for that will simply be this: In addition to having a Propensity to remain Blue, our Blue Sphere has a Propensity to continue to have *that* Propensity. And, beyond being Propensitied to stay Spherical, our Blue Sphere *is Propensitied to continue to be Propensitied* to stay Spherical.

In the very simplest situations of *that* sort, there will obtain (at least) two related conditions.

First, the entity (in focus) will be *Propensitied to retain all its Propensities*, each of them just as it is (and just as it's been), *including this very Propensity itself*, of course, which we may call its *Comprehensively Propensitive Propensity*. Or, in metaphysically more perspicuous discourse, the entity will be *Propensitied to continue to be Propensitied just as it is* Propensitied, and just as it's *been* Propensitied. (There's no paradox in any of this; not even anywhere in the neighborhood.)

Second, the entity's Propensities will all be Completely Unconditional. A Blue Sphere will continue to be Blue, and it will continue to be Propensitied to be Blue, no matter, for instance, how far the Sphere is from the nearest Cube, and no matter whether or not there are ever any Green Cones, and so on. Though there will be many Blue-Annihilators, I'm inclined to agree, none will be so "situated" as to have its salient Propensity manifested, leastways not in any interaction with our considered Blue Sphere. Just so, no Blue-Annihilator will exist at any time during our Blue Sphere's Eon or, maybe, even during any of its many successive Eons. (Leastways, except if it might exist in a different World from our Blue Sphere's World, there'll never be any Blue-Annihilator existing when our Blue Sphere exists.) Nor will there ever be, in our Blue Sphere's World, and in any of its possibly very many Eons, any Sphere-Annihilators, or any Blue-Color-Changers, and so on.[18]

As I imagine, certain Neo-Newtonian Particles might (be supposed to) satisfy these simple conditions or, at the least, some Decently Qualitied Newtonian Particles might (be supposed to) do so. Here's how that might go: At the World's start, maybe an Almighty God created ever so many Dark Grey Spherical Neo-Newtonian Particles—each a certain small length in diameter, each perfectly solid (with respect to all

---

18. As readers may notice, there's a certain tension between my saying that a Blue Sphere may have a Propensity for Continued Existence that's Completely Unconditional and, then, my saying that any Blue Sphere must be vulnerable to annihilation by Blue-Annihilators. And, if taken strictly, maybe there's a contradiction in that. So, to relieve the tension, and to avoid contradiction, understand my use of "Unconditional" to mean the same as *Categorical*, or *Absolutely Real*. Thus, there's then no implication as to the Blue Sphere's continuing to exist in absolutely all conditions, including all that never obtain in our Blue Sphere's World.

others), each with a certain small mass (or gravitational power), and so on, in respect of absolutely everything as to how each Particle is intrinsically Propertied. What's most salient in this "and so on"? Well, in respect of absolutely all its intrinsic Properties, each Particle's Propensitied to stay just the way God first made it—saliently including, among these intrinsic Properties of a Particle, its being *just so Propensitied, for ever so much intrinsic Monotony.* And, after he created the Neo-Newtonian World, the Almighty God may have Annihilated Himself, so that he exists no longer. Or, he may have irrevocably set Himself against ever altering anything about how it is, intrinsically, with any of His created Particles, just so suitably Changing His Own Propensity Profile, in the very process of forming that momentously irrevocable resolution. At all events, as we're supposing, nothing in our Neo-Newtonian World can ever mean, from this point onward, any cessation of, or any intrinsic change in, any of our Neo-Newtonian Particles. (Please, don't get upset by any of this; it's just a small attempt at vivid illustration.)

Anyhow, in more complex Worlds things won't be as simple as that. So, for one thing, in some such Worlds, even the very most basic entities won't be Propensitied for Monotony. Rather, insofar as they're Propensitied, they may be, for the largest part, Propensitied for Change, even as regards their most intrinsic Properties, or features. And, for another thing, maybe there won't be any entities with Self-directed Propensities. Rather, how it next will be with an entity Propensitively (as opposed to how it is quite currently) will depend on its (often-changing) relations to other entities. And, for a third thing? No; enough with all this unattractive complexity. Let's get back to some elegantly simple situations.

Right now, I'm going to focus on a certain salient sort of Self-directed Propensity. This is a (supposedly) basic entity's Propensity for (its) Continued Existence. Suppose that a Single Field is (or it constitutes all of) a certain wholly material World; it always has done, and it always will do. Then, as we may naturally suppose (though it's not required that we suppose this), the Vast Concretum will always be Propensitied for Monotony as regards (its) Existence, and it will always be Propensitied for Monotony with regard to *that* Propensity, its Propensity (for itself) to Continue to Exist. This will be a most natural supposition, and it will certainly be a quite coherent supposition, even if we should go on to suppose, as well we might, that, in ever so many other respects, the Vast Spatial Concretum is Propensitied for Change—for example, it may be Propensitied for Change as regards the spatial distribution of (its Variegated) Spatially Extensible Quality.

Somewhat similarly, I'll suggest, we should proceed with paradigmatic Particles, say, with Democritean Atoms. Perhaps, as I'm suggesting, it also may be simplest to conceive them as being just so Self-directly Propensitied. At every moment, they're each Propensitied for Monotony as regards existence, *and* for Monotony as regards that *very Propensity*. What's more, it's also natural to suppose with such Atoms, that this Propensity is Completely Unconditional (or something close to it). At least, no matter what the arrangements among a Democritean World's Atoms, each Atom will continue to exist, just as it's Propensitied to do, and just as it always *was* Propensitied to do.

A couple of Chapters down the road, I'm gong to advocate, quite cautiously and tentatively, nothing less than a Quasi-Cartesian Interactionist Substantial Dualism.[19]

On the Interactionist Substantial Dualism I'll advocate, each of us is an immaterial soul, a mentally Powerful individual that's wholly nonspatial. (Or, at the least, and not very different from that, each of us has, as her only essential part, aspect, or feature, just such a single and distinct immaterial soul.) On one Form of this View, which I'll call an Emergent (Interactionist) Substantial Dualism, each us was generated, in the first place, by the mutual manifestation of certain soul-generating Propensities, many trillions of them, each the Propensity of a (numerically different) basic material concretum, say, a distinct elementary particle. In a certain human mother's womb (or wombs), each of these soulfully-productive particles came to be arrayed, along with trillions of others, in a suitably healthily normal brainy way. How suitably? Suitably enough for there then to arise a certain single one of these nonspatial souls, complete with its power to experience, a power possessed by the soul right from its very first moment.

Substantial Dualism, whether Emergent or not, is very unfashionable, nowadays, in the most respectable academic philosophical circles (as is, for that matter, anything else that's very different from our dominant Scientiphical Metaphysic). But, as I surmise, some sort of Substantial Dualism is the preferred View of very many nonphilosophers,

---

19. It's not that, still later in the book, I'll be abandoning the advocated Dualism. No; I'll see it through, right to the end. Indeed, in the book's last Chapter, I advocate several very novel Forms of such a Substantial Dualism, one of which will be a Quasi-Platonic Dualism, as much as it's a Quasi-Cartesian Dualism. So, rather than suggesting any abandonment of any Dualism, my qualifying words indicate only that, in my advocacy of a Substantial Dualistic Metaphysic, whatever its precise Form, I won't ever be expressing any great confidence on my part, simply because I won't ever *have* any great confidence in any Substantial Dualism. But, then, neither will I so much believe, either, any rival View.

maybe saliently including many Protestant Christians. I just surmise here; I really don't know.[20]

Anyway, about any such advocated immaterial soul, we may ask much the same existential questions as we can ask about ever so many material things, including even very many (supposed) quite basic physical individuals. So, we may ask why, given that it did exist, just a moment earlier, a particular immaterial soul still does exist, just a moment later, and then another moment later, and so on. One sort of answer, especially simple and elegant philosophically, is in terms of the soul's having a self-directed Propensity for Monotony as regards (its) existence. Or, perhaps more perspicuously, just such an elegant answer might be put in these terms: The reason the soul exists later is that, just a moment earlier, it was Propensitied for Monotony regarding (its) Existence, as well as being Propensitied for Monotony as regards (its) being just so Propensitied. And, as there was nothing to prevent, or to obstruct, these Propensities from being manifested, nor anything even remotely like that, they *were* manifested, first at the noted early moment and, then, manifested again, just a moment later, and so on. With that being so, the continued existence of our considered soul was very well secured. So, our soul's continued existence was, throughout, very far from being even remotely like any purely random matter, or any utterly happenstantial happening.

In the previous paragraph, there may be the seed of a metaphysically plausible account of how it may be that, even with the human likes of us, there may be mental life, or Mentally Propensitied Existence, after biological death, and bodily disintegration. As seems appropriate, at least to me, this account may be a model for, or it may provide a model for, what might be called *an Optimistic Form* of an Emergent Quasi-Cartesian Dualism of Minds and Bodies. But, beyond just giving you this little signal, for me to say more about this matter, in our present Section, would require me to get very far ahead of myself. And, even as I shouldn't do that, I won't do it.

---

20. Just recently, I read a bit of a new book I bought, written by the psychologist Paul Bloom. The book is *Descartes' Baby*, Basic Books, 2004. As far as I can tell, Bloom himself is as much of a Scientiphicalist as is almost any other highly educated Western contemporary of ours. Quite certainly, he's no great shakes as a philosopher. But, so what? After all, he's really a psychologist, and not a philosopher. Anyway, the point of this note is that, at least, according to Bloom, we're all, quite naturally, Substantial Dualists, whatever else we also might be. Just so, here are two (consecutive) sentences from the book's Preface: "We can explain much of what makes us human by recognizing that we are natural Cartesians—dualistic thinking comes naturally to us. We have two distinct ways of seeing the world: as containing bodies and as containing souls."

20. Thinking about OTHERONS: A Good Long-Term Investment for Substantial Dualists?

With my upcoming Dualism in mind, though not for that reason only, I'd now like to notice some Individualistically-directed Propensities that, in a most salient way, are *diametrically opposite* to (what I've called) Self-directed Propensities. For most of us, myself included, these will be, quite apparently, some very peculiar Propensities. Trying to be a pretty gentle soul—pun very much intended, I'll do this in a couple of steps, not forcing us to confront, all of a sudden, such very peculiar Propensities.

For a big first step toward our appreciative end, I'll rehearse some passages about some suitably supposed entities, possibly even some quite basic individuals. Right there, my sentences all concerned matters of existence and nonexistence, as well as certain Propensities to just such radical effects, but none that are any Self-directed Propensities. Just so, recalling them from our Section about Basic Concreta, Propensity for Annihilation and Propensity for Continuation, I'll have us again encounter these potentially helpful sentences:

> We want to get just as clear, I trust, that there's a huge difference between something's being Propensitied with respect to itself, or its having a Self-directed Propensity, and its having a Propensity for Monotony as to (its) Existence. Well, we may consider a Yellow Cube that's Propensitied to continue to Exist, with this Propensity directed at, or with respect to, any Purple Sphere that's within a mile of it. For the longest time, the Yellow Cube has been well within a mile of many Purple Spheres. But, finally, it comes to be more than a mile from any and, straightaway, it ceases to exist. Why did that happen? Well, without further specifications, this can be only very partially explained. But, by way of explanation, there's already this to be said: It came to be that the Cube was no longer in conditions where there would be manifested its Propensity for Monotony as to (its) Existence; it came to be that it was no longer within a mile of even just one Purple Sphere. So, if the Yellow Cube continues to exist anyway, that's a sheer accident, a random happening. And, as we've been supposing it *not to have a Propensity for Change* as to (its) Existence, if the Cube should cease to exist, when first it's far from any Purple Sphere, well, that's also a sheer accident.
>
> But, of course, the main point here concerns what happened with our Cube *before* it got so dangerously distant from Purple Spheres. For all *that* time, it *continued to exist*. And, it's temporally protracted persistence, we may suppose, *wasn't any sheer accident*. Rather, it was the

manifestation of the Cube's Propensity for Monotony as to (its) Existence. And, as we said when first contriving this case, that's *no Self-directed* Propensity of the Cube. Rather, this Propensity for Monotony as to (its) Existence is directed at, or it's with respect to, suitably sustaining disposition *partners*, none of them the Yellow Cube itself, of course, as any of them is, instead, a Purple Sphere.[21]

To be sure, the Yellow Cube considered just above, which we may call *Yuval Corpus*, certainly *doesn't* have a Self-directed Propensity as regards (its) Continued Existence. And, for present purposes that's a plus, a step in the right direction. On the other hand, this Yuval Corpus *isn't Individualistically* Propensitied, at all, as concerns (its) Continued Existence. Rather, we've assumed that, as concerns any such existential issue, it's just Generalistically Propensitied. And, for present purposes, that's not a plus; it's a minus. So, we should do better.

With all that in view, it's very easy, right now, to take a big step in just the right direction: Just so, we'll now consider a very different Yellow Cube, one *Yuval Carnal*, whose Propensitive profile includes just this: Yuval Carnal will continue to exist when, but only when, it's (still) within a mile of just a *certain particular one* Purple Sphere, whom we may call *Peter Sellers*.

Well, with Yuval Carnal, we've got a Cube that *is* Individualistically Propensitied as regards (its) Continued Existence, which is a plus; and, at the same time, this *isn't* a Self-directed Propensity, which is another plus. So far, so good; plus and plus. Still and all, even with our Yuval Carnal's noted Propensity, for (its) Continued Existence, there's not everything we might wish. Well, there's not everything that *I'd* like to see. So, for a little while longer, please bear with me.

What more would I like to see? Well, maybe I can best begin by saying this: To my mind, at any rate, there's something obviously *self-involving*, as we might say, about this Yuval's Propensity for (its) Continued Existence and, what's very much more, it's self-involving in a way that *completely transcends the (obviously needed) fact that it's Yuval's* Continued Existence that the observed Propensity concerns. No; quite beyond anything like that, what we have, in this case, is something self-involving in, or about, the (nicely Individualistically-directed) Propensity's *conditions of manifestation*: The Propensity for Monotony as to this Yuval's existence will be manifested when, but, of course, only when, *Yuval itself* is (externally) related in a certain way to just a certain other individual, our Peter Sellers. (Or, as it might similarly be,

---

21. The quoted passage is from Section 18 above.

another Yellow Cube, one *Yolanda Companionable* may be Propensitied to Continue to exist just precisely when it's (externally) related, in a certain way, to some certain other individuals, say, our Peter Sellers and, another particular Purple Sphere, say, one *Paul Silas*, and a third individual, as well, one *Patti Smith*. Though Yolanda's dependent on a plurality of other individuals, and not just one, still its Propensity for Continued Existence is also self-involving.)

By contrast with all that, let's now imagine a certain *OTHERON*, a very peculiarly Propensitied individual whom we'll call *Yuval Carte-sianeton*. Also a Yellow Cube, what's so peculiar about this Other Yuval is *how it's Propensitied* for (its) Continued Existence. Just so, this Yuval is Propensitied to Continue to Exist providing (only) that certain *Other individuals* are, and they continue to be, in certain appropriate external (sustaining) relations—*not* with Yuval itself, mind you, but, by contrast, or instead—*just with each other*. One of these Other individuals may be, again, our same peculiarly potent Purple Sphere, Peter Sellers. And, the other will be (not Yuval itself, of course but, say) a certain particular Green Cone, whom we may call *Gary Cooper*. So, as it may be, or as we'll suppose, our Yuval Cartesianeton will (continue to) exist when, but, of course, only when, Peter Sellers and Gary Cooper are (quite as they long have been) *no more than a billion light-years apart from each other*. As far as Yuval Cartesianeton's future existence goes, *that's* what's re-quired. It *doesn't* matter, by contrast, where this Yuval itself is. Just so, that concretum may be in an alien galaxy, terribly far, perhaps, from where it's ever been before. Or, alternatively, it may always be nearly adjacent to Peter, maybe on an opposite edge, so to say, from any that's closest to Gary. None of that matters; nor does anything even remotely like that matter. Quite the opposite, for this Other Yuval's future ex-istence, the situation is this: *All that matters is that Peter and Gary be appropriately (spatially, and thus externally) related*. As long as *they're* within a billion light-years of each other, Yuval Cartesianeton is still in busi-ness. But, just as soon as *they're farther apart* than that, well, that's just how soon that our Yuval's no more.

All that being so, this also might well be so: For eighty years al-ready, Peter Sellers and Gary Cooper have been well within a billion light-years of each other. But, sometime in the next decade, they will (come to) be more than a billion light-years apart. Just as soon as that happens, then Yuval Cartesianeton (already an octogenarian OTHERON) will cease to exist, completely and forever. No matter what subsequently happens with Peter and Gary, no matter how close they later become, it'll all be over for Yuval Cartesianeton. (By becoming closer again, Peter and Gary may come to generate, and they may then come to sustain, a genuine OTHERON. And, maybe, this will be an OTHERON that, in ever so many ways, is just like Yuval C. is, or was. But, still, that will then be *another* OTHERON, numerically different from Yuval Cartesianeton.)

As I'm sure some will have sensed, but as I'll now make perfectly explicit, it's not for nothing that we've considered this Other Yuval, whose Individualistically-directed Propensity, especially as to (its) Existence, is entirely Other-involving, and not the least bit Self-involving, as concerns the conditions for its manifestation: In our philosophic theorizing, we may easily think to replace our considered Yellow Cube, Yuval Cartesianeton, by a particular *nonspatial soul*, maybe one *Nina Simone* or, more shortly, just *Nina*. And, in parallel, we may replace our Gary and our Peter, just two particular basic physical individuals, by very many more elementary particles, a certain trillion billion trillion of them, perhaps. And, then we may think this: So long as just *these* productive Particles are nicely enough arrayed, then the nice Nina they first generated will continue to exist. But, just so soon as *they* become rather less nicely arrayed, well, then, that's the *end of our Nina*.

(For the sake of completeness and clarity, I'll offer these thoughts, even if some should take them to be a bit of a digression. The idea that a certain concreta may have Propensities whose conditions for manifestation are fulfilled when, and only when, certain other individuals are aptly externally related, well, this idea is hardly confined to Propensities as regards Monotony as to Existence, and Propensities as regards Change as to Existence. So, for example, a certain other Yellow Cube, one Yuval Colorchanger, may be Yellow, and may stay Yellow, when, but only when, our Peter and our Gary are within two billion light-years of each other. When they're further apart than that, this Yuval may become Light Blue, quite as it was always Propensitied to do, and to become. With no need for more examples, I end these clarifying thoughts. So, it's back to the main line.)

With our discussion of OTHERONS, as with our Nina Simone, we're pretty close, I do believe, to having a very nice model for what we might call *a Pessimistic Form* of an Emergent Quasi-Cartesian Dualism of Minds and Bodies. In a quite obvious way, I think, this nicely complements, even as it clearly opposes, *The Optimistic Form* of Dualism we've so lately observed, in the just previous Section. But, with just so many words now offered, to just such a tantalizing philosophical effect, I'd better not offer any more such stimulating badinage. Mindful of that, I'll now try to treat only some very different matters, hoping to observe some interesting connections among several points we've already encountered in this Chapter.

21. The Confused Idea of a World's Default Setting

As we've discussed, there's a real difference between temporal Monotony and, on the other side, temporal Change. (That's true both overall, and for any of the many respects in which there may be temporal Change.) Concerning that real difference, there's this to discuss: Is Monotony always a *default setting* for things, both overall and in any absolutely specific respect? By contrast, does temporal Change always call for an explanation?

With us humans, there's a tendency to think that Monotony's the more natural state of things, and that Change must be a departure from Monotony's natural default position. But, such preferential thinking prevented us, for millennia, from better appreciating the ways of our actual world. Here, it's a lesson from Galileo and Newton that makes the salient point. Most naturally, we're given to think that, when there are changes in the places of massive material objects, then there's a *departure from the default setting for* those *resting* material things. But, at least so long as the changes in place proceed at a constant rate, then *that* may have a better claim to be their default, at least in the actual world. In this actual world, anyhow, we'll need something to explain the slowing down of a stone rolling on a horizontal plain; maybe, it will be some friction between the stone and the plain. What we're to explain, it turns out, isn't why a the moving stone keeps moving, but, rather, why the stone slows down and, eventually, why the stone comes to rest on the plain.

Pursuing this line, I'll suggest that we should reject the idea that Monotony is, or must be, the default setting for a World. What do I mean by this suggestion, at once feisty and abstruse?

Pretty often, I've had us consider Worlds whose basic physical things are Blue Spheres, and sometimes Red Spheres, but, in either case, Monochromatic Particles temporally Monotonous as to how they're Extensibly Qualitied. Now, as we humans may naturally think, such temporal Monotony as regards Quality must be the default for any quite clearly conceived basic Particles, no matter what sort of World the Extensibly Qualitied Particles may inhabit. But, instead of thinking in such "default setting" terms, we may consider the matter far more clearly, I'll suggest, when recognizing how very various may be even the utterly basic Propensities of a World's very most basic physical things.

In this connection, we'll consider two Worlds that differ markedly as regards how their basic concreta are Extensibly Qualitied Monochromatically.

First, consider yet again a World whose basic physical things are just so many (Monochromatic) Red Spheres, always (temporally) Monotonously Qualitied, and, in addition to them, just so very many Blue Spheres, also always (temporally) Monotonously Qualitied. Both with the Red Spheres and with the Blues, the Monotony in how they're Qualitied is a *manifestation of how they're Propensitied*. The Red Spheres each have a Propensity for Monotony with respect to (Color) Quality; and, in their case, this amounts to each having a Propensity (for it) to remain Red, a Propensity that's continually manifested. And, the Blues are also Propensitied for Monotony with respect to (Color) Quality; and, in *their* case, that amounts to a Propensity (for *them*) to remain Blue, a Propensity also continually manifested. Well, that's mostly old hat. What's next is more novel.

Second, consider a World whose basic concreta are two sorts of Spheres that, as *their Propensities* serve to promote, enjoy certain temporal *Changes as regards their Extensible Quality*. On the one hand, there are Spheres that, while at every moment they're Monochromatic, undergo a certain sort of regular Change as to Color: These Particles *oscillate Qualitatively*, perhaps about as continuously as can be, from Red, through Purplish Red, through Reddish Purple, to Purple, and then Qualitatively back again, from Purple to Red, and then back to Purple *again*—over and over, ad infinitum. Far from any random happenings, our supposition has it that these Qualitative Changes are *manifestations of each Sphere's Propensity for Change with respect to its Extensible Quality*. Well, that's one sort of Sphere. Now, some words about the second sort: Like Spheres of the first sort, they're also each always Monochromatic, and also each always Qualitatively oscillating. But, unlike the first, they oscillate through a quite different range of Color Quality, from Red, through Orangish Red, through Reddish Orange, through Orange, and then Qualitatively back again, and then back *again*—over and over, ad infinitum. Far from random happenings, our supposition also has it, *these other* oscillating Qualitative Changes are manifestations of *these other* Spheres' Propensity for Change with respect to *their* Extensible Quality. With each of these Spheres, too, we suppose that its Qualitative Changes are *manifestations of its Propensity for Change with respect to its own Extensible Quality*.

Is the first World, with its denizens all *Qualitatively Monotonous* Spheres, a better candidate for having a *Default Setting* than the second World, whose concreta are *Qualitatively Changing* Spheres? Myself, I can't see anything to favor an affirmative answer.

When we abandon thoughts of Default Settings, we may be much clearer about how it is with these two considered Worlds. The first

World's basic physical occupants are Propensitied just as *they* are, saliently including a *Propensity for Monotony as to how they're Qualitied*, and *that's that*, as fundamental as anything can be, regarding any such matter. And, the second World's basic denizens are Propensitied just as *they* are, saliently including a *Propensity for Change as to how they're Qualitied*, and *that's* that, as fundamental as anything can be, regarding such a matter.

Well, we've just made some progress, I'm pretty pleased to think. By pursuing our progressive line further, maybe we'll make some more. Let me elaborate on my optimism.

Once we're clear of the confusions occasioned by thoughts as to a World's having a Default Setting, we can better appreciate our account of the continued existence of basic entities. As things certainly seem to me, the philosophically fashionable treatments make less sense of these matters than does our Quasi-Lockean approach, with its suggestion of how a currently extant concreta really may be Propensitied for (its) Continued Existence. Emboldened by that appearance, I mean to finish the Section with comments on a couple of more fashionable treatments, these more favored approaches to be conveniently placed under two heads.

First, there's what may be called the *Silent Treatment*, probably the approach that's now most fashionable: With our question of continued existence, for basic concreta there really can't be any explanation, not even any quite partial and incomplete account. And, so, we should be silent about any such metaphysically basic existential matter. Well, that's all very respectable, I imagine. But, still, the discussion we've been having doesn't let this fashionable Treatment look very good. Rather, as it now appears, our Quasi-Lockean approach *does* say something substantial about our metaphysically basic existential matter, even if nothing that's ever very detailed, let alone anything that's quite complete and full. Just so, our approach serves to rule out, quite intelligibly, the thought that each particular's continuing to exist may be mere happenstance, as might happen with an *Existentially Humean World*, wherein what exists at any given time *doesn't* serve to determine, or even provide *any help* toward explaining, at all, what exists just after that. By contrast, the Silent Treatment leaves things neutral between, and indeterminate between, a World's being an Existentially Humean World and, on the other hand, a World's being, at least to a certain degree, an Existentially More Stable World. So, however fashionable it may be to give the basic existential matters the Silent Treatment, we shouldn't continue to do that.

Second, there's what may be called the *Default Treatment*, which will have us thinking this: Given that a World's currently basic denizens now *do* exist, which we certainly may take as given, it's simply part of the World's Default Setting that now *there do* exist these perfectly basic worldly constituents. Just so, unless something *special* happens, the World's basic objects *simply* continue to exist. And, generally, *nothing* so special *does* happen. And, that's that. There's not any need for, nor is there any chance for, even a most modest *account of why* any basic concreta continue to exist.

But, as we've been arguing, and as it's just so easy to argue, very effectively, the idea of a World's having a Default is more confusing than illuminating. For a minute, think about Particles that are Probabilistically Propensitied to Annihilate. Just by itself, that's enough to crushingly clarify the deeply confused Default Treatment, though we could go on, indefinitely, with adducing other crushingly clarifying considerations.

Better than either the Silent Treatment or the Default Treatment, or any other approach that conflicts with it, we should continue to embrace our Quasi-Lockean Treatment of these matters. On our Quasi-Lockean approach, we will explicitly distinguish between an Existentially (Somewhat) Stable World, which is something we take the actual world to be, and, by contrast with that, an Existentially Humean World.

Instead of either of those terribly pessimistic fashionable approaches, or any view even remotely like either, we should prefer the Quasi-Lockean approach on offer: When a basic concretum continues to exist, then, typically and usually, that's not any merely random happening. Rather, it's a manifestation of the concrete particular's Propensity for Monotony as to (its) Existence. Because this Propensity is indeed manifested, the concretum does continue to exist, from time, to later time, to later time still.

22. Time without Change

While I'm not very sure about this, it strikes me that many philosophers favor ideas, at least implicitly, according to which there can't be any Time (maybe in some considered possible World) unless there is Change (in the considered World). Or, many may hold that, unless it's to be understood in terms of Change, any understanding of Time is bound to amount to no more than a quite empty and barren conception. Or, many may hold something else in this neighborhood, thus giving Change, in one way or another, an especially central place in respect of questions concerning Time, far more central, it would seem, than the place they give Unchange or, in my preferred lingo, than the place that's given to *Monotony*.

Myself, I suspect that, with anything much like any of that, there's precious little but some confused philosophical dogma. And, as I further suspect, this may be just a special case of the Confused Idea of a World's Default Setting.

By contrast with many other philosophers, I guess, I don't think there's anything to the idea that, for most possible Worlds, or for paradigmatic possible Worlds, there's a default, for the Worlds, that's something like Wholesale Monotony. For them, the Default is Monotony. And, with that being so, without there being some shifts away from this Default, or some Change, there won't be any Time or, at the least, there'll be no Time that's ever conceivable, even at all, by us human thinkers.

As I've been suggesting, all that's just some pretty nonsensical prejudice. By contrast with it, here's something that's more sensible, at least somewhat more sensible: First, with any World that's worth its salt, or that's really real, there's at least one concrete individual, propertied just as it actually is propertied. And, just a bit more specifically, the considered concretum is Propensitied just as it's Propensitied. Now, many Worlds each have many such individuals, while many others just have one. Maybe most satisfying, with these others there's a vast Field, perhaps. Anyhow, there's nothing that's any Default here. There just are Worlds of certain sorts, and also Worlds of other sorts. That's a nice start with some sensible thinking; now, let's go on with it.

In some Worlds, all the individuals are Propensitied just for Monotony. Quite Deterministically, or quite Nonprobabilistically, they're all Propensitied for Monotony in every conceivably relevant respect or regard. In these Worlds, in many ways very various, there will always be all sorts of Monotony, and there'll never be any Change at all. And, throughout eternity, that won't ever be the least bit accidental, or inexplicable, or anything of the kind. Rather, it will just be the continual, or the continuous, manifestation of how it is that all the World's individuals, always the same in number, and so on, are always Propensitied, including the manifestation of their Propensity to retain all their Propensities, even including this very Propensity itself. Though there will never be any Change, in any of the Worlds, there will always be Time. Throughout all Time, in a certain one of these Worlds, there'll be an infinity of Blue Spheres, each a meter in diameter, and each two meters from four other Blue Spheres, always the closest concreta to it. In another of these Worlds, throughout all Time, there will always be just two Red Cubes, each a meter on a side, and each twice as far from the other as each is wide. As I said, in ever so many ways, each of these absolutely Monotonous Worlds will be very different from ever so many other absolutely Monotonous Worlds. But, in this one respect, at least, they're all exactly the same: Though they're all infinitely enduring temporally, and though they all endure forever, and forevermore, none are ever involved in any real Change at all.

Any position much opposed to the approach I'm advancing is, I believe, little more than a metaphysical prejudice. It's a prejudice in favor of Change and, in the bargain, I guess, it's also a prejudice favoring Propensity for Change. But, any positively favoring prejudice is, in the nature of the case, also a negatively discriminatory prejudice. Just so, any position that's much opposed, in these matters, to the perfectly neutral view I'm advocating is a position that, without any discernibly strong reason, discriminates negatively against Monotony and, also, I guess, against Propensity for Monotony. But, though it's terribly boring, of course, a perfectly Monotonous way of being is, as even any merely human thinker can understand, a perfectly proper way for many Worlds to be.

So, this is what I now say to you: Just as we shouldn't discriminate against Monotony, so we shouldn't hold, on pain of being quite negatively discriminating, that Time requires Change, or that Time is to be understood in terms of Change, or anything even remotely like any of that.[22]

23. Do Our Reciprocal Propensity Partners Present a Cosmic Miracle?

It would be nice and neat for this Chapter to end with the Section just concluded. But, that's not to be. Instead, we'll end with some disturbingly problematic material, and some speculative ideas prompted by it. As is my hope, these ideas may help clarify the scope of the Humanly Realistic Philosophy we should seek, as well as its limits.

To set the stage for the problematic material, I rehearse a central thought about Propensities: First, the Propensities of a concretum are all *intrinsic* properties of the substantial individual. In other words, by contrast with any *relation* between any individual and any other

22. See Sydney Shoemaker's interesting essay "Time without Change," *Journal of Philosophy*, 1969. This essay is reprinted in the valuable collection of his essays *Identity, Cause and Mind: Philosophical Essays*. The expanded edition of this work, now available even in paperback, came forth from the Oxford University Press in 2003.

concretum, an individual's Dispositions are, every last one of them, *monadic* properties of just that substantial thing itself. (We should never confuse an individual's *Propensity for* interaction with other things, on the one hand, and, on the other hand, an individual's *actual interaction with* other things, which may be the *manifestation* of the Propensity in question. It's only the manifestation that requires a *relatum* for our considered individual, a partner that's related to our pondered entity. The concrete particular's Propensity for interaction doesn't require there to be, in actual fact, any partner for the Propensitied particular.)

In *this* metaphysical respect, there's no difference between how a concretum is Propensitied and how it's Qualitied. So, just as a basic physical concretum's being Blue is an intrinsic feature of the entity, so its being Propensitied in a certain way—whatever way it be—that's also perfectly intrinsic to the concrete individual. The point is, of course, entirely general. It holds not only for whatever physical things may be basic concreta—whether basic Particles, or basic Fields, or basic whatnots; it also holds, just as well, for mere physical complexes, or for whatever *nonbasic* physical things there may be. And, equally, it holds for all *mental* individuals—*whether or not* the mental particulars should be (just a certain sort of) physical entity.

Have I rehearsed ingredients for a metaphysical mystery? Well, let's see.

Early in a certain World's history, we may suppose, or in an assumed Eon's history, there are very many electrons, each of them a Small Blue Sphere with a certain characteristic profile of Propensity. In this profile, we're supposing, there's a Propensity to strongly repel any of the World's other Small Blue Spheres, or its other electrons, each so similarly Propensitied with respect to any others. Now, even with just this much supposed, it can seem that the envisioned World is so filled with perfect matches as to be almost *miraculous*. Or, better, there's this thought: Should the *actual world* be anything like as *wonderfully Propensitied as that*, with so many electrons each so similarly matched for dynamic interaction with all the others, then *this* may be almost miraculous. (Unlike me, you might never feel any such amazement. Don't worry. The next few paragraphs will be more stimulating.)

As we may imagine, we just supposed a World as it was in a relatively early Eon. As we'll now suppose, after that Eon the World's very many continuing electrons are joined by very many newly existent basic physical concreta, all of them of a very *different basic kind*. Still, just as with the electrons, *none* of which *Changed* (Propensitively) upon the arrival of these new Particles, each new Particle is, in all intrinsic respects, precisely similar to all the others. Well, *what* kind of new Particles should these be?

Evidently, there's an enormous (infinite) variety of possible kinds of basic Particles. Well, for specificity's sake, let's suppose that our new Particles, we may call them *legons*, are all precisely similar Large Green Ovoids, each with the same Propensity profile as all the others. (For one thing, each may be Propensitied to repel any other legon there may be, much as each electron is Propensitied to repel any other electron. But, of course, that's old hat.) Now, with this question, we enter new territory: Are our *electrons Propensitied for dynamical interaction with the legons; are our electrons suitable reciprocal disposition partners for regular dynamical interaction with each of our newly existent legons?*

Unless the answer's affirmative, our supposed World (or Eon) won't be any World (or Time) where there's impressive physical activity. For, as we've been supposing, those are all the basic concreta there are. So, for our supposed World to be anything much like the actual world, our electrons and legons must be nicely matched disposition partners. For the actual world is, evidently, a World where there's lots of interesting physical activity, at least enough to have it be that there's lots of chemical activity, and lots of biological activity, and so on.

For our supposed World to be much like the actual world, with so much physically promoted nice activity, its old electrons must be, and they *must have been*, Propensitied for happy dynamical interaction with its legons, so much more newly existent. (Remember, we're supposing that, even with the advent of the legons, *none* of the Small Blues *Changed* (Propensitively); rather, each remained the same.) But, now, it seems utterly miraculous that, even long before there are any legons, our electrons should be Propensitied for (just a certain specific sort of happy) dynamical interaction with possible Particles of precisely *that* specific sort—possible Particles Shaped as just the legons are Shaped, and Qualitied just as they are, and so on. Why does this seem so miraculous?

Well, there are *enormously many* diverse kinds of *possible* basic Particles, maybe even infinitely many kinds: So, on the one hand, we may take our supposed electrons to be fairly like, overall and relevantly, our actual world's real electrons. But, on the other hand, it seems absurdly profligate to think that our electrons, actual or even just supposed, should be Propensitied for happy dynamical interaction with *each and every (possible) member of each* of the enormously many diverse kinds of basic entity. How can our electrons be so *terribly richly* Propensitied, so *very variously* Propensitied, for such happy interactive Change? Any positive answer boggles the mind.

Now, it's far more comfortable, I think you'll agree, to take our electrons as being very significantly limited, as regards their Propensity profile. But, if an electron *isn't* terribly richly Propensitied for such various dynamical interaction, it will be almost *miraculous*, it seems, that the electrons should be Propensitied for such nice interaction with Particles of any *given specific sort* of basic physical things, as with some supposed hooligans, for instance. In particular, it seems miraculous that our Propensitively *quite limited* electrons should be Propensitied for nicely dynamical interaction with, not just so may Large Green Ovoids, but, what's more, with just the precise basic sort that we've supposed our "later-arriving" legons to be.

And, apparently, these next points are even more marvelously miraculous: that our electrons should be Propensitied, in advance, for just such dynamical interaction with the (subsequent) legons as will contribute (along with interactions with members of still other basic physical kinds) to there being an impressive variety of chemical complexes and, what's more, to there being myriad biological complexes, and so on. Yet all of this is so. There *are* an impressive variety of chemical complexes, and there *are* many biological complexes, and so on. So, in the most relevant imaginable scenarios, there will eventually obtain, among what are then the World's (basic) reciprocal disposition partners, just such a match of Propensities as is required for there to be "chemically generative interaction," and also "biologically generative interaction," and also "interaction generative of us thinking experiencers."[23]

Finally, and in a liberally Cartesian spirit, let's suppose there are nonphysical mental beings, each endowed with nonphysical mental powers, including a power to think, and a power to experience. As we'll suppose, I'm one of these mental beings, and you're another. Now, how might I communicate my innermost thoughts to you, or communicate how it's just been with me experientially? Well, barring extreme implausibility, there must be, in the first instance, a happy match between *my own* Propensity profile and, on the other hand, the Propensity profile of some *physical* thing, or things, *through* which I may (be allowed to) *communicate to* you how I've just been experiencing. This

---

23. The apparent miracles of Propensitive match aren't confined to considerations of Particles possible interacting dynamically (or possibly failing to interact dynamically.) In the blatantly physical realm of various Plenumate Worlds, just maybe including the actual world, Parallel miracles appear concerning how it might be that a given Field might, or might fail, to interact dynamically with another Field, possibly a later arrival in the World than the former Field. This requires, of course, a nice match between the Propensity profile of these two Fields. Also, apparently most miraculously, a similar match must obtain for there to be dynamical action between a given Field and, perhaps first existing only subsequently to it, any given Particle, or Particles.

must be so whether the Propensities involved are Individualistically-directed Propensities, as they really should be, or whether, as may be (perhaps confusedly) presumed, they're Generalistically-directed. As well, there must be a correlatively happy match between *other* (Individualistically-directed) Propensities of a *physical* intermediary, or intermediaries, and, on the still further hand, *your* (Individualistically-directed) Propensities. To my mind, this seems extremely lucky for us soulful experiencers, who would otherwise each be a terribly isolated person.

Because I'm uncomfortable with the thought of there being ever so many miracles, occasioned by all sorts of terribly mundane matters, this Section's material presents, to my mind, a pretty disturbing problem. What can be said to resolve this problem, or, at the least, to have it properly appear less disturbing? Though nothing's extremely satisfying to say, a few things may be usefully said.

In the *first* place, there's nothing very peculiar here. Indeed, what seems like miraculously unlikely matching attends a wide variety of cosmic issues and hypotheses, many of them quite speculative, to be sure, but also many not so speculative. For example, those familiar with Lewis's view of infinitely many Worlds may also be familiar with an objection, in the literature, to the effect that, on such an extremely generous metaphysics, it seems *miraculously* lucky (and maybe *incredibly* lucky) that we should live in a World, the actual world, where ordinary inductive thinking isn't just reasonable thinking, for most folks most of the time, but, to boot, it's *usually quite successful* thinking. Myself, I don't think any such objection to be very telling. Agreeing substantially with Lewis, on this matter, I think that an encounter with his view just makes it vivid for us, for the first time in a long time, that, concerning inductive thinking, there are acute philosophical issues still largely unresolved. When we first encountered these issues, as may have happened when we first read some passages from Hume, the issues were quite disturbingly vivid. But, as time passed, what was disturbingly vivid faded so much as to appear almost a dead issue. And, then, when first encountering Lewis's metaphysics, this nearly dead issue may become, at least for while, a live issue once again.

In the *second* place, there's this to be said. Always something of an issue for many philosophically sensitive souls, there's the question of why the world is, *even in its most basic* features, *just precisely the way* that, in fact, the world *actually is*. (In the neighborhood of this issue, there's a very famous question that may be, really, just a central part of this same issue. As most commonly expressed, the famous question goes like this: Why is there something, rather than nothing? Somewhat more precisely, it goes like this: Why is there ever any concrete being, instead of never any concrete beings at all?) When first confronting the question of why the world is just as it is, many thinkers, myself included, find it a vividly disturbing question. But, much as with questions of inductive thinking, as time passes this also fades so much as to become almost a dead issue. And, then, when encountering problematic material like what we've just confronted, with discussion of "miraculously matched" disposition partners, this nearly dead issue may become, at least for a while, a live issue once again.

A *third* thing to say mirrors, pretty closely, something often said in response to the question why the actual world is as it is—a world with many systematically related enduring things, a world with experiencers pondering philosophical questions, a world with many thinkers communicating their ideas with many others, and so on. Well, suppose that there's a real concrete World, or at least one, for each of the infinitely many absolutely specific sorts of (possible) World, or perfectly specific (possible) ways for a World to be. Now, as it certainly seems, *in the vast majority* of the real concrete Worlds with basic physical things, the basic physical concreta won't ever be well enough behaved to subserve even the simplest living things, much less will they be fit to subserve experiencers who ponder cosmological questions. This may very well be true even if, or even though, not only is the vast majority infinite in its membership, but so is the comparatively tiny minority.[24] So, let us

24. There's a nice joke that, in my view, very neatly makes this point, a joke I first heard from Larry Temkin: A terrible sinner and a generally quite saintly person both die and, together, they come before a Quasi-Cantorian God. On just one day of his life, the sinner behaved very well, helping a blind old lady cross a busy street, and so on, whilst on all the other days he behaved quite badly, even cruelly. So, his record isn't all negative, entirely deserving of punishment only. And, quite the reverse holds of the generally saintly person. With a record of his deeds that isn't entirely positive, but which does include only a very few venal deeds, it's not entirely deserving of reward only. So, our Quasi-Cantorian God says this. One of you will spend a day in hell, and then a thousand days in heaven, and then a day in hell, and so on. And the other of you, you'll spend all your time, forever and ever, in a reverse sequence: A day in heaven, and then a thousand days in hell, and then a day in heaven, and so on. But, as Georg Cantor has taught us, each of you will, thus, spend not only an infinite number of days in each place, but, indeed, the same number of days. And, so, either way, you'll be spending just as much time in the one place as in the other—an infinite amount of time. So, it really doesn't matter, which of you enjoys, or suffers, which of the sequences. So, I'll just flip a perfectly random coin, and let it decide, so to say, which of you undergoes which of the two sequences.

To my mind, at least, this Quasi-Cantorian God is as nutty as a Christmas fruitcake. Quite obvious, at least to me, for justice to prevail, it must be the saintly guy who undergoes, and who enjoys, the first-mentioned sequence, with a thousand days in heaven for each day spent in hell, while the sinner undergoes, and suffers, the reverse sequence. Well, with just that much said, I reckon that, about the relative sizes of various infinite groups, there's been enough said. So, it's now back to the body of our text.

proceed: Though almost all these Worlds will lack such thinking beings, it may not be very surprising that *this actual world, with us now
asking questions (about the cosmos)* has such physical concreta as are very
well suited to support complex mental activity, such as asking questions
(about the cosmos.) For, *we actually do* exist, and, we actually do ask
such questions. So, for us right now, at least, the existence of wondering thinkers is an undeniable *given*. Well, this "anthropic" thinking,
as I'll call it, may not do a very great deal toward dispelling appearances of miraculous Propensity matching, or any other apparent cosmic coincidences. But, especially in combination with other relevant
considerations, it does do something. (As may be worth noting, there's
a parallel response to the correlative question concerning the Eons of
just this one world: Why is the *present* Eon *just the way that it is;* why are
there *now* basic physical concreta so well suited to subserve thinking
beings, now asking questions about all the Eons?)

A *fourth* thing to say will be deemed, by some, to be excessively
speculative: It may be that each of our actual world's basic Particles, or
whatever are its most basic (physical) things, have very many Propensities that, for lack of there ever being any suitably matching Propensity
partners in our world, are always unmanifested. As it may be, each of
our world's basic concreta, say, its electrons, should be Propensitied for
dynamical interaction with *very many sorts* of basic concreta, but kinds of
concreta that, in this actual world, are never actually instanced. Is this
too speculatively profligate? Well, here's one way for things to be on
which, to my mind, that's not such a terribly profligate speculation:
Along with what we've posited, it may be that, with regard to *many more
such sorts* for basic concreta, our electrons *aren't* Propensitied for dynamical interaction.

(As it may be, with many of these enormously many sorts of possibilia, our electrons are Propensitied *for static coexistence*. In such an
event, we can see how, in a World with both such "static possibilia" and
things just like our electrons, it will *be no accident that*, between those
electrons and these static possibilia, there's never any dynamical interaction. And, in the bargain, it will be no accident that there's never
any "very interesting" spatial arrangements of basic concreta, as there
is, in the actual world, with the basic constituents of a DNA molecule,
for instance, or, again, with those of a snowflake. And, as it also
may be, with many of these very many sorts of possibilia, our electrons
aren't Propensitied at all, neither Propensitied dynamically nor, even,
Propensitied statically. Now, in a World whose only basic entities
are particles like our electrons and, on the other side, such "utterly

unmatching basic possibilia," well, whatever happens there, among the possibilia of the two main sorts, it *will be sheer happenstance*. And, so, if it should come to pass that, in such a World, there come to be diverse individuals arranged very interestingly, as with the quarks and electrons of one of our actual world's snowflakes, then *that* will be sheer happenstance.)

Once we realize all this, we may think that, in a most relevant way for reckoning these matters, it's *really not so many* sorts of possible concreta for which, on our positing speculation, we've supposed our electrons to be Propensitied dynamically. And, so, we may well think that it's *not an excessively* speculative posit that we need to make here.

A *fifth* point is, in a certain sense or way, almost opposite the fourth: In addition to all the basic physical things Propensitied to interact dynamically with us, whether directly or only quite indirectly, there may also be, even in the actual world, very many *other basic concreta*, many of them basic spatial bodies, perhaps, but none Propensitied for dynamical interaction with any of our basic constituents, nor with any Propensitied dynamical interaction with our quarks and electrons. Though they're all spatiotemporally related to us, or to our bodies, none will ever be even the least bit detectable, not by the human likes of any of us, anyhow. (Some may be just statically Propensitied with respect to all our interaction partners, in such a way as to be utterly unnoticeable by us. And, very possibly, there may be many others, maybe all "utterly unmatched Propensitively" with respect to all our interaction partners, that will also be unnoticeable by us.) So, not even very indirectly will we ever have any concrete indication of their existence. And, so, even while our electrons (for example) are Propensitively well matched for dynamical interaction with concreta of *certain* basic kinds, they may be, at the same time, not the least bit well matched for any such interaction with actual concreta of *other* basic kinds, and maybe *enormously many* other kinds. Never harmed nor benefited by any of these concreta, of course, we shall never have even the least clue, not empirical clue, anyway, as to the existence of any of them, however numerous, and however various, they should be.

Now, as a *sixth* thing, perhaps we may say that each of the five prior points can complement all the others. Still, I can't help but feel that there should be something more to say. But, of course, this is how it so often is in philosophy, especially when, as we're now doing, there's an attempt to deal with a most basic metaphysical question.

For a *seventh* thing, we'll have to wait till very near the end of our work, when we're well into the book's Tenth Chapter, its very last Chapter.[25] As I really do hope, and as I also suspect, you may think this seventh thing is more penetrating, and maybe also more plausible, than any of the six things just presented. But, to do any more than just expressing the hope, and the suspicion, well, that will have me getting very far ahead of myself. So, I won't do that.

Unlike most of this Chapter's Sections, I'm sure you'll have noted, the present one has been manifestly speculative and, even among metaphysically speculative writings, it's been a fairly far-fetched business. By my lights, maybe all too idiosyncratic, that's philosophically refreshing. But, in any event, it's now time to start another Chapter. And, with that fresh start, it's time to confront some thoughts that certainly aren't any such very speculative propositions.

25. In offering this so-called seventh thing, I'll eventually put forth a very considerable effort. Just so, toward the end of Chapter 10, when the stage will have been set, for my making such an effort quite productively, I imagine, I'll there devote two whole Sections to addressing this present Section's titular question, Do Our Reciprocal Propensity Partners Present a Cosmic Miracle? Specifically, I'll address it, first, in Section 21 of the book's last Chapter, "Recalling and Addressing the Question of Nicely Matched Propensity Partners." And, then, I'll further address the question in the very next Section, too, namely, the Tenth Chapter's happily labeled Section 22, "Our Hypothesized Dualism and the Question of Nicely Matched Propensity Partners."

6

IS FREE WILL COMPATIBLE
WITH SCIENTIPHICALISM?

With a fair lot of philosophical work, just some of it fairly speculative, we have a pretty fair grasp of our dominant Scientiphical Metaphysic. And, much of Scientiphicalism appears to comport well with our developing Humanly Realistic Philosophy. All that's been the upshot, apparently, of the three preceding Chapters. In this present Chapter, by contrast, I'll change course. Here, I'll expose difficulties with our accepting the Scientiphical View.

In much of this Chapter, I'll argue that Scientiphicalism is *incompatible* with our having a power really to *choose*. But, as you know, when introducing our Humanly Realistic Philosophy, in Chapter 2, we agreed that sometimes we really do choose; at the very least, sometimes we choose what to think about. That happened when I intentionally imagined a Red Sphere, because I chose to do so.

As we've been using the term "Scientiphicalism," the most salient form for the Scientiphical View is materialism, nowadays often called "physicalism." For decades, this has been the dominant position on questions of mind and body. (Weak forms of dualism, as with Dualistic Epiphenomenalism, are less salient sorts of this Scientiphical View.) Well, I'll signal that the incompatibilist considerations offered against Scientiphicalism, in this Chapter, will also count against a physicalist position on mind and body.

In discussions of mind and body, the main objection to physicalism has been that this view is incompatible with certain uncontroversial facts of our conscious thinking and experiencing. This has been true at least since Descartes; indeed, recent objections to physicalism don't differ greatly from a certain aspect of the Cartesian paradigm.[1] When it's this sort of incompatibility that's claimed, the conscious episodes in focus are purely passive events involving the experiencing subject. Or, so far as the offered objection goes, they may as well all be passive. At

---

1. All these recent arguments find their basic impetus, I think, whether in one way or whether in another, from Descartes's old idea that he could conceive of himself existing even without there being any material bodies in existence. For a pretty recent example, see Saul A. Kripke's argument for thinking that pain isn't any physical phenomenon, in lecture 3 of his *Naming and Necessity*, Cambridge, Mass.: Harvard University Press, 1980. For a more recent example, see David J. Chalmers's argument for thinking it possible for there to be experienceless zombies, each a physical duplicate of a human experiencer, as in his book, *The Conscious Mind*, Oxford: Oxford University Press, 1995, and also as in some subsequent essays. And, for references to other somewhat similar arguments, as well as an overview of these currently salient antimaterialist pieces of reasoning, see Chalmers's "Consciousness and Its Place in Nature," in Stephen P. Stich and Ted A. Warfield, eds., *The Blackwell Guide to Philosophy of Mind*, Blackwell, 2003, pp. 104–108.

As many Descartes scholars apparently agree, that famous idea was not, for Descartes himself, the only strong reason to think that his mind was, or that he himself was, something not material, or something not bodily. Rather, while Descartes did think that argumentation was sufficient to establish that thought, he also thought he had another sufficient argument. Equally, sufficient, at least for Descartes, was this piece of reasoning: He himself was absolutely (spatially) *indivisible*, as was intuitively quite evident. But, as was also intuitively evident, even as anything bodily was a (spatially) extended entity, of course, so any material being, by contrast, was a (spatially) *divisible* concretum. So, quite evidently, he himself wasn't any material being.

In the recent literature, there seems rather little interest in this argumentation, though I myself find it a very interesting line of thought, just as impressive a line for favoring the idea that Descartes, himself, really wasn't any material being—and that, like him, neither am I, myself, any physical concretum.

Well, I've just honestly expressed my rather high assessment of both of Descartes's central arguments for his Substantial Dualism (given the proposition that there are some material things, or at least one such). At the same time, I won't offer, here and now, any discussion in support of these perennially seminal arguments. But, Descartes devotees, do not worry. Late in my last Chapter, I'll do something to discuss these time-honored thoughts of our modern master.

In this present place, at any rate, the main point to notice is that, with any of these arguments for dualism, there's no important role to be played by anything like our belief that we really do choose, from actual alternatives for our thoughtful activity. By contrast, with what this present Chapter will offer, against both Scientiphicalism and against materialism, the central points are, precisely, points about the real choosing we all believe ourselves to engage in, or to instance, at least on occasion. So, not only is our upcoming argumentation very different from the salient (apparently peripheral) antimaterialist arguments stemming from Descartes, it's also just so different from the largely ignored (apparently central) anti-physicalist reasoning flowing from modern philosophy's seminal father.

any rate, this objection *doesn't* concern whether a wholly material being, whose powers are all physical Propensities, can ever really *choose* to do anything. But, as I'll be arguing, it's precisely this conflict with our really choosing that's such a huge problem for any materialistic philosophy. So, the considerations I'll offer against materialism differ markedly from those antithetical thoughts that, to date, have dominated this discussion.

That said, I notice that there's certainly no contest between the traditional objections to materialism and, on the other side, those I'll be offering in this Chapter. Indeed, each may best be taken as complementing the other. At any rate, that's what I believe.

Anyway, each of these two challenges has its distinctive strong point, along with, on the other side, an aspect that's certainly no dialectical advantage.

The advantage of the challenge dominating discussion is this. A very few radicals aside, nobody has even the least inclination to doubt that, from time to time, he is involved in conscious experiencing. And, any attempts to motivate doubts about *that* seem far more confused than compelling. Well, that's its strong point. On the other side, it's hard to make compelling the thought that there's a genuine incompatibility, in this area, between one's consciously experiencing and one's being a wholly physical entity. Just so, many are the prominent physicalists who think all episodes of our experiencing are purely physical episodes, each involving just so many purely physical changes in us purely physical complexes. What of our *power* to experience? Though few have explicitly considered this particular question, there's little doubt as to how they'd treat it: Our power to experience may well be—indeed, it must be!—a purely physical power of us wholly physical complex entities. Quite like your power to walk, your power to experience is a physically derivative Propensity, physically deriving from the physical properties of your physical constituents, saliently their physical powers, and from the physical relations among them. At least at this late date, it may be hard to argue, very convincingly, that there's a real incompatibility between experiencing and physicality.

Perhaps it's fortunate, then, that my impending challenge's strong point lies oppositely. For, it's *not* so hard to make problematic the thought that the power in question, the power to *choose*, is a physically derivative power, or any physical power at all. Well, that's *its* strong point. On the other side, what's less strong about my challenge also lies oppositely: Quite a few, I imagine, have some small inclination, at least, to think that nobody really does choose to do anything. Any appearance of real choice is, they might think, just an illusory appearance. Well, something like that. Anyway, it's more obvious, to me, that I experience, I certainly grant, than it is that I ever really do choose. But, as we've early and often agreed, for our present project, that difference doesn't much matter: As our Humanly Realistic Philosophy sensibly holds, it's *plenty clear enough* that, at least occasionally, we do really choose.

Beyond its forcefully presenting my new objection to physicalism, and to any Scientiphical Metaphysic, our discussion should engage philosophic issues that, from time immemorial, have been of substantial interest: From time immemorial, there have been very vexing challenges to our thought that, at least occasionally, we humans *choose what to do from among actual alternatives* for our own activity. In the present Chapter, I'll look to explore some of these traditionally vexing challenges, with a view to seeing how we may meet them, most fully and fairly, within the compass of a Humanly Realistic Philosophy.[2]

As I said a moment ago, it's *plenty clear enough* that, at least occasionally, we do really choose. In keeping with this, there'll be no serious question, in our discussion, as to whether we're to take vexing challenges to be negatively decisive. On the contrary, we'll say that, where a certain proposition is offered as incompatible with our truly

---

2. In the upcoming Chapters, I plan to put considerable pressure on the idea that Scientiphicalism, or anything very like it, is an adequate worldview. In this present Chapter, I'll argue that, by contrast with what I'll call *Nonentity Emergentism*, the Scientiphical Metaphysic is incompatible with the idea that you choose from among alternatives actually available for your thoughtful activity. At least for that reason, Scientiphicalism should be rejected.

Among at least modestly conservative alternatives, this leaves our Emergentism and, not so conservatively as that, (certain sorts of) Substantial Dualism. (By contrast with Dualism, Idealism isn't even a modestly conservative option to Scientiphicalism.) As Emergentism is more conservative than Substantial Dualism, initially there's reason to prefer Emergentism. And, as we've just been observing, Emergentism does better than Dualism, at least somewhat better, with the Problem of Our Unconscious Quality, even if, perhaps, not very much better. So, by the time we get to this Chapter's end, Emergentism should appear as our preferred view.

But, in the Chapter directly following this one, I plan to uncover problems that, as it seems to me, are quite devastating to our Emergentism, even as they are also devastating what's by then a terribly beleaguered Scientiphicalism. Some of these problems concern what would appear to be a repugnant plethora of experiencers, right where you take yourself to be the sole sentient being. The most blatant problem, however, involves what would seem to be—right where you take yourself to be the sole chooser, making just one single choice—an absolutely absurd enormous abundance of choosers, many make a certain choice while many others then make, instead, a very different choice.

Apparently, these problems undermine totally both Scientiphicalism and Emergentism. By contrast, the problems are treated far better by Dualism, as well as by yet more radical departures from our accepted worldview. With all that before us, I'll find myself quite at a loss, and quite unable to find acceptable any available worldview. But, maybe you'll fare better.

choosing from among real options—a thesis known as *Determinism* has often been the challenging statement of choice—there are only two live options: Either the proposition (for example, Determinism) really isn't incompatible with our truly choosing for ourselves, however much that may first seem so, or else the proposition isn't really true, however much *that* may first seem so.

Until recent decades, the preferred way to think about such challenges to our choosing, preferred among respectable philosophers, has been the first of these two ways: However much a certain appealing proposition, say, Determinism, may seem incompatible with our truly choosing, there's really no conflict between the statement's being true and our choosing from among actual alternatives. Lately, with far fewer believing Determinism to be true, the tide has turned. So, at the present time, quite a few hold that there really is the conflict claimed by the challenge, but, then, and at the same time, they hold that the conflicting proposition, Determinism, or Inevitabilism, isn't really true. Well, I guess that I'll be among these newly respectable *Incompatibilists*. But, the challenging statements on which I'll mainly focus won't be any Deterministic theses. Though I'll spend some time discussing some of those traditionally discussed views, I'll spend more discussing certain Scientiphical propositions.

1. A Few Points about Real Choice

Much as you do, I deeply believe that, at the very least, sometimes I choose what I'll *think about* from among actually available options for my thoughtful activity. As sometimes happens, I choose to think about metaphysics, even while there are other alternatives available for me, including an option to think about meat and potatoes. When I think about metaphysics *because I chose that alternative*, from among several available, there may be an especially clear instance of what's usefully called *real choice*.

I mean to use the term "real choice" to express our most central conception of choice: So, real choice must be *nonderivative* choice—which may be also called, more positively, *basic* choice. By contrast with that, a mere committee may make choices, from among the alternatives available to it, but these will be only derivative choices and, so, not real choices. Derivative because a committee, which isn't even any concrete individual, makes choices only when, in a more central way, some of its members, individual concrete conscious beings, each nonderivatively choose.

Yet more of what I mean can be seen in these considerations: Some people may set things up so that a certain mindless machine, perhaps fitted with randomizers, makes "choices" for them, or for other people. Even if the determinations made by the machine can be loosely called choices, they will not be what I call real choices. For, again, the selections will be derivative choices, dependent on the more basic choices of those who installed the machine, or, perhaps, on the choices of people choosing to be guided, in their behavior, by the machine's mindless determinations.

Here are further features of real choice. First, to make a real choice you must choose from at least two actual alternatives for you, each something that's actually available for your selection. And, each of these options must be something that, in some significant sense, you have in mind. It may be too much to require that, whenever you really choose from your available alternatives, you must actually consciously consider some of them, including the option you really choose. But, something similar, and a bit less stringent, doesn't seem too much to require for real choice: To really choose from among alternatives, you must have, at least, *the capacity to consciously* consider some of the options. So, if you really choose to think about colors rather than to think about sounds, you must have the capacity to consciously consider colors and, as well, you must be able consciously to consider sounds. There should be at least that much of a connection, it seems, between real choice and, on the other side, the most rudimentary sort of effective conscious consideration of alternatives, effective enough to eventuate in the choice of just one of the alternatives.

Second, and on the other hand, our making a real choice doesn't require that, when choosing, we have a special experience as of choosing. No doubt, with many people something like that sometimes does happen. And, with a few, it may often happen. But, after consciously considering whether to think about baseball or about basketball, I may simply choose to think about baseball, without my having an experience as of embracing that alternative, or rejecting the other option. Even so, I may now be thinking about baseball because I really chose to think about that. Indeed, it may be that, with some folks, all real choice is that way.

Third, in a most basic and central sense of the term, a real choice is an *independent* choice. When I really choose a certain available option, for my own thoughtful activity, my so choosing must be independent of how it is that anyone else chooses. Of course, I can choose, just as others can equally choose, to undertake a joint venture with others. But, then, while much of my subsequent activity won't be independent of much of theirs, my original *choice must be independent of all their similarly initial real choices*, if that choice of mine is to be a genuine instance of my *really choosing* to participate. Here's another point that may clarify this requirement: The two of us, you and I, may be privy, somehow or other, to the investment choices of the savviest money-man, Warren Buffet, the so-called Oracle of Omaha. Just a second after he (anonymously) buys some shares in a given company, we're the only folks who know which company that is, suppose, whilst anyone else who ever learns of it comes to know only five minutes later, or even later still. By contrast, right away, the two of us can be certain of what's gone on. Then, each time I learn of one of these purchases, I'll buy some shares, too, even if that can't be, of course, as many as Buffet himself just bought. And, as I'll suppose, so will you. For vivid specificity, let's say that, at 11:27:26 AM, on a certain Tuesday, Buffet bought 600,000 shares of Boeing. And, then, doing just as I chose, at 11:29:08, I bought 600 shares of Boeing. And, similarly, at 11:29:41, you bought 500 shares. Now, it's evident, I should think, that my choice to buy my 600 shares was independent of your choice to buy your 500 shares. What may be less obvious, but what's still true, nonetheless, is that my choice was independent of Buffet's very influential real choice, just previously, to buy all his shares of Boeing. Or, at least, that must be so if I really chose to buy my 600 shares of Boeing aircraft. Now, it may well come to pass, eventually, that my following Buffet's lead, or your doing so, should become automatic, or reflexive, or something of the kind, no longer being, as it once was, any independent act. Well, in such an event, by clear contrast, we won't, in this matter, still really be choosing.

Fourth, and finally, at least for the meanwhile, there may be many real choices that are entirely lopsided, the diametric opposite of situations where agents are indifferent as to their available options. So, it may be that I must choose between two possible punishments, for being caught parking in a no-parking zone. Quite bizarrely—but, it's a crazy world, after all—I must either pay a fifty dollar fine or else go to jail for a full year. As the judge so truly says, suppose, it's up to me; it's my choice. No surprise, I fork over the fifty bucks. In a restaurant, the next week, after hearing me relate the episode, but maybe mishearing several key words, a friend may ask me why I gave the city fifty dollars. As well might happen, I may say these words in reply, "I really had no choice in the matter." But, supposing that I ever really choose to do anything, it's almost certain that this reply isn't really true. Rather, I really did choose here, choosing the only option that was even the least bit reasonable, or the least bit attractive, and so on.

See here, philosophy fans, questions of real choice are very important issues, and not just philosophically, but also personally, too: If we didn't engage in real choice, at least from time to time, our lives would lack much of, maybe most of, the significance we commonly suppose our lives to have. In very central respects, they'd be no more significant than the lives of happy clams—for philosophy's sake, we suppose there to be such clams that, while they do consciously experience, never really do choose. So, should gripping considerations pose a threat to our deep belief that we engage in real choice, they'd threaten our belief that our lives are, in just such central respects, far more significant than those of such choiceless happy clams. It seems fair, then, to say that "real choice" expresses (the heart of) what many philosophers mean by "free will." All this being so, it's hardly too much, even in such a seriously ambitious book as this one, to devote a Chapter to this topic, and, I think, a pretty protracted Chapter, at that.

2. Free Will and Determinism, Real Choice and Inevitabilism: Not an Urgent Issue

In many traditional discussions of whether we "have free will," the central issue is whether the proposition that we really choose what to do is consistent with, or whether it's really *incompatible* with, a thesis of Fatalism, or Determinism or, as I like to label the threatening doctrine, *Inevitabilism*.

According to what may be called *All-Too-Full Inevitabilism*, any event in which any of us is centrally involved, like your imagining a gray triangle an hour or so ago, was inevitable from times long before any of us first existed, even if perhaps not from a time long before, when, say, an Almighty God made (the rest of) the universe.

Many will note that, in what's just been said, I've not mentioned any laws of nature, much less said anything like: "Deterministic natural laws take the state of the world at a given specific time and yield, or determine, the state of the world at other specific times." Recently, it's been common to think about Inevitabilism under the rubric of Determinism, and to state a Deterministic doctrine in some such terms as those. But, that's too limiting to do justice to the thesis.

Better, I'll suggest, for us to think of the matter like so: In several recent centuries, *most of the reason to believe* in an All-Too-Full Inevitabilism derived from reason to believe that the world was "governed by deterministic natural laws," in the sense indicated in the just prior paragraph. (The reason was always far from conclusive, but it may have been pretty impressive.)

Toward gaining an appreciation of Inevitabilism, we may notice what we commonly think about the past and, by contrast, what we think of the future: The past is absolutely settled and closed, in every real respect; by contrast, the future is at least somewhat unsettled and open, at least in some real respect. So, it's absolutely settled whether yesterday one thing that happened was your imagining a gray triangle; either that happened yesterday or else it didn't happen, and *that's that.* Right now, there's simply nothing to be done about such a purely past matter. By contrast, it's at least somewhat unsettled and open whether tomorrow one thing that will happen is your imagining a gray triangle; presumably, it's *not* true that either this will happen or else it won't happen, and *that's that.* Rather, at least so far as we can tell, it's perfectly *possible for you to* imagine a gray triangle tomorrow and, equally, it's *possible for you not* to do it.

Now, according to Inevitabilism, this ordinary thinking is all wrong: Just as it is with the past, so the *future* is absolutely settled and closed, in every real respect and regard. Just as it's absolutely settled what happened yesterday, so *it's also absolutely settled what will happen tomorrow*; just as it's absolutely settled whether one thing that *happened yesterday was* your imagining a gray triangle, so, it's also completely settled whether one thing that *will happen tomorrow is* your imagining a gray triangle. That's Inevitabilism for you, laws or no laws.

At all events, most current readers won't see much reason to believe Inevitabilism, or Determinism. For, nowadays, few will believe any "physical proposition" even remotely like a statement to the effect that, say, the distribution of matter at earlier times fully determines the distribution of matter at later times. In line with that, few will think that *anything* fully determines that there be, or has it as inevitable that there be, a certain distribution of matter at a certain later time. And, in line with *that,* few will think that, for each future time, there's a wholly specific way that, even as of right now, is the only way for the world then to be.

Why so? Well, nowadays, few will hold with classical physics or, for that matter, with any science that has what's most plainly physical in our world be subject to complete antecedent determination. Rather, accepting "indeterministic" physics with the same "objectivist" interpretation favored by most current physicists themselves, most agree that, even with what's plainly physical, there's plenty of room for purely probabilistic events, whether or not there's any room for really chosen activity. Just so, since few philosophers now believe a thesis of Determinism, or Inevitabilism, few have an *urgent* interest in a thesis of (Deterministic) Incompatibilism, on which a comprehensive Determinism is inconsistent with our really choosing for ourselves. (A fair number still have a *non-urgent* interest in this Incompatibilism, with able thinkers on each side of the issue.)

3. A Widely Disturbing Argument Presents a More Urgent Issue

More philosophers now take an urgent interest in another issue concerning real choice that, at least nowadays, may be the real heart of "the problem of free will." This more urgent issue may be presented by way of an argument that's strikingly forceful for reasoning so sketchy and bare:

> *First Premise*: If Determinism holds, then, as everything we do is inevitable from long before we existed, nothing we do is anything we choose from *actual alternatives* for our activity.
> *Second Premise*: If Determinism *doesn't* hold, then, (while *some* things we do *may* be inevitable from long before our existence and, so, it's never within our power to choose *them* for ourselves) it may also be that *some* things *we do aren't* inevitable—but, as regards any of *these* things, it will be a *matter of chance* whether we do them or not, and, as nothing of *that* sort is something we *choose* to do, (here, too) nothing we do is anything we choose from actual alternatives for us.
> *Third Premise*: Either Determinism holds or it doesn't.
> Therefore,
> *Conclusion*: Nothing we do is anything we choose from actual alternatives for our activity.

This argument is quite disturbing. Indeed, nowadays, able thinkers often take it to suggest that our concept of real choice is an incoherent idea, never true of any reality at all.

Such a severe judgment threatens to put us in the same bad boat as our choiceless happy clams. As I believe, that judgment's unduly pessimistic. But, then, what's wrong with our sketchy argument, and so badly wrong as to place it beyond repair?

Well, there's little point in questioning the relation of the argument's premises to its conclusion; anything amiss will just call for a small reformulation. Nor is there a deeply serious objection to the argument's Third Premise, to the thought that either Determinism holds or it doesn't. So, for philosophical profit, we should consider just the argument's first two premises.

At least at this point, it's easier to get clear on the First Premise, about the implications of Determinism's holding, than on the Second, about the implications of Determinism's failing to hold. Mainly for that reason, I'll next discuss, very briefly, the appealing First Premise. Then, I'll spend more time exploring what's promoting the appeal of the Second.

4. Real Choice (Free Will) Is Incompatible with Inevitabilism (Determinism)

Though I'm not absolutely certain of it, I feel fairly sure that Inevitabilism, which I've argued is the heart of Determinism, is incompatible with real choice, or free will. What fosters my belief is a line of thinking that's exceptionally simple and, to my mind, quite obviously correct.

Basically, it's just this: Let's suppose that, as regards anything that happens after a certain time long before I ever existed, at least from that time onward it's absolutely inevitable that it happen. Then, for each time throughout my existence, and forever after, there's really *just one* (perfectly specific) way for the world then to be. For any of the times when I exist, then, there won't even be as many as two ways for the world to be. But, for any time at all, I will then have actual alternatives, as regards what to do, or, as regards anything else, for that matter, only if there really are, at that time, or, maybe, at the very next moment, *at least two different* ways for the world to be, and *not only one way* that's possible for the world. After all, for as long as I exist, I'll always be just a part of the whole world. And, if there's only one way for the whole world to be, at any given time, then, surely, as must needs be, there'll be only one way, too, for each of its parts to be, at that same time. (For some folks, this little bridging thought may be helpful here: Suppose there are as many as two ways for the world to be, at a given time. Well, then, one of these different ways *for the world to be* may represent, or it may provide, or it may just plain be, one alternative *for me to do* something, and another may provide *another* alternative *for me*. But, if there *aren't even as many as two ways* for the world, *then it simply can't be that anything*—anything at all—may represent, or may provide, or may just plain be, *an alternative* for me to do anything.) Well, with all that being so, this must then also be so: Throughout my existence, *I'll never have any actual alternatives* at all, and, in particular, any alternatives as regards what I do. So, nothing I ever do is anything I choose to do from *alternatives for my* activity. Of course, there's nothing here that's special to me. So, if Determinism holds, none of us will have any real choice, or, what's here the same, any free will.

Many philosophers will think this simple reasoning to be badly objectionable. In response, they may resort to one or another philosophical story from the highly inventive work of David Lewis, maybe much as I myself once did.[3] Or, they might object in other ways. But, as I suspect, any of this will produce a thought more happily wishful than deeply convincing.

Of course, I can't support this suspicion with ideas that all sensible readers will find conclusive. Realizing that, I won't try to say more toward establishing the proposition that Determinism, or Inevitabilism, excludes real choice. Anyway, we'll make more progress, as I've suggested, by exploring the appeal of our argument's Second Premise. That's what we'll next do.

5. Is Real Choice Incompatible with the *Denial* of Inevitabilism?

Fancy clauses aside, the thrust of our Second Premise is this. If Determinism *doesn't* hold, then some things we do, even as they may *not* be inevitable, will all then be a *matter of chance*—and nothing of *that* sort is something we *choose* to do. So, this Premise says that the *denial* of Inevitabilism (Determinism) is incompatible with our ever doing what we really choose, from actual alternatives for our activity.

Now, on the face of it, that seems wildly implausible. But, then, why have so many thinkers found our Second Premise, or statements much the same, to be so appealing?

3. Lewis offers the basis for two sorts of response. On the one hand, there's his metaphysical system of many mutually isolated worlds, with counterparts of us in many of them. This can encourage one way of looking at matters of choice in terms of which nothing so metaphysical as what I'm trying to promote will ever seem to be both something truly real and any life-enhancing big deal. For a full treatment of this system, see his *On the Plurality of Worlds*, Blackwell, 1986.

On the other hand, his semantic ideas about the context-dependence of ever so many judgments can make it look like, in essays like this present paper, the author is just raising the standards for judgments about our choice to heights that are as unrealistic as they're divorced from our ordinary concerns for our lives. For this, see his "Scorekeeping in a Language Game," *Journal of Philosophical Logic*, 1979, reprinted in his *Philosophical Papers*, Volume 1, Oxford University Press, 1983. In my *Philosophical Relativity*, University of Minnesota Press and Blackwell, 1984, reprinted by Oxford University Press, 2002, I try to apply this semantic idea to the issue of this present Chapter, especially in "A Problem of Power and Freedom," which is Section 2 of Chapter 3.

As I'm advancing in the present Chapter, both of these "Lewisian" ways of playing down what's required for us to choose from actually available alternatives must be ways of being misguided, as must be any other ways of playing that down.

When pondering this Premise, which has chance be the only contrast with inevitability, we may bring to our thinking some powerfully constraining metaphysical assumptions. To see how this may happen even with able thinkers, we look at this passage from Peter van Inwagen:

> What happens if we reject determinism?... the quantum-mechanical world of current physics seems to be irreversibly indeterministic.... Let us suppose for the sake of argument that human organisms display a considerable degree of indeterminism. Let us suppose in fact that each human organism is such that when the human person associated with that organism... is trying to decide whether to do A or to do B, there is a physically possible future in which the organism behaves in a way appropriate to a decision to do A and there is also a physically possible future... appropriate to a decision to do B. We shall see that this supposition leads to a mystery. We shall see that the indeterminism that seems to be required by free will seems also to destroy free will.
>
> Let us look carefully at the consequences of supposing that human behavior is undetermined. Suppose that Jane is in an agony of indecision; if her deliberations go one way, she will in a moment speak the words "John, I lied to you about Alice," and if her deliberations go the other way, she'll bite her lip and remain silent. We have supposed that there is a physically possible future in which each of these things happens. Given the whole state of the physical world at the present moment, and given the laws of nature, both of these things are possible; either might equally well happen.
>
> Each contemplated action will, of course, have antecedents in Jane's cerebral cortex, for it is in that part of Jane (or of her body) that control over her vocal apparatus resides. Let us make a fanciful assumption about these antecedents, since it will make no real difference to our argument.... Let us suppose that there is a certain current-pulse that is proceeding along one of the neural pathways in Jane's brain and that it is about to come to a fork. And let us suppose that if it goes to the left, she will make her confession, and that if it goes to the right, she will remain silent. And let us suppose that it is undetermined which way the pulse will go when it comes to the fork....
>
> Does Jane have any choice about whether the pulse goes to the left or to the right? If it goes to the left, that *just happens*. If it goes to the right, *that* just happens.... it would seem that there is no way in which anyone could have any choice about the outcome of an indeterministic process. And, it seems to follow that if, when one is trying to decide what to do, it is truly undetermined what the outcome of one's deliberations will be, then one can have no choice about the outcome ....[4]

4. Peter van Inwagen, *Metaphysics*, Westview Press, 1993, pages 191–193. My page references are to the first edition of the book.

Where I talk of what's a *matter of chance*, van Inwagen writes of what *just happens*; but the suggested thought's the same.

As will be worth attention later in the Chapter, what's quoted above is just as forceful where the behavior in question is purely mental activity, as with Jane's thinking more about lying. So, equally, it seems that, with Determinism's not holding, Jane won't really choose even what to think about.

Anyway, before the passage quoted, in his text our author argued for the statement that free will is incompatible with determinism. So, shortly after he has us thinking about ourselves in much the same terms we've just thought about his Jane, van Inwagen presents a disturbing dilemma for free will that, in all essentials, is quite the same as what's suggested by our own three-premise argument:

> But now a disquieting possibility suggests itself. Perhaps free will is...incompatible with determinism. But perhaps it is also incompatible with *in*determinism....If free will is incompatible with both...then, since either determinism or indeterminism has to be true, free will is impossible. And, of course, what is impossible does not exist.[5]

When we think about ourselves much as we've just thought about Jane, which we often feel compelled to do, then, I suggest, we're all but forced into such a disturbing dilemma. And, we're then all but forced, as well, into the disturbing dilemma suggested by our three-premise argument: Either what we do is quite inevitable, from times long before we existed, or else it's just a matter of chance what we do. So, in any case, we never do what we choose, from real options for our activity.

But, *must* we think of ourselves in such terms as we've just thought about Jane; or, are there alternatives available?

To give the question a philosophically satisfying answer, we must think hard about what, exactly, are the metaphysical assumptions we're bringing to bear when we think of ourselves much as we've just been thinking about Jane. In subsequent Sections, we'll do that.

Right now, here's just a usefully suggestive answer. From the history of modern philosophy, we may recall metaphysical views that are very different from the Scientiphicalism now so prevalent. First, we may consider such a radical departure from our customary metaphysical thinking as Berkeley's Idealism.[6] For Berkeley, there's a world

---

5. Van Inwagen, *Metaphysics*, page 195.

6. With or without embracing Berkeley's theistic thoughts, his Idealism is, I think, a coherent view of reality, though I won't bother to argue that large point here.

of many minds and, maybe ontologically parasitical on each, the ideas of each mind. Now, as it certainly seems, the finite minds of this world, maybe you and me, can exercise our powers to choose, if only to choose what to think about: We can choose to think about metaphysics and, alternatively, we can choose to think about music. If we think about metaphysics, not music, that needn't be anything inevitable, and it also needn't be a just matter of chance. Rather than either, we may do that *because we really chose to think about matters metaphysical*.

To feel free from false dilemmas, we needn't go so far as to be Idealists. Recalling nobody less than the father of modern philosophy, we may entertain the Substantial Dualism of Descartes. (Both in its historical Theistic Version and also in Nontheistic Versions, with this seminal metaphysician's Dualism there is, I think, a coherent conception of concrete reality. In several later Chapters, I'll aim to advance some Forms of Substantial Dualism that are, each of them, quite a lot like a Nontheistic Version of this seminal thinker's own Dualistic View.)

Indeed, in the most relevant respects, Descartes's view of us—we're each a distinct temporally enduring nonphysical mental subject—is quite the same as Berkeley's. (Here, we put aside Descartes's remarks that conflict with his main view. According to these remarks, you're a special unit, comprising both your mind and your body, wonderfully intermingled. Well, as I said, we place them aside.) At all events, I needn't now repeat much from the previous paragraph. Rather, I'll simply say that, for the old Dualist, as much as for the old Idealist, there seems plenty of room for real choice. So, our conception of real choice, or free will, doesn't itself seem incoherent, contradictory, or otherwise absolutely unsatisfiable.

6. Our Scientiphical Metaphysic and the Currently Dominant Conception of Ourselves

Far from the tenets of Substantial Dualism, any view now deemed intellectually respectable, by almost all prominent philosophers, will have each of us be just an especially interesting physical complex. On their view, you're one physical complex and, quite separate and distinct from you, even spatially quite separate, I'm another mentally impressive physical complex. Give or take a nuance or two, whatever Propensities, or "powers," you have will derive, in a fully physical fashion, from the physical Propensities of whatever far simpler physical things serve to compose you and, of course, the physical relations among your simple physical constituents. Proceeding along the lines of whatever are the basic physical laws, the derivations will be, in all essentials, quite the same as the fully physical derivations of the powers of your more complex physical constituents, as with your heart's powers, and as with your brain's Propensities. Just as the powers of these organs physically derive from the Propensities of the far simpler physical things that compose them, say, from their constituent protons, neutrons and electrons, so all *your* powers will be quite fully derivative physical dispositions. In this metaphysically most central respect, all your powers will be the same as the powers of obviously choiceless physical complexes, as with even such geysers and volcanoes as are commonly reckoned to be "very active." The differences concern only details. While the details are, of course, far more complex with you, there's no philosophically notable difference between the derivations of your powers and, say, the derivations of the powers of your car.

So it is that, when I think about myself in what seems an intellectually responsible way, my thoughts must comport with our Scientiphical Metaphysic. With an eye to how this dominant worldview may bear on questions of our real choice, I'll now rehearse some of this Scientiphicalism.

First, insofar as it's determined by anything at all, and it isn't merely random, the spatial distribution of all the world's matter at a time (including what wholly composes all the world's physically complex entities) is determined by the distribution of the matter at earlier times. (We understand this, I suppose, so that it allows there to be, but it doesn't require there to be, a time before which there isn't any matter.) All this determination proceeds in line with the world's basic natural laws, which are its basic physical laws.

Second, owing to the variety in these material distributions, at certain times, like right now, much matter composes complex physical structures or systems, many of which are stars, for example, and some of which are, say, planets. Salient among the systematic physical complexes, and relatively rare in our physically vast world, are those that are alive. Yet more salient, and also still rarer, are the highly complex living physical entities that are feeling and thinking beings.

Third, on the Scientiphical Metaphysic all living human people are highly complex physical entities, each with many physical parts, but no other substantial parts. These people include me myself and, so far as I can tell, everyone with whom I'll ever communicate any of my thoughts or experience; each of us is a physical entity *ultimately wholly constituted* of just so many basic physically simple things, like quarks, maybe, or maybe like superstrings. (On a Nonstandard Version of the Scientiphical

Metaphysic, there aren't any absolutely basic entities; rather, there's an infinite sequence of "more and more basic physical constituents." As I suspect, a Nonstandard Scientiphical Metaphysic cannot be sustained. Whether or not that's so, it won't do anything toward having us be entities with important mental powers, including the power to really choose. In a later Section of the Chapter, this matter will be discussed.) Just so, and at all events, none of us ever has any constituents except all those that are .fully and wholly physical entities.

Fourth, all our powers and Propensities are physically derivative dispositions, whether or not they're probabilistic. And, all our behavior and activity, even our most refined mental activity, physically derives from the behavior of our physical parts (and of other nonmental physical things, physically simpler than us, that "serve to compose our environment"). Thus, even as physically simpler things are governed by physical laws, insofar as their behavior's not random, so, even if indirectly, we ourselves must be governed by these laws, insofar as our behavior isn't random.

When thinking only in the terms of this dominant Scientiphical Metaphysic, can I think of myself as an entity that really chooses from actual alternatives? As it usually seems, I can't do it. Why is there this unsettling appearance?

Certainly in this one Chapter, and even in the book as a whole, I won't try exhaustively to explore the conflicts, or the apparent conflicts, between our belief in our real choice and, on the other side, our Scientiphical Metaphysic. Rather, I'll focus on the seeming conflict between this belief and the proposition that all our powers are physically derivative Propensities. And, then, much nearer the Chapter's end, I'll address the apparent clash between the belief and, on the Scientiphical side, the proposition that we're subject to, or governed by, laws of nature.

7. Simple Physical Entities and Their Basic Properties

If we're to make any sense of our Scientiphical Metaphysic, then we'd better be able to make good sense of what seem its metaphysically simplest forms, and its conceptually clearest forms. So, we do well to focus on a form of the view where the constitution of physical complexes has a basis in some physically basic entities, or entity. What's more, we do well to focus on forms of the view where there are many basic physical entities, as with many Particles, and where each belongs to just one of a very few basic physical kinds, these kinds being mutually exclusive for, and jointly exhaustive for, the basic entities.

To have matters be vivid, from Chapter 3 we recall this nicely focused question: How might we quite limited human thinkers intelligibly differentiate between a World of Spherical Newtonian Particles moving about in an absolutely empty void and a World that's mainly a material plenum, or a field, but with absolutely empty Spherical regions whose trajectories (of motion) precisely parallel the paths of the Newtonian World's Particles? For a helpful answer, I proposed that, in addition to two sorts of basic property for physical objects long recognized, one well enough called *Spatials*, as with Shape and Size, and the second called *Propensities*, as with solidity, we should recognize a third sort, aptly called *Qualities*. More specifically, there will be those Qualities fit for pervading space, the *Spatially Extensible Qualities*. These will be Extensible Correlatives of experiential color qualities; so, we may label one *Red*, another *Blue*, and so on. While a Particle's spatial properties may be at least precisely mimicked by a counterpart void in the Plenumate World, and while its Propensities might possibly be pretty well mimicked, not so with its Extensible Qualities.

With Blue as our supposed Quality, we may contrast our "problematically mirroring" Worlds as follows. In the Particulate World, there will be many Small Blue Spheres, each with a gravitational Propensity to attract each of the others, moving about in the vast empty space of the World. This empty space will be completely devoid of Quality, even as it will also lack real Propensity. In the Plenumate World, there will be Blue instanced *everywhere except* where there are the Small Spherical voids. Wherever there's the Blue plenum, there'll be, say, the plenum's "Propensity to pulsate in such-and-such a way." With the manifestation of this Propensity, an epiphenomenal upshot will be the "movement of the voids."

Applying this framework, we may contemplate vividly a World with electrons, and protons, (and neutrons), pretty much as such Particles were first conceived. So, we'll suppose there to be many Small Blue Particles—very tiny physical Spheres serving as the World's electrons, and also many Large Red Particles—not quite so tiny Spheres serving as the World's protons. As we may also suppose, each Particle may have a certain Propensity to attract each of the others. With a Propensity that's proportional to its Size, each Particle attracts every other to a degree that's inversely proportional to (the square of) the distance between the centers of the Colorful objects. This Propensity, we're supposing, is a disposition of each Particle *with respect to*, even if not otherwise directed at, the Sizes of other Particles. In a rough way, we've just expressed the World's gravitational feature.

As well, each of the Small Blues may be disposed to repel, much more strongly, each of the others, while each Large Red is disposed to repel, just as strongly, any other Large Red. And, each Small Blue may be disposed to attract strongly any Large Reds, while each of the latter are, reciprocally, disposed to attract any Small Blues. This quite different Propensity, we'll suppose, is a disposition of each Particle *with respect to* the Qualities of other Particles. Roughly but well enough, we've now just described the World's electrical feature. (For a nice supposition about neutrons, we may suppose many Large Yellow Particles each with gravitational Propensity, but no electrical Propensity.)

As will be supposed implicitly anyway, but as I'll now make explicit, each of these Particles will be impenetrable by, or with respect to, all the other Particles. In other words, all our supposed material Particles do very well by the feature of impenetrability, or solidity.

With suitable Propensities supposed for our Particles, well beyond what I've just specified, they may be well suited for constituting the World's physical complexes.

8. Reciprocal Propensities and Physical Laws

In conformity with a plausible conception of the physical that's broadly like our actual conception, what sort of further Propensities should we be supposing?

Not that they'll do anything interesting toward promoting impressive complexes, but, for an orderly presentation, I'll first note the Propensities that a basic Particle has with respect to itself, which I've seen useful to call the Self-directed Propensities of the basic physical Particle. So, a Particle that continues to exist may do so as the manifestation of its Self-directed Propensity for Monotony with respect to its existence, and a Particle that ceases, may do that as a manifestation of its quite opposite Propensity, for Change with respect to its existence. And, as I've also noted in the Chapter just previous, a Particle may have a Self-directed Propensity for Monotony, or else for Change, with respect to less fundamental matters, as with a Propensity for Monotony with respect to its Spatially Extensible Quality. Still, for your having a power really to choose, these Propensities of your Particles, these so-called Self-directed Propensities, won't do very much.

We turn, then, to consider just such Dispositions of our Particles as are their Propensities for interaction with other Particles (certainly those that are actual and, maybe, those that are merely possible Particles). Well, consider how it may be that a Particle (of a certain basic sort) may manifest its Propensity to have another Particle (of another basic sort) spin faster. Then, just as there's that power manifested on the part of the first thing, to increase spin on the part of the second, there must be, on the part of the second, the manifestation of a "receptive" disposition, to *have its spin increase* through just such interaction. In a (humanly intelligible) Particulate World with physical complexes, each of a complex's (basic) physical constituents will be Propensitied for interaction with others of its (basic) physical constituents. In other words, each (basic) constituent of a complex physical entity is a *reciprocal disposition partner* for other (basic) constituents.[7] What's just been offered entails this: A (basic) physical Particle behaves in accordance with (basic) physical laws. That's how our terms, "*physical Particle*" and "*physical* law," are to be understood. But, what's this business about *behaving in accordance with laws*? What does that really amount to?

It's no great exaggeration to say that *all a physical law amounts to is* that, as concerns such entities as are (best said to be) governed by the law, they *have certain Propensities*. And, if we go on to make a provision for the singular case, as with a simple Plenumate World, what we've said might be no exaggeration at all. Where there's just one physical entity involved in a vast physical reality, as with Descartes's material plenum, to say there's a physical law governing the entity is to say that the thing has certain Propensities. Just so, governing the plenum there may be a law to the effect that, whenever the Field becomes Purple, a second later it will become Orange, and whenever it becomes Orange, a second later it will become Purple. As I'm suggesting, this law amounts to *the plenum's having the Propensity* to become Orange a second after it becomes Purple and *its having the Propensity* to become Purple a second after it becomes Orange. So, the law "responsible for" the very regular cyclical change of the Color of our plenum isn't anything that governs the plenum from on high, or from anywhere else at all. Rather, as it amounts to the plenum's having these Propensities, so the law inheres in the plenum itself.

---

7. As in Chapter 2, where I introduced this notion into our inquiry, I'm again greatly beholden to the compelling Neo-Lockean thoughts of C. B. Martin.

For a good example of Martin on these matters, see his contributions to D. M. Armstrong, C. B. Martin and U. T. Place, *Dispositions: A Debate* (ed. Tim Crane), Routledge, 1996, perhaps guided by the index entries for "reciprocal disposition partners." A nice new exposition of this idea, and its connection with other fertile Neo-Lockean conceptions, can be found in C. B. Martin and John Heil, "The Ontological Turn," *Midwest Studies in Philosophy*, 1999.

For a Particulate physical reality to be fairly intelligible to us, we should understand its governing laws in a similarly perspicuous ontological manner. For instance, the gravitational law governing all the Particles in a Newtonian Particulate World will inhere in that World's many Particles, each of which has the gravitational Propensity for interaction with each of the others. Even better, the situation is this: It's the *Propensitied Particles that are ontologically fundamental,* and such laws as may be said to "govern" these Particles are all, really, ontologically parasitical on (how it is with) the Propensitied Particles in question. And, with a Plenum, or a Field, the situation is this: It's the Propensitied Plenum that's ontologically basic, and such laws as are said to "govern" the Field are all, really, just ontologically parasitical on (how it is with) the Field. For an adequate discussion of real choice, this point is of the first importance. Indeed, what may be only a small extension of the point is, I suspect, the crucial key to a most adequate discussion. Well, more on that later.

Now, let's suppose that a notion of *objective probability* is applicable in properly metaphysical considerations.[8] At all events, our Scientiphical Metaphysic accommodates the thought that, rather than being deterministic, our World's basic physical laws may be *objectively probabilistic.* In terms we may find as ontologically perspicuous as any in this neighborhood, what does that mean? Well, the fact that our Particulate World's basic physical laws are probabilistic, which we're now supposing, will amount to the fact that the World's basic physical entities have (at least some) probabilistic Propensities. For instance, instead of all the Particles having a Propensity simply to promote an increase in the speed of spin of others, certainly and always, some may have the Propensity to promote *with a certain degree of objective probability* an increase in others' spin speed, with those others then having a reciprocal receptive Propensity that's probabilistic, a disposition to *have their* spin increased with *just that degree* of probability.

Whether the derivations be deterministic or whether they be probabilistic, Scientiphicalism has all your powers derive, in a fully physical fashion, from the Propensities of your basic physical constituents, and the physical arrangements among them. (If the basic Propensities are all deterministic, so too will be all the derivative powers; if some are probabilistic, there'll be some probabilistic derivative powers.)

8. As I said in an earlier Chapter, I can't really make much sense of probabilistic Propensities. But, in what follows, I'll just suppose, for the sake of the arguments, that this is all simply a deficiency of my own understanding.

How do these ideas affect the question of whether Scientiphicalism allows us real choice? In the next Section, we'll explore this question.

9. Objective Probabilities, Random Happenings, and Real Choices

To make a manageable start, we suppose that, whether the basic physical Propensities be deterministic or whether probabilistic, the conditions favorable for their manifestation are such straightforwardly physical ones as the relative spatial positions of our Particles, and their relative velocities. And, we suppose that all your simplest constituents may be combined in ways spatially and dynamically very complex, with the upshot that they'll then wholly constitute you in a fully physical fashion. There'll then be, of course, a very complex derivation of all your powers. But, it's a fully physical derivation.

With that in mind, let's again consider our Scientiphical Jane. Composed of very many Particles, and nothing else metaphysically basic, all Jane's powers must derive, in such a straightforwardly physical fashion, from the basic Propensities of her quite simple physical constituents—now, probabilistic Propensities—along with the physical arrangements of these Probabilistically Propensitied Particles. As it appears, none of these derivative dispositions will be Jane's power to *choose* her course of activity, from actual alternatives for her.

Just as Jane won't ever be making any real choice or decision, it also seems that, contrary to what van Inwagen would presume for this philosophically useful character, she can't ever really be in any state of *indecision*, or deliberation. So, I doubt we'll then have a truth expressed with this sentence of his, which I've lately displayed: "Jane is in an agony of indecision; if her deliberations go one way, she will in a moment speak the words 'John, I lied to you about Alice,' and if her deliberations go the other way, she'll bite her lip and remain silent."

By contrast, it's not so doubtful that a truth may be expressed with this other lately displayed material from the same passage:

> there is a certain current-pulse that is proceeding along one of the neural pathways in Jane's brain and...it is about to come to a fork....if it goes to the left, she will make her confession, and...if it goes to the right, she will remain silent. And...it is undetermined which way the pulse will go when it comes to the fork.

As we may well suppose, the neural pathway is wholly composed of just so very many Blue and Red (and Yellow) Particles, impressively arranged, while a current-pulse consists of fairly few streaming Blue Particles. Now, when we imagine that our current-pulse comes to our neural fork, and it then goes to the left, what are we to suppose? Need we suppose, with van Inwagen, that if it goes to the left, and Jane speaks the truth, that *just happens*?

Well if by "it just happens" we're to mean that the current's going left isn't a matter of real choice, and Jane's consequent confessing isn't really chosen, then, as it surely appears, we must suppose that these things just happen. For, as it surely seems, this *isn't* someone choosing from real options for her thoughtful behavior—not with such an entirely Scientiphical Jane, with all her presumed powers being just so many physically derivative Propensities. So, on the central question, we agree with our author's pessimistic suggestion.

That said, we note that, with a natural use of "it just happens," we may well mean that the event in question is a *purely random happening*, quite beyond the reach of any probabilistic considerations. And, in *that* case, we *needn't* suppose there's a truth that's expressed with "it *just happens* to go left," or with "Jane just happens to speak the truth." For, our electron-stream may have derivative probabilistic Propensities. And, the neural fork may have derivative reciprocal probabilistic Propensities. Just so, even as (some of) the former may be (directed) with respect to the neural-fork, so (some of) the latter may be (directed) with respect to the current-pulse. Since that may be so, it also may be that, in the circumstances prevailing at the supposed time, there is, for instance, an objective likelihood of 0.7 of the electron-stream's going to the left of the neural fork (and a 0.3 chance of its going to the right, and no chance of any other logical possibility's obtaining). So, then, if the current does go left, that will be the *objectively likely outcome*, not just a random happening. And, so, when Jane consequently speaks the truth, *that's* the objectively likely outcome, not just some purely random happening.

Jane's making a confession may be an objectively likely outcome. But, even so, it also seems that, for all the world, her doing that isn't something Jane here can choose to do, from what are actual alternatives for her. After all, whether or not Jane confesses all depends, quite wholly and fully, on whether the current-pulse goes left or not. And, what happens here will be just the manifestation of certain reciprocally directed probabilistic Propensities, on the part of the pulse, and the fork, and maybe some other wholly physical things as well. Being just the upshot of how it is with the manifesting of those reciprocal probabilistic Propensities, our Scientiphical Jane's speaking her mind, even if objectively quite likely, isn't something that, from among real options for her own activity, she really chooses to do.

And, just as plainly, Jane also won't choose if she *doesn't* say any-thing, becoming involved in what's here the *unlikely* behavior for her. For, as we're supposing, that will just be a consequence of the current-pulse's going right, instead of left. Though this is the unlikely outcome, still, if this *does* happen, then *it* will be the manifesting of the very same aforesaid reciprocal probabilistic Propensities. And, of course, this, too, won't ever amount to anything Jane chooses to do.

Well, we've just noted a disagreement with van Inwagen. But, for questions of real choice, as we've also noted, our difference with him is unimportant. Even if Jane's behavior here is a properly probabilistic matter, and may be contrasted with *random* events that *just happen*, still, as regards the question of her having any real choice, our probabilistic Scientiphical Jane is in quite the same bad boat as her deterministic counterpart.

10. Can Inhering in a Field Help Us Have Real Choice?

In considering physical things with probabilistic Propensities, we de-parted from the very simple form of Scientiphicalism, and the very comfortably clear intuitive form, with which we began our exploration of how the View comports with our belief in real choice. Now, that depar-ture certainly didn't help a Scientiphically Respectable Jane to really choose anything. But, might some *other* departure do much better?

The most obvious move, toward a less manageable Scientiphical-ism, will have us consider a Plenumate View, on which there's just one fully physical basic entity, almost all of it doing nothing, right now, toward subserving mental activity. (As this Plenum, or Field, occupies all the world's space, even if that space be impressively infinite, so nowhere is there, on this smoothly simple view, any physically abso-lutely empty spatial region.)

In such a Fieldy Scientiphical world, what goes on with a Scienti-phical Jane will be determined, insofar as it's determined by anything at all, by what goes on with the Field, in which she "inheres." This will also be true of each of Jane's familiar parts, like her brain and heart. Indeed, just as are her so-called parts, even Jane herself, will be, on this View, just an exceptionally complex persistent pattern of pretty stable per-turbations of the Field, or something very like that. About such a completely inclusive situation, perhaps we may say that Jane will be *patterned in* the Field in which she inheres. And, perhaps, we might go on to say that such a Fieldy Jane will be *wholly constituted of* just that much of the Field as that in which she inheres, or in which she's patterned.

Whatever the best characterization of the relation between our Fieldy Jane and her constituting Field, she doesn't fare any better than her Particulate counterpart, as concerns her really choosing what to do. Or, so it certainly seems to me. For, with a Jane who's always wholly inhering in a purely physical Field, the situation seems to be just this: Should the Field *evolve in one of certain ways*, then, only as an aspect of that whole evolvement, there'll be a mere pattern as of someone speaking, for example. And, if the Field *evolves in one of the other* ways presumed possible for it, there'll be, as a mere part, aspect, or feature of *that* evolvement, a mere pattern as of someone not speaking. So, *however* the inhering Field evolves, there won't be any Scientiphical Jane who's any real individual at all, it surely seems, much less anyone who's really choosing to do something.

11. Can an "Infinitely Deep Hierarchy" of Physical Powers Help Us Have Real Choice?

What may be the most radical attempt to depart from a comfortably clear form of Scientiphicalism, while still trying to uphold a Scientiphical view, comes with the suggestion that there's no basic entity at all, but, instead, there's an "infinitely deep hierarchy" of physical entities. This radically uncomfortable position is the Nonstandard Version of Scientiphicalism that, when introducing Scientiphicalism near the book's beginning, I adumbrated parenthetically. Anyway, on this Nonstandard Version, there aren't any basic physical entities. Rather, the supposition is that there's an infinite sequence of "more and more basic physical constituents," *none* of these constituting entities having *any nonderivative* Propensity or power. Just so, each physical Propensity of a concrete entity will physically derive from *other physical Propensities*, maybe mainly those of its physical constituents, along with complementary physical factors.

By contrast with the idea of a Propensitied physical field, discussed just above, this Nonstandard supposition might not really be coherent. Anyhow, whether coherent or not, the conception is a familiar enough idea, common even in the daydreams of children. Here's a pretty detailed way for Nonstandard Scientiphicalism to go: Within each of your atoms, there are galaxies upon galaxies, many of them having planets inhabited by, amongst other things, little philosophers each constituted of quadrillions of atoms. And, each of *these* atoms contains galaxies upon galaxies, and so on, ad infinitum. (But, there's also nothing that's at the top, so to say. So, we may all be contained in an atom that's one of many quadrillions serving to constitute, say, a button on the pants of what's, to us, a very vast philosopher. That said, let's pay no more attention to this "upward direction" of the compositional fantasy.) At all events, the powers of the planets in a given galaxy should physically derive from the powers of their atoms, which derive, in turn, from the powers of the atoms in the galaxies in *those* atoms, ad infinitum.

Is this fantasy a coherent conception? Or, have we conflated presumably coherent thoughts about spatial inclusion with incoherent ideas as to powers? I suspect it's the latter. Trying to think of it as the *physical behavior* of a *physical entity*, we may try to think of the waving behavior of a certain little shirt, on a certain windy day, on a planet in a galaxy that's in one of the oxygen atoms now in your bloodstream—with *all of it* being "infinitely high up" in an infinitely deep hierarchy. How might this really be the *physical* behavior of a *physical* thing?

That doesn't seem possible. On one side, we're barred from thinking of the waving of the shirt as a manifestation of nonderivative Propensities of a physical field. On another, we're barred from having it be the upshot, in any sense, of nonderivative powers of Particles that constitute the shirt and its environs. Indeed, as it appears, with all physical powers presumed to be derivative Propensities, there's nothing more than an "infinite hierarchy of buck-passing," with nothing really having any power at all, not even any "power to pass a buck." For there to be any physically derivative Propensities, it seems to me, there must be *some nonderivative* dispositions, from which (along with other factors) derivative powers might derive.

Rather than an infinitely deep hierarchy of physical powers, what we've envisioned might more plausibly be taken as a world that's really quite devoid of all physical Propensity and power. What we've managed to imagine, I'll suggest, may be a world with an infinite nesting of pure Quality patterns. (Here, I place to the side our Antinomy of Extensible Quality, discussed in Chapter 3.) As regards the so-called infinite hierarchy of physical Propensity, there seems no possibility, I suggest, for any real interaction among things each suitably set for just such interaction with each other. Rather than anything so nicely "Lockean" as that, what we have here is, rather, a perfectly "Humean" world. So, perhaps our imagined World might be Qualitied in an impressively regular pattern. But, that's not enough for the world to have any real Propensity or power. So, with such an "infinitely deep hierarchy," there'll really be *nothing*, it seems to me, with any real Propensity.

For our present discussion, however, we needn't establish anything like that.

Indeed, let's now grant that all of the foregoing may be just a confused quest for overkill, and that the Nonstandard Version is, in fact, a fully coherent form of Scientiphicalism. Even so, for this Chapter's main matters, our skepticism concerning this Nonstandard View will be little worse than a harmless digression.

We may see that to be so, I submit, by thinking, once again, in terms of a Scientiphically Respectable Jane. After all, our Jane's powers still will be physically derivative Propensities. Indeed, now they'll all be, if anything, more thoroughly derivative than we've previously recognized.

So, once again, we consider a Scientiphically Respectable Jane, with her current-pulse heading toward her fork. And, we again suppose that, if the current goes left, Jane will confess. And, again, we suppose the pulse does go left and, in consequence, Jane confesses.

For being in an infinitely deep hierarchy of Propensities, will *this* Scientiphical Jane fare *better* than her previously pondered counterparts, as regards her choosing to confess? I can't see that. Indeed, it may seem that an "infinitely derivative" Scientiphical Jane will fare even worse as regards really choosing for herself. For, here, everything about this Jane seems just so *completely epiphenomenal*. But, even if she doesn't fare worse, in respect of real choice, than her previously discussed counterparts, neither will an "infinitely derivative" Scientiphical Jane fare any better than they do. So, like them, she won't ever really choose.

Let's take stock.

Well, if we're to hold a Scientiphical Metaphysic, we must hold either a Standard Version or else a Nonstandard Version. Now, if we hold with a Standard Version of Scientiphicalism, then, as our inquiries in prior Sections indicate, it may be quite impossible to think of ourselves as having real choice. And, as we've just observed in this present Section, it seems equally impossible should we hold with a Nonstandard Version of the widely accepted Metaphysic. As long as we hold with the Scientiphical Metaphysic, then, it seems impossible to think of ourselves, coherently and intelligibly, as really choosing what to do.

With our confronting this gloomy appearance, which threatens to have us all be choiceless, perhaps we should seriously notice, if only fairly briefly, some alternative metaphysical conceptions.

12. Radically Emergent Beings with a Radically Emergent Power to Choose

Not much concerned with positive proposals, this Chapter's mainly aimed at presenting some Incompatibilist propositions, each concerning a conflict between a widely accepted Scientiphical supposition and, on the other side, our deep belief that we engage in real choice. Still, I'd like to provide some sketchy suggestions as to how, even in what's mostly a nonmental physical world, we might have real choice.

First, I'll offer a Quasi-Cartesian suggestion. To be sure, this means a considerable departure from our Scientiphical worldview. Still, to put things in a properly wide perspective, the suggested Substantial Dualism will be a far more conservative option, for shaky Scientiphicalists, than is any Idealist metaphysic. And, anyhow, in the Section directly following, I'll offer a metaphysical suggestion that means a (still) smaller departure.

On my Quasi-Cartesian suggestion, we're *radically emergent beings*: Even as each of us is generated by a different physical complex, each of the complexes spatially separate from all the others, so we're each an enduring *nonphysical* mental being, *nowhere in space*. Each of us has her own *radically emergent mental powers*, including her own power to really choose. At the same time, and even though we each may have *plenty of mental powers*, still, each of us may be a metaphysically simple entity, with *no substantial parts* at all.

Toward vividly contemplating some such perfectly partless yet radically powerful beings, imagine a World where all the most basic physical entities are Small Blue Particles. And, suppose this to be so: When a quintillion Small Blue Particles are all within a Sphere of a certain fairly Small size, say, a centimeter in diameter, then there will come into existence a metaphysically simple, richly Powerful experiencer. The same point put differently: Each Small Blue has the Propensity to generate, and then to sustain, a Cartesian self, or an immaterial soul, when it's in a Smallish Sphere with about a quintillion others, with each of them also serving to generate, and each then serving to sustain, an immaterial soul. When the point's put this way, there needn't be, I think, even so much as the appearance of any objectionable magic. Why? Well, the emergence of a nonphysical mental being will be, after all, just *the manifestation of a Propensity of our Particles for a certain sort of generative mutual interaction*.

(Now, against what's just been written, it may be objected that, when a being is generated wholly by the mutual interaction of just so many basic physical entities, then the generated being *is also a physical* entity and, so, it *can't* possibly be a *nonphysical* mental being. To this objection, we should concede the point that, with such a generation, there's something in common with the standard physical derivation of a complex physical entity's physically derivative properties, as with such common matters as the solidity of an ordinary brick. That being so, we may concede that, in a very undemanding sense of "physical entity," the nonspatial Cartesian souls I consider will be physical entities. But, insofar as we allow such an undemanding sense to be the dominant sense of "physical," well, then there *won't be much claimed*—by any so-called physicalists, or materialists, or anyone else, for that matter, when it's said that all concrete individuals are *physical* entities (whether of one sort, or another, or another, or yet another). And, correlatively, when many Substantial Dualists express their opposition to more fashionable, more materialistic views, they'll have to resort to somewhat artificial locutions, not being able to say, well enough for their purposes, that plenty of concrete individuals, or some at least, aren't any physical individuals. So, in these pages, I won't let any such undemanding sense of "physical" be the dominant sense. Rather, I'll employ a rather more demanding sense of expression. So, in the sense of "physical" I'll find most useful, physically generated Cartesian souls *won't be physical* entities.)

Though I said this Quasi-Cartesian suggestion means no bad magic, sometimes I feel it means something like magic. But, I think we may see this to be a baseless prejudice, which I share, no doubt, with many others of my place and time. Toward our attaining a rationally more liberated frame of mind, let's think of a World where things proceed very much as in the World just supposed, except that the entity generated by a quintillion neighboring Small Blues *is* a *physical* entity, even in a quite demanding sense of the term, though it's otherwise quite novel for the World. We may suppose that what's generated is a Large Orange Sphere, with distinctive basic physical Propensities, quite different from those of its Small Blue generators. In this newly supposed wholly physical World, there's the radical emergence of a spatial Orange being—not any nonspatial mental being—that's just *the manifestation of a Propensity of the (Small Blue) Particles for a certain sort of generative mutual interaction*. And, though this may sometimes look too much like "getting something from nothing," we should swallow that presumed pill. For, on our present supposition, the Small Blues always did have this generative Propensity, its manifestation awaiting enough of them becoming nicely enough arranged. So, quite readily enough, I suggest, we may accept the emergence of these Orange spatial beings.

But, if the radical emergence of novelly powerful Orange beings isn't a badly magical idea, then why should it be so bad to countenance the emergence of novelly powerful mental beings? Is it that the Orange beings are spatially extended entities, whereas the mental beings aren't spatial? I can't see that this should mean any very severe discrimination. Is it that the Orange beings are physical, and nonmental, whereas the mental beings are mental, of course, and nonphysical. Again, I can't see a basis for severe discrimination. Anyhow, this isn't the place to *defend* a full-blooded Emergentive Substantial Dualism. Just so, I'll just sketch a bit more of a Quasi-Cartesian Dualistic View.

For a palatable sketch, I'll try to model, in a very sketchy way, some of our ordinary thought about the generation, sustenance, and prospect of human mental beings, as well as some central conditions of our (human) existence: From the first moment of her existence onward, and for just so long as she exists, each nonphysical mental being will be in exceptionally close causal connection with the physical Blue Particle that, at the moment of the being's emergence, was nearest the center of the relevantly crowded Smallish Sphere, that being her *Central Small Blue*. (This may happen some seven months after the event known as "the conception of the being," by which time the fetal brain, in the mother's womb, has become a suitably complex structure. Anyhow, we may suppose the Central Small Blue is always in the midst of those many small Blues that, at any moment, serve to constitute what's then the being's suitable brain.) So long as she has any close causal connection with any physical individual, then, each emergent Cartesian being will always be in closer causal connection with her Central Small Blue than with any other basic physical thing. As we may further suppose, our experiencer will be in somewhat less direct causal relations with many other Blue Particles, each of them interacting, pretty directly, with her own Central Small Blue. That being so, certain of these interactions may constitute the workings of our being's sensory system, even as they may aptly affect the experiencing of the mental being. This models our conscious perception of our physical environment. And, making a few further such suppositions, we'll have this: The relevant quintillion (or so) Small Blues constitute *the physical body of* the nonphysical being who's so closely tied, causally, to the body's original center.

About the World now imagined, two quite opposite further speci- fications seem salient: *First*, we may suppose that, once a mental being exists, her continued existence is *not dependent on* what takes place with Blue Particles; even if there occurs the utter annihilation of them all, the experiencers always will exist. This supposed nonphysical mental being may be *immortal*, even if the being isn't, and it can't possibly be, necessarily immortal, or essentially immortal. So far as I can tell, it's a *perfect paradigm* of what we should mean by "a radically emergent mental being."

Second, we may make this quite opposite specification: With the complete dissolution of the body of a Cartesian being, with the dispersal of all her Sphere's Small Blues, the being will cease to exist, completely and forever. Though such a *mortal* mental being won't be a perfect paradigm of an emergent entity, still, for present purposes she'll also qualify as a radically emergent being.

Though it's not really necessary for me to do this here, I'll now give you a helpful preview of some work I mean to do, only a Chapter or two down the road, in connection with the two possibilities I've just mentioned: That of immortal generated souls and, alternatively, the possibility of physically generated souls that are merely mortal. So, please do recall now, if only for just some several minutes, our discussion of OTHERONS, in the just previous Chapter. You'll remember, I trust, that our first OTHERON was an *otherwise* unproblematic physical individual, a certain Yellow Cube, one Yuval Cartesianeton, by name. But, maybe rather problematically, this Yuval's existence depended (*not on how he* was spatially related to, or on how he was physically related to, other physical Particles; but, rather, it depended) *only on how certain other physical concreta*, a Peter S and a Gary C, were spatially and physically *related to each other*. That's where our perplexing discussion began. But, quite quickly and nicely, indeed, the discussion turned to focus on a *nonphysical* OTHERON, one Nina Simone, by name. And, once we so nicely replaced our spatial Yuval with our nonspatial Nina, at the center of our attention, we then went on, just as nicely, to notice this. In parallel with that, we may replace our Gary and our Peter, just a mere twosome of basic physical individuals, with vastly many more elementary particles, by a certain trillion billion trillion of them, perhaps. And, then, without going in for complications that don't, in any event, affect any central issue, there'll be the likes of this to contemplate, for those who think well of any OTHER-ONISH entities: For only so long as just *these* productive Particles are *nicely enough arrayed*, these Nina-generating basic physical individuals, that's how long that Nina herself will exist, and not one moment longer.

Tipping my mitt just a bit, I'll be quick to admit this: Largely in Chapter 8, but also in Chapter 10, I'll be urging that, from a purely philosophical perspective, there's more to be said for our being immortal souls, who aren't any nonphysical OTHERONISH entities, than may be said for our being merely mortal souls, or nonphysical OTHERONS needing continual sustenance by nicely arrayed physical promoters.

But, at least for the meanwhile, nothing in any such dispute need trouble us much. For, either way, as we're now supposing, it will be true (in the sort of case we're presently considering) that varying arrays of Small Blues will have various effects on the experiencing of an emergent experiencer. Just so, and either way, we're supposing that each emergent mental being will have, among her Propensities, a passive power to have her course of experience influenced in certain ways. But, of course, since it's so passive, this receptive power is very different from a power to choose.

When our purely mental being has certain experiences, she may have certain thoughts occur to her. For instance, suppose she has a strong desire to have some experience as of a cube. Then, typically, upon having such an experience, it will occur to her that she's having a quite satisfying experience. But, just as typically, this thought will be quite unbidden. Her Propensity to have such unbidden thoughts is, again, far more passive than the power to choose.

How might our emergent being really choose to *think about* metaphysics or, alternatively, choose to think about athletics? For starters, it must be possible for her to think about metaphysics *and also possible for her* to think about athletics. And, she must have in mind, at least in some sense of "have in mind," both possibilities for her activity. Further, she must be undecided, and unsettled, between them. Further still, she must have the *power to determine what will be her settled state* in this matter, whether it will be a state in which she (starts and so) is thinking just about metaphysics, and not about athletics, or whether a state where she's thinking just about athletics. Then, our emergent experiencer may exercise her power to choose what to think about. In doing that, she chooses to think about metaphysics, we suppose, and, for this reason, she starts thinking about that. As it seems, here's a perfectly possible case of a being making a real choice, between actually available courses for her thoughtful activity. Quite unlike what goes on with our Scientiphical Janes, with a Radically Emergent Cartesian Jane, by contrast, there's no impossibility, it seems, in the thought that she really chooses. Rather, it seems perfectly possible for her situation to be this: She can choose to have it that she'll be just a certain way, where she'll think about metaphysics, and she also can choose another way, where she won't.[9]

---

9. In the first instance, it was Dean Zimmerman's trenchant comments that made me realize I must consider, as a serious candidate view, a Nonentity Emergentism like that next presented in this Chapter.

In his book *Persons and Causes*, Oxford University Press, 2000, Timothy O'Connor presents an Emergentist View not very unlike what I'll next sketch.

13. Physical-and-Mental Complexes with a Radically Emergent Power to Choose

With less of a departure from Scientiphical Metaphysics, than we made with our suggested Dualism, here's a second sketchy suggestion: Each of us may be a complex constituted of simpler physical entities, and each may have many physically derivative powers; but, unlike many more boring physical complexes, we'll each *also* have *radically emergent mental powers*, powers with *no* physical derivation. Salient among these powers, there is our power to *choose what to do from among actual alternatives* for ourselves, and, in particular, our power to *choose what to think about*.

On this view, it's a misleading simplification to say, with no amplification, that we're *physical* complexes, though it's true that we all will be physical beings. For, we may be mental beings just as much as we're physical entities, even while our mentality is no more reducible to our physicality than the latter is reducible to the former. Thus, among our very most central and peculiar powers, there'll be mental powers that have no physical derivation from our physical features. To avoid misleading, maybe we should say we're *physical-and-mental complex beings*: As with mere rocks, it's true, we'll have physical powers that don't (physically or mentally) derive from anything mental. But, unlike rocks, and much more peculiarly, we'll have mental powers that don't (mentally or physically) derive from anything physical.[10]

About the suggestion that we're such radically powerful physical-and-mental complexes, this may be the main point: A complex being's many physical Propensities, and many other physical features, may be *in no conflict with* her having, as well, many purely mental features, none of which has any physical derivation at all. In particular, a complex's having spatial extension, and its having many physical Propensities, may present no problem for that very entity's having, at the same time, a radically emergent mental power of real choice.

Mightn't it be, further, that a complex entity's nonmental powers derive, but don't wholly derive, just physically, from certain unobvious Propensities of the physical-and-mental being's basic physical parts?

---

10. Somewhat well motivated, there may be a very broad sense of "physically derive," and of "physical Propensities," on which the mental powers of these complexes do physically derive from the physical Propensities of their basic constituents, along with the physical relations among them. But, we may also employ a more restricted sense, on which that won't hold. Towards the end of the next Section, when we discuss physically effective choice, this may become much clearer.

These Propensities will be, my suggestion runs, Dispositions of a Particle for serving, when it's in some apt physical conditions, to help constitute, along with so many other Particles, a complex entity with both physical powers and also radically emergent nonphysical mental powers. It is somewhat unclear, I guess, what this suggestion amounts to. But, perhaps, I can do something to help remedy the situation.

By contrast with the World of Small Blues supposed in the previous Section, in another World whose physical realm is exhausted by basic Blue Particles, there may be, inhering in each of its Small Blues, a Propensity toward serving to constitute physical-and-mental complexes. So, inhering in each of a quintillion well-arrayed Small Blues, there may be made manifest this Propensity for interaction with each of the others: the Propensity to be a constituent part of a mental-and-physical whole with the radically emergent mental power to choose.

We've just been observing a View that (perhaps somewhat humorously) I'll call *Nonentity Emergentism*. Well, as that's a mouthful, I'll often call it by just its last name, *Emergentism*. Anyhow, before closing this Section, it's crucial to notice that, in entertaining this Nonentity Emergentist View, I'm doing all I can to forestall a move toward so much as a Substantial Dualistic Metaphysic. Now, as I should say very clearly, and in no uncertain terms, I have significant doubts about whether this Emergentism is, at bottom, a truly coherent position. Though I'm very uncertain in the matter, both in the one way and in the other, I have significant suspicions that what I've been sketching isn't really a view that's both truly distinctive and fully coherent. Maybe, this so-called Nonentity Emergentism is what many philosophers would call an "unstable position." So, for all I can really tell, it may be that, with many articulations of this allegedly new view, what we'll really end up with is just a very complex articulation of Scientiphicalism. And, it may be that, with all the other articulations, what we'll find ourselves formulating is a much more Radical sort of Emergence. That is, we'll then find we've formulated a View where there'll be emergent powers, all right, but only when, in the bargain, there are *radically emergent beings*, as with a newly generated Spherical Particle, or as with a materially generated immaterial soul. Maybe, it's only such emergent beings, as such a more fully articulated and coherent View will have it, that can ever truly possess radically emergent powers. Or, the same point put more perspicuously, it's only radically emergent beings that will ever be radically emergently powered.

In this book's central dialectic, whatever may be the ultimate status of our offered Nonentity Emergentism, well, it's all neither here nor there. Why? Well, by *supposing* this observed (and conservative)

Emergentism to be a fully coherent view, we force ourselves to give it a good run for the money. And, by doing *that*, we only make it harder, not easier, to provide an persuasive case for some sort of Substantial Dualism, indeed, for *any sort of Substantial Dualism*, including *the Emergentive Substantial Dualism*, as I'll call it, the likes of which I've just lately been sketching.

14. The Scientiphically Supposed Causal Closure of the Physical: How Much a Side Issue?

The most central problems of real choice, or free will, concern our belief that we choose what to think about quite as much as they concern our belief that we choose how to behave bodily. So, questions concerning only the second of these deep beliefs can't be the very most central problems of free will. Even if that's already clear, the point warrants some reflection.

For poignancy, let's imagine ourselves as Cartesian immaterial beings who may choose, deeply and freely, to move our bodies in certain ways—to wiggle our Blue thumbs, for example. So, our imaginative thought runs, we're nonphysical radically emergent mental entities that, at least from time to time, influence the course of physical reality. Now, this thought conflicts with a proposition that's accepted by almost all philosophers who, in recent decades, have written prominently on central questions of mind and body. Often going under the name "the causal closure of the physical," it's the proposition that, insofar as anything determines the course of (any of) physical reality, it's always only some sort of purely physical things that do so. But, if we Cartesian beings succeed in wiggling our thumbs, perhaps because we choose to move our bodies in that way, then there'll be some *nonphysical* things—we Immaterial beings—determining (some of) the course of physical reality. So, then, there'll be the failure of the causal closure of the physical. And, even if less poignantly, there'll also be that failure if we're physical-and-mental complex entities, each with an emergent mental power to choose her bodily movements, that she sometimes exercises effectively.

Is this thought much more disturbing, for presently prominent philosophers, than the thought that a *nonphysical* concrete being may (causally) determine (some of the course of) *nonphysical mental* reality, providing that (some of) mental reality is nonphysical? I don't think so. Philosophers endorsing the causal closure of the physical are also committed, by and large, to the thought that, insofar as *anything* determines the course of *any* concrete reality, whether or not the determined concreta be physical, this will always be just (some of concrete) *physical* reality. While that may sound like a mouthful, what I'm expressing is, really, a pretty simple idea.

For a moment, consider Dualistic Epiphenomenalism. On this View, the mental isn't anything physical. Still, as this Epiphenomenalism says, it's only the physical that causally determines the course of what's mental, insofar as anything ever determines that, whilst the mental, for its part, *doesn't* (even begin to) determine the course of any concreta at all, not even any purely mental concreta, much less any concretum that's physical. Well, nowadays, this Epiphenomenalism certainly isn't any very fashionable view. But, even so, it's far from being outrageously outlandish, or outlandishly outrageous. Compare it, for a moment, with any View that says that, even if physical reality sometimes determines the course of (even nonmental physical) concrete reality, so, at least at some other times, some concrete reality is determined, at least in part, by concreta that aren't any physical entities. Now, in the current intellectual climate, *that's* an utterly unrespectable idea, outlandishly outrageous and outrageously outlandish.

So, it's a bit misleading, I think, to say that Scientiphically-minded philosophers, who are actually almost all the most recently respectable philosophers, are *especially* concerned with the causal closure of the physical. No; that's not really it. Rather, or to the contrary, what grips them is, in point of actual fact, a thought that's a much more comprehensive idea.

Where central questions of real choice are our focus, I've just said, we shouldn't narrowly train our sights on the causal closure of the physical, focusing on what's *something of a side issue*.

But, of course, the question of causal closure *isn't entirely* a side issue. And, even if it may not be, or it should not be, of any truly special importance to the Scientiphically-minded, it represents an important Scientiphical commitment that does run, as I've been urging, contrary to deep commitments of commonsense thinking. And, as I've also been suggesting, these commitments should be some central tenets of our developing Humanly Realistic Philosophy. Just so, our Philosophy should comport, very well, with such apparent philosophical data as this: Sometimes I've picked up a pen because I chose to lift the cylindrical physical object, even while my leaving it lie was an actual alternative for me. Then, my real choice was physically effective; the pen was lifted *because I chose to* lift it. So, there's an effect on physical reality that's wrought through the effective exercise of a nonphysical mental power of mine, not any physically derivative Propensity. Or, ever so commonly, we very deeply believe.

As concerns large questions of mind and body, our developing Humanly Realistic Philosophy should be an Interactionist Metaphysic. To see that clearly, we may proceed in any one of many favorable directions. For continuity of exposition, I'll choose a path already well trod, in Chapter 2's discussion of my communicating to you, often quite successfully, how it is with even my innermost thinking (and, correlatively, of course, your successfully communicating to me). After really choosing to imagine a Red Sphere, we agreed, I can also really choose to communicate, to you, the fact that it was just such a thing, a Red Sphere, that I was just imagining. In this way, I'll ensure that you know how it was with me, just recently, experientially and imaginatively. But, I cannot accomplish this in any very direct way. Rather, I do it in some such indirect way as this: I utter some such sentence as, say, "I just imagined a Red Sphere," speaking loudly and clearly enough for you to gather my meaning. So, the choosing experiencer who is me affects nonmental physical reality, as with my moving lips and, yet more certainly, as with the air between our bodies. And, various physical disturbances that I produce, well, they affect how things are with you, another experiencer, including even how things are experientially and thoughtfully. And, of course, I could go on and on about things like this. So, as I just said at this paragraph's head, our Humanly Realistic Philosophy will be an Interactionist Metaphysic.

Maybe, and pretty conservatively, our Philosophy will be an Interactionist Nonentity Emergentism, wherein purely physical entities affect mental-and-physical complexes while, just as truly, mental-and-physical complexes affect purely physical entities. Or, at the least, this now seems a viable alternative for us.

Maybe, less conservatively, our Philosophy will be an Interactionist Emergentive Substantial Dualism—not wholly unlike Descartes's philosophy—wherein purely physical entities (in no wise mental) affect purely mental entities (in no wise physical) even while, just as truly, purely mental entities affect purely physical individuals.

But, in either event—whether it's to be an Interactionist Nonentity Emergentism or whether an Interactionist Substantial Dualism—either way, as I'm suggesting, our Humanly Realistic Philosophy certainly will be at odds with the so-called causal closure of the physical. Well, then, so much for the so-called causal closure of the physical.

Now, even whilst agreeing with me on these just previous points, some philosophers might be quite content just to subvert the dominant Scientiphical Metaphysics. And, for them, a serious discussion of the physical's alleged causal closure may be little more than an optional exercise. But, for more positively inclined thinkers, like we who seek to develop a Humanly Realistic Philosophy, there's more to be done. Accordingly, we've been seriously discussing this currently popular doctrine known as the causal closure of the physical; for us, this is more than an optional exercise.

According to the causal closure of the physical, at least as I understand the fashionable dictum, physical reality isn't ever affected by any truly radically emergent mental power (that is, by any power that's not a physical power). To the contrary, all that ever affects physical reality is something that's itself just some part of, or some aspect of, or some feature of, physical reality. But, as I've been arguing, that dictum is, then, in conflict with the idea that we engage in *physically effective* real choice.

Because we see this conflict, we can be clearer about the thrust of our offered Emergentism, with its claims of physical complexes that have, along with their physically derivative powers, *nonphysical* mental powers. Unlike the manifestation of any of your fully physical Propensities, which may all be quite fully in line with the causal closure of the physical, the physically effective exercise of your nonphysical power to choose won't always be so fully in line. Sometimes, when you chose to wiggle a certain finger, well, that *does contravene* the fashionable doctrine of causal closure. When we believe, quite as our Emergentists do believe, that we exercise this nonphysical mental power, then our belief is that we're *not* just some very complex physical thing, all of whose powers are each just one or another physical power. Rather, we believe ourselves to have, or our *Emergentists* believe themselves to have, in *addition to* just so many fully physical Propensities, various *nonphysical* powers. And, with the nonphysical exercise of (at least some of) these nonphysical powers, sometimes there'll be a certain effective interference with, or a certain effective contravention of, the properly physical Propensity of our world's actually existing individuals. Not only is this a deliverance of reflective common sense, but, quite as well, it's equally endorsed by our noted Emergentists: There's more to our behavior, both our overt activity and our covert activity, than the manifestation of all our purely physical powers, derivative and nonderivative.

(How are we to understand the origination of a physical-and-mental being, with its radically emergent nonphysical powers? For a decent understanding, the key point here is, in its essentials, much the same as what we observed before, in connection with the origination of a radically emergent Immaterial being. The emergence of a physical-and-mental being will be just the manifestation of a Propensity of its constituent Particles, or of whatever are its basic physical constituents, for a certain sort of generative mutual interaction. In this instance, each constituent Particle will have a Propensity for interacting with just so many other Particles, when they're arranged in any of such-and-such ways, so as to compose a complex that has, along with its physically derivative physical powers, the nonphysical mental power that's the entity's power to choose. In that each Particle has such a generative Propensity, each has a disposition toward composing a whole that can do things that conflict with, and that will sometimes prevail against, the manifestation of the basic constituent's physical Propensities. In contrast with anything I find comfortably familiar, this is an amazingly strange Propensity. But, without such amazing Propensities, all the powers of physical complexes will be some physically derivative Propensities.

A parallel point will hold for a basic Field. The Field has, along with its purely physical Propensities, a Propensity to generate beings with nonphysical mental powers. When (some part of) the Field is configured in a way conducive to such generation, then there'll be generated one of these impressively empowered beings. Presumably, this generated being will have, and will continue to have, a special (quasi-causal) relation with (some of) that part of the Field most directly involved with its origination. Presumably, but not necessarily.)[11]

15. Are Physically Effective Choosing Souls Compatible with Physical Conservation Laws?

When I studied some science, well over forty years ago, I learned about what were called "Conservation Laws." When studying chemistry, I learned of something called the Law of Conservation of Matter. To my mind then, that made a fair amount of sense. When you put some massive materials through some chemical reaction, some materials whose masses were first weighed, or measured, and when you then collected, and you weighed, all the materials resulting from all the chemical activity, you should wind up with materials that, together, weighed just precisely the same as, and were just exactly as massive as, all the materials that were initially involved in the chemical process. It's not that I was absolutely clear about what it was, exactly, that this

---

11. Well, in broad strokes, that's about the best I can do. Am I confident that, at least broadly speaking, it's really delivering us the goods? No; I'm not. Remember this: I'm very uncertain whether our offered Nonentity Emergentism is, in the first place, a properly comprehensive and fully coherent metaphysic.

Conservation Law said. (And, quite beyond that, I was never anything like quite certain that, whatever it might say, exactly, the time-honored Law really was perfectly true.) But, as I noted, I had a fair idea of what it said. Or, so it seems to me. And, I was more than willing to suppose that, at least for practical purposes—not the least of these being my own scholastic promotion—this was a perfectly true proposition, governing absolutely all material stuffs and things. No doubt, in these regards, I hardly differed from most of my readers, or most who took such science courses.

Anyway, that's little more than a friendly preamble to what's soon to be related. Why is this, really, all quite innocuous material, fit for little more than just such a preamble? Well, even right now, when I'm far from innocent of formal philosophy, I can't see that any Law of Conservation of Matter is likely to bear importantly on questions of real choice. Even if some such Law should be perfectly true, there won't be much plausibility, it seems to me, in the idea that it should pose a threat to anyone's belief in real choice. Indeed, it doesn't appear to threaten even a belief that, by choosing from among real alternative options for herself, a nonphysical soul may alter the course of physical reality. For, I don't feel the slightest temptation to think that this might ever be accomplished by some nonphysical soul's causing there to be, in the physical realm, some additional matter (without its destroying some equivalent matter) or by a soul's destroying some matter (without its producing some equivalent matter). Nor do I think that, to engage in some physically effective real choice, a soul would need there to be, for any other reason, any more matter in the world, or any less matter in the world, than otherwise—say, than if she was always paralyzed with indecision. Indeed, among those of my acquaintance, I know of nobody with even the least inclination toward anything along any such very strange line. Wanting soon to consider a quite different intellectual situation, which dramatically contrasts with the boring business I just laid before us, I now hasten to move far beyond my friendly preamble, beyond all this boring business that's now quite fully concluded.

A bit later in my career as a student, when learning basic classical physics, I learned something called the Law of Conservation of Energy. Except as a bunch of heuristics helpful for choosing which equations to manipulate in which circumstances, this never made much sense to me at all. I remember being told, as if it were only last month, about someone throwing a stone up onto a high cliff. First, there was some chemical energy stored in the athlete, in his caloric fuel, so to say. As he went into motion, this was transformed into kinetic physical energy on the part of the athlete (whatever, exactly, that might mean). Then, much of the athlete's kinetic energy, well, for instructive simplification, let's suppose all of that energy, was communicated to the stone being thrown by the athlete. Or, maybe much the same, the athlete's kinetic energy was transformed into the thrown stone's kinetic energy (whatever, exactly, any of *that* might mean). Well, even as all good things must come to an end, so the stone stopped moving when it landed on the top of the cliff, not very far from the cliff's edge. Energetically speaking, so to say, what happened then? Get this: With little energy lost—for elegance, we may assume none at all—the moving stone's kinetic energy was transformed into (something called) *the potential energy of the (now resting) stone*. So, by just exerting the very little energy needed to roll the stone over the cliff's edge, just by providing the resting stone with only a very little (kinetic) energy, which he would thereby be adding to the considerable potential energy of that selfsame stone, a weak little mouse could, indirectly but strikingly, crush someone's skull at the base of the high cliff. (Let's not be so cheaply ironic as to say it's our athlete whose skull gets crushed. Or, as with some movie cartoonists, we might be so cheaply ironic.)

Being less elegant, and less cleanly instructive, we might allow that, as our story progressed, there were certain losses of energy. For example, to overcome the friction of the air, the thrown stone would have to lose some of its kinetic energy. So, at least for that reason, when later resting on the cliff, the stone's potential energy would be somewhat less than the kinetic energy it had upon just leaving the athlete's hand. But, then, if we add back any energy that was lost, in the progression of our story, we'd end up with precisely the amount of energy at the start, when there was just so much energy stored as caloric fuel. Well, it went something like that, with the upshot being something like this: In any closed physical system, there's no energy ever lost, and none ever gained.

(Even when innocent of philosophy, I took it that such stories, apparently about a something that was called "energy," must be a way of saying something quite useful, and probably something roughly true, about something more evidently real. Thinking much the same thing right this minute, nowadays I'd put the point more colorfully: Insofar as there is any energy, it's ontologically very parasitical, certainly not any real individual, physical or nonphysical.)

However rich, or poor, may be anyone's understanding of what's said by the (so-called) Law of Conservation of Energy, none of that much matters here and now. What does matter, rather, is this: As concerns what bearing it may have on questions of how an immaterial soul might affect physical reality, with *this* (so-called) Conservation

Law, there's a feeling, at least, of real relevance. And, maybe there's even a feeling of some truly threatening relevance. This is a very different kettle of fish, I take it, from how things (even just) seemed with the (so-called) Law of Conservation of Matter. In marked contrast with that bore from before, with the presently putative proposition there does seem to be, at least, a real conflict between its holding true and, on the other side, somebody's belief that an immaterial soul may, in exercising some radically mental nonphysical power, affect how it is that things proceed in physical reality, as with affecting the course of some (presumably) moving physical particles. (For whatever it's worth, and I suspect it's not worth very much, here I do feel a temptation to think that this might be accomplished by, and maybe accomplished only by, some nonphysical soul's causing there to be, in the physical realm, some additional energy (without its destroying some equivalent energy) or by a soul's selectively depleting some energy (without its producing some equivalent energy). And, as I certainly suspect, quite a few other folks feel something of the same temptation.)

Though certainly not always, sometimes a little knowledge is a dangerous thing. And, as I'll suggest, this may be one of those many instances. In order to minimize this danger, for myself and for quite a few readers, no doubt, I'll quote the most pertinent parts from the entry on "Dualism," in what may well be the most comprehensive, authoritative and up-to-date reference work of philosophy, the *Routledge Encyclopedia of Philosophy*. In the section of that entry called "Objections to Dualism," the prominent *materialist* philosopher David Rosenthal writes:

> Although the character of physics underlies one major argument, a specific principle of physics is sometimes thought to show that dualism is wrong. That principle states that in a closed physical system (that is, closed to other physical systems) the total energy remains constant. But if mental events are nonphysical, then, when mental events cause bodily events, physical motion occurs uncaused by anything physical. And this, it seems, would result in an increase in the total energy in the relevant closed physical system. Mental causation of bodily events would conflict with the principle of the conservation of energy.
>
> No such problem arises, even if dualism is true, when bodily events cause mental events. When bodily events cause mental events, presumably they cause other physical events as well, which enables energy to be conserved....
>
> But [also] the dualist need not adopt the unintuitive idea that mental events never cause bodily events. Conservation of energy

dictates only that the energy in a closed physical system is constant, not also how that energy is distributed within the system. Since mental events could effect bodily changes by altering that distribution of energy, the conservation principle does not preclude minds' having bodily effects.[12]

So, whatever the exact import of the Law of Conservation of Energy, there appears no good reason to think that it's incompatible with the claim that, at least from time to time, the radically free choices of wholly nonphysical souls affect the course of physical reality, even unto how it is with altering the motions of certain minute Particles.

Equally, whatever the exact import of the Law of Conservation of Energy, there appears no reason to think that it conflicts with the claim that, from time to time, the radically free choices of mental-and-physical complexes affect the course of purely physical reality, even unto how it is with altering the motions of certain minute Particles, perhaps including the electrons comprising a certain current-pulse in a certain brain. Maybe, sometimes that happens in, or with, your brain, and sometimes with my brain, and sometimes with the brain of a real-life Jane.

As a closing shot at this issue, I'd like to say something that, to my mind, very nicely complements what's so recently come before: In the light of all the evidence mankind's so far accumulated, at the time of this very writing, I'd endorse the idea that, at least on occasion, we really do choose, from among actually available options for our intentional movement, or the intentional movement of our bodies, just such bodily movements as we then do make. And, just as unabashedly, I'll say that, at least on occasion, we make these intentional movements, or we intentionally make our bodies move as they do, *because we really choose* to make those things happen.

Now, if the weight of (philosophical) argument should favor the thought that this can happen, in the actual world, only if each of us is an emergent mental-and-physical complex, then so be it, say I. And, with this said, I'll then be that much friendlier to the thought that I'm a mental-and-physical complex.

But, if the weight of argument should favor the thought that this can happen, in the actual world, only if each of us is an immaterial soul, then so be *it*, say I. And, with *this* said, I'll be that much friendlier to *this other* idea.

12. David M. Rosenthal, "Objections to dualism," which is section 4 of his encyclopedia entry "Dualism," in E. Craig, ed., *Routledge Encyclopedia of Philosophy*, Routledge, 1998. I retrieved this from the *Encyclopedia*'s electronic version, on November 29, 2003, from this Web address: www.rep.routledge.com/article/V011SECT4.

As well, whether it's in favor of our Interactionist Nonentity Emergentism, or whether in favor of an Emergentive Interactionist Substantial Dualism, I'd be at least somewhat unconfident of the argument, however strong it might appear. And, I'd also be a little bit unconfident of my making any physically effective real choices—even if, about this matter, it's only just a very little bit. (Well, you already knew all that. Even so, I think I should be perfectly explicit here.)

So, I'm happy to find, I'll admit, that our developing Philosophy is, evidently, quite compatible with anything about conservation that physics actually requires. But, even without any such happy finding, I'd advocate this Humanly Realistic Philosophy anyway, to be perfectly honest with you. At the same time, I should also say most sincerely, in such an unhappy circumstance, I'd be advocating the Philosophy even less confidently than I now do.

16. Are Physically Effective Choosing Souls Compatible with Other Physical Principles?

So strong is our allegiance to Scientiphicalism, I imagine, that many will barely be touched by anything said in the previous Section. Very possibly, they may think something like this: Even if there's no conflict between physical conservation laws and, on the other hand, physically effective choosing by particulars that aren't fully physical, well, there *must be some other conflict* between physics and, on the same suspiciously other side, any such spookily effective choosing.

Well, as one who's ignorant of contemporary physics, there's little that, with any confidence or propriety, I myself should direct at that insistence, beyond saying that it certainly strikes me as very badly dogmatic. So, much as I did in the just previous Section, I'll again quote from another reference work, intended for both many philosophers and also many others. In this case, I quote from David Chalmers's contribution to *The Blackwell Guide to Philosophy of Mind*:

> By far the most influential objection to interactionism is that it is incompatible with physics. It is widely held that science tells us that the microphysical realm is causally closed, so that there is no room for mental states to have any effects. An interactionist might respond in various ways. For example, it could be suggested that although no experimental studies have revealed these effects, none has ruled them out....
>
> By far the strongest response to this objection, however, is to suggest that far from ruling out interactionism, contemporary physics is positively encouraging to the possibility....

In fact, one might argue that if one were to design elegant laws of physics that allow a role for the conscious mind, one could not do much better than the bipartite dynamics of standard quantum mechanics: one principle governing deterministic evolution in normal cases, and one principle governing non-deterministic evolution in special situations that have a prima facie link to the mental. . . .

All this suggests that there is at least room for a viable interactionism to be explored, and that the most common objection to interactionism has little force. Of course it does not entail that interactionism is true. There is much that is attractive about the view of the physical world as causally closed, and there is little direct evidence from cognitive science of the hypothesis that behavior cannot be wholly explained in terms of physical causes. Still, if we have independent reason to think that consciousness is irreducible, and if we wish to retain the intuitive view that consciousness plays a causal role, then this is a view that has to be taken very seriously.[13]

Now, the alert reader will surely notice that, in what's just above, Chalmers speaks of consciousness, whereas this Chapter's focus is on choice, or choosing. But, in this connection, I'm happy to have several things to say.

First, as I've been arguing in this Chapter, even as we may have, so far, some independent reason to think that consciousness is irreducible to anything physical—or that the power to experience (consciously) isn't a physical propensity, neither physically basic nor physically derivative, we have, so far, *stronger* reason, or more *forceful* arguments, for thinking that real *choosing* is so irreducible—or that the *power to really choose* is irreducible—to any wholly physical power, or powers. What's more, even while it's intuitive that consciousness (or possibly passive conscious experience) plays a causal role, or that's an intuitively quite credible idea, it's *at least as credible that our choosing*, for ourselves, from real alternatives for our behavior, plays a causal role as regards our behavior. And, then, of course, it will be just as credible, really, that our choosing often plays a causal role in, or has an influence with regard to, a fair bit of physical reality that's quite obviously external to ourselves. (This happens, no doubt, when someone whimsically chooses a pink shirt to put on.)

Second, and on top of all that, there's this: In the very next Chapter, I'll offer arguments for thinking that, just as much as with the power to choose, the power to experience (consciously) isn't any

13. David J. Chalmers, "Consciousness and Its Place in Nature," in Stephen P. Stich and Ted A. Warfield, eds., *The Blackwell Guide to the Philosophy of Mind*, Blackwell, 2003. I've cited selections from pp. 125–127.

physical power, certainly not any basic power of basic physical individuals, but also not any physically derivative power, either. In the
bargain, I'll be arguing that consciousness, or conscious experience, is
irreducible—whenever it occurs, it's always the activation of a power, or
the manifestation of a Propensity, that's no physical power. At the same
time, everything I'll say there will be, just as everything I've said here
has been, completely consistent with the Humanly Realistic idea, and
the eminently sensible idea that, in the development of physical reality,
conscious experience plays a crucial causal role. (This happens, no
doubt, when, upon seeing another wearing a pink shirt that he likes,
someone goes out and buys a similarly likeable pink shirt.)

Well, freeing us from Scientiphical dogma is one thing, I'm sure,
while getting ahead of myself is quite another. That admitted and
acknowledged, let's get on with this Chapter's argumentation.

17. Radically Self-directed Power

In just a short while, I'll be arguing that there's this terribly serious
conflict between what Scientiphicalism holds and, on the other side,
what's required by real choosing: As I'll argue, a choosing being can't
be wholly subject to natural laws, neither deterministic nor even
probabilistic. But, according to Scientiphicalism, the behavior of every
concrete being, insofar as it's determined by anything at all, *will be*
governed by natural law, whether deterministic or whether merely
probabilistic. About the seriousness of this conflict, I've become pretty
well convinced.

Right now, however, I want to discuss another seeming conflict,
between our being real choosers and the Scientiphical View of ourselves. About the genuineness of this other apparent conflict, I'm not
quite as fully convinced. But, I do suspect, at least, that it means real
trouble and, in any event, it concerns a matter of considerable philosophic interest.

For a being to have the power to choose, from among actual alternatives for her activity, the being must have the *power to direct herself*
to a particular one of her actual alternatives. And, as it seems to me, we
may understand this suggestion in a very strong sense of its terms. So,
for a being to direct herself *to* a certain particular option, in this very
strong sense, she must *then also be able*, at the very same time, to direct
herself in *another* way, which is *not to* that option. Now, for all that to be
so, the being must have an apparently quite radical power: It must be
within the being's power to take up that option and *also within its power not*

to take it up. Can such a radically self-directed power fully derive from just the Propensities of basic physical things to interact physically with other basic physical things, and the physical relations among them? I don't think so.

To be sure, we do talk of complex physical things in terms of self-direction, in terms of their directing themselves to do certain things. For example, we may consider a heating device controlled by a thermostat that's part of the device itself. After the complex heater has done a fair bit of heating, its thermostat will register the surrounding air to be hot to such-and-such a degree. Due to the thermostat's registering that temperature, and due, as well, to the control system that's guided by the temperature's registration, the device stops heating. Why did it stop? Well, as we may say, the heater directed itself to stop heating. And, later, when the temperature's dropped a lot, the thermostat will register a certain lower temperature and, in due course, the heater will start heating. As we may also say, the heater then will direct itself to start heating. Yet, all the while, we accept that all the heater's powers are just so many physically derivative Propensities.

But, then, do we really think there's terribly much in common here, between your power to direct yourself on a certain course of activity and, on the other side, the heating system's Propensity to direct itself? I don't think so. After all, we don't really think that, in the full way that there are actual alternatives for your action, there are actual options for the heater's behavior. Just so, we certainly do think that, quite as it's within your power *to* think about metaphysics, it's also within your power *not to* do that. But, we certainly *don't* think that, even as it's *within the heater's power to* produce heat, it's also within its power, then and there, *not to* do so. Again, while we think that it's up to you, right then and there, whether or not you'll think about metaphysics, we don't think that, right then and there, it's up to the heater whether or not it will produce heat. So, along with all this, it's only in a quite weak sense of the terms, I submit, that we may speak of the heater, or of any such physically derivative complex, as having the *power to direct itself*.

Now, what of the power to choose? For a being to have the power to choose to do a certain thing, it must have the power to direct itself in a very strong sense. So, if you have the power to choose to think about metaphysics, then you must have the power to direct yourself to do that and, at the same time, you must *also* have the power to direct yourself in *another* way, where you *don't* think about metaphysics. And, this requires, of course, that you have it within your power *whether or not* you think about metaphysics. So, a being with the power to choose must be able to direct itself as to what it will do, in a very strong sense of those terms, a sense far stronger than any that's satisfied by our physically derivative thermostatic heater.

In this very strong sense, required for real choice, Scientiphicalism won't allow that *you direct yourself*: On the Scientiphical View, all your powers are just so many purely physical Propensities, all deriving from the basic physical properties of your simple constituents, saliently including their basic dispositions for interacting physically with other such simple concrete particulars. And, no such physically derivative Propensity can have it be within your power *whether or not* to think about metaphysics. Just so, no such physically derivative power can be your power to really choose.

18. An Exemption from Natural Law Is Required for Real Choice

It's now time to discuss a most serious conflict between what Scientiphicalism holds and, on the other side, what's required by real choosing. This is the conflict between the Scientiphical thought that the behavior of every concrete being is determined in accordance with natural law, insofar as the behavior isn't merely random, and, as I'll argue, the requirement that a choosing being can't be wholly subject to natural laws, neither deterministic nor even probabilistic.

This great conflict, I suggest, transcends any issues concerning whether or not a materialistic metaphysic holds true. Just so, even if we should be purely mental partless beings, as perhaps with Immaterial souls, that's not enough, by itself, for us to have real choice. For it may be possible for some such simple nonphysical beings to be *wholly subject to natural laws*. But, for a being to have real choice, she *must not be* so subject to natural laws. Let's discuss the matter.

We've already agreed that an entity's being subject to *physical laws* amounts to its having certain Propensities. In an extreme case, as with an infinitely vast material plenum, there may be just a single physical thing (without any substantial parts, but) with Propensities to go from certain states into certain other states. In one such simple case, a plenum may lawfully alternate between being all Orange for a second and being all Purple for a second. In a slightly more complex case, when Orange a plenum might have a 0.7 chance of next being Purple and a 0.3 chance of next being Green, and when Purple a 0.7 Chance of next Green and a 0.3 chance of next Orange, and when Green a 0.7 chance of next Orange and a 0.3 chance of next Purple. Wholly subject to a certain physical law as to its Qualitative state, it may go through an always somewhat unpredictable sequence of Color states, perhaps infinitely lengthy. But still, in all that there'll be just the manifestation of the (probabilistic) Propensities of the mindless material being.

It's equally possible that there should be purely mental Immaterial experiencers (each without any substantial parts, but) all wholly subject to certain natural laws. One of the laws might be to this effect: When a being is experiential orange (and no other experiential color), there's a 0.7 chance of her next being experiential purple (and no other color) and a 0.3 chance of her next being experiential green (only); when being experiential purple, a 0.7 chance of next experiencing green and a 0.3 chance of sensing orange; and, when experiencing green, a 0.7 chance of next orange and a 0.3 chance of purple. With those being an experiencer's mental Propensities, we may then say this: Subject to a natural law as to its experiential state, an immaterial mind will go through an always somewhat unpredictable sequence of experiences, perhaps infinitely lengthy. But still, in all that there'll be just the manifestation of the (probabilistic) Propensities of the bodiless mental being.

Of course, there may be far more complex laws governing a partless mental being's experience. As well, though having no substantial parts, a mind may have a complex endowment of dispositions as to its contentful thought processes. Accordingly, a certain soul may be subject to laws governing her thinking, which may be deterministic or, equally, which may be probabilistic. So, when a certain soul is consciously thinking that yellow is more like orange than like purple, there may be a 0.3 chance she'll next consciously think that blue is more like purple than like orange.

Now, with certain immaterial souls, it may be that all their activity is determined, insofar as it's determined by anything at all, by just such wholly lawful Propensities, that is, by natural laws that (thus may be said to) govern the nonphysical individuals. But, as far as real *choosing* is concerned, a partless mental being that's so *wholly subject* to laws, whose *dispositions are all such perfectly* lawful Propensities, well, the being is utterly unsuited to be a real chooser. To make real choices, I'll notice, even a perfectly Immaterial mind must be, at least to *some* degree, exempt from laws of nature. The laws must leave *some things open to her*. Maybe it's left open to her to choose to increase the chance that she'll experience orange, or maybe to choose to decrease the chance she'll think that yellow is quite like orange. Anyhow, there must be some powers she has that *aren't wholly lawful* Propensities, or else she won't have a power of real choice.

Now, according to Scientiphicalism, we're each wholly subject to natural laws, unless we should be involved in just some purely random happenings. But, of course, our being involved in *purely random* happenings can't mean our ever *really choosing* what we do.

This is a genuine Incompatibility, it seems to me, between the dominant Scientiphical View and our belief in real choice. Indeed, to my mind, this is the most deeply disturbing conflict between the dominant metaphysic and, on the other side, our belief in our power to choose.

How might we best adjudicate this deeply disturbing conflict?

19. The Real Reason Why an Exemption from Natural Law Is Required for Real Choice

In previous Chapters, I've spent many words propounding a Humanly Realistic Philosophy. In doing that, I've often talked of how concrete things may be Propensitied or, as I'll now also say, how concreta may be Powered. Much less often have I talked of natural laws. There's a reason for that difference in presentation. On the metaphysic I'm concerned to advance, it's Propensitied individuals, or Powered particulars, that are more basic metaphysically, more fundamental ontologically, while the likes of laws are metaphysically more derivative, and they're ontologically more parasitical. Indeed, just as we avoid reifying Propensities (or any other so-called Properties), so we should also avoid reifying laws, while we should always focus, instead, on substantial individuals. So, at least for us, it's no great exaggeration to say that *all a natural law amounts to is* that, as concerns such concrete particulars as are said to be *governed by the law*, and as are said to be *subject to the law*, they're so regularly Propensitied just as they *are*, in fact, just so nicely Propensitied.

In explaining why there's a conflict between our being wholly governed by natural law and, on the other side, our having real choice, we'll conceptualize matters in a way that, as it seems to me, is quite the reverse of how so many philosophers often treat natural laws, and such entities as are said to be governed by those laws. On our approach, it's not that, in the first place, something agreeable must be happening with natural laws so that, in the second place, we may (have the chance to) really choose. Not at all. Rather, insofar as it makes sense to speak of a conceptualizing order here (not any ordering, of course, in concrete reality itself) it's better to say that, in the first place, we sometimes really choose what to do and, so, in the second place, *whatever natural laws obtain must be compatible with our doing what we really choose to do*. But, of course, I should do more to explain what I mean by this.

Let's suppose that certain particulars, maybe even some meta-physically basic individuals, do have the power to choose from among actual alternatives for their activity. As we'll suppose, you may be one of these; and I may be another, distinct from you. So, as we're supposing, you have the power to choose *whether or not* to think about metaphysics (in a moment or two), and, quite distinct from that, I have that power to choose whether or not to think about metaphysics.

Now, let's consider a rather general statement about you that concerns not just your past and your present, but your future as well. Well, given what we've just agreed, about what powers you possess, we should have agreed, I think, that you have the *power to determine whether or not* this rather general statement holds true. It's really up to you whether or not, in just a moment or two, you'll be thinking about metaphysics; and, so, it's up to you whether, or whether not, your whole pattern of thinking serves (to continue) to instance the offered generalization. So, rather than there being any *generalization governing you*, in any interestingly strong sense of such terms, it's really you, the choosing subject, who will determine whether the general statement holds true, or whether only some other statements, conflicting with the offered generality, will be truer descriptions of your whole history of thoughtful activity.

So far, so good. Now, suppose that, in sequence, you make several real choices and, as it adventitiously happens, a very simple and elegant generalization (consequently) holds true of you. And, suppose I also make several choices and, as it just as accidentally occurs, some very simple generalization (consequently) holds of me. Indeed, we may suppose that the very same generalization holds of both you and me. And, what's more, we'll suppose that you and I are the only thinking beings. So, our nice generalization holds true of all thinking beings. For its great elegance and simplicity, and for its holding for its whole purported domain, will *this* generalization be a *natural law*? No; it *won't* be any law of nature. For, as we've usefully been supposing, it's *only quite adventitious* that the generalization holds of you, at least insofar as your past (and present) may be concerned; and, it's *only accidental*, too, that it (only) similarly holds true of me. Being only such an accidental generalization, the considered proposition can't be any law of nature.

It's for just such a reason as that, I suggest, that it can't be that we really do have the power to choose and, at the same time, we're wholly subject to, and we're wholly governed by, laws of nature.

As I said just moments ago, it's logically required of our being real choosers that we (not be wholly subject to the laws, but) be exempt (whether wholly or whether just partially) from natural laws. And, as I'll now say, more perspicuously, I think, *it's required of a natural law that it not exhaustively concern any beings that really choose what to do.*

As I believe, we've just noticed a pretty satisfying explanation of why it is that an exemption from natural law is required for real choice. And, with that, we see further support for thinking there's a genuine conflict between Scientiphicalism and, on the other side, our belief in real choice.

20. Apparent Scientiphical Incompatibilisms and Further Philosophical Explorations

Central aspects of Scientiphicalism, I've been suggesting, are incompatible with our having real choice, or free will.

First, there's this: For a person to choose what to do, from among real alternatives for her, the person must be able to direct herself toward each of the alternatives and, at the same time, she must be able, as well, to direct herself, instead, toward any of the others. Can this ability be a physically derivative Propensity? I've argued that it can't be. Again, for a person to choose among real options, it must be within her power to choose any one of the options and, at the same time, it must be within her power, as well, not to choose that option. Can this power be a physically derivative Propensity? Again, I've argued that it can't be. Now, according to Scientiphicalism, we're all purely physical complexes, whose powers are, really, all just physically derived, from the fully physical Propensities of the simple physical things (or Fieldy Thing) that wholly compose us (and from other physically fundamental factors). So, as I've been arguing, the Scientiphical Metaphysic is, for this reason, incompatible with the thought that people choose what to do, from real alternatives for them.

Second, there's this: For a person to choose what to do, from among available options for her, it must be that, beyond anything concerning purely random happenings, the person *not be wholly governed by* laws of nature. But, according to Scientiphicalism, each of us is wholly governed by natural laws, whether deterministic or whether probabilistic, except insofar as there may be some purely random happenings. So, as I've been arguing, the Scientiphical Metaphysic is, for this other reason, incompatible with the thought that people choose what to do, from real alternatives.

It's useful, I think, for us to call these apparent conflicts, and others relevantly like them, *Scientiphical Incompatibilisms*. Each of these Incompatibilisms, if it's a genuine conflict, means that, in some central way or respect, we'll be scarcely more significant than happy clams. At the least, that's how the matter appears. So, it may be quite important for us to consider these Scientiphical Incompatibilisms.

For further philosophical exploration of these apparent conflicts, three avenues all but present themselves. Each avenue might be, I hope, taken by some of us. I'll now note each explicitly, though it's only the last of them that, in the rest of this book, will see much of my effort.

First, some should explore the (for all we know) possibility that, though there's an *apparent* clash between some Scientiphical statements and our belief in real choice, there *isn't a real* incompatibility here. Of course, those still wanting to uphold the Scientiphical Metaphysic should explore this avenue most energetically. No doubt, there'll be many to take this avenue, as there'll still be many Scientiphicalists. But, just as you expect, I won't be among them.

Second, some might explore how to see, more fully, what it is about the Scientiphical suppositions, and what it is about real choice, that may mean a real conflict between the two. I don't know who'll take this unfashionable avenue, though I do hope some readers will. Since I've just offered my own explanation of the conflict, in the just previous Section, I won't do this, either.

Third, there should be attempts to develop philosophical alternatives to the Scientiphical Metaphysic, worldviews that may be more open to our having real choice. And, along with that, there should be attempts to adjudicate among the alternative views developed. With this Chapter's offer of a Nonentity Emergentist position, and its sketch of an Emergentive Substantial Dualism, we've already taken some steps along this third avenue. In the next Chapter, we'll take more.

7

WHY WE REALLY MAY BE
IMMATERIAL SOULS

By observing apparent conflicts with our believed power to really choose, we've advanced a pretty strong new challenge to Scientiphicalism, a metaphysic that has all our powers be physically derivative Propensities. Not wanting to be simply negative in matters metaphysical, we observed that some other worldviews, each an alternative to Scientiphicalism, might do better by our belief in our real choice, or our free will. And, not wanting to be very radical, we observed that we certainly needn't become idealists to meet this challenge to our power to choose. Rather more conservatively than that, we may adopt a Substantial Dualism, not terribly unlike Cartesian Dualism. Yet more conservatively still, we sketchily advanced a Nonentity Emergentist Metaphysic that, as it seemed, would also emerge unscathed from our challenge to Scientiphicalism.

In this present Chapter, I mean to develop another new challenge to Scientiphicalism. As I suspect, this new challenge will mean much trouble for the noted Emergentist View, maybe as much as it means for the beleaguered Scientiphical Metaphysic.

By developing some old ideas of mine, in a newly disturbing direction, and by advancing arguments suggested by the new developments, I'll advance a challenge to the Scientiphical Metaphysic that complements the one we advanced in the previous Chapter. And, unlike the last Chapter's challenge, with this present one you'll see Scientiphicalism to comport very poorly even with your central beliefs as to your own apparent conscious experiencing, as well as comporting quite terribly with your central beliefs as to your own believed choosing.

For reasons related at the last Chapter's start, this may be important. Let's rehearse those reasons.

By contrast with my offered challenge to Scientiphicalism, and to any Respectable materialism, a drawback of the currently dominant sort of challenge is this: It's hard to make compelling the thought that there's a real incompatibility between your consciously experiencing and, on the other side, your being an entirely physical entity. At the same time, it's less hard to make compelling the thought that there's a conflict between your choosing from actual options for you and, on the other side, your being an entirely physical individual. So, that comparison favors the sort of challenge I presented, over the sort that's been more dominant. But, another comparison pulls the other way: Just so, it's hard to make compelling the thought that you don't really ever consciously experience. Right off the bat, we may see that it's darned near impossible for *you* to find this at all compelling in *your own* case. And, it's nearly as hard *for me* to think that you're never really experiencing. At the same time, it's rather less hard to think that you don't ever really choose. And, with that being so, there's this to consider: Perhaps convinced of a genuine conflict between her Scientiphicalism and her presumed choosing, a staunch Scientiphicalist might come to deny that she ever really does choose, despite her feeling, from time to time, *as if* she really chooses. Now, what can we say to such a staunch Scientiphicalist?

Well, in this present Chapter, I'll present a Problem, I'll call it the *Experiential Problem of the Many*, that may be deeply disturbing for such a staunchly Scientiphical philosopher. Quite apart from any question concerning her very apparent real choosing, she'll see conflicts between her Respectable worldview and, on the other side, some of her most central beliefs concerning her own experiencing. For those of us more interested in developing a Humanly Realistic Philosophy, and not so interested in any modish Respectability, this may be a most interesting development.

(More fully, in this Chapter, I'll present two main Problems that, along with others quite like them, I call the *Mental Problems of the Many*. First, I'll present the Experiential Problem of the Many. And, once that's in place, I'll then present what I call the *Problem of Too Many Choosers*.)

In the bargain, there may be other interesting developments. Due to the particular way I'll argue against Scientiphicalism, we'll also be encountering a challenge to the Nonentity Emergentism we've lately observed. To embrace an adequate philosophy, all this will suggest, we must adopt a worldview that differs from Scientiphicalism much more radically than does that Emergentist View.

Well, insofar as our new arguments are persuasive, they may provide motivation to take seriously a metaphysic not very unlike Descartes's Substantial Dualism. For all sorts of operative reasons—even social pressure may operate strongly here—I can't so much as *believe* any Substantial Dualism much like that. Indeed, being so largely a product of my place and time, I can't really believe *any* metaphysic differing much from our dominant Scientiphicalism, for instance, almost any view departing from it substantially more than does the Emergentism we've lately considered. But, though I've almost no control over what I believe, nor more than you do, we have more control over what we take seriously.

During the several years these pages were composed, including all the many revisions, any view departing so much from Scientiphicalism as much as Substantial Dualism does, in absolutely any of its main Versions or Forms, has been extremely unfashionable among mainstream academic philosophers, at least among those prominent professors whose primary language is, just as mine is, the English language. Indeed, any Philosophy anything much like Descartes's Substantial Dualism has been scarcely less fashionable, in these circles, than a Philosophy like Berkeley's Subjective Idealism. Curiously interesting relics of bygone times, historically important but, otherwise, nothing to be taking very seriously. Indeed, that's been the prevailing view for something like fifty years, now, and there's little sign that it won't continue to prevail for another fifty years, or more.

All right now, philosophy fans, THIS PARAGRAPH PROVIDES YOU SOME MARVELOUS TIME-SAVING TIPS, very useful, indeed, when confronting such a dauntingly long Chapter. (Why is this Chapter so long? Well, owing mostly to the enormous force of the fashions just lately noted, almost all respectably seasoned philosophers will, I confidently predict, have a very hard time aptly attending to what I've really written in this Chapter, conflating my offered sentences, all quite unwittingly, with various far more problematic messages. Largely for that reason, a great deal of this Chapter, by now the book's longest, comprises an almost overly generous attempt, even so likely futile, to avoid just so much pointless misunderstanding. Well, enough about all of them, so sadly enslaved by formidable fashion. Now, as promised, here's some goodies for you.) Folks happily innocent of most recent philosophy, as with undergraduates new to the subject, and as with folks whose university education encompassed only some other fields, well, you folks may skip, quite safely and very comfortably, half of this Chapter. While I'm not absolutely certain what's best for you to ignore, I'll make three pretty safely useful time-saving suggestions. First, there's this whopper: Even as the Chapter has some 23 numbered Sections, many may skip, I guess, these eleven Sections: 2, 5, 7, 9, 10, 11, 14, 17, 18, 20 and 23. Second, there's this pretty obvious advice: *Don't* bother to read the notes to the Chapter. (Actually, for many most innocent readers, this advice applies to every last one of the book's Chapters. But, as this present Chapter may have the most notes, and also the longest notes, right here this time-saving tip may be especially welcome.) Third, and finally, this is the only Chapter with an appendix. Innocent lambs, *don't* read that, either.

Well, that's enough with providing time-saving tips for many dear readers. And, for the meanwhile, I've also said enough about Substantial Dualism, the View that the Chapter aims to advance. Before attempting any strong moves in that direction, I'll wax happily nostalgic.

As I said only some several moments ago, I'll proceed by developing some *old* ideas of mine, and by advancing challenges suggested by some new developments of the old thoughts. As a lead-in for the Chapter's first numbered Section, I'll say something about my old ideas.

Many years ago, I blush to recall, I published some arguments against the existence of all sorts of commonly supposed entities—against rocks and desks, plants and planets, stars and salt shakers, human brains and bodies, and, perish the thought, even against us human thinking experiencers, including the one who's me.[1] By contrast, now I'm trying to develop a Humanly Realistic Philosophy, wherein my existence, and yours, has the status of an undeniable

---

1. In chronological order, the most directly nihilistic of these papers are: "There Are No Ordinary Things," *Synthese*, 1979; "I Do Not Exist," in G. F. MacDonald, ed., *Perception and Identity*, Macmillan, 1979; and "Why There Are No People," *Midwest Studies in Philosophy*, 1979. All three essays are reprinted in the new collection of my (selected) previously published papers, *Philosophical Papers, Volume 2*, Oxford University Press, 2006.

The main thrust of these papers is the articulation of a nihilistic approach to various *sorites* arguments. Typically, these arguments trade on the idea, for all I really know perfectly correct, that a tiny difference between two ordinary entities—minute as regards Propensities as well as all sorts of other things—will never mean the difference between one of them being a rock, for example, and the other not being a rock, nor the difference between one a thinking being and the other not a thinking being. In the third, and the last, of those papers, "Why There Are No People," I provide a detailed diagnosis of what I call "vague discriminative terms," terms like "rock" and "person," according to which all such terms are, so far as their semantics goes, as completely inconsistent as "perfectly round cube," though they're not nearly so obviously inconsistent.

philosophical datum. How can ideas from those old nihilistic arguments impact the positive present effort?

As it seems to me now, certain *trying ideas* deployed in such nihilistic
reasoning may bear importantly on the question of *what sort* of Humanly
Realistic View we should adopt. On a first pass, one trying idea is a
thought to the effect that, where I'm apt first to think that there's just
this one human body, "my body," seated in just this one chair, "my desk
chair," there are, more accurately, billions of human bodies, each seated
in billions of chairs. And, where I'm first given to believe that there's just
one healthy active brain, "my brain," promoting someone's mentality,
there may be billions of brains, each of them largely overlapping so
many of the others, and each serving, quite equally, to promote a
thinking, experiencing and choosing human being, or a human self.
Maybe each brain promotes the very same mind, or self, as do each of
the others, in which case there's just one mind, or self, who's promoted
(perhaps, with some redundancy) by them all. Or, maybe each promotes a numerically distinct conscious individual, in which case billions
of experiencers may be, in my situation, simultaneously promoted.
And, what's more, maybe each promotes a numerically distinct conscious real chooser, in which case there may be billions of real choosers,
right now, all in what I take to be just my own situation. When they're so
starkly suggested, as I've just done, these remarks should seem no
better than cryptic comments. But, pretty soon, their import should
become clearer.

1. Recalling the Problem of the Many

In a paper called "The Problem of the Many," I pondered a peculiar
problem for our ordinary thinking. As I saw only years later, it's a

---

Less directly nihilistic are a few other papers, including "The Problem of the Many,"
Midwest Studies in Philosophy, 1980, also reprinted in my *Philosophical Papers*. In this last
publication, none of the key ideas has anything much to do with any sorites arguments, or
with "discriminative vagueness," though a casual glance at these key ideas may often give
such an erroneous impression. Right now, I'll warn you against conflating these two very
different sorts of nihilistic reasoning. And, in the bargain, I'll warn against mistaking, for
any sorites argument, or any reasoning at all concerning discriminative vagueness, the
trying thoughts I'm about to supply in this present essay.

Finally for now, I signal that, while several of this present Chapter's key ideas do
arise from issues central to "The Problem of the Many," some presently central ideas go
far beyond anything considered by that old paper. (While there are great differences
between the thoughts of this new book and the ideas of that old paper, an attempt to
detail the differences looks to be more distracting than instructive.)

trouble quite distinct from anything mainly concerning the ancient sorites paradox, the so-called paradox of the heap. Indeed, it's distinct from any problem that involves, in any essential way, any "vague discriminative" terms, or conceptions, as with our ordinary conceptions of sticks and stones, tables and chairs, plants and puppies.

Insofar as my old Problem of the Many strongly resembles a still older problem, it's a problem first pondered, perhaps, by Peter Geach.[2] (To be fair to myself, I contrived my Problem, or I discovered it, quite independently of Geach's influence; indeed, I learned of his earlier effort only after I'd written "The Problem of the Many.") Here's a quick rendition of Geach's problem: We're to contemplate both a certain ordinary cat, one "Tibbles," and also a rather cat-shaped material entity, sort of "nested" in Tibbles, and slightly smaller than the (presumably unproblematic) cat. This smaller entity isn't composed of all the matter composing Tibbles; rather it may be composed of all the matter composing Tibbles *except for* the matter that serves to compose Tibbles's tail. Or, for another case, all Tibbles's matter except for just the matter composing a certain one of Tibbles's hairs. Let's call this slightly smaller entity "Tib." We may now ask interesting questions, including this: Along with Tibbles, isn't Tib also a cat, a cat that's slightly smaller than Tibbles?

There's an obvious way to secure the commonsense thought that, though Tibbles is a cat, Tib isn't any cat: Just as Tibbles is supposed to have a pretty clear natural boundary, so it's supposed to be pretty clear what's all the matter that's constituting a cat in Tibbles's situation. This is precisely all the matter that's within Tibbles's boundary, no more matter than that, of course, but no less matter, too. So, *it's just that* matter that composes the only *cat* in Tibbles's situation. At the same time, it may be that certain large portions of that matter compose some (merely) *felinistic* entities, to coin a new term, with many of these felinistic beings overlapping many of the others. But, even as none of the nested entities is a *properly feline* entity, so none of them may be properly counted a cat. Perhaps we may usefully say that each (merely) felinistic being is a *schmat*, to coin another new term, correlative with "felinistic." So, in Tibbles's situation there's just one cat, however many schmats might be there, with Tibbles himself being that sole cat. Our commonsense thinking is secured.

2. See P. T. Geach, *Reference and Generality*, 3rd ed., Cornell University Press, 1980. My present citation of Geach is taken from Brian Weatherson's useful entry, on the Problem of the Many, in the generally useful Stanford Encyclopedia of Philosophy, a fine Internet resource. The entry's address is: http://plato.stanford.edu/entries/problem-of-many/

By contrast with Geach's considerations, what fuels my Problem of the Many means more trouble for this commonsense thinking of ours. In presenting these more troublesome considerations, I'll begin here, as I did before, by considering certain *ordinary clouds*, as with those we seem to see, on some very sunny days, each apparently separated from the others by cloudless stretches of blue sky. As often viewed by us from here on the ground, such puffy "picture-postcard" clouds give the appearance of having a nice enough boundary, each lovely white cloud sharply enough surrounded by the same blue sky. (In marked contrast, on other days it's a wonder we don't simply speak singularly of "the cloud in the sky," where each visible cloudy region is so messily "merged together with" so many other cloudy regions of sky.) But, as may happen when you're in an airplane, on closer scrutiny even the neatest clouds don't seem, to you, to be so nicely bounded at all. And, this closer look seems, quite surely, to be a more revealing encounter. For, quite as science seems to say, even our neatest clouds are composed of, for the most part, very many tiny water droplets; and, the dispersion of these droplets, in the sky, or in the atmosphere, is always, in point of fact, a very gradual matter. With almost any outward route that starts from even a prettily puffy cloud's presumed center, or from any point quite near the center, there's no stark stopping place ever really to be encountered. Rather, when anywhere near anything presumed to be a possible boundary, in moving outward along any such route, there's only a quite *gradual* decrease in the density of droplets fit, more or less, to be constituents of our pretty cloud.

This being so, we may see there to be enormously many complexes of droplets each as fit as any other for being a constituted cloud. Each of the many will be a cloud, we must suppose, if there's even as many as just one constituted cloud in the presumed cloud's situation, where it first seemed there was exactly one cloud. How is that? Let me explain.

For starters, I'll sketchily describe just two cloud candidates, each greatly overlapping the other, one to be called Clarence and the other Clarice. Though Clarence and Clarice have very many components in common, they won't share either of *two* "widely opposing" water droplets—one of them, to be called Dan, is a droplet that's way over there on your left, and the other, one Donna, is way over on your right. Except for Dan and Donna, the two candidate clouds, our Clarence and our Clarice, may wholly overlap each other, at least as far as water droplets goes. Just so, leftward Dan is a constituent of just candidate Clarence, and it's no component of candidate Clarice. Equally, but by contrast, rightward Donna is a component of just Clarice, not Clarence.

Each of these two candidates will have, then, exactly the same number of constituent droplets as does the other. And, each *may* have exactly the same mass, and precisely the same volume, as the other does, though it's likely there'll be small differences here. And, given that a water droplet has very many molecules, it's most likely that Dan will either have more molecules than Donna, though not vastly more, or else he'll have less molecules than she, though not vastly less. And, also most likely, the droplet with more molecules will be the more massive droplet, though not vastly more massive. So, it's only by the small difference between the masses of Donna and Dan that there'll be a small difference, that same small difference, in the masses of Clarence and Clarice. I can't believe that this difference can do much for Clarence's candidacy over Clarice's, or vice versa. And, along the same relevantly egalitarian line, I have the obvious more general belief: Clarence won't have anything to favor his being a cloud over a claim for Clarice to such a successful effect, even while Clarice won't be any more qualified for cloudhood than Clarence.

Now, all around the outer portion(s) of a supposedly single cloud, what obtains is a gradual change of droplet density, along ever so many paths from the considered cloud's central portion(s) to what's merely its droplet-infested environment. In actuality, there's not just one "problematic pair of opposing droplets." It's not that our only Problem concerns what to think, differently as regards cloudhood, for just our Clarence and our Clarice. Rather, there'll be very many *distinct* such pairs, that is, many pairs of peripheral droplets each of which has no droplet in common with any of the other pairs. Indeed, either droplet from any one of very many opposing pairs might be coupled equally well, instead, with at least one of the two droplets from (almost) any other one of these very many pairs. This being so, the mathematics of combinations has it that, where one first supposes just a single concrete cloud, there are *billions* of clouds present. Each of these billions of cloud candidates has precisely as many droplets as does each of the others. And, in every way plausibly relevant for cloudhood here, each of our billions of candidate clouds is no better qualified than any other.

(Though it's not needed to expose our peculiar Problem, it can be fun to combine what's just been offered with some considerations concerning vagueness. So, in the case we've been considering, the extremely good cloud candidates aren't limited, of course, to the exactly equally good ones that differ only as regards two such opposing peripheral constituent droplets. In addition, there's another candidate, also a quite good candidate for cloudhood, that *lacks not just one of, but that lacks both of* the peripheral opposing droplets first considered. If there are any real clouds here at all, this candidate, which I'll call Claudia, will be a cloud that's just one "droplet's worth" less massive than either of our first two candidates, than either Clarence or Clarice, and that's just slightly smaller than them volumetrically, too. At the same time, but now "going in the other direction," we may notice a slightly larger good cloud candidate, a certain Clyde, that *has not just one of, but that has both of,* Dan and Donna, among its water droplet constituents. As regards both mass and volume, Clyde will be just one droplet *larger* than Clarence, and than Clarice; and, so, Clyde will be *two* droplets' worth larger than Claudia. Still and all, both Clyde and Claudia will be good cloud candidates. Or, at the least, both of them will be mighty good candidates if Clarence is, or if Clarice is.

With even just this much thrown into our cloudily explosive mix of considerations, our situation's recognized cloud population greatly rises.

While there should be limits on how far such "numerically differential highlighting" can be taken, lest sorites arguments here lead to nihilistic ideas, we won't be anywhere close to approaching those limits with differences of just two peripheral droplets in the cloudy complexes we're considering. Indeed, even with differentials of *six* such peripheral droplets, even six on *either* side of our initially chosen "tied clearest current cloud case," we won't be close to threatening any such limits.

Well, these matters concerning vagueness have been, as I predicted, some fun to consider. But, they're peripheral to the currently central issues, to which main matters we return.)

Now, as I'll be the first to admit, there isn't an absolutely perfect parallel, or a fully complete parallel, between a common cloud and its constituting droplets, on one hand, and, on the other, a water droplet and (at least some of) its constituting molecules, or atoms, or elementary particles. But, in relevant regards, there's enough of a parallel. We may grant, if need be, that there are many routes from a single droplet's aqueous center to its own mere environs, with breaks that are quite clean, and maybe even perfectly abrupt. Even so, with many *other* such routes, matters will be much messier, enough so for there to be plausibly opposing pairs of minute droplet constituents. As it may well be, at one "end" of a troublesome route out of droplet Donna, there'll be a certain pretty peripheral water *molecule*, one Moe; and, at the opposite "end," there'll be an *opposing* peripheral molecule, one Max. From this opposing pair of water molecules, Moe and Max, and from many other similarly opposing pairs, we may reason, quite in parallel with our just previous thinking, to the idea that, where there first seems to be just one water droplet, there are actually billions of water droplets—should there really be even so many as just one. (So, rather, than our having used the name "Donna" to label just a single droplet, what we did was something quite different. If we succeeded in bestowing the name on any real droplet, we bestowed it, equally, on billions.)

Of course, the point just made for water droplets is hardly peculiar to that presumed sort of ordinary entities. In all relevant regards, the same point holds with rocks and bricks and desks, with plates and planets and plants, and with human brains and bodies. Right here, then, where there first seems to be just a single human body, which is just "my body," there may really be very many human bodies, supposing that there's any real human body here. And, over there, where I casually take there to be your one brain, ensconced in just your one head, there may be very many human brains, each equally "yours," all similarly ensconced in vastly many human heads, each equally "yours."

Now, it's pretty obvious, I think, that this is a quite cheerful way to put a certain problem, apparently a difficulty that's quite a problem for much of our common thinking. Originally, I put the difficulty in less cheerful ways. For instance, this is less cheerful: If there really are any human bodies, then, right where you take your own single body to be, there are actually billions of human bodies. And, so is this: Either there are billions of bricks where you take just one brick to be or (else) there really aren't any bricks anywhere. And, even while I invited folks to avoid the thought of there being the billions, so I suggested that we conclude that there really aren't any bricks, say, or any human bodies, either. But, right now, I'm not in any mood to advocate any such nihilistic propositions; since it's only the development of some positive metaphysics that presently most interests me. (Well, just between you, me and the lamppost, while I'm quite confident that there's you, and I'm certain that there's me, I'm still pretty darned suspicious about there really being any lampposts. But, at least for the meanwhile, I won't plague you with any peculiar suspicions, neither mine, nor yours, nor, most certainly, any lamppost's.)

2. A Couple of Comments on That Comparatively Uninteresting Problem

Since that old paper's publication, many philosophers have written replies to its Problem of the Many. In this materialist age, almost all saw the Problem as a challenge even to our own existence, quite as I myself first did. But, now that I'm quite ready to reject materialism, along with our dominant Scientiphicalism, I no longer see it as such a very comprehensive challenge. For, even as I might be a nonspatial immaterial soul, maybe an individual entirely without any substantial parts, it might well be that there's no such Problem that's threatening, at all, my quite obvious thought that I myself exist. Nor need there be any that's threatening my thought, to me not quite *that* obvious, I suppose, that you exist, dear student, or reader.

Anyway, for a whole host of reasons, only a few concerning anything like their allegiance to materialism, many were much exercised by this Problem, even so much as to publish proposed solutions to the difficulty. And, evidently, very many more were similarly exercised, though not to quite the same degree, evidently, as they took no very (favorably refereed) public action. (Less widely public, this was also evident, from many conversations, and other personal communications.) Much more than any deep proclivity toward any metaphysical view, what prompted all this agitation, I feel sure, was that, with quite a few philosophically educated folks, there's a great attachment to what philosophers call "commonsense thinking." And, at least as it appears, even the judgment that there are billions of bricks right there—where you seem to see only one brick—blatantly conflicts with this commonsense thinking. Just so, many feel compelled to avoid even that judgment, almost no matter what might be the intellectual cost of this avoidance.

Let me try another tack, almost starting all over again. Forget about planets, and plants, and rocks, and even clouds. And, in the bargain, forget about bricks, too. Instead, think only of physical complexes (if such there be) as are like this: In shape, they are rectangular solids—not perfectly rectangular, of course, but only about as much so as is, say, a typical brick. What (physically derivative) Propensities do these pretty rectangular complexes have? Well, they're pretty rigid, and solid, and sturdy. By contrast, they aren't highly magnetized, or very fragile. To make a long story short, let me just say this: Propensitively they're very much like bricks are. Are these nicely Propensitied rectangular complexes very useful to people? Well, they're not as important to us as water is, or air, or food. But, on the other hand, they're not entirely useless, either. Especially when you can stick them together, as when using a lot of mortar, they're pretty useful for building walls, for one thing.

When I do some "Problem of the Many Reasoning" in terms of one of these pretty useful, nicely Propensitied, roughly rectangular physical complexes, I don't find there to be much intellectual disturbance. Right over there, I say to myself, quite complacently, there may well be billions of these overlapping rectangular complexes. Of course, none prevents any of the others from being roughly rectangular, or from being sturdily Propensitied, or from being useful for building walls. But, then, who should ever think there's ever any such untoward prevention. Not me and, I'm sure, not you, either. So, there's no problem here at all, not even any pretty superficial problem, not even a problem for the commonest of human thinking, enjoyed even by many human two-year-olds, and maybe many mature human morons.

With many overlapping rectangular complexes, why is there nothing here that's very disquieting, even despite the acknowledged multitude? Do you think it's because these are very "simplistic" complexes? Do you think it's because I haven't told you enough about them? OK, Buster; let's have another think, or two.

OK, Buster, so you want to know a lot more about these supposedly simplistic rectangular complexes? Fine. I'll let you know whatever you might like.

Would you like to know that, with each of them, or with many of them, there are certain indeterminacies. Would you like that to be true? OK; fine; let's have it that way. Then, with each of our overlapping rectangular complexes, there are elementary particles such that it is indeterminate whether or not that particle is a constituent of, or a part of, that overlapper. It will just be, of course, that each of many different overlappers each may have a (very slightly) different group of such "indeterminate particles." And, in the bargain, it will also be that many different overlappers will each have a (very slightly) different group of "determinately constituent particles." On top of all that, it may be that, even as some overlappers differ only in the first of these two ways, and others differ only in the second, still others differ in both at once. So, if appeals to indeterminacy do anything effective here, which I doubt, they may serve only to *increase*—and increase very greatly, indeed—the vast number of roughly rectangular overlappers rightly recognized, in a situation where, at first blush or first glance, we'd take there to be only one usefully sturdy rectangular physical complex. For, in such an event, there'll be a lot more for us to reckon, with apt employments of the mathematics of combinations. And, so, from (wrongly?) recognizing (only?) many billions, we should go to (rightly?) allowing that there are many trillions; or from (wrongly?) allowing that there are (only?) trillions, we should go to (rightly?) recognizing that there are many quadrillions. As best as I can tell, then, a really close look at how appeals to indeterminacy may play out, in these matters, is more likely to highlight our Problem than to rectify any genuinely erroneous Scientiphically inspired reasoning. Anyhow, enough with appeals to the likes of indeterminacy, a dead horse if ever there was one.

Would you like to know that, with each of our overlapping rectangular solids, the physical complex has certain interesting "persistence conditions"? Goodness knows why you'd now like to know this; very far from our discussing any *allegedly spatially coincident* objects— where ideas of "persistence conditions" might seem to have some useful application—we're talking about *spatially overlapping* complexes here, which *obviously aren't* spatially coincident. But, as it appears, among the philosophically very educated, even a most innocuous sort of Problem of the Many stuns the intellect, even as it appears to mandate importing an entire arsenal of technical distinctions (and correlative philosophical apparatus). Well, you want a nice little story involving so-called persistence conditions; so, I'll do a little something in that direction, enough for our present very limited purposes. Just so, I'll have you know this about our fairly rectangular physical complexes: One of these pretty rectangular complex entities can become a little rounder—as with the rounding of its so-called corners, and yet it may still exist. But it can't become just any old shape and still exist. For instance, and for one thing, the complex's matter may be gradually rearranged to form something very, very thin, and very, very long—a tubular object that's only about a millionth of a millimeter in diameter and thousands of miles long. Somewhere during that Shapewise transformation, we may suppose you to know, the complex in question will cease to exist, for want of there no longer being, right there, a complex whose shape satisfies our "brickish" complex's persistence conditions. Maybe, nobody can ever know exactly when, or precisely where, that will occur. But, for our present very limited purposes, that doesn't matter. Is that a nice enough (partial) persistence condition? Who knows; and, who cares? It's just a for-instance, just an illustrative example. The point, of course, is just this: Whatever the persistence conditions of our rectangular complexes, they'll all be "had" by *very many overlappers*, in anything like an actual "brickish situation." And, quite typically enough, they'll all be "met" by very many overlappers (providing that even just a single one physical complex ever succeeds in doing that). So, for a "commonsensibly comfortable" resolution for our Problem, anything about persistence conditions will be utterly irrelevant, a result rightly anticipated at this paragraph's beginning.

(No; you don't like this persistence conditions business; you think it's only a shadow of your own practices and proclivities, merely appearing to give yourself a say-so as to how things are with objective external reality. That's also fine. Again, you can have whatever you like here. Again, none of it will make a particle of difference—pun very much intended.)

No matter how complex we make our descriptions of our rectangular overlappers, and no matter what the sort of complexity, we may still employ our "Problem of the Many Reasoning," without much disturbance at all. As the upshot, of course, we have an overlapping multitude, right where, with a casual take on things, there should appear to be just one. But, very far from there being, with just that, anything that's terribly disquieting, there'll be only a big yawn here, or just a big so-what. Or, in my most deeply metaphysical moods, so it certainly appears to me, your deadly serious author.

Now, let's forget about being very deeply metaphysical or, indeed, philosophically very serious in any way, shape, or form. In this more lighthearted mood, let's return to remember just plain old bricks themselves, after having temporarily forgotten about these supposed satisfiers of our ordinary common noun "brick."

Well, when I do some parallel "Problem of the Many Reasoning," involving the very common word "brick," or the very familiar concept of a brick, or anything of that "comfortably familiar ilk," then, to my otherwise (suppose) quite lighthearted self, things often seem quite bad. In *this* event, it seems—even to lighthearted old me, I'll have you know—that all hell just breaks loose: What?!? Billions of *bricks* right over there, all of them just two feet away from me!?! That's preposterous; it's outrageous; we just can't allow anything like that to stand!! Bring in the logicians; bring in the philosophical technicians. And, do it right away. Heck, with our very bricks at stake, we're on the verge of a philosophical crisis!

Look, things have gone very wrong here. What's gone wrong? While I've offered something toward diagnosing this situation, in some several much earlier writings, it's only a very partial diagnosis that, even now, I can provide.[3] But, whatever the best diagnosis, the trouble doesn't involve any deep philosophical difficulty. So, to my mind at least, my old Problem of the Many is a comparatively boring problem. Compared to what? Well, compared to more purely metaphysical problems, or at least to some of them. Which ones? Well, I

---

3. Both directly to the point and reasonably accessible, you might look at may paper, "Toward A Psychology of Common Sense," *American Philosophical Quarterly*, 1982, reprinted in my *Philosophical Papers, Volume 1*. Not quite so directly pertinent, but possibly helpful as well, you might take a gander at another old paper, pretty happily related to the piece just mentioned, "The Causal Theory of Reference," *Philosophical Studies*, 1983, also reprinted in my *Philosophical Papers*. Finally, somewhere in my overloaded office files, there's a long manuscript—well, over one hundred pages, anyway—where I tried going more deeply into these matters. But, for a variety of reasons, I lost interest in completing that project.

certainly don't know about all; but a few are some that this book aims to address.

Right now, I'd *like* to engage in a Problem of the Many that's a pretty interesting problem, perhaps an interesting descendant of my old Problem of the Many. For that to happen, we should confront a Problem that *doesn't* apply to the likes of mere bricks as much as, or in the same way as, it applies to the more important likes of you and me. As a very small first small step in that direction, I'll rehearse these words, from the just previous Section:

> Right here, then, where there first seems to be just a single human body, which is just "my body," there may really be very many human bodies, supposing that there's any real human body here. And, over there, where I casually take there to be your one brain, ensconced in just your one head, there may be very many human brains, each equally "yours," all similarly ensconced in vastly many human heads, each equally "yours."[4]

Well, as I must admit, all that does sound rather strange. But, maybe there isn't anything in it that should be more than just very mildly disturbing. (So long as we're clear as to what are the main relations among the many billions of brains proposed, and among them and the billions of proposed bodies, maybe there needn't be any serious problem. For instance, we can be clear enough about what we may correctly express when saying that none of your brains is in, nor is any of your brains a part of, any of my many bodies. And, we may be similarly clear about saying that each of my brains is in, and each is a part of, all of my bodies. And, of course, while each of your brains overlaps many other brains that are yours, none of your brains overlaps any of my brains, nor any of my billions of human bodies. At the same time, of course, none of my many bodies ever overlaps any human body that's yours.) Anyway, if that's right—if there isn't anything right here that should be more than mildly disturbing, then we must take some further steps toward confronting a relevantly more interesting Problem of the Many.

3. The Experiential Problem of the Many

In this philosophical neighborhood, inhabited more by brains than any bricks, maybe there will be a philosophically serious issue. This might happen, I'll suggest, with the thought that, in what I take to be just my

---

4. The quoted passage is from Section 1 above.

own situation, there are really very many experiencing thinkers. Really, now, can anything like *that* possibly be right? The very suggestion is, I think, a terribly disturbing idea.

Right here and now "in my situation," are there vastly many experiencing thinkers, each with a protracted illusion of being, in this very situation, quite singular and unique? In the *least incredible scenarios of that sort*, I suppose, each of the many will be experiencing ever so similarly to each of the others, each having its own conscious mental life, so to say, running in parallel, simultaneously and qualitatively, with each of the others. Well, at least in my case, this idea defies belief. Am I being, perhaps, overly self-centered here? I don't think so. When I consider a similar "experientially explosive" suggestion that has you be the experiencer in question, I find the thought of billions of like-minded experiencers just about as incredible as in my own case. And, the matter in question doesn't seem to be any merely semantical issue. Rather, with an *Experiential Problem of the Many*, it seems that there's nothing less than a metaphysically serious problem.

Just a few sentences make clear how very much such an experientially explosive supposition flies in the face of even our commonsense thinking about ourselves. And, far more important, by my lights, they show how much it flies in the face of a Humanly Realistic View of Ourselves. For one thing, each of the (supposed) overlapping experiencers will believe that, among all the folks on earth right now, he alone is experiencing (immediately, complexly, qualitatively and totally) in just the *perfectly precise way* that, right at the moment, is the perfectly precise way *he is* experiencing. Just so, I believe that *you're not* experiencing in a way that's precisely like the way I'm experiencing right now, even though we're near each other, and we're in the same room, and we're each looking in much the same direction as is the other. For one thing, I have a tingling condition "in my left foot" that, as I believe, is quite different from any slight suffering of yours. For another, even my perspectival visual experiencing is qualitatively different from yours, at least slightly different. Or, at the least, so I certainly do believe and, as I suspect, you do, too.

Matters quickly go from bad to worse; incredible thoughts compound incredibly. Am I to think that, with vastly many experiencers promoted by vastly many brains in my situation, each may be communicating his innermost thoughts to very many other experiencing thinkers, each promoted by one of the many brains in your situation?

Something's badly wrong here. And, as we're dealing with the likes of you and me, what's gone wrong must be central for a Humanly Realistic Philosophy.

Part of what's puzzling may concern what's been modishly called, in recent years, the "subjectivity of experience." This so-called subjectivity is closely related to—heck, it might even be the very same thing as—what was once fashionably called, in certain earlier years, the "privacy of experience." No expert on fashion, I don't much care about that. But, at all events, I'll try to say something useful here, maybe more useful than what's said with the noted phrases.

Right off the bat, I should make perfectly explicit an unproblematic thought that's so far been just implicit: The experiencing I'm discussing is, of course, nonderivative experiencing. So it is that we're properly exploring only the experiencing of substantial individuals, each of them a perfectly concrete particular, and not the (so-called) experiencing of any quasi-abstract entities, as with committees, and countries, and corporations. Even as a committee can choose only when there's choosing enjoyed by, at least, some of the committee's individual members, so a committee can experience only when there's experiencing enjoyed by some of its individual members. If a committee is wholly composed of just you and me, then this committee can experience satisfaction, say, at a job well done, only if you and I experience in some such way, or at least one of us does. With that made explicit, we further amplify.

The thought that there are, in my situation, many individuals all experiencing is far more disturbing, to my mind, than the thought that, in this situation, there are many entities each chewing, or many each digesting. With the digesting of some chocolate candy, say, there seems little more at stake than just a matter of our choosing what forms of words to use: Following common sense, even if perhaps speaking somewhat loosely, we may say that, in just the part of the world where I am, there's now just one process of digesting going on. Or, paying less to common thought, and more to certain principles of differential constitution, we might instead say that, with many similar overlapping entities each engaged in a very similar digestive process, there are occurring many very similar overlapping digestings. As it seems, this latter description is just somewhat less palatable.

An individual's digestive power is, we should allow, just a physically derivative physical Propensity of the physically complex being. As such, it's a metaphysically superficial power that's ascribed (perhaps, in each case quite properly enough) to each physical complex that's a human body, or, perhaps, that's a human organism. Indeed, each digester might have only such powers as are each a physically derivative Propensity. But, then, each complex may be only an ontologically superficial being, after all, an entity that's quite as derivative, physically, as is any of its powers.

With an experiencing being, by contrast, matters seem very different. By contrast with a mere power to digest, a power to experience must be, at the least, a radically emergent mental Propensity, in no wise any mere physical power, neither derivative nor nonderivative. For some, this contrast will be both evident and also pretty profound. But, for others, more discussion may be useful.

For the sake of a vividly engaging discussion, let's suppose that a Substantial Dualism holds. And, further, let's similarly suppose that, immaterial soul that I be, yet I causally interact, quite directly and equally, with each of very many overlapping complex bodies, each thus one of *my bodies*. Must there be many *other* Cartesian thinkers, in addition to me, who also causally interact, quite equally, with (so many of) these same bodies, the bodies with which I'm so directly interacting? Apparently not. Indeed, it may be a great advantage of Dualism that it will have things be quite different from that: All the bodies in my situation, however numerous and overlapping, will serve to promote only me myself, and not any other sentient self. And, it may be that just this one causally promoted self is the only experiencer directly interacting with any of these promoting bodies. So, on such a Substantial Dualism, there's that motivation to treat *each* of very many bodies as being *one of my bodies*. And, in the same bargain, there's the wanted related motivation, to treat *none* of these bodies as being the body of *any other* sentient being.

At least tolerably well, we may allow that I should have very many human bodies, none of which is anyone else's body. And, we may allow, equally well, that I should have many *digestive systems*, each overlapping many others. To be sure, this sounds like it goes against commonsense thinking, and against typical biological thinking. And, very possibly, it does. Still, there's nothing terribly problematic in it. And, there's nothing deeply disturbing, either, in each of several further ideas, each thought also a "materially explosive" conception. For instance, without any very deep disturbance, we may also think that each of my many digestive systems is engaged, right now, in digesting chocolate candy, with each digestive process very similar to the many others. Though it's somewhat unnatural for us to say such a profligate thing as that, still, there's no great philosophic difficulty, I think, in our being so liberal about what occurs with many material complexes.

Think about this for a minute. For much the same reason I might be said to have billions of digestive systems, I may also be said to have vastly many *nervous systems*, each largely overlapping many others, and each sharing most of its basic physical constituents with the others. Much as we might readily tolerate the thought that my many digestive systems are engaged in overlapping digestive processes, so we might also easily tolerate the thought that my many nervous systems are engaged in overlapping neural processes.

But, can we similarly tolerate the idea that each of these nervous systems may undergo, or each may be engaged in, a process of *experiencing* distinct from the experiencing engaged in by overlapping nervous systems? I don't think so. Rather, what seems truer is this: Each of the many nervous systems in my situation, or each of my many nervous systems, causally *promotes just the same single experiencer, just a certain single being that's engaged in just a single (present process of total) experiencing, namely, my total experiencing.* Of course, this experiencer is nobody but me.

How might that happen? Briefly and roughly put, here's how: Each of my electrons, quite like each of my quarks, is a basic concretum that's Propensitied to promote, when nicely configured with ever so many reciprocally Propensitied basic concreta, just a single (nonphysical?) experiencer. When so many of them are so nicely configured—quite enough of each kind, but, as well, not too many—then they simply must promote an (immaterial?) experience. And, even as they must promote at least one such, so, and at the very same time, they can't possibly then promote more than just one. Even when they're arranged optimally for promoting conscious experiencing, there's a *singular resolution* as to *what experiencer* my nervous systems' basic components can all promote, optimally interacting altogether. And, so, there's a singular resolution, too, as to what experiencing they can then promote, it's just all the experiencing that's then ontologically parasitical upon that single experiencer they're all promoting, just as she is at the time in question. Or, more colloquially put, it's just all the experiencing that's then *the experiencing of* that single experiencer they're all promoting, just as she is at the time in question. Even as they can't promote more experiencers than just one—now, in fact, just the one who's me—so they can promote, even altogether, only just so much experiencing as is this single experiencer's experiencing—now, in fact, just my experiencing.

For some several minutes, we've been supposing that the correct metaphysic is a Substantial Dualism, not terribly different from Descartes's classic view. Now, let's drop that supposition, and let's suppose, instead, that a "more materialistic" view of mentality is correct. For example, we might suppose that what's correct is the Nonentity Emergentism we've been discussing, on which human experiencers are physical complexes that have radically emergent nonphysical mental powers.

Well, just *insofar as* we may comfortably maintain some such view, just to *that extent* we might be comfortable in thinking that, even in my situation right now, there are billions and billions of experiencing thinkers. But, as our discussion has been suggesting, this mightn't be very far at all.

4. How the Singularity of Experiencing May Favor Substantial Dualism

To deal with puzzles about our experiencing, it may help to adopt, if only tentatively and skeptically, a Substantial Dualism. On this view, each of us is a nonphysical experiencer who *interacts with* a certain physical thing, or some certain physical things.

Within the compass of such a robust Dualism, there may be a singular resolution for our Experiential Problem of the Many. So, in my situation, we may plausibly enough conjecture, there may be many overlapping brainy complexes that, altogether, serve to promote a single nonphysical experiencer. But, of course, each of these overlapping complexes will do its promoting in what's really only quite a derivative way, even as each has a Propensity to promote that's only a physically derivative Propensity. Just so, with each mentally promoting physical complex, the derivation will proceed from the basic physical components of the very complex in question, especially insofar as each of them is basically physically Propertied, and from the (sufficiently basic) physical relations obtaining among those basic components. And, so, in each of many worldly derivations, it may be just the very same sentient self, or experiencing mind, that the complexes in question each serve (derivatively) to promote.

In a happy enough sense, then, the (physically derivative) promoting of this single mind, *by any one of* these physical complexes, will be a *causally redundant* promoting. Of course, there won't be any complex that's doing any of this derivative promoting without there being, at the same time and all at once, many others also promoting the selfsame mind, all of them physically derivative entities, all engaged in physically derivative promoting. More basically, and not so derivatively, the basic constituents of these complexes will be, altogether, promoting the single experiencer.

In any very direct sense or way, it will be just this single promoted mind itself—in my own case, just me myself—that has a power to experience, rather than any of the promoting physical entities. So, it will be only in a much weaker sense or way that any of these physical things may be said to experience.

Nowadays, it's hard for academically respectable philosophers to believe in mentally powerful nonphysical beings. But, even for us academics, this may be less incredible than the thought that *precisely one* of our many considered complexes itself has this power. Who can believe that, each of them so terribly like all the others, somehow there's just one brainy physical complex that's really experiencing, in my situation right now, while all the others are experientially powerless? To me, *that's* incredible. And, the idea of nonphysical minds is also less hard to believe than the proposition that just one of the basic (enough) physical entities in my situation, say, a certain particular quark, has the power to experience richly, while all the other quarks here are quite powerless in any such mentally rich regard. And, it's certainly less incredible than the thought that a mere abstraction, or abstractum, should be the sole entity that, with me right now, is experiencing. Purely abstract objects don't experience at all. And, quasi-abstract objects, we've explicitly observed, don't engage in nonderivative experiencing, which is, quite properly, the only experiencing our discussion concerns.

Nowadays, it's hard for us to believe we're not each a spatially extended being, a physical complex that's the size of, and the shape of, a human organism. Indeed, it's hard to believe anything very different from how our Scientiphicalism has us be. So, it's hard to get further from the dominant Metaphysic than the nearby Emergentism that, only lately, we've been trying to take quite seriously. Yet, as I've suggested, this Emergentism is as deeply embroiled as Scientiphicalism with the Experiential Problem of the Many.[5]

---

5. This is a very good place, I think, about as good as any, for us to recall what's really been, all along, this beleaguered Emergentism's dialectical status (in the context of this book.) Toward that end, I can't do better than to rehearse, verbatim, this paragraph from Section 13 of Chapter 6:

[B]efore closing this Section, it's crucial to notice that, in entertaining this Nonentity Emergentist View, I'm doing all I can, to forestall a move toward so much as a Substantial Dualistic Metaphysic. Now, as I should say very clearly, and in no uncertain terms, I have significant doubts about whether this Emergentism is, at bottom, a truly coherent position. Though I'm very uncertain in the matter, both in the one way and in the other, I have significant suspicions that what I've been sketching isn't really a view that's both truly distinctive and fully coherent. Maybe, this so-called Nonentity Emergentism is what many philosophers would call an "unstable position." So, for all I can really tell, it may be that, with many articulations of this allegedly new view, what we'll really end up with is just a very complex articulation of Scientiphicalism. And, it may be that, with all the other articulations, what we'll find ourselves formulating is a much more Radical sort of Emergence. That is, we'll then find we've formulated a View where there'll be emergent powers, all right, but only when, it the bargain, there are *radically emergent beings*, as with a newly generated Spherical Particle, or as with a materially generated immaterial soul. Maybe, it's only such emergent beings, as such a more fully articulated and coherent View will have it, that can ever truly possess radically emergent powers. Or, the same point put more perspicuously, it's only radically emergent beings that will ever be radically emergently powered.

Among the available metaphysical views that aren't so embroiled with the Experiential Problem of the Many, Substantial Dualism departs *least*, so far as I can tell, from our dominant Scientiphical Metaphysic. That's a less radical departure, certainly, than what's afforded with a fully mentalistic metaphysic, whether such a completely mental view be called "idealism," or "phenomenalism," or, as may be more fashionable nowadays, "panpsychism." Wishing not to be so radical, I'll suggest that, in the face of this Experiential Problem, we should take seriously Substantial Dualism.

5. Many Overlapping Experiencers, but Only One of Them Now Experiencing?

Most of us academics are, nowadays, so gripped with our Scientiphicalism that we'll do almost anything to avoid departing from it. Grasping at straws, almost any thought may occur to us, as a possible alternative to abandoning this dominant view.

However desperate it may be, here's one idea that's occurred to me: In my situation right now, there are very many mentally powerful physical complexes, each overlapping many others. (As well, there are *very many more* physical complexes that *aren't* mentally Propensitied, with many of them overlapping many others.) Now, maybe each experientially Propensitied complex is just a physical complex, with an experiential power that's just a physically derivative physical Propensity. Or, against that materialistic idea, and more as our Nonentity Emergentism offers, maybe each is a mental-and-physical complex, with a Propensity to experience that's not physically derivative. At least for now, the difference between these two proposals doesn't matter. So, either way, what may be happening is this: While there are very many experiencers in my situation, right now only one of them is actually experiencing. With just that one, its Propensity to experience is *now manifested*, or exercised, or activated. With each of the others, in marked contrast, the power to experience is now unmanifested, or unexercised, or unactivated. So, in my situation right now, there is not any overabundance of experiencing,

---

In this book's central dialectic, whatever may be the ultimate status of our offered Nonentity Emergentism, well, it's all neither here nor there. Why? Well, by *supposing* this observed (and conservative) Emergentism to be a fully coherent view, we force ourselves to give it a good run for the money. And, by doing *that*, we only to make it harder, not easier, to provide an persuasive case for some sort of Substantial Dualism, indeed, for *any sort*. ...

as with billions of extremely similar streams of experience. No; nothing like that at all. Rather, there's just one individual stream of experience or, more perspicuously, one individual who is experiencing. And, at least at first glance, that doesn't seem so bad!

Well, I don't know about you; but, when I look hard at this idea, on second glance it seems *very* bad, and on third glance, and fourth glance, too. Just dwelling on the idea itself for awhile, before thinking about any ramifications, the idea seems preposterous. It seems perfectly preposterous to think that, sitting in my chair(s) right now, or in any special connection with my brain(s), there's a multitude of sentient beings (with just one of them actually experiencing, while many are sleeping deeply and dreamlessly, or while many are involved in something rather like deep dreamless sleep).

With only a few moments reflection, problems appear to escalate alarmingly.

Here's one immediately obvious difficulty: Just as each of the presumably powerful overlappers is so extremely similar to each of the others, so, too, each confronts disposition partners that, even all taken together, are just so *extremely* similar to those that confront each of the others. Much the same, with each presumably powerful complex, there will obtain conditions for manifesting its presumed power, its posited Propensity to experience, just so *extremely* similar to those obtaining with all the others. How is it, then, that there's just this one experiencer now actually experiencing here, and just so very many perfectly dreamless sleepers? While anything's possible, as we say, including such an inexplicably perfectly discriminating circumstance, the idea fairly defies belief.

Really, what have we done here? As I see it, we've just taken one preposterous proposition, a statement concerning certain considered complexes and their putative mental powers, and we've traded it for a correlatively preposterous proposal, a statement concerning the alleged single manifestation of, and the alleged very many nonmanifestations of, those putative mental powers. With a trade like that, who can really believe that there's any advance? Not me; that's for sure.

Here's a further difficulty: Just like you do, from time to time, I go to sleep. During some of the time I sleep, I'm experiencing, as when I'm dreaming very vividly. But, during much of the time, my power to experience is quite unmanifested. Or, going against Descartes's official position, so most of us believe. Anyhow, soon enough, there will once again occur, in my situation, a being who's experiencing, whether the being's just dreaming, and he's still asleep, or whether the being fully awakens. So, we've got billions of sleepers here, in my situation. Soon, on the proposal we're discussing, just one of them will awaken, to enjoy some conscious experiencing. But, with so many well-Propensitied sleepers, it's most unlikely that the one soon awakening, and *next* experiencing, will be the very same complex as the one that was *last* experiencing. Offhand, the chances look to be one out of billions. But, then, almost certainly, any deep sleep will be my very last sleep.

Can it really be that, before going to sleep, I am just a certain one of these complexes and, even though that very complex *is still in existence*, upon someone's awakening, I won't be any waking complex, but, instead, I'll be only a *different complex*, one that *hasn't* ever been experiencing? This is perfectly incredible. Can it be that, while I now am a complex who's experiencing, before I awakened, this morning, I never before was experiencing? That's also perfectly incredible.

While I could go on with this Section's theme, I doubt that my doing so would accomplish much more than what's already been achieved, however modest that might be. Anyway, with the hope that the Section's been helpful to some readers, I turn to consider complementary themes.

6. Some Cases of Singular Causal Resolution

A little while ago, I said this: We can tolerate, even if only tolerably well, the idea that, in my situation right now, there are many digestive systems. And, we can tolerate the further thought that, with each of "my" many systems, it's now engaged in a numerically different digesting. But, we can't similarly tolerate a parallel thought about "my" many nervous systems, each of them being involved, all at once, in a numerically different *experiencing*. No. Rather, about each of the many overlapping nervous systems now in my situation, we should say that it causally *promotes just the same single experiencer, who's engaged in just a single (present process of total) experiencing*, (the present process that's) *my total experiencing*, the same lone experiencer causally promoted, quite equally, by each of the others. Of course, this single experiencer is me. How might that happen?

Well, each of my electrons, or my quarks, or whatever, is a basic concretum that's Propensitied to promote, when nicely configured with ever so many reciprocally Propensitied concreta, just one single experiencer. One they simply must promote; more than one they can't possibly promote. Even when they're arranged optimally for promoting conscious experiencing, there's a *singular resolution* as to what experiencer, and as to what experiencing, my nervous systems' basic components can all promote, optimally interacting altogether.

(Impressed by the research of R. W. Sperry, and others, on split-brain patients, some philosophers have suggested that, at least from time to time, there might be as many as two experiencers in my situation.[6] While I find their essays stimulating, I suspect they may be confused.[7] But, for the present discussion, that doesn't matter. After all, as all of them also agree, there are, in what we take to be just my situation now, far fewer than seven simultaneous experiencers and, so, a fortiori, there are far, far, far fewer than billions.

We may accommodate these philosophers, as a matter of course, by advancing a slightly more cautious idea concerning causal resolution: In what's ordinarily taken to be just my situation, "my many brains" all together promote, or their many basic physical constituents all together promote, at least one experiencing being, but not more than two experiencers. For the aims of this book, it makes no difference whether we advance the logically stronger idea, and the happily simpler idea, that I favor, or the logically weaker idea, that accommodates the authors so impressed by split-brain studies. So, I'll consider the simple thought that, in my situation, there's a singular causal resolution, with just me as the sole experiencing being.)

At this point, it will be useful, I think, to explore some thoughts concerning singular causal resolution. My little exploration will confront only a few cases of singular causal resolution, with each case a bit easier to grasp than its successor, but each progressively harder successor more directly relevant to such singular causal resolution as may concern the singular promotion, by many material entities, of a single immaterial soul.

---

6. For nice examples of Sperry reporting on his research, and offering his overly imaginative (I think) interpretations of his experimental findings, see R. W. Sperry, "Brain Bisection and Mechanisms of Consciousness," in J. Eccles (ed.), *Brain and Conscious Experience*, Springer-Verlag, 1966, and also R. W. Sperry, "Hemispheric Deconnection and Unity in Conscious Awareness," *American Psychologist*, 1968.

Even some of the ablest contemporary philosophers may go berserk (I think) when offering their own enjoyably stimulating interpretations of Sperry's findings, and other scientists' findings. For a couple of essays produced by a couple of the most able, see Thomas Nagel's "Brain Bisection and the Unity of Consciousness," *Synthese*, 1971, and Derek Parfit's "Divided Minds and the Nature of Persons," in Colin Blakemore and Susan Greenfield (eds.), *Mindwaves*, Blackwell, 1987. Happily, Nagel's essay is reprinted in his collection, *Mortal Questions*, Cambridge University Press, 1979; and, also happily, Parfit's is reprinted in Peter van Inwagen and Dean Zimmerman, (eds.), *Metaphysics: The Big Questions*, Blackwell, 1998.

7. Not so confused, a more plausible interpretation is offered by Roderick M. Chisholm in his very short paper, "Questions about the Unity of Consciousness," in Konrad Cramer, Hans Friedrich Fulda, Rolf-Peter Horstmann and Ulrich Pothast (eds.), *Theorie der Subjektivität*, Frankfurt: Surkamp, 1987, especially at pages 98–101.

As least as far as what science seems to allow, our first case will be highly realistic. Suppose that, in a perfectly symmetric fashion, two precisely similar television cameras are taking pictures of a solid gold sphere. And, also each in a precisely similar manner to the other, each camera beams its picture to a precisely similar television station, though a numerically distinct station. And, accordingly, each of the two stations features a boring broadcast that's precisely similar to the other's. But, in all the land where this takes place, there's just one television set, and there are no other broadcasts. (Since the set always receives the same boring broadcast from both stations, there's no question of changing channels, and it has no mechanism for that.) Owing to the entire setup, each of the two stations does quite well enough, by way of affecting the TV set, so that what it broadcasts will be displayed on the TV's picture tube, even without the operation of the other station. As far as modifying this TV set goes, the working of each station is causally redundant, in this circumstance where both stations are broadcasting. (Of course, in the absence of any broadcasting from the other station, a station's broadcast will be needed to produce the TV picture, and, in such a circumstance, a single broadcast will, quite alone, do just that.) As almost goes without saying, even if we were to have a billion similar TV stations at work here, the situation is essentially the same, with just the one picture produced on the one TV set. Very easy for us to grasp, I think this is one case of a singular causal resolution.

Now, I'll set the stage for my next illustrative example, presenting the case itself right after setting the stage for it.

In recent decades, the philosophic literature on Personal Identity has saliently featured various science-fictional cases of so-called *Teletransportation*. In certain of these cases, someone enters a Sending Teletransportation Booth and, after some buttons are pressed, the device records exactly information as to which basic sorts of physical thing are each of his basic physical constituents, or those of his body, as well as complete information as to their relative arrangement, in his body. At the same time, and in this very process, the device so radically alters how that body's particles are all related that it destroys, at least for the meanwhile, the body in question. Just a moment later, the device sends the destroyed body's matter, in a stream of elementary particles, to a complementary Target Booth, where all those material particles are well received, along with a fine reception of all the information as to how, in the body so recently destroyed, each particle was related to all the body's other basic physical constituents. Just a bit later still, the Target Booth arranges the received particles so that each has just the same physical relations, in what's at least a precisely similar human body, that last it had in the body at least temporarily destroyed. As we suppose, when all this arranging is completed, there's an experiencing person in the Target Booth, someone who's perfectly similar, at least, to the person last in the Sending Booth. Maybe that's because, upon their becoming nicely arranged in the Target Booth, these particles (once again?) causally promote a new (possibly immaterial?) experiencer. Or, maybe it's for another reason, possibly much more materialistic. For the present discussion, none of that matters. Anyhow, by this point, the stage is set for my next illustrative example.

For the illustrative case I'm now starting to present, what matters is this: In an expansion of our fairly familiar sort of Teletransportation case, we may have two people each enter a distinct Sending Booth, each Booth precisely similar to the Booth that the other enters. If you like, we may have each of these entering people be a precise Generalistic duplicate of the other. (In that each person may have an immaterial soul with Individualistically-directed Propensity to interact with just his own body—and each may have a body that's reciprocally Individualistically-directed, it might not be possible to have each be a complete perfect duplicate of the other, though each may be perfectly symmetric with the other.) Shortly, each body is destroyed, at least temporarily, and its elementary particles are sent to, and they're received by, the very same Target Booth that receives all the other's particles. In the Target Booth, all of one body's particles are all together, on one side, along with the information as to how they were arranged in a human body, and all the other body's particles are on the opposite side. Then this Target Booth probabilistically selects, or it randomly selects, which of these two batches of particles to use to form a human body (whether this body be counted the very same as an earlier body, or whether it be counted only a duplicate of an earlier body). Upon the completed construction of this living body, we may suppose, there's an experiencing person in the Target Booth. As we're supposing, there's then a single person in the Target Booth (maybe someone who's numerically identical with a person who was in one of the Sending Booths, and maybe not, but, at all events) someone who's terribly similar to such a Sending Booth person. This is another case of singular causal resolution.

Why should there have occurred such a case of singular causal resolution?

Well, as there's a purely probabilistic occurrence here, with the Target Booth's selection of which batch of matter to employ in an organic construction, there's only so much to be said by way of an explanation. But, there's this to say: The particles serving to compose the Target Booth are so Propensitied that, when they're in a certain physical arrangement, there will be a probabilistic selection of particles on one of the Booth's sides, or else there'll be a probabilistic selection of particles on another side. It may be that, with just two sides involved, there's a probability for each of exactly one half, and with precisely three sides, a probability of exactly one third, and so on. Or, so we may Propensitively suppose. Anyhow, whichever (stream of) particles will be selected for timely productive arrangement, their selection will be the manifestation of that Probabilistic Propensity of all those Target-Booth-constituting physical concreta. Beyond that, the humanly productive process of arranging is the manifestation of further Propensities. Some of these will be the Propensities of particles serving to constitute the Booth, those being Propensities for precisely just such productive activity. And, the others will be the Propensities of just so very many selected particles, for being so arranged as to form a living human body, and, then, for quite directly promoting a human experiencer, should they be so happily arranged.

With any manifestation of those Propensities, the Target Booth must promote at least one experiencer, all right, but, then also, not more than one experiencing being. This will hold true even for a greatly expanded case, where a Very Large Target Booth will be bombarded, simultaneously, with streams of particles coming from billions of Sending Booths, each stream containing just the particles that, just previously, composed a numerically different human body, a body distinct from any composed by the particles in any of the other streams. Even with all that, there'll be only one experiencer generated, while billions of unemployed material batches will each rest in a distinct storage drawer, one of billions of these drawers, all in the Very Large Target Booth.

Well, that's enough, I think, about our second illustrative case of singular causal resolution. Now, it's on to our third case, and our last illustrative case.

The third case will have three Versions; there'll be an Evidently Material Version, and a Reminiscently Emergentist Version, and an Evidently Dualist Version. That sounds like we'll be in for a lot of complexity. But, actually, it will all be pretty simple. For one thing, with each of the three Versions, we begin just like this: Much as we've done many times before, we'll again imagine a World where each basic physical individual is one of many Small Blue Spheres, or else it's one of many Large Red Spheres. Though this World, with these Spheres, existed for an extremely long time (maybe even infinitely long) so far there hasn't been, in the World, a single individual that's Propensitied to experience. Nor has there been any Extensible Yellow spatial individual. But, very soon, there'll be Yellow Particles. Here's why.

For there to be a Yellow individual in this World, it's required only that some of the World's Blue Spheres, and also some of its Red Spheres, manifest their Propensity for just such mutual interaction as will promote, or generate, or bring into being, a Yellow spatial physical object. And, for that to happen, it's just this that's required: At least one hundred Small Blues must each be within one inch of the same single Large Red, though any given Red will do. So far, of course, this has never happened. But, right now, two hundred Small Blues all move so that, simultaneously, they're all well within an inch of Ralph, a certain Large Red. Well, as that's just happened, there just came into being a certain Small Yellow Sphere, one *Yolanda*, as we'll call it. Now, even as all the Large Red Spheres each have certain characteristic physical Propensities, each the same as all the others, and correlatively with the Small Blues, so Yolanda, too, will have a fine physical Propensity profile, a profile quite different from any Large Red, and also different from any Small Blue.

In the Evidently Material Version of this case, which is the easiest for me to conceptualize, Yolanda won't have any mental Propensities; in particular, it won't have any power to experience. All the powers in Yolanda's Propensity profile, all its Propensities, are just some evidently physical Propensities.

As should be made plain, this is a case of singular causal resolution. While fully two hundred Blues came to be close to the same Red, and only one hundred needed to be so close for a Yellow Sphere to originate, all the Reds and Blues are so Propensitied that, even in such a situation as is most conducive for generating Yellow objects, there'll be generated no more than one Yellow thing. Thus, as regards their generational interaction with Red Ralph, there was, on the part of each of our two hundred Blues, a certain causal redundancy. Easily grasped quite well, that's the Evidently Material Version of our third illustrative example.

For the Reminiscently Emergentist Version of our third case, we just specify, differently, that, when it's generated, Yolanda will have, for as long as it exists, not only the noted profile of physical Propensities, but, just as well, a fine profile of mental powers, including a rich power to experience, a nice power to think, and even a significant power to choose. Now, to many readers, these suppositions may seem disturbingly strange; no doubt, we're not used to thinking of an individual that's both quite simple physically and quite complex mentally. But, though it may strike us as strange, it still may be that it's all completely coherent. And, what's more, it's an illustrative example that's pretty easy, really, to grasp.

Finally, and at last, we consider our third case's Evidently Dualist Version. Here, there's never any Yellow individual that's ever generated, and, indeed, the World we're now supposing may never, ever include any spatial object that's Spatially Extensible Yellow. With the Reds and the Blues of *this* World, they're all entirely lacking any Propensity ever to promote, or ever to maintain, any Yellow concrete particular. Rather than anything like that, they have a certain Propensity to promote an immaterial soul, richly endowed with mental powers, including ever so many that are aptly Individualistically-directed Propensities. They may be so productively Propensitied, even if they're not Propensitied to promote any new physical concretum, or any new spatial individual. Quite as you might now expect, the conditions for manifesting these soulfully promotional Propensities, these Powers of the Red and the Blue Spherical Particles, will all precisely parallel the conditions specified for our case's two previous Versions. Just so, when it comes to be, in our Evidently Dualistic World, that there are at least a hundred Small Blues within an inch of the very same Large Red, then there'll come to be, in this World, and at long last, the World's first immaterial soul, the very soul, of course, who's the World's first experiencer, and its first thinker, and, for good measure, even its first chooser, too. (Let's say that, in the generating of such a first soul, whom we may call Sally, the Large Red so centrally involved is one Raphael. Then, we might say that, from the first moment of her existence, and for as long as she exists, Sally will have, among her Propensities, various Individualistically-directed Propensities to interact with Raphael. And, for his part, of course, Raphael will be Propensitied, reciprocally, for interaction with Sally. But, naturally enough, Raphael won't ever interact with any other immaterial soul.)

Now, this Evidently Dualistic Version may also seem a terribly strange example. But, it's not substantially stranger, I imagine, than the Reminiscently Emergentist Version, considered just before. At any rate, quite like that Emergentist Version, this Evidently Dualistic Version might be a case that is completely coherent. And, beyond that, it may be an illustrative example that's reasonably well understood. In particular, even as we may understand that, in the Emergentist Version, there's a singular causal resolution as to the promotion of a mentally powerful Spatially Extended experiencer, so we may similarly understand that, in the Evidently Dualistic Version, there's a singular causal resolution as to a mentally powerful Nonspatial experiencer.

(In bracketed paragraphs earlier in the Chapter, I noticed philosophers who hold that, where we're usually given to think that there's just one human experiencer, it may be more accurate to think there are actually two experiencers, quite as certain experimental results with some split-brain patients suggest to some philosophical thinkers. As I said, my own belief is quite the opposite, but, still, my aim is to

accommodate the more unusual view. In just such an accommodating
spirit, I'll now notice that, correlative with each example that I've used
to illustrate the idea of singular causal resolution, there's a case to
illustrate the correlative idea of dual causal resolution. For the case
concerning a television, for instance, we can observe an example
where, all at once, each of billions of stations serve to promote a certain
image on both of two televison sets. In all the most central respects, the
relevant points will be the same.)

7. An Immaterial Experiencer's Causally Resolved Singularity Is a Relevant Singularity

In many of this book's passages, I've offered some quite unusual
thoughts—well, at least by the conventional standards of these quite
conventional times, they're rather unusual. So, for one thing, I've said
that our talk of an individual's experiences can often be metaphysically
misleading, by comparison with talk of the individual herself just
variously experiencing. Is such seemingly most sensible talk as that
somehow responsible for our Experiential Problem of the Many?

Somewhat strangely, to my mind, there are some ideas, en-
tertained by intelligent people, to just that effect, quite as terribly
desperate as it's perfectly irrelevant. At least roughly, those ideas go
like this: Against your nominalistic treatment of what goes on with
experiencers, maybe the real truth is better expressed by saying that,
in any episode of her experiencing, an experiencer *has* a certain
mental item, that's an item of hers, of course, and which mental
whatnot is, of course, *her experience* (or, if not quite that, then, at the
very least, it's one of her experiences). Well, ordinarily, and in most
philosophical works, too, we take it that each individual's experience is
perfectly private to, or is enjoyed only by, just that very individual.
Even if I'm now having a certain experience (as) of red and, quite
simultaneously, my perfect twin is having a precisely similar experience (as) of red, still each of us is having an experience that is numerically distinct from the other's experience. But, for both so many
philosophers and so many philosophically innocent thinkers, that may
be no more than an enormously widespread and deeply ingrained
error. In point of fact, the real situation may be that each of these
experientially similar individuals is similarly related to the very same
single experience—we can call it "Edwina." So, even while I'm (experientially) having the single mental item that's Edwina, my perfect twin
is *also (experientially) having* just that very same mental item, Edwina.

Well, perhaps that might not happen with me and my perfect twin, maybe owing to the very different causal histories of our respective experiences. Perhaps, and perhaps not. But, with the multitude of overlappers in what's presumably just my own situation, that's not so; with all of us there's no notable disparity as to causal histories. Thus, with me and all my overlappers, it really may be that each of us is having—in the way of having quite peculiar to experiences—one and the same individual experience, Edwina itself. Now, if that should be so, then, even amongst all the messy flux of our notably overlapping brains and all the rest, yes, even among all that temporarily disturbing plurality, there will still be, in point of actual fact, a notable singularity with my experiencing. And, even as we now notice that notable singularity, well, maybe we won't ever be much bothered by the so-called Experiential Problem of the Many.

(Look, before replying to this passage, I'll observe that, in its neighborhood, and very much like it, there are many other passages that, instead of this one, I might have related, to much the same soothing effect. Indeed, and as we'll soon see, what's to be replied to any one of the neighboring would-be soothers, including the passage I've actually related, is the same as what's to be replied to any of the others, at least as regards all of the essentials.)

Well, we've just read through a passage meant to quell any disturbance caused us, even if only temporarily, by encountering our Experiential Problem of the Many. Is there anything much that's wrong with it? Well, for starters, the (deeply silly) suggestion asks us to help ourselves to a whole passel of what are, to put the point most charitably, just so many terribly suspicious sentences. At the very most, that will provide us, as Russell said, with all the benefits of theft over honest toil. But, actually, the real problem here is far worse than any of that. Look, what's the real problem, or the main problem, that we've encountered with our so-called Experiential Problem of the Many? Pretty obvious, when you come to think of it, it's really just this: What we typically take to be just my own situation, with *me alone* as the only *experiencer* involved, seems so much to be, on anything like a Scientiphical Metaphysic, or on anything like a materialist worldview, a situation where there are billions of *people* or, at the least, *very many* conscious *individuals*. *That's* the real problem, it should be clear. Look, anything else in the neighborhood is, by comparison, a side issue, or little more than a family squabble. So, if a certain philosophical view suggests we should think that, just when you're enjoying the taste of a very rare wine, for example, well, billions of other folks are, just then, also enjoying the taste of such a very rare wine, then, as I suggest, we should abandon that view, whether or not we're in a position to replace it, with any more adequate view. For just that reason, I'll go ahead and now suggest, we should reject our Scientiphicalism, and any known form of materialism. And, quite as much as with them, we should also reject the noted Emergentism that, in the previous Chapter, initially looked like a pretty promising alternative to a Substantial Dualism.

In this Section, I've discussed a certain claim, concerning your experiencing, that alleged there to be what we might well call a putative singularity: Each of the many presumably overlapping experiencers has, or suffers, or enjoys, or experiences, just a certain single "token" experience. What I've said about the claim is this: Even if it should somehow prove true—which it won't do—the sort of singularity it posits, or claims, is quite an irrelevant singularity. Irrelevant to what? It's irrelevant to what's mainly at stake, philosophically and otherwise, with our Experiential Problem of the Many.

By contrast with what's been the focus of this Section's discussion, in the previous Section we encountered, and we discussed, a truly relevant singularity. When we considered how it may be that many overlapping material complexes should generate just one single experiencing individual, then we considered something that, insofar as there's some truth to it, can provide a reasonable resolution for the Experiential Problem of the Many. By contrast, when observing the soothing passage presented in this present Section, we observe something that's just so irrelevant to our Problem. When noticing how marked is that contrast, we may appreciate, quite fully and clearly, these two things: First, our ideas about singular causal resolution may be some very substantial philosophical thoughts, and, second, those substantial ideas may be highly relevant to resolving, quite reasonably, what's mainly at stake with our Experiential Problem of the Many.[8]

8. These Are Metaphysical Matters, Transcending All Purely Semantic Issues

What we've just observed, over the last couple of Sections, should give us a fair appreciation, I think, of our Experiential Problem of the Many. (And, as I've just suggested, it may do something, too, for helping us appreciate how we should best resolve this philosophically important Problem.) Coming at the matter from other directions, I'd

8. In writing this Section, discussion with Don Garrett was most usefully stimulating.

now like to provide, in this present Section, a bit more to help us appreciate the depth of, and the importance of, this Problem.

The Experiential Problem of the Many is a genuine metaphysical difficulty, concerning how it is with matters in concrete reality. Though it may interface interestingly with certain semantic problems, both some questions concerning vagueness and also some other semantical issues, the heart of this Experiential Problem goes beyond any merely semantic difficulties. By this stage of our discussion, that should be very clear. But, nowadays, some philosophers think they see all manner of philosophical matters to be issues of vagueness, if not entirely, then at least in large measure. And, along with many other philosophers, they (rightly) think that issues of vagueness are semantical matters, at least primarily, and maybe entirely. So, it may be useful, I think, to show that the Mental Problems of the Many, including the Experiential Problem, *aren't* mainly issues of vagueness, nor are they mainly matters of *any semantical* sort.

To this useful end, I'll make (what I take to be) a quite incredible supposition. I'll suppose that our term "experiencer," like our expression "is experiencing," has semantic conditions that serve always to select, from all the physical complexes in my situation, just one single complex to be the sole entity, or to constitute the sole entity, to which the term properly applies. For very many other complexes, overlapping the sole complex that's somehow so singularly selected, the term will just barely fail properly to apply. Or, so we may pretty charitably suppose. (And, then, of course, the term will more than just barely fail to apply, and may dramatically fail to apply, with yet many more complexes, also overlapping.) Along with this, we'll make parallel suppositions, of course, for each of our very many other terms in the relevant neighborhood, for "real chooser" and "really chooses," for instance.

Now, even with such a singularly selective semantic supposition in force, our Emergentist should say, along with our Scientiphicalist, that there are billions of overlapping complexes right now, in what I'm wont to call my own situation, each with a power to engage in *something extremely like experiencing*. So, even if it should be true that, in my situation, there's only one complex that, with perfect propriety, can be said to have a power to experience, even then, there'll still be billions of complexes that each can be said, quite properly enough, to have a very similar power, with a very similar manifestation. As we might say, quite properly enough, each of these billions will have a power to *schmexperience*; and, when that's manifested, each of them will be *schmexperiencing*.

But, as far as any first philosophy goes, about all of that, what can we think except a big so-what? As far as can be discerned, by any human thinker, at least, there's nothing of much metaphysical moment

in any alleged difference between conscious experiencing and conscious schmexperiencing.

Of course, the thought that, right here with me right now, there
are many consciously schmexperiencing beings is, apparently, also
quite preposterous. And, what's more, this preposterous thought appears more disturbing than innocuous. So, our Nonentity Emergentist,
as much as our Scientiphicalist, will be fully embroiled in a deeply
disturbing thought. This will be so, apparently, even if it's not quite
correct to express the disturbing idea by saying that, in my current
situation, there are billions of overlapping *experiencing* beings.

As I imagine, it should now be pretty plain that, quite apart from
the incredibly selective semantics it posits for our ordinary mental
terms, the noted approach doesn't engage what's mainly at issue with
our Experiential Problem of the Many. But, as is my hope, these next
remarks will make that still clearer.

Recall our discussion of the thought that, in my situation right now,
there are billions of overlapping human organisms, and billions of
overlapping human digestive systems. Though this also seemed quite
incredible, you'll recall, there didn't seem any deep philosophical
difficulty with the apparently preposterous suggestion. As much as
anything else, it seemed a suggestion to the effect that certain of our
locutions, "human organism" and "human digestive system," really
have a rather liberal semantics. Just so, if someone seeks to raise a
philosophical question by saying "I wonder whether there's just one
digestive system, right here with me right now, or whether there are
very many overlapping digestive systems, right here right now," well,
right then and there, it's hard to believe there's a metaphysically meaty
issue he's placing on offer. By contrast, if someone similarly seeks to
raise a question with the words, "I wonder whether there's just one
conscious experiencer, right here with me right now, or whether there
are very many overlapping conscious experiencers, right here right
now," it's *not* hard to think he's advancing a question of real metaphysical significance. And, as I've been suggesting, of course, this
proclivity of ours may be a philosophically appropriate propensity.[9]

---

9. A couple of Sections ago, as you'll recall, I considered the suggestion, however
empty it might really be, that, right now in my situation, there may be billions of experiencers all enjoying, or having, the very same token experience, or experience-trope,
or whatever. As I then went on to argue, even if it should be a very substantial thought,
this idea is perfectly irrelevant to our main problem, which is, and it always has been, just
this: On anything even much like Scientiphicalism, and on any standard sort of materialism, there are, right now in my situation, so very many *experiencers*, just billions and
billions of *people*. Well, that's just a lead-in to this note's main point.

9. These Problems Transcend Questions of Spatial Boundary: On Complex Complexes

When I first presented the old Problem of the Many, all those many years ago, I used examples of clouds to provide a very vivid entree into the Problem. And, as I've long imagined, it's hard to find a more vivid entree into *any* philosophical issue, whether the problem it posed should be, after all, only a pretty superficial trouble or where it should be rather more profound. So, partly for that reason, and partly to regale readers with a happily nostalgic sample of my early authorial efforts, I again did that here, near this Chapter's beginning. While there were those benefits in doing that, there are also some dangers attending that presentation; and, when it's the Experiential Problem that wants posing, there even might be some downright drawbacks. Well, by this late point, in our current text, the attendant dangers may all have been, already, quite fully forestalled. And, for most of my readers, the aforesaid drawbacks may have been fully nullified. But, at least for a few of those following the Chapter's progress, I'll now try to be particularly helpful.

With "my cloudish presentation" there's the suggestion, of course, that many Problems of the Many, if not quite all such Problems, are Problems mainly concerning spatial boundaries. And, what's more, it may be suggested that the Problems mainly concern what we might well call "spatially external spatial boundaries." With some who've been reading this Chapter, I guess, they may still be under some such

---

Just so, and in the midst of that Section's discussion, I offered this following bracketed paragraph, here indented and truncated as well as bracketed:

(Look, before replying to this passage, I'll observe that, in its neighborhood. and very much like it, there are many other passages that, instead of this one, I might have related, to much the same soothing effect. Indeed, and as we soon see, what's to be replied to any of the neighboring would-be soothers ... is [in all essentials] ... what's to be replied to any of the others.)

Anyway, and now quite obviously, one of the salient neighboring would-be soothers is this: Even while, right now in my situation, there are very many experiencers, billions and billions, we may say that they're all involved in the same single (process of) experiencing. As what I've just said in the text suggests, as will much of what's upcoming in the Chapter, this is also a quite senseless idea, really, just as senseless as the (now familiar) thought that, in my situation, billions of folks are all having the same single token experience. What's more, what applied before applies here once more: Even if *this* should be a very substantial thought, the present idea is also perfectly irrelevant to our main problem, which is, and it always has been, just this: On anything even much like Scientiphicalism, and on any standard sort of materialism, there are, right now in my situation, so very many *experiencers*, just billions and billions of *people*.

On this matter, I'm indebted to stimulating discussion with Elizabeth Harman.

impression, even as concerns the Experiential Problem of the Many. But, quite as many will have realized, that's very far from the truth of the matter.

How should I help some to see—if they should really need any help here—how very far that is? Each in its own way, I imagine, several complementary thoughts each may be of use. Though it will mean a little lengthier exposition, I'll choose to proceed in a very gentle manner.

At least for the meanwhile, forget about such relatively homogeneous complexes as clouds and bricks, all of which are, comparatively, quite boring physical complexes. Instead, let's consider only some much more *complex complexes*, as we may call these other ontologically dubious candidate entities. For one example of such a complex physical complex, we'll consider a certain (supposed) complicated watch, one that's happily old-fashioned and thoroughly mechanical. For another example, we'll consider a human brain, say, your brain. First, we do the watch.

By the reckoning of skilled watchmakers, and also expert repairmen, a certain watch might be considered to have, say, 176 parts. As it might be, this complicated old wristwatch is a wonderfully working collector's item. It's worth hundreds of thousands of dollars and, in keeping with that, it's worn proudly by its billionaire owner. Well, anyway, among this watch's 176 "watchmaker's parts," it might be that, say, 45 are little more than just so many decorative components, or protective parts. At any rate, each of them is quite inessential to the watch's being able to run, and for its running quite regularly. So, our pricey watch will then have, we're imagining it to be, 131 essential watchmaker's parts, that is, 131 parts each of which is essential to its being able to run regularly. As we may more specifically suppose, 21 of these parts will be 21 little jewels. And, while none of the others are, then, any jewels, 43 of them may be 43 little gear wheels, and so on. Of course, I'm just pulling these details out of thin air. But, of course, none of my cockamamy specifications matters a jot, or a fig. Anyhow, even while our assumed timepiece is telling time very nicely, the pricey watch sits right there, on the lefthand wrist of our proud billionaire, quite clearly apparent, and quite aptly placed, for all his watchcollector friends to examine and admire.

Now, just as we may do well to suppose, each of the 21 jewels, all so essential to the watch's working, is an internal part of the watch, each of them surrounded by some several watchmaker's parts spatially external to the jewel. Some of these surrounding parts will be at the watch's socalled surface, or, if not that, then it will be closer to the aforesaid so-called surface. Quite the same, I imagine, such a part will be, then, at least somewhat closer, than is the jewel, to the watch's so-called (so-called by me) spatially external spatial boundary.

At any rate, just as is true for each of the watch's 43 gears, and for each of its other watchmaker's parts, too, there's a Problem of the Many for each of the watch's 21 jewels. Indeed, even if we consider only the elementary particles of a certain single supposed jewel—or a certain single supposed *candidate* jewel—there's a Problem of the Many. So, supposing that there really are any of these 21 jewels—in effect, supposing that there really are such things as jewels, at all—well, then, wherever it is that, quite casually, we should take there to be just one single jewel, this will be, apparently, a more accurate reckoning as to the presumably jewelish situation: Right in that very little vicinity, there are billions upon billions of jewels, each of them overlapping very many others.

With so very many jewels all internal to our imagined timepiece, quite as we're doing so well to continue to suppose, what are we to say of our billionaire's watch-situation, so to put the question? Just so far as these jewelish considerations go, should we conclude that he's wearing billions upon billions of watches, each of them overlapping, *at least internally*, with each of the others? We might possibly do that. Or, alternatively, and quite desperate to appease the quasi-philosophical horde of commonsense enthusiasts, we might think to claim that there's some external-boundary-maximality rule already nicely in force, wonderfully governing the semantics of the word "watch." (Myself, I suspect that's just a lot of ad hoc nonsense. And, of course, any such alleged rule won't be to any avail, anyhow, as whatever Problems we've now found with a so-called watch's "internal boundaries," we've already encountered, several times over, with the so-called external boundaries of, or the alleged surfaces of, the likes of presumed watches, and supposed brains, and what-all.) But, really, who can care, or care very much, about any of this (mostly, or wholly) semantic business? Not any philosopher who's mostly concerned with truly substantial matters, quite as any very serious philosopher ought to be.

Let there be only one watch on the billionaire's lefthand wrist, albeit that's a watch, of course, with many billions of jewels, certainly far more than just the 21 first advertised. Let that be so; who cares? Or, alternatively, let there be billions of watches on his watch, each of them a watch with precisely 21 jewels, so that, quite as was advertised, he's wearing a 21-jewel watch—well, even better, he's wearing billions of such very nice watches, rather than just a single watch with 21 jewels. Let *that* be so; again, who cares? Or, still another alternative, I guess, let matters be generous all the way round, so that, on our billionaire's wrist, there are billions of precious watches, and, with each and every one of these fine watches, the nice timepiece has billions of jewels. If you prefer, I'll let *this* be the case—or, at least, I'll do my level best in just such an attempt. Who can care very much, really, about any of this business, all of it being concerned, evidently, with just so much *ontological superficilia*?

Maybe there's more here than just *playing* with words. But, there's not very much more than just a lot of fancy semantics. Now, with a certain fancy semantics assigned for the term "watch," perhaps we can speak of certain of the supposed complex physical complexes as watches. (Well, I *guess* that might be all right—*whatever* it is that we might then be *saying*, pray tell, especially if, as I suspect, there never are—anywhere and anyhow—any real complex physical complexes. And, how about—what shall I say?—simple physical complexes, like clouds? Ontologically, are they *better* off? Fat chance. But, enough of this; lest this book turn into a joke book.)

Moving right along, I should say that, or maybe I should just suppose that, with another esoteric semantics *also* in mind, one that's not quite so liberal as to what, when and where something can be properly reckoned a watch, we may speak of *other* complex complexes—those that don't quite make it all the way to watchhood—as *schmatches*. And, then, with *still another* fancy semantics *also* in service, we may speak of *still other* complexes—which fail on a couple of more quite trivial counts—as *schmatchaches*, and so forth, and so on.

Even with all these billions of internal jewels in mind—or, maybe, it's billions of internal *shmewels*; I don't care—anyhow, there's still regular timekeeping going on, right over there, in the little vicinity of our billionaire's left wrist, or his billions of left wrists, or his billions of left *schmists*. Indeed, with ever so very many complex complexes all involved, each so terribly similarly as all the others, in ever so many saliently temporal processes, it appears that, in our considered situation, there's a very great deal of timekeeping occurring, or obtaining, each instance of timekeeping in ever so close a parallel with all the other instances. Or, if there's a wonderfully selective semantics working on a word like "timekeeping"—which, to my mind, is also quite desperately absurd (but, really, who cares very much about that?)—well, then, there's a very great deal of quite parallel *schimekeeping* that obtains in our considered situation. For all you folks, who've all read the just previous Section, I certainly needn't say much about schimekeeping.

So much for watches, and schmates, and schmatchaches, and so on. Now, we'll consider your brain or, at least, your supposed brain.

Well, as we ordinarily think about the matter, you've got just one brain, of course, and it's an extraordinarily complex physical complex. Among your brain's many physical constituents, we suppose, are some several billion wonderfully complex nerve cells, or neurons. Now, as it may be, for all I know, quite a few of these neurons may be reckoned, by folks supposedly knowledgeable in such matters, as "external neuronal constituents" of your brain—well, something like those neurons that are at, or nearest to, your brain's outer surface, or maybe something like those that are nearest to your brain's ensconcing skull. (I don't know. But, while it may be inordinately difficult to have any of this be precise, or maybe even have it be coherent, none of that, surely, is one of *my* problems. Nor should it be, I'm suggesting, one of your problems, either.)

At all events, very many of your neurons *won't* be such external constituents of your brain. And, accordingly, we may consider them, well enough, to be your brain's *internal neurons*. Well, just as with any other neurons, and just as with any of your brain's other cells, for that matter—as with all your brain's multitudinous glia—well, with each of these very many internal neurons, many millions upon millions of them, it will have a Problem of the Many. Indeed, even just *insofar as its* "most external constituents" are concerned, there will be that Problem. Just so, and getting quite basic very fast, with each of these many millions of neurons, this will obtain with the neuron's "most external quarks," and it will also obtain with the neuron's "most external electrons." Well, then, whenever it may seem that there's just a single internal neuron, here, when there's just so much commonly casual observation and, maybe, just so much happily loose thinking, too, there will really be—heck, a bit closer to the real truth of the matter, anyway—billions and billions of neurons.

With so very many neurons all "internal parts of" your supposed brain, what are we to say of your brain-situation, so to put the question? Just so far as these internal neuronal considerations go, and forgetting about any of your brain that's nearer your skull, so to say, should we conclude, now, that you've got billions of brains, each of them overlapping, at least internally, with billions of others? As with our old-fashioned watch, we might possibly do that. Or, as with our watch, we might not. But, really, and once again, who can care, very much, about any of this business? Not any philosopher who's mostly concerned with truly substantial matters, quite as any most serious philosopher ought to be.

Just with all these billions of internal neurons in mind, or billions of internal *schmourons*, if you prefer, there's occurring very regular control of your breathing, just for one thing. Or, if your prefer, there's very regular schmontrol of your schmeathing.

Now, with each of these very many brains, or with each of these very many schmains, each of them so similarly involved in a saliently temporal process that's ever so like very many other processes, each process involving another one of the billions of other schmains, might there also be, in your situation, billions of processes of *experiencing* that occur, or that obtain, with each experiencing the experiencing of a numerically different *experiencer*? That defies my belief. Or, if some fancy semantics may just possibly settle that singularly—as I most certainly doubt—then what I simply can't believe will be better put, much as it was before, in terminology that's devoid of just such fancy semantics. Contrary to that, what I believe will, then, be better put like this: There *won't* be, in your situation, billions of simultaneous schmexperiencers, each of them simultaneously schmexperiencing, or each concurrently schmexperiencing, or anything importantly like that.

10. Problems of Propensitively Redundant Propensitive Contributors

With the previous Section's discussion, we've done a fair bit, I think, to dispel any suggestion that the Experiential Problem of the Many mainly concerns, or that it even very largely concerns, just so many questions as to presumed spatial boundaries. In this present Section, we'll do more.

Consider, for a moment, any one of your brainy complexes that, for promoting any of your experiencing, or any of your schmexperiencing, does at least as well as does any complex physical complex. Well, this very complex brainy complex, the one we're just now considering, comprises billions of trillions of billions of constituent elementary particles, including very many trillions of quarks, let's say, and also very many trillions of electrons. Now, consider as well, everything that's there excepting a certain one "deeply internal" quark and, an inch away from that quark, a certain single "deeply internal" electron. Now, as I'll suggest, what we're just *now* considering may also be a brainy complex—one that's "got a certain little gap in it," where there happens to be a certain single electron, and, to boot, it's a complex that's "got a certain *other* little hole in it" wherein there's ensconced a certain single quark, a *second foreigner to* our just newly considered complex. Or, there'll be that, I should suppose, *providing there are*, really and truly, any brainy physical complexes at all.

(When I began to discuss candidate brains, do recall, I specified candidates each of which had exactly as many (basic) physical constituents as did each of the others. So, for instance, each had precisely as many quarks as did any other 'tied best' brain candidate. And, similarly, with any other basic components, say, with constituent electrons. Well, the "deeply internal" reckoning we've just engaged in, that means a shift from this starting thought, where there's exactly equality concerning the components. But, for several different reasons, the shift doesn't matter. Here are two.

First, there's this. Let's begin by returning to consider our two-gap complex physical complex. Now, we may imaginatively add to it, so to say, just one of the electrons that, for both this two-gap complex and for its non-gappy complex predecessor, is one of the supposedly *barely too peripheral electrons*—barely too peripheral, that is, for us to have *arbitrarily reckoned it* as one of these considered complexes basic constituents. And, similarly, we may add a barely too peripheral quark. OK; now that's been done. Well, then, at *this* point, with those two peripheral particles taken as constituents of a *just newly considered* brainy complex, we're now considering a just slightly bigger two-gap complex than the two-hole complex first considered. And, with this just newly considered two-gap complex, we're pondering a complex that has exactly as many quarks, and also precisely as many electrons, as does each of the *non-gappy* brainy complexes considered at the very start of this whole (parenthetically presented) discussion. All by itself, just all that has our so-called shift seem utterly unimportant, for any matter of any metaphysical moment. So, that's one thing; and here's another.

Second, and as you'll likely recall, in the midst of our much earlier discussion, back there some several Sections ago, we allowed that there should be a certain amount of leeway, even if never very much, as regards how many possibly peripheral particles, so to say, and even how many possibly peripheral droplets, may be included among the constituents of a sufficiently felicitous candidate cloud. And, as well, we allowed, or we might just as well have allowed, that there should be some such little leeway, too, concerning how many possibly peripheral particles may be included in a good enough candidate brain—good enough to be an instance of true brainhood (indeed, good enough to be a paradigmatic instance of true brainhood). Now, as we may do very well just to continue with at least this little bit of agreement, rather than suddenly not allowing any such leeway whatever, we can hardly help but realize this. Though we did the job ever so nicely, in the just previous paragraph, we never really needed to make the nice adjustments there essayed, so as to have, nicely juxtaposed for consideration, brainy complexes each with precisely as many basic constituents as the other, and even for every sort of basic component. Rather, as concerns the issues at hand, all that was a *perfectly supererogatory effort*, above and beyond the call of philosophical duty.)

Anyway, whatever experiencing may be promoted by our non-gap brainy complex, and whatever experiencer, that may be promoted, just as well, I'll suggest, by our two-gap brainy complex. Or, for those doubtful of our developing dualism, there'll be this to consider: Even as the *non-gap* brainy complex is perfectly sufficient to sustain an experiencer, or to subserve an experiencer, or to realize an experiencer—or to do *whatever* you here most favor—so our *two-gap* complex is *also* perfectly sufficient to do just that, even if the latter should sustain, or whatever, a numerically different experiencer from that which the former sustains. Or, for those who're still embroiled with semantical niceties, what we'll have to confront is some such statement as this, scarcely any more palatable a proposition: Even as the non-gap brainy complex is perfectly sufficient to sustain an experiencer—or whatever you most favor—so our two-gap complex is perfectly sufficient to sustain a schmexperiencer, a numerically different entity from that which the former sustains. Of course, and quite as we've already agreed, even as schmexperiencing is just so enormously like experiencing, and even as it's no different in any metaphysically meaningful manner, so a schmexperiencer is just so enormously like an experiencer, and *they're no different in any metaphysically meaningful manner*.

In a nutshell, what does this mean? It means that, as concerns anything in this neighborhood that's metaphysically significant, well, all by itself, just one single electron—*any* single electron—it just won't make even the least particle of difference (pun intended).

Even as concerns pretty mundane processes, like the regular control of breathing, that's clearly true. And, it's clearly true, too, for our old-fashioned watch, or our overlapping mechanical watches, particularly insofar as regular timekeeping is concerned. One single electron more, or just one less, that won't make any difference as to how (well) the watch is keeping time, or how all the overlapping watches are each keeping time. Rather, so far as any of these mundane processes are concerned, each electron, and each quark, too, is a *Propensitively redundant Propensitive contributor*. In the concrete context of all those other quarks all so nicely arranged and aworking, and all those electrons also so nicely aworking there, too, well, anything that any single quark might be doing, heck, it's utterly unnecessary for there to occur the specified Propensitive manifestation.

Basically, here it's just the most basic physical particles we're talking about, just those physical concreta whose ontological credentials are least problematic. When what's in focus is just these perfectly basic Propensitive contributors, then this sort of situation, a scenario with Propensitively redundant Propensitive contributors, is a terribly pervasive sort of situation. But, it's not universal. What's that, now? Let me explain. If you want there to be a hydrogen atom, in a certain situation, for a nice example, and what you've got there is just one electron, and just one proton, with the former characteristically circling the latter, then—providing there's no illicit shenanigans, say, no sneaky electron importing—heck, then you'd better make sure that, in this situation, you've still got your electron. You've got to have that electron there. You need it to have a hydrogen atom, or anything even much like a hydrogen atom—for all that can be much like a hydrogen atom, right there in your situation, is your single hydrogen atom itself. And, you need your electron for there to be that little circling process, however mundane and unexciting it might be. Those are the plain facts. That's how the actual world really is, at least during this present Eon.

But, with supposed mechanical watches, and with presumed human brains, too, just one single electron, whether one more or one less, that *really doesn't* make any significant difference, not to any of the issues we've rightly been considering. While those are undeniable facts, they contrast starkly with many other facts. And, just as well for our purposes, they similarly contrast with many properly supposed suppositions. Let me amplify.

Recall what, in the just previous Section, we specified for most of our supposed mechanical watch's watchmaker's parts: While 131 of these parts are each absolutely necessary for the watch's running, in the context of our perfectly proper supposition, some 45 others are, more or less, just so many decorative components. At any rate, each of them is utterly unnecessary for the watch's running regularly, and, for what's here much the same, for the watch's being able to run. Now, these 45 parts, as you should certainly realize, *aren't* Propensitively redundant Propensitive contributors—so far as concerns this watch's running, or so far as concerns anything else in focus, or apt for current consideration. Rather, as concerns anything we've been contemplating, they're *not Propensitive contributors at all*. In a way, that's one of the two central points to be made with our old timepiece example,

And, the other main point? Well, cutting to the chase, it's this. So far as this watch's salient Propensities are concerned, each of 131 different watchmaker's parts makes a distinctively necessary contribution. Whatever Propensitive contribution is made by even the tiniest and most peripheral gear, well, on our specified assumptions, that's really needed; it's needed for the watch to run, and it's needed for the watch to be able to run, and so on. (There's no mystery in any of that, of course. For, putting it all pretty compendiously, the basic situation is this: When you've got a *so-and-so* aworking arrangement of *thus-and-such* quintillions of quadrillions of elementary particles, then you've got a running mechanical watch. When you take away *this-and-that* particles from the arrangement—the taking away is just illustrative, of course— then you're left with a mere *thingamabob* array of basic particles. And, very unlike what's there with a *so-and-so* array, so sufficient for so much to be so nicely aworking, well, with a mere *thingamabob* arrangement, there's certainly no watch there that's able to run, much less any actually running watch. Well, I'm sure you get the hang of it.)

Quite unlike our watch's 131 individually necessary watchmaker's parts, and *quite like* each of our watch's quintillions of electronish parts—that is, each of its quintillions of electrons—every last one of your brain's (or your brains') individual neuronal parts—that is, each of the neurons—well, each is just a Propensitively redundant Propensitive contributor. That's a fact. There's no specially Propensitive neuron ever present, in any brain, of any human being. None of your neurons is, any more than even any of your mere electrons ever is, any Propensitive contributor that *isn't* Propensitively redundant, for there to obtain any of your mental powers, and for there to occur any of your experiencing. As with your mere electrons, each neuron has millions of others as "backup object," so to say, and each is, itself, such a "backup object" for millions of others.

(As I've been told, and as I've no reason to doubt, when you enjoy an alcoholic beverage then, typically, you lose about a hundred or so neurons, without any replacement. Oh, the exact details don't matter. Anyhow, with some small neuron loss, there's no loss in your power to experience. With the loss of very many neurons, by contrast, you may lose, for instance, your power to experience visually; that will happen if all the neurons lost, or almost all, are in a certain part of your brain. Unfortunately or not, that's a fact. But, with just one or two fewer neuron contributors than you have right now, there *won't be any change* in, say, your power to experience visually, no matter where it is, in your brain, that the very few neurons may be lost.)

And, of course, what holds here for each of your individual neurons, well, it holds in spades, and it holds far more certainly, for each of your individual electrons, and for each of your individual quarks, too.

Anyway, so little does our Experiential Problem of the Many concern external spatial boundaries or, really, any spatial boundaries at all, that it just enormously concerns, quite enormously more than any of that spatial boundary business, crucial questions as to whether there are, or whether there aren't, "for your main mental situation," many Propensitively redundant Propensitive contributors. Well, we know, plenty well enough, how you fare with those crucial questions: As concerns the promotion of any of your experiencing, and as concerns even the promotion of any power you may have to that experiential effect, extremely often, in fact, *there are* just so very many Propensitively redundant Propensitive contributors, at least when the contributors in question are as ontologically unproblematic as the likes of quarks and electrons. And, so, it's extremely often that there actually does arise, in fact, for your own power to experience, nothing less perplexing, philosophically, and even metaphysically, than our deeply disturbing Experiential Problem of the Many.

11. Our Experiential Problem Doesn't Presuppose Any Suspicious Identifications

Crazy as it seems to me, quite a few current academic philosophers are quite prepared to live with the idea that, right now in my situation, there really are very many experiencers, with I myself being just one of the vast multitude. Though I don't have a whole lot of respect for this cockamamy and complacent reaction, still, in just a little while, I'll say some things that, for those Complacentists who bother to pay attention, should be highly disturbing propositions. Perhaps, they'll be disturbing enough, I should hope, for a few such Complacentists to take seriously a reasonably well worked out Substantial Dualism. But, right now, I'll address some quite opposite reactions.

To all appearances, most current academics aren't at all prepared to live with the idea of there being such a cockamamy multitude of overlapping experiencers. Well, thank goodness for that! So, quite as expected, those in this great horde will deny that, in anything remotely like what I'm calling "my situation," there's ever more than just one experiencer, the one who's me, of course. Fair enough, I myself deny that. But, unlike my denial, theirs is meant to comport well with a materialistic metaphysic, and with our dominant Scientiphicalism. (At the very least, and most certainly, it's meant to comport well with our Nonentity Emergentism.)

What is it that we hear from these pretty common commonsense enthusiasts. Generally, it's something like this: To get to the idea that there are billions of experiencers in my situation, I must be identifying an experiencer, quite crudely and wrongly, with something else. Though I certainly didn't do that intentionally, or even at all wittingly, I must have been doing it nonetheless. Or, at the least, that's what they're wont to say. But, in saying that, what can they possibly have in mind here, beyond just a lot of very dubiously relevant technical chitchat?

For a handy sampler, we might go to a currently standard textbook, or anthology, in what's called "the philosophy of mind," apparently an area of philosophy that's to be much more manageable than the overly ambitious likes of good old metaphysics. In the first small part of such a book, generally there's presented something on behalf of Dualism. Typically, an anthology will feature Descartes, of course, and then offer a couple of other fellow-travelers. And, a text will paraphrase some Cartesian arguments, and then some more contemporary Quasi-Cartesian considerations, none of them all that different from Descartes's original ideas, at least so far as I can see. And, with just this little smidgeon up front, that's almost all the motivation provided for reading through the rest of the (to my mind) pretty boring volume. What's in all the rest? Well, in a nutshell, it's just this: a variety of proposals each aiming, somewhat differently from each of the others, to "make the world safe for materialism"—or, at the least, for something very like materialism.

(One thing that you *won't* find is any worry, at all, about how we might best conceive of anything that's material, or that's physical. Far from being anything much like a Bertrand Russell, your inappropriately optimistic author will be, almost certainly, quite perfectly complacent about the truly basic questions in the presumed neighborhood. And, with very few exceptions, *another thing you won't* find is anything arguing for an idealistic philosophy, or any mentalistic metaphysic, not even a page from such a marvelously stimulating philosopher as Berkeley. This will be sadly so, despite this evident fact, with which your typical textbook author, or anthologizer, will fully agree: With the obvious exception of Descartes, scarcely any of the work your text or anthology presents, if any at all, is *anywhere near* as important, philosophically, as each of many nice selections from Berkeley's Dialogues, each arguing for the view that all of concrete reality is just so many *minds* and, maybe less fundamentally, their ideas, or mental modifications. As I said, what passes for an instructive book in the philosophy of *mind* is, almost entirely, just the presentation of just so many hopeful proposals about how we might make the world safe for materialism. Shameful, you say? Well, there are mitigating circumstances here or, at least, for serious philosophy, these are hard times: All of it generated by just so very much highly effective social pressure, it's a dense intellectual fog, indeed, that's the relentless environment serving to determine the very narrow range of reading you'll find offered, not to mention the surpassing superficiality of almost everything presented for your edification.)

Anyway, in your philosophy of mind book, there'll be a veritable smorgasbord of *verbally* diverse material, I guess, almost all of it mainly aiming to make the world safe for physicalism, or materialism. Among the verbiage provided to this end, some of it will be just so hopelessly bad that it doesn't bear even the least bit of serious discussion, as with the "logical behaviorism" of Gilbert Ryle. (An aside, this is the same Ryle whose writing on Dispositions has led to more philosophical confusion than even I can appreciate, and not just about matters of mind, mind you.[10] If ever there have been writings just filled with horribly influential philosophical garbage, with Ryle's work we're pretty close to a Prime Mover.) What any of this behaviorist bullticky may have to do with anyone's ever *experiencing* anything, well, it all just beats the heck out of me. And, for sure, it doesn't appear to have the least bit of relevance, either, for questions about anyone's really *choosing* to think about anything, from actual alternatives for her up-coming thoughtful activity. Well, even while this behaviorist bull is just so much utterly hopeless nonsense, some of the book's other verbiage, provided later in your instructional publication, is a little better than that. Or, a bit less misleadingly put, it's not quite *that* bad.

For example, right after your confrontation with logical behavior-ism, you may well encounter something that's often called the Identity Theory (of the mental and the physical). In most of its most favored forms, this doesn't aim to identify some plainly physical individual with, or as, any sentient entity, or with any conscious experiencer, or, heaven forfend, with any real chooser. Oh, no; that would be much too crude, it

---

10. Almost certainly, your selection from Ryle will be excerpted from *The Concept of Mind*, Hutchinson of London, 1949, a book whose intellectual influence may be exceeded only by its philosophical fatuity. About as representative as anything else, I suppose, I'll display this salient little tidbit, from page 123:

To say that this lump of sugar is soluble is to say that it would dissolve, if submerged anywhere, at any time and in any parcel of water.

Even to many folks innocent of all philosophy, it's obvious, for at least four independent reasons, that this sentence is wildly false. What's much worse, I fear, are contextual implicatures of Ryle's wildly false sentence, provided by many other sentences, including this more "theoretical-sounding" little item from page 125:

Dispositional statements are neither reports of observed or observable states of affairs, nor yet reports of unobserved or unobservable states of affairs.

Now, unlike David Armstrong, for example, Ryle doesn't mean much by "states of af-fairs." Rather, this is his way of saying, in effect, that a statement *apparently* asserting that a certain electron is disposed to attract protons, well, *that doesn't really* say anything about how it is with that electron. And, to think that, when I was a teenager, I thought that *The Concept of Mind* was a remarkably fine work in philosophy, quite as full of profound philosophic truths as it was replete with nice stylistic turns. Well, that's teenagers, for you. But, as I now fervently hope, not very many philosophers will continue to be so much like a certain mere teenager once was—so terribly impressed by just so much false and even fatuous philosophy.

would seem, for these sophisticated authors. (Or, maybe, it would be much too hopeless for them to spend much effort on.)

Rather, and much more typically, it's a certain mental *process*, or a certain experiential *event*, that's said to be the very same *process*, or the very same *event*, as some (quite obviously) physical event. (Sometimes it's a certain *kind* of mental event (or process) that's identified with, or as, a certain *kind* of physical event (or process)—as when, for instance, and just roughly, the event-kind *being in pain* is said to be the very same event-kind as is the event-kind *electrical firing of neural C-fibers*. As most authors (rightly enough) agree, that's not very plausible.) A tad more plausibly, and far more commonly, it's something like this that's said: A certain particular mental event, say, your suffering this very pain right now, is the very same event as a certain particular plainly physical event, say, these very 7,123 C-fibers—all of them in your head, I guess—firing electrically, right now. Well, anyhow, it's something like that. Heck, by now, you must be getting the hang of this stuff.

For our Experiential Problem of the Many, what are we to make of any of that?

Now, unless *you're* a certain particular *process*, a process sometimes *intensely elated*, and unless *I'm* an *event* that's sometimes quite *painfully depressed*, well, unless that's so, I just can't see that any of this has any relevance, at all, to our Experiential Problem of the Many. And, unless there are processes and events that are richly mentally Propensitied, events that possess a Power to experience and a Power to really choose, these alleged critters, these (ontologically suspect) processes and events can't have anything to do with the subject we're discussing. But, as it certainly seems to be, whatever processes there may be, well, none of *them* ever experience, and none of *them* ever choose. Indeed, no such "item" even has the least little power to do anything remotely like that. So, it's a pretty safe bet, I'll wager, that you're not really any process, or any event, no more than I am. So, even as may be easily anticipated, *these* alleged identities have no relevance to our present Problems.[11]

---

11. It's been many years, indeed, I now realize, since I first employed arguments of just this sort. Heck, it's even been many years since I got up the nerve to publish some such arguments. For one pretty early publication utilizing the idea that I'm not any event, nor any events, see my paper, "Impotence and Causal Determinism," *Philosophical Studies*, 1977, reprinted in my *Philosophical Papers, Volume 2*. In large measure, key ideas for this paper were applications of, or specific instances of, certain far more general points that I published elsewhere, but at about the same time, in "The Uniqueness in Causation," *American Philosophical Quarterly*, 1977, also reprinted in my *Philosophical Papers*.

Hold your horses, Buddy, I know what you're thinking. Quite rightly, you're thinking something like this: Who cares whether I'm right, or whether I'm not? Who cares about what's properly called a *process*, and what's not properly so-called? And, similarly, who cares about what's properly called an *event*? Fine, fine; I fully agree with you, there. It's of very little importance who gets the rights to these terms, or to these expressions—quite as it is with (almost?) any other terms and expressions. So, the real main point must be this: If I am an event, then I'm a specially interesting one, so to say. I'm an event that sometimes experiences just very joyously, and other times experiences only very unhappily. And, when I did experience just joyously, I was able to experience just very painfully—or, at the least, I then had the capacity to experience only so very painfully. So, then, what *sort of event am I*? Well, I tell you this much. *I'm not* any event that's even anything remotely like the actual event of the electrical firing of just this-and-that neural fibers, whether it's just the firing right now, whether a firing that's gone on all this year, or, (just maybe?) more plausibly, whether it's a firing that's *gone on for over sixty years!*

So, OK, buddy, let's agree to say that you're a process and I'm an event. But, then, the events and processes we're now discussing, well, *they aren't ever discussed* by our currently considered instructional writers. (Not unless an event much like the electrical firing, right now, of a certain 7,123 C-fibers—all of them in your head, I guess, sometimes choose to think mainly about food, and so on. But, of course, even as those suggestions are quite perfectly absurd, there really *isn't* any *unless* here.) Rather, with our eventfully-oriented authors, there's just so much pretty implausible baloney, I think. And, much more importantly, there's this: Whether it's only baloney or whether it's some genuine Genoa salami, here's something about it that we don't just think, but that we know full well: It's all utterly irrelevant to our present Problems.

In just a moment, I'd like to return to questions of identification. Right now, I'll make a quick pass, very effective, I'm sure, at putting the rest of your instructional book to bed, where it can bore itself to sleep, instead of boring you and me. This won't be very scholarly, of course, but I don't think what's here really deserves all that much serious scholarship. For a representative additional sample, likely to pop up a bit later in your text, there'll be various forms of "functionalism" that you'll encounter. But, whatever the advantages of, and whatever the (far greater) drawbacks of, this further make-the-world-safe-for-materialism material, none of it has much relevance, you can be sure, for our present Problem.

Just cursorily confronting functionalism, I'll just say this: First, there's a Problem of the Many for Coke Machines, whose function is, roughly, to take in money and give out drinks, canned or bottled or however. Just so, where we take it that there's just one machine, sometimes taking in just one paper bill, there are actually (if there actually are any Coke machines at all) some several billions of overlapping such Machines, each taking in, during just a certain second or two, some several billions of overlapping bills. (But, of course, this isn't any terribly interesting problem, and it's certainly nothing that's metaphysically serious.) And, next, there's a Problem of the Many for Functional Experiencers. (Or, there would be such a Problem, if it made any sense to speak of anything remotely like Functional Experiencers.) Just so, where we might take it that there's just one Functional Experiencer, doing whatever it needs to do (for it) to feel very depressed, there are actually (if there are any real physical complexes at all) some several billions of overlapping such Experiencers, each doing whatever it needs to do (for it) to feel very depressed, with each of them doing that, presumably, just ever so similarly to all the others involved. (Now, even as this makes the Experiential Problem of the Many seem much less interesting, it's yet another indication of the inadequacy of functionalism, as a philosophical treatment of experiencers, or of experiencing, or of experience, or of anything of the like. Not that more indications are needed or, really, ever were needed.) Well, that's more than enough, I guess, about all of this sorry-sad functionalist business.

Look, I'm getting a bit tired of all this standard stuff in (what's called) the philosophy of mind. So, even if it may be a bit unfair now, I'm not going to pursue anything more in our paradigmatic instructional text, or our hopefully helpful anthology. Partly, that's because, as I think, once we've gotten past Descartes, we've left behind the philosophically most interesting material and, certainly, the most substantial material. (In fact, most of what remains is perfectly consistent with Berkeley's Idealism, even as nothing in the book presents the slightest reason, I think, for denying his brilliantly intriguing philosophy. But, let's pass over this now, since little good will come, I fear, from our dwelling on all the sadness of this whole sorry business.)

Anyhow, that's hardly the main reason, for my neglecting to further remark on those typical instructional volumes. Rather, the main reason is just this: I want to return to discuss some material that may be *much more relevant to* our present Problems. At the least, I don't want to discuss verbiage that is obviously all perfectly irrelevant. A big waste of time, that.

OK; let's suppose, if only for a moment, that materialism is true. Well, then, we're supposing that everything that really exists is something that's material. And, now, not being any nutty Eliminativists, let's agree that I exist, and you, too. So, then, we must conclude that I am a material thing and, not being me, you are another material entity. So far, so good; or, at least, so you might well think. But, now, let's look really hard, and very closely, to see what sort of material thing I might plausibly be.

It's not at all plausible to think that I'm a certain elementary particle, I should suppose, say, a certain particular electron. Nor is it the least bit plausible to think that I'm any much more complex physical entity, as with a certain water molecule, but none so complex that there'll arise any troublesome Experiential Problem of the Many. Rather than anything like that, I should be, for the sake of even just some initial plausibility, a tremendously more complex material thing than is any mere water molecule, constituted of many trillions of trillions of elementary particles (whatever else, also plainly material, might also serve to constitute me). But, then, *which* such constituted material entity am I?

Of course, we're now on the verge of just rehearsing, all over again, our Experiential Problem of the Many. Well, now looked at in what may be one pretty illuminating light, that problem is this: Apparently, there isn't any single material complex—and it had better be a single one, just as I myself am a single being—with which I may be plausibly identified. Heck, there's none that admits of anything like even just a halfway plausible physicalistic identification. Futility is followed by nothing so much as just yet more futility.

Here's another way of seeing the futility. Suppose that, as much as anything ever is, I'm a physical individual that's experiencing redly now. Fair enough. And, suppose that, in virtue of that, there's an event that's my experiencing redly now. And, suppose that, wonder of wonders, this event is the very same thing as a certain physical event, namely, the firing, right now, of a certain 8,999 R-fibers. Look; just suppose; OK? Well, as it surely appears, I won't be all alone in this. Rather, quite as much as with me, there will be billions of other physical individuals, too, each of them overlapping me greatly, and each of them very similarly involved with the firing of these very same 8,999 R-fibers. (Or, at the very least, and only if R-fibers are really terribly tiny things, there'll be billions each similarly involved with some 8,999 R-fibers now firing, with each of those firings serving quite as well, it certainly seems, for each of these others to be experiencing redly.) Well, then, what do we have here? Obviously, what we have is, all over again, our Experiential Problem of the Many. It's not that this Problem has been resolved, of course, not even in the least little bit. Rather, it's only been recast, and recast only very slightly, at that.

Well, that's enough about all this identification business. So, very quickly, let's take stock and, then, let's move on: In the last several Sections, I've argued that we should abandon our dominant Scientiphicalism and, in the bargain, we should also reject our initially promising Nonentity Emergentism. But, as I'm such a highly educated academic, that's very hard for me to do. Apparently, I need a good deal more help, psychologically, than what's afforded by the Experiential Problem. So, in what's next, I'll confront further thoughts that, as I hope, may help me become less fully embroiled with Scientiphicalism.

Of course, I'm hardly the only philosopher who, about matters lurking in our neighborhood, may need quite a lot of help. Who else do I have in mind? Well, for our mutual benefit, I'll now rehearse the words that began this Section:

> Crazy as it seems to me, quite a few current academic philosophers are quite prepared to live with the idea that, right now in my situation, there really are very many experiencers, with I myself being just one of the vast multitude. Though I don't have a whole lot of respect for this cockamamy and complacent reaction, still, in just a little while, I'll say some things that, for those Complacentists who bother to pay attention, should be highly disturbing propositions. Perhaps, they'll be disturbing enough, I should hope, for a few such Complacentists to take seriously a reasonably well worked out Substantial Dualism.[12]

So, quite as much as I seek help for myself, I'll also be seeking help for the philosophical folks that, without meaning them any truly terrible offence, I've called Complacentists. Anyway, with a wish to benefit both myself and others, I'll now aim to offer another Mental Problem of the Many.

12. The Problem of Too Many Real Choosers

For the Scientiphical View, and also for our noted Nonentity Emergentism, there's a mental Problem of the Many that's yet more unsettling, I imagine, than the Experiential Problem of the Many. I'll call

---

12. The quoted passage is from the first paragraph of this Section.

it *The Problem of Too Many Real Choosers*, and I'll turn to address this related Problem.[13]

Quite as with other folks, I'm more prone to imagine certain sorts of things than things of certain other sorts. For example, I'm far more prone to imagine a pretty woman than an ugly plant. But, with many sorts of things, there's little difference in my imaginative proclivities. For example, this may happen with my imagining a disc, or else a cube, or else a sphere, each option to exclude the others. Equally, this may occur with my imagining something wholly red, or else something all white, or else something just blue. With many groups of alternatives for imagining, I've no dominant disposition toward just a certain one of the options for me.

What's more, even with something I'm strongly prone *not* to imagine, often I can choose to imagine it nonetheless. For just a minute, think about that. Well, during that minute, I did some imagining: Counter to my proclivities, I just chose to imagine an ugly plant. And, because I chose that option for my imagining, I actually imagined a pathetic weed, very dry and brown. Dramatically put, the point of that is this: My power to choose effectively comprehends a very great deal of my power to imagine experientially.

In an easier area, I may choose among options for my imaginative activity where my proclivity for each *is* about equally strong, even if there might not be absolute equality. Well, just to provide an illustrative example of this sort, I'll soon choose to imagine experientially either a disc, or else a cube, or else a sphere. And, also for the sake of a helpful argument, let's suppose that the conscious experiential imagining I'm about to perform will be a *purely mental* act of mine, entirely isolated from the world's physical realm. Not only will this imagining not be anything physical, we'll suppose, but, as we're further supposing, it won't have any physical cause. And, as well, it won't ever have any physical effect, or consequence, or Propensitive manifestation. (Later, we'll drop this pretense of isolation.)

---

13. I should note that at least one other philosopher has noticed this Problem, or at least has noticed a quite similar Problem. After first properly crediting my old paper, "The Problem of the Many," Hud Hudson presents a Problem he calls "The Threat of Many-Brothers Determinism." This presentation is provided as Section Five of his First Chapter, a Chapter he names "The Many Problematic Solutions to the Problem of the Many," in his book *A Materialist Metaphysics of the Human Person*, Cornell University Press, 2001. As his book's title indicates, Hudson is concerned to deploy the somewhat different considerations he entertains to a very different effect from any I should choose to pursue. Oh, well, not to worry: Show me two philosophers and, on at least some philosophical issue, I'll show you two conflicting positions.

All right, I'm now imagining just one of the three mentioned sorts of simply shaped solids. Make a guess, please, as to which of the three I'm imagining. You might guess, I suppose, that I'm imagining a cube. Or, you might guess that it's a sphere I'm imagining. Or, you might guess it's a disc. Whatever you may have guessed, I'm now done with that bit of imagining. Now, as you'll recall, I said my chosen imagining won't have any physical manifestation, not even in its distant future. Sticking with that supposition, I won't ever communicate to you, in my (physically manifested) writing, what sort of shape it was that I actually did just imagine. At the same time, however, and just for the sake of instructive reasoning, we may make the mere *supposition* that it was a cube I just imagined. Let's proceed to reason from that mere supposition.

For the sake of helpful reasoning, I ask some questions: When I just put the question of this three-way choice as a little exercise for myself, did billions of very similar people, all of them in my situation, each similarly put the question to *himself*? And, when I made a choice among my three specified options for imagining, each an alternative to exclude the others, did each of them also effectively choose? How many of them effectively chose to imagine a cube experientially, the alternative that we're merely supposing I myself effectively chose?

If there really are vastly many people in my situation, then the only plausible thing to suppose about them is that, just like me myself, each of them has his own power to really choose. And, since this is a power to choose fully, and freely, from among actually available alternatives, *each* thinker's power may be exercised in a way that's *independent of the exercise of each of the others*, including, of course, my own choosing of what to imagine. This is a perfectly general point, and a completely intuitive point, about any real choosing. It applies just as much here as in any other circumstance, including one where, as you may recall, I chose to follow Buffet's lead and, so, I chose to buy some shares of Boeing. Just as my choosing, in that case, must be independent of Buffet's, in order for it to be some real choosing that I do, so, in the present case, each thinker's choice must be independent of all the other (overlapping) thinkers, in order for it to be any real choosing that any of these thinkers does (myself, presumably, just a certain one of these real choosers). So, it's only plausible to suppose, further, that when I made my effective choice to imagine a cube experientially, each of them made an equally effective choice to imagine, with each of the choices *made quite independently* of my choice, and each *made independently* of all the others.

Given just these apt assumptions, it would be an astounding coincidence, and not any credible occurrence, should all these billions of supposed people imagine a cube, each freely choosing to imagine the very sort of shape that, of the three specified exclusive options, I myself freely chose to imagine. (After all, we've been supposing that, no more than I myself am, *none* of these billions of overlappers is *much more* prone to imagine a cube than he is to imagine a sphere, or a disc.) Indeed, it would be extremely unlikely should there be, among the billions of choosers in my situation, under ten million real choosers who imagined a sphere, when I myself was imagining a cube. And, equally, it would be extraordinarily unlikely should there be, among the billions with independent powers, under ten million who chose, quite effectively, to imagine a disc experientially. With *any less* diversity of chosen shape images than *that*, among my overlapping physical-and-mental cohort of independent real choosers, there'll be *far* too little diversity for the outcome to be at all credible.

The point here is, in its essentials, quite the same as a point about choice concerning me and you, and billions of other relevantly independent choosers, thinkers who *aren't* largely overlappers, thinkers who *aren't* "in numerically the very same situation." For this case of "spatially separated choosers," or choosers with spatially separate bodies, and brains, we may playfully consider the most suitable two billion subjects, for a very widespread but temporally brief psychological experiment, selected from among the world's current population, which numbers over six billion. Now, as we may well suppose here, very few of these two billion has a tremendous proclivity toward imagining cubes, as against discs or spheres. The great majority has a roughly equal Propensity in each of the three specified directions. Well, let's suppose all those choices are made. Now, if it's proposed that under ten million of us chose, freely and effectively, to imagine a sphere, while almost all of us choose to imagine a cube, there's proposed an unbelievably great coincidence. Myself, I wouldn't believe in such an alleged outcome. Better than that overly coincidental nonsense, I'd go back and question various propositions that we were supposedly holding true. Was there, perhaps, mass mesmerization going on globally, so that almost all of us were made to imagine a cube, with hardly anyone really able to exercise his power to choose?

Whether the freely independent beings are overlapping or whether not, it's absolutely incredible, then, that *every last one of billions of real choosers should all* really choose to imagine a cube experientially, with *none* opting for a sphere, or a disc, when those two are, quite as forcefully, also presented as appropriate options. But, at the same time, it's not really credible, either, that there really was, in my situation, truly substantial diversity in conscious experiential imagining, when I was (supposedly) imagining only a cube. So, it's just incredible that, over-lapping with me right now, there are many other entities, many physical- and mental beings, who each *really do* choose.

In objection to what I've been saying, it might be proposed, there must have been something in my situation that prevented any of the overlapping choosers from effectively choosing otherwise than I myself did. Well, with this objection, there's just a refusal to accept the sup-positions of our discussion, a move that's quite inappropriate in this context. But, let's be very concessive to the objector, anyway. Being so very concessive, we'll be led to thoughts like these: Perhaps there may have occurred the barest beginnings of an attempt to imagine other-wise, to imagine a sphere, for example, but none of these came to anything. But, then, we should expect *some* difference between me, on the one hand, and the overlappers who barely began to choose oth-erwise. Perhaps they might feel some small surprise at how their imagining eventuated, when they found themselves imagining a cube, and not a sphere; or perhaps there'll be some frustration on the part of each of them, or whatever. At all events, there's to be expected, on the supposition of many overlapping independent real choosers, *some* real difference between those who quite directly choose to imagine a cube, and find themselves just so imagining, and those who make an effort, or a move, or a start, however small, in another imaginative direction. A perfect congruence, among all the real choosers, will be a quite incredible outcome, as each of the very many, we must continue to suppose, will proceed quite independently of the others. So, even if we make a great concession here, the objection still won't do anything more than take a question of incredible diversity away from one domain, where there's a diversity among what's successfully imagined, and move it to another domain, maybe making it a bit less conspicu-ous, but, still, leaving it all as just so very problematic.

In a couple of its variations, we've just observed the Problem of Too Many Real Choosers. As I suspect, for the dominant Scientiphical Metaphysic, this Problem is a quite insuperable difficulty. As I similarly suspect, the Problem also thwarts the Nonentity Emergentist View.

13. Wholly Immaterial Souls Favored over Emergentist Physical-and-Mental Complexes

On the Nonentity Emergentism we've been exploring, each of us is a physical-and-mental complex. By contrast with our severe Scientiphi-cal View, which has all our powers be physical Propensities, on this

Emergentism each of us will have, in *addition* to ever so many physical Dispositions, radically emergent nonphysical mental powers. And, each of us will occupy a spatial region different from that occupied by any other mentally potent physical complex, even those that greatly overlap the thinker in question. What this means is that our Mental Problems of the Many, and, in particular, our Problem of Too Many Choosers, has our Emergentism be an incredible view, just as much as with our beleaguered Scientiphicalism.

In the previous Chapter, we argued that Scientiphicalism is, in several ways, incompatible with our thought that we really choose, from among real alternatives for our thoughtful activity. Then, after offering those arguments, we observed that, at least apparently, our noted Emergentism was perfectly free of such Scientiphical Incompatibilisms, quite as much so as was Substantial Dualism. At the same time, this Nonentity Emergentism was a more conservative view, as it meant less of a departure from our Scientiphicalism than did a Substantial Dualist Metaphysic. So, as it seemed at the time, our Emergentism might be a more tenable position than any such Substantial Dualism, at least for the likes of us erstwhile Scientiphicalists. But, that was then; and, this is now.

In light of our current discussion, there appears a great difficulty for our Emergentism: On this Emergentist View, there'll be, in your situation right now, billions of physical-and-mental complexes, each overlapping many of the others, and each of them a real chooser, relevantly independent of all the others. But, as we've been observing, such a suggestion utterly defies belief, even when it's only the Experiential Problem that's born in mind. And, the suggestion becomes nearly intolerable when we confront the Problem of Too Many Choosers, and we realize the almost perfectly certain consequence that, from time to time, there'll be qualitative diversity in the chosen mental lives of very many (overlapping) physical-and-mental beings, with a certain one imagining an object with just a certain shape, and with another physical-and-mental complex imagining only very differently.

For our Nonentity Emergentist View, there's no credible response to this philosophic difficulty. Especially in such a "messily gradual" world as ours is, it's not credible that, among so many extremely similar physical-and-mental complexes, each of them a physical complex that so greatly overlaps so very many others, there should be just a single one that's endowed with real mental powers, including a power to really choose. Nor is it credible that, while each of very many complexes is endowed with such a power to choose, there's just one, alone among them all, that exercises his power to choose, at the time of a certain episode of conscious experiential imagining. What could it possibly be, pray tell, that's so selective in

favor of just the one that gets to choose? At least to my mind, any suggestion to any such effect is quite incredible. Nor is there any way, on this
Emergentism, for there to be a suitable singular resolution of this matter,
favoring just one of many overlapping physical-and-mental complexes, all
posited to be present in my present situation. But, without any such singular resolution, we've observed, there's a plurality of present conscious
experiencing, right now in my situation, that's perfectly incredible. And, as
our Problem of Too Many Choosers makes plain, there's even a qualitative
diversity, utterly incredible, in the chosen conscious experiencing, in this
selfsame situation. So, as far as we *now* can tell, in this present Chapter, the
Nonentity Emergentist View really *isn't*, for us, a tenable alternative to
Scientiphicalism. Among articulated options to Scientiphicalism, it certainly seems, a Substantial Dualism is the most conservative metaphysic
that, as of right now, is even the least bit tenable.

14. A Singular Physical Manifestation of Many Choosers' Powers to Choose?

In presenting the Problem of Too Many Choosers, I had us suppose,
for our consideration, only such choosing as was purely mental activity,
in no way at all physical, and even such purely mental activity as is
always causally isolated from all physical occurrences. That may have
allowed, I hope, for a presentation that was helpfully vivid. At all
events, it may now be good for us to explore situations where the
chooser *is* involved with physical occurrences. Apparently, this happens when an agent typically *communicates to others* what she effectively
chose to imagine.

    As before, I'll again choose to imagine either a disc, or else a cube,
or else a sphere. Well, I've just made my choice, and I'm now
imagining a geometric figure of just one of those three sorts. Well,
while that's still going on, I'm going to choose to produce a physical
signal of what it is that, because I just chose to imagine it, I'm now
imagining experientially. (Pretend, now, that I'm communicating by
writing on a pad, in your plain view.) So, it's an obviously physical
inscription I voluntarily produce, and which you then read, when I
effectively tell you it's just a sphere that I'm imagining, and neither a
disc nor a cube.

    In producing a physical inscription of the sentence form "I'm
imagining just a sphere, not a disc or a cube," I made a certain change
in physical reality. Before I did this work, we may suppose, there was

exposed an entirely blank sheet of paper; whereas, in consequence of the work, the paper came to have a certain inky inscription on it. And, this physical change I wrought was a real result, as we're sensibly supposing, of a choice I just made to just such an effect, my choosing to produce an inky inscription of that readily intelligible form.

Placing aside our previous worries, and that's placing aside a whole lot, maybe we can somehow make it palatable to ourselves that, in my situation, there were many millions of people choosing to imagine a disc, quite effectively, and millions of others effectively choosing to imagine a cube. Or, maybe we can't make it palatable. I don't know. But, in any event, let's now simply *suppose* that there just recently were, in my situation, very many overlapping choosers. Each quite independently of the others, and each doing so very effectively, many chose to produce a mental image of a disc, and many chose to imagine a sphere, and also many chose to imagine a cube. If such a supposition were to hold true, will *that* vindicate our offered Emergentism, with many overlapping physical-and-mental complexes?

No; it won't. Rather, even with that supposition, there'll still arise, or there'll still remain, this parallel Problem: With each of our shape options chosen by many millions, each independently of all the rest, *how is it that just those who chose to imagine a sphere* managed to produce a signal, a physical inscription, aptly conveying what (or how) *they* chose to imagine—while none of those who imagined a disc did anything much, in this regard, nor any of the millions who imagined a cube? Here's one specific suggestion, offered just as a sample: Maybe it's a matter of the numbers, as with a voting procedure; and, maybe more chose to imagine a sphere than chose a cube, or than chose a disc. Well, this suggestion may occur more frequently, or to more people, than most equally specific alternatives. But, even so, this "voting-thought" isn't any less absurd, I think, than other specific ideas, each apparently conflicting with it. Why not have it that, among all the sorts of imaginings of solid figures, the one that gets reported, or expressed, is the imagining of a figure with the highest ratio of volume to surface area? That's also quite absurd, but maybe not much more absurd.

Here's a little argument against the thought that there really might be some voting going on here, guided by whatever sorts of laws, or rules, or whatnots, with me myself always on one or another side of the outcome, and with many others each voting for each of the other salient outcomes, many of them voting along with my side and many others voting otherwise. (Or, maybe it's little more than a philosophical joke; I don't know. Either way, it may be good for you now to hear it.)

Well, all you political junkies, what about how successful I am, or at least appear to be, when I try to (supposedly vote to) physically express what I've just chosen to think imaginatively? Now, as I blush to admit, here's how all the allegedly relevant votes have, so far, appeared to me, all those where (along with each of so many (other overlappers) I've tried (or willfully "voted") to express just what it was (or how it was) that, in the instance concerned, I myself successfully chose to imagine. With very, very few exceptions, I seem to be entirely successful in the whole endeavor. Of course, once in a blue moon, I express something other than what I should mean to express, as happens with a slip of the tongue. But, in the attempts to express my chosen thinking, that's really quite rare with me. And, more to the present point, it's not any more common here than it is with attempts to communicate my thoughts and experiences, to you, where there's nothing even remotely like choosing ever involved. For instance, I'll make some slips of the tongue, or other useless noise, when telling you in detail, maybe on the telephone, about a passing Halloween parade, comprising many exotically costumed folks below me, that I see from my nicely placed Greenwich Village windows.

Anyhow, if there really is any voting with our conjectured many overlapping communicators, whatever the form or character of the conjectured procedure, I seem to be on the winning side in almost every instance, even if not quite absolutely every one (as I sometimes make slips of the tongue, and so on). Over long sequences of trials, my rate of success is nearly perfection. But, this will be a tremendous coincidence, tremendously lucky for me, I guess, and pretty unlucky, by contrast, for many choosers presumably overlapping me. Silly Willies are they all? Did they just choose to imagine like I did—however they might be presumed to know how I chose—so that, in following their charismatic leader(?), they'd have a wonderfully accurate record of thoughtful expression, quite as I myself do? Of course, that suggestion is absurd. Well, then, *how should it be* that, *unlike* the great majority of overlapping choosers, I'm almost always so very successful here? While what's just suggested may be a logically possible state of affairs, as we philosophers like to say, it's really not anything that's very credible.

Well now, it may be (jokingly) replied, somebody's got to have a long string of successes, with hardly any failures. Instead of any of your overlappers, or very many of them, anyway, why shouldn't you be the lucky stiff? But, really, dear reader, am I luckier here than you are, who are apparently so much more successful than are (the vast majority of) your overlappers? Am I vastly more successful than is your favorite aunt? No; give or take a trial or two, we're all very successful here.

Everyone we know is very successful. I'm not really a lot like a lottery winner in this—it's not that someone's got to win. So far as we can tell, there are almost all winners, and almost no losers.

For astutely remembering readers, the previous passage will resonate with passages that, in this very Chapter, they've already read. Indeed, from just the Section actually entitled "The Problem of Too Many Choosers," where our currently discussed Problem was introduced, they'll be able to remember, I reckon, (the main thrust of) some helpfully rehearsed words, all aimed at discussing a matter where, just as it was certainly specified, all the many choosers (presumably overlapping with me then) were each engaged only in trying to imagine something perfectly mental. As it was specified, you may recall, none of the choosers was ever to be involved, not in the least little bit, so far as his choosing was concerned, with anything physical. So, we were then confronting a different question, albeit a related issue. With that observed, please peruse these helpfully rehearsed words:

> Perhaps there may have occurred the barest beginnings of an attempt to imagine otherwise, to imagine a sphere, for example, but none of these came to anything. But, then, we should expect *some* difference between me, on the one hand, and the overlappers who barely began to choose otherwise. Perhaps they might feel some small surprise at how their imagining eventuated, when they found themselves imagining a cube, and not a sphere; or perhaps there'll be some frustration on the part of each of them, or whatever. At all events, there's to be expected, on the supposition of many overlapping independent real choosers, *some* real difference between those who quite directly choose to imagine a cube, and find themselves just so imagining, and those who make an effort, or a move, or a start, however small, in another imaginative direction. A perfect congruence, among all the real choosers, will be a quite incredible outcome, as each of the very many, we must continue to suppose, will proceed quite independently of the others. So, even if we make a great concession here, the objection still won't do anything more than take a question of incredible diversity away from one domain, where there's a diversity among what's successfully imagined, and move it to another domain, maybe making it a bit less conspicuous, but, still, leaving it all as just so very problematic.[14]

Now, with this passage before us, we'll articulate an obvious parallel: Where there's a sequence of many trials of choosing among options, to simply imagine, how should it be that, unlike so very many choosers

---

14. The quoted passage is from Section 12 of Chapter 7 above.

supposedly overlapping with me, unlike the vast majority of my many overlappers, I myself should find things, almost always, to flow so smoothly in the matter, with nary a hitch. As long as what's an option is within my known range—a six-sided figure, say, and not a sixty-six-sided figure—I always quickly succeed in imagining anything I make a start at imagining, or make any effort toward imagining. With so many supposedly choosing so variously, why am I among the select few easy-streeters? And, as I'm sure, you're on this easy street, too, along with your Aunt Sadie, your Uncle Joe, and also most others you know. Is there really such widespread good fortune? While this, too, might be a logically possible state of affairs, as we philosophers like to say, it's also not very credible.

So, listen up folks! Isn't it becoming pretty plain to you, and to you, and even to you, way over on the side, that there's no neat trick that will resolve, at all adequately, our Mental Problems of the Many. All that any neat maneuver ever accomplishes, so far as I can see, is nothing very different from this: The neat move takes one form of these Problems and, dressing it up, or dressing it down, it presents us with another form of the Problems. Nothing problematic is ever really resolved with any of that. Indeed, if anything transpires, it's just that we see ever more (forms) of our Mental Problems of the Many.

At least to my old and weary mind, all this brings home how incredible is the idea that, in anything like my present situation, there are very many real choosers or, for that matter, very many real experiencers, whether experiencing choosers or whether, say, just much more apathetic experiencers. Indeed, it's absurd to believe any proposition anywhere in that neighborhood: It's absurd to think that there are many overlapping people here—but only one of them has the power really to choose, or only one has the power really to experience. It's also absurd to think that there are many with the noted power, or powers, but, at any given time, only one sentient being gets to exercise the power. And, it's also absurd to think that there are many who exercise the power, but there's only one, or only a tiny minority, who regularly succeeds in (attempts at) saying how she exercised her power; and, so on; and so forth.

15. Do These Problems Favor Substantial Dualism over Its Most Salient Alternatives?

Recall our remarks about how *each of many* overlapping nervous systems, in my situation, might be one of *my* nervous systems: In what serves to constitute my overlapping nervous systems, there are Propensities to the effect that there's to be a limit placed—a limit of just one—on how many (consciously) experiencing particulars may be promoted by these overlapping systems. How so? There's a pretty plausible way for that to happen, I think, and, quite as we've already anticipated, it's this: Each of a system's simple physical constituents, as with each of its constituting quarks, has marvelous Propensities regarding how it may interact with very many other simple physical things, so that, in optimal arrangements for promoting conscious experience, there's an effective *singular resolution* as to what conscious *experiencer* they promote. And, in the same bargain, there'll be an effective *singular resolution* as to what conscious *experiencing* is promoted by them all.

It's hard to believe, we said before, that the single conscious experiencer thus promoted should be a complex physical thing, whether or not the complex should have radically emergent purely mental powers. For, as it surely seems, any good candidate for being the single conscious experiencing complex, in the situation, isn't a better candidate than each of many others, all massively overlapping and extremely similar. It's hard to believe that, somehow or other, *just a certain one* should have the power to experience, whilst all the others should lack the power. (And, it's *also* hard to believe that, in parallel with me right now, there are *many* highly similar conscious experiencers promoted, rather than just me consciously experiencing alone. And, it's *also* hard to believe that, in parallel with me, there are so many highly similar complexes promoted, with each of them doing something that's *very like conscious experiencing*, rather than there being just me alone, right here right now, who's doing anything much like that.)

Still and all, let's just suppose that, somehow or other, a certain single one of these many physical complexes is the only conscious experiencer, right here right now. Well, with that supposed, we should then ask this: What happens when, as will happen so soon, this experiencing complex loses one of its very many pretty peripheral constituents? Does this sole conscious experiencer go out of existence? That's incredible. Does it, rather, come to coincide with a just slightly smaller complex, previously "nested" in it, whilst becoming very slightly lighter than before this very slight loss? Even at first blush, this is hard to believe. And, almost directly, there arise further questions: With this hypothesized coinciding, will there then be an *experiencing* complex that's perfectly coincident with an *insensate* complex? That's not credible.[15] Alternatively, will there then be *two consciously experiencing* complexes, one previously experiencing and one, just now, only newly experiencing? This is also incredible. Is there a still further alternative that's much more credible than any of the suggestions we've just observed? Well, anything's possible, as we say; but I can't see anything that's very credible. With both our entrenched Scientiphicalism, and with our observed Emergentism, I'll submit, there's no credible resolution for the Experiential Problem of the Many. For folks so inclined to Scientiphicalism, myself included, this Experiential Problem is a quite disturbing difficulty.

And, in certain salient ways, we habitual Scientiphicalists might find the Problem of Too Many Choosers to be a still more disturbing difficulty: On the one hand, it's blatantly absurd to think that, at certain times, in my situation, there are many effectively choosing to imagine only a cube and, in consequence, they imagine just such a figure, whilst many others choose, just as effectively, to imagine only a sphere and, in consequence, they imagine in just such a different conscious experiential way. [This may be yet more disturbing, I've suggested, than the thought that there are, in my situation, very many conscious experiencers all experiencing very similarly.] But, it's also absurd to think that there's a *single physical complex* that's here the only real chooser,

---

15. Pretty much like this, though not entirely the same, a similar question is asked, and a similarly negative argument is offered, in Eric Olson's valuably lucid book, *The Human Animal: Personal Identity without Psychology*, Oxford University Press, 1997 (paperback, 1999). As the book's subtitle indicates, it's main thesis is that each of us is, most essentially, a physical complex that's a certain sort of biological animal, a human animal. Just so, how it is that you're Mentally Propensitied is, on this thesis, an accidental feature of yours; you lacked Mental Propensities when you first existed, when you were a quite early fetus; and, should you come to be in a persistent vegetative state, Olson thinks, you'd still exist, while entirely lacking (what I've been calling) all Mental Propensities.

Having little to do with considerations like that in the text and, so, on various very different grounds, I argue against any such "animalist view" in "The Survival of the Sentient," *Philosophical Perspectives*, 2000, reprinted in my *Philosophical Papers, Volume 2*. In that paper, I'm neutral between a psychologically-oriented materialist view of ourselves and, on the other side, a Substantial Dualist View.

For an extremely recent essay concerning questions of wholly coincident physical complexes, and very critical of any arguments like Olson's, and like this very most recent reasoning of mine, up there in our text's true body, there's Sydney Shoemaker's difficult and ambitious unpublished paper, currently called "Microrealization and the Mental," likely to be publicly available in the near future, whether with that same title or, just possibly, another. Unlike my essay "The Survival of the Sentient," which is no more friendly to materialism than to Substantial Dualism, Shoemaker's piece is meant, at least in largest measure, to advance only materialistically-friendly propositions.

with all the overlapping others being, somehow or other, quite choice-less here, or ineffective in their choosing.

In contradistinction to both our dominant Scientiphicalism and our observed Emergentism, I've recommended that we adopt, or at least we take seriously, a Substantial Dualism, not wholly unlike Des-cartes's seminal metaphysical view. For a few, I hope, this recom-mendation will appear, at this late juncture, to be at least a modestly sensible proposal. But, for more than a few, I fear, it will still seem, even at this late juncture, to be absurdly retrograde. In due course, I'll try to fuel the hope, and to diminish the correlative fear. But, right now, I'll be content to do little more than ask this question: What alternatives to Dualism remain for us as viable options now, each of them less of a departure from Scientiphicalism than is Substantial Dualism, and, maybe for just that reason, each of them a more palat-able option for erstwhile Scientiphicalists?

16. Some Less Salient Options to a Quasi-Cartesian Substantial Dualism

Let's now consider an option, or at least an alleged option, that may be associated with a name no less eminent than John Locke's, whether or not such a specific idea was actually Locke's own view. Anyway, on this alleged option, the idea is that, while each of us is spatially located, always at one or another spatial point, no one is ever spatially extended in space.

Well, I don't know about you, but I can't make much sense of this Lockean suggestion. For even as I must always be a real concretum, whether spatial or not, so any real spatial concretum will always be, in contradistinction to a mere empty spatial place, an entity that's Spatially Extensibly Qualitied, say, Transparent Red, for example. But, for something to be so Extensibly Qualitied, for it to be Transparent Red, for example, it must be spatially extended, with its Spatially Extensible Quality, its Transparent Red, pervading it. So, even if there should be spatially nonextended somethings, none of them will be any concrete individual (unless it be deeply analogous to a spatially extended thing and, thus, it be a *non*spatially (space*likely*) extended entity).[16] None will

---

16. Here I'm adverting to some analogically speculative ideas, quite nice ones, I think, that I barely sketched in Section 8 of Chapter 4: Maybe, just as Extensible Colors are suited for pervading Space, Extensible Sounds, even while they're not suited for Space pervasion, might be suited for analogously pervading, say, Sone, as I'll call it, a Spacelike dimensional aspect of concrete reality for which, conversely, Colors aren't suitable pervaders. Or, something like that.

ever be you, and none will ever be me. I'm sorry, but, at least to my mind, this alleged option isn't an intelligible alternative to Substantial Dualism.

Well, especially because it may help us segue into another option that we should also discuss, it's useful to say a bit more about this "Lockean ostensible option," if I may so label the suggestion. And, in this connection, I'll have us confront some comments from Chisholm, beginning with these:

> What if we suppose that the concept of an extended thing presup-poses the concept of ultimate nonextended things which, somehow, make up the extended thing? Could we then identify the person with such an unextended thing? I believe that this hypothesis would con-tradict the assumption *entia per se*. For I would say that the unextended things (boundaries, lines, points, surfaces) that are said to be pre-supposed by extended things are ontological parasites and not instances of *entia per se*: they depend for their own properties upon the extended things which are said to presuppose them.[17]

Just so, I can conceive, quite well enough, how there may be a Transparent Red Cube, with eight perfectly pointed corners, this Red spatial object then being a concrete entity "in its own right." But, by contrast with this pointy Cube, each of its eight corners is a mere ontological parasite, not any substantial individual. By contrast with anything like these mere corners, *I am* a real substantial concretum.

Now that we're in the business of quoting Chisholm, let's make use of some further sentences from the same metaphysical selection:

> The theory would be, then, that I am literally identical with some proper part of this macroscopic body, some intact, nonsuccessive part that has been in this larger body all along. This part is hardly likely to be the *Luz* bone, of course; more likely, it would be something of a microscopic nature, and presumably something that is located within the brain.[18]

Much later in the book, in its very last Chapter, there's a much fuller discussion of all this. But, anyhow, I doubt that Locke ever came within a country mile of thinking about these speculative matters. So, in this part of the book, right up there in the text, you don't really need me, I guess, to make the noted qualifications. Perhaps through unhelpful zealotry, I do it anyway, in the interests of greater potential metaphysical completeness and (maybe pedantic?) philosophical accuracy.

17. My quotation is taken from Roderick M. Chisholm, "Which Physical Thing Am I?" an excerpt from "Is There a Mind-Body Problem?'" which is selection 34 in Peter van Inwagen and Dean Zimmerman (eds.), *Metaphysics: The Big Questions*, Blackwell, 1998. According to those editors, this selection comprises sentences from two of Chisholm's publications, "Is There a Mind-Body Problem?" *Philosophic Exchange*, 1978, and "Self-Profile," in Radu J. Bogdan (ed.), *Roderick M. Chisholm*, Reidel, 1986.

18. See note 5 to this Chapter.

What point would there be in the hypothesis that certain individual things have the property of being nonphysical? How could that help us in explaining anything?

If I am a physical thing, then the most plausible hypothesis would seem to be that I am a proper part of this gross macroscopic body, even if there is no way of telling from the "outside" which proper part I happen to be.

I would suggest that, if this philosophic hypothesis seems implausible to you, you try to formulate one that is less implausible.[19]

On the hypothesis Chisholm's here considering, what sort of physical thing might you be? Well, at the very least, you're to be a physical thing that, throughout your uninterrupted existence, is always perfectly intact; for years and years, presumably, this physical thing hasn't lost any of its parts, however small and seemingly inessential, and, presumably, it also hasn't gained any parts, and, presumably, it hasn't suffered any great rearrangement of parts, either. Now, for you to be such a physical thing as that, then, as our scientific understanding of these matters has it, you should be a microscopic entity, maybe an elementary particle, like an electron. Or, more ambitiously, maybe you might be a hydrogen atom, very unlikely to lose, quite completely, any of its very few elementary particles. Or, still more ambitiously, perhaps you might even be something as complex as a particular water molecule. But, in any event, it would appear, you're to be a microscopic part of your gross macroscopic body, presumably one that's somewhere in your brain, or in many of your many overlapping brains.

(While what's in the present parenthetical passages will be just a digression for some, for other readers it may be very usefully helpful. For, though it's quite sad for me to say so, it's still true, as I'll depressingly note, that many professional philosophers cling to the notion that common parlance just so terribly often expresses commonsense belief and, what's more, almost all commonsense belief is true, or correct. So, quite as happens with some very smart undergraduates, largely innocent of philosophy, these philosophers think that when I standardly use the words "I weigh over one hundred pounds," or "I am over three feet long, or tall," I must be uttering the literal truth, contrary to any thought that I may be a certain atom. Or, much more commonly much more to the point, I must be contravening any soulful Cartesian thoughts, like the idea that I may be a nonspatial immaterial soul.

Now, as I'll far more happily notice, on this little matter, we may receive some help here, from each of many other philosophers, just

19. See note 5.

one of whom is Roderick Chisholm: After presenting his delightfully eccentric view, Chisholm presents five numbered objections, and replies. Anyhow, in this sadly commonsensical and drearily unimaginative climate, it may be worth reproducing here, I think, the briefest of Chisholm's five items, after which I'll make some remarks of my own. First, here's Chisholm:

> (3) "You say I'm identical with some microscopic particle or some subparticle. But I am 6 feet tall and weigh 175 pounds. Therefore your theory would imply that there is a certain microscopic particle which is 6 feet tall and weighs 175 pounds. But this is absurd and therefore your theory is absurd."
>
> The argument, of course, errs in taking too literally the premise expressed by saying "I am 6 feet tall and weight 175 pounds." For what the premise actually tells us is that I have a body which is 6 feet tall and weighs 175 pounds.[20]

Well that's Chisholm for you. Now, here's something from me.

While I'm in basic agreement with Chisholm here, I think he's too definite in saying that, with the words "I am 6 feet tall" I must be referring, if only obliquely, just to my body. Rather, the situation is much messier, I imagine. So, while I just might possibly be doing that, it's equally possible that I might be referring, quite indifferently, both to my body (or to my bodies) and also to the matter that constitutes it (or them). Or, as might happen on certain occasions, I guess, I might be referring only to the matter. Or, as might sometimes happen, I might be referring, indifferently, to physical things of, say, some six different gross sorts. Who knows? And, for serious philosophical issues, who cares?

Anyway, even while none of that very much matters, it can lead us into some instructive entertainment: Just so, I may say to you "Someday, maybe some billions of years from now, I'll be nothing more interesting than just so much interstellar dust." What am I referring to there, so that what I convey can be at least roughly right? Not my body, surely; not literally and quite truly so. For, at the time I reference, my body won't really exist anymore—supposing that it ever did. Or, as we *say*, "Then, my body will be nothing more interesting that just so much interstellar dust." Do I refer just to the matter that's now constituting my body? Or, maybe better, I may be referring to most of, or maybe just much of, that matter. For instance, maybe much of the relevant matter will be, someday distantly in the future, transformed into energy—a la Einstein, I guess—even while much of it will be, just as truly, just material

---

20. In *Metaphysics: The Big Questions*, this material appears on pages 293–294.

interstellar dust. If so, then I'll want to have it that my off-the-cuff remark turns out to be a correct prediction, or correct enough, *whatever* it is, exactly, that the remarkable prediction may mainly concern.

Moreover, and as Chisholm himself notices, urban car owners say, very frequently, the darnedest things. For instance, I might well say something like "Today I got lucky; I'm only about a block away, much better than last week, when I couldn't find anything nearer than eight blocks from here." Far more than conveying something that's just about myself, or even that's mainly about me, I'm commonly referring to my car, with such common words, and I'm saying something about where, in space, *it* is. This will be the correct interpretation of my centrally intended thought whether I be a Materialist car owner, or whether I be a Dualist car owner. And, with the Dualist, of course, *enormously more other* sentences will also be interpreted, somewhat messily but quite well enough, anyway, so that there's an apt oblique-ness to the message the thinker mainly conveys.

Very obviously, none of this is peculiar to just someone's talk about himself, or about anyone else for that matter. Just so, you have little trouble with understanding me when I say "Someday, maybe some billions of years from now, your car will be nothing more interesting than just so much interstellar dust." Since you're no dope, you don't have me telling you that, as I believe, there'll be a car that's just so marvelously lacking in cohesiveness, rigidity, and so on.

Well, that's the end of our little lesson or, for some, maybe just a tedious digression.)

As I was saying, just before I (parenthetically) digressed, it appears that, on the likes of Chisholm's eccentric view, you're to be a micro-scopic part of your gross macroscopic body, presumably one that's somewhere in your brain, or in many of your many overlapping brains. Why so? Well, a couple of things. First, and for what most worries Chisholm, if you were to be more complex than that, and so larger than that, you wouldn't last very long, as you'd lose one of your very many tiny simpler parts, which would be enough to do you in. Second, and for what most worries us here, things will also be very bad, even if not for quite the same reason. For, should the physical thing that's supposedly you be any much larger physical individual, or should it be anything that's physically very complex, then we'll cer-tainly have you be, as a matter of fact, very badly embroiled in the Mental Problems of the Many. So, on either sort of worry, there's this: If you should be a gross macroscopic part of your body, as with a healthy heart, perhaps, or, more plausibly, as with an active brain, there'd be very serious problems to be faced, just as serious as those confronting the thought that you may be a whole healthy human organism.[21]

As I'll now suggest, the hypothesis that you're a microscopic physical thing usefully divides in two. In turn, I'll consider both of the more specific ideas.

On the first of these thoughts, you're a physically simple thing, a certain electron perhaps, that hasn't any substantial parts, really, and, for that reason, you've got no part to lose. Now, even if we consider only such an electron as may be somewhere within your brain, and never one of those that's in one of my toes, this idea is, nonetheless,

---

21. At least in a note, I should say that Chisholm does offer considerations to motivate our rejecting the Scientiphicalist thought that you're a macroscopic physical body (even if, just perhaps, a big body that's specially "associated with" various non-physical Epiphenomenal episodes), and for preferring, over that thought, the hypothesis that you're always a certain intact microscopic physical object. First, he presents worries about the persistence of any sort of alleged macroscopic ordinary material thing, as with an alleged ship, or an ostensible rock, or a putative river. Any such thing as any of those, it's clear, loses some of its original parts, at least and in fact, over any time interval lasting longer than just a very few moments. As such, there may be a grave difficulty in thinking that any such thing persists, or continues to exist, in anything more than a loose and popular sense of "persists," or "continues to exist." Even for friends of ships, and friends of human brains and bodies, such things will be, in a important way, mere ontological parasites, parasitical upon more basic things, that continue to exist in a much stricter sense of the terms. Just so, in another selection, Chisholm writes this:

> In other words, persistence, in the loose and popular sense, through time ... presupposes persistence, in the strict and philosophical sense, through time. For it presupposes what I have called intact persistence. It is not implausible to say, therefore, that if there is anything that persists, in the loose and popular sense, through any given period of time, then there is something (perhaps not the same thing) that persists intactly through some subperiod of that time.

(This passage is from Chisholm's "Identity through Time," in H. Keifer and M. Munitz (eds.), *Language, Belief and Metaphysics*, State University of New York Press, 1970, reprinted in van Inwagen and Zimmerman (eds.), *Metaphysics: The Big Questions*, where the cited passage appears on page 181.) So, there that is. And, what's more, in quite a lot of his work, Chisholm makes clear his thought that none of us is any such "ontological parasite," to use his nice term. Rather, and as his idea has it, when you persist, from one day to the next, it's not that you persist only in the loose and popular sense. Far beyond anything like that, you exist in the strict and philosophical sense.

Now, if you're a physical thing, then this may mean that you must exist intactly, without the loss of even the smallest part. And, at any rate, it will mean that you're not any macroscopic physical thing, as any such thing as that, will, in fact, loose myriad parts, even from one day to the next.

Myself, I'm uncertain how much force to accord these motivating thoughts of Chisholm's. I don't find them to be directly compelling, I should say. Yet, neither do I find them to be wholly without force, as once I did, and as does the currently common assessment of such stringent ideas, quite as complacently commonsensical as it's leniently liberal. To my mind, all this wants protracted reconsideration, in one venue or another. But, this is not the place for that.

quite extraordinarily implausible. What's far more plausible is the thought that you can survive the loss of, and even the utter destruction of, any particular single electron, or any one quark, or any (other) quite basic microscopic material thing. Just so, the idea that I'm an electron is so very implausible that, rather than embracing such a thought, I *would* try to formulate a less implausible hypothesis, even if it might be, perhaps, an hypothesis along a Quasi-Cartesian nonphysical line.[22]

Though that's the obvious way to pursue the first specific idea, we may also pursue the thought far more speculatively. Perhaps you're an unknown sort of physical thing, maybe an elementary particle of a sort that's yet to be discovered, or that may never be discovered. So, you might be a certain *souletron*, let's say, a simple spatial concretum of a very special sort. And, spatially quite separate and distinct from you, I may be another souletron. Now, except insofar as they're spatial things, these souletrons are, in almost every other way, utterly unlike all the known elementary particles. Propensitively, this is blatantly the case. On the one hand, these souletrons aren't Propensitied in any pretty simple way, for interaction with any other physical things. They don't have any mass (or gravitational Propensity), or any electric charge (or electrical Propensity), and so on. It's because of this that they've never been discovered and, as we're supposing, they'll never be discovered. (Or, at the least, that will be so if we forego such Dualistic arguments as might, just possibly, serve to indicate the existence of souletrons.) And, on the other hand, unlike all the other elementary particles, both known and, presumably, also unknown, the souletrons, quite alone, will have special nonderivative (mental) Powers, including the Power to think, and the Power to really choose, and the Power to experience. Supposedly, it's only through some physically effective exercise of one of these special powers that, through protracted philosophical argument, we may reasonably arrive at the idea that there exists a certain souletron. So it may be, for instance, with an argument that starts from the thought that, in choosing to move a certain finger, a certain souletron may influence, quite peculiarly but utterly directly, a certain few electrons, each in the souletron's brain, whereby there's produced, further down the causal line, a stream of electric impulses aptly sufficient for moving the finger in question.

Well, I don't know about you, but, at least to my mind, the positing of these so-called souletrons strikes me as the worst sort of ad hoc thinking,

---

22. This idea can't be improved by saying I might be a simple physical-and-mental thing. For, any such entity must be a simple physical thing, of course, whatever else it also might be.

or very nearly the worst sort. And, in any event, the idea that I'm a certain single souletron is so very implausible that, rather than embracing such an idea, I *would* try to formulate a less implausible hypothesis. That's enough, I think, for suggestions that you really are, or that I really am, a certain quite simple microscopic physical individual.

Well, as I've already suggested, there's another thought being offered here, complementing the idea we've just abandoned, as to how you might be a certain microscopic physical entity. On this second idea, you're a physical complex, an individual with substantial physical parts, all right, but, still and all, you're a complex that's always perfectly intact, never losing any of your real parts (nor, presumably, gaining any such) for years, and years, and years. On this second thought, then, you might be, for instance, a certain continually intact oxygen atom, presumably, an atom that's long been somewhere in your brain, or in your brains, and that's always had the very same constituent particles. Or, you might be, just perhaps, something as complex as even a certain water molecule. But, to my mind, these suggestions aren't any more credible than the idea that you're a particular quark, or some other quite basic physical thing. Indeed, they're also so implausible that, rather than embracing the ideas, I *would* try to formulate a less implausible hypothesis, even if that might be, as I've suggested, an hypothesis along a Quasi-Cartesian nonphysical line.

Well, let's turn to consider physical entities each much more complex than water molecules, *so much more* complex that, at *first* blush, at least, it's *not* implausible that one of these complexes should be you, an individual who thinks, and who experiences, and, presumably, who really chooses. Imagine that there should be, in your situation right now, a certain very complex physical individual who's never lost any of his basic constituent parts, not even so much as a single electron.

But, then, what's the upshot of this hopefully helpful supposition? Well, unfortunately for those who would hold with the Scientiphical Metaphysic, or with any of its close cousins, the real result is nothing less than this: If there's at least one such individual (as we'll now be supposing) then, quite as we've been observing, there'll be very many such experiencing complexes. In your situation, all with you right here and right now, there'll be many of these experiencing complexes, if there's any of them at all. So now, this appears as the upshot of the hopefully helpful supposition: What's been gained in plausibility, at *first* blush, is lost, quite quickly, at *second* blush, so to say.

In contradistinction to suggestions about my being some sort of physical thing, and to suggestions about my being spatially located but not spatially extended, there's the further thought, yet to be pondered, that I'm a *spatially extended entity that's not physical*. As with the physicalist suggestions taken, or borrowed, from Chisholm, this hypothesis also nicely divides in two.

First, there's the idea that I might be a *simple* spatially *extended non-physical* concretum, without any substantial (spatial) parts. On this suggestion, I might be some sort of simple ghostly being, I guess, perhaps comprising some sort of Nonphysical Ghostly stuff, even if not, perhaps, comprising any ectoplasm. Nowadays, in any very respectable philosophical circles, a Nonphysical Ghost View, like this, if I may label it such, is hardly ever proposed. Indeed, in academically respectable circles, it's never taken at all seriously. Myself, I think more philosophers should take a Nonphysical Ghost View more seriously, well, at least somewhat more seriously, even though the View is more peculiar than it's plausible.[23] So, even while we may take this View more seriously, we should, at the same time, try to formulate, and try to develop, a somewhat less implausible hypothesis. We should do this even if the formulated conjecture might be, as it turns out, an hypothesis along a Quasi-Cartesian nonphysical line, where I won't be any spatially extended concretum.

Second, there's the idea that I might be a *complex* spatially extended nonphysical concretum, who *does* have various substantial (spatial) parts, though *none is any physical* part. On such a View, I'd be something like a ghostly "water molecule," perhaps, whatever that might be like. Though I should not reject such a view out of hand, I find it even less attractive than the pretty implausible Nonphysical Ghost View, just previously floated.

Then there are Hybrid Views. Indeed, it might be said that, along with his most official view, Descartes sometimes advanced a Hybrid, as when he said he was a *unit*, or some such, *comprising both* a certain single nonextended mind and some one particular extended body, suitably interacting. Of course, this Cartesian Hybrid contradicts Descartes's Official Substantial Dualism, on which he himself is only a perfectly nonspatial being.[24] Now, even as this Official Dualism avoids the Hybrid's blatant difficulties, it's to be preferred, I suggest, over the

23. See William Hasker, *The Emergent Self*, Cornell University Press, 1999, especially pages 189–192. Hasker offers an analogy with a magnetic field. But, then, as he insists, it's only an analogy. So, it's hard to know what's the actual view here, in any usefully positive and specific terms.

24. Look, little more than a big fan of Philosophy's Canonical Modern Figures, I'm certainly no Historian of Modern Philosophy, not even a very mediocre interpretive scholar. So, what I'm calling Descartes's Hybrid View may be vastly more simple than any position Descartes actually endorsed, with any real seriousness. But, in these pages, that doesn't much matter. For, the Hybrid View that I'm entertaining is, I think, a position that's instructive to consider. And, as I hope you'll agree, my consideration of it, in the text, leads us to some usefully instructive constructive ideas about which views may be, at this present juncture, among our most plausible options and, equally, which may be rather less plausible.

Cartesian Hybrid. That may be gleaned from only the bare beginning of a Q&A concerning the problematic Hybrid: Is my physical part just a certain physical simple, say, a certain electron? That I am partly a certain one electron and, in addition to it, the rest of me is just a certain nonphysical thing, well, this thought seems a quite incredible idea. Or, is my physical part, or parts, perhaps, ever so many largely overlapping neural structures, all somehow combining with my soul to constitute me? To me, that's also quite incredible.

For all I can tell, what I've called the Cartesian Hybrid View might even be an unintelligible position, inasmuch as it may claim that my soul and my body (or my bodies) are related constitutively, so as to compose me, in a way that involves more than just how it is that they are Propensitively interactive. Or, at the least, it might be unintelligible that this Hybrid is a truly distinct and distinctive View, substantially different from the Official Cartesian Dualism. Though I'm uncertain of that, it often does seem to be so. Being quite at a loss here, I am very skeptical.

But, suppose this skepticism's misplaced and, somehow or other, it's perfectly intelligible how some such Cartesian Hybrid should be a truly distinctive position and, what's more, a position that's completely coherent. (Or, at the least, let's pretend to suppose that much.) Even so, such a Hybrid certainly won't be a much more *credible* view than the quite unbelievable thought that I'm just a certain single electron. Indeed, I can't see that it will be even the least bit more credible. So, recalling what I said when closing our discussion of Chisholm's "Electron Self Hypothesis," I'll

---

For those who want a fair idea about just how simplistic is my take on Descartes, here, it may be useful to see some sentences from someone who really does know a lot about the central texts themselves, and really does have the ability to engage in adequately comprehensive textual interpretation. Just so, upon reading my passages about "Descartes's Hybrid View," my able colleague Don Garrett had this to say: "I don't think Descartes's Hybrid view makes the relations between my mind and my body to be more than causal, but they are special causal relations. Not only do my mind and body have powers individualistically directed toward one another, he thinks, but the mind has further powers to change what some of these powers are. The result of these individualistically-directed powers is that the mind-body complex has a 'nature' that goes beyond the non-relational nature of each. This warrants thinking of the mind-body complex as a complex substance with a more-than-accidental unity. It also allows him, for purposes of conciliation toward Catholics, to say that the human being is a kind of hylomorphic compound, with the soul constituting the form and the body the matter." Well, as you well know, like Descartes himself, I'm also very friendly to the idea of Individualistically-directed powers, and, come to think of it, I'd like to be friendly to many Catholics, too, at least the many who are reasonably tolerant of others' views.

Anyhow, some good news is this: However much I simplify, or mangle, the views of Modern Philosophy's seminal father, Descartes's exalted position in history will remain secure, long after all of us are dead and gone, dear readers—after it's all over for me, and for you, and for all the most able interpretative scholars who're now alive.

now say the same again, in closing our discussion of this Cartesian Hybrid View: It's so terribly implausible that, rather than embracing the View, I *would* try to formulate a less implausible hypothesis, even if it might be, perhaps, an hypothesis along a Quasi-Cartesian nonphysical line.

(Other Hybrids are, it seems to me, even less attractive than the one just discussed. Am I to think that I'm a wonderfully intelligible combination of a simple nonphysical soul and, say, a complex physical thing, a certain particular water molecule, perhaps? Rather than that, you can sign me up for the project of developing a Quasi-Cartesian Substantial Dualism that's not any Hybrid View.)

Besides a Dualism on which I'm a nonspatial immaterial soul, what else remains to consider, that's not so radical a departure from Sci-entiphicalism as an Idealist View? What are the other available meta-physical options? Though I certainly can't tell you anything much about any of them, perhaps there may be various almost-inexpressibly-far-out Views. Well, maybe so. But, at least until I complete this present work, where I mean to give Substantial Dualist Views a real run for the money, I think it quite fair not to worry, at any great length, about any such far-out claims as I'm not yet able to so much as sensibly entertain, or contemplate the least bit clearly.

17. Aren't Immaterial Souls Really Just Eliminable Middlemen?

Despite all I've so far said, some will still harbor the idea, I'm sure, that any wholly immaterial soul must really be an eliminable whatnot. In our philosophical economy, they'll be thinking, we're asked to pay quite a lot, while we get very little or, maybe nothing, in return. But, as I'm pretty sure, and with a pretty pun most certainly intended, this thought represents only what's a quite *wholesale* misunderstanding. Please let me explain.

As I've been allowing, each of very many largely overlapping brains, or largely overlapping bodies, may serve to sustain, in existence, a single wholly immaterial soul, a single experiencing real chooser. Wholly non-spatial, the sustained soul is really nowhere at all, quite literally. But, none-theless, she causally interacts, quite variously and quite often enough, with (at least many of) the material overlappers that sustain her. Well, then, why don't we get very economical here? Why don't we just take all the basic constituents, of all of these sustaining material overlappers, and simply say that they just constitute a certain happily fat material complex, rather rich in all sorts of (commonly believed) mental powers? Why not "go maximal" about all this, materially and, in that way, just have everything be a material thing or, at the least, have everything be nicely spatial?

Maybe doing nothing more than trying to turn a truly metaphysical issue into just some semantic spat, these self-styled economists haven't the least idea, really, as to what are the possibilities for any sensible philosophical investment. In reality, and as I've been repeatedly reminding folks, the actual situation is just this: In the case of each real human being, ever so many of her relevantly considered elementary particles, each of her electrons, say, serves as a backup body for, or as a tiny fail-safe for, each one of ever so many similar particles, or other electrons. Just so, there's not a single one of her electrons that's ever needed, really, for there to be an experiencer in her situation.

So, look folks, don't be fooled. Your own real situation is this: In any given second, for instance, at least one of the electrons in your "maximal brainy object" will be lost; indeed, quite a few will be lost. (And, generally, there'll be more electrons lost, in the second, than are gained; so, generally, folks, what we're here talking about are net losses.) Indeed, in such a long period as that, a full second, quite a few electrons will come to be too far away from the rest, or too poorly positioned. Because they've so strayed, they'll no longer be at all helpful, toward the generating of any experiencer, or any experiencing. Well, then, in the last several seconds, just while you were reading just a part of this very paragraph, that's happened with you, and with your electrons. Indeed, it's already happened, just so recently, some several times over. But, did there cease to be experiencing in your situation? Of course, not. And, in point of actual fact, it's for just precisely the reason we've noted: Every last one of your electrons serves simply as a (relevantly redundant) little backup body for, or as a tiny "fail-safe system" for, each of just so many other electrons of yours. Likewise, each one of your quarks similarly backs up, and is similarly backed up by, each of your other quarks. And, so it goes, too, for any other basic physical constituents, beyond your quarks and your electrons. Well, now, what we generously assumed to make good sense here, if only for a moment's pleasant pretense, heck, it really doesn't make any sense at all. Or, much the same, the maximalist suggestion from our self-styled economists hasn't any relevance for resolving our Chapter's central Problems.

Well, then, what will our self-styled economists do now? As persistently indefatigable as they may be unhappily immaterial, they might suggest that, perhaps, we should now move in the opposite dialectical direction. Maybe, they'll suggest, we should think that, among all the elementary particles said to subserve a single soul, there's a certain minimal group that's really doing all the relevant work. So, instead of saying that this "minimal brainy object" sustains a wholly immaterial experiencer, or a mentally powerful nonspatial soul, why don't we do this? Why don't we just take these comparatively few constituents,—oh, nothing like billions, mind you, and, maybe just around only 78 million, or so—and then say, quite economically, that they constitute a happily thin material complex? Of course, we'll then also say that, in addition to it's being so nicely materially thin, this svelte complex is nicely rich in all sorts of (commonly believed) mental powers. As they say, you can't be too thin, or too rich! Just so, why not "go minimal" about the material matter and, in *this* way, just have everything be a material thing or, at the least, have everything be quite nicely spatial?

But, of course, this is just baloney or, at the least, it's not any good salami. In the first place, it's extremely implausible, right off the bat, to think that there's any such unique barely sufficient group of basic physical constituents. Heck, it seems nuts to think that there's a just barely sufficient group of neurons, or nerve cells, whilst each neuron is constituted of billions of atoms, and of yet many more elementary particles. As compared with this, it's only slightly more nutty to think that you might be, really, just a certain water molecule, presumably one that, as we say, is somewhere in your brain. On this matter, here's the bottom line: As far as any real plausibility goes, in the first place we're already quite near the last place.

And, as only a second or so passes, things just go from terribly awful to even worse: In a short fraction of a second, typically you'll lose—as a net loss here—some several of your brainy basic constituents. But, on our "minimalist" hypothesis, currently considered, before this net loss you had just barely enough electrons to be a real experiencer—one less and you're out of the experiencing business. So, what are we to think here? Do you really think that you last for only a split second? Nah; far worse than even mediocre salami, that's just baloney.

In this short Section, we've considered, so far, only the Experiential Problem of the Many, not even so much as mentioning the Problem of Too Many Choosers. Well, that just changed. But, I won't change things much now, leastways not enough to turn this into any long Section. Rather, I'll just close by saying this: Were we to consider, in any detail, the Problem of Too Many Choosers, the clearly quite untenable lines of our self-styled economists would become, in pretty short order, even yet more clearly untenable maneuvers, all perfectly irrelevant to resolving the Mental Problems of the Many.[25]

25. In writing this Section, I've been aided by comments from Don Garrett and from Michael Raven.

(Though this isn't the best place to press the point, it's worth noting, even here, that there's also available a very different reply to those who say, confusedly, that our hypothesized souls are eliminable middlemen. In a nutshell, it starts like this: Even though it may comport less well with a (merely?) apparently scientific take on our world, still and all, some strong philosophic considerations favor the view that, once generated by brainily arrayed particles, immaterial souls need no sustaining by their generating brains, nor by any other physical entities. Now, in this present Chapter I'm being only quite moderately ambitious, as regards the sort(s) of *Emergentive Substantial Dualism* being advanced. So, it's only parenthetically that, right here, I sketchily start this very different reply. And, though it's no very great wait, we'll have to look to the next Chapter for me to give such a more robust Emergentive Substantial Dualism a decent run for the money. At the same time, and polishing off this present Section, I'll say that, as it seems to me, this is a good place to signal what we'll encounter in the Chapter next upcoming.)

18. Wholly Immaterial Souls Are Generated Abruptly, Not Gradually

In the previous Chapter's Twelfth Section, on Radically Emergent Beings with a Radically Emergent Power to Choose, I provided a very crude sketch, far too crude to be believable, as to how an immaterial soul might be generated by the interaction of material bodies, and as to how the selfsame soul, once generated, might interact with just a certain single body, or just certain bodies. At this point in the text, when we've more motivation for taking an Emergentive Substantial Dualism seriously, it's time, I think, to provide a somewhat more credible story.

To begin, I'll rehearse some words from the crude sketch I gave: When a quintillion Small Blue Particles are all within a Sphere of a certain Smallish Size, say, a centimeter in diameter, there will come into existence a metaphysically simple conscious experiencer. The same point put differently: Each Small Blue has the Propensity to generate, and then to sustain, a Cartesian self, or an immaterial soul, when it's within a Smallish Sphere with very nearly a quintillion others, each of them similarly serving to generate, and then serving to sustain, an immaterial soul. The emergence of a nonphysical mental being will be just *the manifestation of a Propensity of the Particles for a certain sort of generative mutual interaction*. What's more, from the first moment of her existence onward, and, maybe for just so long as she exists, each nonphysical soul will be in exceptionally close causal connection with just that one Blue Particle that, at the moment of the being's origination, was the physical concretum nearest the center of the crowded Smallish Sphere, that is, with just her sole *Central Small Blue*. (This may happen some seven months after the biological event known as "the conception of the being," by which time the fetal brain, in the mother's womb, has become a suitably complex structure. Anyhow, we may suppose the Central Small Blue is always in the midst of the many Small Blues that, at any moment, serve to constitute what's then the being's suitable brain.)

Moving along with our illustrative exposition, we recall that, for so long as she has any close causal connection with any physical individual, then, each emergent Cartesian being will always be in closer causal connection with her Central Small Blue than with any other basic physical thing. (As we may further suppose, our conscious experiencer will be in somewhat less direct causal relations with many other Blue Particles, each of them interacting, pretty directly, with her own Central Small Blue. That being so, certain of these interactions may constitute the workings of our being's sensory system, even as they may aptly affect the conscious experiencing of the mental being.) Thus, the soul's Central Small Blue will have Individualistically-directed Propensities, for affecting just that soul, as with affecting it perceptually. And, for its part, the generated soul will be reciprocally Individualistically-directed Propensitied, for being affected by that Central Small Blue, as with its being experientially affected as a manifestation of perceptual interaction.

On something like the other side of this same coin, the willing soul may quite directly affect its Central Small Blue Particle, less directly affecting, thereby, such other Particles as the affected Central Small Blue may itself, in turn, affect. Thus, this generated radically emergent soul will have Individualistically-directed Propensities, for affecting that Central Small Blue Body, as with affecting it willfully. And, for its part, the Small Blue Body will have reciprocal Individualistically-directed Propensities, for being affected by that nonspatial soul, as with its being affected so willfully, maybe ensuring no causal closure of the physical realm.

As I've so recently remarked, this sketch is incredibly crude and, in just a few moments, I'll replace it with a more complex sketch that's rather more credible. But, before that, I should notice a point that holds true, I think, whether the more complex sketch is more accurate or whether, alternatively, it's a very simple sketch that does most justice to our hypothesized Dualistic nature.

That central point is this: For any Emergentive Substantial Dualism to be properly credible, it should hold that there are some absolutely abrupt conditions for the generation of a generated soul, and for the sustained continuation of a generated soul. Here's an illustrative example of how that might happen: Right before our quintillion Small Blues are all in our one-centimeter Sphere, when there'll be conditions conducive for their generative interaction, there may be as many as a *quintillion-minus-one* Small Blues in the one-centimeter Spherical region. But, that's *not* yet enough, not *quite* enough, for (any of) the Small Blues to engage in soulfully generative mutual interaction. And, right before our quintillion Small Blues are all in our one-centimeter sphere, there may be a quintillion Small Blues all in a Sphere with a diameter of 1.0000001 centimeters. But, that's *also not* yet enough, also not *quite* enough, for (any of) the Small Blues to engage in soulfully generative mutual interaction. Just so, unless conditions are *just* right, in all sorts of relevant ways, there's simply *no soul* generated in the considered situation. But, *once conditions are* right, then, all at once, a single soul *is* generated. In this strong sense, the conditions for generating souls are *abrupt* or, equivalently, they're *all-or-none*.[26]

This is very different from what happens with the building of a house, for example. Without quite enough bricks arranged housewise, say, on a certain site, there won't be, on that site, a complete brick house. Still, there may well be *something of* a house there, and even quite a lot of a house. Perhaps, there may be only an incomplete house, so to say. But, then, it's *not* true that there's *nothing of a* house there. With our immaterial souls, as I've said, there isn't any comparable incompleteness, nor anything like the gradualness found in the case of any such ordinary house. Rather, without there coming to be a real soul, in any given situation, there *won't be anything of* a soul, in that situation. Quite certainly, there *won't* be any merely *partial soul*, or *incomplete* soul, whatever any of that might mean.

Even with a soulless natural object, indeed, even with one that's alive, there's much the same gradualness, it appears, as what's found with our artifactual brick houses. Consider a seed, even a seed that's properly taken to be more alive than dead. Since our seed is nicely ensconced in fertile soil, recurrently well watered, and so on, it will grow, eventually,

---

26. At very considerable length, and offering all sorts of interesting passages, Parfit argues that the conditions of our existence aren't all-or-none, which is a central theme of Part Three of his *Reasons and Persons*, Oxford University Press, 1984. Myself, I follow suit, in that respect, in my *Identity, Consciousness, and Value*, Oxford University Press, 1990. As I now believe, the both of us may have just wasted our time, and our energy, even while we enjoyed so much energetic philosophical activity.

into a mature plant, say, a mature rose bush. But, all of this is gradual. There's no single second when, so far as there being anything of a bush in our situation, everything's generated. Rather, as the developmental processes gradually occur, there gradually comes to be more and more of a bush. (Or, if nihilistic sorites arguments are really as powerfully undermining as sometimes they appear, then, maybe only something only very roughly like that will be true.) By contrast, on the Substantial Dualism I offer, nothing even remotely like that can be said, in truth, of us immaterial souls, myself included.

So it is too, with the relevant sustaining of us souls, myself again included among them. As it might be, in certain possible Worlds, maybe including this actual world, what goes on when what's bodily serves to sustain a soul is, in its essentials, rather like this: For just so long as there's (at least) a quintillion Small Blues all together in a one-centimeter sphere, they'll mutually serve to sustain the soul that, when (at least) so many of these Small Blues were first in the sphere, was the single soul then generated by the Small Blues, through their soulfully productive mutual interaction. And, at least for such souls as may be mortal, complementary statements also may be truly made, perhaps including a judgment much like this one: Should there come to be *less* than a quintillion in the noted one-centimeter spherical region, then it will be true, in this World we're considering, that there's *no* soul sustained. Rather, in just such an abrupt event, the single soul that (as we're supposing) they produced, and they later sustained, well, it will abruptly cease to exist. And, just precisely at that moment, there'll be the absolute the end of that very soul, quite utterly out of the existence business, completely and forever.

In the present context, sustained continued existence is the opposite of soulful cessation. So, even as the sustaining of a soul will be abrupt in many ways, or along many dimensions for consideration, so it will also be, quite equally, for the cessation of sustained souls. If there should come to be, for instance, a quintillion Small Blues in just a *very slightly larger sphere*, say, in a sphere with a diameter of 1.0000001 centimeters, then it will (also) be true, in this World we're considering, that there's *no* soul sustained, not by any of these Small Blues we've been contemplating.

Just before, we observed that, without there coming to be a real soul, in any given situation, there *won't be anything of* a soul, in that situation—not any merely partial soul, nor any merely incomplete soul, nor anything of the like. This is very unlike what happens with the gradual growth of a brick house, and even a living rose bush. On the other side of the coin, we'll now observe, much the same obtains. Just so, when a soul ceases to be, that's also absolutely abrupt; there's *never* any situation when there's *just something of* a soul present. This is utterly unlike what may happen with a brick house, as when, say, just some several of its pretty peripheral bricks are removed. And, it's utterly different, as well, from what may happen with a living rose bush, as with one that's very heavily pruned, but, still, not fatally pruned.

Let's be terribly clear about all this: When a certain number of a certain house's bricks are removed, far more gradually than explosively, then it might be true that there's *just something of* a brick house in the situation [assuming, of course, that there really are some brick houses]. This will be so, in certain circumstances, even when there's no longer any brick house in the considered situation. But, with our immaterial souls, I'll repeat, there isn't ever any such happy gradualness, nor anything even remotely like it. When a certain soul ceases to exist, it can't be that, even so, there's then *something of* the soul. No; that's perfectly absurd.

(As I'll be happy to grant, it may be that there are immaterial souls that will exist forever more; in that sense or respect, they'll be immortal. But, for the present discussion, it should be obvious, that's neither here nor there.)

With such immaterial souls as may ever cease to be, their cessation must be perfectly abrupt. Quite absolutely, then, the existence of all our contemplated souls is always an all-or-none matter, never anything like a merely gradual affair, whether happy or unhappy.

In several earlier publications, I'll hasten to admit, I argued that, even as the actual world was a pretty thoroughly gradual world, so the conditions of our own actual existence were relevantly gradual conditions (even if not conditions requiring, for their satisfaction, some completely continuous phenomena).[27] But, that was then; and, this is now. When I advanced those old arguments, I assumed, I now realize, something much like the Scientiphical Metaphysic. Or, at the least, I assumed that some such Scientiphical View was more nearly right than was any Quasi-Cartesian Dualist Philosophy, with its advocacy of nonphysical mentally potent individuals. (Much less did my assumptions allow any truth for, say, a Berkeleyan Idealist Philosophy, a View affirming that all real individuals are nonphysical mentally potent individuals.) Having done all that way back when, I wish now to be perfectly clear as to my present very different view. We should place to the side all such Scientiphical endeavors, as well as any fairly conservative Nonentity Emergentist work.

---

27. Heck, I did this in about half a dozen earlier publications. To list them here now would serve little purpose, I think, so I'll spare you this bit of tedium. Besides, in other notes to this Chapter, there's occurred, or there will occur, more than enough mention of my own earlier writing.

And, at least for the meanwhile, we should undertake, in their stead, such endeavors as may help develop a highly intelligible Emergentive Interactionist Substantial Dualism.

Before closing this Section's discussion, concerning the conditions of our existence, I'll notice that our most *intuitive* idea is that these questions must always receive a clear-cut, yes-or-no answer. And, equally, concerning the nature of these questions, our most *intuitive* idea is that they're very substantive issues, as deeply metaphysical as you please, in no wise any merely semantical questions, or logical questions, or anything of the like. For example, the question of whether, in some certain situation, a soulful you actually exists, well that's always utterly unlike any query concerning whether, in this or that apparently puzzling quasi-residential situation, there's a certain brick house still existing. And, very likely, it's also utterly unlike any query concerning whether, in this or that apparently puzzling horticultural situation, there's a certain bush still existing.

Though he's famously opposed these most intuitive ideas, and he recurrently opposes them, Derek Parfit takes great pains to observe that these intuitive thoughts strike us, over and over again, with very great force, and not any force that ever very much dissipates, no matter how much argumentation we may ever attempt to bring against the ideas.[28] In line with this, and at least since Descartes, many philosophers have observed, quite rightly, I think, that the burden of argument certainly lies with those wishing to hold otherwise. In earlier publications, as I've admitted, I tried to shoulder this burden.[29] But, as I'll repeat, I now believe I didn't attain any success at all. And, as I also believe, nobody else has attained, even at this late date, significantly more success.

So, in closing this Section, I'll suggest that these deeply intuitive ideas, whose great force hasn't ever been successfully displaced, may be yet another consideration forcefully favoring a Quasi-Cartesian Substantial Dualism over of its more fashionable rivals.

---

28. An excellent example of this is Derek Parfit's extremely engaging thoughts about himself in Part Three of his *Reasons and Persons*. It's not for nothing that he titles that Part's first Chapter (Chapter 10) "What We Believe Ourselves to Be" and its second Chapter (Chapter 11) "How We Are Not What We Believe." Another clear example of this, I now realize, comes with much of the work I myself offered, when struggling with central themes of my *Identity, Consciousness and Value*.

29. Trying to exploit an idea to the effect that (something like) gradualness attends the existence of sentient beings, I wrongly tried to make one sort of big deal out of this, very negatively, in my old essay, "I Do Not Exist," in G. F. MacDonald, ed., *Perception and Identity*, 1979, reprinted in my *Philosophical Papers, Volume 2*. Trying to make another sort of

19. Our Own Souls and the Wholly Immaterial Souls of Nonhuman Animals

With very few and sad exceptions, as with the brain-dead, and as with an infant born without a developed cerebrum, we human beings are relevantly powerful experiencers, able to experience very variously indeed. By contrast with oft-repeated remarks to that effect, I've said very little in this book, so far, about other sorts of experiencers, as with such canine experiencers as those we call *dogs*, for example, and as with such "chimpine" experiencers as we call *chimpanzees*. Well, right now, it's high time for a big change.

Unlike most of my philosophical contemporaries, I think that, in his most central philosophical writings, Descartes upheld only a very few truly nutty beliefs (and, most of the time, I believe, he had pretty interesting reasons for affirming even these few looney propositions). Anyhow, among Descartes's truly fruitcake philosophical ideas was the thought that, even where you can't help but think there's a cat before you that's feeling terrible pain, there's actually only a fleshy entity that's never involved in any feeling at all. Intellectual genius though he most certainly was, I'd say that, as regards this matter, it's Descartes himself, and not the poor cat, who wasn't sufficiently involved in feeling. But, heck, nobody's perfect.

Anyhow, quite as fervently and firmly as you do, I believe that, very often, very many cats experience very painfully, and, very often, too, many cats consciously experience in other ways—often experiencing visually, often experiencing tactilely, and so on. And, so it is too, I'm quite confident, with many dogs, and many mice, and, most certainly of all, with our distant cousins, the chimpanzees.

Well, now, just as the Experiential Problem of the Many obtains in the case of us humans, so it also obtains, and for perfectly parallel reasons, in the case of them there cats, all over our neighborhood. That's pretty certain, I believe. And, quite certainly indeed, it obtains

---

big deal out of the same misguided idea—this time very positively, but, of course, just as wrongly—I took a quite opposite approach in my just somewhat less old book, *Identity, Consciousness and Value*, Oxford University Press, 1990. Now thinking myself to have erred both times—and, each time erring quite oppositely from the other's unsuccessful effort—how much confidence do I have in this present book's position? Not much, you can be sure; not much at all. But, it's not the main purpose of philosophy, I believe, to arrive at the full truth about any central philosophical questions. If that were the main purpose, then almost any really active and truly distinctive philosophical thinker, should she have even the least bit of a sensible perspective on her overall activity, should give up the field quite early in life, generally not very long after turning thirty.

in the case of our chimpine cousins, whose bodies are no further from me than is the widely celebrated Bronx Zoo. Now, whether or not you think the Problem of Too Many Choosers also arises, for these chimps—and I, for one, certainly think it does arise for them—there can be little doubt that, just as with you and me, so, with them too, there arises, at the very least, our Experiential Problem of the Many.

Now, as I've been arguing, for the case of us human experiencers, the best resolution of this problem, or the intellectually most attractive so-lution, is that, wherever there are very many healthily normal over-lapping human brains and bodies, as with the billions of them apparently right there in your very own house (or in your overlapping houses), each group of relevantly overlapping bodies, or overlapping brains, serves to sustain, in existence, just a single immaterial experiencer. In your case, of course, it's the single immaterial soul that's you (or, as some might prefer to say, it's the single soul, your sole soul, that's the most essential part of you, or aspect of you, or whatever). Equally, I'm now suggesting, we may also argue, in a perfectly parallel manner, and with very nearly as much force, that, wherever there are very many healthily normal canine brains and bodies, with each brain so largely overlapping just so many others, well, all these (overlapping) canine bodies, or all these (overlapping) canine brains, serve to sustain, in existence, just a single immaterial ex-periencer. This may happen, for instance, with your neighbor's dog, providing only that you have a neighbor who has a dog. So, in such a circumstance, the single immaterial soul is what's really your neighbor's dog. Or, at the least, it's just this soul that your neighbor should care most about, so far as his concern for his dog is concerned. For, it's just *that*, the single soul that's interacting with all those canine brains and bodies, that feels weary when, as we say, your neighbor's dog feels weary. And, it's just *that* which, when the canine bodies are badly injured, will so typically feel severe pain.

From very many established perspectives, both philosophical and otherwise, this Section's main point is, I think, a quite radical idea. After all, folks, that point is nothing less than this: *Not just* where we ordinarily take there to be an organism that really chooses, and, what's yet much more, *not just* where we ordinarily take there to be an organism that really thinks, in anything like the ordinary sense of "thinks," but, *even* where there's only (what we typically take to be) an organism that *merely feels*, it's an immaterial being, a wholly nonspatial soul, that's the feeling concretum. So, if a lobster feels great pain when placed in a pot of boiling water, then, at least at those times (and, presumably at other times, too) lobsters have souls, to use a nicely colloquial expression.

How "far down" must we go here, if there's to be a rightful recognition of all "this planet's" immaterial souls? Do earthworms have souls; or, much the same, are there earthwormy experiencers that, as with other suitably singularly resolved beings, really are nonspatial immaterial beings? For the philosophy we're advancing here, it's not crucial that we answer these questions. Rather, for present purposes and endeavors, we should take our arguments as pieces of reasoning for just so many merely conditional propositions. Which conditionals? Here's an obvious representative: *If* it's true that, in what we ordinarily take to be a situation where there's an earthworm impaled on a hook, there's something feeling pain, *then* there'll be, interacting with just so much earthwormy matter, a perfectly immaterial and nonspatial experiencer. Or, to put the point more colloquially, we may say that, if that there worm's feeling pain, then it's a worm with an immaterial soul.

20. Metaphysically Material Ruminations about Extraordinarily Different Gestations

Just a couple of Sections back, I'm sure you'll recall, I argued for the idea that Wholly Immaterial Souls Are Generated Abruptly, Not Gradually, and I went on to explain, in just a bit of detail, why that should be so. And, in the Section just following that one, which this present Section itself directly follows, I advanced the idea that, among all the immaterial experiencers closely (Propensitively) associated with this planet, the earth, we human beings are hardly alone. To the contrary, there are both Our Own Souls and also the Wholly Immaterial Souls of Nonhuman Animals. Thinking about both recent Sections at once, some may think to make, at this present juncture, certain objections to the happily generous Emergentive Substantial Dualism I've been placing on offer.

Each much like the others, a representative objection runs like this: "At reasonably early stages, in the development of the human fetus, what's in the mother's womb (or what's in the overlapping wombs of the overlapping maternal bodies) resembles, in deeply striking ways, what's in the mother's womb (or the overlapping mothers' overlapping wombs) of a chimpanzee fetus, at certain *correlatively early* stages of *that* gestational development. And, come to think of it, at *quite* early stages, what's in the human mother's womb (maybe just an embryo, but maybe even so much as a very early fetus) resembles, in striking ways, what's in the mother *mouse's* womb, at certain *correlatively early* stages of *that mousey* gestational development. Now, even as the gestational period for mice is quite short, it may well be that, just after a very few weeks, a mouse fetus is (neurally) developed enough to experience pain. So, in the case of the mouse, on your view, there'll be a soul generated just a few short weeks after the mousey zygote's formation—that soul's being generated, of course, by the fetally arrayed matter that's then in the mommy mouse's womb.'

Well, at least for the sake of an instructive argument, with that much I'll allow myself to agree. Why? Well, with my agreeing to just that much, I don't think that, in my generosity, if that's what it is, I've become embroiled with any philosophically serious difficulty. But, then, of course, our objector won't yet be finished. What more might he say?

Our objector may now continue rather like this: "Though it may take somewhat longer in the case of human gestational development, than in the case of the mouse, it won't be very much longer until there's a human fetus that, in striking ways, resembles what was in the mommy mouse's belly when her mousey little fetus (supposedly) first generated a mousey soul. Pretty plausibly, I guess—I certainly don't really know much about these things—in the human case it may take about twice as long. At any rate, something roughly like this will be true: After just a couple of months of human gestation, there'll be, in the human mommy's belly, a little fetus that resembles, in striking ways, what was in the mommy mouse's belly when, after just about a month, say, her developing fetal matter first generated a wholly immaterial soul. Well, then, on your Dualistic View, it now seems we should suppose that, after just a couple of months of human fetal development, the fetally arrayed matter, that's then in the human mommy's belly, will similarly first generate a wholly immaterial soul. But, in point of fact, in the course of human gestation, that's far too early for there to be generated, with any significant degree of plausibility, a human soul. Rather, *if* a human soul is *ever* to be generated, in the course of a human's gestation, it will be a good six or seven months after the human zygote first formed, and maybe even longer. So, even just so far as you've already specified the position, or you've already developed the view, the Emergentive Substantial Dualism you're offering can't be even the least bit plausible."

For philosophers not much stupefied by their philosophical education, it should be quite obvious what's gone greatly wrong with the objection we've been considering. Let's suppose that, quite as I've allowed myself to agree, at a pretty early stage of its development, the experiencing mouse fetus resembles, in striking ways, a quite early human fetus, say, one that's just two months from conception. Well, even if this should be so, it may also be true that, in various *other* ways, the two fetuses will substantially differ. And, if we believe that the two-month old *human* fetus is *not* yet an experiencer, and doesn't interact with any immaterial experiencer, then, of course, something quite like this must also be true: Concerning what a fetus may need for *any involvement with experiencing*, the human fetus is *quite different from* the mousey fetus. So, look, this objection really isn't about the generation of souls per se. It should offend any sensible materialist, for goodness sakes, quite as much as it should any decent dualist. So, with *either* sort of metaphysician—or, really, with any intelligent reader—they'll reject it almost right off the bat, or nearly quite out of hand. As far as this Chapter's main issues go, I'm sure, this objection is premised on material that's all utterly irrelevant material.

What's more, it's premised on badly false (utterly irrelevant) material. Lacking a good biological education, I've long thought there was some important truth, whatever exactly it might be, expressed by the famous slogan (wrought by one Ernst Haeckel) "Ontogeny recapitulates phylogeny." But, apparently, there's naught but crap anywhere in this famous slogan's vicinity, which neighborhood is, evidently, a big garbage dump. Indeed, about all that, biologists at Berkeley say nothing less than this:

> Ernst Haeckel, much like Herbert Spencer, was always quotable, even when wrong. Although best known for the famous statement "ontogeny recapitulates phylogeny," he also coined many words commonly used by biologists today, such as phylum, phylogeny, and ecology. On the other hand, Haeckel also stated that "politics is applied biology," a quote used by Nazi propagandists. The Nazi party, rather unfortunately, used not only Haeckel's quotes, but also Haeckel's justifications for racism, nationalism and Social Darwinism.
>
> The "law of recapitulation" has been discredited since the beginning of the twentieth century. Experimental morphologists and biologists have shown that there is not a one-to-one correspondence between phylogeny and ontogeny. Although a strong form of recapitulation is not correct, phylogeny and ontogeny are intertwined, and many biologists are beginning to both explore and understand the basis for this connection.[30]

But, anyhow, for our inquiry, Haeckel's errors are hardly a main item. For, as I recently remarked, just before providing the displayed tidbits from California, the sort of objection this Section's discussing is all

---

30. These quotes are from the Web pages of the University of California Museum of Paleontology, which is part of the University of California at Berkeley. Within those Web pages, the specific address is: www.ucmp.berkeley.edu/history/haeckel.html.

According to its Web pages, the museum's mission is this: "The mission of the University of California Museum of Paleontology is to investigate and promote the understanding of the history of life and the diversity of the Earth's biota through research and education." Well, I don't know about you; but, my citations from this source seem quite credible to me.

perfectly irrelevant to any interesting questions about the existence of, or about the nonexistence of, any alleged immaterial souls. In particular, then, it's irrelevant to questions concerning such immaterial souls as may comport well with the Emergentive Substantial Dualism that, on recent pages, I've been advancing. Indeed, it's utterly irrelevant to any claims for emergent immaterial souls made by any even halfway decent Dualism. It's irrelevant to any decent dualistic claims for such souls as may be interacting with our human brains, and our human bodies, and, quite equally, it's irrelevant to correlative claims for such souls as may be interacting with many chimpine brains, and many chimpine bodies, saliently including those in the Bronx Zoo.

21. People and Nonhuman Animals Again: Might All Souls Be Equally Powerful Individuals?

Against the claims of anything like an Emergentive Substantial Dualism, where each and every soul is a substantial immaterial individual, what impresses ever so many folks, I fear, are facts like these: When there's a lot of alcohol in your blood, including, of course, the blood in your brain, you can barely think straight—indeed, with a very great lot, you'll pass out, becoming quite unconscious. When people suffer certain lesions, or wounds, to certain parts of their brains, they appear to lose certain of their mental powers, including even some quite central mental powers. So, with certain areas damaged, you'll no longer be able to enjoy, or to suffer, any more visual experiencing. With others damaged, you'll no longer be able to experience auditorally. And, then, there are even sadder cases. On a PBS program, concerning cognitive functioning and the brain, I saw, at considerable length, the plight of a man whose brain had been attacked by a certain virus, years ago, the attack itself lasting, I think, for just about five days. In consequence, this man, previously a concert pianist, was quite unable to consciously remember his past personal life and, to boot, he was also unable to form new memories (going forward, so to say) from his currently ongoing experiences and activities. While he certainly remembered how to write, and he even quite compulsively composed a journal, he kept writing (what was essentially) the same paragraph over, and over, and over again. Pathetically, it went something like this: "I'm going to keep a record of my activities now. I must remember to write specific things down, so that later I'll be helped to recall what's recently happened to me." Time and time again, on one page after the next, that's all he wrote. In keeping with all that, there was this: While he could still play the piano beautifully, and remembered the most difficult pieces from the classical repertoire, he was perfectly unable to recognize his nurse, as anyone at all familiar, though he'd seen her just several minutes ago, before she left his room to get him some food or drink. Nor was he able to recognize his own wife, who visited him on a daily basis, even though they had been married for years, quite devotedly, well before the onset of his viral attack. Who can observe the likes of this and be an Interactionist Substantial Dualist? Doesn't all this show, very well, indeed, that there's nothing more to anyone's mind than whatever his brain allows or, more broadly, than what's allowed by an almost all-powerful physical reality?

For those who've read quite this far in my book—heck, even for those who may have been skipping over most of its previous pages—it should be obvious that such facts as I've just related are entirely irrelevant as to whether, or whether not, any Substantial Dualism is true. Particularly at this late stage, I sure won't sing any long song about this for you. But, here's a short little something that, even if it's only for a few needy souls, might prove instructively helpful.

Look, having been heavily involved with professional philosophers for over forty-five years, now, I've come to know a great many learned academics and, in the bargain, thank goodness, a couple of actual philosophers. Well, let me tell you something. Even among the most modestly talented of my many academic acquaintances—not any very tiny group, to say the least—there's hardly anyone dopey enough to think that, with facts like the stunners related near the Section's start, it's a short step to a convincing case against *Berkeleyan Idealism*. Of course, there's nothing remotely like that ever to be found, not anywhere in the neighborhood, folks, including even the outermost psychological and physiological boroughs. Fair enough?

Well, think about this for a minute: While being perfectly neutral with respect to a Berkeleyan metaphysic, how will such supposedly stunning truths be devastating to a Cartesian philosophy? Indeed, how will they to be so much as the least bit problematic for any Substantial Dualism that's even just moderately ontologically serious? No way; it's just not possible. Indeed, it's only the most complacent confusions that should ever have matters so much as appear to be otherwise.

But, then, if they're all just so completely irrelevant here, why did I mention these undoubted truths? Why, then, did I relate these facts about how greatly someone's experiencing, and her remembering, and her other "psychological activity," so to put it, all depend on what she's got—and, correlatively, on what she's *not* got—by way of anything like a healthily normal human brain? Well, as I see it, dear reader, it's a potentially effective way of getting you to be involved, along with me, in contemplating certain neglected philosophical propositions that, at least to me, appear enormously interesting.

What ideas are these terribly neglected thoughts, currently all quite thoroughly ignored by almost all possessed of philosophically respectable academic credentials? Roughly put, they're some thoughts to the effect that each soul might be, as regards its own Propensities, or powers, the exact equal of every other soul. (Well, maybe that's a *bit* too much; but, just as well, maybe it's *just* a bit too much; and, just maybe, it isn't too much.)

(Thinking about this possibility, or this apparent possibility, can be, I believe, a great deal of philosophical fun. For that reason alone, I think it's well worth my trying to get you involved in it, even if it may be only quite slightly involved.)

Now, as my own experience here seems to show, it may be helpful to approach these potentially enjoyable philosophic ideas, very gently, and only quite obliquely. So, rather than directly engaging the soulful ideas themselves, I'll start by discussing some other ideas that, while they're evidently terribly different thoughts, may still serve, even so, as an approach to the intriguingly elegant idea that all souls are Propensitive equals (and to the somewhat intriguingly elegant idea that each soul is, at the least, quite nearly the Propensitive equal of all the other souls).

Well then, you may well recall that, just some several Sections back, I discussed a delightfully eccentric view of Chisholm's, a view on which Chisholm himself was a certain microscopic physical individual—say, a certain electron. (Presumably, and as plausibly as possible—but not necessarily—this mentally powerful electron will be an electron that's always in Chisholm's brain, well, at least from the date of his birth until the time of his death. Or, on our more considered reckoning, it will always be, at each moment of Chisholm's existence, in each of his very many overlapping brains.) Now, while this is an outstandingly implausible view—at any rate, to my mind, it is—well, even so, it has a certain undeniable charm. What's more, and as you'll also recall, Chisholm considers five numbered objections to his eccentric view, replying to each one right after it's mentioned. Here's his second numbered objection, along with most of Chisholm's reply to it:

> (2) "Persons, being thinking beings, must have a complex structure. But no microscopic entity that is known to physics has the equipment that is necessary for thinking. After all, you can't think unless you have a brain. And *those* little things don't have brains!"
>
> The hypothesis being criticized is the hypothesis that *I* am such a microscopic entity. But note that I do have a brain. And therefore, according to the hypothesis in question, the microscopic entity has

one, too—the same one that I have, the one that is inside my head. It
is only a confusion to suppose that the microscopic entity—which in
fact may be inside my brain—has *another* brain which is in fact inside
of it.

The brain is the organ of consciousness, not the subject of
consciousness—unless I am myself my brain. The nose, similarly, is
the organ of smell and not the subject of smell—unless I am myself
my nose. But, if I am one or the other—the brain or the nose—then, I
the subject, will have some organs that are spatially outside of me.[31]

Well, as this reply is silent on matters of how the specially personal
electron is Propensitied, it's only the barest beginning for what might
be a more fully adequate reply. But, still, it is, I think, a pretty nice
start. And, with a couple of small alterations—going more lightly on
how people themselves must have a complex structure, and dropping
the bits about what's spatially outside what—a pretty parallel passage
may serve pretty nicely, I think, toward starting to say how a soul, like
you yourself, perhaps, may use its brainy equipment, or interact with its
brain(s), so that it may engage in thinking, even including some pretty
impressive philosophical thinking.

Pretty nicely, I said, not wonderfully well. But, that's all right. Look,
all I'm trying to do, right now, is get us to entertain some ideas; I'm not
claiming the ideas are any very credible propositions. That's it; that's all.
So, let's just entertain this thought, or think about this bare possibility:
Much as all the currently actual electrons may be very similarly Propensitied, each one Propensitively quite like every other electron—well,
at least as concerns all their Generalistically-directed Propensities—so it
may be, too, that all souls may be very similarly Propensitied, at least as
concerns *their* Generalistically-directed Propensities.

Approaching it all from a very different direction, here's another
way to get the hang of the idea: In a certain world, there may be very
many talented musicians, each exactly as talented as all the others. As
far as her Propensitive profile goes, each can play excellently, or as
excellently as the instrument will allow, on any of a hundred different
sorts of musical instrument. Just so, one of our musicians may have,
available to her, a grand piano, while another may have, available to
her, just a kazoo. Now, in such a case, the first musician will engage in
far more complex music-making than will the second musician, and
in much more impressive musical activity. But, that's not owing to
her having greater and more impressive musical powers. Rather, it's
owing to the better musical equipment, or the more complex physical

31. Again, see note 5 to this Chapter.

music-making partner, with which she has the chance to interact. Both musicians are extremely good, and they're equally able, at making music with a grand piano. And, similarly, they're both very able at making music with a kazoo—well, at that, they're both just as good as anyone can be. So, it's just because *she has a better interaction partner*, in her having a grand piano, that the first musician will be able, in fact, to make much more impressive music than the second, whose only relevant chance lies with her available kazoo.

What I've just offered is meant to be a helpful analogy, nothing like any full and perfect parallel, nothing like any sort of identity. Even so, it may have been helpful enough for me to proceed.

Now, as I'm going to suggest—heck, this really *is* just a suggestion—it might just possibly be that your soul, or the soul that's really you, is Propensitively profiled much the same as is the soul of your neighbor's dog (or the soul that's really your neighbor's sentient pet). No doubt, you're able to engage in much more complex reasoning than that soulful pet can manage, and in reasoning that's much more impressive ratiocination. No doubt about that, I'm happy to agree. (As is only appropriate, *this isn't* any discussion about epistemological skepticism concerning other minds, I hope I needn't remind you. And, as I'll also hopefully observe, that hopefully quite gratuitous reminder *isn't* any suggestion that all such other discussions are philosophically unimportant, or uninteresting. Quite to the contrary, I'm happy to agree that some are very interesting. Still and all, that's no reason to change the subject. And, accordingly, I won't change the subject.)

Why is it that you engage in much more complex reasoning than that soulful pet ever manages to do? As I'll boldly suggest, it might *not* be because, so far as reasoning goes, in your soulful Propensitive profile you've got more reasoning power than what's that soulful pet's Propensitive mental nature. Rather, as I'm suggesting, it's just because (or it's mostly because) you've got a much better brain to interact with, so far as engaging in reasoning goes, than does the soul that's set to interact with what's only a canine brain. (You've got a grand piano, so to say; she's got just a darned kazoo. Especially as compared with the guy nicely set to interact with his concert grand, what are we to expect from the poor soul who's got, available for interacting, just a kazoo?)

So, in its most extremely elegant form, here's the suggested deal: Propensitively, each and every soul is just enormously well-endowed, and each equally so. Some get generated by pretty powerful human brains—so, they may come to have, over the course of anything like normal human learning opportunities, a very good array of matter to interact with, for engaging in quite a lot of interesting thinking. Others get generated by mouse brains. So, being Individualistically-directed with respect to just those puny brains, these materially deprived souls never come to engage in much interesting thinking.

(It takes no great imagination, at this juncture, to see that these enjoyable ideas may fit neatly with certain doctrines about reincarnation. There's a lot more to do, of course, if we're to have available, in any articulate form, any such serially spectacular view that's a fully coherent position, and a view that's pretty impressively comprehensive. For one thing, and very importantly, it must be worked out how, surviving the demise of your brainy body, and no longer having Individualistically-directed Propensities with respect to any material thing, the immaterial soul who you then are may come to have, maybe after a long period of "disembodiment," and maybe only some several years later, such singularly directed Propensities with respect to some quite distinct matter, say, some largely Asian particles that come to be, some several years from now, the basic physical constituents of a baby cow (or overlapping baby cows) somewhere in Hindu India. Well, this Chapter isn't the best place for that. (In the next Chapter, however, I will discuss these difficult issues.) Just so, I'll now turn to consider some very different questions concerning how we're Individualistically Propensitied. Unlike anything needed for the far-out likes of reincarnation, these issues really must be addressed now, if we're to have, any time soon, a decently plausible Humanly Realistic Philosophy that's a Emergentive Substantial Dualistic Philosophy.)

22. Bodily Flexibility as Regards Individualistically-directed Soulful Propensity

For a Substantial Dualism that's even just modestly credible, about as much as can be expected in the current intellectual climate, I must provide more than the starkly crude sketch (first offered in the prior Chapter and then rehearsed in this present one) featuring a so-called Central Small Blue Sphere. What we want here is, of course, a sketch that comports much better with certain main lines of our received scientific belief. In this Section, I'll take a couple of steps toward that goal.

Right off the bat, we'll do better to think that, when your soul first existed, say, some seven months after "your biological conception," there wasn't just a certain one elementary particle, or a certain single atom, that, among all the physical concrete particulars, was alone in being Individualistically Propensitied with respect to you, a certain particular nonspatial immaterial soul, with just these two quite simple individuals aptly Propensitied, reciprocally and Individualistically, for a nice variety of mind-body interactions. Instead, we do better to think that, upon the generation of your soul—or upon the generation of you yourself—there were very many elementary particles each one of which was Individualistically Propensitied with respect to just that nonspatial mental being who was you, when first you existed. We do decently well to think, I'm suggesting, that when (at least) a certain minimal number of these nicely Propensitied particles (and maybe, as well, no more than a certain maximal number) were in one of some certain range of physical spatial arrangements, then you first felt pain, which may have happened, just suppose, exactly 0.1156 seconds after you first existed. And, when a certain (perhaps different) minimal number of them were in one of a certain other range of arrangements, well, that was when you first felt warm; let's say, or let's happily enough pretend, that was exactly 0.0437 seconds after you first existed. And, similarly, with your first experiencing in other rudimentary ways.

Well, right there, we've taken a big step, I think, toward offering a more palatable Dualistic story, more plausible than what we had with talk of your having a Central Small Blue Sphere. But, we now need to take, toward this same end, at least one more big step in the same scientifically informed direction. Quite directly, I'll say what that is.

With the exception of your nerve cells, you lose many cells every year and, in the gradual process, you gain new cells in their place, at least by and large. Over the course of something like seven years, there's a complete cell-for-cell replacement of all your cells, other than nerve cells. That's widely known, of course. What's not so widely known, I imagine, though it isn't a very recondite fact, either, is this: Even with your neurons, there's a mammoth changeover of constituting matter. So, each of your neurons loses, over time, almost all its original electrons, for example, even as it gains ever so many new constituting electrons, by way of a gradual replacement process. In a palatable Dualist story, which is to be a suitably conservative sketch, of course, facts like this must be accommodated. How might that be done?

To advance the discussion, we should now say something like this: While serving to help constitute your brain, or many of your overlapping brains, each of very many electrons, for example, is Individualistically-directed with respect to you, an immaterial nonspatial entity, quite as are many similarly constitutive protons, and also neutrons. But, as I've indicated, when time goes on, your brain(s) will lose many of these nicely Propensitied electrons, even while gaining other electron constituents in their stead. Now, at our scenario's outset, each of the eventually gained electrons *isn't* Individualistically Propensitied with respect to anything; in particular, each isn't so Propensitied with respect to (the immaterial soul that's) you. But, for a palatable Emergentive Substantial Dualism, the matter shouldn't remain this way. So, what are we to do?

As we may usefully speculate, when a previously "outside electron" comes to be in apt proximity with enough electrons (and other basic physical whatnots) that have been constituting your brain(s), and still are doing so—or, much the same, when such an erstwhile outsider comes to be close enough to enough electrons (and other basic physical whatnots) that are each Individualistically-directed with respect to you—well, what then happens is that this erstwhile outsider comes also to be Individualistically-directed with respect to you, quite as so many of its new neighbors still are. In this way, there may always be, in suitably nice physical arrangements for soul sustaining (and for apt mentally modifying interaction with the soul sustained) plenty of electrons (and other basic physical whatnots) each properly Propensitied. Just so, there may thus be, in apt arrangement, more than enough electrons to sustain a wholly immaterial you, and to interact nicely with this nonspatial you, throughout (almost) all your body's (or your overlapping bodies') long biological lifetime(s).

With electrons that *move far away from* those constituting your brain(s), so that they're no longer among those so nicely arranged for that, they'll cease to have any of the Individualistic Propensities, with respect to you, that they previously enjoyed. Or, so we may usefully speculate. Given what the previous paragraph's already provided, it may then be ensured, in this way, that there'll always be a nice number of electrons (and a nice number of quarks, and so on), each Individualistically Propensitied with respect to you. Not only will this be a number that's nice for any such soul sustenance as you might require, but, as well, it will be a number that's nice for interesting both-way mind-body interactions. Just so, for anything of interest here; there'll be neither too many aptly Propensitied electrons for the interesting item, nor too few, either; and, there'll be neither too many quarks nor too few, either; and so on.

In a couple of upcoming Chapters, I'll be offering various other Forms of Interactionist Substantial Dualism, some also Emergentive, some others not. On some of these other Forms, whether Emergentive or not, you'll long survive the utter death, destruction, deterioration and dissemination of everything about you that's even the least bit organic, or biological. On these Dualistic Views, you'll survive even if it should happen that, quite suddenly, all your body's matter, or all your many bodies' matter, should become naught but widely scattered elementary particles, as with the least cohesive sort of "interstellar dust." But, quite as much as does the sort of Emergentive Dualism being advanced right here and now, in the present

Chapter, each of these other Dualistic Views will also require, if it's to be at all palatable, or plausible, a story much like what's being sketched right here and now, in the present Section. For, whatever form of Substantial Dualism we should ever adopt, it must comport, very well, indeed, with propositions to the effect that, right now, you're an *embodied soul*, so to speak. Or, much the same, it should comport, very well, with statements to the effect that, right now, you're a soul that *does have* a body (or that does have overlapping bodies). At least during times like right now, when you've got a "biological life," you'll be, on any plausible Substantial Dualism, an immaterial soul *who's engaging in much mind-body interaction*. So, for all these "biologically lively" years of yours, on any attractive Substantial Dualism something like this will be required: For your experiential modification in conscious perception of physical complexes, for example, there mustn't be too many electrons that are each Individualistically Propensitied for modifying you in appropriate experiential ways, and there shouldn't be too few, either. Sound familiar? It certainly should. So, even if you should be truly immortal, still, very much of the account now wanted will be similar, in all essentials, to what we've provided just above, for souls each presumably quite mortal indeed. In point of fact, except for a lot of the business about sustaining, of course, what's wanted by any decent Substantial Dualism will be something that parallels, very closely indeed, the sort of metaphysical story I've been suggesting.

Well, that's quite enough of this, for now; with much more I'll be getting far ahead of myself. So, I'll now get back to what's currently our main track, even while I say that, much of what's next upcoming, on this main track, should be incorporated into quite a wide variety of Substantial Dualist Views, if any of those Views is to be any very plausible Metaphysic.

With just so much as what's been so far presented in this Section— which isn't very much, at all, I reckon—there's been provided the central thrust of a pretty palatable Emergentive Interactionist Substantial Dualism, plausibly enough dovetailing with what we take to be the emergence, in human gestation, of such sentient beings as we ourselves may be. But, then, the central propositions already offered should, themselves, all be well integrated with the serious sort of ontology that, in much of this book, we've been felicitously developing. And, so far, that's not been done. So, directly, I turn to that task.

Now, quite as a matter of accident, an electron may gain certain Propensities, including certain Individualistically-directed Propensities. (And, quite by coincidence, an electron may lose certain Propensities, too.) But, in the sketch we've just been providing, that's not what I've supposed to have happened. Rather, when an electron first came to be Propensitied in a certain way, perhaps even Individualistically, its coming to be so Propensitied was *itself the manifestation of a certain Propensity already possessed by the electron*; presumably, it's a Propensity possessed, quite equally, by all electrons (or, at the least, by very many electrons). So, each electron (or ever so many of them, at least) will be Propensitied in some such way as this: Should the electron come to be in one of certain conducive conditions, as when nicely arranged with neighbors that are already Individualistically Propensitied with respect to a certain soul, then that electron will also be, even if for the very first time, similarly Propensitied with respect to that selfsame soul. Even as (just about) any electron is already replete with *this* Propensity, so it will be that, whichever electron should happen to be "gained by a certain nerve cell," so to put it, well, that electron will have been, all along and from time immemorial, ready-to-go in just the respects that are here so crucial. So, quite for *that* reason, it will partake in apt reciprocal interaction with neighbors already so nicely Individualistically Propensitied. And, then, as a manifestation of just such interaction, this newly gained electron will come to have (and, so, then, it *will* also have) the appropriate Individualistic Propensities for interacting with just the very soul in question, the selfsame soul that its nice neighbors have been sustaining (and the selfsame soul they've been mentally modifying, and so on).

Eventually, and as may be expected of a two-year-old soul, let's say, there'll be a radically emergent nonspatial being with the power to really choose and, to boot, the power to make many physically effective real choices. When that happens, the nonspatial chooser may influence, quite directly, some of the electrons that are Individualistically-directed with respect to it, each already Individualistically Propensitied, quite aptly, to be affected by it. Now, when this happens, then some of the electrons, now so directly affected so soulfully, will be pretty newly acquired; they *won't* be among those that served to generate the soul, say, some seven months after the biological conception in question. But, of course, quite along lines like those sketched just above, they'll have come to be aptly Individualistically Propensitied, in just such a way that, right now, they're each well suited to be wilfully influenced by just a single nonspatial real chooser.

For this present quite exploratory work, which is, really, just so terribly exploratory, this is enough, I trust, to provide a pretty palatable sketch of a decently plausible Emergentive Interactionist Substantial Dualism.[32]

32. In writing this Section, discussion with Matthew Kotzen was usefully stimulating, as was discussion with Michael Raven.

23. Taking Stock and Moving On

Both in the previous Chapter and in this present one, we've been offering arguments against Scientiphicalism, and also against any Materialist Metaphysic. As far as I can tell, the arguments placed on offer are entirely novel pieces of reasoning, quite unlike anything already available.[33]

Now, it's not because I think there's no force in any of the older arguments that I've bothered to articulate new considerations against the aforesaid metaphysical conceptions. On the contrary, I still find some force even in Descartes's famous old argument for his own distinctness from everything bodily, an argument from his ability (but, maybe, from what's merely an apparent ability) to really imagine himself existing, even without there ever existing anything that's bodily, or that's material, or that's concretely spatial.

And, I find some force, too, in this less famous thought of his: Though all material individuals are (spatially) divisible, and, though he

33. For far more standard pieces of Dualist reasoning see, first, of course, Descartes's argumentation, as it was Descartes who set the Dualistic standard for almost all subsequent authors who've subsequently written on behalf of Dualism, including almost all those in our present day and age.

On behalf of his Substantial Dualism, concerning mind and body, Descartes offered two main arguments. Renditions of both may be found in his *Meditations*; and, more specifically, both may be found in the Sixth Meditation. For that, those who don't know languages beyond just English, myself included, will do well to see *The Philosophical Writings of Descartes*, trans. J. Cottingham, R. Stoothoff, and D. Murdoch, Volume 2, Cambridge University Press, 1984. In this volume, the more influential of Descartes's two main arguments, which might be called his "Conceivability Argument," it may be found on p. 54. And, the less influential argument, which might be called his "Indivisibility Argument," that may be found on p. 59.

In the first note to this present book's Sixth Chapter, I notice a couple of recent Dualistic arguments that, in my view, aren't all that different from Descartes's Conceivability Argument, including arguments by Saul Kripke and by David Chalmers.

In some several of his writings, Richard Swinburne also offers an essentially similar argument for Dualism. Perhaps, it's in his multi-edition book, *The Evolution of the Soul*, that Swinburne argues most thoroughly for Dualism, the first edition appearing in 1986, from the Oxford University Press. According to Dean W. Zimmerman, an expert assessor of Dualist Argumentation, in this first edition, Swinburne's Cartesian arguments mainly appear on pages 145–160 and pages 314–315. Anyway other students of such Argumentation will do well to see Zimmerman's engaging essay, "Two Cartesian Arguments for the Simplicity of the Soul," *American Philosophical Quarterly*, 1991.

In the revised edition of *The Evolution of the Soul*, Oxford University Press, 1997, though there is little change in the body of the text, there are added some seven New Appendixes. As concerns argumentation for Dualism, the most salient is the new appendix C, "The Modal Argument for Substance Dualism," comprising pages 322–332. In addition to setting out an unabashedly Dualistic piece of reasoning, this Appendix replies to some critics of the first edition, Zimmerman among them.

himself is a perfectly paradigmatic individual, still, he really isn't (spatially) divisible; all that being so, he's an *im*material entity, an individual who isn't anything material at all. (Indeed, I still find *some* force even in some of Berkeley's arguments, against the existence of anything nonmental—though that's lately been diminished, with my coming to think about individuals as Spatially Extensibly Qualitied.)

At the same time, however, I also find some force in certain *objections* to the previously available arguments against Materialistic Metaphysics (and against the Scientiphical View)—available previous to the time when I first brought myself to compose the book you're now reading. Not only do I find some force, I should be clear, in objections to Descartes's original pieces of reasoning, but I find force, as well, in objections to much more recent reasoning against materialism. (These much more recent efforts are fairly few and far between, I should say, and they're all much less original argumentation, of course, than the Cartesian efforts inspiring them.)

For me, that's reason enough, I suppose, to offer some novel negative contributions to these disputes. So it is that I've offered these Singularly Peculiar Arguments, leveled against both our dominant Scientiphicalism and against (all sorts of) materialist metaphysics.

We should all be curious, I imagine, to see how forceful are such Scientiphical replies as may be made to our Singularly Peculiar Arguments, or such materialist objections as may be made against our Substantially Dualistic Resolution for the Mental Problems of the Many. Equally, but from the dialectic's other main side, we might be just as curious to see how weak, in point of philosophical fact, the objections might be. How will things turn out here? I don't know. Right now, anyway, I doubt that anyone can say anything very substantial,

---

By contrast with Kripke, Chalmers, and most of the other few recent arguers for *any* sort of mind-body, but, then, very like Descartes himself, Swinburne argues for a robust Substantial Dualism. In this scholastically materialistic era, it takes some considerable intellectual courage, I think, even if it's here me who's saying it, for a prominent academic philosopher to do that. Apparently, Swinburne wouldn't disagree with this judgment, as is evidenced by these sentences from the first page of his Prolegomenon to the revised edition:

> The central theme of the book [the first edition] was the theme of substance dualism—that humans consist of two separate substances, body and soul. Plato thought this, and so did Descartes, and so did many other thinkers of the last three millennia. But, in 1997, as in 1986, few philosophical positions are as unfashionable as is substance dualism. These days one gets a far more sympathetic hearing for arguments to the existence of God than for arguments to the existence of the soul.

Almost needless to say, in the just-noted respect, things are scarcely different in 2005 from how they were in 1997, and in 1986.

one way or the other. So, I doubt that, right now, there's anyone in any decently clear position to predict the long-term course of the dialectic.

But, of course, in these last two Chapters, we've offered much more than just some arguments for some very negative conclusions, however novel the arguments, and however unpopular the conclusions. Much more positively, and culminating only in the present Chapter, we've been arguing for an Emergentive Interactionist Substantial Dualism. Let's be excruciatingly clear about this. What I've been arguing is that, for us right now, right after reading just some seven Chapters of this deadly serious dissertation, the least implausible worldview may be an Interactionist Substantial Dualism, maybe not very greatly unlike Descartes's traditional Dualism, placing aside his conception of matter, and his ideas about a God, and his thoughts about animals, and some several other Cartesian doctrines and dicta. Why? Well, such a Substantial Dualism may represent, among all actually available views right now, the least radical departure from our dominant Scientiphicalism—well, the smallest departure that's not yet run horribly afoul, apparently, of quite intractably serious difficulties.

Near this Chapter's outset, you'll recall, I said I can't actually believe in a metaphysic that departs from Scientiphicalist orthodoxy as much as does any Substantial Dualism, including even a nicely Emergentive Interactionist Substantial Dualism. As I suspect, you're in the same boat. So, what are we to do?

Three main courses strike me as available.

First, we may reconsider our investigation, and look for serious errors. Then, we may come to think, perhaps quite rightly, that there aren't any Mental Problems of the Many, or, at any rate, there's none that's any great difficulty for our widely accepted Scientiphicalism. And, we may come to think, as well, that there's no great Problem for Scientiphicalism, of any kind at all. Truth to tell, I hope that you'll all take very seriously this line of inquiry. And, I hope that some of you, at least, will seriously pursue a most intensive reconsideration. But, as for myself, by now I've done this several times over, during the eight years preceding this book's completion. And, in the wake of all those labors, I've little energy left to expend in that direction. So, for me right now, that leaves two courses more fully open, for future investigative activity.

Second, we may ask ourselves what are the most disturbing aspects of a Cartesian View, or a Quasi-Cartesian Metaphysic. After trying to articulate them, we might endeavor to show how they might really mean far less intellectual disturbance than they first appear to do. In the rest of the book, that's one thing I'll aim to do.

Third, and finally, we may try to develop a variety of Interactionist Substantial Dualistic Views. As this book progresses further, my main efforts will lie in this third direction.

Appendix: Beyond Discriminative Vagueness,
Safe from Nihilistic Sorites

Ever so many of our ordinary terms are what I've called *vague discriminative terms*, as with "ship" and "star," and "planet" and "plant" and, I suppose, as with "people." (I introduced this expression, "vague discriminative terms" or, equivalently, the term "vague discriminative expression," in an old paper of mine, "Why There Are No People."[34] Both in that old essay and subsequently, I've found it to be a memorably useful expression.)

Each vague discriminative term purports to discriminate the items to which the term properly applies, the ships, for example, from all the other items, for instance, from all the nonships. This means trouble for the terms, it appears, as many of the nonships, for example, may be placed on a gradient with the ships, so that only very small differences separate some of the ships from some of the nonships.

Now, as it surely seems, there are certain physical complexes, each composed of about a thousand wood planks, that are each a ship, providing anything is. But, as it also surely seems, each of these ships will withstand the removal of, and the destruction of, only one of these planks. Or, at the very least, such an episode won't leave *no ship*, at all, in the contemplated situation.

What's more, with any ship obtained with such a small and innocuous removal, it equally appears, the same procedure may then be employed, with no more upsetting an upshot, so far as the existence of ships is concerned. And, so it goes, without limit: At any place in the destructive spectrum, the innocuous removal of just one plank won't take us from there being at least one ship on the scene, to there being no ship there at all. But, of course, with just one plank in the situation, or no planks at all, there won't be any ship on the scene. So, as it finally appears, maybe there wasn't any ship in the first place, not even with over a thousand wood planks, all "nicely arranged shipwise," as some philosophers may be wont to say. (As should be clear, on the diagnosis presently presented, not only aren't there any ships, but, quite as well, and for perfectly parallel reasons, there aren't any planks, either; and, what's more, nothing's ever correctly said to be arranged *shipwise*. But, no matter.)

Quite notoriously, I guess, I've long embraced all that, nihilistically maintaining, as I've long done, that, owing to the incoherence of

---

34. This was first done, I believe, on page 181 of my paper "Why There Are No People."

"ship," nothing can ever satisfy the term and, so, there never are any ships. Equally, one may maintain that, due to the parallel incoherence of "star," "planet," "plant" and, maybe "people," too, nothing ever satisfies any of those terms, either. And, so, there never are any stars, or planets, or plants, either, and, maybe, no people, too. In this present text, I don't mean to defend that position, or any other position on those issues. Rather, I mean only to do some very different things.

Some of what I'd like to do requires that I discuss, if only very briefly, a certain partial account of the semantics of vague discriminative terms. When I first provided this account, it's true, it was by way of supporting the notorious nihilism I'll now neglect. But, as I said, in this present work, that's neither here nor there. Anyway, on my partial account of the matter, any vague discriminative term is governed by two apparently trouble-making conditions, even if, perhaps, they may also be governed by some several other conditions (all of them perfectly powerless, evidently, to resolve, to avoid, or to otherwise nullify, any of the trouble made by the two governing trouble-makers). Very briefly, I'll now notice these two apparent trouble-makers, one of them being:

> 1. THE VAGUENESS CONDITION. Along any *dimension(s) of difference for the term*, there are suitably small differences, and *none* of them *means the difference* as to whether or not the term properly applies.

For a little illustration here, consider the ordinary word "red." There are many (possible and even actual) color patches, of many colors, many of which differ only quite slightly, as regards color, from many of the others. And, quite a few are readily called "red." Well, we may notice one dimension of difference for color, that's readily called *chromatic hue*. Along this dimension of difference, there'll be some patches that are only a very little more orangey, to coin a term, than patches *most* readily called red. Well, since these patches differ in color only a very little, that difference doesn't matter, as to whether they're red. So, they're red, even if they may be a very slightly orangey red. (Color patches, or colored patches, many also differ as regards there shape. But, then, *shape is not* a dimension of difference for "red," a fact that, in some sense, at least, is known by most American three-year-olds.)

In addition to being governed by the Vagueness Condition, each vague discriminative term is also governed, quite equally, by this markedly different condition:

> 2. THE DISCRIMINATIVE CONDITION. Along some dimension(s) of difference for the term, there are suitably large differences, and at

least *some* of them *do mean the difference* as to whether or not the term properly applies.

So, along the aforementioned dimension of difference for "red," consider such color patches as are most readily called "orange" or, better yet, some that are most readily called "yellow." Along this dimension of difference, our dimension of chromatic hue, here there are quite large differences, between such patches as are most readily, and most typically, reckoned to be red and, on the other side, such patches as are most readily, and most typically, reckoned as yellow. Accordingly, that is, according to the Discriminative Condition, here there's a chromatic difference that's so very large that "red" doesn't properly apply to *these* color patches, all of them being, supposedly, *paradigmatically yellow* color patches. Rather, just as regards their color, "red" discriminates against these color patches, that is, "red" discriminates them all from all the red color patches. So, of course, *they aren't* items to which the term "red" properly applies. To the contrary, the term *doesn't* properly apply to them. And, perhaps equally, it's just the term *nonred* that, among the two opposed words in focus, is the only term that applies to these (paradigmatically yellow) patches.

As I believed then, and as I'm still rather inclined to think, these very many ordinary expressions, all these vague discriminative terms, well, they're all governed by these two pretty simple conditions (which conditions, I'll admit, I articulated a bit barbarously). But, of course, if that's so, then the terms won't ever be true of anything at all, no matter what other conditions—maybe much more complex, and maybe much more refined—may also, rather more innocuously, govern the expressions, as well. For, our two apparent trouble-makers are mutually unsatisfiable conditions. This much, at least, should be pretty plain: Even as the small differences *won't ever* mean a relevant difference, still, and at the same time, we may combine them, whether absolutely all of them, or whether just a very impressive lot of them, so that, *when they're so combined*, there'll be, inevitably, *just such a very large* difference as *will* mean the difference between correct application and, on this difference's other side, just a failure of semantic application.

Few will agree, of course, that (what I've called) vague discriminative terms, like "red," and "ship," and all the rest, are governed by any such conditions as those I've proposed. Rather, as they may well hold, instead, the correct thought is that these ordinary terms are governed only by *somewhat similarly sounding* conditions. Readily mistaken for my simple candidates, I can almost hear them say, these more refined conditions won't ever run afoul of each other.

But, really, will those "smarter conditions" be anything quite readily learned by, and pretty fully learned by, enormously many very moderately intelligent three-year-olds, and very many pretty stupid four-year-olds? Myself, I doubt it. But, these little children have very readily learned, and they've pretty fully learned, what's involved in the accepted usage of "red," anyhow, and, with quite a few of the tikes, of "ship," too. Indeed, quite as far as I can tell, there's nothing here, at all central to these matters of common usage, that I've learned, all right, but that, somehow or other, the kids haven't yet picked up on. If not yet, then when will they get it?

Heck, when did I get it, this fancy semantic business that, quite mechanically and unconsciously, somehow allows me to avoid paradox? When I was thirteen, perhaps, just in time for Bar Mitzvah? Up with such nonsense I will not put, said the rightly mocking Churchill, regarding another linguistic business. And, regarding this pack of apparent nonsense, so say I right now, regarding the presently clothesless emperor: Up with *such* nonsense *I* will not put! Anyway, I suspect that any nice replacements for my queerly conflicting candidates, for the Vagueness Condition and the Discriminative Condition, well, they'll be just that: *replacements*, for what's really already in place.

Again, my suspicion—and it really is just a suspicion—is that what many esoteric professors would have us all believe, about what are really some pretty simple semantic matters, well, it's all just a bunch of ad hoc heroics, all tailor-made, from whole cloth, in a hopeless attempt to salvage some so-called commonsense belief. Or, as I prefer to say, it's to salvage just so much very vulgar speech, and just so much very widely popular opinion. Oh, so you actually think well of most very widely popular opinion? Well, then, I hope I haven't offended your sincere sensibility.

All right, that's more than enough nihilistic innuendo. Now, let's notice these presently much more pertinent points.

First, the Problems of the Many *don't* trade on there being any terms that are (as I've called them) vague discriminative expressions. Even the oldest and most superficial of these Problems, it doesn't have anything whatever to do with that, *whether or not* any of those very many expressions—terms like "ship," and like "red"—really do have, for what might be their perfectly hopeless semantics, any such simple and stultifying conditions as those I've proposed. Just so, this point holds even for the most tiresome of the Nonmental Problems of the Many. For instance, we may have a term that will apply only to such physical complexes as are composed of precisely two thousand absolutely elementary particles, in a certain precisely bounded sort of arrangement.

Let's call any such complex as that a "bimillenial botch." Well, in a certain messily gradual World, rather as our actual world seems to be, there may be many such overlapping complexes, each comprising precisely two thousand absolutely elementary constituents, and each having a shape that, quite clearly, falls within the range specified for the candidate complexes. And, this may well obtain in many relevantly problematic microscopic situations. While looking through a powerful microscope, almost all observers will think, even as they're quite casual observing folks, that there's just one bimillenial botch before them. But, in fact, there may be many millions. Anyway, nothing that's at all like this has anything much to do with problems of discriminative vagueness.

Second, and maybe more importantly, none of the terms I've employed centrally in this work is, I think, a vague discriminative expression. Or, at the least, I've taken some pains to ensure that and, so far as I can tell, the work's paid off. Look, there isn't any dimension of difference that the term "space" purports to discriminate with respect to; "spatial" doesn't purport to draw a line between some objects and, differing dimensionally from them somewhat, some nonspatial things. Nor does "immaterial soul" purport to make any such discriminations as that. Nor does "power," or "Propensity," purport to draw a line, in the conceptual sand, between the Propensitied particulars and, what?, the (evidently nonexistent) perfectly powerless individuals? And, as far as I can tell, the same story holds for "real alternatives" for example, and so on, and so forth.

So, even if almost all writing should be, at almost every turn, just positively riddled with incoherence—which may be, perhaps, ever so unlikely; I don't really know—still, all the most metaphysical sentences in this essay, all those most crucial to my central thoughts, well, maybe they're be quite free from that theoretically horrible problem. Or, at the least, I've taken some measures toward ensuring some such splendid end.

8

WHY WE MAY BECOME
DISEMBODIED,
BUT TO NO AVAIL

As I've been arguing, nothing remotely like Scientiphicalism is any acceptable metaphysic. And, neither is any materialist philosophy any true philosophy, leastways none that's ever been made available. Rather, as the weight of relevant philosophic consideration suggests, we do better to pursue a Quasi-Cartesian Substantial Dualism, on which each of us has, or is, an immaterial soul.

When pursuing such an Interactionist Substantial Dualism, certain questions will quickly arise for many readers. In brief, here are several of these questions: May we, each of us, somehow become a disembodied soul, upon the death of, or the destruction of, or the disintegration of our body, or bodies? When we are disembodied souls, if indeed we ever are disembodied, how should things be for us then, and not just as a mere possibility, but as a pretty likely state of affairs, or a pretty plausible proposition or prospect? Is it at all likely that, or at all plausible to think that, many of us will then enjoy some future experience or, at the least, engage in some quite rudimentary experiencing? Or, do we each actually need a body for that—or, perhaps, some several (possibly overlapping) bodies? At all events, what may be the most realistic prospects of your coming to have a body again, after you've been disembodied? And, what might the existence of an

470

Almighty God have to do with any of this, if there should be, in fact, a Supremely Powerful Creator of us all?

In this wide-ranging Chapter, I'll try to address these frightfully difficult questions. Though my speculative attempts will be far less protracted than many other efforts to do that, I have hopes of making a novel contribution to our thinking about these widely important issues. This, despite the fact that most of what I'll propose is advanced only quite tentatively, and very unconfidently.

Hoping to help some folks with these terribly sensitive questions, I'll try not to offend anybody. If you find yourself in great disagreement with me, that might be quite good, actually, especially if your attitude is one of open-minded intellectual inquiry, quite as I resolve for mine to be. Now, let's get down to some real philosophical work here.

1. Why We May Become Disembodied Souls, with the Deaths of Our Brains and Bodies

In the previous Chapter, or two, I've been very friendly to the view that, even as each of us may be quite directly generated by certain material entities, we may each be an immaterial soul, perfectly distinct from any material object that ever exists. And, more particularly, I've been quite friendly to the thought that, throughout our existence, each of us should always have a body (or some several bodies). Here's the same point expressed differently: I've looked favorably on the thought that each of us should always be an embodied soul, lasting only so long as our (complex) sustaining bodies remain normally healthy or, what's much the same, only so long as our (simpler constituent) bodies remain aptly physically related. But, even while I've been so friendly to that idea, I've also been somewhat positive about a very different Dualistic thought, especially in the Twelfth Section of our Sixth Chapter. This is, of course, the idea that, even though each of us immaterial souls is generated by material entities, once generated we don't depend, for our continued existence, on the supposed sustaining activity of our material bodies or, indeed, on any sustaining by any material entities at all.

Very unlike with the Chapter just previous, in this present Chapter I'm going to favor the latter sort of Interactionist Substantial Dualism over the former sort of Dualistic View. Certainly, this is not because I find it easier to believe that I may become disembodied. To the contrary, for me it's easier to think that my existence, such as it is, will always depend on there being some certain concurrent (or just previous) material sustaining of just the immaterial soul who's me. But, as I suspect, that proclivity may be, or it may be owing to, a badly misplaced metaphysical prejudice. And, in any case, there may be this to consider: First, the View on which I'll become disembodied may be a philosophically unobjectionable position. And, second, it may be, as well, a far more interesting sort of Dualistic Metaphysic than the View advanced in the just previous Chapter.

It's quite plausible to surmise, I think, nothing less than this: If you actually are an immaterial soul, then you're an immaterial individual who's not constituted of any real substantial parts at all, neither any material parts, of course, nor even any immaterial constituents. Rather, in this respect, at least, among all the actual physical entities, those most like you are the likes of perfectly simple and basic elementary particles, as with quarks, perhaps. In other words, you may be relevantly quite like just such simply basic physical entities as aren't constituted of, or by, or from, any concreta at all (it being nonsense, on my use of the expressions, to consider an entity as constituted by itself.) So, the most sensible surmise here, regarding how things are with the existence of a particular immaterial soul, may be this metaphysical proposition: Concerning the continued existence of a particular immaterial soul—which we should consider an *elementary immaterial individual*—well, they'll parallel, in all the most general respects, how things are with the continued existence of an *elementary material* individual.

Well, then, in all the most general respects, how *are* things with the continued existence of an elementary material entity?

Now, it's time to recall, from our Section on Propensity for Monotony and Propensity for Change (which was the Twelfth Section in Chapter Five) that many a basic concretum may have a Self-directed Propensity for Monotony as to (its own) Existence. Indeed, at least when we're thinking of basic spatial individuals, or basic material concreta, it's precisely this (Existential) Propensity that we expect an individual to have. And, we expect it to manifest its Propensity for Monotony as to its Existence—or, its Propensity for Continued Existence—on pain of its otherwise ceasing to exist.

(Suppose that, somehow or other, this Propensity isn't manifested? What is it that, in such an unexpected circumstance, we then will expect to take place? Well, as we should then expect, it won't be just sooner or later that the Particle, say, will cease to exist. For, just as we don't expect there to be very many sheer accidents, each occurring right after many others, so we don't expect anything very much like this: In just a moment's time, the considered basic concretum will still be there, just as a sheer accident; and, a moment after that, it will, once again, still be there, also just quite happenstantially; and, just a moment later than that, the very same concretum will, once yet again, still exist; and so forth, and so on. *Nothing but* perfectly sheer accidents, one after another, after another, after another? It's possible, I guess. But, goodness knows, it's extraordinarily implausible. Rather, the much more plausible thought is this: Because it doesn't have any Self-directed Propensity for (its) Continued Existence that's currently manifested—and because it hasn't any *other* Propensity with *that* Existential manifestation—well [that's why] our concretum won't exist anymore.)

For a basic physical concretum, this here's the metaphysically most simple and most satisfactory case, as to how it is with (its) Continued Existence: The basic (material) concretum has the Propensity to Exist in the next moment, along with the Propensity then to retain that very Propensity. And, with nothing to prevent these Propensities from being manifested, the concretum then *does* exist in that erstwhile next moment, complete with its (retained) Propensity to exist in (what's now) the *next* moment; and so forth, and so on. As compared with this simple state of affairs, whatever's next most satisfactory metaphysically (and whatever's next most plausible epistemologically), well, as a candidate for actually obtaining, it runs a fairly distant second. Or, at least, so it seems to me.

Just as it is for basic bodies, I've suggested, so it is for simple souls. So, for basic mental concreta, this *here's* the metaphysically most simple and most satisfactory case, as to how it is with (its) Continued Existence: The basic (immaterial) concretum has the Propensity to Exist in the next moment, along with the Propensity then to retain that very Propensity. And, with nothing to stop these Propensities from being manifested, the concretum then *does* exist in the next moment, complete with its (retained) Propensity to exist in (what's now) the *next* moment. As compared with that, whatever's next most satisfactory metaphysically (and whatever's next most plausible epistemologically), well, it runs a very distant second. Or, at least, so it also seems to me.

2. Even While You May Be an Immaterial Soul, Are You Really an Existential OTHERON?

Of course, we may recognize the possibility of an individual, even a basic physical entity, having *only some other* sort of (or sorts of) Propensity for Continued Existence, as with its having a certain Generalistic Propensity for Monotony as to (its own) Existence. So, for example, we may entertain the idea that, for it to keep existing, a certain basic body needs to be near at least two Blue Spheres—say, within an inch of each such Sphere. To my mind, at least, this is a less plausible state of affairs, far less metaphysically simple and satisfactory than what we've just been considering. But, in this present context, the difference between them is hardly the most notable difference. Rather the most notable difference will be, of course, the difference between the metaphysically most satisfactory case and, on the other side, a possibility (if that's the right word for it) that's metaphysically *least* satisfactory or, quite the same, that's metaphysically *most unsatisfactory*.

What is such a metaphysically most *unsatisfactory* case, of a basic concretum's Propensity as to its Continued Existence? As some of you will remember, we considered this question, or a question quite like it, a fair ways back in our inquiry, in our Chapter on a Plenitude of Power. In that familiar place, we focused, at first, on what we should think about the case of a (metaphysically most unsatisfactory) basic *material* concretum. It was only afterward that we then thought to consider, at all, the case of (Continued Existence for) any immaterial concreta, saliently including, of course, a (possibly) basic soulful concretum. In this present Chapter, our discussion will follow that same old order.

Concerning the continued existence of basic *physical* individuals, the least satisfactory case is, to my mind, the one where the concretum in question is an Existential OTHERON. How's that?

Well, among those who've been loyally reading through my many pages, quite a few may recall, from our familiar Fifth Chapter, the discussion of just such basic physical OTHERONS, including, very memorably, one Yuval Cartesianeton. (Heck, it's not for nothing that I bothered to inscribe that label—the label OTHERON—all in CAPITAL LETTERS.) But, many others, I'm afraid, won't remember that discussion, despite my quite memorable inscriptions of the humorously notable term, *OTHERON*. Anyhow, it may be a good idea, I think, to rehearse some of those old passages:

> ...imagine a certain *OTHERON*, a very peculiarly Propensitied individual whom we'll call *Yuval Cartesianeton*. Also a Yellow Cube, what's so peculiar about this Other Yuval is *how it's Propensitied* for (its) Continued Existence. Just so, this Yuval is Propensitied to Continue to Exist providing (only) that certain *Other individuals* are, and they continue to be, in certain appropriate external (sustaining) relations—*not* with Yuval itself, mind you, but, by contrast, or instead—*just with each other*. One of these Other individuals may be, again, our same peculiarly potent Purple Sphere, Peter Sellers. And, the other will be (not Yuval itself, of course but, say) a certain particular Green Cone, whom we may call *Gary Cooper*. So, as it may be, or as we'll suppose, our Yuval Cartesianeton will (continue to) exist

when, but, of course, only when, Peter Sellers and Gary Cooper are (quite as they long have been) *no more than a billion light-years apart from each other*. As far as Yuval Cartesianeton's future existence goes, *that's* what's required. It *doesn't* matter, by contrast, where this Yuval itself is. Just so, that concretum may be in an alien galaxy, terribly far, perhaps, from where its ever been before. Or, alternatively, it may always be nearly adjacent to Peter, maybe on an opposite edge, so to say, from any that's closest to Gary. None of that matters; nor does anything even remotely like that matter. Quite the opposite, for this Other Yuval's future existence, the situation is this: *All that matters is that Peter and Gary be appropriately (spatially, and thus externally) related.* As long as *they're* within a billion light-years of each other, Yuval Cartesianeton is still in business. But, just as soon as *they're farther apart* than that, well, that's just how soon that our Yuval's no more.[1]

All right; so, now all loyal readers will quite nicely remember. And, even those not so loyal, well, they'll also now get the hang of these pretty unusual ideas.

What do I think about the suggestion that, in the actual World, there are basic physical things that, especially as concerns the question of their continued existence, are just like Yuval Cartesianeton, our legendary Existential OTHERON? Well, to say the least, anything much like this Yuval will be, I expect, an exceptionally unusual and uncommon individual (if ever there should be any such actual individuals at all). Just so, it strikes me as a highly implausible suggestion that, in our actual world, there are many Existential OTHERONS. Certainly, even if there may be some such, there shouldn't be anywhere near as many of them as there are quarks, or electrons, or whatever else might be the basic physical concreta of our world. (Indeed, it's hard for me to believe that there's even a single such OTHERON, anywhere at all in our actual world.) (To be sure, with thinkers quite *utterly* unlike me, well, the suggestion might strike them quite differently. But, even as they're just so terribly unlike me, they won't be, I expect, any merely human thinkers. Well, I'm writing this book for (communication with) human thinkers, not sapient beings utterly unlike us.)

Well now, let's bring these thoughts to bear on our present discussion's central topic, which is, of course, the continued existence of immaterial souls. To do that quite quickly, and to do it most memorably, I'll rehearse a key passage from the just previous Section:

It's quite plausible to surmise, I think, nothing less than this: If you actually are an immaterial soul, then you're an immaterial individual

1. The quoted passage is from Section 20 of Chapter 5 above.

who's not constituted of any real substantial parts at all, neither any material parts, of course, nor even any immaterial constituents. Rather, in this respect, at least, among all the actual physical entities, those most like you are the likes of perfectly simple and basic elementary particles, as with quarks, perhaps. In other words, you may be relevantly quite like just such simply basic physical entities as aren't constituted of, or by, or from, any concreta at all (it being nonsense, on my use of the expressions, to consider an entity as constituted by itself). So, the most sensible surmise here, regarding how things are with the existence of a particular immaterial soul, may be this metaphysical proposition: Concerning the continued existence of a particular immaterial soul—which we should consider an *elementary immaterial individual*—well, they'll parallel, in all the most general respects, how things are with the continued existence of an *elementary material* individual.[2]

Combining these key thoughts with what we've just previously been discussing, I'm led to certain thoughts about the souls of our world, very possibly including both you and me. I'll amplify.

Even as it's most plausible that we're each Propensitied for Monotony as to (our own) Existence, and that this is why we continue to exist, so it's very implausible that we should be even remotely like an Existential OTHERON.

Of course, in just this very Section, the only Existential OTHERON considered was a (supposedly) basic *material* individual. On our Developing Dualism, by contrast, you and I each will be a (presumably basic) *immaterial* concretum. So, how are we to appreciate the purport of this eminently sensible statement—the statement that it's implausible to think we should be even remotely like an Existential OTHERON? Well, to attain such a wanted appreciation, we've some explaining to do, even if our explanatory work should amount to little more than some stage-setting, along with a rehearsal or two.

As we've been doing a fair bit, in this Chapter, we'll once again revisit some memorable passages from Chapter 5, where we first introduced our (basic) material OTHERON, our nostalgically familiar Yuval Cartesianeton. Even at that early juncture, we didn't bring him on stage just for the heck of it, or just to show off how wildly imaginative we could make our philosophical writing. (Heck, on that score, we'd already piled up vast overkill.) No; there was a quite definite method in, or purpose for, our wildness. For, as you'll also be brought to recall quite nostalgically, it was only moments after first introducing him that we went on to employ our Yuval Cartesianeton as a metaphysical model,

2. The quoted passage is from Section 1 of this Chapter.

even if not quite an actual male model. (At this point, some slightly bored reader is sure to ask, What was he then a model for?) Just as we made him be spatially simple—without any substantial spatial parts or constituents, we had him be a model concretum for a perfectly non-spatial immaterial entity. In other words, he was a model for a certain *nonspatial soul*, one that I *initially* dubbed—pun intended—Nina Simone.

To jog your memory most effectively, I'll rehearse the passage where we first encountered this Mentally Propensitied nonspatially soulful Nina:

> As I'm sure some will have sensed, but as I'll now make perfectly explicit, it's not for nothing that we've considered this Other Yuval, whose Individualistically-directed Propensity, especially as to (its) Existence, is entirely Other-involving, and not the least bit Self-involving, as concerns the conditions for its manifestation: In our philosophic theorizing, we may easily think to replace our considered Yellow Cube, Yuval Cartesianeton, by a particular *nonspatial soul*, maybe one *Nina Simone* or, more shortly, just *Nina*. And, in parallel, we may replace our Gary and our Peter, just two particular basic physical individuals, by very many more elementary particles, a certain trillion billion trillion of them, perhaps. And, then we may think this: So long as just *these* productive Particles are nicely enough arrayed, then the nice Nina they first generated will continue to exist. But, just so soon as *they* become rather less nicely arrayed, well, then, that's the *end of our Nina*.[3]

As I'll now explicitly suggest, for those who are both philosophically sensitive and intellectually open-minded, this Nina should also appear to be a very peculiar concretum. Maybe, she should seem about as unpalatable an individual as ever was our paradigmatic material OTHERON, namely, our oft-recalled Yuval Cartesianeton.

To this suggestion, some will object, I suppose. But, as a reply to the obvious analogies I've noted, how can any objection be any genuinely relevant response, much less any truly telling objection?

3. Immaterial OTHERONS Are Just as Problematic as Material OTHERONS

The most obvious and salient fullish reply, by far, begins by noting this difference, or these differences, between our Yuval and our Nina: Yuval,

---

3. The quoted passage is from Section 20 of Chapter 5 above.

a material body, is a spatial, physical individual, well suited for being related spatially with other spatial (physical) bodies in all sorts of ways, or in very many ways. And, he's well suited, too, for being physically related with other (spatial, physical) bodies in many other (physical) ways, as well, beyond what's involved in just being (physically) spatially related to other (spatial, physical) bodies. By contrast, Nina, an immaterial soul, isn't a spatial body, nor any other spatial concretum. Rather, she's just a nonspatial, nonphysical individual, quite unsuited to being related spatially with any (spatial) physical bodies. And, she's quite unsuited, too, for being physically related with any (spatial, physical) bodies in any other (physical) ways, as well, beyond what's involved in just being (physically) spatially related to any (spatial, physical) bodies.

Supposing all that to be so, the salient reply continues like this: Because he's *suited for spatial relations with* other bodies, and for other physical relations with them, any candidate conditions for Yuval's Continued Existence should require him to be in just certain sorts of these relations, and not in objectionable others, on pain of the candidate's failing to provide sufficiently plausible conditions. Just so, with our bodily Yuval, we may have certain plausible expectations, for candidate characterizations as to how he's Propensitied as to (his own) Continued Existence. When a candidate violates these expectations, or when it fails to satisfy them, we may then reject that candidate. (And, when all the possible candidates violate the expectation, we may reject the idea that there really is any such bodily individual, putatively labeled "Yuval" and (Existentially) Propensitied only in some such ways as are all (spatial, physical) bodies. Anything's possible, as we say. But, even when she's nicely undogmatic, the sensibly ambitious metaphysician needn't take very seriously every last one of all the apparent possibilities.)

By contrast, as the salient reply continues, things are very different in the case of our Nina: Because she's *unsuited* for spatial relations with anything, and because she's also unsuited for any purely physical relations with any concreta, the main existential issues are all very different with Nina, so far as anything properly metaphysical goes, from how they are with the nicely spatial likes of our Yuval. Just so, with our soulfully nonspatial Nina, we shouldn't have any expectations, at all, concerning how she may be Propensitied as to (her own) Continued Existence.

Well, I don't know all that much about you. But, as it strikes me, I'll tell you, this salient reply just doesn't cut much philosophical mustard. Indeed, it seems quite weak, to me, even supposing that, in all its subsidiary claims, and in all its underlying assumptions, the reply is entirely correct. (By my lights, much of that isn't entirely correct; but, no matter.)

To make this point poignant, I should be able to regale you with an illustrative little fable. Well, along such fabulous lines, what can I say?

OK; I've got it! Look, suppose that our World has been created by Seven Gods, all perfectly eternal, all quite happily cooperative, all very knowledgeable, each marvelously powerful, even though, of course, *none* of them is any *Supremely* Powerful Being. (They might be spatial concreta, maybe each one permeating all of space; or, alternatively, maybe they're each spatially otherwise. Or, they might be nonspatial concreta; maybe each one extended only in some merely spacelike dimension, scarcely accessible to human experiencers; or, alternatively, maybe they're each nonspatially otherwise. For our presently developing story, it's not very important to specify any of that. But, to be most helpfully instructive, I'll specify that each of our Gods is a wholly immaterial being, in no wise spatial at all, or properly physical in any other respect or regard.)

Anyway, much as many of you ungodly sports fans do, these Gods variously become fans of various baseball teams. Some of them like the Yankees; others greatly prefer the Red Sox. Being Gods, they each see every inning of every game, of course, as well as everything else that any human being ever does, or ever undergoes (not to mention everything that's going on with all the flowering plants, and so on). Just so, it's fully based on a God's own (aptly interactive) perceptual experiencing that each Godly fan of the Yankees sometimes becomes disappointed with their recent play. And, it's for just such a nicely based reason, as well, that, in particular, just every once in a while, and certainly not at all often, at least one of the Gods becomes disappointed in how Derek Jeter's been playing very recently.

Well, as it happens, even as these Seven Gods produced a World where various individuals have some quirky Propensities, so, in particular, and somewhat surprisingly, sometimes even they themselves are Propensitied very peculiarly. And, even if it's only once in a blue moon, still, from time to time, there's manifest one of their quite quirky reciprocal Propensities. Representative of many others, here's one of these queer Propensities, I'll advise you, even though I specify it only quite briefly, roughly, and crudely: Should at least three Gods each be, each at the same time as the others, severely disappointed in the recent play of Derek Jeter, then a certain *other* individual (also always perceived by the Gods, of course) will suddenly die—say, he'll die of sudden heart failure. And, to boot, his immaterial soul will then suddenly cease to be (presumably, quite completely and forever). For specificity, we'll say that this other individual is one *Norman Melman*, as we'll call him, who's your regular mailman, as we'll suppose. As we may certainly assume, if only to be most illustrative, Norman has, or he really is, an immaterial soul, as are all the other experiencers in the World, each of them created by our immaterial Gods, even if, perhaps, it's only in a very indirect way that the Gods managed to create the lesser, ungodly soulful experiencers. (For instance, it may be that it was by creating a largely physical world, maybe a world quite like what I've lately been Dualistically sketching, that the Gods (indirectly) created all the lesser souls: First, the Gods produced ever so many soulfully-productive reciprocally Propensitied Particles, the condition of manifestation, for this Propensity being, of course, that some certain nice number of these Particles become arranged in just such a nice way as will trigger their mutually productive soul-generating Propensity. And, second, the Gods have it that, from time to time, various of these Particles do become arranged just so and, in this very bargain, there's generated an immaterial soul that's Individualistically Propensitied with respect to each of (many of) the Particles serving to generate the soul in question.)

Now, quite beyond any of that, and quite as I quite lately said, these (immaterial) Gods are quite quirkily Propensitied. So, should as many as three Gods each be, all at once, severely disappointed in Derek J's recent play, well, then it's curtains (not for Derek J, mind you, the recently disappointing player, but) *only for Norman M.*, that utterly *other* perfectly Nonspatial Soulful Individual (and, maybe, for poor Norman, it's curtains quite completely, forever and ever).

Well, I don't know about you, my wearying reader. But, with such a weirdly vulnerable Norman as *that*, with such an *utter* OTHERON as we've supposed to bear that name, well, it's darned near impossible, for me, ever to believe in the existence of such an allegedly utterly OTHERONISH Norman. Just so, should someone tell me that things really work anything at all like *that*, like they supposedly do with our utterly OTHERONISH Norman, I should be extremely resistant, I tell you, to take what she says at all seriously. (Get real, I'd say to this OTHERON monger. This is the good old actual world, I'd say, a world where things just ain't anywhere near as quirky as all that.)

Please don't mistake the main point here for one that's less than terribly general. Just so, it would be completely inappropriate to think, about the example just given, that all it's illustrated is, really, something like some badly misdirected anger. For quite equally, really, the main point can be made, in fact, by all sorts of very different examples. In particular, it can be made by cases that, each in a most salient respect, is the diametrical opposite of the example proposed just previously. For what may be one nicely instructive case, we'll suppose that the Quirky Gods strangely arranged things, all quite unwittingly, so that whenever three Gods are greatly *pleased* with Jeter's recent play, well, it's just then that Norman M. will cease to exist. And, for another nice case, we may suppose that, when three Gods are severely displeased by Derek's hitting and fielding, then just something very *nice* happens to Norman M., as with his suddenly feeling quite elated. Perfectly nonspatial though all of it is, still and all, *absolutely none* of this OTHERONISH business sits at all well with me. Logically possible? Sure, I suppose so, whatever it is, exactly, that we should ever mean by those overly employed terms. But, anything much more than just logically possible? No way, I'll say. This is the good old actual world, I'll say, where things ain't anywhere near as quirky as that.

What all this strongly suggests to me isn't, I'll wager, very different from what it does for you. As we'll agree, as far as any alleged Existential OTHERONS are concerned, we may happily apply much the same strict standard with our allegedly immaterial soulful Nina, nonspatial individual that we've always supposed her to be, as we properly apply with, or applied with, our allegedly material bodily Yuval, spatially extended entity that we've always supposed him to be. Apparently, any objection to our doing that is, I suggest, as empty of philosophical merit as it is full of arbitrary bias.

As far as all the main metaphysical considerations may be concerned, the so-called Optimistic Form of Dualism—so-called by me, of course—well, it has a distinct advantage over the correlatively-so-called Pessimistic Form of (Interactionist Emergentive Substantial) Dualism. On the Optimistic Form, the story about how it is that a suitably simple *immaterial* individual should continue to exist runs parallel to the *most* plausible story about how it is that a suitably simple *material* individual should continue to exist. And, that's just what's wanted, I've argued, by any most sensible metaphysic of these matters.

On the Pessimistic Form, by contrast, the story about how it is that such a simple immaterial entity continues to exist, well, it runs parallel to what may well be a *least* plausible metaphysical story. And, even as that's to be avoided by any most sensible metaphysic of these matters, so the Pessimistic Form of Dualism won't be any very sensible metaphysic. Very far from any such apparently cockamamy Dualism as is that poor View, any very sensible metaphysician will do well to prefer our Interactionist Emergentive Substantial Dualism's Optimistic Form: Even though each of us immaterial souls is generated by material entities, still, (once we're generated) we don't depend, for our Continued Existence, on any (supposed) sustaining activity of our material bodies or, indeed, on any material entities at all.

4. Metaphysical Asymmetries and Further Forms of Substantial Dualism

In the line of reasoning just presented, I've urged us to observe certain parallels between presumably simple physical entities, as with quarks, and the presumably simple mental entities we ourselves may be, or that our souls may be. But, along with the parallels, there are also differences. Let's explore what may be some of the most significant differences.

As a first step in this exploration, it may be most useful first to consider a certain sort of friendly objection. Quite nicely, I hope, that objection may be rendered like this:

> Reasonably enough, you note that basic physical entities appear to be Propensitied for Monotony as to their own Existence. And, that's a reasonably weighty reason to expect that immaterial souls would be Propensitied for Monotony as to *their* Existence. But it might also be a relevant question whether basic material entities are *brought into* existence in the manifestation of the Propensities of *other* things, or whether, by contrast, they may be eternal, or whether, by another contrast, they may come into existence, but *not* in the manifestation of the Propensities of other things. If basic material things *aren't* brought into existence through the propensities of other things, then one might argue as follows: As basic material things aren't brought into existence by other things, it's reasonable to expect they're not going to cease to exist, either, as the manifestation of other things. So far, so good. But, on your Emergentive Dualism, immaterial souls *are* brought into existence by particular arrangements of basic material things or, in other words, in the manifestation of Propensities of these *other* things. So, unlike how it is with our presumably *nonemergent* basic material simples, with your *emergent souls*, by contrast, it may not be so reasonable to expect very much. In particular, it may not be so reasonable to expect that, just as a manifestation of *their own alleged* Propensity for Existential Monotony, they'll continue to exist—even when, or even after, their promoting Particles *aren't* conducively arranged, and even after there's no longer, in place, anything material that's been relevantly related, through a nicely gradual history, to the originally promoting Particles.[4]

---

4. What's just been displayed is nearly the same as an incisive comment, and a concise comment, from Don Garrett. Well, with my expansive editing of his concise remark, that virtue's been lost. But, as I'll think you'll agree, the comment remains quite incisive.

Well, to this friendly objection, something substantial should be said, by way of reply. In what remains of this Section, I'll say what, within this Chapter's compass, may fairly be said.

(In the book's very last Chapter, I'll do much more. By that late point, I'll have set the rich stage required for presenting, at all well or clearly, a *Nonemergentive* Substantial Dualism or, as it just might be somewhat better labeled, a *Quasi-Emergentive* Substantial Dualism. This Dualistic Metaphysic will be more like Plato's view on the matter, leastways in certain salient respects, than it's like Descartes's Substantial Dualism. And, I won't stop there, with just that *Quasi-Platonic* Dualism, as we might also aptly call it. In addition, I'll also present other Substantial Dualist Views whose decently clear presentation requires, quite equally, that same rich stage to be set.)

According to current Cosmology, I imagine, what are currently the most basic physical entities, say, something quite like quarks, weren't always around. Rather, somewhat as I've hypothesized souls to be emergent entities, our current quarks—or whatever physical things are now most basic—emerged from (something, presumably physical, that emerged from something, presumably physical, that emerged from) something, very possibly physical, that existed before they did. What was this presumably physical early something? Well, just for the heck of it, let's say that it was an utterly partless plasmatic soup, whatever that might really be. So, some twenty or so billions of years ago, this partless soup exploded in a so-called Big Bang. Well, even if it may be rather more indirect and complicated, on the going Cosmology, the origination of quarks runs something like that.

In any such event as that, something like this will have been so: However else it also may have been Propensitied, that soup—or that physical whatever—was Propensitied to so explode, but, of course—or, presumably—just when there should obtain some suitable conditions for its so doing. (Presumably, neither the explosion itself nor its timing was just sheer happenstance.) Maybe, the world had to wait for its plasmatic soup to become Extensible Platinum, which might itself have been the long-awaited manifestation of certain ways that the soup was Propensitied. Anyhow, the soup was Propensitied so that, upon its becoming Extensible Platinum, say, it exhaustively exploded and, what's more, it did so in just a certain very nice way—very nice, that is, for there coming to be, sooner or later, a physical realm rather like (what we currently take) the current physical realm (to be). So, however directly, or however indirectly, this Big Bang gave rise to (first, such-and-such, and then so-and-so, . . . and then) gadzillions of (precisely similar partless) quarks, and (quite different from all the quarks) goodzallions of (precisely similar partless) electrons. Well, and again, it's something like that. So, from all that there then, we're all here right now.

Well, then, how are things, relevantly, here and now? Presumably, in the whole Propensity profile of each quark, there's the individual's Propensity for Monotony as to its Existence. And, presumably, so it is, too, for all the other most simple physical things, say, for all the electrons.

Even as each quark and electron are physically generated, on our Cosmological story, by the exploding Extensible Platinum plasmatic soup, so, on our pretty conservative Emergentive Dualistic Metaphysic, each immaterial soul is also physically generated. So, given anything much like the going Cosmological story, there's not all that much difference, really, between how it is that the quarks were brought into existence, in the manifestation of a certain Propensity of the (presumably) physical plasmatic soup, and, on the other side, how it is that, even today, some souls may be newly brought into existence, in the manifestation of certain other Propensities of certain (presumably) physical quarks, and electrons, and so on (namely, those constituting, as we say, the recently formed brains of the new souls). In each case, it's something (presumably) physical that serves, Propensitively, to bring into existence a new individual, a perfectly partless particular, quite basic enough for its metaphysically relevant realm of, or for, many concrete individuals—whether it be a purely material, physical, spatial realm, for just such concrete particulars, or whether it be, contrarily, a purely immaterial, mental, nonspatial realm, for just *such* concreta (or whether it be, again contrarily, a *third* sort of realm, for *whatever* concreta).

To be sure, the quarks are (just yet some more) *physical* entities—*as was their presumed generator, or generators*—whereas the souls aren't themselves physical entities, in *contradistinction to their* presumed generators. But, this just amounts to the fact, humdrum in this discussion, that the quarks *are physical* and the souls *aren't* physical. Of course, even at the outset, we knew there *must be some such* humdrummery, as the proposed Emergentive Metaphysic is a Substantial *Dualist* View (of Mind and Body).

Our friendly objector's noted difference, I'll suggest, boils down to this: When it's a physical whatnot that's generating another physical whatnot, then, even however different the two may be, in all other ways, that is, in all ways consistent with the both of them being physical—well, then even the *generated* physical whatnot may well have a robust Propensity for its Continued Existence. But, when it's a physical whatnot that's generating a *nonphysical* whatnot, then, even however similar the two may be in all other ways, that is, in all ways consistent with the first being physical and the second not—well, in *that* case, the generated nonphysical whatnot *won't* have a robust Propensity for its

Continued Existence. This is well worth contemplating, I think. Certainly, this is not a wholly implausible proposition. But, overall, it doesn't strike me as very plausible, either.

While I'm not very confident of the judgment, it does strike me that, even at just this point in our dialectic, our so-called Optimistic Dualism is about as tenable as our so-called Pessimistic View, even if it might not be more tenable. At any rate, the Optimistic Dualism is tenable enough, or plausible enough, to be worth some further development or, at the least, some further inquiry.

(In certain metaphysically significant respects, certain Nonemergentive Dualisms, to be discussed in our last Chapter—maybe better labeled *Quasi-Emergentive Dualisms*, are each more plausible than both of our offered Emergentive Dualist Views and, perhaps, more than any Emergentive Dualism whatever. But, it won't be that, in every metaphysical respect, these impending Quasi-Emergentive Views will be more plausible. And, at all events, what we may learn about our Optimistic Emergentive Dualism can have great relevance, I'll assure you, to developing any adequately comprehensive Quasi-Emergentive Dualistic Metaphysic. With just that being so, there'll be considerable reason, in our development of this whole work, to inquire further into this Dualism. So, in much of this Chapter's upcoming space, that's one thing we'll do.)

5. Some Questions about Disembodiment, and about Reincarnation

Though I don't really believe it to be so—not yet, anyway—let's go ahead and suppose that we do survive the deaths of our bodies, and our brains. Let's suppose that our so-called Optimistic Substantial Dualism is true, or correct.

Indeed, we can make an awfully strong supposition to that general effect: As we'll now suppose, an immaterial soul—you yourself, for example—will continue to exist even if there should be the utter annihilation of all the matter that, at any time during your embodied existence, was the matter of your body (or of one of your bodies). Or, much the same, you'll survive the annihilation of all the matter that is, or that once was, the matter of any physical thing with respect to which you were ever (or, if you like, with respect to which your immaterial soul was ever) Individualistically Propensitied. Alternatively, if we like, we can make this other very strong assumption: Even if there should be an extraordinary *dispersal* of all the matter that, at any time during your embodied existence, was the matter of your body (or of one of your bodies)—as with all those elementary particles becoming just so much monumentally scattered intergalactic particle-dust—well, you'll still continue to exist; you metaphysically simple immaterial soul, you—so nicely Propensitied will you be, for Monotony as to (your own) Existence. Anyhow, with one or another such strong supposition in place, there will arise, almost directly, stimulating questions of (at least) three salient sorts.

For one thing, we're prompted to ask about these matters: Once it's disembodied, how long will the soul continue to exist, before something happens so that it ceases to exist? Or, better, once the soul is disembodied, must it always exist, for all eternity? Or, if not, how should it ever come to be that this disembodied soul—maybe, even you yourself—will some day cease to exist?

For another thing, we should also ask about this: When a soul is disembodied, then which of its Propensities will it still have? And, among the Propensities still possessed, which will ever be manifested with, or in, or by, the nicely Propensitied utterly disembodied soul? A bit more specifically, will a disembodied soul ever enjoy any experiencing; will it ever be engaged in any thinking; will it ever really choose? And, if a disembodied soul ever does experience—or it thinks, or it chooses—then *how will it happen that* the wholly immaterial individual—*not* nicely partnered with any material concretum—ever does come to experience—or to think, or to choose?

And, for a third thing, we'll also be moved to ask about this: Once a soul comes to be disembodied—or it comes to exist without any sustenance by, and without any dynamical interaction with, any material concretum—how might it happen that, still later, the soul should become *reembodied*, or *reincarnated*? How should it come to be that, once again, the soul should dynamically interact with a body, or with some several bodies, perhaps doing it so nicely that it may be said to have *acquired* the body?

Very possibly, in response to these questions, I may not have anything very enlightening to say. Still, I should make an honest attempt in this direction, trying to do the best I can. So, I'll try.

6. Prospects for Disembodiment

First, let me take up the matter of a soul's disembodied existence, and questions concerning how it might be that, even so, the soul might be vulnerable to annihilation, whether or not it should ever actually be annihilated or, for that matter, whether or not it should ever, in any way, come to no longer exist.

Back in Chapter Five, we encountered a couple of passages out-lining, or sketching, how it might be that certain Worlds should be very stable Worlds and, in particular, how they should continue to have, indefinitely into the future, exactly all the individuals that such very stable Worlds will have. Both passages focused on a paradigmatic basic concretum, a certain Blue Spherical Particle, in such a very stable World. Anyway, whether or not you've read that Chapter, it now will be useful for you, I think, to focus on these two paragraphs from there, happily rehearsed here right now:

> First, the entity (in focus) will be *Propensitied to retain all its Propensities*, each of them just as it is (and just as it's been) *including this very Propensity itself*, of course, which we may call its *Comprehensively Propensitive Propensity*. Or, in metaphysically more perspicuous discourse, the entity will be *Propensitied to continue to be Propensitied just as it is* Propensitied, and just as it's *been* Propensitied. (There's no paradox in any of this; not even anywhere in the neighborhood.)
>
> Second, the entity's Propensities will all be Completely Uncon-ditional. A Blue Sphere will continue to be Blue, and it will continue to be Propensitied to be Blue, no matter, for instance, how far the Sphere is from the nearest Cube, and no matter whether or not there are ever any Green Cones, and so on. Though there will be many Blue-Annihilators, I'm inclined to agree, none will be so "situated" as to have its salient Propensity manifested, leastways not in any inter-action with our considered Blue Sphere. Just so, no Blue-Annihilator will exist at any time during our Blue Sphere's Eon or, maybe, even during any of its many successive Eons. (Leastways, except if it might exist in a different World from our Blue Sphere's World, there'll never be any Blue-Annihilator existing when our Blue Sphere exists.) Nor will there ever be, in our Blue Sphere's World, and in any of its possibly very many Eons, any Sphere-Annihilators, or any Blue-Color-Changers, and so on.

Well, as you can hardly fail to see, this (nicely illustrative) stable World had just so many simple *material* individuals, at least one Blue Spherical Particle, of course, maybe a couple of Yellow Cubes, without having even so much as a single immaterial individual. But, at this juncture, we should extend our considerations, along as parallel a path as is pos-sible, to cover, as well, such immaterial souls as may be the inhabitants, in some Eons, of a (sometimes) very stable World.

Well, as it seems to me, pretty much everything we then said, for Blue Spheres, and everything that's relevant to our presently primary purposes, we can now say, just as well, for immaterial souls, including such nonspatial souls as may be (sometimes, or always) disembodied basic mental individuals. And, to my mind, at least, this may be a very useful thing to do. For, it may help us toward pretty clearly conceiving how there may be a World, not only quite replete with souls, but, quite as well, replete with such souls as always retain, at least for Eons and Eons, their central mental Propensities, or Powers, as with the power to experience, for example.

For help with conceiving some very nicely stable immaterial souls—and maybe, just maybe, each soul the Propensitive equal of all the others—the first of the two paragraphs, just lately displayed, may be employed just as it is, without even the least little alteration:

> First, the entity (in focus) will be *Propensitied to retain all its Propensities*, each of them just as it is (and just as it's been) *including this very Propensity itself*, of course, which we may call its *Comprehensively Propensitive Propensity*. Or, in metaphysically more perspicuous discourse, the entity will be *Propensitied to continue to be Propensitied just as it is* Propensitied, and just as it's *been* Propensitied. (There's no paradox in any of this; not even anywhere in the neighborhood.)

Now, as far as the second paragraph goes, it's clear that we need to change some wording. But, it's also pretty obvious how we should do that. For instance, if we want all our souls always to be each other's Propensitive equals, we may have that by saying they're each just *Basically Mentally Propensitied* and, having said that, we may then go on to reformulate the displayed passage so as to convert it into this suitably new companion paragraph:

> Second, the entity's Propensities will all be Completely Unconditional. A Basically Mentally Propensitied Soul will continue to be so Propensitied, and it will continue to be Propensitied to be so Propensitied, no matter what its relations to any other simultaneously actual individuals. Though there will be many Soul-Annihilators, I'm inclined to agree, none will be so "situated" as to have its salient Propensity manifested, leastways not in any interaction with our considered Soul. Just so, no Soul-Annihilator will exist at any time during our Soul's Eon or, maybe, even during any of its many successive Eons. (Leastways, except if it might exist in a different World from our Soul's World, there'll never be any Soul-Annihilator existing when our Soul exists.) Nor will there ever be, in our Soul's World, and during any of its possibly very many Eons, any Experiencer-Annihilators, or any Experiencer-Incapacitators, and so on.

With this conversion, we now have displayed two passages that may provide a good start, I think, toward understanding what we're after. So, we now have a good start toward grasping how there might be, in some certain very stable Worlds, some genuinely everlasting immaterial souls, each always Basically Mentally Propensitied.

To get most of the rest, and maybe all that relevantly remains, we just need to add something like this: When we're talking of a Soul-Annihilator, say, or when we're speaking about, say, an Experiencer-Incapacitor, we needn't be referring to a single individual, leastways not just to any particular basic concretum. Rather, almost anything may be counted, in this context, as a Soul-Annihilator, just so long as it has the Power to annihilate souls: It might be a very complex entity, for example, comprising many simpler individuals. In some cases, each constituent of the contemplated Annihilator may itself be an immaterial soul; in other cases, each may be a basic physical concretum; in still others, there may be some material constituents of our supposed Soul-Annihilator and, as well, some immaterial constituents. Heck, almost anything's fair game here. Just so, it might be that the "dangerous" situation is just like this: There's an intermittently angry immaterial God, one who destroys all concurrent finite souls when, but only when, he's in one of his rare anger episodes, each episode lasting just for a minute, and any such episode occurring, on average, only once in ten billion years.

But, whatever the "possible threats" to our considered souls' continued existence, this may be both most safely and most relevantly said: So long as our immaterial souls *aren't in any such soulfully dangerous World*—that is, so long as the actual world *isn't so (Propensitively) soulfully dangerous*, any given soul may well continue to exist, forever and ever, always replete with all its Basic Mental Propensities, forever and ever.

As I see it, here's a nice way to summarize, or to present very perspicuously, what we've just suggested. No immaterial soul is quite essentially, or is quite necessarily, any everlasting entity, leastways not in any very strong sense of "essentially" or "necessarily." But, just as well, none of our souls need be, either, only a temporary entity, so to say, lasting only for some finite period of time. Nor need any soul retain its Basic Mental Propensities—or be Basically Mentally Propensitied—for only a finite future period. Rather, so long as the conditions for its doing so remain conducive for its so doing, which may be infinitely long into the future—or, forevermore—a soul may possess its Power to Experience, along with whatever else is comprised in, or by, its being Basically Mentally Propensitied.

Well, so far as what might be called the *strict possibilities*, that's pretty much the whole story, I suspect, concerning our future existence (supposing, of course, that we may each become, in the actual World's future, a Basically Mentally Propensitied disembodied soul).

But, more pertinent to most people's personal concerns, what are the relevantly *realistic prospects* concerning the matter? Well, to be honest, I've hardly a clue. But, even in my woeful ignorance, I'll try to say something useful—maybe, even, something that's at least halfway plausible. At least, I'll try to say something that's helpfully stimulating. All right, here goes.

Even as our actual World may go through an infinity of Eons, including, for example, an (almost?) endless series of big crunches and big bangs, so, with a certain one of these Eons, there may come to be (maybe as a product of its formational big bang, whether directly or only more indirectly) some entities that are Soul-Annihilators, entities with Annihilational Power-directed Powers. Now, given all our earlier suppositions, this may be, I suspect, something like a halfway plausible cosmological conjecture. Anyway, at least for the purposes of an interesting discussion, let's suppose that some such conjecture as this holds true: Our prospects are pretty good, at least, for continuing to exist for some several billion more years. And, what's more, our prospects are pretty good, at least, for our continuing to be, throughout all these years, Basically Mentally Propensitied. In these respects, time's on our side, at least, a whole lot of time, even if, perhaps, not all the time in the world.

But, as regards the prospects for your future *experiencing*, how much is time on your side?

7. Even If We Disembodied Souls Last for Eons, What Are Our Prospects for Experiencing?

For the sake of a potentially instructive discussion, I'm going to stipulate, without argument, that the prospects are very good for your soul's retaining, for Eons and Eons, all the mental Propensities it enjoys when it will last be embodied, say, at the time of your biological death or, at any rate, most of this richly variegated complex of mental propensities. (Remember, on most of what's been suggested most lately, the soul of a person with advanced Alzheimer's disease is still very richly Propensitied. It's just that, for having been ravaged by her disease, her brain has become (or her many brains have all become) no decently productive interaction partner for her soul. Accordingly, she'll no longer manifest very much in way of mental Propensity, however richly endowed she may still be, even by way of just such mental Propensity. So, in the present context, the stipulation just suggested isn't any very wild stipulation. But, anyway, let's get on with some newer business.)

However richly you may be mentally Propensitied, it won't be of much use to you or, maybe better, it won't really benefit you much, except insofar as these Propensities, or some of them, are actually manifested. So, suppose someone said that if you should take a certain drug, right there in his outstretched hand, you'll live for another hundred years, almost all these years in excellent biological health; and, suppose he backed it all up with exceedingly good evidence to just that effect.

Well, if that's the whole story, it's a darned good offer. And, even just out of sheer self-interest, you'd be a fool not to take him up on it. Or, for the sake of potentially instructive reasoning, let's agree on that much. But, now, let's go on to consider this: Suppose he also said that, as your price for taking the drug, you'd have to agree to go into a terribly deep coma, starting just a year from now, and lasting, say, ninety-eight years. So, you'd have a year of normal experiencing, and then ninety-eight years of no experiencing, and, finally, another year of experiencing. He's offering you a very long biological life, to be sure, leastways long by contemporary human statistics and standards. But, as there'll be so little (time when there's) manifestation of your central mental propensities—and, in particular, your power to experience—it's a bad offer. Without much experiencing for someone and, more generally, I should think, without much mental activity of any sort (however overt or, alternatively, just covert) there's very little value in a very long life, or in an exceedingly protracted existence, however long should be the existence. (This must hold whether Scientiphicalism should be true, or any form of materialistic position, or any Dualistic metaphysic, or any decent Idealistic philosophy, or anything else you may care to mention.)

As it is for all us earthly human beings now (whether or not we should now be embodied souls) so it will also be for any disembodied souls that may ever exist: However long a soul may ever exist (whether embodied or disembodied) there will be little of any benefit in its existence, even for the selfsame soul herself, unless there should also be, at a bare minimum, a quite considerable amount of time when she's experiencing. So, even assuming that all your great-great-great-grandmothers still exist, as disembodied souls—or, that the souls of your great-great-great-grandmothers all still exist, or however you want to put it; by itself, so to say, none of that matters much at all, not even to them, or as far as just they're concerned. Rather, if there's to be something of value here, for these female ancestors of yours, in all these many years of disembodied existence, so to label the temporal period, it must be the case that, during some of this period of disembodiment, they're experiencing. Or, at the very least, all these disembodied years will be of very much less good to any of them than just a single typical day that they really enjoyed, when they were healthily alive, or their bodies were, and when they were normally embodied souls, pretty normally experiencing.

All that being so, we must surely hasten to ask: Even assuming that she's retained ever so much of her Propensitive nature, how likely is it that, or how plausible is it to think that, a certain one of your great-great-great-grandmothers, one Gertrude, perhaps, has been experiencing pretty recently? (If you like specificity, you may ask: How plausible is it to think that, say, Gert's experienced, or she's enjoyed some experiencing, on at least one day during the last five decades?)

Myself, I think that, even with all our suppositions firmly in place, or taken as givens, this is very unlikely for poor Gertie. In my view, it's quite implausible to think that, even given all that, Gert's been experiencing at any time lately, really, at any time since the day she (or her body) biologically died, all those many years ago. Why is that my view? Well, nothing very esoteric, really. Rather, it's just due to the impact, on my system of belief, of the available real empirical evidence (discounting, as quite negligible, just so many fabricated reports that, almost certainly, are the products of just so many terribly wishful thinkers or, what's much worse, the products of variously deceptive individuals, preying on the wishes of others, far less deceptive folks who're far more gullible individuals).

Even if it may be only indirectly relevant, evidentially, to questions concerning when an immaterial soul may be experiencing, in any way at all, still, there's some pretty impressive evidence available concerning just those important questions. This impressive evidence includes facts like those I related some several Sections ago, when remarking on a quite different question, a question for which they had precious little relevance. But, as they're all very relevant to what's presently our primary question, I'll now relate these facts all over again, and I'll do it very saliently:

> When there's a lot of alcohol in your blood, including, of course, the blood in your brain, you can barely think straight—indeed, with a very great lot, you'll pass out, becoming quite unconscious. When people suffer certain lesions, or wounds, to certain parts of their brains, they appear to lose certain of their mental powers, including even some quite central mental powers. So, with certain areas damaged, you'll no

longer be able to enjoy, or to suffer, any more visual experiencing. With others damaged, you'll no longer be able to experience auditorally. And, then, there are even sadder cases. On a PBS program, concerning cognitive functioning and the brain, I saw, at considerable length, the plight of a man whose brain had been attacked by a certain virus, years ago, the attack itself lasting, I think, for just about five days. In consequence, this man, previously a concert pianist, was quite unable to consciously remember his past personal life and, to boot, he was also unable to form new memories (going forward, so to say) from his currently ongoing experiences and activities. While he certainly remembered how to write, and he even quite compulsively composed a journal, he kept writing (what was essentially) the same paragraph over, and over, and over again. Pathetically, it went something like this: "I'm going to keep a record of my activities now. I must remember to write specific things down, so that later I'll be helped to recall what's recently happened to me." Time and time again, on one page after the next, that's all he wrote. In keeping with all that, there was this: While he could still play the piano beautifully, and remembered the most difficult pieces from the classical repertoire, he was perfectly unable to recognize his nurse, as anyone at all familiar, though he'd seen her just several minutes ago, before she left his room to get him some food, or drink. Nor was he able to recognize his own wife, who visited him on a daily basis, even though they had been married for years, quite devotedly, well before the onset of his viral attack.[5]

So, at least as regards *what sort* of thinking and experiencing a soul will actually enjoy, it seems clear that there should be appropriate interaction between that soul and, on the other side, (the basic physical constituents of a normally healthy brain (or overlapping brains). Little doubt, but that, for there to be conditions conducive to such interaction, it's required the basic constituents of the soulful being's brain (or of his brains)—say, just so many quarks and such—are so spatially arrayed, or are physically related, in just certain ways (and, so, not in certain other ways). Just so, in the sad cases of total blindness, utter deafness, both-ways amnesia, and so on, there's only a very modestly conducive array of such constituents. That's not conducive to modifying the Propensitively partnered soul mentally, I'm sure, anywhere nearly as richly as is the case, thank goodness, with the soul who's you and, yet more certainly, with the soul who's me.

To this we may add many other undoubted facts, each rather more directly relevant to our currently considered question: Whenever someone's brain is rendered relevantly inactive, as with a very heavy

5. The quoted passage is from Section 21 of Chapter 7 above.

general anaesthetic, that person then goes through a period when she's not experiencing, not experiencing *at all*, a period that lasts just as long as the anaesthetic's still modifying her brain very effectively. What means this "very effectively"? Well, the substance is modifying the brain, or the brains (by modifying how the appropriate elementary constituents are related, presumably), in such a way that, for having the soulful patient be an experiencing patient, the brain, or the overlapping brains, won't then be an aptly dynamically Propensitied reciprocal Propensity partner.

Maybe even more impressive, evidentially, there's this: Many people have fallen into very deep comas, their comas lasting, in many cases, for years and years. From such deep comas, some people have eventually awakened. Even after awakening, they never reported any experiencing, during the years that they were deeply comatose. To the contrary, in very many of these cases, each was under the distinct impression that, during her deeply comatose years, she didn't experience at all. (Many others, of course, died while still deeply comatose. Who can think that, while in their terribly deep comas, these moribund people were, each of them, actually experiencing? Not me, buddy; and, as I more than suspect, not you either.)

And, then, even more extremely, there are those people who've gone into, or, maybe better, whose bodies have gone into, what's called *persistent vegetative state*. Here, the neurons of their upper brains have died and, so, these people, or their bodies, no longer have any living cerebrum, while their lower brains, by contrast, are still alive, and are functioning pretty normally. With a living and functioning autonomic nervous system still at work, their vital organs are still well controlled, the heart pumping the blood around regularly, the lungs regularly breathing air in and out, and so on. Suppose that these people's souls are somehow still involved with their bodies. Even on such a supposition, who can believe that these souls are then experiencing? Nobody that's anybody, that's who. Suppose, contrarily, that their souls are now disembodied. Is it any more credible, now, to think they're experiencing? Not by my lights; nor by the lights of anyone else in his right mind.

There's *nothing absolutely incoherent*, of course, in this idea:

(DE)   A disembodied soul engages in ever so much experiencing.

Indeed, there's nothing intrinsically absurd in the thought that this may happen even as a manifestation of a soul's Self-directed Propensity for (its) experiencing, the condition of manifestation for this Propensity being—what else?—that the soul should be disembodied (or, here quite the same, that the soul should lack any (actual) material reciprocal Propensity partners for any dynamical interaction). But, even while this idea may be perfectly *coherent*, there is, at the same time, nothing suggesting, evidentially, that it's *true*. And, as I've been urging, there's plenty suggesting that it's *untrue*.

Am I being unfair here, or wrongly conservative in my views? I don't think so. Look; there's also nothing absolutely incoherent, of course, in this related idea:

> (DE*^?!) A disembodied soul engages in ever so much experiencing, with all of it comprising just so much experiencing as of undifferentiated and unaccompanied aquamarine, inasmuch as there's a visual aspect to the experiencing, and with all the experiencing being, in its auditory aspect, as of undifferentiated and unaccompanied belltone.

Indeed, there's nothing intrinsically absurd in the thought that just *this* may happen even as a manifestation of a soul's (Self-directed) Propensity for (its) experiencing, the condition of manifestation for this Propensity being, of course, that the soul should be disembodied. But, even while this *obviously cockamamy* idea is perfectly *coherent*, there's nothing to indicate that *it's true*. And, as I'll hardly have to urge, I trust, there's plenty indicating that it's *untrue*. Finally, let me now say this: The first of our two lately labeled propositions (DE) isn't *as* incredible, and it isn't *as* cockamamy, as is the more specific second statement (DE*^?!). But, even if it's to a much lesser degree than the utterly ridiculous (DE*^?!), still, and nonetheless, the proposition (DE) is a quite incredible proposition.

By the way, or maybe not so by the way, there's this to say: So far as questions of any real benefit go, here's a point that may be as important as it's apparently undeniable: For Gert to experience in a way that's at all beneficial to her, she can't be experiencing in just such a way that, all the time, insofar as her experiencing is visual, it's always just so much experiencing as of undifferentiated and unaccompanied aquamarine, and insofar as it's auditory, it's just so much experiencing as of undifferentiated and unaccompanied belltone, and there's precious little else as regards the character of her experiencing. Nor will it be enough, either, for there to be Change as regards Gert's experiencing. Suppose, for example, her experiencing visually goes from her experiencing just aquamarinely to her experiencing just maroonly to her experiencing just orangely, to her experiencing aquamarinely again, and so on. That's not much good for Gert. And, suppose that,

in addition to that, as well, her experiencing auditorally goes from experiencing belltonely to her experiencing bangingly, to her experiencing belltonely again, and so on. Even so, that's not much good for Gert
either. Look, I'd be among the last to say that all that's important to
having a good (embodied or disembodied) existence is something that's
experiential.[6] Still, I'll be among the first to espouse, I should hope, this
nicely complementary proposition: For someone's existence to be any
good for her, *quite a lot is required experientially* (whatever may be required,
as well, that's nonexperiential). Well, then, without ever again having any
physical interaction partners, what are the prospects for disembodied
Gert's not only coming to experience again, but, what's much more, her
coming to experience in one of those total ways of experiencing, or one
of those ways of total experiencing, that will be quite beneficial for that
dearly departed soul? Very bleak, indeed, are the prospects of anything
really beneficial for our dear old disembodied Gertie.

Anyway, all our undisputed experience with all humanity strongly
suggests the truth of this very bleak proposition: Even if each of us
should have a perfectly immortal immaterial soul, still, except insofar
as that soul is interacting with some conductive physical Disposition
partner, or partners, the soul won't ever be manifesting any of its central mental Propensities. In particular, it won't ever manifest its power
to experience and, so, it won't ever be experiencing. For a presently
disembodied soul, then, a soul that currently lacks any experientially
productive physical Disposition partners, the experiential prospects
look utterly bleak, quite as all the really hard evidence indicates—heck,
quite as all the *real* evidence so strongly suggests. So, if Gert's now
disembodied, well, she'd better get a body, if she's ever again to be
someone who's experiencing. And, what's more, she'd better get a
body that's an appealingly apt interaction partner for her, if she's ever
again to enjoy any experiencing, or experience in some such way as
may be, at least for her, even the least bit beneficial.

8. What Are Our Prospects for Reincarnation?

Well, how in tarnation is Gert ever gonna get a body, so that, just
possibly, *she'll have an apt experientially productive physical Propensity
partner*? In just a single word, how's she going to get *reincarnated*, for

---

6. Though hardly attempting an exhaustive exploration of the matter, I go into all
this at considerable length in "The Appreciation of Our Actual Values," which is the last
Chapter of my *Identity, Consciousness and Value*, Oxford University Press, 1990.

goodness' sake, so that there'll be some physical thing, or some physical things, quite suited, at the very least, to *triggering her power to experience*? Or, maybe expressed a bit better, she'll come to have something physical, once again, that's so suited for some nice Gert-directed interaction, so nice that there'll then be the *manifestation of* that power of hers, so that she'll *experience* again?

Articulating a consistent metaphysic for reincarnation is, I think, a piece of cake. But, by itself, mere consistency means very little, philosophically.

Consider this consistent but mostly crazy metaphysic: During the years when it first existed, the immaterial soul of a certain famous horse, one *Trigger*, by name, was Individualistically-directed with respect to trillions upon trillions of elementary constituents, including all the electrons it "had," when first it was generated, and, including the quarks it "had," when last alive or, maybe better, when last embodied. Now, we may instructively suppose that, ever since Trigger died, some few decades ago, he's been just a disembodied soul or, here much the same, there's existed the disembodied soul that (when it was embodied) was Trigger's soul. (As I've heard tell, though I can't vouch for it, Trigger's carcass was taxidermically prepared, or attractively stuffed, and then saliently placed in his owner's mansion, that being the main home of the multimillionaire Western movie star who was Trigger's owner, the late Roy Rogers.) Well, then, how shall Trigger's soul— which might be the real Trigger (that is, it might be the all-time best candidate for bearing his name, "Trigger")—how shall this once-equinely-embodied-soul, so to say, ever get a body again, or become embodied again? Heck, let's just say this: First, and just for expository convenience, we may say, perfectly unobjectionably, and even quite elegantly, that any of the elementary particles that *ever were* Individualistically directed for interaction with Trigger's soul, is one of *Trigger's Erstwhile Basic Constituents*. (I've always thought "erstwhile" a quite elegant-sounding word, though it means little different from the commonplace "former.") Then, second, and quite out of the blue, we might say something like this: Once Trigger becomes disembodied, or once he became so, then, just as soon as at least 106 of Trigger's Erstwhile Basic Constituents come to be constituents of any complex of constituent elementary particles, where the particles are suitably related for there to be either soul-generation or, alternatively, some reincarnation, well, then, Trigger's got a shot at getting a body again. What are such bodily complexes as will be so suitable? Well, as far as we can tell, anyhow, they will be just those that are living healthily functioning brains; or that aptly include such healthily functioning brains. Or, at the least, they'll be something a lot like that, whatever may be, exactly, the most apt description of the nicely functioning brainy physical complexes.

All right; so that's when Trigger will have some sort of shot at getting a body again. But, then, when will he have more than just a shot? Well, let's just say that, providing his Erstwhile Basic Constituents outnumber the Erstwhile Basic Constituents of any other formerly embodied soul. So, then, it's a bingo! And, Trigger's a winner! Rather than all *those* particles generating any genuinely new soul, and rather than their coming to be Individualistically directed with respect to any formerly embodied soul that's not Trigger, these particles come to be physical Propensity partners for just our soulful Trigger. More colloquially, and pretty roughly, they all come to be the basic constituents of Trigger's new body (or overlapping bodies).

As our stipulated metaphysic has it, the same sort of condition that holds for Trigger holds, just as well, for all the other disembodied souls, including, say, our dear old Gertie. Just as soon as at least 106 of *Gertie's* Erstwhile Basic Constituents come to be constituents of any complex of constituent elementary particles, where the particles are suitably related for there to be soul-generation or, alternatively, some reincarnation, then, *Gertie's* got a shot a getting a body again. And, when will *she* have more than just a shot? Well, let's just say that, providing *her* Erstwhile Basic Constituents outnumber the Erstwhile Basic Constituents of any other formerly embodied soul. So, then, it's another bingo! And, *Gertie's* a winner!

Now, it may be quite a while until anything like this happens, anything that's so experientially productive for, and so beneficial for, our disembodied and experienceless soulful Trigger. During a long period, it may be that only some such events as these take place.

First, while some seventy three of Trigger's erstwhile Particles came to be in the fetal brain that, just over a year ago, generated your little nephew's brand-new soul, Trigger's soul just languished, as it most certainly did, a couple of years before that, when only fifty six erstwhile Particles came to be arrayed, with trillions of others so that (suppose) a brand-new soul was generated for a shrimp, Individualistically Propensitied for interaction with that shrimp's "brainiest" Particles. For, this brainy complex didn't have at least 106 of Trigger's Erstwhile Basic Constituents as components (even as it also didn't have at least 106 Erstwhile Basic Constituents of any other disembodied soul). So, for that reason, Trigger's soul didn't then get to "have" any (new) healthily brainy body, or bodies.

Second, Trigger's soul also languished, still disembodied, when, just a month ago, 109 of its Erstwhile Particles came to be the basic constituents of the brain of a certain fetal camel. Why? Well, they were beaten out by 112 of Gertrude's Particles, whose disembodied soul came, just right then, to be embodied camelly. Or, more colloquially, Gertie's soul then came to have the body of (or the many overlapping bodies of) a certain camel fetus, or fetal camel. For Trigger's many fans, all this was pretty discouraging. Even more discouraging was this: Just three days ago, 113 of Trigger's Erstwhile Particles came to be basic constituents of a fetal pig. But, at the same time, so did 113 Erstwhile Particles of one canine Lassie, the last of the Lassies ever to appear on the old TV show. As there was a tie here, there wasn't, of course, any old soul winning any Erstwhile Particle competition. So, just as our metaphysic has it, in this "exciting" event, there was an entirely new soul generated, for interaction with the developing piggish body, or bodies.

Well, now, after all that, let's have our soulful Trigger get much luckier: Just yesterday, as we'll further suppose, 106 of Trigger's Erstwhile Particles came to be basic constituents of the ripe fetal brain of a certain little human female fetus and, as Trigger was there the High Scorer— with more Erstwhile Particles contributing that any other formerly embodied soul—so, just right then, this once-equinely-embodied-soul became embodied once again. As it happens, we'll suppose, this late-fetal little girl was the preinfant daughter, or maybe even the infant daughter, of one Mr. and Mrs. Rabinowitz, both of them longtime fans of old Roy Rogers movies. Knowing that the mom was carrying a girl fetus, something very easy to know, nowadays, the Rabinowitzes named their tiny daughter "Dale Evans Rabinowitz." (As my younger readers may not yet know, Dale Evans was Roy Rogers's wife, and she starred opposite him, often in just such a role, both in movies and on their TV show.) Wrapping things up now, and projecting happily into the future, we may instructively say that, throughout the rest of her earthly life, say, throughout the next ninety years, Dale Evans Rabinowitz will have Trigger's soul and, in the bargain, Trigger, or Trigger's soul, will have the body of Dale Evans Rabinowitz. Once (the body of, or the bodies of) D. E. R. are no longer alive, of course, at the end of these ninety years, this soul will become, once again, a disembodied soul. But, until that time, and thanks to the aforementioned reincarnation, it will be an embodied soul, often interacting with very many Particles in the body of this Dale, especially very many of those that are in (and that serve to constitute, as we say) this Dale's brain.

All this being so, Trigger's soul, or the being that's really, really
Trigger, will thus come to enjoy quite a few years of (typical human)
experiencing, as well as quite a good deal of rather impressively intelligent (typical human) thinking and, to boot, some real choosing, I
suppose, at least from time to time. For even as this old soul was always
richly mentally Propensitied, now it's got a really fine physical interaction partner, so that these Propensities are very *impressively manifested*,
quite directly, in the very human sort of mental activity just mentioned
and, a little less directly, in quite a bit of intentional overt, and physical,
characteristically human behavior. Not that Dale R. won't be enjoying
all this; to the contrary, on the suppositions in place, she most certainly
will. After all, and as we properly Cartesian metaphysicians will properly observe, the really, real Dale Rabinowitz, is nobody but a certain
soul, the sentient being that, quite colloquially, we call "her soul." And,
also after all, this soul is, of course, the same sentient being as was, and
as is, nobody but that once-equinely-embodied-soul who's Trigger, that
is, the sentient being that, also quite colloquially, we call "Trigger's
soul." So, most strictly, really, and truly, Trigger (the soul) is the very
same individual as is (the soul) Dale Evans Rabinowitz. That's reincarnation, for you.

(Here's what may be only a digression, even if, perhaps, a helpfully
friendly digression: Pretty thoughtlessly, I think, many people assume,
and some real philosophers suppose—well, (at least) one real philosopher, anyway—that a reincarnated soul should have memories of how
things were with it, or at least some several salient such things, when it
was previously embodied.[7] I can't think of the slightest reason to believe anything even remotely like that, or anything even remotely like
any philosophically decent reason. Why is anything like this, apparently, quite widely assumed and, maybe, even widely believed? About
any of the specifics here, I'm quite uncertain and agnostic. But, in
general, I should think it's mainly the product of one, or of another,
sad sort of wishful thinking. Anyhow, digression or no, that's the last
of these tidbits. So, it's back to the main track.)

Now, the metaphysic I've just sketched for you is a perfectly consistent scheme. And, it's even got lots of things properly Propensitied

7. For this bit of silliness, see Derek Parfit's *Reasons and Persons*, Oxford University
Press, 1984. More specifically, see the book's Section 82, How a Non-Reductionist View
Might Have Been True, on pages 227–228.

Actually, this sort of thinking seems pretty widespread, and not just among tabloid
readers and seance fans, but also among academic philosophers. Why do I single out
Parfit for mention? Well, just for one thing, he's among the few living philosophers who,
overall and for the most part, I really do find to be philosophically admirable.

toward a reincarnational upshot, so that things don't have to be just so utterly happenstantial, time after time after time. Since this latter holds true, the sketched reincarnational metaphysic is far less crazy, you can be sure, than very many other things I could have placed before you. Just so, I'm afraid, it's far less crazy than almost anything else, to any genuinely reincarnational effect, that's available in the literature—including the philosophical literature, the religious literature, and, usually the most entertaining of all, the just-plain-crackpot literature. Check it out! There's just tons of silliness out there, and there's darned little else.

So, relative to what I just *might* have said, and compared with what most others actually say, what I presented, with Trigger and Dale and all, isn't even so much as half bad—not by any seriously systematic metaphysical standard. But, that's saying very little, as just about all that other stuff, including stuff left unsaid by me, is utter hogwash. Anyway, that's enough of this depressing negativity. Let's get back to a main track.

As compared with almost all the other metaphysical offerings, in this lengthy book's jampacked pages, how does my reincarnational story stack up? Myself, I think it stinks. It's got so many perfectly arbitrary propositions, each at a place that's just so absolutely crucial, that it can't even begin to make a bid for any credibility. And, what may be worse, for those of us plagued with much philosophical sensibility, its far more embroiled with intellectual ad-hoc-ness than with metaphysical elegance, or with intuitive plausibility, or with anything else that's philosophically important.

As I've been suggesting, even if we should be, for many trillions of years, just so many perfectly disembodied souls, these will be our prospects, leastways our nontheistic prospects, for ever enjoying any reincarnation and, in the bargain, for ever again experiencing, after (first) we cease being embodied souls: Slim, dim and none. (This really isn't any greater than the more commonly enunciated *slim and none*; it just sounds funnier, partly because it sounds like there's a bit more.)

9. The Question of Disembodied Souls and the Question of an Almighty Creator

Many are the readers, I'm sure, who've noticed the telltale term "nontheistic" just above. For, as I'm quite prepared to agree, our prospects might be far better, if only there should be an appropriate God—that is, of course, an *appropriately Propensitied* God—in the picture. Or, far better, if there's an aptly Propensitied God in actual concrete reality.

Well, then, *is* there such an Almighty Helper here, in what's really and truly our actual world?

Among prominent academic philosophers, nowadays, there aren't many who, in their publications, address this question, or any question much like it. And, among the few who do address it, almost all of them are theists. Well, I'm certainly no theist. So, why should I address this question?

By way of providing a responsive answer, I'll rehearse the first, second, and fourth sentences of Bertrand Russell's preface to his last systematically serious work in philosophy, *Human Knowledge: Its Scope and Limits.*[8] Famous for his articulate atheism, as well as for some six hundred or so other things, Russell addressed our current question in several of his philosophical publications, though not, so far as I can tell, in *Human Knowledge* itself. Still and all, these Prefatory words of his apply, quite nicely, to my own current project and purposes.

> The following pages are addressed not only or primarily to profes-sional philosophers but to that much larger public which is interested in philosophical questions without being willing or able to devote more than a limited amount of time to considering them. Descartes, Leibniz, Locke, Berkeley, and Hume wrote for a public of this sort, and I think that it is unfortunate that during the last hundred and sixty years or so philosophy has come to be regarded as almost as technical as mathematics.... Philosophy proper deals with matters of interest to the general educated public, and loses much of its value if only a few professionals can understand what is said.

Well, though my prospects for achieving the goal are far less than Russell's were, I'm also interested in addressing the general educated public, a public that hasn't changed much, in the ways Russell deemed most relevant, over the last sixty or so years. And, just as I've tried to make this book a pretty accessible work, avoiding extensive use of any highly technical terminology, so I'm also trying to address, in this same work, quite a few philosophical questions that interest the general educated public. Now, perhaps especially when it's the English-speak-ing public that's in question, as it surely was for Russell then, and for me now, too, well, with this big group, few questions interest them more than do issues concerning the existence of, and the nature of, an (at least alleged) Almighty Creator. With my project's purposes just made quite clear, it's to these questions that I now turn.

8. Bertrand Russell, *Human Knowledge: Its Scope and Limits*, Simon and Schuster, 1948.

First, I'll lay my cards on the table: From the general tone of this book, I suppose, it may have occurred to many readers that, on questions concerning the existence of an (alleged) Almighty God, I'm agnostic. But, there are agnostics and agnostics. So, what sort am I? Well, I'm an agnostic who inclines toward the atheistic side of the issue; not overwhelmingly, I guess, but, still, decidedly more than I incline to the theistic side.

Unlike many imbued with atheistic leanings, I'm very uncertain that there's anything wrong with being much more theistically inclined than I myself am. I can't tell, really, whether the weight of all the evidence, and of all the philosophic arguments, is anything like decisive on the matter. To my mind, at any rate, there's some considerable intellectual appeal in certain Arguments from Design, despite the fact that, on the other side, there have been several intellectually appealing critiques of these Arguments. So, as best as I can tell, there may well be—though there also may well not be—some pretty winning Arguments for some such theistic view as this position:

(UNIQUE) ALMIGHTY CREATOR. A single Supremely Powerful Concrete Individual, who's both an Always Existing Entity and also a Paradigmatically Personal Individual, created all the (actual world's) other concrete individuals, whether doing it all quite directly or whether, more plausibly, doing much of it rather indirectly. (In just doing that, of course, He didn't create Himself, of course, which would involve us in perfectly nonsensical notions; but, rather, He created *all the rest of* concrete reality.)

While I don't so much as believe this proposition, I'm not extremely confident it's false, either. More likely it's false than true, I say, whatever that exactly means here. (Well, I've already told you I'm an agnostic who's atheistically inclined, so you know what, in this present context, *I mean by* that sentence, even if none of us knows, exactly, what the sentence itself actually means.) Anyhow, even as I've already admitted, there may well be some pretty winning Arguments for (UNIQUE) ALMIGHTY CREATOR, as best as I can tell. So, even though I think it more likely false than true, I have quite considerable intellectual respect for this view, whose shorter name will be, I now say, ALMIGHTY CREATOR.

But, however things may fare for ALMIGHTY CREATOR, it's an enormously long step from that proposition to the idea that, even if we all should become disembodied souls, many of us will, some day, become reincarnated. And, it's also a giant step to the thought that, after we may first become disembodied souls, we'll come to have, once again, apt physical interaction partners, apt for manifesting our power to experience, much as we experiencing embodied souls apparently have right now. To be sure, it might be terribly nice for us, I imagine, if some such circumstance should some day befall us, even if it should be quite long after our (initial) disembodiment. Or, at the least, this might be very nice providing that, in such a circumstance, much of our experiencing should be pretty pleasant experiencing, or reasonably satisfying experiencing, or fairly fulfilling experiencing—well, you get the idea. But, why should anyone think that anything like this should ever come to pass? Certainly, by itself, ALMIGHTY CREATOR doesn't give us much reason.

For there to be an Almighty Creator who'll give us good prospects for nice reincarnation, and for nice experiencing long after first-bodily death, there should be the right sort of Almighty Creator, so to put it. Anyway, not just any old Supremely Powerful and Productive Personal Being will turn the trick, or should be expected to do so. No; not by a long shot. What we need here is a God who's a pretty nice Guy, so to say. Less colloquially, what we need is a Powerful Creator, and Arranger, who's moved, or motivated, by a favorable concern for the long-term plight of us actual human beings, saliently including you and me (whatever might be our metaphysical nature). In more traditional terms, there should be a terribly Powerful Creator Who is a Benevolent Being, concerned about the prospects of, or for, the infinitely less powerful sentient beings that, on our hypothesis, He bothered to create. He can do whatever He wants, we may grant. But, then, what *is* it that He wants? What concerns Him? What does He care about, even the least little bit, perhaps, even so much as just half a little shit? If it's mainly His own amusement that concerns Him, say, then it's hardly likely that He'd bother to have set things up so that we should have a terribly nice time of it all. After all, what would be so amusing about anything like that—about just so many pretty smoothly painless lives, or just so many pretty painlessly smooth paths, for just so terribly many pretty powerless feeling souls? Even to such a pathetically powerless person as myself, that seems a quite boring state of affairs, rather lacking, I should think, in dramatic surprises and surprising dramatics. In creating a world that works out well for the very limited likes of us, He'd be behaving in a way that, at least for the most part, did very little to satisfy His presumed primary interests.

To make a long story shorter, for it to be credible that you should have a nice afterlife—heck, even any afterlife at all—not only must

ALMIGHTY CREATOR be quite credible (or else something very like that proposition) but, very far beyond anything like just that, some such traditionally familiar dictum as this must be very credible:

> BENEVOLENT ALMIGHTY CREATOR. A single Supremely Powerful Concrete Individual, who's both an Always Existing Entity and also a Paradigmatically Personal Individual, created all the (actual world's) other concrete individuals, whether doing it all quite directly or whether, more plausibly, doing much of it rather indirectly. (In just doing that, of course, He didn't create Himself, of course, which would involve us in perfectly nonsensical notions; but, rather, He created *all the rest of* concrete reality.) And, what's very much more, thank goodness, He is a deeply, and widely, Benevolent Creative Arranger, working in ways that really benefit, far more than ever they harm, every last one of all His very many sentient creations, each and very one of the terribly many mentally Propensitied individuals that He has created.

No doubt, as you'll observe, my formulation of this traditional dictum, or doctrine, is a very shoddy and sloppy formulation—overgeneralizing in some certain ways, maybe undergeneralizing in some others, and rife with yet other deficiencies, too. But, for our present discussion's primary purposes, that's all just by way of nicety and nuance, in no wise affecting the central thrust of the proposition. Just so, our displayed dictum is quite as clear to raging atheists, provided they have even the barest acquaintance with Western culture, as it is apparent to the most devout of traditional theists, and the most traditional of devout theists. Let us not quibble, then over what's bound to be little more than a family squabble.

No quibbles, no squabbles; let's get on with what are, right now, the main matters.

Now, even for those who may doubt that there really are any facts as to what things, or which beings, are truly good, or are good in and of themselves, there shouldn't be a problem with the factual credentials of BENEVOLENT ALMIGHTY CREATOR. This is not any claim to the effect that there's a Powerful Individual Who is good. No; not at all. It's a claim about whether there is such a One who is very decently concerned about, and quite effectively concerned with, the plight of sentient beings, presumably, all of them beings that He has created (even if, perhaps, He's done that all quite indirectly). So, these doubters should have no problems right here, however many difficulties they may (think they) see with various other claims, relevant only to various other discussions. So, as I lately just said, I'll say once again: Let's get on with what are, right now, the main matters.

Well, really, now, how credible do you find BENEVOLENT ALMIGHTY CREATOR? Or, for that matter, how credible do you find any proposition even just remotely like that traditional, or traditional-sounding, doctrine? Well, you can put me down for a big loud "*Not Very!*" And, boy, it's a veritable landslide here, as the case for a negative answer is almost absurdly overwhelming.

First of all, there's this. Nowadays, it's true, almost all childhood suffering and death is, in some sense at least, preventable by human intervention. Sadly, much of this intervention goes undone, as folks in wealthier lands do very little, even as compared with what we're well able to do, for those in the poorest countries (which are, in large measure, now African countries). So, many young children suffer and die. In all this, where, on God's good green earth, is the Benevolent Almighty Creator? Nowhere, that's where. And, why's that? Well, as some may well hold, He's just putting us all to a big moral test, to see how well we exercise our power to choose, all us pretty wealthy (to very wealthy) potential benefactors. But, that's just crazily outrageous. He's content to let all these little kids suffer so terribly just because, or largely because, He wants us to be presented with a big ongoing moral test? *That's* certainly no *Benevolent* Power. And, I'm just starting to warm up.

So, let's think back a little ways, say, just a single century, or so. Back then, hardly anybody could do much to help anyone in absolutely awful straits—even the finest doctors were helpless against the likes of mere *influenza*—that's just a long name for the flu—with epidemics killing many millions of all sorts of folks, including millions of innocent little children. So, with nobody on earth even the least bit at fault, millions upon millions of innocent little children suffered and died—not just in Niger, mind you, nor yet just in Nigeria, but even in, and maybe especially in, my native New York City. Quite obviously, this wasn't any moral test, not even any moral test the giving of which was, itself, just so much morally outrageous activity—the furthest thing from any benevolent behavior. Not even the finest doctors could do anything, for Christ's sake! Whoever arranged a world with all this presumable optional suffering, but not any humanly preventable suffering, well He's not even any moderately concerned Intelligence, much less any truly Benevolent Power.

But, let's not limit ourselves to human beings, especially as, on all the philosophically most plausible conceptions of embodied immaterial souls, the bodies involved aren't just the (normal healthy) human bodies. No; not by a long shot. A cute little puppy will have, or she'll be, a perfectly real immaterial soul, even if she is, or her soul is, embodied caninely, rather than humanly. Well, if it costs you little or nothing, would you let a little puppy suffer? Of course, not; you're far too benevolent for that; you're far too caring a person to just sit on your hands here. But, every day, of course, and for very many millions of years, there've been very many little puppies each suffering mightily. A Benevolent Almighty Power, you used to say? Get real, buddy. This is the planet Earth we're talking about, not a world that never was.

With that in mind, let's go back a ways, in our imaginative historical journey, or exercise, long before the advent of humankind or, for that matter, even any of our fellow primates. So, just think, for a moment, of all the many millions of sensitive creatures, all the little fawns, for instance, that, over millions of years, were all painfully burned, just excruciatingly roasted, in ever so many forest fires, all of them "naturally occurring" forest fires. (None of these fires was ever, of course, the fault of any negligent camper, let alone any careless smoker, as there didn't yet exist, leastways anywhere here on earth, any campers or smokers at all.) How horrible is *that*, I ask you, all you who dare to uphold, quite as heartlessly propounded as it's brainlessly affirmed, any claim that's even the least bit like the utterly incredible BENEVOLENT ALMIGHTY CREATOR? It's certainly too horrible, I tell you, to have anyone believing, even the least bit reasonably, or the least bit intelligently, anything remotely like that extremely dubious doctrine.

Are any of you, all you readers of mine, at all surprised here, by any of this? There's not the slightest reason for that, you know; never has been, never will be. Look here, now, let's think a bit, just a little bit, even, about how things are with ever so many *nonsupreme* individuals. You know who I mean here; I'm talking about just so many flesh-and-blood human beings or, maybe metaphysically better, the souls embodied in these active, healthy, normal human beings, or human bodies. Well, I still don't know about you; but, I'll tell you something about my own experience with earthly people. Not just from what I've seen directly, sort of up front and personal, but also from the much broader perspective that the media provides us—that it provides even to such pathetically powerless people as you and me—well, it's just plain obvious that there's no very strong correlation, for goodness sakes, between how powerful a thinking being is, or how influential is the individual, and, on the other side, how benevolent, or caring, is the individual in question. Nor, have I noticed even so much as *any* strong correlation that might plausibly be deemed *relevant* here—say, between how intelligent an individual is, or how knowledgeable, and, on the other side, the degree to which the being is a kindly soul, or she's an altruistic individual, or he's concerned for others. As anyone can easily see, no extrapolative inference will do much for our badly beleaguered BENEVOLENT ALMIGHTY CREATOR.

10. Why Our Long-Term Prospects May Be Very Bleak Prospects

In the previous couple of Chapters, I argued that each of us is, or each of us has, a distinct immaterial soul, in no wise physical or material. And, in this present Chapter I've argued that, though each of us may well have been generated by some material body, or bodies, or each of our souls may well have been, still, once an immaterial soul is generated, and it exists, it will continue to exist, even if there should no longer exist any of its generating body, or bodies. And, I've argued that, maybe after his or her brain dies, each of us will become a disembodied soul, retaining all the soul's Basic Mental Propensity.

Still, unless a soul enjoys substantial further experiencing, this won't be of any great benefit for any of us immaterial souls, disembodied or not, even if we should last for all eternity. And, without apt interaction with apt physical Propensity partners, none of a soul's mental Propensity, saliently including her Power to experience, will ever be manifested. And, without just such a manifestation, or just such manifesting, there won't be any future experiencing that's *her* experiencing. What are our prospects for such future experientially productive interaction? To put the same question in more familiar terms, what are our prospects (presumably after our disembodiment, but maybe just straight off, without any such nonspatial hiatus) of future reembodiment or, more familiarly still, for our reincarnation?

Unless there's a Supremely Powerful and Benevolent Creative Arranger, the prospects are, I've been suggesting, very bleak indeed. Well, then, *is* there, in actual fact, such a Benevolent Powerful Creator?

While anything's possible, I guess, it's most implausible, I've argued, to think that, in this sorry actual world of ours, there's a Benevolent Almighty Creator.

But, wait a minute. Maybe I've been a bit too fast with all of this. Might we make do with something much less than that, much less than a Supremely Powerful and Loving Arranger? Well, theoretically, we might well do all right with a much lesser being, or a much less caring being. For example, if He was quite benevolent, even if not Supremely so, we might make do with a far less than Supremely Powerful

Creator-Arranger. And, if He was very powerful, though not Supremely so, we might make do, in another way, with a far less than Supremely Loving Creator-Arranger. But, either way, how much less would really suffice? And, in what sorts of way, or ways, might there be some quite tolerable deficiency, or diminution, on the part of the world's most powerfully creative concretum?

Not in any way, I imagine, that's both likely to be in the cards and that's likely to be very beneficial for us, for us pitifully puny soulful beings.

Look, it's no very great shakes to arrange the actual world—and mainly just this solar system—in some such way where it doesn't happen that, over many millions of years, very many millions of fawns painfully die in many quite natural forest fires. One way to do that may be just this: Have it that, just as soon as some smoke is inhaled, a fawn becomes insensitive to fire and, in the bargain, it no longer can feel much pain at all. Another way may be just this one: Have it that there's always enough moisture in the forest for there never to be any very big forest fire. And, of course, that's just a start. By comparison with any of that, it's a very big deal, indeed, for even a wonderfully powerful being to arrange things so that disembodied souls, or at least very many of them, later become embodied souls and, once again have happy interaction partners, so that, once again, they come to experience substantially (and they do so even pretty interestingly, or enjoyably).

Don't misunderstand me, please. It's not absolutely inconceivable, I grant, that there should be a benevolent God who created us all, and who arranged for us, or for many of us, eventually to become reincarnated—even though He's not quite up to it to spare each of so very many of His little fawns, just such protracted and excruciating pain. And, it's not absolutely inconceivable that He shouldn't quite manage to spare very many innocent human infants very great suffering, and early biological death, through dehydrating diarrhea—quite unheard-of in many wealthy countries, but still very prevalent in the poorest parts of the world. But, while all this isn't absolutely inconceivable, it is, nonetheless, almost perfectly incredible. In an obvious enough way, I think, this would be like having our world be the product of a sort of incredibly elite savant. Maybe he'd be quite kind enough, or quite impressively benevolent. But, at the same time, then, he'd be, quite queerly, indeed, both very able, in certain matters, and yet terribly unable, in certain others. Can you and I really be the products of an immaterial *Rain Man*, so to say, a nice example for those who've seen that entertaining movie? Anything's possible, I guess, in some sense of that often-abused term. But, actually, really and truly? I simply can't believe that we're all the products of such a kindly but only so queerly able savant. And, supposing that you're in your right mind, neither can you.

Where, then, does all of this Chapter's discussion leave us? Well, at least so far as we can tell, it leaves us thinking that, most likely, this is the human condition: Though we may well all become disembodied, that will all be to no avail.

9

THE PROBLEM OF OUR UNCONSCIOUS QUALITY

In the last couple of Chapters, I've offered considerations to favor Substantial Dualism over its salient more conservative rivals, whether the favored Substantial Dualism be only a Pessimistic Form of the Thesis or whether it be an Optimistic Dualism that's favored. In either event, we should want a Substantial Dualism that is, in the best sense of the expression, a *Humanly Realistic Philosophy*. For that to transpire, we should articulate a Substantial Dualism that does well by the Problem of Our Unconscious Quality, a nice difficulty that I introduced quite early in this book, as early as in our second Chapter, where I also first observed our goal of developing a Humanly Realistic Philosophy. As you may remember, this Problem concerns how it may be that, even as we should always be qualitied individuals, we should, even so, survive lapses in our conscious experiencing, or at least apparent lapses.

Now, at that early stage of our work, we didn't yet have much discussion of Quality, or even much about quality. And, we certainly didn't have very much motivation to develop any Substantial Dualist Metaphysic. So, at that early stage, there wasn't much point in an extensive discussion of the Problem of Our Unconscious Quality. At this later stage, however, that may be much more productive: With a heightened awareness of this Problem, and of how it may impact any Substantial Dualism, we may better appreciate such Dualist Hypotheses as can, in due course, allow for an apt Dualistic answer to the proposed

Problem. In this shortish Chapter, I'll aim for a heightened awareness. Then, in the Chapter to follow, the book's last Chapter, I'll advance a Hypothesis that allows Substantial Dualists to answer, quite nicely, the Problem of Our Unconscious Quality.

As I just said, this is a shortish Chapter. But, it isn't minute. So, excepting readers who just can't ever get enough metaphysics to ponder, you may want to skip most of this Chapter. Without your incurring any crucial loss, and with your acquiring enough to appreciate what's in the long last Chapter, you can read just a couple of Sections here. As good a choice as any, I think, many might want to peruse just Sections 3 and 4, here, and then proceed, directly, to the last Chapter.

1. Physical Objects Aptly Qualitied, Experiencers Differently Qualitied Just as Aptly

In a very brief and crude rendition, here's a Scientiphical story as to how an imagined World might come to include some nonphysical experiencing thinkers, and maybe even how, in some Eons, the actual World might come to include some. Though we needn't suppose a storied World to be Particulate, for a nicely neat exposition I'll make that tidy assumption. So, we allow ourselves a World happily populated with a nice variety of elementary particles, saliently including Blue electrons, Red protons, Yellow neutrons, and your own favorite Particle, which we may suppose to be Extensibly Qualitied Purple. At all events, we'll have many Particles each replete both with Spatially Extensible Quality and, as well, with appropriate physical Propensity.

As time goes by, our supposed Particles become arrayed in a wide variety of physical complexes. Intricate bonding occurs; turbulent oscillating obtains; all manner of physical growth and transformation have their turn. Eventually, there's you or, at least, there's your body, that's right over there (or, maybe, there are your many bodies, all right over there). And, right here, there's my quite different body (or, maybe, there are my many bodies, each of them quite different from yours).

Now, your body is constituted of many billions of little Reds, and Blues, and Yellows, and Purples. So, it's a complex physical object whose Qualities are just all those Extensible Colors: a little Blue in this place, a little Red in that one, again a little Blue, though now in this other place. Thus it is that your body is Qualitied in such-and-such a variegated Extensibly Colored way. Of course, that's very sketchy and speculative. But, for our having a fairly clear conception of how *your body* may be complexly Qualitied—or how your many bodies each may be Qualitied—it will suffice.

What about *how it is that you yourself are experientially qualitied?* In a world so replete with physical things whose space is all Qualitied Extensibly, it may seem quite impossible for there to be, as well, genuinely experiencing beings, each with Nonextensible experiential quality. How so? Well, with great physical change in your brain, there may be wondrously dynamic arrays of Spatially Extensible Quality, marvelous spatial patterning of Extensible Red, Blue, Yellow, and Purple. Still, if *that's all* that's qualitative concerning you, then, as it seems, there'll be nothing in the World that's ever your experiential quality. For, as it seems, none of those changing patterns of Blue, and Red, and other Spatially Extensible Qualities, will ever amount to the experiential quality that you yourself have when, for instance, you're experiencing a pure sound, as with your experiencing belltonely. To have a World where it's very clear that you're experientially qualitied, we should make, it seems, some additional substantive assumptions.

As I've been suggesting, maybe these should be Substantial Dualistic assumptions, on which you're a well-qualitied nonspatial experiencer and real chooser. Now, as it appears, you should be able to conceive, at least tolerably well, how things are with you qualitatively, at any moment when you should exist. But, as it also appears, at some moments of your existence you're utterly unconscious. And, at some of these moments, at least, you'll have no experiential quality. Or, so it appears. Well, at least apparently, we're fast rubbing up against a problem here, the Problem of Our Unconscious Quality. In a patiently methodical fashion, let's move to discuss the matter.

2. Every Individual Is Qualitied, Including You and Me

In our discussion of physical concreta, we agreed that, at least insofar as they may be clearly conceived by us human beings, each is propertied in three naturally basic ways: First, each will be Spatially propertied, as with having a certain shape or size. Second, each will be propertied Propensitively, as with having a certain mass or solidity. And, third, each physical individual must have some Spatially Extensible Quality, or Qualities, suited to *pervading the space of* the individual, as with Extensible Color. By now, all that should be, I hope, philosophically pretty appealing.

Comporting well with those familiar thoughts, I'll now offer ideas somewhat less familiar. Though they're less familiar thoughts, they might be still more appealing ideas.

For a moment, suppose that our Quasi-Cartesian account is roughly right. Then, first, your body will be propertied in the three mutually complementary ways rehearsed just above, even though it may be just derivatively that this physical complex will be so triply propertied. But, then, second, there's also this. Being a nonspatial mental particular, you yourself won't be propertied in those three ways. While you may be Propensitied, you won't be Spatially propertied. And, at least for that reason, you won't have any Spatially Extensible Quality.

Now, though a nonspatial mental particular won't be Qualitied in *that* way, it must be qualitied in *some* way or other. For, as it seems, *any* concrete individual must be qualitied in some way or other, whether it be physical, or mental, or both, or neither. Well, at least any concretum *our human minds can conceive*, at all fully or clearly, must be qualitied in some way or other.

Look, as I'm quite sure, *you can conceive yourself*, fairly fully and pretty clearly, much as I can conceive myself, quite well enough. So, still supposing that we're nonspatial beings, and still agreeing that we'll have no Spatially Extensible Quality, we should then conclude that we're qualitied in some *other* way, not that we're not qualitied at all.

At least somewhat realistically, how might this happen? When taking that question seriously, it's not long till we confront, very squarely, the Problem of Our Unconscious Quality.

3. We Reconsider the Problem of Our Unconscious Quality

Whenever I'm conscious, or experiencing, I'll have some *qualitative character*. Sometimes I'm experiencing in a rather painful way; and sometimes in a way that's not painful. Sometimes I experience visually and not auditorally; sometimes the converse holds; sometimes I experience in both ways at once. And, just perhaps, sometimes I may be experiencing, but not in either of those two familiar ways. Lying in perfect darkness and absolute silence, perhaps I might be experiencing just insofar as I'm feeling certain bodily sensations.

In these situations, and in indefinitely more, I'm *experientially qualitied*. This will be so, whether *or not* I'm then Spatially Extensibly Qualitied. So, *that's* how I might be richly endowed qualitatively, *even if*

I should always be lacking Spatially Extensible Quality. (Well, at the least, that's one way.) Thus, so long as I'm conscious, it may be unproblematic how it is that I'm a substantial concretum, a nicely qualitied individual, even if I might not be a spatial particular. And, it may be unproblematic, as well, how it may be that, so long as I'm conscious, I'm apt to be quite well conceived, even by the likes of such a quite limited human thinker as, no doubt, I myself am.

But, what of the times when, as it appears, I'm *wholly unconscious*, as with my deepest sleep between dreams? It might be, I'll suggest, that these are times when, even though I'm utterly unconscious, nonetheless I still exist. As far as it goes, that's well and good. But, wanting some pertinent understanding, we should now ask about this. When I'm utterly unconscious, how is it *then* with me qualitatively? What's *then* my qualitative character? As it certainly seems, at least at first blush, a Substantial Dualist will draw only a depressing blank here.

Whether or not it really is so very bleak, a Substantial Dualist's situation does appear, at least, to be quite as depressing as all this: Since we're entirely lacking in spatiality—by contrast with our spatial bodies—well, then, when we nonspatial souls are utterly unconscious, we have *no* qualitative character at all, neither Extensible nor Nonextensible. Will we have, then, *only powers*—or have Propensities *only*—*without any quality whatsoever*? Such a suggestion seems, at least to my mind, to be a disturbingly empty proposal. To those of us who've labored on the Mystery of the Physical, it's certainly, and at the least, a pretty depressing suggestion.

How might one try to make this depressing idea a rather more palatable proposition? Here is a representative effort: Almost always, we can allow that certain Propensities I have when unconscious, whether constant or changing, may manifest themselves as to quality upon my regaining consciousness. So, before going into soundest sleep I may be stumped by a hard problem. Upon awakening from this deep sleep, a solution may occur to me in a burst of conscious thought. In the dreamless interim, I may have been thinking unconsciously about this problem. At that time, I may have manifested my power to *think*, but I might *not* have manifested my power to *experience*. When I awaken, then, once again, my power to experience may be manifested. And, when I again experience, then, of course, I'm again experientially qualitied.

That effort does nothing, really, for the Problem of Our Unconscious Quality. To make this very clear, we consider cases of people who died in deepest sleep, when wholly unconscious. As we might usefully suppose, and quite as Pessimistic Dualists will uphold, these people then ceased to exist, completely and forever. Anyhow, they never again awakened, or will awaken, and they never again experience. Now, with any of these unfortunate people, after they went into that deep sleep, there wasn't any opportunity for them, nor was there any real chance for them, ever again to manifest their power to experience. So, as a matter of course, after going into that deep sleep, none of them had any experiential quality. Consider just a certain one of these unfortunate people, any single one of them at all. Well, when *she* last existed, in just the very deepest sleep, did she have *experiential Propensities only*, and no quality at all? The thought is, I think, extremely unfortunate.

But, there's no deep difference, of course, between these poor people and we who awaken from deepest sleep, again and again, and, upon our awakening, enjoy more experiencing, again and again. Their case only serves to make more dramatic a problem that, for a Substantial Dualist's attempt to conceive herself clearly, arises with all deep sleepers, including us luckier guys: When you were quite unconscious sometime last night, as we should allow actually did happen, didn't *you* still have *some* qualitative character? I certainly think so. But, on a Substantial Dualist View, without there being any experiencing on your part, how can you possibly be qualitied at all?

There are some similarities, of course, between the problem I'm discussing and certain more familiar, smaller problems. For example, someone may experience a headache that, as we say, has a certain character: it's fairly severe, it's apparently centered behind her eyes, and so on. For a while, our sentient subject is distracted by wonderful news and, apparently, she then doesn't feel any headache. Then, having become accustomed to the news, she again feels a headache of just the same character. Now, as we're inclined to say, this is a recurrence of the selfsame headache, which never went away entirely. But, during the interim period, was there still a feature of her qualitative aspect that, except for experiential awareness of headache, was very like her qualitative aspect when experiencing the considered headache? During the interim, when she had no experience as of headache, how could there be any headachy quality at all involved in this person's qualitative character? Even with this smaller problem, it's hard to know what's a satisfactory answer.

There are several reasons why this familiar problem is a lesser difficulty than the one we're mainly discussing. Here is one: In that our headachy subject is always experiencing, it's always clear that she's *always qualitied in some* way. So, it's not that she's supposed to be an entity with powers only, without any qualities at all. And, here's a closely related reason: In that she's always consciously experiencing in some way or other, her losing consciousness of the headache raises no serious question regarding whether, or when, she'll cease to exist. For, all during the considered period, she'll always have some experiential quality, even if not always quality that's characteristically headachy. With our sound sleeper, by contrast, we do suppose that she comes to lack experiential quality completely. And, when supposing Substantial Dualism to hold, there's then the suggestion that, in losing consciousness, she comes to lack qualities altogether. That does raise a serious question regarding whether, and when, she'll cease to exist.

Here's a bit more about how our Problem is a more substantial difficulty: It hardly matters whether (we say) our headachy person has just one headache, which in the middle period goes unnoticed, or whether (we say) she has one headache before the interim and another after. Being scarcely any very substantial matter, this latter just might be, perhaps, the sort of issue that we might decide for ourselves. Perhaps we may decide it by effectively deciding to say the first thing, and getting it to stick that we say headaches to be so continuously persistent. Well, maybe that remark implies impossible verbal magic. Still, what's true about the headache issue doesn't seem to matter much. With sound sleep, by contrast, what's right seems to matter a lot. With the question of whether our deep sleeper continues to exist, or whether it's someone else who freshly awakens, a real thinker's very existence is, evidently, right on the line.

In much of our present presentation, we've taken some Dualist propositions to be our background suppositions. That's helped us, I think, to appreciate the Problem of Our Unconscious Quality. But, at the same time, it may obscure how very broad is the scope of this Problem. Directly, I'll try to indicate its broad compass.

Without our "Qualitative" resolution of the Mystery of the Physical, provided only after we first introduced the Problem of Our Unconscious Quality, this Problem would be a serious difficulty for Scientiphicalism, and for any previously available Materialist Metaphysic, and for our beleaguered Nonentity Emergentism, as much as it is, and as it may continue to be, for any available Substantial Dualism. To my mind, that point is of great importance. There are two related reasons, at least, for this great importance. On the one hand, the point drives home how crucial it is, for any view remotely like Scientiphicalism, that there be Qualitied physical individuals (or, at the least, one such well-Qualitied physical concretum). These will be spatially extended individuals whose space is pervaded with *Quality fit for spatial pervasion*. On the other hand, the point highlights these further issues: Once we do take there to be physical things with (Spatially Extensible) Quality, then, at least at first blush, we may take Scientiphicalism to offer fair prospects for the development of a Humanly Realistic Philosophy. (And, at a later stage of inquiry, our observed Emergentism may seem, at first blush, to offer fair prospects.) Now, quite as Substantial Dualist Views seem so badly beset by the Problem of Our Unconscious Quality, well, in this one respect, at least, our Enlightened Scientiphicalism—and, maybe even more so, our Nonentity Emergentism—may seem a philosophically superior position, however much trouble the View (or the Views) may have in other respects, and however numerous may be those more troubling respects.

In having us be spatially extended entities, pervaded with Extensible Quality, Scientiphicalism allows for, I've said, a nice resolution for this Problem. By contrast, Substantial Dualism can't offer that resolution. (Nor can it be offered, of course, by any other view on which we never have any Spatially Extensible Quality, as with, for example, a Berkeleyan Idealism.)

Well, then, *how can* this Problem be nicely resolved, with just the resources of a metaphysic, *any* metaphysic, on which you're *not a spatial* being of any sort? This is, I think, an intriguing question. Our discussion of it starts with thoughts flowing from Descartes.

4. We Notice How Descartes Heroically Denies This Problem

Recall Descartes's reply to the objection that, in deepest sleep between dreams, we're apparently utterly unconscious, not experiencing at all, and yet we survive to tell more tales. Famously holding that you must be conscious whenever existing, and your existence isn't an interrupted affair, he just bit the bullet, and spit it back whence it came. Against common sense, Descartes simply *denied that there are* any periods of sleep when you *aren't* conscious; it *only appears that way*. Contrary to your impression of a long night's full sleep, Descartes says, what really occurred is that you kept consciously experiencing all night through, but, as concerns most of it, you completely forgot your conscious thinking and experiencing, maybe right after it occurred, and certainly before you finished your sleeping.

In saying all that, Descartes heroically denies our proffered Problem. Now, using terms of quality, the Cartesian denial may be put like this: Because you always have some *experiential* quality, *there really is no Problem*. (In service of truth and fairness, I should say that I'm coopting Descartes, or creating a Descartes who's interested in questions of quality. In fact, Descartes seems not to be much concerned with phenomenological considerations. And, when it comes to physical reality, generally it's just geometric features that he finds important, apparently not even recognizing any characteristically physical powers, or Propensities, much less any need for Spatially Extensible Quality. So, where I'm talking about Descartes, you may take it that we're discussing a Cartesian philosopher, possibly contrived, who's very concerned with questions of quality.)

In opposition to this denial, which really is rather heroic, a Humanly Realistic Philosophy offers a more plausible stance on the matter, or at least a part of that. When you come to be completely unconscious, as may well happen in deepest sleep, it may happen that, while you still do exist, your power to experience isn't manifested.

But, this can be only part of a more plausible approach. For, as we've agreed, a concrete entity can't have powers only, or just Propensities, leastways not if it's to be adequately conceived by human thinkers. Rather, it must have quality as well. It can't be, then, that when you're in deepest sleep, and apparently not experiencing, absolutely all that goes on with you is the persistence of mental powers, with some of them manifested, perhaps, but with none that's manifested experientially, or qualitatively.

As it holds that you're composed of spatially extended things, an Enlightened Scientiphical Metaphysic may hold that, even when you're utterly unconscious, you may have whatever Spatially Extensible Quality, or Qualities, will pervade the simple spatial things that serve to compose you. In this way, Scientiphicalism may allow you to be utterly without experiential quality, as might happen in deepest sleep and, even so, you may still be well qualitied. (And, in just the same way, our Nonentity Emergentism also allows that.) As you may be qualitatively well-endowed, of course, just for your being Spatially Extensibly Qualitied, well, you certainly won't have no quality at all. And, so, it won't seem incomprehensible to us, or almost utterly unintelligible, that you should exist even while, as may sometimes happen, you'll be utterly unconscious.

Here's a bit more of what an Enlightened Scientiphicalist might say: After you awaken from your deepest sleep, and also when you experientially dream during some less deep sleep, you'll be both Extensibly Qualitied and also experientially qualitied. So, according to an Enlightened Scientiphicalism, you'll then have an *abundance of quality*. But, of course, that's no problem. As concerns any alleged concrete entity, a problem will arise, at least for us, only with the thought that the considered individual will have no quality at all. By contrast, no problem will arise, at least not for us, with any thought that the concretum may be quite *abundantly* Qualitied, or very *richly* qualitied.

In its ability to provide a decently sensible treatment of the Problem of Our Unconscious Quality, Scientiphicalism has an advantage, at least apparently, over Substantial Dualism. And, of course, it will also have this advantage, at least apparently, over certain still more radical departures from the dominant Scientiphical Metaphysic, like, for instance, a Berkeleyan Idealism.

5. A Quasi-Humean Substantial Dualist May Heroically Deny the Problem

As I did in the book's second Chapter, I'll again display this sentence from Hume: "When my perceptions are remov'd for any time, as by sound sleep; so long am I insensible of *myself*; and may truly be said not to exist."[1] And, as always, it's interesting to notice the great difference between Descartes and Hume, as concerns your existence and your consciously thinking or experiencing.

Descartes holds that, even as our existence isn't temporally intermittent, so there actually *aren't* any periods of unconscious sound sleep. It may seem to us, even often, that, in each of our lives, there really are many such absolutely experienceless periods. But, as Descartes holds, what really happens, with each of these periods, is that the sound sleeper just *completely forgets* her experiencing *directly after* she enjoys the forgotten experiencing.

By contrast, Hume holds that our existence *is temporally intermittent*. You exist *before* dreamless sleep, and *also after* perfectly sound sleep, when there's again experience that's yours. But, during the interim period, you're not consciously thinking or experiencing. So, then, even though we may say that you're sleeping, the reality is that, in this interim, you *don't* exist.

(In discussing Hume, we saw that he wasn't a Substantial Dualist. Indeed, so far from holding that your experiences are ontologically parasitical on you, the individual experiencer, Hume held that it's "your perceptions" that are ontologically primary; for Hume, you're just a "bundle of perceptions." For Hume, then, you're ontologically parasitical on your perceptions, or on your experiences. But, in the present discussion, I'll ignore that unfortunate feature of Hume's philosophy.)

1. Hume, *Treatise*, page 252.

Right now, I'll focus on Hume's thought that each of us has temporally intermittent existence. This Humean idea can be appropriated by certain pretty peculiar Substantial Dualists. In response to our Problem of Our Unconscious Quality, such a *Quasi-Humean Substantial Dualist* may say that, even while your body may have continuous existence, you yourself will have intermittent existence. For this new Dualist, at every moment of your existence you're conscious and, thus, you're replete with experiential quality. And, when you lose consciousness, then, lacking such quality, you cease to exist. Now, when there's again experiencing by the mental individual that's subserved by your body, or your bodies—or that's interacting with your body, or with your bodies—well, then you'll exist once again. But, during the interim period, you won't exist. In this middle period, as between dreams in deepest sleep, it's only your body, or your bodies, that exist.

From the perspective of common sense, this Quasi-Humean position is scarcely any better than a more thoroughly Humean approach. It may do better, I suppose, in explaining away certain common beliefs. But, in seeking to develop a Humanly Realistic Philosophy, that can't count for very much.[2] So, we must seek a better position than any such Quasi-Humean Substantial Dualism.

6. A "Compositist" Substantial Dualist May Similarly Deny the Problem

The Quasi-Humean Dualism just discussed suggests a *Compositist Substantial Dualism*, as I'll call the position. In its simplest claim, this Compositist View is similar to Descartes's idea that you are a union of a spatial body and a nonspatial mind, or soul, often interacting with each other, and with no further parts than just those two (and, perhaps also, such bodily parts as may be, in turn, constituent parts of your body, or your overlapping bodies). Beyond that simple claim, the presently proposed Compositism may be ambitious in either of two most salient ways.

---

2. Look; I'm not promoting the idea that, for me to exist from an earlier time to a much later time, I must exist at absolutely every time intermediate between the two. Maybe, even as much as that really is true; I certainly don't know. The point here, however, is just this: We shouldn't be forced to allow any more temporal discontinuity, insofar as our existence is concerned, than seems forced upon us by some pretty compelling evidence to such an effect.

In my *Identity, Consciousness and Value*, Oxford University Press, 1990, I take a fairly flexible line on these questions, especially as on pages 110–112.

First, the Compositist Dualist may hold, most implausibly, I think, that it's just your body that's your really essential part, whereas your mind is quite inessential for your existence. This is the exact opposite, I imagine, of what Descartes himself should hold, or any right-minded Cartesian should hold, when proposing that you're a composite, or a union, comprising both body and soul. Anyway, on this Compositist View, you may exist, even while your mind doesn't exist. So, on this Compositism there's no real challenge from the Problem of Our Unconscious Quality. Just so, and as is quite obvious, on this View you'll always be Spatially Extensibly Qualitied, both when you're consciously experiencing and when you're utterly unconscious. Quite as with an Enlightened Materialist Metaphysic, or with an Enlightened Scientiphical View, so also on this Compositist Metaphysic, you'll be very well qualitied—presumably, quite continuously—for years, and years, and years.

This highly implausible Compositist View has several serious difficulties. Right now, I'll observe that, on this View, the best that can be said for your mind, or your soul, is that it has intermittent existence, quite as much so as, on Hume's old view, you yourself have intermittent existence. That's no great advance, beyond Hume. (Or, alternatively, our Compositist may say that, after you suffer a period of unconsciousness, you awaken with a new soul, or a new mind, numerically different from the mind, or the soul, you had when last you were conscious. But, at least to my mind, that's scarcely a real improvement.)

Well, so much, I say, for the first way for our Compositist to be ambitious. Now, let's look at the second way.

Second, our Compositist Dualist may say, more liberally, that neither of your component parts is essential for your existence. As long as at least one of your two metaphysically salient parts has continuous existence, whether it be your body or whether it be your mind, well, then that's enough for you yourself to exist quite continuously, and quite protractedly. Indeed, as he may go on to add, it may be that, in fact, sometimes the continuous existence of your body will be the reason for your own continuous being, whilst at other times that may be owing to the fact that, during those other times, it's your soul that continuously enough exists.

As best I can tell, all the most serious difficulties observed just before, well, they also befall this more liberal version of the Compositist View. Or, at the very least, some of them do. At any rate, we should certainly seek a better position than any Compositist Substantial Dualism.

7. Will Unconscious Experiential Quality Provide a Less Heroic Dualistic Answer?

By taking a page from materialism's book, and by adapting the material to suit his own purposes, a Substantial Dualist may look to provide our Problem with a still different answer.

Recall our woman with a headache who, when distracted by wonderful news, didn't feel any headache. Then, after accustomed to the news, she again felt a headache of just the same character. Now, we're to entertain what may be claimed, on her behalf, to be a real possibility as to her qualitative character throughout: All along, she was *qualitied headachely*, even when she was so struck by the wonderful news. At that middle time, she was experiencing similarly—but she wasn't *consciously experiencing* headachely. What can I mean by this expression?

Throughout this book, it's been my resolve to use the terms "experience" and "conscious" in a way that has any talk as to experiencing be just some talk as to conscious experiencing, and vice versa. For me, the term "consciously," as it occurs in "consciously experiences," for instance, has served as a sort of emphasizer word, so to say; anyhow, the term has been, for me so far, scarcely more than an entirely redundant modifier. But, at this juncture, I'll allow myself to change my usage.

Here and now, I'll allow a usage of these terms, "consciously" and "experience," on which it may be consistently said that, sometimes at least, a person may experience, even while the person doesn't consciously experience. What might motivate this usage? Well, the idea is to allow for the possibility, if there should really be any such possibility, that a person might *be* experiencing without the person being at all *conscious* of the experiencing, or of herself experiencing, or anything of the like. Now, as I'm well aware, whatever's being offered here may be an almost unimaginably far-fetched idea. But, let's try to take it seriously, at least a little bit seriously.

(In an obvious way, the thought now suggested is similar to the Cartesian response to the Problem of Unconscious Quality. On Descartes's response, we always consciously experience; it's just that, at certain times, we experience but we don't remember any of the experiencing. On the newly offered idea, we always experience, it's just that, at certain times, we experience but we're not conscious of any of the experiencing.)

When we discussed introspection, in our Fifth Chapter, we observed that a person's having his beliefs, or the person's believing as he does, amounts to his being Propensitied in certain ways. Well, as I'll now observe, there's not much difference between these two states of affairs:

(1)   A certain person's being conscious of currently experiencing

(2)   That person's believing, perfectly certainly and completely correctly, that she's currently experiencing, all of that being *the manifestation of her Self-directed Propensity*, toward just so believing just such a thing, the condition of such manifestation being just that she *is* currently experiencing

That being so, we may understand someone's being conscious of currently experiencing to involve a lot more than just her being someone who's experiencing. To be conscious of currently experiencing, the person must, at the very least, have some such self-directed Propensity. And, as well, there must obtain conditions conducive to the Propensity's manifestation. And, what's more, the Propensity must be manifested for those reasons; and, maybe, much else also must hold true.

With anything like these notions in play, there's plenty of room, at all events, for a nonspatial soul to be modified experientially, for the whole time that said soul should exist, presumably for years, and years, and years. (Or, at the least, there's plenty of room for the soul to be so modified, for as long as it's properly paired with some appropriately brainy physical interaction partner. Or, at the very least, something quite like that.) Anyhow, at these times, the soul certainly will be qualitied, all right, even as *it then will be experientially qualitied*. Now, consider those times when the soul is in deepest sleep. Well, on our offered idea, the deeply sleeping experiencer may never have even the least inkling that, at any such times, it's ever experiencing, or it's experientially qualitied— leastways, not unless the soul engages in some very penetrating philosophizing! Much less will this deeply sleeping experiencer ever be, at those times, or, at any other times, for that matter, consciously aware that, right then, it's an experientially qualitied individual.

There may be some slight evidence, I suppose, in favor of the idea that, even when we're utterly unconscious, we may still be experiencing. What I have in mind are considerations like these: In the olden days, there were often shown, in movie theaters, double features; then, you could see two films for the price of one admission. Generally, in between the two films, there was an intermission. Now, only in some relatively few instances, I understand, there was some foul play involved, at least with the first of the featured films. Into the film, there was spliced, here and there, a single frame showing a tub of buttered popcorn, or maybe even a couple of consecutive frames. (Or, maybe it showed a big cup of Coca-Cola; it doesn't matter.) Anyway, these inserted frames went by so rapidly that none of the viewers was ever aware of her experiencing popcornly. Or, putting the point less barbarously (but also less perspicuously) none was conscious of having any experience as of popcorn. During the intermission, however, quite a few viewers bought popcorn, several times more viewers than when, in a more ordinary showing, there were no film frames that featured any popcorn. Now, here's one pretty natural interpretation of all that: Though none of the viewers was conscious of visually experiencing as of popcorn, still, very many of them did so experience, maybe even all the viewers. And, among those easily moved to purchase popcorn, their nonconsciously experiencing as of popcorn moved them to buy some popcorn, when there was the intermission. (Well, what went on in some movie showings, way back when, may not have been exactly as I've described things here. But, in all respects most relevant to our discussion, some of these instances of *subliminal advertising*, as it was called, were quite as I've described them.)

During many years, more recently, there have been many psychological experiments indicating similar findings, or strongly suggesting similar interpretations. So, perhaps it may be said, very fairly, that there's considerable evidence to favor the idea that, when people *are consciously experiencing*, they are, *at least some* of the time, *also nonconsciously* experiencing.

Now, even if that should be perfectly true, I hasten to admit, it's quite a leap to my present speculation: When people *aren't consciously experiencing*, they are, *even all* of the time, *just nonconsciously* experiencing. But, even if that might be a pretty big leap, it's not, I think, an inference that's utterly without any motivation at all.

In some moods, this speculative response seems significantly less heroic, to my mind, than Descartes's somewhat similar answer. At other times, however, I ponder certain questions and, then, the response seems a terribly dubious answer. What are these questions?

Whenever I'm experiencing, there must be some *specific way in which* I'm experiencing. Right now, my total experiencing, so to say, is largely visual, and also largely kinaesthetic, whilst not so impressively auditory, and hardly worth mentioning so far as concerns any olfactory or gustatory experiential features. Insofar as I'm experiencing visually, there's rich variegation as to my experiencing. When I'm nodding off to sleep, there's much less variegation. Well, now, what happens when I'm most soundly asleep, and not dreaming at all? Insofar as I'm visually experiencing, is it only blackly that I'm experiencing, and that's it, or is it partly blackly and partly dark-grayly, and *that's* it? Or, alternatively is it partly blackly, partly dark-grayly, and partly mid-night-bluely, and, by golly, *that is* it? Now, there must be some absolutely specific way I'm experiencing, when I'm most deeply sleeping, providing that I'm experiencing, at all, when I'm in deepest sleep. But, the mention of any such specific way seems utterly absurd.

The absurdity here is not, I think, that I have no reason to suppose, for myself then, any one specific experiential modification, in contradistinction to all the others, all equally possible for me then. Rather, the silliness looks to be more fundamental. Just so, the merest thought of *any* specific suggestion has the whole idea look to be an absolutely ad hoc conception, quite as heroic as anything else we've lately canvassed. In other words, what each specific suggestion brings home to me is, I think, just this: But for my being faced with a certain perplexing philosophical Problem, I'd never come to so much as attempt any thought to the effect that, at certain protracted times in my life, I'm continually experiencing, all of it without my having even the least idea to the effect that, during any of those times, I'm actually experiencing.

What's more, we may consider people, as sometimes I do, who've been in deep coma, for years and years, and years. When I think about those who've just recently awakened, well, then, if anything, there seems even less to recommend the idea of very protracted, quite continuous nonconscious experiencing.

Am I being dogmatic about this? I don't think so. Anyway, even if I should be a bit off on this matter, it's not by any very great deal that I'm missing the mark. So, it's with some considerable confidence that I'll say this much: Though it may be possible that the thought of nonconscious experiencing should do something positive for Substantial Dualism, with respect to allowing our Dualists a proper answer to our posed Problem, we should still seek, on behalf of the Dualists, another response to the Problem of Unconscious Quality. Maybe, it will be in addition to what's just been proposed, and not instead of the idea of nonconsciously experiencing, that this other response will serve Substantial Dualism. But, at all events, we should hope to notice, as available to a Substantial Dualist, some stronger answer to the Problem of Our Unconscious Quality.

In the next Chapter, that will be one thing I'll hope to do.

8. How Fully May Dualists Offer a Speculative Answer to the Problem?

Concerning its conflict with our belief in real choice, we've found deep difficulties with our dominant Scientiphical Metaphysic. And, with the

Mental Problems of the Many, we've found difficulties with the thought that, departing only slightly from our entrenched Scientiphicalism, we may comfortably move to accept an observed Nonentity Emergentist View, on which each of us is a physical complex, all right, but a complex with radically emergent mental powers (and not only with just so many physically derivative propensities). What's more, in our discussion of those Problems, we found it difficult to sustain any view on which each of us is a spatially extended entity, fit to be Spatially Extensibly Qualitied. All that was followed by two further developments. On the one hand, and quite positively, we sketched decently palatable Forms of Dualism, first a Pessimistic View and then an Optimistic View. On the other hand, and not all so positively, we noticed that, in any Form, Substantial Dualism seems troubled by a difficult Problem of Unconscious Quality. To address this problem, the best we could do so far, quite in this present Chapter, was to advance the speculation that, contrary to commonsense belief, each of us is always experiencing, even when the experiential subject is utterly unconscious, as we say, and she's utterly unaware that she's experiencing. About that strange proposal, who knows? At all events, we should hope to notice, for the sake of Substantial Dualism, a substantially better answer.

In the next Chapter, our main concern will be with some very different challenges to Substantial Dualism. To meet these challenges, I'll propose a quite novel speculative idea, the Hypothesis of Spacelike Extension. And, in particular, I'll propose that we take seriously, very seriously, the Dualistic Form of this speculative Hypothesis. With an acceptance of a Dualistic Hypothesis of Spacelike Extension, however tentative and unconfident that may be, there'll be available, for the Substantial Dualist, another answer to the Problem of Our Unconscious Quality. It will be this: Even as spatial bodies may always have Spatially Extensible Quality, which isn't any experiential quality, so nonspatial minds, or souls, might always have *Nonspatially Spacelikely* Extensible Quality, which *also isn't* any experiential quality. Now, this other answer will be, of course, a quite speculative response to our Problem. But, as we may come to see, all in due course, of course, a metaphysical speculation may be a philosophically stimulating conjecture, and, just maybe, it might be quite fruitfully stimulating, too.

10

HOW RICH IS
CONCRETE REALITY?

Quite as we've often done before, let's consider some clearly distinct basic bodies, as with some spatially separate Spherical Red Particles. It's in conceiving such clearly spatial bodies as are so spatially separate, I'll suggest, that we humans may have our clearest conception as to how it is that, all at the very same time, there may be several distinct concrete individuals and not, say, just a single concretum multiply conceived. Indeed, it's in just this way that we can quite clearly conceive how it is that there may be numerically distinct individuals even when, at every moment of their existence, each concrete particular is precisely like each of the others in all intrinsic respects (well, all those that aren't Individualistically-directed Powers, anyway) and even when, in all their external relations (and in all their Individualistically-directed Powers, too) they're all perfectly symmetric. Think of a World whose only concreta are always just two perfectly congruent spatially separate Red Spheres, each always just like the other intrinsically, and each always in perfectly symmetric spatial (and any "other possible external") relations with the other.

By contrast, we do poorly in attempts to conceive how it is as with Nonspatial Cartesian minds, or souls; and, also, of course, with Nonspatial Berkeleyan minds, or souls. So, we do pretty poorly with conceiving how it may be that, always at the very same time, there are several distinct nonspatial minds, and not a single mind multiply conceived.

And, especially without any analogical aid, we do very poorly, indeed, when trying to conceive distinct nonspatial minds, all perfectly alike at every moment of their existence, and each always perfectly symmetric with all the others insofar as any of them may be externally related to any other concrete individual, or individuals.

Now, in several previous Chapters, I've urged you to take seriously a couple of Interactionist Substantial Dualist Views, despite some difficulties with, or some challenges to, the suggested Emergentive Dualisms. In early parts of this present Chapter, I'll observe some further challenges to any Substantial Dualist View, whether Emergentive or not, on which each of us is a distinct nonspatial mind, or soul (or, just a bit different, on which each of us *has* a distinct nonspatial mind, or soul). For Scientiphical philosophers, these challenges may seem, at first, to be welcome windfalls. For more uncertain philosophers, like me, they do more to signal some real work that needs doing than any real reason to reject Substantial Dualism.

1. Sameness and Difference of Concrete Individuals

During the first days of many metaphysics courses, there's offered a distinction between diverse concrete particulars, however similar they may be, and a single individual, however diversely conceived.[1] Often the teacher provides the students with a pair of technical terms: With perfectly resembling concrete particulars, precisely similar in every

---

1. A few words about the phrase *concrete particulars*, as used in this essay: There's a view, often called "trope theory," on which a basic category for analytical ontology is that of *abstract particulars*: Consider two qualitatively identical white balls, one to be called "the first" and the other "the second." There'll then be *the whiteness of the first ball*, which is one thing, and, precisely resembling that first abstract particular, there'll be a diverse thing, another abstract particular, *the whiteness of the second ball*. Whether there are any such things as abstract particulars I don't know; and, in our present context, I don't care. Anyway, I won't try to talk about any of that. So, maybe all that my use of "concrete" does here is to signal a possible limit for my discussion. At all events, readers may take my use of "concrete" to be little more than simply an emphatic term; so a concrete particular will be just a genuine particular, as opposed to, say, a particular quality, which isn't any concrete particular at all, or, say, a particular set, or number, which also isn't a really, real particular.

For what a metaphysician might do with the canonically contrasting technical terms "concrete" and "abstract," see "Concreteness," which is Section 1.7 of David Lewis's book *On the Plurality of Worlds*, Blackwell, 1986. Even a master metaphysician, it becomes clear, can't do very much to make clear what will be the terms' philosophically most helpful uses. But, as with the main conceptions of Lewis's boldly radical book, this essay's main thoughts also may be grasped, well enough, I trust, without any very refined use of, or any essential reliance on, "concrete" or "abstract."

qualitative respect, there's *qualitative identity*, it's technically said. With a single individual, by contrast, we're to say, just as technically, that there's *numerical identity*.[2] Derek Parfit's words, in *Reasons and Persons*, nicely typify recent writing on sameness and difference in concrete particulars. His Section "Qualitative and Numerical Identity" starts like this:

> There are two kinds of sameness, or identity. I and my Replica are *qualitatively identical*, or exactly alike. But we may not be *numerically identical*, or one and the same person. Similarly, two white balls are not numerically but may be qualitatively identical. If I paint one of these balls red, it will not now be qualitatively identical to itself yesterday. But the red ball that I see now and the white ball that I painted red are numerically identical. They are one and the same ball.
>
> We might say, of someone, "After his accident, he is no longer the same person." This is a claim about both kinds of identity. We claim that *he*, the same person, is *not* now the same person. This is not a contradiction. We merely mean that this person's character has changed. This numerically identical person is now qualitatively different.[3]

No accident, Parfit offers us two sorts of illustrative example. No surprise, the first concerns ordinary physical complexes, or complex bodies, while the second concerns an ordinary person.

As with most mainstream philosophers lately writing on these topics, Parfit's examples of qualitative difference in a single individual, or in one enduring concrete particular, each involves an entity's undergoing some temporal change, or changes. Just so, his unfortunate accident victim first has a certain character, a certain propensity profile, we might say; then, after he undergoes a dramatic temporal change, due to his unfortunate accident, this person has a quite different character, a quite different propensity profile. (As some Substantial Dualists may well say, this may be, more deeply and truly, a case where

●

2. As should be clear, this use of "qualitative" is very different from all my uses of "Qualitative" and, in most of the book, my uses of "quality" and "qualitative." Consider two congruent Red Spherical Particles, spatially separated, each with (a profile of) Propensity differing from the other. Now, just as there's no difference in the intrinsic Spatial features of these two supposed Spheres, there's also *no difference* in their Quality. Yet, there is an intrinsic difference between them, of course, a difference as regards Propensity. With them in mind, we may clearly note the two uses of cognates of "quality." Though the Spheres *are* precisely alike Qualitatively, they *aren't* precisely alike intrinsically and, so, in the philosophically prevalent use of the expression "qualitatively identical," the Spheres *aren't qualitatively identical* entities. In what follows, context should make clear, at any point in the text, what is the use of "qualitative," and of its cognates, that's most appropriate there.

3. Derek Parfit, *Reasons and Persons*, Oxford University Press, 1984, pages 201–202.

there's change in a certain soul's Individualistically-directed propensity partners, each a perfectly physical individual, rather than in the soul itself. But, for the meanwhile, let's pass over that.) And, so it is, too, with the insensate ball, a ball that's no person at all. At the case's start, the ball is white and, then, after it undergoes a change that it survives, or several such temporal changes, the selfsame ball is red (we're invited to suppose) and not white any more.

Though useful enough, such examples may create the impression that qualitative difference in a single particular must involve that particular's undergoing, and surviving, some temporal change. That's an unfortunate impression. To get quite clear of any such possibly misleading impressions, we'll increase our stock of homey illustrative cases.

Many statements concern the numerical sameness of an object exhibiting qualitative difference *without any real temporal* change. Even about questions as to who's who, or what's what, some are as usefully informative as any statements about the numerical sameness of an object, over time, that survives many real temporal changes: With both ends of each tube visible to you, there may be two (temporally) *unchanging* tubes whose lengthy middles are entirely obscured by a rectangular solid. On your left you may see the very blue end of one tube, and the very red end of another. And, on your right, you may also see the blue end of one tube and the red end of another. As you may be correctly informed, the tube that's blue on your left is the very same tube as the one that's red on your right and, as well, it's numerically different from the tube that's blue on your right. How might that be? Well, of course, it's no big deal: In the obscured regions of these two tubes, as you may learn, even if, perhaps, only indirectly, there's qualitative difference, or qualitative variegation, from blue to red or, what's here the same, from red to blue.

At all events, sometimes we do quite well in conceiving, as diverse concrete particulars, two numerically different spatial bodies, even when, at every moment of their existence, the two bodies are precisely similar, or "qualitatively identical." What's more, we can conceive, fairly fully and quite clearly, *how it is that the two individuals are externally related to each other.* And, of course, we may do this not only when we're conceiving two humanly perceptible particulars, as with two physically complex white billiard balls—now instructively presumed as precisely similar. Just as well, we may do it when we're conceiving two truly basic bodies, as with a pair of perfectly congruent White Particles, both inhabitants of the same World. To do all this quite well, or, at least, as clearly and fully as ever we can, we must engage in conceiving that's highly experiential, whatever may be, at the same time, our conceiving's importantly intellectual aspect.

Happily, sometimes that's perfectly possible, even for us quite limited human thinkers.

With conceiving that's highly experiential, how may we do best at conceiving two precisely similar basic spatial bodies? Not seeking a complete answer, a start of the story is this: We should conceive each body as occupying space that's wholly distinct from the space of the other body, with neither body spatially overlapping the other. And, for good measure, we do well to conceive each body as *spatially separate from* the other. That precludes, most clearly for us, any question as to whether we're conceiving two perfectly contiguous things in perfect contact, or whether it's just one spatial body conceived that, at its thinnest place, so to speak, is only "imaginatively bisected." (With qualitatively different bodies, say a White Cube and a (spatially congruent) Black Cube, this question might not arise, not even for our most highly experiential conceiving. Maybe each of these conceived cubes may be experientially conceived as perfectly contiguous to the other: Just where there's Black pervading a relevant space, that's where one Cube is. And, just where there's space pervaded with White, that's where the other Cube is. Maybe, and maybe not. But, for present purposes, it's not important to explore that issue. Here, we're mainly concerned with qualitatively identical (precisely similar) bodies, not with qualitatively different (quite dissimilar) bodies.)

Even with bodies always precisely alike, we can conceive each as spatially separate from, and as spatially apart from, all the others. (And, to do this, we needn't think, of course, that there is any such entity as empty space, or as an empty space.)

None of this is to say that two basic spatial bodies are distinct individuals *in virtue of* their diverse occupied spaces, or in virtue of their spatial apartness, or anything of the like. Indeed, as far as I can discern, it's *not in virtue of anything at all* that any one spatial body is diverse from, or it's simply *other than*, any other spatial body. So, I'm not trying to suggest any "metaphysical ground" of, or for, the diversity of spatial bodies, which I think to be just a misleading gesture. Rather, my point concerns the scope of, and the limits of, certain of our most central human conceptions.

2. Conceiving Nonspatial Simultaneous Souls, Always Precisely Alike

Nowadays, almost all academic metaphysicians are Materialist metaphysicians or, at the least, so like materialists as makes little difference.

Just so, they're almost all Scientiphicalists, as are also the far fewer halfway respectable Epiphenomenalist metaphysicians.

As all these Scientiphicalists hold, Materialists and Epiphenomenalists alike, every actual sentient being is, in fact, a spatially separate physically complex entity. (For the most part, they're ignorant of our Mental Problems of the Many. And, even among those who are aware of these Problems, most are perfectly undisturbed by the Problems—so rigidly solid is their deeply habitual Scientiphicalism.) Well, some might worry, just a tiny bit, about the likes of Siamese twins. And, some might be upset, maybe more than just a tiny bit, by their thoughts about so-called split-brain patients. Still, even those a little leery of the formula I've provided— "every actual sentient being is, in fact, a spatially separate physically complex entity"—well, they all hold, at least implicitly, something that's pretty much like it. On their view, at any rate, whatever its precise formulation, this will be the verdict about you and me: I'm a certain single physical complex who's spatially separate from you, and you're another single physical complex, just so spatially separate from me.

Already in this Chapter, I've suggested an advantage these philosophers may possibly enjoy, as against those opponents who hold that we're nonspatial minds, or souls. It's this. On the view that we're each a physical entity, each of us spatially separate from other concrete individuals, or from each spatial concretum that's not among one's own real parts, there's little difficulty in clearly conceiving how it is that two distinct thinkers are externally related to each other. Apparently, there's no more difficulty here than there is in conceiving how two (white billiard) balls may be externally related. But, on views where we're each a nonspatial entity, there might be, perhaps, a very great difficulty. (Of course, with the actual physical world being so messily gradual, there are problems of the many, which may befuddle us thoroughly, both with physically complex thinkers and with physically complex unthinking (white billiard) balls. In this present context, however, we pass over those problems.)

Among contemporary philosophers, I'm not the first to notice this relative advantage. With hopes of making progress beyond my predecessors, I'll discuss some sentences in Ernest Sosa's nicely stimulating essay "Subjects among Other Things." Strikingly, the first part of its blatantly negative Section, "Against Souls," is the boldly ambitious Subsection "The Argument from Individuation." And, the first part of that is this:

> Against souls as nonspatial particulars it might be argued that they are unacceptably deprived of a principle of individuation:

Call a property qualitative if its exemplification does not entail with regard to any concrete particular that it specifically must exist. Two distinct spatial things can conceivably share all their qualitative properties, as shown by Max Black's universe populated only by two identical spheres. The distinctness of such spheres must hence be understood in terms of their differing spatial locations. Absent spatial location, as with souls, we lack any way to understand the distinctness of allegedly distinct but qualitatively identical souls.

Let's call this The Argument from Individuation.[4]

Almost immediately, we may see that this needs at least a bit of tinkering: For, two minds may exemplify just exactly the same qualitative properties, even in a completely congruent manner, though they do so at different times. Indeed, there are many different ways for that to happen. In a usefully extreme instance, it may happen with one mind going through a rich qualitative history and then ceasing to exist, completely and forever, before another mind, first existing only much later, then goes through a precisely similar qualitative history, whereupon it then also ceases to be.

By making just a small adjustment, we have a more instructive form of the Argument from Individuation (against Souls): With both existing at precisely the same times, two numerically different spatial things can be, at every moment of their existence, qualitatively alike in every respect. This is shown by a universe with just two spheres that, always simultaneously, and always just as a manifestation of each one's Self-directed Propensity for Change as to (its) Quality, change their "Spatially Extensible Quality," as I'll put it, from Red to Blue, then from Blue to Red, and so on. The distinctness of such simultaneously changing spheres must hence be understood in terms of their differing spatial locations. Absent spatial location, as with nonspatial souls, we lack any way to understand the distinctness of allegedly distinct but always qualitatively identical simultaneous souls. Let's call this the Fuller Argument from Individuation (against Souls).

As an argument against the very existence of nonspatial souls, even this Fuller Argument isn't anything even remotely like any decisive piece of reasoning. Rather, the Argument can establish, at the very

---

4. Ernest Sosa, "Subjects among Other Things," *Philosophical Perspectives*, 1987, page 160. As you'll quite likely recall, in our First Chapter (specifically, in its Sixth Section) we actually cited Black's presentation of his well-known example. (Of course, our purposes there were very different from those of Sosa's here, or from any of Black's own purposes. In fact, as I feel sure, our own purposes never crossed their minds. But, for this present discussion, none of that really matters. So, don't worry about any of that; don't again become involved in our Mystery of the Physical.)

most, only that, in certain respects, *we can't conceive how it is* with distinct (contemporaneous) nonspatial individuals very well at all; we can't do this nearly as clearly as, or nearly as fully as, we can conceive *how it is with* distinct (contemporaneous) spatial entities. So, let's suppose that each of us is a nonspatial mind. And, let's also suppose this: Though you can quite clearly conceive yourself, you can't so clearly conceive (there being) other nonspatial minds, especially not others meant to be, at every moment of your existence, qualitatively just like you. (I'm not saying that's right; I'm just having us *suppose* there to be such a difference in what we can very clearly conceive.) Well, even if that should be so; so what? As almost goes without saying, there might very well be a *great variety* of concrete entities, *none* of which we human thinkers can conceive very well. In particular, among the very various concreta each only very modestly well conceived by us, there may be many nonspatial sentient beings, each always qualitatively just like many others.

Even when being very generous to the Fuller Argument, maybe even more generous than I've just been, we can see it to be, as an argument against the existence of nonspatial thinkers, minds, or souls, only a rather weak argument. OK? Anyhow, right now, after having been quite generous, it may be more useful, for making some philosophic progress, for us to be less generous.

Well, as it seems, I don't do all that badly at conceiving (there being) some several nonspatial minds, each distinct from myself, each always just like me, and, in the bargain, each just like all the others. What I do very badly at, in this neighborhood, is conceiving how these simultaneous minds may be externally related to each other, that is, related in any way that goes relevantly beyond their qualitative similarities and dissimilarities. (Or, I do very badly in conceiving how these minds may be related in any way that, as many philosophers technically say, is a way that doesn't (wholly) supervene on just how it is, qualitatively, or intrinsically, with each mind individually.) Just so, I do very much better, indeed, at conceiving how it is that two simultaneous bodies, which are *spatially separate* spatial individuals, may be externally related. (For, I can conceive, rather clearly, how they may be *spatially related*.) Of course, this doesn't even begin to make problematic the apparently coherent idea that there might really be many distinct nonspatial minds, with some of them always precisely just like some of the others.

Well, I don't want to be dogmatic about any of this. And, anyway, what's most interesting about these questions may lie in a somewhat different direction. Just so, I turn to discuss how pondering these issues, and closely related ideas, may shed some light on what may be involved

in our (pretty meager) understanding of certain philosophically prominent and time-honored ideas.

3. Berkeleyan Idealism: Even If Just Modestly Grasped, It Might Be True

So indecisive is the Fuller Argument, I'll suggest, that it doesn't disrupt
even the Berkeleyan Idealist thought that *every* concrete individual is a
nonspatial soul, even while there are, at the very same time, a great
plurality of perfectly distinct nonspatial mental beings. This is the situation, it seems clear, with the Historical Version of the Berkeleyan
View, on which there's a single infinite mind, a single God, in addition
to very many finite minds, or souls, all of them about as severely limited
as you, or I. And, it's just as true with an Atheistic Version of Berkeleyan
Idealism, or an Atheistic Version of a Subjective Idealism, on which
each of the world's many minds is a very limited being, and on which
each quite finite mind is perfectly distinct from each of the others.

Now, even if a Berkeleyan view is true, or correct, it may be that we
can conceive only very modestly the full import of the Subjective Idealism. For, rightly placing aside confused thoughts as to "causal relations," we seem quite unable to conceive, even the least bit well or
clearly, how it is that any one of the many (finite) nonspatial individuals
is externally related to any of the others. But, as also seems sure, how
well we grasp the import of an Idealism is quite independent of whether
the view is correct. So, whether or not a Berkeleyan view is correct, we
seem quite unable to conceive clearly the full import of such a Subjective
Idealist Metaphysic.

As best I can tell, these same difficulties attend any idealistic philosophy, or purely mentalistic view, that's really intelligible to us, but
that denies the existence of any spatial concrete particulars. Consider a
certain *particular feeling of elation*. Now this must be a feeling of just
exactly *one particular sentient being*. It must be the feeling of at least one—
for it cannot simply float free, quite unfelt by anyone or anything. And,
it must be the feeling of at most one, too—for it cannot be experienced,
or shared, by some several sentient beings. So, we can conceive our
considered particular happy feeling, at all fully and clearly, just insofar
as we can conceive, fully and clearly, the sole mental subject whose
happy feeling it is. But, for this subject to be conceived so clearly and
fully, it (so far) seems, the subject must be conceived as a spatial being,
spatially separate from other spatial entities. (Well, just so far in our
text, that's certainly how it *seems*.) None of this is to suggest that, for

having you not be a spatial entity, standard idealist views must be false. Rather, and once again, the point is this. Even if such a view should be true, it's only very modestly, perhaps, that (so far, at least) we grasp the full import of the metaphysical position.

4. Cartesian Dualism: Even If Just Modestly Grasped, It Also Might Be True

Idealistic philosophies have been horribly unfashionable for decades, as have been all sorts of purely mentalistic views. So, nowadays, the points just made may not interest many philosophers. What may be somewhat more widely interesting, I imagine, are certain similar thoughts concerning a Substantial Dualism. Though any such robust Dualism is also, of course, very unfashionable, it's not widely taken, it seems to me, to be so very far beyond the pale as is a Metaphysic that denies the existence of, or denies the materiality of, all allegedly material entities.

On a Substantial Dualistic View, whether in the Historical Cartesian Version or in an Atheistic Version, there's a nonmental physical being, or maybe many insensate physical entities, that *are spatial* concrete particulars. (On Descartes's actual philosophy of matter, as I take it, the world's physical realm is really just one vast plenum. But, when I refer to a Cartesian Metaphysic, I won't be making that assumption. Rather, it's left open whether physical reality is a plenum, or whether it's much more disjoint and particulate.) And, in addition to what's perfectly spatial and material, there are nonspatial mental beings, perfectly immaterial souls. Now, what are we to think of such a Substantial Dualism?

Well, in the first place, it's obvious that among *nonspatial* souls, or nonspatial concreta of any sort, there *aren't any spatial* relations. That's absolutely impossible. But, without thinking in terms of spatial relations, how can we conceive diverse mental particulars that are always precisely alike? Unless we can find a decent answer to this question, we won't have any more grasp, really, of what Cartesian Dualism implies about how it is with us, collectively, than we do with Berkeleyan Idealism. We won't have any more grasp of how we're externally related to each other, really, than we do with such a Subjective Idealism.

Well, maybe that's an exaggeration. Maybe, and maybe not. But, even if that should be so, still, it won't be any very great exaggeration. Let me explain what that means.

To tell a short story that seems to favor Dualism, over Idealism, I'll suppose a material reality that's replete with spatially separated material bodies, many of them causally interacting with many others. In addition, I'll suppose there to be systematic causal interactions between each of many nonspatial souls and, aptly aligned with each soul, its body (or, a bit less nicely, its many overlapping bodies; or, also less nicely, all the Particles that are Individualistically-directed just with respect to it, and not with respect to any other nonspatial concrete individual). Now, as we might very easily think, such Dualistic suppositions will secure, for us, a quite clear conception of each one of these minds, however similar the minds always may be, and however similar also might be the interacting bodies. My mind is just the single mind that's (clearly conceived as) causally interacting with just a certain one spatial body, my body. And, as for my Generalistically precise duplicate, if such there be, and his single mind? It's causally interacting only with the spatially distant body that's his body. So, there's my duplicate's rather similar mind, maybe differing intrinsically from mine only in its Individualistically-directed Propensities, that's (clearly conceived, quite differently, as) causally interacting with just a certain other spatial body, his body, spatially separate from my body. Well, then, this may be just perfectly fine. For, just as I can clearly conceive each of these minds as causally interacting only with its own body, or with its own overlapping bodies, so I can clearly conceive myself and my so-called duplicate to be related externally in just such a quite indirect way, by courtesy of the spatial separation of their respective bodily interaction partners. Though that (external) relation may be quite indirect, still, it does seem that, in all of this, everything is very clearly conceived.

That short story first seems to be a perfectly fine story. But, is that really so? Maybe it is. As I can't really tell, I'm somewhat uncertain.

Here are some thoughts that make me uncertain: We may *say* "This clearly conceived body has such-and-such nice causal relations only to this one nonspatial mind, and not to any other nonspatial being." But, even with our saying some such apparently excluding words, how much of a conception will any of us humans have, really, as to how a particular nonspatial mind externally relates to its spatial body, much less how any mind externally relates to any other nonspatial mind?

Let's suppose, or maybe let's just pretend, that I can clearly conceive how it is that you, a particular nonspatial soul, are causally related to just one particular spatial body, which may thus be duly dubbed "your body." But, this idea of mine seems to be a terribly bare idea, with nothing that serves to meet the gaze of the mind's eye. So, let's next suppose, or let's pretend, that I have a change of heart and, now being less agreeably cooperative, I say something like this: Gee; I first thought I was conceiving how it was with just a single nonspatial mind being in a certain sort of causal relation with just one particular body. But, now, I'm very unsure that's what I was conceiving. Maybe, I was conceiving how it was that each of several nonspatial selves, maybe both you and also some others, each always precisely like you, were, *all at once and all together, enjoying precisely parallel causal relations* to, or with, the very same spatial body, or the very same cluster of overlapping bodies. In perfect parallel, each of these nonspatial minds may be Individualistically Propensitied with respect to just that one body, or just that one body-cluster. And, for its part, the body, or the cluster, may be Individualistically Propensitied, reciprocally, with respect to *each of those several* minds, in each case the Individualistically-directed Propensity being, precisely parallel to, or perfectly symmetric with, all of the others.

Can I distinguish, at all fully or clearly, between what I was supposedly doing the first time round, when there was, allegedly, only a single nonspatial soul conceived in the pretended causal mix, and what I was supposedly doing the next time round, when there was, allegedly, some several nonspatial souls? Well, maybe so; maybe, I *can* do quite well here. And, maybe not; *maybe I can't* do at all well. It's just so very hard to tell.

For the most part, I'm inclined to think that, in these attempts at individuating conceptions, I'm doing well enough, even if I may not be doing very well. If that's so, then, in certain Dualistic frameworks, at least, there'll be a decently good reply, or a reply that's good enough, to the challenge we've extracted from Sosa's writing.

But, still, I should like to do rather better than that, if it's at all possible. And, I should like to do it along lines that allow even Berkeleyan Idealists to meet the noted challenge. Certainly, this is a tall order. But, as best I can, I'll try to fill this tall order.

Nor is this just an isolated philosophical challenge I'm proposing. No; not at all. And, here's why: Later in the Chapter, I'll offer some radically new forms of Substantial Dualism, perhaps most notably one that I'll call a *Quasi-Platonic Quasi-Emergentive Substantial Dualism*. Now, on these radically new forms of Substantial Dualism, there may be many nonspatial individuals that won't ever be involved in any interaction, at all with any spatial body. So, quite distinct from supporting any Idealist View, it's with a strong long-term aim that I'll try to help us better grasp a Berkeleyan Metaphysic, on which none of the world's many distinct concreta is any spatial individual.

To do this even the least bit well, as you can imagine, we must proceed pretty patiently, and sufficiently soberly. So, that's how we'll proceed.

5. Substantial Individuals and Our Conceptions as to Such Concrete Particulars

In many attempts to conceive how things are with distinct spatial bodies, we'll do better than with any attempts at conceiving how things are with distinct nonspatial souls. But, this shows little about the existence, or the nonexistence, of any such souls. Though we've already advanced that sensible idea, it's so central to our Humanly Realistic Philosophy that we should approach it from several directions. More sentences from Sosa's essay open more avenues for our discussion:

> The problem with supposed nonspatial particulars like souls is simply that no pure relation can be found to play the role for them that spatial apartness plays for spatial particulars. We have no inkling of any relation that can help us grasp the diversity of two souls alike in every qualitative respect. The universe with infinitely many identical spheres, all equidistantly arrayed on a straight line, still permits some further understanding of the distinctness between any two of the indiscernible spheres, for each and every one of them is spatially apart from every other sphere. Consider a world with infinitely many souls all indiscernible in every qualitative respect.... How are we to understand the diversity of all these identical souls? ... Is there anything that can do for them what spatial apartness does for spatial entities?[5]

It may manifest a confusion, I think, to ask: Can anything do for distinct qualitatively identical souls what spatial apartness does for distinct qualitatively identical bodies? For the spatial separation of two (precisely similar) bodies, clearly conceived by us as numerically diverse, doesn't really *do something for the bodies themselves*. In particular, it doesn't provide for them their numerical diversity. Nor does anything else provide them with their distinctness. But, then, there's no need for anything to make any such provision. Now, I'll amplify on those remarks.

Sometimes there may be something, of course, that causally explains why there are several bodies in a situation. For instance, there may be an explosion that explains a certain subsequent dispersion of matter, the explosion resulting in the formation of several spatially separate bodies. So, when some contiguous matter's exploded and, in consequence, there's a more disjoint material situation, (adverting to) the explosion explains, quite well enough, why later there are the several diverse bodies. At any rate, it adds nothing to say that, with these bodies, their spatial apartness has them be several bodies, or it has them be diverse individuals.

---

5. Sosa, "Subjects among Other Things," pages 162–163.

Since it's such a pervasive confusion I'm trying to uncover, I'll press the point with an example that comes at the issue from an angle absolutely opposite to the one that so attracted Sosa and that, years before that, so attracted Max Black. Instead of a world populated by just two perfectly similar spheres, let alone an infinity of such spheres all aligned so symmetrically, we'll consider a world populated precisely by just a White Sphere and a Black Sphere, each spatially separate from the other. As they're Qualitied differently, these spatial bodies aren't, of course, qualitatively identical.

Now, it might be wondered, I suppose, whether there's something that "does for" these two spatial bodies what sheer spatial apartness "does for" two precisely similar spheres. To this possibly misplaced wonderment, there may be these beguiling answers, replies that apparently conflict. Maybe, the diversity of these objects is grounded in a complex consisting of both their qualitative difference and their spatial apartness. (This may be presumed analogous to a complex cause of something, comprising two different events, for instance.) Or, maybe, their qualitative difference, quite by itself, grounds their diversity and, equally, quite by itself, their spatial apartness also accounts for their diversity. (This presumably parallels causal overdetermination, wherein each of two distinct items is causally sufficient for the result.) Or, it may be that, quite by itself, their qualitative diversity does the job; though, if that wasn't so, then their spatial apartness would ground the diversity of the bodies. (This presumably parallels a certain sort of causal preemption.) Or, on the other side of this apparently silly coin, it might be that the spatial apartness actually does all the work, with qualitative difference being no more "efficacious" than any other mere "epiphenomenon," and so on.

These ideas, every last one of them, really, are just so many quite silly suggestions. And, as their silliness may help make clear, there can't be any substantial response to the question they're suggested to answer. Nor are matters the least bit different in the original case, where we have two precisely similar spheres in mind. Just as it fosters confusion to ask, in the case of our white and black spheres, what has the spheres be two individuals, and not just one single concrete particular, so it also fosters confusion to ask, in the case of the two perfectly similar spheres, what has the spheres be two substantial individuals.

We should avoid all quests for what may "ground" numerical difference in concrete particulars themselves, or what may "ground" numerical sameness. All such quests are futile. Steering clear of them, we more clearly focus on *our own conceptual abilities*: In conceiving (basic) bodies as spatially separate from one another, *we ourselves* may have an adequate conception of (even so much as) how two distinct bodies may be externally related to each other, no matter how alike they are, at every moment of their existence, no matter how symmetric may be all their relations to each other.

6. We Prepare an Analogy between the Properly Spatial and the Relevantly Spacelike

It's quite impossible, I think, for humans to conceive *very fully* how simultaneous *nonspatial* individuals—for example, Cartesian souls—may be externally related to each other. We can't ever conceive that anywhere near as fully as, quite often, we so clearly conceive how spatial bodies are externally related to each other. But, with great effort, perhaps we can do moderately well or, at least, somewhat well.

For us to do even just that much, we should engage, I'll suggest, in some radically analogical thinking. And for that, we want an analogy that provides a parallel, more or less strong, with how it is that distinct spatial bodies are spatially related. No doubt, the wanted analogy should be of this very general form, here expressed as crudely as it's displayed briefly: Spatial bodies are to space as nonspatial souls are to something that's relevantly like space.

What can this something possibly be, that's relevantly like space? (Please don't think that, at long last, I'm going in for reifying, both with space itself and, then, with a wanted spacelike cousin. That would be a quite perverse interpretation of my present suggestive sentences, serving only to distract us from what must be their real point.) Well, space doesn't just allow for spatial relations among spatial objects; space, or portions of it, are occupied by, or are pervaded by, spatially extended particulars. So, this something must be extensive in much the same way that space itself is extensive. Or, at the least, it must be extensive in a way that's strongly analogous with spatial extension: So, first, it must allow for there to be *spacelike* relations, as we may call them, among *spacelike* objects, as we may call these utterly real, even if only quite modestly conceived, substantial individuals. And, what's more, it must allow for its different spacelike regions to be pervaded by, or to be occupied by, different spacelikely extended particulars.

Now, if souls are to partake of the wanted analogy, then they must each be some such (merely) *spacelikely* extended particulars. Then, rather than its being spatially extended, a nonspatial soul will be *extended in a way relevantly like how it is that a basic body is spatially extended*. But, in concrete terms, what is *this way*?

To make progress on the matter, we rehearse some thoughts about our clearest conceptions of spatial bodies: When we conceive a spatial body most clearly, and most fully, we conceive all the space of the extended individual to be perfectly pervaded with some single (Absolutely Specific) Color, a Transparent Color that's *its* single Spatially Extensible Quality. For our very best cases of such conception, the Transparent Color should be a Quality that's suggested by, or that's the objective correlative of, some (absolutely specific) experiential transparent color. So, I do best at conceiving a spatial body to be Spatially Extensible Transparent Red, for instance, when I myself am experiential transparent red—that is, when I'm experiencing transparent-redly. As I feel sure, you're starting to get the hang of this.

Next, let's recall some thoughts from our Fourth Chapter, concerning a Cornucopia of Quality. Well, first off, there's this thought about familiar Families of Qualities: Maybe more so than any other Quality Family, it's the Family of Colors that has, in addition to many experiential members, *many Spatially* Extensible members, as well. Just so, Extensible Red, for example, is intrinsically suited to pervading spatial objects and regions.

Well, as I've hypothesized, some Spatially Extensible Colors actually are exemplified in basic physical entities. For my hypothesis to be very credible, we must allow, of course, that these actually exemplified Colors (probably) aren't the Extensible Correlatives of any experiential quality that's exemplified in human experiencing.

What does that mean for us? Well, let's grant that the Colors actually exemplified aren't any Qualities that we can conceive at all directly, or very clearly or fully. Let's call one of these analogically conceived Absolutely Specific Extensible Color Qualities *Col*, and we'll call another *Lor*. Now in Respect of Mode of Exemplification, Col is precisely like our Red and our Blue. And, of course, so is Lor. For each Extensible Color pervades space in just the same way as does any other. What of the *other* Central Respect for Resemblance, the Respect of Pure Quality?

Even in Respect of Pure Quality, a spatial object's being Qualitied Lorly isn't all *that* different from its being Qualitied Redly. In Respect of Pure Quality, that difference is very much less than the difference between me now, when (pretend) I'm qualitied just redly and myself yesterday, when (pretend) I was qualitied just belltonely. In the first comparison, both Qualities, both Red and Lor, are members of the same Quality Family, the Family of Pure Color. By contrast, in the second comparison, only one of the two qualities, experiential red, is in the Color Family, while the other, experiential belltone, is in a quite disparate Family, the Family of Pure Sounds.

(That said, I'll remind you of these points: It's required by the character of an Extensible Color that any of its exemplifications be *spatial* exemplifications. And, with an instance of Extensible Color, the exemplified Quality must pervade something spatially extensive. And, just as each different Color is a different Extensible Quality, so no region that's pervaded by any one Color is also pervaded, anywhere within, by any other Color.)

Now, it's no part of this approach that the Colors are the *only* Qualities pervading space, much less that they're the only Qualities intrinsically suited for spatial pervasion. But, I do think that, at least *for us* human thinkers, the (Transparent) Colors provide the *clearest instances* of how it may be that spatial bodies are pervaded by *Spatially Extensible* Quality, especially for the many cases of quite insensate basic bodies, quite as we suppose, say, quarks and electrons to be.[6]

The forgoing thoughts accord well with these further ideas, also recalled from our Fourth Chapter: First, an Extensible Color is intrinsically fit to pervade what's spatially extended and, reciprocally, what's spatially extended is intrinsically fit for pervasion by Extensible Color. Now, second, a Sound, in marked contrast, just *can't* pervade a spatial body or, for that manner, any strictly spatial region. For, a Sound is *intrinsically unfit* to pervade what's spatially extended and, reciprocally, what's spatially extended is unfit for pervasion by a Pure Sound. Regarding strictly spatial extension, I've suggested, Colors and Sounds are opposites. Colors also contrast, in this way, with Odors, and with many other presumed Qualities, that is, presumed Extensible Correlatives of experiential qualities.[7]

---

6. As you'll recall from Chapter 4, we also seem to do quite well when, say, you conceive your own feeling body as being more elongated, head to toe, as compared with, along any line perpendicular to that, how lengthily you're extended, or you're elongated. But, with anything like this conception, even in our conceiving itself, we're requiring the spatial body conceived to be an experiencing individual. That won't generalize at all well, of course, to what we take to be most of the world's spatial bodies, including all of its much more basic physical individuals.

7. Because I've enjoyed reading about Sounds in the philosophical literature, it's on these *Spatially Nonextensible* Qualities that I'll focus in proceeding toward our wanted Analogy. (Of course, in the literature there's much more about colors than there is about sounds. Still, several prominent thinkers have written influentially on sounds, even what I'm calling the Pure Sounds, and even in just the twentieth century alone.)

Among these writings, as it seems to me, it's Peter Strawson's Chapter "Sounds," in his book *Individuals*, Routledge, 1959, that's been the most imaginative and, I imagine, also the most influential.

But, my aims here are very different from what Strawson's were. Using Sounds as his central Quality, he wished to see how robust a conception we could have of a *nonspatial* concrete reality. (Of course, that's only a very crude statement of his aim.) By contrast, here my aim is to see how there might be, in addition to space, *dimensional aspects of concrete reality correlative with space*. (And, of course, that's only a very crude statement of my aim.)

Now, let's make this speculation: It may be that, in concrete reality, spatial extension isn't the only sort of (nontemporal) extension. For some, the speculation may seem insufficiently intelligible. But, why? Well, we humans have a rather clear conception of *spatial* extension. But, we haven't any decent idea, not even just very modestly decent, of any other sort of (nontemporal) extension. That is, we haven't any decent idea as to how a concretum may be extended in any other (nontemporal) way. (From now on, I'll usually omit qualification as to what's nontemporal.) But, as I'll now suggest, by employing apt analogical thinking, we might come to have a modestly decent idea.

By their very nature, Sounds are metaphysically precluded from pervading anything that's (strictly) *spatial*. But, that doesn't preclude Sounds from pervading *nonspatial* regions of concrete reality. Thus, it might possibly be that there are concreta, each Qualitied with Extensible Sound, and each occupying a distinct nonspatial region, much as spatially separate bodies, each Qualitied with Extensible Color, each occupy a distinct spatial region. Ontologically and metaphysically, each of these nonspatially extended concreta may be on a par with the spatial bodies. For philosophers with an adventurous spirit, these thoughts may be a promising start for some interesting speculations.

7. The Hypothesis of Spacelike Extension: An Analogical Speculation

It's time for our analogical speculation as to what may be relevantly spacelike. In the spirit of our essay, we want the speculation to be as conservative as possible. That is, as long as it's rich enough to help with the philosophical Problems we've encountered, we want the speculation to require as small a departure as possible from our currently dominant metaphysic. (Well, at the very least, we want to start off in that way. And, for the most part, we'll want to stick with that. But, occasionally, we should allow ourselves to make some quite far-fetched and expansive speculations. After all, who knows where we may find our most interesting philosophical thoughts and, perhaps, our most fruitful thoughts, too?)

Anyway, at least for starters, we want a speculation that may comport well with a Substantial Dualistic metaphysic, not wholly unlike the Emergentive Dualisms we've already been considering. (The plural word "Dualisms" seems annoyingly barbarous to me. So, from now on, I'll just use the singular term, "Dualism," even when I'm discussing some several Dualistic Views.) To this end, I'll explore a speculative conjecture on which the actual world has, besides space itself, just one spacelike dimension of concrete reality. This conjecture is the *Dualistic (Form of the) Hypothesis of Spacelike Extension*.

How shall I express this hypothesis? Well, as I'll agree, sometimes it's confusing to use "spacelike" both for what's relevantly *like* space and *also for space* itself. But, sometimes this inclusive use will be handy. Speaking just so handily, I'll say that, on the Dualistic Hypothesis of Spacelike Extension, our actual concrete reality has exactly two spacelike dimensions, or precisely two spacelike dimensional aspects.

Quite familiar to us, space itself is one of the two spacelike dimensions. In supposing a simple Particulate World, we suppose distinct regions of space each to be occupied by distinct *spatial concrete objects*, most basically by distinct Particles. And, of course, we suppose that no Particle is located in any other spacelike dimension, other than space itself.

Quite unfamiliar to us, and only very analogically conceivable by us, perhaps there's another spacelike dimension, we may Dualistically hypothesize, that's ontologically on a par with space. Now, many separate regions of this other spacelike dimension—I'll call it *sone*—are each occupied by separate *sonal concrete objects*, most basically by distinct *Sonicles*, if you will. As we're now Dualistically hypothesizing, each of these distinct sonal objects, each of these so-called Sonicles, may be a distinct nonspatial mind, or a numerically different purely sonal soul. In a parallel with basic spatial individuals, on a nicely Dualistic form of our Hypothesis, no sonal individual is located in any other spacelike dimension, other than sone itself.

To conceive *spatial bodies*, at all well or clearly, we must conceive each to be pervaded with *Spatially* Extensible Quality. And, to do that, quite well, we should conceive each to be pervaded with Extensible *Color*, a Quality that's so nicely fit for *Spatial* pervasion. And, then, to conceive quite clearly how several separate bodies may be spatially related (and, thus, spacelikely related) we conceive each to be *spatially separated*, from each of the others, by some absolutely empty *space*, that is, by some space that's wholly without any (Spatially Extensible) Quality at all.

To conceive *sonal minds*, at all well or clearly, we should conceive such souls in a relevantly parallel manner. Thus, we should conceive each to be pervaded with *Sonally* Extensible Quality. And, as we've agreed to suppose, for our illustrative exposition, the Sonally Extensible Qualities are (or they saliently include) the Pure Sounds—much as the Spatially Extensible Qualities are (or they saliently include) the Pure Colors. So, to do this pretty well, we should analogically conceive each soul to be pervaded with Extensible *Sound*, a Quality that's so nicely fit for *Sonal* pervasion. (As I'm fully aware, of course, no Sonally Extensible Quality is available in human imaginative experiencing; and, so, our thinking in terms of them will be heavily analogical thinking, unlike our thinking in terms of Spatially Extensible Quality.) At all events, to conceive pretty clearly how several nonspatial souls may be sonally related, or to conceive it as clearly as we humans can do, we should conceive each sonal soul to be *sonally separated*, from each of the others, by some absolutely empty *sone*, that is, by some sone that's wholly without any (Sonally Extensible) Quality at all.

A Sound, I've suggested, even a nonexperiential Sound, is intrinsically unfit to pervade what's spatial, and, correlatively, what's spatial is intrinsically unfit for pervasion by a Sound. For a helpful Dualistic Hypothesis of Spacelike Extension, that suggestion is helpful. For, on the other side of the analogy that's wanted, there's this: A Color, even a nonexperiential Color, will be intrinsically unfit to pervade what's sonal, or whatever's spacelike but nonspatial, even while what's sonal (and spacelike, but nonspatial) will be intrinsically unfit for pervasion by a Color.

Using some pretty specific terms, we may illustrate our speculative analogy quite vividly. At the same time, our illustrative formulation may have it, quite rightly, that *everything that's real is a substantial individual*. Right here and now, let's do just that.

A spatial object, in particular a basic body, *may be* Extensibly Qualitied Redly. And, it *must be* Extensibly Qualitied Colorly, somehow or other. But, it *can't be* Extensibly Qualitied Belltonely; indeed, it *can't be* Extensibly Qualitied Soundly at all.

A sonal object, by contrast, and in particular a basic sonal soul, may be Extensibly Qualitied Belltonely. Or, so we speculatively and instructively conjecture. And, along this instructively speculative line, we may say that a sonal soul *must be* Extensibly Qualitied Soundly, somehow or other. But, of course, a sonal soul can't be Extensibly Qualitied Redly or, for that matter, Qualitied Colorly at all.

For an Hypothesis of Spacelike Extension that's clearly Dualistic, these will be, I suggest, very apt assumptions.

At all events, we humans are disposed to conceive spatial concreta quite fully and clearly, even as to how each may be externally related to just so many simultaneously similar others. But, even if there should be very many sonally separate sonal souls, we're *not* Propensitied to conceive their like anywhere near so fully, or so clearly. Indeed, even if all their Sonally Extensible Quality should be the Extensible Correlative of a very familiar experiential sound, that will certainly be so. Perhaps, this may seem an unsettling consequence of the Quasi-Cartesian Dualism we've been contemplating. But, then, we've known all along, really, that this is plainly so: Any of *our* thinking that's conducted in merely spacelike conceptions, and that's not conducted in any truly spatial conceptions, won't be any very full or terribly clear thinking. That is, it won't be nearly as clear, or nearly as full, as the common thinking we do that, quite direct and not just analogical, is conducted in just such (spacelike) conceptions as are strictly spatial ideas.

8. The Deflationary Approach: An Apparent Alternative

Our Hypothesis of Spacelike Extension is, I know, an extremely strange philosophical conjecture. Indeed, it's so strange that, even at this point, it will be unclear to many readers. To make matters clearer, I'll now contrast the conjecture with what may seem a more down-to-earth alternative for addressing the issues it's meant to confront. I'll call the offered apparent alternative the *Deflationary Approach* to these issues.

We've been agreeing, for some time now, that my power to be visually qualitied experientially sustains my power to conceive spatial bodies, quite fully and clearly, as Spatially Extensibly Qualitied concrete particulars. And, we've also agreed that, by contrast, my power to be auditorally qualitied experientially *doesn't* sustain, in me, a similarly helpful power to conceive.

My power to be auditorally qualitied experientially doesn't help me to conceive, at all fully and clearly, any *spatially* extended concreta. And, as it seems, we may quite safely go beyond that, at least this far beyond: This auditory experiential power doesn't help me conceive, very fully or clearly, any (nontemporally) extended concreta at all, neither any that's spatially extended, nor any that's merely spacelikely extended, nor any that might be (nontemporally) extended otherwise, whatever this last might possibly mean. My power to be qualitied belltonely, for instance, doesn't enable me clearly to conceive concrete individuals to be extended in a "merely spacelike" way. Much less does it enable me to conceive them as being extended in, or through, space itself. Of course, this isn't just some idiosyncratic limitation. It's quite the same, I imagine, for other human thinkers. But, what about much further-fetched thoughtful beings?

In advancing our speculative Hypothesis, I relied on certain intuitively appealing thoughts. One was the intuitive idea that, owing to the intrinsic nature of the Extensible Colors and the character of space itself, those Qualities are suited for pervading space and, reciprocally, space is suited for pervasion by Extensible Colors. With that, I suggested certain strict limits on how concrete particulars may be clearly conceived. What limits? Well, quite in parallel with your conceiving some basic particulars as being Qualitied with Extensible Color, there might exist a being—call her "Sheila"—who conceives some basic concreta as being *Qualitied with Extensible Sound*. My restrictive suggestion requires that, in this concrete thinking, Sheila *won't* be conceiving individuals to be extended *spatially*. Since she's conceiving concreta as Qualitied Soundly, it's only with respect to some other spacelike dimension, not space itself, that Sheila's conceiving any concreta as spacelikely extended.

That should help clarify, I trust, the contrast between our offered Hypothesis of Spacelike Extension and, on the other side, the Deflationary Approach to our topic. Let me amplify.

On the Deflationary Approach, there *isn't* anything about the Extensible Colors, and there *isn't* anything about what's properly spatial, that has each be peculiarly well suited to the other. Indeed, on the Deflationary Approach, the Extensible Colors *aren't* more suited to pervading what's properly spatial than are, for example, (what I've been calling) Extensible Sounds. So, much as *my* experiencing *bluely* may sustain *my* power to clearly conceive a spatial body as Qualitied *Bluely*, so, on this Deflationism, our *Sheila's* experiencing *belltonely* may sustain *her* power to clearly conceive a spatial body as Qualitied *Belltonely*. When all these matters are understood, our Deflationist holds, there's no indication of any metaphysically important difference, at least so far as extension goes, between the Pure Colors and the Pure Sounds. All that's really going on here is just this: On the one hand, there's *me* conceiving a spatial object as Extensibly Colored, exercising *my* power to conceive even insensate concreta as *spatially extended*. And, on the other, there's *Sheila* conceiving a spatial object as *Extensibly Sounded*, exercising *her* power to conceive such substantial particulars as *spatially extended*. Even as Sheila is very different from me, so her power to conceive particulars, as spatially extended, is very different from my power to do so, with each of our very different powers having very different sorts of mental manifestation. Just so, there are just such differences in these conceivers, and in their conceptions, but not in what they're then conceiving: Though the spatial extension of conceived individuals may be quite differently conceived by quite different thinkers, still, all so-called spacelikely extended individuals are just so many spatially extended entities. Maybe excepting temporal extension, that's the only way a concretum can ever be extended.

What are we to think of this Deflationary Approach? To me, it's only in a weak sense of "intelligible" that this Deflationism is even so much as a barely intelligible position. And, so, it's only in a weak sense of "alternative" that it's an alternative to our Hypothesis of Spacelike Extension. Myself, I can't make much sense, really, of the suggestion that a Pure Sound can pervade a spatial object or region, little more than I can make of the notion that a Shape, like Sphericity, might be a Color, like Blue. So, of course, I can't make much sense, either, of a being who can clearly conceive a spatial object as being pervaded by a Spatially Extensible Sound.

Not wanting to be dogmatic about these matters, it's without any alleged certainty that I'll make my suggestion about our Hypothesis of Spacelike Extension: For us human thinkers, at least, this Hypothesis makes enormously much more sense than does the Deflationary Approach. To be sure, this Hypothesis is plainly a very speculative conjecture, whereas that Approach may appear to be far more down to earth. But, all that may just be a certain initial appearance. All things considered, and as best I can tell, our considered Deflationism is no real alternative to our speculative proposal.[8]

9. An Hypothesized Dimension Far More Like Space Than Like Time

In any Form, our Hypothesis holds that concrete reality actually has, in addition to space and time, at least one other dimension. And, on this Hypothesis, any other such further dimension is far more like space than it's like time.

The Hypothesis of Spacelike Extension may take a Dualistic Form, as we've been repeatedly observing. For the Hypothesis to be helpful in articulating a Dualism between mind and body, even while allowing us to be fairly conservative in our speculations, it will posit that reality's sole further dimension must be enormously more like space than it's like time: Unlike the enormously accommodating dimension of time, the hypothesized further dimension should be as unaccommodating as space is, or as selectively accommodating as is space. Indeed, to serve

8. Much more modest than what I've just been calling the Deflationary Approach, there are other positions that thus may be called, maybe much more aptly, "Deflationary Approaches." For instance, it may be denied that there are any beings, even possible beings, who can conceive any spacelikely extended individuals in a way that's (even remotely) on a par with our conceiving spatial bodies as Extensibly Qualitied. But, these are such very modest positions that, in the present context, it's pointless to discuss them.

Dualism best, perhaps we should have the hypothesized spacelike dimension be *just precisely as* selectively accommodating as space is, not any more and also not any less, even while it's *oppositely* selective, from how it is with space itself, as regards *which Extensibly Qualitied* concreta it accommodates. And, we're Dualistically Hypothesizing, that will go hand in hand with this: Just as space itself *is* fit for *spatial bodily* location, and for occupancy by *spatial bodies*, and space *isn't* fit for *mindily* location, so to speak, or for occupancy by *nonspatial souls*, so the *hypothesized spacelike* dimension—we're calling it *sone*, I'll remind you—well, *that will be* fit for *mindily* location, and for occupancy by *spacelikely sonal souls*. And, to complete the parallel, we add this: Our hypothesized spacelike sone *isn't* fit for *spatial bodily* location and, of course, it *isn't* fit for occupancy by *spatial bodies*.

To have a clear idea of what's just been said, and a decently clear idea of our Dualistic (Form of the) Hypothesis of Spacelike Extension, we must have an understanding of space, and of time, on which each is very unlike the other. This goes against the current philosophical orthodoxy concerning time, prevalent throughout most of the twentieth century (though, perhaps it's now somewhat waning—or, so it may be hoped). On this orthodoxy, time is treated in very much the way that space has always been treated. Can we reject this orthodoxy?

Of course, I think we can have a tolerably clear idea of our speculative Hypothesis. And, I think this may suggest that the truest way to conceive space and time, which does most justice to each, is to conceive each as very unlike the other. Anyhow, toward seeing how we might well think space and time to be greatly different, I'll consider four aptly related examples.

First, we'll imagine a spherical solid whose innermost regions are always Transparent Red, and whose outermost regions are always Transparent Blue. As regards the distribution of Color Quality, in this case there is a spatial difference, but there is no temporal difference. (In the middle, it might be, or it might not be, that there are regions that are Purple. And, it might be, or it might not be, that there is continuous differentiation, from Red through Purple to Blue, and vice versa. For present purposes, these matters are all secondary issues.)

Second, we'll similarly suppose a similar solid all of whose regions are always Transparent Red. As regards the distribution of Color Quality, in this case there is no spatial difference and, as well, there is no temporal difference.

Third, we'll suppose a similar solid whose regions are, at first, all Transparent Red, and whose regions are, at last, all Transparent Blue. As regards the distribution of Color Quality, in this case there is a temporal difference, or a *real alteration*. But, even at every moment of time, there isn't any spatial difference, any real qualitative *variegation*. (In the middle, it might be, or it might not be, that these regions are all Purple. And, it might be, or it might not be, that there is continuous alteration, from Red through Purple to Blue, but not vice versa. For present purposes, these matters are also all secondary issues.)

Fourth, we may suppose a spherical solid whose regions are, at first, just as are all those of the first of our four supposed solids, some regions being, at first, Transparent Red, while others are, then, Transparent Blue, and not Transparent Red. Well, all this fourth solid's regions are, at last, different Qualitatively from how they first are. So, a region that's first wholly Red will be, at last, wholly Blue; and a region that's first fully Blue will be, at last, pervasively Red. As regards questions of Color Quality, in this case there are, throughout and quite truly, *both a temporal* difference, a *real qualitative alteration*, and *also a spatial* difference, a *real qualitative variegation*.

As these four examples illustrate, not only are temporal alteration and spatial variegation perfectly independent of each other, but, as well, each is enormously unlike the other.

With our Hypothesis of Spacelike Extension, I've said, the further dimension we posit is enormously more like space than it's like time. And, what's more, it's rather like space, all things considered, even while, all things considered, it's utterly unlike time. So, we should ask: Might a dimension that's very like *time*, maybe even time *itself*, be enough to afford us an *Extensional Hypothesis* that, especially for us human thinkers, has a quite intelligibly relevant *Dualistic* Form? I think not.

All over again, let's try to prepare for a helpful Extensional Hypothesis. So, we again note the mutual suitability of spatial concreta and Extensible Color. And, again, we hypothesize that there may be a similarly mutual fit between certain *nonspatial* concreta, maybe especially some nonspatial *souls*, and some other Extensible Quality, maybe Nonspatially Extensible Sound.

Now, in the philosophic literature, it's sometimes said (incorrectly, I think) that, just as colors are fit for pervading space, so sounds are fit for pervading time. That occasional statement suggests this proportionality: Colors are to space as Sounds are to time.

Is *that* (putative) proportion what we want for our analogical thinking? Well, we want something that's suggested by our experiencing, whether it be Sounds or whether not, that will help us get a better grasp of *how it is that nonspatial souls may be externally related to each other*. Well, being reminded of *time* can't possibly help us with any such quest as *that*.

For this reason alone, we want a very different analogy, where Sounds serve to indicate something *utterly different from time*. Indeed, it seems that what Sounds should serve to indicate, if it's to help us at all in this matter, must be both utterly unlike time and, what's more, enormously more like space than like time. So, at least in this sense, this Sound-indicated dimensional candidate should be pretty much like space itself, at least enough for it to be aptly labeled a *spacelike* candidate.

There's another reason that, for our analogy, we want a dimension that's quite like space and utterly unlike time: To all appearances, space is *asymmetric* with regard to Colors and Sounds, suitable for pervasion only by the former Qualities. But, as it's susceptible to pervasion *both* by Colors *and also* by Sounds, time *isn't* asymmetric. Rather, quite equally and symmetrically, just as time accommodates Extensible Colors—or any concreta that may be Extensibly Colored—so time will also accommodate any Extensible Sounds that might ever be instantiated—or any concreta that may be Extensibly Sounded (now coining a usage of "Sounded" to parallel a familiar usage of "Colored"). Indeed, utterly unlike how space certainly seems to be, not only *may* time accommodate absolutely all of concrete reality, however vast that reality ever should be, but, indeed, time *must* accommodate absolutely all concrete reality.

Here's another statement of the same reason: We want an analogy where Sounds—or, at any rate, where some Nonspatially Extensible Quality, or Qualities—are (somewhat) peculiarly suited for some central dimensional aspect of concrete reality much as Colors are (somewhat) peculiarly suited for space. And, much as space is suited for (pervasion by) Color, so this dimensional aspect should be suited, somewhat peculiarly, for (pervasion by) Sound. Or, at any rate, it should be so suited for (pervasion by) *some* Extensible Quality that, *unlike* Extensible Color, *isn't* suited to pervade space itself. Well, then, what's wanted for this analogy won't be time, of course, nor anything very like time (whatever that might precisely mean). Rather, we want a dimension that's quite like space and, in the selfsame bargain, that's enormously much more like space than it's like time. Of course, in offering our Hypothesis of Spacelike Extension, it's just this that we're suggesting.

As I hope, these next words may also be helpful: Quite as space accommodates only entities Qualitied *only in certain* ways, as with those that are Extensibly Colored, so another *spacelike dimension* may accommodate only entities Extensibly Qualitied *only in certain other* ways, as with those that might be Extensibly Sounded or, perhaps, say, Extensibly Odored. In this large regard, spacelike dimensions, including space itself, are *selectively accommodating*. With time (or with any other dimension that's very timelike, if any such there be) there's nothing so *selectively* accommodating. Rather, there's only what's nonselectively accommodating or, using a more positive label, there's only what's *absolutely* accommodating.

For a most intelligible and amenable Dualistic speculation, I've been suggesting, it's *just a selectively* accommodating dimension that's wanted, a dimensional aspect that's relevantly quite *spacelike*. Happily, I think, that's what's offered with our Dualistic Hypothesis of Spacelike Extension.

10. Our Fullest Conceptions of Spatial Bodies

The Hypothesis of Spacelike Extension may allow us, I'll suggest, to conceive nonspatial souls in something of a parallel, more or less great, with spatial bodies. Now, for a fullest conception of such analogically conceived souls, as full as may be humanly available, we may want, very likely, a conception of souls that parallels, quite closely, and in very many respects, our fullest conception of spatial bodies. Or, maybe we can make do with a little less of a parallel. But, at all events, for a most useful discussion of how we may most fully conceive souls as externally related to each other, we should first observe our fullest conceptions of how spatial bodies may be externally related.

To make a good start on this, we should look to conceive *basic* spatially extended entities: Though a basic body may have different spatial parts, in a very weak sense of "part," roughly synonymous with "region," still, each basic body will be, throughout the whole region of space it occupies, a relevantly simple particular, with no other spatial bodies serving to constitute it, nor even anything remotely like that. In a word, a basic spatial body won't have any *substantial* parts.

Each most fully conceived basic body will have properties of three basic sorts, we've now long agreed, the first two of which we can quite fully, and quite clearly, conceive the body to have: First, the body will have certain spatial properties, as with the Spherical Shape of a Transparent Red Sphere. And, second, the body will be spatially Qualitied pervasively, as with the Transparent Red Color of a Transparent Red Sphere. Well then, with that said, we're two-thirds of the way home, as it were. What's the final third? To conceive bodies quite fully and clearly, we should also conceive such spatial concreta as aptly Propensitied.

For our fullest conception of bodies, what's a bodily Propensity that we might take to be salient? Well, to conceive our bodies quite fully and clearly, we should be able to conceive, as clearly as we can, how they may be externally related over time, and not just momentarily. And, at least in the most usual case, this will include such periods of time as those when the bodies move.

Now, to do all that quite well enough, we should conceive our moving bodies as always remaining spatially separated, so that there's never even the least danger of our confusing a conception of some perfectly absolute mere contact with any idea of some most marginal bare overlap. And, to do *this* quite well, perhaps we shouldn't conceive each body as staying spatially separate from the others by just some happy accident. Maybe, we'll do better if we conceive that to transpire, or to occur, as a veritable manifestation of the Propensitive natures of the simultaneously spatially quite separate bodies themselves.

Wishing all this to be satisfied, quite as we do, we may see the bodily Propensity of absolute *solidity* to be especially salient, for our present conceptual purposes. And, we may well want, even so, to go quite beyond that especially salient Propensity. How's that? Please, let me explain.

When it's spatial bodies that we're most fully to conceive, as fully as ever we humans can do, then we should conceive each individual as Propensitied to maintain its spatial separation from any other spatial concretum that there may be: We conceive each body as strongly *Propensitied to preclude any spatial overlapping with*, and any penetration by, any other spatial body. And, for *extra* good measure, we might conceive each body as strongly Propensitied to preclude (even just so much as any) *spatial contact with* any other body.

A nice little example may illustrate our point: Again, consider a World with many Large Blue Spherical Particles and many Large Spherical Reds, too, and with all the Particles the very same size. Now, each Red is perfectly resistant to penetration by each of the other Reds, we suppose, and, what's more, each Red is Propensitively precluded even from any real contact with each of the other Reds. And, we suppose similarly for the Blues. But, we'll suppose—or maybe we'll just pretend— that the Reds and the Blues may penetrate each other, often even quite perfectly and completely. Whenever this happens, then, quite as we'll keep supposing, there'll be a Purple Sphere, just the same Large Size as is, or as was, each of the Large Reds, and also each of the Large Blues. And, apparently quite aptly enough, any such Purple Sphere will be intermediate in Color between Red and Blue.

In a bit more detail, here's what's supposed to happen in such a "fusing change." Before the penetration is complete, there's a gradual change of shapes, through a bulbous three-dimensional "figure eight," having a central region that's Purple and, protruding symmetrically from the 3-D figure eight's center, there's both a Red region and also a Blue region. Or, so we're now supposing or, at the least, we're now pretending. Anyhow, that goes on, and on, for however long you please. At any rate, by the end of the supposed fusing change, there's a perfectly Spherical Purple Particle, with a Size the same as the Red's first was and, so also, the same as the Blue's original volume.

Now, we may have certain inclinations to think that certain things have happened here. For instance, we may have an urge to think that, at the end of such a fusing change, there remains the Red that fused and there also remains a Blue Particle, which also fused. Along with the Purple Particle to which they both contribute, they both occupy a certain spherical region of space. But, of course, we also have quite different inclinations. Anyhow, whatever our urges or inclinations, in whichever directions, one thing now seems quite safe to say: We can't conceive very fully, nor can we conceive very clearly, *how it is* that, in this one spherical space, there's more than just one basic spherical body.

For our fullest conceiving of simultaneous spatial bodies, as I've said, we should conceive each to be effectively Propensitied to remain *spatially separate from* all others.

In much of this suggestive discussion, we've conceived bodies that moved and, what's more, that moved toward each other. But, we may also conceive, very fully and clearly, bodies that never move, neither toward each other, nor away from each other, nor in any other fashion. In certain of these clearly conceived cases, it's the Propensities of the bodies that's always at work. Each body may have a Propensity for stasis, or for spatial monotony—maybe even absolutely, or maybe just with respect to any other bodies. As a manifestation of these reciprocal Propensities, there's the continual stasis of the bodies, each always spatially separate from all the others.

(At all events, it's quite interesting, I think, to observe that, for all we really know, this may well be the actual world's material situation: It's very far from clear, I'll submit, that there's really a plurality of basic physical things, in the actual world, much less that there's a plurality of such basic spatial objects each really moving, or each truly moving with respect to ever so many others. Rather than that, and so far as anyone can really tell, basic physical reality is perfectly Plenumate, and nothing much like Particulate at all. Well, with just a Single Plenum, or with only one Single Substantial Field, there isn't any real plurality of distinct spatial concrete particulars. Nor will it ever be clear what "motion" can really mean, or what motion can really be, in respect of such a Perfectly Plenumate Cosmic Circumstance. For, what appears as something that's moving—say, a moving *modification of* the Field—will really be just a certain qualitative change occurring, in a certain spatially and temporally well-ordered way, with respect to the only real spatial entity, the Plenum itself, of course. We can *call* such an orderly change "movement," and, no doubt, we all have some inclination to that effect, even if it may be no very great urging. But, now speaking most strictly, and truly, and seriously, it's not the real thing.)

11. An Analogical Conception of Nonspatial Souls

On a Humanly Realistic Philosophy, there'll be a plurality of distinct souls, in whatever realm of concrete reality, or whatever realms, these diverse souls should be. In particular, and specifically, I'll be one of these several souls; and, you'll be another. On our presently proffered suppositions, as I'll remind you, these distinct souls will be sonally separate sonal individuals. But, of course, the main point is a perfectly general proposition.

At all events, this situation with souls differs dramatically, you can be very sure, from our conception of a nonmoving spatial Plenum, where there's just a single spatial concretum involved, perhaps spatially infinite in all directions.

Of course, and also at all events, it's easy enough to suppose a realm of nonmoving spatial concreta, at least a possible realm, that *doesn't* differ so dramatically, not nearly as dramatically as does just a Single Nonmoving Spatial Plenum, from an hypothesized realm of distinct nonspatial souls all of which are always nonspatially stationary. Just so, and very simply indeed, we may have quite a clear conception of some several spatially separate spatial bodies, with none of them ever moving. And, so, we may clearly conceive there to be some several spatial bodies, with each of them always spatially separate from all the others. (This is some nice news, I'll suggest, for those who want, much as I do, for us to have a decently clear conception of distinct nonspatial souls, including even an idea as to how each of them may be externally related to each of the others.)

What's more, we can have a clear conception on which none of that is any accident, none of that persistently static spatial separation amongst all our supposed spatial bodies: Each body may have a Propensity for stasis, or for spatial monotony—maybe even absolutely, or maybe just with respect to any other spatial bodies. Even as a veritable manifestation of all these Propensities, among all the bodies, there may be the continual spatial stasis of the spatially separate spatial bodies, with each body always remaining, spatially, just as it was just before. (This is more nice news, I'll suggest, for those who want, quite as I do, for us to have a decently clear conception of distinct nonspatial souls, including even an idea as to how each of them may be externally related to each of the others.)

On a nice analogy with the aforesaid conception of perennially separate spatial bodies, we may have a pretty decent conception, anyway, even if it's not, of course, quite so clear a conception, as to sonally "nonmoving" nonspatial sonal souls. In parallel with our spatially static spatial bodies, we may conceive each sonal nonspatial soul to be strongly Propensitied for (nonspatial) *sonal* monotony—maybe even absolutely, or maybe just with respect to any other sonal souls. Even as a veritable manifestation of all *these* Propensities, among all the souls, there may be the continual *sonal* stasis of the sonally separate sonal souls, with *each soul always* remaining, sonally, *just as it* was just before.

With just that conception in place, I think, we may have all we want, without yet taking it upon ourselves to go in for conceiving how things may be with "sonally moving perennially sonally separate sonal souls." Of course, if you like, you can go in for just such a conception as of that, without the slightest real problem. As almost needs no saying, that will be an idea that's closely analogous, in sonal terms, to our quite clear conception of how things may be with spatially moving perennially spatially separate basic spatial bodies. With what we've already observed, in connection with the latter conception, this will require no extraordinarily new novel thinking.

For us to obtain a nice idea of sonally separate sonal souls each sonally moving—maybe each of them sonally moving just with respect to all other sonal entities—well, we just mimic our fullest conceptions of spatially separate spatial bodies spatially moving. What is that conception?

For a start on an answer, we may say, very roughly, something very general about what it is for spatial bodies to move: A spatial body moves spatially—whether absolutely or whether just relative to other spatial things—when there's a temporal change concerning how it is that the body is spatially located—whether absolutely or whether just relative to other spatial things. So, for a matching start of a statement about sonally separate souls sonally moving, we do little more than substitute, in our rough spatial statement, some sonal terms for its spatial terms. So substituting, we may say, also very roughly, something very general about what it is for sonal souls to move: A sonal soul moves sonally—whether absolutely or whether just relative to other sonal things—when there's a temporal change concerning how it is that the soul is sonally located—whether absolutely or whether just relative to other sonal things. Well, easy as pie, that's a decent start at articulating what may be our best conception of how it is with sonally separate sonal souls that sonally move.

For our fullest conception of sonally moving souls, what more do we want? Well, we want something to parallel, analogically, what's involved in our fullest conception of spatially moving spatial bodies.

Well, then, what's involved in *that* conception? For a statement of that, I'll bring forward some material from the previous Section:

> [W]e should conceive our moving bodies as always remaining spatially separated, so that there's never even the least danger of our confusing a conception of some perfectly absolute mere contact with any idea of some most marginal bare overlap. And, to do *this* quite well, perhaps we shouldn't conceive each body as staying spatially separate from the others by just some happy accident. . . . [W]e conceive that to transpire, or to occur, as a veritable manifestation of the Propensitive natures of the simultaneously spatially quite separate bodies themselves. . . .
>
> [W]e should conceive each individual as Propensitied to maintain its spatial separation from any other spatial concretum that there may be: We conceive each body as strongly *Propensitied to preclude any spatial overlapping with*, and any penetration by, any other spatial body. And, for *extra* good measure, we might conceive each body as strongly Propensitied to preclude (even just so much as any) *spatial contact with* any other body.[9]

With all that in place, we agreed, we can clearly conceive some several spatial bodies all spatially moving around and about, with each always ensured, Propensitively, as spatially separate from all the others.

Quite automatically, for our best conception of sonally moving sonal souls, then, we may do little more than substitute, in the likes of our lately displayed verbiage, some several sonal terms for the several salient spatial expressions. By doing that, we'll obtain this: We should conceive our sonally moving souls as always remaining sonally separated, so that there's never even the least danger of our confusing a conception of some perfectly absolute mere sonal contact with any idea of some most marginal bare sonal overlap. And, to do *this* quite well, perhaps we shouldn't conceive each soul as staying sonally separate from the others by just some happy accident. Rather, we should conceive that to transpire, or to occur, as a veritable manifestation of the

---

9. The quoted passages are from Section 10 above.

Propensitive natures of the simultaneously sonally quite separate souls themselves. Just so, we should conceive each soulful individual as Propensitied to maintain its sonal separation from any other sonal concretum that there may be: We conceive each soul as strongly *Propensitied to preclude any sonal overlapping with*, and any sonal penetration by, any other sonal soul. And, for *extra* good measure, we might conceive each soul as strongly Propensitied to preclude (even just so much as any) *sonal contact with* any other sonal individual.

As I'll suggest, all that will yield us humans a pretty decent conception of sonally moving sonal souls, each always sonally separate from all other sonal individuals. Of course, this decent idea won't ever be as clear, or as full, as is our far more direct conception of spatially moving spatial bodies. But, of course, that was always to be expected. As expected, our ideas as to how nonspatial souls may be externally related, each to all the others, isn't as clear an idea, nor is it as full an idea, as our best conceptions as to how spatial bodies may be externally related, each to all the others.

At all events, let's now look to observe what may be some benefits of such an evidently analogical conception of nonspatial souls.

12. Our Hypothesis Allows More Fully Conceivable Substantial Dualist Views

Toward providing a vividly specific exposition of the Dualistic Form of the Hypothesis of Spacelike Extension, and toward providing such Substantial Dualistic Views as this Hypothesis makes Humanly quite available, we'll continue with our suppositions: Nonspatial souls, we'll suppose, are simple sonal concreta, much as basic spatial bodies, say, some Particles, are simple spatial concreta. Just so, we're now conceiving our spatial bodies to be *nonsonal*, just as much as we're conceiving our sonal souls to be *nonspatial*.

To further our parallel of entities in a (merely) spacelike dimensional realm, we're supposing each sonal soul to be sonally separate from every other soul, much as each spatial body is spatially separate from every other body. On this conception, no soul is *spatially* apart from any other soul, of course, just as none is spatially contiguous with any other. All that almost goes without saying. But it does help to remind us of this. Quite in parallel, no spatial *body* is *sonally* apart from any other body, of course, just as none is sonally contiguous with any other body. Very nicely, I'd say, that's how things are, according to our potentially quite helpful Dualistic Hypothesis.

Indeed, for our sonal souls, we're supposing much more than that. Just so, we're further supposing at least as much as all this: It's as a veritable manifestation of the Propensitive natures of the sonal (non-spatial) souls that there's ensured, for as long as the souls should exist, the real sonal separation of each basic nonspatial mental being from all of the others. It's thus *Propensitively ensured*, in other words, that each soul is, and it always will be, sonally apart from, or sonally separate from, every other sonal soul. So, not only is it ensured, ever so perfectly Propensitively, that there'll never be any sonal overlap among, or between, any of the souls; but, what's more, it's even ensured, quite as Propensitively, that there'll never even be any (potentially confusing) sonal contact between any one sonal soul and any other basic sonal experiencer.

All this parallels, quite happily, central propositions concerning well-conceived bodies, nicely related to each other in ways also quite well-conceived: It's as a veritable manifestation of the Propensitive natures of the spatial (nonsonal) bodies that there's ensured, for as long as the bodies should exist, the spatial separation of all basic spatial physical beings. It's thus *Propensitively ensured*, in other words, that each body is, and it always will be, spatially apart from, or spatially separate from, every other spatial body. So, not only is it ensured, ever so perfectly Propensitively, that there'll never be any spatial overlap among, or between, any of the basic bodies; but, what's more, it's even ensured, quite as Propensitively, that there'll never even be any (potentially confusing) spatial contact between any one spatial Particle, say, and any other basic spatial concretum.

Beyond what we've already observed, we may go on to enjoy still further conceptions in parallel. So, even as we customarily think of each spatial body as occupying a spatially voluminous region of space, quite as we consider it to be a body with a certain spatial volume, so we may conceive each sonal soul as occupying a sonally voluminous region of sone. For, analogously, or in parallel, we may consider each sonal soul to be a (*non*spatially) extended concretum with a certain *sonal volume*. And, even as we conceive each body's spatially voluminous region to be spatially separate from that of any other spatial body, so we may conceive, in parallel, each soul's sonally voluminous region to be sonally separate from that of any other sonal soul.

And, even beyond all that, we may go on to enjoy still further conceptions in parallel. All in all, I'll suggest, we may have, quite nicely available, even for us mere human thinkers, a very substantial parallel, between nonspatial sonal souls, on the one hand, and nonsonal spatial bodies, on the other hand. As I'm suggesting, along the lines of this quite considerable parallel, we may do pretty well at conceiving numerically distinct nonspatial souls. We may even do pretty well, as I'm further suggesting, at conceiving how the sonal souls might be, all at once, externally related, each to all the others. With just this much of a parallel, we may have an "almost bodily" conception of souls.

With rather less of a parallel, might we still attain, analogically, a conception of souls that's pretty decently full and clear? To some, it might well seem so, at least initially. But, I'm not so sure that it's really true. Let me amplify.

Consider a conception of souls, for instance, on which each nonspatial soul has a sonal location that's sonally separate from that of any other soul, but, on which, nonetheless, none of the souls are sonally voluminous. On this suggestion, each soul will be at a quite separate sonal point, but not at any point that's sonally extended. To specify this a bit or, at the least, to make an attempt to do so, we might say that, between any two sonally extensionless points (of sone) where there's a soul, well, there's *at least one* extensionless sonal point where there *isn't* any soul, nor any sonal concretum at all. With each such intermediate extensionless sonal point, we're trying to say, there'll be a perfectly empty part of sone, or an empty place in sone, or something of the sort.

If a soul has no sonal extent, then how can it be Qualitied with Nonspatially *Extensible* Sound, which is, on our supposition, just *Sonally* Extensible Sound? For any analogical thinking that's to be humanly helpful, there's a serious problem here. After all, whenever a *Spatially* Extensible Quality is instanced, as with an Extensible Color, there must be a spatially extended concretum that is thus Qualitied. So, to have an analogy that's decently clear here, we seem driven back to a more body-like conception for sonal souls. We seem forced back to a conception where, in other words, not only is each sonal soul located in sone, but, quite as well, each sonal soul is sonally voluminous. So, for a decently rich conception of nonspatial souls, we should have at least this much: Even as the spatial region that a certain simple body occupies is pervaded by just the (Spatially) Extensible Color of just that very body, so the sonal region occupied by a certain simple soul will be pervaded by just the (Sonally) Extensible Sound of just that very soul.

Unless we allow quite a strong parallel between sonal (nonspatial) souls and spatial (nonsonal) bodies, I'm suggesting, we may be saddled with a Mystery of the Mental that's quite as debilitating as was our Mystery of the Physical. Along with due respect for our rich Propensity, full attention should be paid, I'm suggesting, to such Sonally Extensible Quality as each of us also might have. Or, if it's not Sonally Extensible Quality that you have, then some other sort of Nonspatially Extensible Quality, relevantly on a par with Nonspatially Extensible Sound. For a Substantial Dualistic conception of concrete reality that's even just moderately full, then, or even just decently clear, we should allow quite a strong parallel between our simplest nonspatial souls, whether sonal or otherwise, and, on the other side, our simplest spatial bodies.

For quite awhile now, it should have been clear that all the Dualistic ideas we've been developing apply to both our so-called Pessimistic Dualism—a View on which, putting it roughly, a soul *doesn't* survive the death of its body, or its (overlapping) bodies—and also our so-called Optimistic Dualism—a View on which a soul *does* survive such death, or such deaths. With the Optimistic Dualism, it may be more obvious, I suppose, that we need something like sonal separation, or some sort of merely spacelikely separation, for a conception of souls that may relevantly parallel our best conceptions of spatial bodies. Even if it's not quite so obvious as it is with those "Optimistic souls," still, the point also holds true, just as nicely and fully, with the nonspatial souls of the Pessimistic Dualistic View, each always sustained by just its own spatially separate body (or its own spatially separate cluster of bodies.)

What's more, all these developing Dualistic ideas, regarding the likes of merely Spacelikely Extensibly Qualitied Individuals, will also apply, and with just as much justice, to various further forms of Substantial Dualism, which we've not yet considered. What's this last string of words? Well, you can believe me when I say that it's not any idle sentence that was just offered, nor any idle promise. In just a short while from now, we'll consider some further forms of Dualism, focusing on just such forms as are, to my mind, philosophically most significant. To prepare for that discussion, I'll first briefly address, in just the next Section, some extremely general ideas about how things may be, in this Eon or that, and, perhaps, in this World or that.

13. Nondualistic Forms of This Hypothesis: Integrated and Nonintegrated Dimensions

So far in this Chapter, the Hypothesis of Spacelike Extension has been employed, in largest measure, towards making most available, to us human thinkers, a Substantial Dualist Metaphysic. For obvious reasons, this has been very appropriate. And, in much of what remains, that will prevail, for much the same good reason. But, in this present Section, I'll venture a much more general discussion of this speculative Hypothesis. As will become apparent very soon,—indeed, as soon as the very next Section—some of this very general discussion will serve to make pretty plausible, or at least pretty palatable, a few new sorts of Substantial Dualism, which I'll soon place on offer, starting in the very next Section.

For a Dualistic Metaphysic, involving nonspatial minds and spatial bodies, we've wanted a conception of concrete reality as comprising, of course, precisely two distinct realms. Some concreta are in just a certain one of the realms, so to floridly speak, and the others are in just the other realm. This is how it is even on a fully Interactionist Substantial Dualism, on which some concreta in each of the realms influence, and are influenced by, some concreta in the other realm. Wanting to provide well for a Substantial Dualistic Metaphysic, we were moved to hypothesize, for nonspatial souls, a merely spacelike dimension, we called it *sone*, which served as a distinct realm for all the souls. Even while we hypothesized this sone to be quite devoid of any spatial bodies, so, in that same hypothesizing, we took it that space should be devoid of any sonal souls.

But, of course, in the service of general metaphysical theory, we needn't be so exclusively concerned with any such Dualistic Metaphysic.

When we broaden our focus, in the service of general theory, we may aim to articulate a broad variety of dimensional conceptions. With some of these conceptions, perhaps, we might never entertain them at all well, or clearly. But, when trying to chart new philosophical terrain, it may be badly stultifying to concern ourselves with that.

What I'll now suggest, for our consideration, is what might be called a Monistic Form of the Hypothesis of Spacelike Extension. On such a Monistic Form, each concretum (in any considered Monistic World) will be located in, and it will exist in, every last one of the world's spacelike dimensions, as well as existing in (what I still feel compelled to presume is) the world's single timelike dimension, that is, time itself. For a very simple Monistic World, and a World quite clearly conceived by us, we may consider a World with only one spacelike dimension and, what's more, have that dimension be space itself, a spacelike realm so suited for pervasion by Extensible Color. For a Monistic World that's just as simple, but that's not so clearly conceived by us, we may again have a World with only one spacelike dimension, all right. But, now, we should have that dimension *not* be space itself, so suited for pervasion by Extensible Color. For an example of that, we might suppose that the World's sole spacelike dimension should be sone, a spacelike realm that's so suited for pervasion by Extensible Sound, and not by Extensible Color.

Less simple Monistic Worlds, or Monistic Worlds more complex, will be richer in respect of their spacelike dimensional aspects. Thus, one (sort of) richer Monistic World may have exactly three spacelike (dimensional aspects or) dimensions: Space itself may be one of the three; our introduced sone may be another; and, a third might be, say, a dimension suited for pervasion by Pure Odors, but not suited for Colors, or for Sounds, at all.

How should such a World be Monistic? Well, the idea is this: First, each concretum of the world will be a spatial entity, certainly located in space, and, just a little less certainly, even occupying some space. And, second, each concretum will be, as well, a sonal concretum, certainly located in sone, and, just a little less certainly, even occupying some sone. And, third, each individual will also be an odoral concretum, located in our third-mentioned spacelike dimension and, presumably, occupying its own region of that spacelike dimensional aspect of concrete reality. Just so, in this supposed Monistic World, as in any Monistic World, any concretum that's located in even so much as one of the world's spacelike dimensions is located in all the world's spacelike dimensions. In this regard, each of these dimensions is *fully integrated with* each of the other spacelike dimensions.[10]

In trying to conceive the objects of this Monistic World, I won't be very successful. At best, I'll do well in conceiving how it may be that they're Colored, or Spatially Extensibly Qualitied. I'll do much less well, of course, in conceiving how it may be that they're Extensibly Sounded, or Sonally Extensibly Qualitied. And, I'll also do much less well, of course, in conceiving how it may be that they're Extensibly Odored, or Odorally Extensibly Qualitied. What may be worse, I suppose, is this: I can't attain even a modestly clear conception of how it should be that a single individual is ever, all at once, Extensibly Colored, and Extensibly Sounded, much less how it may be that, along with all this, the entity is also Extensibly Odored. Partly for that reason, I'm terribly unconfident that it's really possible for a single object to be Extensibly Qualitied, all at once, in three such radically disparate ways. But, in attempting to conceive an unusually rich Monistic World, with each entity located in each of some several spacelike dimensions, what alternative do we have here, each of us merely human thinkers?

10. A few words about time and dimensional integration: In any world, any concretum that's located in any spacelike dimension must also exist in time, even if it should be something of a metaphor to say that it's located in time. On the other hand, it's less certain that any concretum in time must also be located in a spacelike dimension. To be sure, any temporally existing concretum that we can conceive at all clearly must have some Extensible Quality and, so, it must be extended in a spacelike dimension that's suited to its Quality. But, of course, it might be, for all we can tell, that there are some temporally existing concreta we can't conceive at all clearly. And, some of these might not be in any spacelike dimension. So, as far as we can tell, while each spacelike dimension must be fully integrated with time, maybe time needn't be fully integrated with any spacelike dimension.

Anyway, things are not entirely bad, with the unusually rich Monistic conception we've been attempting to attain. On the bright side, there's this: I have a very clear idea, even from my own case, of how a single concretum may be, all at once, experientially colored, and experientially sounded, and experientially odored, too. So, that's some basis, anyway, for some extrapolative analogical thinking here. (Of course, for all I really know, this basis might be hopelessly inadequate. But, as our general metaphysical theorizing is in its earliest infancy, we should not be deterred, I think, by our enormous ignorance.)

Providing that these imaginative conceptions are decently coherent ideas, all sorts of related speculations arise almost automatically. So, for instance, we may contemplate a Dualism, with two distinct realms of distinct concreta, wherein some of the concreta exist in just a certain two spacelike dimensions, say, space and also sone, and wherein the rest exist in, and only in, just some certain other spacelike dimensions, none of them either space or sone. (But, so far as I can tell, every single one of these concreta must exist in just the same single timelike dimension, that is, of course, in time itself. By now, these reminders, about time, have become boring. So, I won't provide more.)

Also automatically available are various forms of *Tripleism*, or *Trialism*, and, for that matter, *Seventeenism*. On one sort of Trialism, there'll be a lot of individuals each in Space, but not in any other spacelike dimension, and there'll be a lot of others each in sone, but not in any others, and there'll be a lot of *still* others each in, say, exactly ten *other* spacelike dimensional aspects. The third sort of concreta will be, in a salient respect (that's only pretty poorly conceived by us humans) far richer than any concretum of the first sort, or any of the second sort. Existing in as many as ten spacelike realms, these concreta will be, presumably, extraordinarily richly Extensibly Qualitied. Of course, they won't be Spatially Extensibly Qualitied. But, they will be, at the very least, Ten-Ways Otherwise Extensibly Qualitied.

Just with this much, you'll know, well enough, I imagine, how to obtain ever so many of these (possibly quite dubious) almost automatically attained Isms, or Realmy Metaphysical Views. Now, there's much more to explore in this quite general philosophical area, concerning the most general matters suggested by the whole full-blown Hypothesis of Spacelike Extension. But, there are better places to do that than in this present study, mainly aimed toward developing a Humanly Realistic Philosophy. So, in these pages, I won't pursue many further thoughts as to the great variety of ways for concrete reality to be very rich Qualitatively—perhaps in various Worlds, perhaps in numerous Eons. Rather, trying to do best by this present work's main project, I return to address just those many metaphysical concerns most pertinent to that endeavor.

14. How Might We Nonspatial Souls Precede Even Our Initial Physical Embodiment?

In the sorts of Substantial Dualism so far considered, an immaterial soul first comes into being, or it initially *emerges*, through the mutually generative interaction of certain basic physical things. Roughly, these soulfully productive physical interactors, all of them mutually Propensitied to just such a richly generative effect, will be just those richly Propensitied elementary particles that, at the time of the soul's generation, serve to constitute the soul's then-current body (or its many bodies) or its then-current brain (or its many brains). Thus, these have been called, quite aptly, I think, *Emergentive* Dualist Views.

In certain ways, these Emergentive Dualist Views are, for us erstwhile Scientiphicalists, the most conservative forms of Dualism. For one thing, they require only a relatively modest departure from our dominant Scientiphical Metaphysic, which is still psychologically quite gripping, however numerous, and however deep, its philosophical inadequacies. And, it's only a relatively modest departure from our Scientiphicalism coupled with, or elaborated in terms of, the "scientifically accepted view" about the origination of, and about the development of, us human thinkers, along with, as I've sensibly suggested, many canine thinkers, and many feline thinkers, and so on. (A useful reminder: In the noted ways, the Pessimistic Emergentive Dualism seems more conservative than the Optimistic version, precisely because, I think, the Pessimistic View seems more easily coupled with the aforementioned "scientifically accepted view" of our origins and, thus, it seems to require a smaller departure from Scientiphicalism, than what our Optimistic View requires.) Owing to this apparent conservatism, these Views may be more appealing, to us erstwhile Scientiphicalists, than other versions of Substantial Dualism, which others aren't (so aptly called) *Emergentive* Substantial Dualist Views. (And, for much the same reason, our Pessimistic Dualism may be more appealing, to us, than our Optimistic Dualism.)

What's this? There are Substantial Dualist Views that *aren't Emergentive*? Yes. And, what's more, in certain ways, some such further Substantial Dualism may be philosophically superior to, and intellectually more appealing than, Emergentive Dualist Views.

Now, for heaven's sake, why haven't I, already in this long book, even so much as mentioned any such Nonemergent Dualist View or, maybe better, any such *Quasi-Emergentive* Substantial Dualism? Well, actually, I have done that, if only parenthetically. Specifically, I did it in the Fourth Section of Chapter Eight. And, as I parenthetically there promised you I'd do, I'll discuss that, here and now, a good ways into the book's very last Chapter. For unlike how it was for us before, we now have rich enough resources, quite nicely available, to provide a happily accessible statement of such an interestingly different Dualism. Why? Well, it's mainly because, at this point, I've provided us with our Dualistic Hypothesis of Spacelike Extension, developed richly enough to serve that purpose. And, it's also because, at this point, we can have a decently clear conception, as well, concerning how there might be, at certain times, some very rich concretum, or concreta, existing in two spacelike dimensional aspects of concrete reality (at least) both space itself, perhaps, and (at least) one merely spacelike dimension, in addition to space itself.

Making heavy use of our Dualistic Hypothesis of Spacelike Extension, I'll present, in this Section, what may be called a *Simple Quasi-Emergentive Dualism*. Pretty aptly, it also may be called a *Quasi-Platonic Substantial Dualism*, as it is, in some of its key features, *reminiscent of*— pun certainly intended—that eminently seminal ancient philosopher. Now, unlike in some other recent philosophic writing, my calling the impending position a *Simple* Quasi-Emergentive Dualism certainly *isn't* an indication that, whether in these pages or anywhere else, I consider this Substantial Dualist Thesis to be an extremely deficient philosophical position. Quite to the contrary, I'm inclined to think that, all things considered, it may well be the best view, on the largest questions of minds and bodies, that's anywhere available.[11] And, in no small measure, I think, this may be owing to the fact that, on this view, a soul is always a Simple Substantial Individual.[12]

11. Here, let me record a hope. As I hope, there may become available, for human thinkers, a still better Substantial Dualism, quite possibly far better than any I can now place on offer. Heck, I'm no hog about any of this. Indeed, by my lights, the sooner that happens, the better.

12. In the Sections to follow, I'll present a couple of other Substantial Dualist Views that make just as heavy use of our Dualistic Hypothesis of Spacelike Extension. And, as concerns the question of how souls may originate, they'll share quite a few features with the Simple Dualism this Section features, but, even in that very respect, they'll also be quite different. For this difference, and maybe for other reasons, too, they're not so aptly called a Simple Quasi-Emergentive Dualism and, with at least one of the two, it may not be called, very aptly, any sort of Nonemergent Dualism. Why? Well, in certain respects, these more Complex Views may be somewhat more credible positions, at least to me. Well, as this longish note keeps growing, I keep getting further ahead of myself. So, it's back to the body of the text.

It's philosophically fruitful, I've suggested, and it's pretty plausible, too, to think of our world as being infinitely temporal, both pastward, so to say, and also furtureward, too. In particular, we may suppose, somewhat speculatively, that our world has existed for an infinity of (nonoverlapping) Eons, maybe with infinitely many of them each being only a pretty short period, but, as well, with infinitely many others each lasting for, at least, quite a few billion years. Indeed, it was along just this line of thought that, in Chapter 8, I told a speculative story that, as I then suggested, didn't run very far afoul of what's agreeable to contemporary Cosmologists or, at the least, to some among them.[13] To jog your memory a bit, and to set the stage for several far fuller speculations, or speculative conjectures, I'll now rehearse that material:

> According to current Cosmology, I imagine, what are currently the most basic physical entities, say, something quite like quarks, weren't always around. Rather, somewhat as I've hypothesized souls to be emergent entities, our current quarks—or whatever physical things are now most basic—emerged from (something, presumably physical, that emerged from something, presumably physical, that emerged from) something, very possibly physical, that existed before they did. What was this presumably physical early something? Well, just for the heck of it, let's say that it was an utterly partless plasmatic soup, whatever that might really be....
>
> In any such event as that, something like this will have been so: However else it also may have been Propensitied, that soup—or that physical whatever—was Propensitied to so explode, but, of course—or,

13. Much as with the Emergentive Dualist Views already offered, for the physical side of our Quasi-Platonic Dualism's presentation, I'm to relate matters in a Particulate manner. For an accessible exposition, this is far more helpful than describing our wanted realm of concrete physical individuals, or our wanted spatially voluminous concreta, in Plenumate terms.

On such an alternative description, I'll remind you, there'll really, really be, in any Eon featuring a realm like that, just a single (presumably vast and marvelously heterogeneous) spatially extended concretum, the Eon's Single Substantial Spatial *Plenum*, to use a Cartesian term, or, in more modern lingo, a Single Spatial *Field*, but, of course, a Single *Substantial* Spatial Field. Now, in my heart of philosophical hearts, so to say, I believe that the weight of all the most philosophical considerations will favor a Fieldy story, over a Particulate version. But, as it's very hard for us to think, in Fieldy terms, about anything even remotely like spatially separate spatial bodies—including any such bodies for us humans ourselves—I won't try to offer, in even the least detail, a Plenumate Version of (the physical aspect of) *any* sort of Substantial Dualism. Just so, and in particular, I won't try to do it for the Quasi-Platonic View just upcoming.

Well, I'm well aware that you know all about that, as I've already offered, in this book, words to much the same effect, some several times over. Still, it now seems to me, your friendly hard-working author, that it's helpful to do it again now, right at this present juncture.

presumably—just when there should obtain some suitable conditions for its so doing. (Presumably, neither the explosion itself nor its timing was just sheer happenstance.) Maybe, the world had to wait for its plasmatic soup to become Extensible Platinum, which might itself have been the long-awaited manifestation of certain ways that the soup was Propensitied. Anyhow, the soup was Propensitied so that, upon its becoming Extensible Platinum, say, it exhaustively exploded and, what's more, it did so in just a certain very nice way—very nice, that is, for there being, sooner or later, a physical realm rather like (what we currently take) the current physical realm (to be). So, however directly, or however indirectly, this Big Bang gave rise to (first, such-and-such, and then so-and-so,...and then) gadzillions of (precisely similar partless) quarks, and (quite different from all the quarks) goodzallions of (precisely similar partless) electrons. Well, and again, it's something like that. So, from all that there then, we're all here right now.

Well, then, how are things, relevantly, here and now? Presumably, in the whole Propensity profile of each quark, there's the individual's Propensity for Monotony as to its Existence. And, presumably, so it is, too, for all the other most simple physical things, say, for all the electrons.[14]

As some timid souls may think, that's all far too speculative to be very interesting. But, that's just timid souls, for you. By my lights, quite the reverse is true. That's not nearly speculative enough to be very interesting or, at the least, to be of much peculiarly philosophical interest.

To make matters much more interesting, for us peculiarly philosophical people, I propose to vastly enlarge on the speculative ideas just rehearsed. To begin things, I'll first speculate that, before the onset of this present Eon, say, some twenty or so billion years ago, the world was radically richer than any merely physical realm could be, or any purely physical world. During that just earlier Eon, I'll suppose, every concretum that was Spatially Extended—and maybe there then was just one vast Spatial concrete individual—was also Nonspatially Extended. Perhaps, it was extended in a dozen merely Spacelike (dimensions or) ways, each as different from all the others as every last one of them is from proper Space itself. But, at the very least, the multinatured soupy individual (or however many proto-soupy individuals) existed in two Spacelike dimensions, as we might say. (Or, as the ontologically most scrupulous might similarly say, it was (or they were) Spacelikely Qualitied in, at the least, two radically different ways.) Presumably, and for

14. The quoted passage is from Section 4 of Chapter 8.

one thing, it existed in Space itself and, in that bargain, it was Spatially Extensibly Qualitied; presumably, it was, at the least, Spatially Extensibly Colored. But, at the same time, that was, at the very most, only half the story. It was also Extensibly Qualitied in another way, beyond, or besides, its being Spatially Extensibly Qualitied. For the purpose of providing a reader-friendly illustration, we may suppose that, specifically, this proto-soupy concretum was (or these proto-Particulate concreta were) Sonally Extensibly Qualitied, too, in addition to being Spatially Extensibly Qualitied. (And, as I said, maybe more than that, too; maybe it was also Odorily Qualitied, thus being Dimensionally Extensive in yet another way. But, also maybe not any more than that. Beyond making a specification for proper Space and for (at least) one merely Spacelike dimension, we leave matters open.) Look, in all sorts of ways, I'm trying to be *pretty* conservative with this, so that, once the first part's on board, I then needn't tell any extraordinarily interesting story about how there came to be, (later) in our own Eon, some quite simply spatial concreta, each existing only in space itself, and not also in any other (merely) spacelike dimension. This is, I think, a pretty interesting start for an appropriately speculative story. But, it's just a start. Now, let's take on some rather heavier metaphysical material.

In the manifestation of its Self-directed Propensity, our proto-soup changed, and it changed, and it changed. Along with its changing greatly in various other ways, it changed Qualitatively, over and over, and over again. At all events, with the occurrence of certain of its Propensitive manifestations, our proto-soup came to be, at a certain time, both Monochromatically Spatially Extensible Platinum and, as well, *Monosonatically* Sonally Extensible Belltone. (With this specification, I've just offered you a friendly for-instance, a happily illustrative specific possibility, to so say. For those this doesn't suit, pick your own specific proto-soupy state, so to put it, one that does more to float your boat.) Well, all along, we were hoping for this to happen! Why? Well, as I'll now nicely specify, our strangely-spacelikely proto-soup was Propensitied in just such a way that, just as soon as it should be THUS Qualitied, then— with a bang, and a boom, and a bam—it should shatteringly explode in an extraordinarily radical way. And, so—bang, boom, bam—there occurred just such a shattering that, from this Singularly Spatial and Sonal Concretum, there explosively came to be just very many purely Spatial concreta and, in addition, just very many simply Sonal concreta, without any individual being both Spatial and Sonal.

After this hypothesized shattering, let us speculatively say, there were, just as far as purely Spatial concreta are concerned, just so many individual quarks and particular electrons, maybe infinitely many of each. (Or, maybe, just a very large finite number of each. Apparently, whichever it should be, we may have there be plenty of physical concreta around, more than enough for the rest of our speculative story.) Maybe, these Particles came directly from the shattering or maybe, and perhaps more plausibly, they eventuated only rather later. (That's another thing that, for rest of our speculative story, really doesn't matter.) Whenever it was that there first came to be all these quarks and electrons, say, well, right off the bat, each of the particles was Propensitied for Monotony as to its Existence, and all the rest of *that* familiar business. And, so, for that familiar reason, and for reasons familiarly correlative to it, there *are*, right now, just so many quarks and electrons.

Well, at the same time, and just as far as purely *Sonal* concreta are concerned, we'll similarly speculate like this: Also ensuing from the same shattering explosion, there came to be (at least sooner or later) just so many individual sonal souls (maybe even infinitely many.) And, as each of *them* was Propensitied for Monotony as to *its* Existence, and all the rest of *this relevantly similar business*, so there *are*, right now, just so very many *individual souls*.

Well, that's almost the whole first part of my present speculative proposal. For the rest of it, there's just to say: Whatever the central Propensities of the spatial quarks initially, that's what they are right now, too, mostly owing to the manifestation of the quarks' Propensity to retain their Propensities. And, similarly, whatever the central Propensities of the sonal souls initially, that's what they are right now, too, mostly owing to the manifestation of the *souls'* Propensity to retain *their* Propensities.

Now, it's on to the second big part of our speculative metaphysical story. So, we ask: What are these importantly retained Propensities, both on the part of the sonal simple souls and on the part of the spatial basic particles? Important for our story, most of what's wanted for the particles are just the same old blatantly basic physical Propensities, whatever they are. No doubt, they're responsible for there being so much chemical order, and so much biological order—and for there being this old hat, and that new shoe. Well, you've got the hang of that much, I'm sure. Most saliently, though, there's the Propensity of these elementary things to become, in certain circumstances, very nicely arrayed brainily, so to say. And, when *that* happens, then there's dynamical interaction between a certain "group" of these Propensitied Particles or, better, between each of the many Propensitied Particles "in the contemplated group" and, on the other side, a certain single sonal soul, that's then reciprocally Propensitied, Individualistically, with respect to each of the very many nicely arrayed Particles. The same point put a bit differently: Between each of those many Particles, on the one side, and this (presumably) new "initially embodied" soul, on the other, there are, right then, all the wanted Individualistically-directed Propensities. And, whether it's right then or whether it's only a little later, when there's the manifestation of certain of those Propensities, then the soul will start to experience.

But, then, how is it that a certain one particular soul comes to be the single soul of a certain newly formed brain, or new overlapping brains? Much the same, how does a single soul become the only one that's Individualistically Propensitied with respect to each of just those very many newly brainily arranged Particles? Absent sheer accident, this must also be some Propensitive play-out, or Dispositional manifestation. Of course, that almost goes without saying. Even so, can we relate, if only quite speculatively, something that's helpfully more specific?

Well, as far as *that* goes, what we should suppose will be only the very sheerest sort of speculative material. Here's a sample: In our Eonically originating explosion, there was a terribly slight temporal difference as to when each soul was produced, maybe a trillionth of a trillionth of a trillionth . . . of a nanosecond. And, in all the resulting souls and all the offshoot particles, there may be Propensities tuned to that. So, as a manifestation of these Propensities, it might happen that, for instance, the first adequately formed brain gets the soul that was first produced; and, then, the next gets the next, and so on. Or, it might be the reverse: The last soul from the shattering is the first up for service as an embodied soul and, once it's embodied, then the next to last is up for such service, and so on. (Either first-come first-serve or last-come first serve, it may be that, in the case of ties—as when ten souls origi-nated simultaneously—there's a probabilistic Propensity ready to work. Soon enough, it plays out, and each brainy-array becomes Propensi-tively paired with one, and only one, sonal soul.)

Equally well, we may speculatively suppose quite different specifics: It may be that the explosion was slightly Spatially asymmetric, and also slightly Sonally asymmetric. Then, as we may speculate, there are, with the spatial bodies and the sonal souls, Propensities sensitive to these original asymmetries, presumably importantly Individualistically-directed, in some almost unimaginably interesting fashion. In the manifestation of these happily sensitive Propensities, there may be a singular assignment of just a certain sonal soul to a certain newly formed brain, or brain-cluster.

Among all the indefinitely many specific possibilities, what actually happened? I don't have any idea. But, as I'm merely a human meta-physician, that's just how it should be. Anything much about the details of all this, or anything quite specific put forward really seriously, well, that can't be anything more than just the sheerest pretension, gaining us nothing worth any sustained attention.

As compared with what I've offered in earlier Chapters, under the name *Emergentive Substantial Dualism*, there are large advantages, I think, to this Simple Quasi-Emergentive Dualistic View. Much the same, as compared with it, the previously offered Dualistic Views appear to have large drawbacks. For one thing, it seems almost unduly extravagant, I must admit, for us to think of actual simple physical concreta— say, quarks and electrons—as being Propensitied for the generating of mentally powerful immaterial individuals, the presumably simple souls who are, among others, you and me. Rather better, I imagine, to think that some exceedingly rich concretum, an individual at once both Spatial and also Nonspatially Spacelike, too, gave rise to just so very many simple Spatial concreta and, in the selfsame bargain, also so many (merely) Spacelike concreta. (Or, maybe it was some several such exceedingly rich concreta that gave rise to the present cosmic situation; for us right now, this difference doesn't matter much.) With all that posited speculatively, the only metaphysically serious issue that remains may well be the question of how it should be that a particular single soul ever gets to be just the one that interacts with just some certain simple particles, whilst, at least at that time, some other single soul will, at the very most, get to interact with just some certain other simple particles. To my way of thinking, at least, this *Quasi-Platonic Substantial Dualism*, as I call it, is a metaphysic that should be taken very seriously (even while several alternative views, its metaphysically serious rivals, should *also* be taken seriously).

This Quasi-Platonic View may have, I'll suggest, some very considerable philosophical merit. Nonetheless, the View is, at least for any of us, almost impossible to believe. Who can really believe, in the current intellectual climate, that he should have existed for very many years before his so-called conception, maybe billions and billions of years? I certainly can't. Well, for would-be Quasi-Platonists, can that proposition be readily avoided? I don't think so.

It won't do, really, for us to say that, in each person's case, it's only her soul that has so long existed, with the person herself coming to exist only much later, and quite recently, when the soul first becomes embodied, or first interacts with (her) physical body. It won't do, really, to say that it's only my soul that has so long existed, while I myself came to exist only much later, when my soul first became embodied. For, with any human person, myself included, there are, apparently, very many bodies that he has, at least as many as he has nicely brainily

arrayed elementary particles. (Indeed, with the mathematics of combinations working as it does, he'll have far more complex bodies, and
complex brains, than he has, or than any of his bodies has, constituent
elementary particles.) Well, then, how many sonal-and-spatial complexes will there be, each of them comprising just a single soul, all
right, but, quite as well, each comprising just a single one of the many
billions of (overlapping) brains, or bodies, in my current situation?
There will be, evidently, quite as many one-soul-and-one-complex-
body complexes, each a numerically different sonal-and-spatial complex, as there are (overlapping) brains, or (overlapping) bodies, in my
situation. So, there will be, in my current situation, billions and billions
of them. (While each of the complexes comprises the very same sonal
soul as do all the others, each comprises a numerically different body
from the body that any of the others comprises.)

What have we just learned? Well, on pain of our embracing, all
over again, some thorny Mental Problems of the Many, rather than
having it that you are a complex comprising both a simple soul and
also a very complex body, we should have it you really are just a certain
immaterial thing, the single one that, rather vulgarly, or habitually, we
may be wont to call "your soul." During its "interactive period," so to
say, this single soul, who is really you, will have billions of overlapping
bodies, with which it then interacts. That being so, we then must realize
this: On our Quasi-Platonic Dualist View, we really should uphold the
idea—however antithetical to common sense it may be, that *you yourself*
have existed for a very long time indeed, for many, many years before
the event commonly known as "your conception."

(Now, I'm not saying that the thorny Problems of the Many to which
I've just adverted are any very deep problems, or anything as fully
metaphysical as certain other difficulties encountered when doing first
philosophy. No; not by a long shot. As it might be, perhaps, *these* Mental
Problems of the Many, just so recently briefly pondered, well, they
might be on a par, or almost on a par, with the pretty superficial issues I
highlighted in my old paper, "The Problems of the Many," by now quite
familiar to my most devoted readers. Just so, here we may have only
some Problems that are rather like the difficulty, for our everyday
thinking, of "our having to allow that" there should be billions of human
bodies in an ordinary situation—a situation where, at least at first blush,
there would seem to be only one. But, even if the newly spotted problem
isn't any very deep metaphysical issue, still and all, it's a thorny problem, all right, and one that we want avoid. So, in order that we do avoid
it, it's really best, I think, that we do just as I've recommended: Rather
than having it that you are a complex comprising both a simple soul and

also a very complex body, we should have it that you really are just a certain immaterial thing, the single one that, rather vulgarly, or habitually, we may be wont to call "your soul."

The idea just stressed is, I believe, a point with quite general application: In expressing any decent Dualist View, we do well to say that each of us *is* a soul. By contrast, we do less well when saying that each of us *has* a soul, even while the latter form of words is far more commonly employed.)

As I said just moments ago, our Quasi-Platonic Dualism is, at least for any of us, almost impossible to believe. But, still, for many of us, it may be no harder to believe than is our Optimistic Emergentive View, on which you'll exist long after the event commonly considered "your death," presumably, for many billions of years after that. Or, maybe better, our Quasi-Platonic View is scarcely any harder to believe. (Of course, on any decent development of our Quasi-Platonic View, you'll not only exist long before your so-called birth, and your so-called conception, but, just as well, you'll also exist long after your so-called death. Still and all, there's this to say: While the Quasi-Platonic View will be, of course, a logically much more ambitious View than is the Optimistic Emergentive Dualism, it's scarcely any harder (for me, at least) to believe the former than it is to believe the latter).

By contrast with both of those two Views, our Pessimistic Emergentive Dualism isn't, at least so far as I'm concerned, anything that's very hard to believe. For, as it happens, I've long thought that, with the death of my brain and my body, it's almost certain that I myself will cease to be, completely and forever. But, maybe, that's mainly owing to my upbringing. Or, maybe it's mainly due to the intellectual climate dominating my peer group, throughout most of my life. By contrast, as far as the philosophy goes (and trying my darnedest to place aside my long-standing psychological proclivities in these matters) this Pessimistic Position might be the least satisfactory of these three competing Substantial Dualist Views, while the Quasi-Platonic View may be the most satisfactory.

15. Do Immaterial Souls Ever Change Propensitively?

Toward the end of our Seventh Chapter, in its Twenty-First Section, I made a few comments concerning that Section's titular question, Might All Souls Be Equally Powerful Individuals? On the affirmative answer, the response that I most favored, there was never any difference among souls as regards their Propensitive nature. Or, more perspicuous ontologically, each soul is always Propensitied, for however long it should be that the soul exists, just precisely the same as that soul is ever Propensitied; and, what's more, the soul is always Propensitied just precisely the same as any other soul is Propensitied, for however long *it* exists. On this nicely simple idea, it's apparent, there's never any Change in the Propensitive nature of any soul. Or, more perspicuously, there's never Change in how it is Propensitively with any soul.

How, then, is this simple view, even if it's so nicely elegant, to explain change in the *mental life* of a soul, to use a term long fashionable with philosophers? Well, for just a minute, think about it. Surely, you'll readily realize, what will play the key role here, crucial explanatorily, will be Change in, or changes in, how things are with the (Individualistically Propensitied) soul's (reciprocally Individualistically Propensitied) physical interaction partner, or partners. So, just for instance, a certain soul may always be Propensitied to experience just *yellowly* and belltonely when it's Individualistically partnered with exactly *yeah-many* Particles that are physically arranged precisely like *this-and-that*, whilst the selfsame soul may always be Propensitied, as well, to experience just *orangely* and belltonely when it's Individualistically partnered with exactly *yo-many* Particles that are physically arranged precisely like *such-and-so*. Well, then, when there's a change *in this soul's physical Propensity partners*, a change *from* yeah-many Particles that are arranged like this-and-that, *to* yo-many Particles arranged like such-and-so, that's the ticket. And, what's the ride? Of course, it's the change that there'll be in how it is with the soul experientially: Whereas *before this* change the soul was experiencing just *yellowly and belltonely*, so *with this* Change the soul comes to be, and it is, experiencing just *orangely and belltonely*.

Well, I don't know about you, but, as for myself, I quite like that nicely simple metaphysical explanation. Indeed, I find myself, now, quite enamored of the Simple View I've proposed, the Doctrine of Propensitive Equality among All Souls. But, heck, that might be just me.

Realizing that my infatuation may be quite idiosyncratic, I should do something, at least a little something, towards articulating some alternative positions or, at the very least, some apparent alternatives. That's been a good idea, I suppose, for the space of what's, by now, some several Chapters. But, without our Quasi-Platonic View to serve as a fine focal point, there wasn't available to us, until just lately, such material as might be most conducive to a good execution of the good idea. But, now, of course, our Quasi-Platonic View certainly is just so happily available.

As it appears, at least, here's one alternative position on this Propensitive matter. Suppose, if only for the sake of a simple exposition, that all souls first came into existence, or first existed, absolutely simultaneously, perhaps owing to the soulfully productive shattering of a multidimensional originating entity. Right then, at the first moment of their existence, it may be that each soul is Propensitively just like every other soul. What's more, on this presently presented position, each soul has the same Propensitive *Potential* or, more perspicuously, each has the same *Potentiating Propensity*—each soul precisely the same, of course, as every other soul—this being, of course, a Propensity for a great deal of Propensitive Change. Or, putting matters very positively, each soul has the same Propensity for a great deal of Differentiating Propensitive Development.

Now, how is it that any given soul Changes Propensitively, or undergoes (Differentiating) Propensitive Development? Well, that will depend on, far more than it depends on anything else, what sorts of physical Propensity partners *become the (Individualistically Propensitied) partners of just that soul*—just how many Particles it first becomes partnered with, and just which kinds of Particles those are, and just how those Particles are first physically related, and so on. (Now, even with that "and so on," what I've just very sketchily enumerated, is, of course, just the barest beginnings of starters, so to say.) Well, as time goes by, the soul's progressive Propensitive Development will depend on, far more than it depends on anything else, various changes as regards its varying physical Propensity partners—varyingly as to number, and varying as to kind, and varying as to how physically related, and so on.

As this alternative View has it, and it might be reckoned an advantage of the position, the soul that's you may have become, quite literally, very differently Propensitied from how it is that I myself am now Propensitied—me and you now being, of course, two numerically different souls, each perfectly distinct and separate from the other. In ordinary talk, part of this may be that, say, you believe that you've enjoyed experiencing (your body's?) ingestion of many meals mainly comprising pasta, but haven't been experiencing much in the way of soul music—think Otis Redding—whereas I, for my part, may believe quite the converse to hold, for myself, and for how it's been with me experientially. Here, it's really the souls themselves that have become so differently Propensitied, one of these souls being me, of course, and the other soul being, of course, nobody but you.

(While there are, no doubt, correlative differences in these souls' respective Propensity partners, still, it's *not only* in their physical partners that there's developed an important difference. Rather, and quite *in addition to that*, each of the two souls *itself* has become Propensitively different from how it was at first and, in the bargain, from how it now is with the other soul.)

Equally, part of all this soulful Propensitive change may be, or one Propensitive upshot of it may be, something like this: You're now Propensitied to pursue much more pasta, and much more experiencing of pasta, and much more experiencing as of pasta, even as *you're not yet* Propensitied toward seeking any *change for yourself in that* regard, whereas I, for my part, may now be Propensitied to pursue operatic arias, and experiencing them, and not much soul music at all. For, as it may be, even as I'm Propensitied to Change Propensitively, in certain ways, that's been manifested as just specified, with my having effectively sought substantial *change for myself*, in just *that* regard. Well, maybe I'm not expressing this very clearly. But, still and all, I feel sure that you're getting the hang of this alternative position or, at the least, this apparent alternative.

Supposing that what I've been sketching amounts to a coherent alternative position, we'll say that those who uphold this different view, all of them Substantial Dualists, of course, affirm the *Doctrine of Propensitive Variety among Embodied Souls*.

Now, many friends of this Doctrine may be *Optimistic* Substantial Dualists. They'll affirm, as you'll recall, that many embodied souls may each become, sooner or later, a disembodied soul. Well, then, as concerns the Propensitive nature of the disembodied souls, what should be thought by these friends of the Doctrine? For them, two views will be, I think, most salient.

On one salient view, each disembodied soul will retain whatever Propensities it had when last it was embodied. Or, pretty much the same, each will retain some significant portion of, or aspect of, her last embodied Propensitive profile, so to say. Maybe some such souls will be, at least when first they're disembodied, Propensitied precisely the same as when last they were embodied. Close to an opposite extreme, maybe other disembodied souls will retain only so much, Propensitively, as a slight semblance of the Propensitive profiles enjoyed when last embodied. We can allow for quite a lot of variation here. Even with a great allowance, we may still say, very well, I think, that those taking this further view will be affirming, along with our observed Doctrine, a certain companion Doctrine, namely, the Doctrine of Propensitive *Variety among Disembodied* Souls. There's little doubt, I should think, but that many members of our own society, perhaps most saliently many devoutly Christian thinkers, accept a view very like this companion Doctrine.

Other Optimistic Dualist friends of our first observed Doctrine, the Doctrine of Propensitive Variety among *Embodied* Souls, may take this very different salient view: Once an embodied soul becomes dis-embodied, it's Propensitively just like it was when first it was an em-bodied soul. Just so, they will *deny* the Doctrine of Propensitive Variety among Disembodied Souls. And, supposing them to hold a positive view on the matter, as we do well to suppose, they'll uphold, in its stead, a Doctrine of Propensitive *Equality among Disembodied* Souls.

Recall, now, our Quasi-Platonic Substantial Dualists, maybe in-cluding me, come to think of it. We'll affirm that, before a soul is ever embodied, it's a *nonembodied* soul, utterly lacking any physical Pro-pensity partner. Just so, for such savvy Quasi-Platonists as adopt this currently considered salient alternative, their elegantly symmetric idea will be this: When a soul becomes disembodied, not only is the soul Propensitively just like it was when first it was an embodied soul, but, what's more, it's Propensitively just like it was long before that hap-pened, when it was (even as again it now is) a nonembodied soul. Any-how, many who may wish to affirm a doctrine of reincarnation, whether or not they're Quasi-Platonists, well, they'll want to affirm the Doctrine of Propensitive Equality among Disembodied Souls.

In addition to the Views I've barely sketched, in this Section, there are still further positions that one may take on the matter of Pro-pensitive Change, and on the question of Propensitive Variety, as re-gards immaterial souls. As I've admitted, I don't much like *any* of these Views, both those I've barely sketched and those I've not even barely sketched. So, I'm not going to go on with this business. Is that owing to just some dogmatism, on my part, or, perhaps, just some laziness? No: I don't think so. Rather, at least so far as anything like metaphysical elegance goes, no competing Dualist Doctrine does anywhere near as well, in my book, as the View that All Souls are Equally Powerful In-dividuals. And, as I'm sure you're well aware, this book is my book.

As I'll take just a moment to remark, the View that All Souls are Equally Powerful comports extremely well, to my way of thinking, with our Quasi-Platonic Substantial Dualism. And, also to my way of think-ing, at least, that's all well and good. For, even as the former View is my preferred position on the question of how things are with souls Pro-pensitively, so the latter is my favorite Form of Substantial Dualism.

With my favoring these two mutually agreeable Views, am I in-volved in just so much wishful thinking, the famous bane of ever so many intellectually ambitious systematic philosophers? Perhaps, but I don't think so. Why? Well, while I can't cover all the bases here, I can, at least, say a little something to address the question.

As may hardly need saying—though maybe it does need to be said—our Quasi-Platonic Dualism *isn't* a View on which there'll be any value for you, not even the least little benefit, in your existing for billions and billions of years. First, there'll be no value, for you, in all your existence that's before (what's commonly called) your birth or, more certainly, before (what's commonly called) your conception. Second, of course, and, of course, for much the same reason, there'll also be precious little value, for you, in all your existence that's after (what's commonly called) your death. Or, given the great bulk of available evidence on these matters, that's what we Quasi-Platonists should accept. Why? Well, just so very much evidence all indicates that, as you'll then be bereft of any apt (physical) interaction partners, both before your so-called conception and also after your so-called death, your power to experience won't ever be exercised, or ever be manifested. Rather, during all that (infinitely) long early period, you'll never be engaged in any experiencing at all, nor will you experience, at all, during all the (infinitely) long period after you die, or your body dies.

While that's well worth noting, it does little to explain, I'm sure, why it's so hard, for the little old likes of me, to believe our Simple Substantial Dualism or, as I've been calling it, our Quasi-Platonic View. Even so, I don't want to spend much of my effort, and have you spend much of your time, seeking a more adequate explanation. After all, who am I, that we should be so terribly interested in my doxastic difficulties? Rather, I'll attempt to express a more credible Substantial Dualism—maybe just slightly more credible—that's not wholly unlike our Simple Substantial View. (Though the Substantial Dualist View I'll try to express may be a slightly more credible position, it may also be, for all that, philosophically inferior to our Quasi-Platonic Substantial Dualism.)

16. A More Complex Quasi-Emergentive Dualism: A Constitutional View of Souls

For some serious consideration, from you and me both, I'll next present an interesting sort of *Complex* Substantial Dualism, in two Versions of this Complex View.

In important respects, and in both Versions, this Complex Dualism is quite similar to the Simple Dualism just observed. In certain other central respects, however, it's very different. In observing what makes the Complex View so distinctive, I follow, in largest measure, the lead of my (erstwhile) student Yuval Avnur. As far as I can tell, his thoughts on the matter are as utterly novel as they're happily peculiar. Now, in very large measure, Avnur employed these thoughts to formulate (at least something very like) what I'll now call a *Constitutional Substantial Dualism*. However the position is most aptly labeled, it's this Complex View that I'll first present.

With the beginning of this View's metaphysical story, and for a fair ways after, too, things are just the same as with our Simple Quasi-Platonic Dualism. So, there's much the same multi-realmy proto-soupy individual, a concretum that's quite as fully Sonal as it's nicely Spatial. And, for much the same reasons, this multi-realmy individual eventually explodes, in *pretty* much the same sort of explosion, producing *somewhat* the same sorts of basic concreta. Well, as far as the salient *spatial* upshot goes, the explosion's *precisely the same* as was the just previously considered Big Bang. So, the present story's explosion also produced a simply Spatial realm, comprising ever so many spatially separate spatial individuals, all of them basic physical individuals, as with just so many quarks and electrons.

But, on the *Sonal* side of the matter, this newly considered explosion is *distinctively different*, with distinctively different consequences. To be sure, there's produced a Sonal realm, comprising ever so many sonally separate sonal individuals, all of them basic sonal individuals. But, unlike with our Simple Quasi-Platonic Dualism, not a single one of them is any soul, or any mind, or anything of the like. None of *these* basic sonal individuals is, by itself, richly Propensitied mentally. None has the power to experience, nor the power to think, nor the power to choose. Rather, their situation is this: Even as each of one these separate sonal concreta is precisely like all the others, each of these *mentons*, as Avnur will have me call them, is suited to serve, along with only some several other mentons—indeed, along with exactly six others—toward constituting a sonally complex soul. Thus, when there arise conditions conducive for their so doing, but only then, some seven *nonsoul* mentons will serve, altogether, to constitute a single sonal soul. Hence, just when there obtain conditions most conducive for the manifestation of a menton's soul-constituting Propensity, precisely then will there arise just such a nicely clean sonal arrangement as will provide for a Complex Sonal Soul, a nonspatial being with the power to experience, and other basic mental powers.

Insofar as it's compatible with that—which is, I think, quite a great deal—the story for Complex Sonal Souls now parallels, pretty closely, the story we told just before, for Simple Sonal Souls. So, for one thing, there'll be a close parallel between the conditions most conducive to having a Simple Soul become embodied and, in this presently told tale, the conditions most conducive to having a Complex Soul come to be constituted: That will happen when, and only when, there's formed, from ever so many elementary spatial particles, a suitably active and healthy brain. Or, at the least, it's something very much like that. Just so, a Complex Soul will be formed, from precisely seven nonsoul mentons, just exactly when, or just before, the newly constituted soul first is, or it first becomes, an embodied soul.

When a new brain is formed, in space, what will determine *which* seven mentons come to constitute *its* soul? The same point put more vividly: Should two (or more) new brains (or "brain-clusters") be formed simultaneously—maybe, despite some merely supposed quasi-Einsteinian concerns—well, how should it be determined, *which* brain (or *which* brain-cluster) gets *which* mentons, as the seven sonal constituents of *just its* single soul partner, Individualistically Propensitied for inter-action *just with it*? For the most part, this story will be the same as the one told before, in response to a parallel question for the Simple Quasi-Platonic View.

For as long as a Sonally Complex Soul's brain (or brains) are healthily active, or actively healthy, the Sonal Soul itself is also intact, a happily unified, mentonly constituted immaterial interaction partner for its body (or its aptly Propensitied elementary particles). With the death of that brain, what happens with, or to, the mentonly constituted soul in question? Well, our Complex View should certainly say *something* about that. At least to my mind, the best thing (for it) to say is something that will have the whole current story be a sonally symmetrical tale: Right then, when the body's spatial constituents first fail to continue to be so nicely arrayed spatially, well, then the soul's sonal constituents first fail to continue to be so nicely arrayed sonally. And, in the bargain, right then, they'll cease to constitute that soul—or, for that matter, any soul at all. But, for some cockeyed Optimists, it's still *open* to say, in some sense of that enormously elusive and charitable word, that the sonal constituents remain so nicely arrayed, and so constitutionally unified, even whilst, perhaps forever after, they continue to constitute the soul. Very few, I think, will follow that lead. (Among many others, here's just one reason for that: As it lacks an apt physical interaction partner, such a soul won't ever experience, as all our available evidence indicates. Evidently, then, any such supposed continued existence won't be, even for that Complex Sonal Soul itself, any benefit at all.)

At least for the most part, you've been presented with a modestly plausible rendition of our Complex Substantial Dualism. Certainly, by now, you should have gotten the hang of this view. Accordingly, you may now supply, for yourself, such further features as you may find to

be needed, for a most appealing Form of this Constitutional Substantial Dualism. For instance, to have there be some symmetry with
what happens in space, or on the physical side, you may want there to
be several sorts of basic mentonish individuals. So, even as complex
physical bodies may be constituted of (suppose) spatially (and physically) simple quarks and electrons, you may have it that a Complex
Soul will be constituted of (suppose) sonally (and soulfully) simple
mentons and soulons. That doesn't do much to float my boat; but,
heck, why not let a hundred flowers bloom? If some of them should just
be flowering weeds, or even very many, well, so what? We can always
find the time, sooner or later, to make do with a lot less.

Let's be very clear, please, about what's quite crucial for this
Complex View to be, even in our terribly difficult metaphysical problematic, a workable philosophical position. With the Complex Soul,
every single one of its (seven) constituents is always needed; none of the
constituents is in any way redundant. In other words, nothing importantly soulful is, by way of the soul's menton constituents, at all over-
determined. Or, at the very least, something very like that holds true.
Else there will be, with our Complex Soul, some Sonal Mental Problems
of the Many or, at the least, the beginnings of some such terribly thorny
Problems. And, of course, that will never do.

(With our severe specifications, it's intended that there's no chance
for that; the proto-problems are nipped in the bud. [If the intention
goes unfulfilled, well, then make the specifications yet more severe.]
Supposing that we've been sufficiently severe here, there may arise, in
the minds of some, a question much like this: How much less severe
can we be, and still avoid the Problems? With any real precision, I can't
say. But, even as that much shouldn't be expected, so, for our present
purposes, it's not needed.)

Let's also be clear that, especially as compared with the Simple
Quasi-Platonic View, there are some nice advantages for this Complex
View (especially for the temporally symmetric Version, that is, the
Version where, with the death of a soul's brain, or brains, the Soul ceases
to be). So, even whilst the Simple View requires that you will exist for
very many years before your (so-called) birth—otherwise, it would foster
its own Sonal Mental Problems of the Many—that's *not* how things are
with this *Complex* View. Rather, before there's your active brain (or
brains) you yourself won't yet have existed. Rather, before there's your
active brain, there's only such mentons as may serve toward constituting you. Just so, it's only when, in the spatial realm, there's first a
certain aptly active brain (yours, of course) that there'll first be, in the
sonal realm, you yourself, a truly immaterial sonal soul, even if a duly

constituted soul. (And, on this temporally symmetric Version, what eventually happens with, or to, you? Well, with the death of your brain, of course, there'll no longer be, on the sonal side, any sonally nice meld of seven mentons. As your erstwhile mentons won't then constitute any soul, you'll no longer exist.)

As it seems to me, there are some real advantages enjoyed by this Complex View. Quite as common sense has it—or maybe it's just (most of) atheistic common sense—you'll exist just about as long as there's your healthily active brain around—certainly not much before that, and, quite as well, not much afterward, either. In this respect, this Complex View is on all fours with the first sort of Substantial Dualism we placed on offer, our Pessimistic Emergentive Substantial Dualism. But, in contrast with that Pessimistic Position, this Constitutional View features a nicely salient metaphysical symmetry: In all the metaphysically most important respects, on this new Constitutional View, *the mental and the physical are on a par*. Or, if not quite that, then, at the least, they're pretty nearly on a par. Just so, our currently considered Complex Dualism *doesn't* hold that just the one of these concrete domains—the physical realm—is that from which all concrete reality flows, or the rest of the real concreta flow, or anything even remotely like that.

Because it has these advantages, and others, I think that this Constitutional Dualism is worth some sustained attention. And, as it may be hoped, it might be provided some pretty considerable attentive development. But, for all sorts of reasons, I'll leave that to others.

17. Drawbacks of This Constitutional View

However impressive the advantages it enjoys, the Constitutional View is not the sort of Substantial Dualism I'm most inclined to favor. By and large, that's because it has some metaphysical drawbacks, especially by contrast with the Quasi-Platonic Simple View. Here are some.

First, on this Constitutional Dualism, we must accept the full reality of complex individuals, each as constituted of its simple constituent parts, with each simple part properly Propensitied. Now, even in the case of commonly acknowledge *physical complexes*, like rocks, and lamps, and brains, I'm inclined toward the thought that what we have is, really and truly, nothing more than what's present with *perfectly obvious onto-logical parasites*, as with a mere *heap*, say, a heap of mutually magnetized iron cubes. Even as I should come quite clean with you here, I'm pretty suspicious about the ontological credentials of supposed ordinary rocks, say, for being any real entities, or any true substantial individuals.

How much better is an alleged rock's credentials, really, if better at all, than those of a heap of mutually attracting less problematic entities?

Throughout much of this work, I've been, at the least, insinuating all that. And, without taking pains to defend the position, I'll be quite explicit about my inclination in favor of a negative, or nihilistic, or skeptical approach to supposed physical complexes. But, in marked contrast with any of that, I'm very far from being even the least bit negative about my own individual reality. Just so, I'm certainly not any mere ontological parasite, I'll have you know, nor am I even remotely like any such superficium, to coin a newly emphatic term. Nor will it help matters here, not even just a jot, to consider myself a complex that, quite unfamiliarly, is allegedly constituted of simple *sonal* concreta, rather than a complex that's allegedly constituted of simple spatial entities. So, right off the bat, I've got some serious metaphysical scruples that go against any acceptance of the Constitutional Dualistic View. (As I suspect, you may share some of these scruples.) And, very quickly, matters go from pretty bad to very much worse.

Second, and apparently worse, on this Constitutional Dualism, we must accept the thought that I'm an *emergent mental complex*, whose powers transcend those of any supposedly physically derivative entity. Or, at the least, so it surely seems. Well, think about this for a minute: Even as I myself have the power to consciously experience, and the power to really choose, none of my constituent mentons has any of these powers. That must be true, if this Constitutional Dualism is to be of any help with these issues, providing any substantial advantage over our Simple Quasi-Platonic view. Otherwise, one of my mentons, at the least, and presumably every single one of the seven, would be, all by itself, a full-blown soul, with no constitutional needs ever to be met (whether by any sonal mentons, or whether by anything else, for that matter). So, for this Constitutional Dualism to provide a usefully distinctive contrast with the Quasi-Platonic View, such Propensities as my presumed mentons possess will fall far short of, say, my own full-blown power to really choose. All right; so far, so good. But, then, what are Propensities of such sonal mentons as may serve, when in such nice sonal arrangement, to constitute me?

Positively speaking, there's little more for me to say. But, as it seems, some negative points may still be made: My mentons' presumed powers *won't* be Propensities of just such a marvelous sort that, just through their possession, and providing only that my mentons should enjoy some nice sonal arrangement, there will *sonally derive therefrom*, quite systematically—or there will *mentally* derive therefrom, quite systematically—my power really to choose. Almost anything's possible,

I guess. That is, there's hardly anything we know for certain. But, to my mind, this would be about as astonishing a development as there being, per impossible, a *physically derivative* power of mine, or of my brain's, that's a power to really choose. Physically, mentally, both, or neither; I simply can't understand, nor can I believe, that my power to really choose is *any* mere systematically derivative Propensity.

Well, what sort of power can it be, then, this power to really choose that's presumably possessed by a complex sonal being? As best I can tell, my power to choose must be, then, a *radically emergent power*. And, rather than being any power of a radically *emergent entity*, as with a relevantly *transcendent* single soul, this radically emergent power—my power to really choose—will be the power of a mere constituted complex. Now, even if some such sonal composite should be a mentally complex concretum, as we'll here allow, it's still impossible for me to make much sense of this situation. Nor am I, it would seem, at all peculiar in this regard. After all, what we're now considering is just *another Nonentity Emergentism*, even if this currently considered Nonentity View is "anchored," so to say, in the sonal domain, and not the spatial realm. And, I ask you, how can *that* difference be of any real help in the matter? As things seem to me, it really can't help at all. So, for us who place much stock in clear metaphysical thinking, there are severe drawbacks to a Constitutional Dualist View.

18. Fusional Dualism

To avoid these very considerable drawbacks, let's consider replacing our Constitutional View with what appears to be a rather similar Substantial Dualism, even if that appearance may indicate, perhaps, no important commonality. What's that?

Well, here's what I have in mind: As before, we start with our menton story. But, now, when seven mentons come together, they don't continue to exist. Rather, it's this that happens: The mentons all sonally fuse together. Just so, each fusing menton "gives up" all its sonal "stuff," toward there being "enough such stuff" for there to be just a single sonal soul, even as it then ceases to exist—maybe forever after, maybe for just so long as that sonal stuff serves to constitute the sonal soul. We may aptly call this position, I'll suggest, *Fusional Dualism*.

On this Fusional Dualistic View, right from the first moment of its existence, a sonal soul will be nicely matched, Propensitively, with a healthy active brain (presumably, with a new brain). And, right from the first, it will be richly endowed with mental Propensity, or with mental power. Suppose that, at first, it doesn't have the power to really choose. Well, if that's so, then, it may have, right off the bat, a Propensity to *develop* that mental power; it may have the *potential* to become a real chooser. In any case, once that soul's physical partners go through aptly normal physical arrays, the Fusional soul will not only develop, but it will then also exercise, its power to really choose. In time, it may choose to think hard about only metaphysics, at least for a certain period.

Both to enjoy a nice metaphysical symmetry and to enjoy (more) agreement with much commonsense thinking, we may advance a *Pessimistic* Form of Fusional Dualism. On this new sort of Pessimistic Dualism, when a sonal soul's brain dies, or her (overlapping) brains die, well, then the soul sonally fissions, or it sonally divides, seven-ways symmetrically. And, upon its sonal fission, the soul ceases to exist. Owing to that, there'll then be, comprising that same sonal stuff, just seven precisely similar mentons, none of which is any soul, and none of which serves to constitute any. (It's not important, here, for us to make such further specifications as may ensure that each of these later mentons is one of the earlier mentons, though that may be done.)

As with both our Pessimistic Emergentive Dualism and with our Constitutional Dualism, this Version of Fusional Dualism yields us our commonsense judgments as to the timing of your existence. Or, maybe better, like those Views do, it also agrees with most of atheistic common sense. For many contemporary philosophers, this will be an advantage of this *Pessimistic Version* of Fusional Dualism.

Another Version of this Fusional Dualism won't be, in the noted respects, so symmetrical. But, this *Optimistic Version* may enjoy another metaphysical advantage. Notice that, whatever Version of the View may be concerned, Fusional Dualism will have you be a *metaphysically simple* sonal individual, devoid of any substantial (sonal or mental) parts. In this regard, this is a Simple Dualism, quite like our Quasi-Platonic Dualism, also like our Emergentive Dualistic Views. On all these Views, you'll recall, in this key respect a sonal soul is quite like a simple spatial concretum, say, a partless quark, perhaps. Well, just as we (rightly) expect a simple quark to be Propensitied for Monotony as to its Existence, so we should expect, analogously, a simple soul to be Propensitied for Monotony as to *its* Existence.

So, on this *Optimistic Version* of Fusional Dualism, there'll be a certain asymmetrical situation. As with the Fission-Ending Version, you'll still start pretty much when (atheistic) common sense says you do. But, unlike how it is with the Fission-Ending View, on this Optimistic Fusional View you won't end when, according to this same commonsense thinking, you're supposed to end. Rather, as this Optimistic Fusional View has it, even well beyond the time of your so-called death, you may exist for billions and billions of years. (As you'll pretty certainly lack apt interaction partners, it's pretty certain that this won't benefit you at all, as you won't enjoy any experiencing.) For many contemporary philosophers, this will be a disadvantage of this Optimistic Version of the Fusional Dualistic View. By my own lights, however, it might not be any substantial drawback.

On a reasonably liberal reckoning, I've provided you, for some metaphysical contemplation, five forms of Substantial Dualism. Among them, the one I most prefer is, I think, our Quasi-Platonic Substantial Dualism. Why? Well, as it seems, I have a very great respect for, or penchant for, cosmically elegant metaphysical considerations. In comparison, I place rather little weight on my habitual penchant for what might be called "current-day commonsense thinking." For those much more greatly concerned with current (atheistic) common sense than I myself am, perhaps their preferred metaphysical view of themselves should be, I'll suggest, the Fission-Ending Version of Fusional Substantial Dualism. No doubt, various readers will feel differently. In this largely exploratory work, largely aimed at encouraging substantially different philosophic views, I won't try to dissuade them.

19. Our Hypothesized Dualism and the Mental Problems of the Many

Over the course of several Chapters, including this present one, I've offered a variety of Substantial Dualistic Positions. Quite obviously, I could go on to offer still more. And, by this point, maybe you could, too. But, at this point, I can't see very much point in any of that. Far better, at this present juncture, for us to observe how well, or how poorly, these Substantial Dualist Views serve toward treating certain Philosophical Problems. Most particularly, those Problems that, earlier in this book, we've worked hardest at exploring.

Well, in our Seventh Chapter, we did a lot of work on the Mental Problems of the Many. In doing that work, we were moved toward Views on which there might be an appealing *singular resolution* for the Experiential Problem of the Many and, as well, the Problem of Too Many Choosers. Let's consider this Problem of Too Many Choosers.

Well, it's incredible that, when I should choose to imagine a sphere, rather than a cube or a cylinder, there are other people "in my situation" that, even as they are really choosing quite independently of me, each imagines a *cube*, not any sphere, while still others each independently imagines a *cylinder*, rather than a cube or a sphere. Now, it appears that, all of them in my current situation, there may be billions of overlapping human bodies, and billions of overlapping brains. Just maybe, some such thought might become credible for us or, at least, may become tolerable. But, not so with the thought that, in this very situation, there are billions of independently choosing people. More tolerable than that will be this: These many overlapping brains, all of them in my situation, all serve to promote a single choosing experiencer, just the generated entity who's me. Just so, I'm really the only person "in my situation," without there being anyone else, anywhere relevantly "around or about," who's making choices just precisely when I do, time after time, after time. So, even as nobody is really constituted by any of these brains, or any of these bodies, so, and always at the same time, I'm really the only experiencer, and I'm the only real chooser, that's ever interacting with them all. Or, maybe better, I'm the only experiencer who's interacting with any of their basic physical constituents.

When I choose to imagine a sphere, rather than a cube or a cylinder, there's nobody else, certainly not in any close connection with *those* noted physical things, who's also choosing to imagine a cube, or who's choosing to imagine anything else, for that matter.

What sort of entity is this single choosing individual, apparently so singularly interacting with all these overlapping brains and bodies? In other words, what sort of being am I myself? For us present human thinkers, there's no philosophically interesting answer, I fear, that's a very credible answer. But, among the pretty incredible answers, some may be more interesting than others.

Now, as we earlier observed, we can consistently answer the question by saying that I'm a basic physical entity, an electron, say, that's on a par, in ever so many respects, with each of the (other) electrons constituting one of, or more than one of, my many (overlapping) brains. Just so far as being an elementary particle goes, this special electron is Propensitively just like any of the other electrons. Or, so far as just avoiding these Problems goes, I might be a somewhat more complex physical thing, say, a certain particular hydrogen atom or, perhaps, even a certain water molecule. But, unlike any ordinary elementary particles, or ordinary atoms, or ordinary molecules, I will have, in addition to all the ordinarily expected physical Propensities, certain much more notable Mental Powers, which won't be any physical powers, at all.

On this view, I myself am somewhere in space. And, I occupy a certain spatial region, presumably a region that's very small, and that's located somewhere amidst my brain, or amidst my many brains. Not only is this view quite incredible, but, as we also earlier observed, it's not a very interesting view, either. Nor is it interesting to have me be some spatially extended entity that's not any physical thing at all and, in the bargain, that's completely eluded scientific observation and theorizing. Now, I'm not quite sure *why* there's so little interest in proposals that have me be a special spatial whatnot. But, here's a suggestive idea. Maybe, the thought that I should be an additional spatial being, specially related to all those more ordinary spatial concreta, well, maybe that thought just isn't speculative enough. Or, maybe better, it isn't sufficiently *imaginatively* speculative. Rather than being an imaginatively exploratory thought, any such strange spatial thoughts seem to be far too "mechanical," in some suitable sense of the word.

For a view that's apparently not so badly mechanical, we may consider, instead, some Form of Substantial Dualism. On a nicely simple form of such a Dualistic view, I may well be an ontologically simple nonphysical thing, entirely without any substantial parts. And, in that respect, anyway, I may be as basic as the most basic (physical constituents of the less basic) physical things that interact with me.

On a nicely simple form of Substantial Dualism, I'll be a metaphysically simple entity, and a quite basic mental individual, that's not any physical or spatial concrete particular. This thought makes salient two possibilities.

First, we may say, following Descartes, that I am a particular that has no extension at all, and no real place or location, whether strictly spatial or otherwise. This sort of view is, of course, quite interesting, even as all Descartes's main lines of thought are quite interesting philosophically. But, for folks well seasoned with philosophy, if we say that, then it won't be any very fresh ideas that we place on offer. And, any Dualism much like the historical Cartesian View won't do all that well, even if it won't do terribly badly, either, at providing us with resources for our grasping how several simultaneous nonspatial souls may be externally related to each other. Just so, we may well want something more.

Second, we may make use of our Hypothesis of Spacelike Extension and, in particular, the Dualistic Form of the Hypothesis. On any such *Hypothesized Substantial Dualism*, I may have *spacelike* location, and even *spacelike* extension, though I *won't* have any strictly spatial extension, or location. On an apt analogy with our best conceptions of separate bodies, with any such Hypothesized Dualism I may grasp something as to how the simple (nonspatial but) spacelike entity that's me is externally related to other similarly simple (nonspatial but) spacelike individuals. Just as I myself am, so each of these nonspatial concreta may also be an experiencer who's *spacelikely located and extended*, but that's not spatially located or extended.

With any Form of our Hypothesized Substantial Dualism, we may provide quite a nice treatment for the Mental Problems of the Many. As indicated, these Views aren't the only metaphysical positions that enjoy this advantage. But, for us humans right now, at least, it may be that they are more interesting positions, and more appealing views, than anything else that allows us a nice treatment of the Mental Problems of the Many.

What I've just been saying, in the course of this Section, applies to all the Hypothesized Substantial Dualist Views that I've offered. It applies to the Emergentive Substantial Dualist Views, both Pessimistic and Optimistic. And, it applies to the Quasi-Platonic Dualistic View. And, finally, it applies to both our Constitutional Dualism and to our Fusional Dualism. Of course, it's no accident that this is so. To the contrary, when offering any of these Dualist Views, a main motivation was to allow a nice treatment of the Mental Problems of the Many.

20. Our Hypothesized Dualism and the Problem of Our Unconscious Quality

In the previous Chapter, we discussed the Problem of Our Unconscious Quality. As we observed, an Enlightened Scientiphicalism provides a fairly straightforward and sensible answer to this problem, as do many enlightened materialistic positions. (And, we observed much the same for our noted Nonentity Emergentism, however questionable, or unstable, this Emergentist View might otherwise be.) Of course, this will hold true for almost any View on which each of us is a spatially extended concretum, and for any on which each of us is always replete with Spatially Extensible Quality. For, on any such View, you may be *Spatially Extensibly Qualitied* at every moment of your existence, at both all the moments when you're experientially qualitied and, quite as well, at all those when you're not.

By contrast with that nice enough treatment of this Problem, the answers available from our offered Substantial Dualist Views aren't as straightforward. Indeed, before undertaking our Hypothesis of Spacelike Extension, the best I could do, on behalf of a Substantial Dualist Metaphysic, was to say something along such apparently lame lines as these: Even when utterly unconscious, each of us always may be experiencing, if only in some very weak or rudimentary way. When you're utterly unconscious, the unlikely line ran, you'll just be utterly unconscious of experiencing—but, still be experiencing, all the same. Now, that may not be quite as heroic an answer, just perhaps, as was Descartes's proposal of continual forgetting. But, even if so, we should still want to provide, on behalf of some Substantial Dualist views, some answer that's less heroic still. Enter, once again, the Dualistic Form of our Hypothesis of Spacelike Extension.

On our Hypothesized Dualist Views, you are a *spacelikely* extended individual, all right; but, you're *not a spatially* extended concrete particular. Now, this allows that you be an Extensibly Qualitied concretum, at every moment of your existence, even if you shouldn't ever be Spatially Qualitied Extensibly. Rather than ever being pervaded with Extensible Color, or with any other Quality suited for spatial pervasion, you may be, on our Hypothesis, a being who's always spacelikely pervaded, at every moment of your existence, with just such Extensible Quality as is suited to pervading whatever merely spacelike realm is the realm containing, or including, you.

This wasn't our initial motivation for offering our Dualistic Hypothesis of Spacelike Extension, this desire to provide a nice Substantial Dualist answer to the Problem of Unconscious Quality. But, it's certainly a very welcome consequence of this Hypothesis, that it does serve to provide that Problem with such a nice Dualist answer. Let's go through this in a bit more detail, making our start by recalling our initial motivation.

When we consider our experiential quality, yours and mine—but we don't (yet) consider any Extensible Quality that we might have—then we consider far too little for grasping anything substantial concerning how we might be externally related to each other. This we've already observed, of course, not once, but several times over. But, by postulating that we each may have Spacelikely Extensible Quality, pervading our separately occupied regions of a (merely) spacelike dimension, our Hypothesized Dualism allows us to grasp, analogically, something significant concerning this conceptually important matter. As also bears repeating, our having Spacelike Extensible Quality plays a key role in this analogical understanding: Because you're Spacelikely Extensibly Qualitied, and so am I, it can be intelligible that we should be concrete individuals, and not mere spacelike vacua, that simultaneously occupy quite separate regions of a spacelike dimensional aspect of concrete reality. Please notice, if you will, that our having such Spacelikely Extensible Quality plays this key role, in our grasping how we might be externally related, even when both of us are fully conscious, each endowed with all sorts of experiential quality. And, now, please also notice this, as well: Quite equally, and in quite the same way, it plays this same key role when *only one of us is qualitied experientially* and the other is utterly unconscious, maybe not experiencing at all. And, of course, it's *also* crucial, for grasping how we may be externally related when we're *both unconscious*, presumably, or very possibly, both of us completely devoid of all experiential quality, and both devoid of any quality of any other sort or kind.

In its treatment of the Problem of Our Unconscious Quality, our Hypothesized Dualist Views closely parallel the treatments given by Materialism and by Scientiphicalism. Of course, it's no accident that there's this close parallel. We've endeavored to develop an idea of souls, or an idea of nonphysical mental individuals, that closely paralleled our clearest conceptions of distinct physical bodies. In the course of such an effort as *this* there was bound to emerge, with our Hypothesized Dualism, a closely parallel treatment of that Problem.

Though it will be little but overkill, for some readers, it may be quite helpful for me now to make a short summation, in parallel with the previous Section's summation. So, I now do that.

What I've just been saying, in the course of this Section, applies to all the Forms of Substantial Dualism that I've offered. It applies to the Emergentive Substantial Dualist Views, both Pessimistic and Optimistic. And, it applies to the Quasi-Platonic Dualistic View. And, finally, it applies to both our Constitutional Dualism and to our Fusional Dualism. Of course, and once again, it's no accident that this is so.

21. Recalling and Addressing the Question of Nicely Matched Propensity Partners

As I'll help you recall, the last Section of our Fifth Chapter was devoted to discussing a very intriguing question, Do Our Reciprocal Propensity Partners Present a Cosmic Miracle? To quite a great degree, this question should be addressed by any very serious metaphysician, even by those who are Enlightened Materialists, or Enlightened Scientiphicalists. But, to an even greater degree, it's important that it be addressed by someone aiming to espouse a serious Interactionist Substantial Dualism. Well, as I'm now in the midst of seriously espousing several such sorts of No-nonsense Dualism, I should certainly address this intriguing question. Though I'll only ever do it pretty briefly and sketchily, I'll still aim to do it fairly usefully.

For serious Substantial Dualists, this question may present a more difficult challenge, I suspect, than the challenge presented to Materialists. At any rate, when a serious Dualist comes to confront the question, there may be a wider range of metaphysical scenarios for him seriously to address, and it's just absolutely clear that none will allow him to provide the question any easy answer. For Materialists, by contrast, the question may be rather easier or, at least, much less complicated. At any rate, for them, matters might not be nearly so complicated.

Mainly for these reasons, I'll first address our matching question, in this present Section, only insofar as it applies to a serious Materialist Metaphysic or, much the same, a serious Enlightened Scientiphical View. This will be worth doing, I'm sure, even for those who, like me, think Scientiphicalism, and Materialism, to be scarcely any Decently Comprehensive Philosophy. Anyway, after finishing my sketchy work with this simpler matter, I'll proceed to examine, in the next Section, what a serious Substantial Dualist might say, by way of providing a happily sketchy answer to our intriguing question.

How might a serious Materialist, or any Enlightened Scientiphicalist, reply to our question, Do Our Reciprocal Propensity Partners Present a Cosmic Miracle? To begin our discussion, I'll remind you how, even just confining our attention to purely physical concreta, it can easily seem all but miraculous that a World's basic physical individuals should be reciprocally Propensitied for interesting dynamical interaction. To induce some apparently appropriate astonishment, I rehearse some passages from Chapter five's aforesaid discussion, used there to a similarly disturbing effect:

> Early in a certain World's history, we may suppose, or in an assumed Eon's history, there are very many electrons, each of them a Small Blue Sphere with a certain characteristic profile of Propensity. In this profile, we're supposing, there's a Propensity to strongly repel any of the World's other Small Blue Spheres, or its other electrons, each so similarly Propensitied with respect to any others. Now, even with just this much supposed, it can seem that the envisioned World is so filled with perfect matches as to be almost *miraculous*. Or, better, there's this thought: Should the *actual world* be anything like as *wonderfully Propensitied as that*, with so many electrons each so similarly matched for dynamic interaction with all the others, then *this* may be almost miraculous....
>
> As we may imagine, we just supposed a World as it was in a relatively early Eon. As we'll now suppose, after that Eon the World's very many continuing electrons are joined by very many newly existent basic physical concreta, all of them of a very *different basic kind*. Still, just as with the electrons, *none* of which *Changed* (Propensitively) upon the arrival of these new Particles, each new Particle is, in all intrinsic respects, precisely similar to all the others. Well, *what* kind of new Particles should these be?

Evidently, there's an enormous (infinite) variety of possible kinds of basic Particles. Well, for specificity's sake, let's suppose that our new Particles, we may call them *legons*, are all precisely similar Large Green Ovoids, each with the same Propensity profile as all the others. (For one thing, each may be Propensitied to repel any other legon there may be, much as each electron is Propensitied to repel any other electron. But, of course, that's old hat.) Now, with this question, we enter new territory: Are our *electrons Propensitied for dynamical interaction with the legons*; are our electrons suitable *reciprocal disposition partners for regular dynamical interaction with each of our newly existent legons?*

Unless the answer's affirmative, our supposed World (or Eon) won't be any World (or Time) where there's impressive physical activity. For, as we've been supposing, those are all the basic concreta there are. So, for our supposed World to be anything much like the actual world, our electrons and legons must be nicely matched disposition partners. For the actual world is, evidently, a World where there's lots of interesting physical activity, at least enough to have it be that there's lots of chemical activity, and lots of biological activity, and so on.

For our supposed World to be much like the actual world, with so much physically promoted nice activity, its old electrons must be, and they *must have been*, Propensitied for happy dynamical interaction with its legons, so much more newly existent. (Remember, we're supposing that, even with the advent of the legons, *none* of the Small Blues *Changed* (Propensitively); rather, each remained the same.) But, now, it seems utterly miraculous that, even long before there are any legons, our electrons should be Propensitied for (just a certain specific sort of happy) dynamical interaction with possible Particles of precisely *that* specific sort—possible Particles Shaped as just the legons are Shaped, and Qualitied just as they are.[15]

With those vividly effective passages, many readers will now feel, I'll bet, some considerable astonishment at the happily dynamical working of our actual world.

In inducing this astonishment, I offered you some passages that were almost trickily designed to just such an effect. What do I mean by that?

Well, just as I intended, I said nothing about how it was that our considered World came to contain ever so many electrons, each so nicely matched for repelling each of the others. Indeed, quite a few may have assumed that, from time immemorial, the World *always* contained all these very happily matched elementary Particles. Or, at any rate, they may have assumed that it was just a happy accident that,

---

15. The quoted passage is from Section 23 of Chapter 5.

for a very long time, the World contained all these Propensitively pretty electrons, without there ever being any Propensitively intelligible origin of the dynamically happy situation. And, with my very bald announcement of the World's later coming to have all those nicely matching (protonish) partners, the aforesaid legons, well, the impression of a huge happenstance then was increased and, as I'll bet, it increased very greatly.

With my intentions now terribly different from what they once were, I'll specify some details that will make things *seem very much less* miraculous, regarding our supposed World with all its prettily matched Particulate Propensity partners. Very forcefully indeed, here's one way for me to do that: First, all the electrons were created by an Almighty Creator, who chose to produce just so very many perfectly similar Particles, all of them of the electron kind, and, so, all of them neatly matched for the noted sorts of dynamical interaction. And, then, this same Creator intentionally produced, quite as he chose to do, just so very many other Particles, all them being of the very different legon kind, with each being quite like a perfectly protonish Particle. Owing to the work of this Almighty Creator, we're assuming, our supposed World then had, as all its concreta, other than the Creator Herself, just so many Particulate individuals as were all so nicely Propensitied for all sorts of interesting dynamical interaction with each other. Well, given all *that*, and also given whatever else he'd need to do, for there to be lots of physically derivative entities and activities, there'll be little wonder, indeed, in the fact that our World should (have come to) contain all manner of physically derivative goodies, as with, say, its having nothing less than oceans, and oceans, of water molecules.

Now, if I believed that our world, the actual world, included some such Creator, a Powerful Being who produced so very much else in the world, beyond just Herself, well, then there'd be little left for me to say here. Or, anyway, I wouldn't need to say much more.[16] But, quite as I've already told you, in Chapter Eight, I really don't believe that. So, for me to do any truly honest justice to our present topic, I really should say something more, if only, perhaps, it's just a little something more.

---

16. Conversely, that very fact gets me to think that, even as our actual world does have so much very nice Propensitive matching—at least for its souls and their physical partner, or partners—so that might be *some* reason to think that (all the rest of) our world *was* produced by such a Craftily Designing Creator. Some reason, as I just suggested. But, maybe also, as I'll further suggest, it might not be very much reason. Anyhow, for what's presently my main theme, that's neither here nor there. And, so, without further ado, it's directly back to the text we go.

Well, even without a designing agent in the mix, we may be helped, in this matter, by thoughts to the effect that, whatever separate individuals our world now does contain—whether these be Particles, or souls, or both, or neither—they may have all originated from some single richly Propensitied individual. For a nice instance of that, return to consider, yet once again, a little passage, itself from Chapter Eight, that sketchily comments on how things may have proceeded, about twenty or so billion years ago, according to conjectures like those of so-called Big Bang Cosmology. As background for the passage, we supposed, properly enough, something like this to have held true: For an Eon or so right before the Great Cosmic Explosion, there was just some peculiar plasmatic soup, whatever that might really be. Herewith, the little passage itself:

> However else it also may have been Propensitied, that soup—or that physical whatever—was Propensitied to so explode, but, of course— or, presumably—just when there should obtain some suitable conditions for its so doing. (Presumably, neither the explosion itself nor its timing was just sheer happenstance.) Maybe, the world had to wait for its plasmatic soup to become Extensible Platinum, which might itself have been the long-awaited manifestation of certain ways that the soup was Propensitied. Anyhow, the soup was Propensitied so that, upon its becoming Extensible Platinum, say, it exhaustively exploded and, what's more, it did so in just a certain very nice way—very nice, that is, for there coming to be, sooner or later, a physical realm rather like (what we currently take) the current physical realm (to be). So, however directly, or however indirectly, this Big Bang gave rise to (first, such-and-such, and then so-and-so,...and then) gadzillions of (precisely similar partless) quarks, and (quite different from all the quarks) goodzallions of (precisely similar partless) electrons. Well, and again, it's something like that. So, from all that there then, we're all here right now.
>
> Well, then, how are things, relevantly, here and now? Presumably, in the whole Propensity profile of each quark, there's the individual's Propensity for Monotony as to its Existence. And, presumably, so it is, too, for all the other most simple physical things, say, for all the electrons.[17]

So far, so good. For, at the very least, we've related, even if just quite sketchily, how our present physical situation, even if it should be, perhaps, a basically Particulate situation, may have originated from some single richly Propensitied individual and, what's more, how all that may itself be, or how it all may itself have been, nothing but the

17. The quoted passage is from Section 4 of Chapter 8.

manifestation of some Propensity, or some Propensities, of that self-same Propensitively rich individual. But, especially proceeding along Particulate lines, that can be only the beginning of anything like an adequate (Materialist) answer to our intriguing question.

For more of the wanted answer, we must say more about the Propensive nature of our explosive peculiarly plasmatic, richly Propensitied individual. Well, then, what should we now say about that? Whatever we say, it should be said, of course, with an eye toward the characterization being fit for explaining, at least to some small degree, an eventuating nice match among just so many eventuating Propensity partners, where each of the eventuating individuals originated, of course, in the explosion of the Propensitively fertile plasmatic entity.

By this late date, you should be right alongside me here, with all this Propensive business. So, quite as you'll be expecting us to do, we explicitly write it into our description of the soup-object's Propensive nature that it be Propensitied radically to explode—under conducive conditions for so doing, of course—into *just such individuals as should be Propensitively matched for this-and-that nicely dynamical Propensive interaction*. Now, suppose, just as a for-instance, that our soup-object should be Propensitied to explode into, perhaps among other basic physical concreta, just so many Large Red Spherical Spatial Individuals—call them Large Reds—and, quite equally, also into just so many Small Blue Spherical Spatial Individuals—or, as we'll say, Small Blues. Well, quite assuredly, that *won't* be the end of that. Quite to the contrary, about all that, at least this much more must now be said. That selfsame explosive Propensity, the originating object's Propensity for exploding into Small Blues and Large Reds, well, that will be a Disposition for the object's exploding into just such Small Blues as will be nice dynamically matched Propensity partners, both for each other and, quite as well, for Large Red Particles. And, it will also be a Propensity, of course, for the object's exploding into just such Large Reds as will be nicely matched Propensity partners, both for each other and, quite as well, for Small Blue Particles.

Well, in just a bit more than a nutshell, that's the sort of story that's wanted, I'll submit, for a richly dynamical Particulate World where, in the present Eon, so to say, the World's physical realm (and maybe its only realm) comprises just so many basic Particles, each a nicely matched Propensity partner for all of, or for pretty much all of, the World's other basic Particles. If we had lots of time to spare, and an almost infinite interest in these topics, we could sketch how the Eons we've just discussed, for our storied World, may themselves have developed, in a Propensitively most satisfactory manner, from how things were, Propensitively, with the individuals that preceded them, in still earlier Eons. As far as I can tell, there's no end to that. But, also as far as I can see, there's no point to it, either.

Noticing the complex story needed to accommodate a World of nicely matching Particles, a materialist can make things much easier for herself, simply by saying that there never are any Particles, nor any other spatially separate spatial bodies, nor even any numerically different physical individuals of any sort. Instead, she can say all that's ever real—all that's *really* real—is a single vast Propensitied Plenum. This Plenum, she may say, is spatially very variegated, certainly as regards its Spatially Extensible Quality, and maybe, too, as concerns how it is Propensitively. (And, as she may very well allow, the Plenum may change greatly, as time goes by, in all sorts of interesting ways.) Now, notice that, with such a properly singular Plenumate physical World, there'll *never arise any* question of nicely matching Propensity partners. For, even as there's always just one individual, in such a World, there's never even any question, really, of there being any real *partners* at all.

While that's certainly interesting for us to observe—and, so, I've just observed it—none of that has any bearing, really, on our current actual concrete reality. For in the actual world, right now, there is a real plurality of sentient *beings*. For example, and at the very least, there's me and, numerically different from me, there's also you, too.

Crackers though it must be, I guess, by this point in our long hard work, let's just suppose, for only a moment, that I'm a material entity and, quite as well, that you're a material individual, too. Given just that, it can't possibly be, then, that the material realm, for our actual world right now, is just a single Plenum, nor any other single individual. Rather, I must be, on our current assumptions, one material object and (presumably spatially somewhat separate from me) you must be another physical individual, numerically different from me. So, as it might possibly be, let's pretend, I'm this certain electron, over there, and, quite distinct from me, you're this *other* electron, say, way over thataway. Or, you might be this one complex molecule, let's suppose, and, quite other than you, I might be another complex molecule. Realism isn't the point here. Rather, the point is that, you and I, we're really two, not one. And, by golly, we do interact, at least from time to time—else I'd never be communicating with you, something that, evidently, I'm most certainly doing. So, if there should be any Materialism worth its salt, which I greatly doubt, very greatly, indeed, well, then, it must be a Materialism that's a Humanly Realistic Philosophy. And, for that, it must be a Philosophy, of course, with a fine story to tell as to how it should be that, Propensitively, you and I, who do communicate with each other are so nicely matched, Propensitively, so wonderfully dynamically matched as, in fact, we actually are.

As regards the Question of Nicely Matched Propensity Partners, and maybe as regards anything else, too, that's enough discussion of anything like a Materialist Metaphysic, or any Scientiphical View. Probably much more useful toward making some real philosophical progress, but, even in any event, we now turn to discuss what our Hypothesized Dualistic Views should say, or what their advocates should say, about that intriguing Question.

22. Our Hypothesized Dualism and the Question of Nicely Matched Propensity Partners

Toward presenting a Decently Comprehensive Substantial Dualism, I should do something toward providing a nicely Dualistic Propensitive answer to our intriguing question, Do Our Reciprocal Propensity Partners Present a Cosmic Miracle? Following some leads observed in the just previous Section, that's what this present Section aims to do. And, look, I'm going to do this just for our Quasi-Platonic Dualism, which is, as you know, my preferred Form of Substantial Dualism. (Once you've observed that, it should be easy to do the same for various other Substantial Dualist Views. Accordingly, I'll spare you just so many details.)

For a nice start, we'll return to consider our proto-soupy multidimensional individual, a key character, you'll recall, in the storyline leading to our Quasi-Platonic Substantial Dualism. As an aid to making that happy return, I'll recall a passage from this Chapter's Section on the question, How Might We Nonspatial Souls Precede Even Our Initial Physical Embodiment? That's the Section where I presented our Quasi-Platonic View, and where I offered this happy speculation:

> To begin things, I'll first speculate that, before the onset of this present Eon, say, some twenty or so billion years ago, the world was radically richer than any merely physical realm could be, or any purely physical world. During that just earlier Eon, I'll suppose, every concretum that was Spatially Extended—and maybe there then was just one vast Spatial concrete individual—was also Nonspatially Extended. Perhaps, it was extended in a dozen merely Spacelike (dimensions or) ways, each as different from all the others as every last one of them is from proper Space itself. But, at the very least, the multinatured soupy individual (or however many proto-soupy individuals) existed in two Spacelike dimensions, as we might say.[18]

18. The quoted passage is from Section 14 above.

Now, when first characterizing this vast multinatured concretum, I didn't bother to say a very great deal as to its Propensitive nature—though, to be fair to myself, I did make a few useful remarks to that effect. Anyhow, this is a very good place, indeed, for me to do a good deal more.

In saying how it is, Propensitively, with our multidimensional soupy concretum, I'll begin by rehearsing some remarks already made to that effect:

> Well, as I'll now nicely specify, our strangely-spacelikely proto-soup was Propensitied in just such a way that, just as soon as it should be THUS Qualitied, then—with a bang, and a boom, and a bam—it should shatteringly explode in an extraordinarily radical way. And, so—bang, boom, bam—there occurred just such a shattering that, from this Singularly Spatial and Sonal Concretum, there explosively came to be just very many purely Spatial concreta and, in addition, just very many simply Sonal concreta, without any individual being both Spatial and Sonal.[19]

With this little passage, I've said that, just as a manifestation of a certain *Propensity of* our originating spatial-and-sonal concretum, there was produced, or there came to be, just so many basic spatially separate spatial bodies and, *dimensionally nonintegrated* with all that, just so many sonally separate sonal souls.

Before I go on to say more about any proto-soupy concretum's Propensitive character, let me offer a "lateral" alternative to the passage just displayed. Maybe this other option isn't any better—hence, I used the word "lateral" here—but, in my heart of philosophical hearts, it's the alternative that I most prefer. So, please, allow me what may be only an old philosopher's indulgence.

Employing a correlative passage that might differ only very mildly, we can say, correlatively, how there should come to be *just a single vast spatial concretum*—as with a spatially infinite Plenum, perhaps—and, quite in addition to that Plenum, just so many sonally separate sonal souls, perhaps even infinitely many. Here's how such a happily correlative passage may run:

> Well, as I'll *now* nicely specify, our strangely-spacelikely proto-soup was Propensitied in a way *just so that*, just as soon as it should be *THUSLY* Qualitied, then—with a zang, and a zoom, and a zam—it should shatteringly explode in an *exceptionally* radical way. And, so,—zang, zoom, zam—there occurred just such an exceptional

---

19. The quoted passage is from Section 14 above.

> shattering that, from this Singularly Spatial and Sonal Concretum, there explosively came to be a single vast spatial concretum, not at all sonal, and, dimensionally nonintegrated with it, just very many sonally separate sonal souls, none at all spatial.

With this alternative passage, I've said how there might come to have been a more Cartesian sort of situation, with just a single entity in our considered World's physical realm.

But, of course, any Humanly Realistic Philosophy must acknowledge *a real plurality of richly sentient beings*—a real plurality of distinct experiencing, thinking and choosing individuals. And, so, in this Humanly Realistic Work, I haven't any interest, none at all, in saying how, from a proto-soupy concretum, there might have come to be (an Eon containing) just a single nonspatial soul. (What's more, of course, and very important to us, on our Humanly Realistic Philosophy, there'll be plenty of interaction among, and between, many of the numerically different sentient beings. Indeed, we may even communicate our innermost thoughts and feelings to each other and, through deeply sincerely and loyally protracted interpersonal communication, we can become, and we can remain, deeply involved, emotionally, with each other.)

(Not that anything really requires me to do it, but, still, it may be useful for me, even at just this place, to comment briefly on two famous systems of philosophy, neither of which has any trouble from any question like our intriguing query, Do Our Reciprocal Propensity Partners Present a Cosmic Miracle?

First, because Spinoza's systematic philosophy allows there to be, really, just one single individual, there's no way for me to be an individual and, along with that, for you also to be an individual, really distinct from me and, most certainly, numerically different from me. As there isn't ever more than just one individual, according to this metaphysic, there aren't ever, of course, any partners. So, with Spinoza, there's never any room, even, for our observed question to arise. Well, that may be a philosophical advantage. But, in almost every other respect, this philosophy may be perfectly repugnant.

No room, in this philosophy, for there to be one individual who's me and, numerically different from myself, somebody *else* who's you? Besides being evidently absurd, that's perfectly repugnant. Of course, Spinoza goes on to say all sorts of things that make sense only insofar as there are some several genuine individuals, and not just one. But, as with anyone else, he can't have his cake and eat it, too. So, by my lights, none of that can really make any decent sense at all. Rather than any of that deeply nonsensical business, let's agree that *you are one* aptly powered individual, nicely powered to think for yourself, and even to choose for yourself. And, let's also agree that, quite separate and distinct from you, *I am another* individual being, also nicely powered to think for myself, and even to choose for myself, all that being quite independent, thank you, very much, from your being so nicely powered. That, I submit, is how things really, really are. It's not just how things appear; and it's not just some superficial whatnot. Rather, it's absolutely real, it's just as real as anything can ever possibly be. So much for Spinoza.

Second, there's Leibniz's philosophy. Well, here there really are plenty of individuals, not only God, but, each numerically different from Him, ever so many distinct mental monads. Well, that's all right. But, little else is all right. For, there's never any real interaction among, or between, any of the individuals. (The closest thing to that, I guess, is what happens when God makes His monads. Well, this last point is just a toss-off.) As there isn't ever any real interaction among any individuals, according to this second metaphysic, on Leibniz's philosophy, too, there aren't ever any *interaction* partners. So, quite as with Spinoza, even if it's for very different reasons, perhaps, with Leibniz, too, there's never any room for our observed matching question to arise.

Anyhow, Leibniz's philosophy is also perfectly repugnant. What horrible loneliness there must be here, as mere illusions of real communication can't ever serve, really, toward having anyone befriend anyone else. In this quite isolationist philosophy, let's face it, there's not even the least chance, or any true opportunity, for any individual to enjoy interacting with any other real individual. Not only is this terribly depressing; but, quite beyond that, there's something deeply pathological about this whole business. No doubt, Leibniz was a true genius. But, so what? By my lights, what that shows is just this. Intellectual power is a vastly overrated attribute. With that duly noted, so much for Leibniz.

Rather than accepting anything much like *any* of this unhappy business, whether Spinozan or whether Leibnizian, we've much more than sufficient reason to prefer a Humanly Realistic Philosophy. With that plain truth expressed, my little semihistorical commentary is over and done. Now, it's back to the main order of present business.)

As you'll remember, I've made some several suggestions as to how it might be that a given newly formed brainy complex (or some given newly nicely brainily arranged Particles, or whatever) should come to acquire just a certain single sonal soul—that is, how it should come to be (or how they should come to be) Individualistically Propensitied with respect to just a certain single sonal soul. For instance, it might be that, rather than all the sonal souls being produced absolutely simultaneously, they came into being in a dense shortish sequence. If so, then, as it just might be, the newest soul might be the first soul to become embodied—that is, it might be the first soul to become Individualistically Propensitied with respect to some apt physical body, or bodies. Well, that's just a "for instance." And, for us here, it doesn't matter what are really the details of the wanted pairing processes. Rather, here's what matters: Happenstance placed aside, as it was with everything we've lately been doing, we may say this. Whatever ordering it is that serves to determine which soul gets paired with which body, well, for one thing, and first, that's all just (part of) a manifestation of how it is Propensitively, at the times when these pairings eventuate, with all the souls and, of course, with all the basic physical concreta, too.

Well, that's one thing to say, as regards what matters. But, still, we should say more, at least this much more: Even as the multinatured object was Propensitied to explode into just so many sonal souls and, dimensionally nonintegrated with them, a spatially bodily physical realm, so it was Propensitied to eventuate in just such souls as should be just so Propensitied as to manifest a certain ordering, as concerns which souls should be paired, in due course, with which part of the physical realm. And, correlatively, the multinatured object was Propensitied to explode, quite as well, into just such a dimensionally discrete physical realm—maybe all just one vast plenum or, alternatively, maybe just so many spatially separate spatial Particles, right here, the difference doesn't much matter—well, just such a physical realm as would be Propensitied in just such a way as to ensure the realization of the aforementioned ordering, as concerns which spatial body, or which physical whatnot, is Propensitively paired with which sonal soul.

Look, I don't want to drive you dizzy with this. I just want you to get the hang of the big picture here (and, maybe, I want you to agree that this big picture isn't hanging way off kilter).

And, listen, I'm not saying that, on our Quasi-Platonic Dualism, everything absolutely must always proceed in fine Propensitive fashion. No; I'm not a sufficient reason zealot. Even though it should offend my philosophical sensibilities—such as they are—well, maybe a lot does happen just as some sheer happenstance. Who am I, after all, that the world shouldn't dare to offend me? There's no guarantee that the world should feature only nicely intelligible occurrences. No; of course not. So, listen, I'm not trying to say how it is that everything simply *must* proceed. Rather, I'm just saying, or I'm just attempting to sketch, how things should be for a happening to be an intelligible occurrence, even if it should be just very broadly intelligible, and, perhaps, even if it should be, as well, just very barely intelligible.

With that said, it should be realized, quite clearly, that all our ambitions, in this work, are just so many quite modest metaphysical aspirations. And, with that well realized, I'll offer only a few more words in just this reasonably modest spirit, toward helping this Section come to a happy enough conclusion.

Confining our attention to Eonic development, and contemplating only what may be an endless sequence of different Eons, we can tell a pretty good explanatory story about how it is that, in very many of these Eons, there is quite nice Propensitive matching. How so? Damning the details, we may think of sequences of explosions, and implosions, and explosions, and so on. And, we may think of all of this endless development as being the manifestation of apt Propensities, or of a vastly complex apt Propensity. None of it happening just happenstantially, quite as we should fervently hope things to be, it *can* be, for all anyone really knows, that whatever comes to pass, in our actual world, should be the manifestation of how it is that individuals are Propensitied. Still and all, for very much of our wanted understanding, the key conception is, of course, this idea: We must allow that some of our world's individuals, at least, are Propensitied in ways that are quite enormously encompassing.

That acknowledged, we turn to discuss some very different questions.

23. Does Our Hypothesized Dualism Make My Current Quality Too Inaccessible?

Descartes, as I've said, didn't think much about matters experiential, or care much about what I take to be qualitative questions. Rather, he was much more concerned about the *content* of his thought, to use a currently fashionable word; famously, he focused on the *content* of *his own present-moment thinking* to that very effect. Reflecting on my own contentful thinking, even when I myself am thinking that I exist, I find that this thinking of mine always has some phenomenology, or qualitative character. Sometimes it's a bit different from other times, but rarely is there very much variance. Though it may proceed differently with quite a few other folks, in my own case, at least, the Cartesian egocentric existential thinking is what some have called "subvocalization." At any rate, when thinking this simple thought, I'm often Qualited auditorally, it appears, even if it's not in quite the same auditory way as when I hear myself overtly speaking. But, quite frankly, none of that really matters now.

What matters, right now, can be put like this: *Qualitatively Concerned Cartesians*, as we may usefully say, are philosophers who hold that, whenever it is that you're experientially qualitied in a particular way—in *any* particular way—then you'll be *conscious that* you're experientially qualitied in just that particular way. So, when I'm experiencing bluely and purply, for example, these Cartesians will take it that I'm *conscious* that I'm experiential blue and experiential purple. Well, even by my lights, that view is too extreme. Sometimes, at least, I may be qualitied in a certain specific way, and yet *not* be aware that I'm qualitied in *that* specific way. But, even though their view is rather too extreme, it still may appear, nonetheless, that our Qualitatively Concerned Cartesians aren't hopelessly far off the mark. And, as it may well be thought, certain Friends of the Qualitatively Concerned Cartesians may be, actually, right *on* the mark. What am I getting at?

When considering our Hypothesized Dualist Views, now that everyone's been exposed to them, some Friends of the Qualitatively Concerned Cartesians will object that it makes our qualitative character far *too inaccessible* to us. On these Dualist Views, they'll observe, what's presumably my most constant and characteristic Quality, exemplified in me even when I'm utterly unconscious, is just some Nonspatially Extensible Quality. And, at least as far as anyone can tell, I'm never acquainted with this Quality at all. Quite certainly, as concerns its Mode of Exemplification, I'm not acquainted with this Nonspatially Extensible Quality. And, presumably, or quite likely, even as concerns its Mode of Pure Quality, I may not be acquainted with it.

At least in certain respects, as I'll admit, this really is a big deal. It's an enormously bigger deal than, for instance, any worries about how it may be with me, as concerns any relevant accessibility, and, say, some "missing shade of Blue"—a shade that's lighter than the many blues I've seen or imagined, but that's darker than all the others I've consciously experienced. Far from anything so piddling as that, with respect to my Hypothesized Spacelikely Extensible Quality, allegedly so characteristic of me, I won't ever have, in all likelihood, even so much as just the merest inkling of any clear idea.

To be sure, these Friends will agree, I needn't always be perfectly transparent to myself, as regards all my qualitative character. But, with these Hypothesized Substantial Dualisms, very much of my qualitative character, including what may be most essential to me qualitatively, appears so terribly far from being accessible to me as to be, for me, an utterly mysterious matter. Better, by far, these Friends will say, to opt for some very different metaphysical view. Or, failing that, better to befriend no metaphysic at all.

At first, this objection may seem quite devastating. But, in point of fact, *most* of what it advances, even if not absolutely all of what it purports, may be employed, with equal effect, against a Scientiphical View of ourselves. Or, this may be done providing only that our Scientiphicalism is qualitatively rich enough to allow us humans, ever to attain, any very intelligible metaphysical conception of physical reality.

Recall the Enlightened Scientiphical answer to the Problem of Our Unconscious Quality: When I'm utterly unconscious, I'm still endowed with my Spatially Extensible Quality, this being, presumably, just such Extensible Quality as I enjoy through being constituted of just so many basic physical things, each of which is Spatially Extensibly Qualitied. In short, I'll have just whatever Extensible Quality, or Qualities, are exemplified in, say, my basic physical Particulate constituents. But, then, what Quality *is* this that I thus exemplify even when utterly unconscious? Or, if there's Qualitative variegation, what Qualities *are* these? Maybe it's all Blue, for all I'll ever know. Or, alternatively, maybe it's Silver, except wherever it's Light Aquamarine. Or, maybe it's a Tutti Frutti melange of Colors none of which has any experiential correlative, leastways none that's ever been enjoyed by me. So, in this central Respect, the Respect of Pure Quality, it's foolish, really, even to hazard a guess as to my nonexperiential Qualitative character.

Not just on our Hypothesized Substantial Dualism, then, but also on our Enlightened Scientiphicalism, what's most essential to me, qualitatively, is so terribly far from being accessible to me. Indeed, it's so very far from that as to be, at least for me, almost utterly mysterious.

Well now, what about the other central Respect of my Extensible Quality, its Mode of Exemplification? On our Enlightened Scientiphicalism, it's true, there's less of a reach than with our Hypothesized Dualism. For we have a quite directly intuitive conception of how a Spatially Extensible Quality may pervade an individual, in that we're so nicely tuned for properly spatial thinking, while we have only an analogical conception, comparatively quite bare and even abstract, as to how things may be with merely Spacelikely Extensible Quality. But, so far as anything like *accessibility* goes, as that notion's generally been understood, things aren't much better with Scientiphicalism, or with any Materialistic View, than with our Hypothesized Dualistic Positions. After all, my conjectural suggestion of some Spatially Extensible Quality, or Qualities, with which I'm endowed, or with which my body (over my overlapping bodies) may be endowed, is just a conjecture, and nothing more. To be sure, it may be that this conjecture is a philosophically illuminating thought—well, at least a little bit enlightening. But, even if that's so, it's nothing I'll ever really *know* to be so. Much less, will I have, with regards to anything like that idea, any such specially direct knowledge as some have supposed is often found with someone's knowledge of his own present experiencing, or his own current experiential character. *Access* as to my *body's* qualitative character? Real *availability*, to me? No way in the world will I ever have that much, not in any sense of the terms figuring in traditionally influential philosophical ideas. So, most of what we said about our Hypothesized Dualist Views we may say, quite as well, about an Enlightened Scientiphicalism, or about any decently enlightened Materialistic View.

When it comes to my *experiential* quality, and not any suggested Extensible Quality, matters are very different. As concerns my experiential quality, how it is with me, qualitatively, is often highly accessible, even if it's not always so very accessible. Well, now, I wouldn't go quite so far as a Qualitatively Concerned Cartesian here. But, still, I'll take a little step in his direction.

Because you're well Propensitied with respect to how it is that you're now experientially qualitied, you'll have some significant awareness, quite often and quite typically, of how it is that you're experientially qualitied. This is true, or something quite like it's true, whether our Hypothesized Dualism (in any of its Forms) is more nearly correct than Scientiphicalism, or whether the reverse obtains.

Speaking first about our Dualism, there's this evident contrast to be made: Of course, you're *not* Propensitied with respect to how it is that, *nonexperientially*, you're now *Nonspatially Spacelikely Extensibly Qualitied*. And, since you're not Propensitied to "register in awareness" your Spacelikely Extensible Quality, or to do anything of the like, you won't be aware of whatever Spacelikely Extensible Quality you may have.

Speaking next of our Scientiphicalism, there's this parallel contrast, just as evident: Of course, you're *not* Propensitied with respect to how it is that, *nonexperientially*, you're now *Spatially Extensibly Qualitied*. And, since you're not Propensitied to "register in awareness" your Spatially Extensible Quality, or to do anything of the like, you won't be aware of whatever Spatially Extensible Quality you may have.

Both in point of fact and on our Hypothesized Dualism, my current experiential quality is highly accessible to me, the experiencer in question. And, both on this Dualism and in point of fact, my current nonexperiential Quality isn't, I suppose, even the least bit accessible even to me. But, both as regards my experiential quality and as regards whatever Extensible Quality I may have, the situation here isn't very different from how our Scientiphicalism will have things be. At all events, I don't see, in any of this, any special problem for our Hypothesized Substantial Dualism, in any of its offered Versions.

24. Two Cartesian Arguments for Some Spacelikely Substantial Dualism

It is quite impossible, I believe, for any human thinker, at least, to form any adequate conception of himself on which he is both an experiencing individual and he's also a truly spatial concrete particular. And, as I also believe, it's impossible, for a human thinker, at least, to have an adequate conception of herself on which she is both a strictly spatial entity and she's also an individual that really chooses. At least as far as the appearances go, that's our cognitive situation. At least for us, there appears an unresolvable conflict between our presumed spatiality and, on the other hand, our supposed experiencing, and our presumed real choosing.

Except for folks entirely innocent of philosophy, everybody knows it. To deny it is, at best, little more than some unduly optimistic self-denial.

Largely owing to just that, there is always great appeal in Descartes's Substantial Dualistic Metaphysic, concerning questions of mind and body, or in Dualist Views much like Descartes's View. This is true, of course, even with those who vigorously oppose Substantial Dualism, even as it's Dualism's appeal that helps to motivate the opponents' energetic activity, as everyone also knows.

In the bargain, there's also some considerable appeal, even if, perhaps, not quite enormous appeal, in Descartes's own arguments for his Substantial Dualism. Let's consider these arguments, if only briefly, with the aim of learning something new from our brief consideration of them, well, at least something just a bit refreshing and novel.

Without much injustice to Descartes, we may say that his main arguments are exactly two distinct pieces of Dualistic reasoning.

What's now the more influential of Descartes's two arguments, by far, occurs, in its considered form, in his Sixth Meditation. At least reasonably well, it may be conveyed in just these very few consecutive Cartesian sentences:

> It is true that I may have (or, to anticipate, that I certainly have) a body that is very closely joined to me. But, nevertheless, on the one hand, I have a clear and distinct idea of myself, in so far as I am simply a thinking nonextended thing; and on the other hand I have a distinct idea of body, in so far as this is simply an extended, nonthinking thing. And, accordingly, it is certain that I am really distinct from my body, and can exist without it.[20]

20. See *The Philosophical Writings of Descartes*, trans. J. Cottingham, R. Stoothoff, and D. Murdoch, Volume II, Cambridge University Press, 1984, page 54.

Now, it's hard for me to know exactly what to make of these words; and it's harder still to relate them to anything argumentative that will resonate with many currently prominent philosophers. But, without going so far as to knock myself out, I'll make something of an effort in that direction.

Using the currently common coin of "conceivability," I'll offer this more trendy rendition:

(1) I can conceive myself experiencing, or choosing, or thinking, indeed, I can even conceive it *most clearly*, without, at the same time, conceiving *at all* anything that's spatially extended.

(2) I can conceive a spatially extended body, indeed, I can even conceive it *most clearly*, without, at the same time, conceiving *at all* anything that's experiencing, or choosing, or thinking.

(3) If 1 is true—quite as it surely seems—and 2 is also true—quite as *it* surely seems, then, given just that I'm an entity that's experiencing (and so on), it follows that I'm not anything that's spatially extended.

But, of course,

(4) I *am* an entity that's experiencing (and so on); that much, at least, really *is* given.

So, at the very least, this much is true:

(5) I'm not anything that's spatially extended; that is, I'm not any spatial body.

Well, for most folks, and for my present purposes, that's all the most interesting stuff, right there. (Just to finish up the business for Dualism, in a short note, just below, I relate the few steps still remaining.[21])

To my mind, at any rate, this argument is pretty persuasive. Now, don't misunderstand me here; it doesn't knock my socks off, certainly not at this late date, with so much philosophically dirty water long since under the proverbial bridge. Heck, to my mind, it's not as persuasive as our Arguments from the Mental Problems of the Many. (Well, it may be

---

21. Now, nearly as surely as 4, there's also:

(6) There are spatial bodies.

So, for another thing, there's:

(7) Spatial bodies aren't any experiencing (or choosing, or maybe even thinking) entities.

So, finally enough, we have:

(8) There's experiencing old me, who's not any spatially extended entity, and there are spatially extended bodies, none of which is any experiencing entity.

Well, with 8, we've gotten the likes of Substantial Dualism. So, it's back to the text.

that, in my case, that doesn't count for very much. For, in my case, the difference in forceful impact, on me myself, may be due to an inclination of mine to be moved more—heaven forfend!—by arguments of my own devising, and be moved less by reasoning received from others.)

Evidently, quite unlike what went on in the *Meditations*—oh, so very long ago—here and now, in this present-day work, this Constructed Cartesian Argument plays no leading part, of course. At the very most, it will play only a supporting role. Well, as reasoning that's no more than a supporting player, I think this Constructed Argument may do quite nicely. But, let's look and see.

You don't think there's much to look at here? Well, then, I'll tell you what I'm going to do, and I'll do it just for you. First, I'm going to observe that, with that Constructed Argument, displayed just above, there's a lot of work done by these two presupposed propositions: First, each of us has a very clear conception of *herself*, or of himself, as an experientially powerful choosing individual. And, second, each of us has a very clear idea, also, with our very best conceptions as to distinct *spatial bodies*. Well, trading nicely on that, what the argument does is, I'll suggest, well, it gets us to think some such thought as this: Whatever properly satisfies the *first* of these ideas, my clearest conception of myself, well, it doesn't really satisfy the second, my clearest idea of a paradigmatic spatial body, and, quite equally, whatever properly satisfies the second fails to satisfy the first conception. I'm not absolutely sure of this, mind you. But, still, that's how matters strike me.

What; you still don't think there's much here for us to observe? Well, once again, I'll tell you what I'm going to do, and, again, I'll do it just for you. I'm going to ask you to run through an argument that's quite *like* the one displayed just above, *but with one very salient difference*. We're going to take certain of our terms, which may express very clear ideas of ours, and we're going to replace them with some aptly different terms, which may express only ideas that are much less clear to us. Just so, we'll replace "spatially extended" with, say, "spacelikely extended." And, we'll replace "spatial body" with "spacelike body." Or, if you prefer terms that are more specific than "spacelike"—quite as the term "spatial" might itself be a relevantly quite specific term—well, then you can replace "spatially extended" with "sonally extended," and you can replace "spatial body" with "sonal body."

Look, with even just that much done, we won't really have to go through the whole argument. Heck, just by looking at the newly obtained first premise, we can tell, plenty well, that we'll never get very far with such an aptly altered business:

1$%#. I can conceive myself experiencing, or choosing, or think-
ing, indeed, I can even conceive it *most clearly*, without, at the same
time, conceiving *at all* anything that's sonally extended.

Well, *that* doesn't strike me as clearly true. Heck, it doesn't *strike* me at
all. For, unlike my clear idea of a *spatially* extended thing, my conception of something *sonally* extended *isn't* any very clear idea. Far
from it. And, with that being so, I've hardly any decent idea, so far as I
can tell, whether I clearly can conceive myself, even as an experiencing
and choosing individual, without at the same time conceiving, if only
doing it terribly unclearly, something (or other) that's sonally extended. Well, I don't know about you, but, with me, at least, there's a
big difference between the Constructed Cartesian Argument, previously placed on display, and the awfully unpersuasive argument I just
didn't even bother to display, displaying no more than just the
hopelessly hapless 1$%#.

Listen, I'm not sure that, when all is said and done, the difference
between these two arguments will really amount to very much. Here's
why: Insofar as I can conceive sonal entities to be similar to spatial
entities—that is, insofar as our analogy between the two is a fully apt
analogy—well, to *just that extent*, it seems like the new first premise
might be all right, after all. But, how apt an analogy do we have here?
To be sure, and on one hand, I hope that it is very apt. But, in that
event, and on the other hand, we may have our transformed first
premise, 1$%#, be rather like 1, Descartes's original first premise.
And, then, we may well have an argument on our hands, quite closely
paralleling Descartes's original reasoning, to the effect that *I'm not any
sonal being*, either, no more than I'm a spatial entity.

This following may be, I suspect, a good way for us to appreciate
my difficulty here: Insofar as sone is really like space, that is, insofar as
there's really something to the idea that *both are spacelike* dimensional
aspects of concrete reality, we may find it quite proper, I suspect, to
take this Section's lead paragraph and use it as a template for con-
structing a potentially disturbing paragraph about our supposedly
sonal selves. Just so, here's what we'll obtain: It is quite impossible, I
believe, for any human thinker, at least, to form any adequate conception of himself on which he is both an experiencing individual and
he's also a truly sonal concrete particular. And, as I also believe, it's
impossible, for a human thinker, at least, to have an adequate conception of herself on which she is both a strictly sonal entity and she's
also an individual that really chooses. At least as far as the appearances

go, that's our cognitive situation. At least for us, there appears an unresolvable conflict between our presumed sonality and, on the other hand, our supposed experiencing, and our presumed real choosing.

This is all a very tricky and difficult business. And, though I wish I could do more to settle this difficult business and, in the bargain, do more toward fully understanding Descartes's enormously influential argument, this must remain, for a while at least, just a wish that I have.

At all events, I now turn to look at Descartes's second main piece of reasoning.

What's now the less influential of Descartes's two arguments, less influential by far, occurs, in its considered form, in his same Sixth Meditation. At least reasonably well, it also may be conveyed in just a very few Cartesian sentences, though they're not quite consecutive sentences:

> The first observation I make at this point is that there is a great difference between the mind and the body, inasmuch as the body is by its very nature always divisible, while the mind is utterly indivisible. For when I consider the mind, or myself in so far as I am merely a thinking thing, I am unable to distinguish any parts within myself; I understand myself to be something quite single and complete. . . . By contrast, there is no corporeal or extended thing that I can think of which in my thought I cannot easily divide into parts; and this very fact makes me understand that it is divisible.[22]

Well, before I comment on this argument, I'll quickly show you just how important Descartes took it to be. In his very next sentence, he comments on it like so: "This one argument would be enough to show me that the mind is completely different from the body, even if I did not already know as much from other considerations."[23]

Don't worry; I'm not going to give you a whole new song and dance here. Rather, I'll try to be as brief as I can decently be. So, very briefly, here's what I think: This argument also strikes me as pretty forceful. Why so? Well, pretty much following suit, I'll now read in a "spatially" both before "divisible" and before "indivisible," and, in addition, as elsewhere seems suitable, say, before "parts." And, I'll read in a "consciously" before the likes of "thinking." As before, what's at work, I suggest, is this: On each side of an offered contrast, we seem to have very clear ideas. And, as it seems to us, what most clearly satisfies the key idea on one of the sides—either one, take your pick—won't satisfy, not even at all well, any key idea on the other side.

---

22. *The Philosophical Writings of Descartes*, Volume II, page 59.
23. *The Philosophical Writings of Descartes*, Volume II, page 59.

Look, let's see how persuasive you'll find this next passage to be, an aptly mangled transformation of Descartes's own (translated) words:

> The first observation I make at this point is that there is a great difference between the mind and the sonal soul, inasmuch as the sonal soul is by its very nature always divisible, while the mind is utterly indivisible. For when I consider the mind, or myself in so far as I am merely a thinking thing, I am unable to distinguish any sonal parts within myself; I understand myself to be something quite single and complete.... By contrast, there is no sonal soul that I can think of which in my thought I cannot easily divide into sonal parts; and this very fact makes me understand that it is sonally divisible.

Well, I don't know about you. But, with me, I'm drawing blanks all over the place. But, what else should we have expected here? After all, how much is there, that's even the least bit clear, in my (enormously analogical) idea of a sonal soul? Accordingly, while the actual Cartesian passage strikes me as pretty persuasive—nothing like conclusive, mind you—this transformation of it doesn't do much for me at all.

While this exercise is, I think, quite interesting, its utility is quite limited. In largest measure, the limitation is due to considerations like we've just lately observed, in connection with pondering a "sonal interpretation" of Descartes's first argument: Insofar as I can conceive sonal entities to be similar to spatial entities—that is, insofar as our analogy between the two is a fully apt analogy—well, to *just that extent*, it seems like a sonal entity should be just as divisible as a spatial individual, though the former will be divisible only sonally, and not spatially, quite as the latter will be divisible only spatially, and not sonally. (Never mind, for this discussion, exactly what it is for a concretum to be *divisible*, whether that be spatially, or whether it be sonally, or whether it be still otherwise. Though that's a very interesting issue, it's not germane to the points presently at issue.) So, quite as with our consideration with Descartes's first main argument, for the real distinction between mind and body, so also with our thoughts as to his second main piece of reasoning, toward that same end. In attempts newly to interpret these Cartesian arguments, wherein conceptions of merely sonal individuals are employed, there's a grave danger of trying to have one's cake and eat it, too. Maybe, there's an adequate way to split the apparent difference here. But, equally, maybe there really isn't any. Myself, I can't tell.

Well, that's enough. I don't mean to make a big deal of what's in this Section. As I've said just recently, my own main arguments for

Substantial Dualism, in any of its Versions or Forms, are utterly different from either of Descartes's main arguments for his Substantial Dualism. So, I'm not counting on those time-honored considerations to do any heavy lifting, on behalf of such Forms of Dualism as I've placed on offer. (Not that I'm all that confident, either, of any reasoning that, newly enough, I've offered for (taking very seriously) some Form, or Forms, of Substantial Dualism.)

Pretty plainly, in motivating a Dualist Metaphysic, I don't heavily rely on Descartes's seminal old arguments, for a real distinction between mind and body. Still and all, I think it's a good idea to present that material here, and to give it a bit of discussion, too. For one thing, it helps to provide a broader perspective, in which we may better develop our Humanly Realistic Philosophy. And, for another thing, it lets us see, more clearly, that we needn't consider every decent sort of Substantial Dualism a Quasi-Cartesian Metaphysical View, or at least not only that. Just so, it's fair enough to call my "favorite" speculative View a *Quasi-Platonic* Substantial Dualism, though we might also lengthily label it, perhaps fairly enough, a *Quasi-Platonic Quasi-Cartesian Substantial Dualism*.

25. Is Reality's Temporal Aspect Uniquely Distinctive?

Our speculations as to further dimensional aspects of reality, beyond the spatial and the temporal, may help us conceive fairly fully, even if only very analogically, what may be a great number of these aspects. On analogy with both (spacelike) sone and (sonelike) space, we may conceive a dimensional aspect of reality that's fit for pervasion by Odors, say, but maybe not by either Colors or Sounds. And, maybe still more analogically, we may conceive dimensional aspects fit for occupancy by only such objects as are Spacelikely Extensibly Qualitied in much further-fetched ways. None of those Qualities will be any Extensible Correlative, so to say, of any experiential quality enjoyed in human experiencing, even if they each may be, metaphysically, quite on a par with the Spatially Extensible Colors. Better still, basic individuals Extensibly Qualitied only just so far-fetchedly may be on a par, ontologically, with the basic physical Particles, each Qualitied Colorly.

Though the number of these analogically conceived dimensions may be very great, their variety may be, in important ways, quite limited. I'll amplify.

The analogically conceivable aspects we've speculatively indicated are all so very much like space as may allow them properly to be termed *spacelike* dimensional aspects of concrete reality. Of course, what's strictly spatial doesn't have any special *ontological* status in any of this, leastways not on our own speculative hypothesizing. Rather, what's special is just something about us and, specifically, about how it is that we're Propensitied for thinking. However it may be with some very far-fetched agents, or subjects, we human thinkers are richly Propensitied for thinking in terms of spatial individuals, both as to how they're propertied and as to how they're externally related. By contrast, we're only very poorly Propensitied for thinking in terms of merely spacelike entities, as with say, our speculated sonal individuals. But, of course, just as much as that speculated sone will be a spacelike dimension, well, just that much will space be a sonelike dimensional aspect of reality.

As just indicated, each of reality's nontemporal dimensional aspects is, metaphysically, rather like each of the others. And, all of them are, each quite equally, utterly different from time. Among our speculated dimensional aspects, as I've been hypothesizing them, there's none that differs even nearly as much from space as each differs from time. And, as best I can tell, excepting time itself, of course, there's no dimension of concrete reality that's fit to be termed a *timelike dimensional aspect*. In a tentative manner and spirit, I propose that, at least insofar as concrete reality's conceivable by us human beings, its temporal aspect is a *uniquely distinctive* dimensional aspect.

It's an old idea, doubtless correct, that we can't conceive of concrete reality's lacking a temporal aspect. For a proposed possible world to be at all intelligible to us, we must be offered a world with some time, at least a little time. I think it's much less clear that the same can be said for us and for space. So, I don't think it's at all clear, to put the point mildly, that this is true: For a proposed possible world to be intelligible to us, we must be offered a world with space, at least a little space. But, I raise those questions here only to get them far out of the way, where others, who may wish to do so, may later explore them. What's of importance to me, here and now, is for us to be clear how very different from those questions are the matters I wish to focus on.

In our current explorations, we're allowing ourselves all sorts of strictly spatial conceptions, and all sorts of strictly temporal conceptions, for conceiving (a World's) concrete reality. As our extrapolative speculations analogically proceed, so that the concrete reality we come to grasp may be richer than what we ordinarily presume, we ask after the status of *further dimensional aspects* of concrete reality, dimensions *beyond* what we ordinarily presume, or *in addition to* them. All of these are rather similar to space, or to the strictly spatial dimensional aspect.

Well, just rather similar, not very similar. How similar is *that*? Well, maybe it's about as similar as Pure Sound is like Pure Color, and, maybe not even quite as similar as that.

By contrast, at least as it appears, none of concrete reality's dimensions is anything much like time, no more than space itself is like time.

In recent decades, the philosophical orthodoxy has been to treat time as being very like space. Putting the matter in somewhat silly terms—though the terms are *only somewhat* silly—the orthodoxy has been to take time as being almost another spatial dimension, different only in that time is much more temporal, I suppose, than are the plainly spatial dimensions, supposedly just three in number. As you can gather, I'm not much taken with this orthodoxy. To my mind, when trying to make sense of time, and even when trying to make sense of space, we do better to focus on the differences between the two than on any alleged similarities or analogies.

Yet, I'm certainly not sanguine about the proposal that's been this Section's focal point, namely, the claim that concrete reality's temporal aspect is a *uniquely distinctive* dimensional aspect of concrete reality. Often, I suspect that any impression to that effect doesn't do much to reflect the richness of concrete reality. Rather, as I often suspect, it may be fostered by, more than anything else, the conceptual proclivities of, and the conceptual limitations of, our distinctively human minds.

So, in short and in sum: I do believe that concrete reality's temporal aspect is a *uniquely distinctive* dimensional aspect of concrete reality. Or, maybe better, I'm strongly inclined to believe that. But, I'm certainly not very confident of any such proposition, nor even anything of the like.

26. Why Are Our Concrete Conceptions of Such Limited Variety?

In very fully and clearly conceiving concrete particulars, individuals truly diverse and several, we humans can't do more than, or do better than, to conceive entities in time and in space. The more clearly separate in space, or in time, the clearer our conception as to truly diverse individuals. So, we begin with what seems an enormously general idea—the notion of diverse individuals, or of a plurality of concrete particulars, no matter how alike all their qualities and how symmetric all their relations. And, in trying for clearly conceived instances of this very general notion, we find little more than a single sort of specific exemplar that, for us, is truly useful: temporally enduring spatially separate voluminous concrete entities. But, then, why are our clear conceptions of diverse particulars of such limited variety?

By way of a general answer to this question, three views seem salient.

First, there is the view that, in the first place, all reality is temporal and, at least near enough, all of it's spatial, and, in the second place, that's about all there is to concrete reality: Not only is our spatiotemporal thinking fairly adequate to reality, but all concrete reality, or near enough all, is comprehended, fairly adequately, in our spatial and temporal modes of conception. For most of us, myself included, that's the only natural view. Certainly, this view dominated mainstream twentieth century philosophy and, among those most likely to read these words, it still dominates the discipline. But, unless philosophers develop alternatives to this position, the field is, I think, likely to remain a quite limited discipline and, just perhaps, a field that's almost as boring as it's sterile.

A second view has it that, beyond the very limited and rather isolated purview of our own experience, what's supposedly spatial, and even what's allegedly temporal, has nothing much to do with concrete reality. This pessimistic view might, for all I know, be usefully associated with the name of Kant. Anyway, even while the first view has all nonmental concrete reality, along with all mental reality, nicely comprehended by temporal and spatial conceiving, this second does not. By contrast, the second view has it that, at the very most, only the most experiential aspect of reality may be conceived in these ways, even just the least bit adequately, whilst any nonmental concretum simply cannot be grasped by means of any spatial ideas, or in terms of any temporal conceptions. Pretty much everything about our modes for conceiving concrete things, leastways beyond what's just our own mentality is, on this view, utterly inadequate to whatever external things there really might be—just so utterly inadequate to things-in-themselves, so to speak. It's only our own thinking and experiencing that's fairly pervaded with purportedly temporal and spatial things. And, if it's really adequate to anything at all, it's only this for which these modes of conceiving, the spatial and the temporal, are at all adequate.

Now, usually, we take it that our spatial ideas, and especially our temporal conceptions, are at least moderately adequate to all of concrete reality, a vast reality of which we ourselves comprise only a very small part. To be sure, there may be much more to this reality than these conceptions comprehend. But, as much of reality as these notions do purport to comprehend, well, to that extent they do at least moderately well by us. Not so on this *Quasi-Kantian View*, if I may be allowed so to label our second approach here. Rather, and by contrast with any of that, on our Quasi-Kantian View we may, almost always, just suffer a terribly comprehensive illusion, as concerns the adequacy of these humanly central conceptions, both our spatial notions and even our temporal ideas. Through penetrating philosophical argumentation, some reasoning of a roughly Kantian kind, we can, perhaps, sometimes transcend this illusion, even if we should generally fall prey to it, habitually and recurrently.

A third view, which I now most prefer, has something saliently in common with Spinoza's philosophy. Reality is very rich, far richer than we're naturally disposed to suppose. So, at least some few of concrete reality's nonmental aspects, and, perhaps, even very many such aspects, *aren't* nicely susceptible to our spatial or our temporal conceiving.

On this third view, this *Quasi-Spinozan Approach*, there's *something* that's illusory in, or about, our spatial and temporal thinking, namely, its *presumption of comprehensiveness* for all concrete reality. But, then, on this Approach, the illusion we suffer isn't anywhere near as debilitating as the one entailed by, or suggested by, our second view, the Quasi-Kantian Approach. No, not at all. For, on our Quasi-Spinozan Approach, our spatial mode of conceiving, and our temporal mode, may serve us fairly well, even in grasping a very great deal as to how it is with concrete reality, both mentally and nonmentally, and both physically and nonphysically, too. It's just that, for an appropriately Comprehensive Philosophy, a Philosophy that does decent justice to the whole of concrete reality, we need to supplement them, these two salient modes, with some additional modes of conceiving concrete individuals—or, at the least, just so many more modes of conceiving one single concrete individual.

In certain respects, then, the Humanly Realistic Philosophy I advocate is rather like such a Quasi-Spinozan Approach (even as in other respects it's Quasi-Platonic, and in still others it's Quasi-Cartesian, and in yet still others it's Neo-Lockean, and so on). As I've been saying, it may well be that, as far as our temporal conceiving goes, there's nothing much for us to supplement it with that's even remotely like this mode itself. But, I've also been saying something much more positive, too. Just so, it may very well be that, for us humans to do even just some decent justice to actual concrete reality, we should supplement our spatial conceiving (and, of course, we'll then be supplementing our temporal mode of conceiving, too) with some *spacelike* modes of conceiving concrete reality—at least one such spacelike mode and, for all I can really say, maybe many more than just the one.

Much more than this, I've indicated pretty vividly, even if, as need be, I've indicated it only analogically, how we might go about doing just that. I refer, of course, to our Hypothesis of Spacelike Extension, and to the discussion provided in connection with the Hypothesis. As is my hope, with speculations like that, and maybe with speculations quite unlike it, too, philosophy may once again become, as it once was, long ago, a kind of human activity that's as engagingly fertile, or that's as positively stimulating, as it's intellectually ambitious.

For this to happen, much of philosophy must deal with, quite as Russell said, "matters of interest to the general public."[24] And, as he said, right after that, it must not be a kind of intellectual activity almost all of whose products are works where "only a few professionals can understand what is said." In this present day and age, not so different from Russell's day and age, it's pretty unlikely, I fear, that anything much like this will, at anytime soon, come to pervade much of this planet's concrete reality. Still and all, in this pretty peculiar book, as properly philosophical as it's openly honest, I hope to have raised, if only a little bit, the odds for such a happy turn of events.

24. Both phrases are from the fourth sentence of the preface to Russell's *Human Knowledge: Its Scope and Limits*, Simon and Schuster, 1948, as displayed in Section 9 of Chapter 8 above.

BIBLIOGRAPHY

Adams, Robert. (1) "Flavors, Colors, and God," in *The Virtue of Faith*, Oxford University Press, 1993.

———. (2) *The Virtue of Faith*, Oxford University Press, 1993.

Armstrong, David M. (1) *Perception and the Physical World*, Routledge and Kegan Paul, Humanities Press, 1961.

———. (2) *A Materialist Theory of the Mind*, Routledge and Kegan Paul, 1968.

Armstrong, D. M., C. B. Martin, and U. T. Place. *Dispositions: A Debate*, Tim Crane, ed., Routledge, 1996.

Berkeley, George. (1) *Principles of Human Knowledge*, 1710, in *Principles of Human Knowledge and Three Dialogues*, Oxford World's Classics, Howard Robinson, ed., Oxford University Press, 1996.

———. (2) *Principles of Human Knowledge and Three Dialogues*, Oxford World's Classics, Howard Robinson, ed., Oxford University Press, 1996.

———. (3) *Three Dialogues between Hylas and Philonous*, 1713, in *Principles of Human Knowledge and Three Dialogues*, Oxford World's Classics, Howard Robinson, ed., Oxford University Press, 1996.

Black, Max. "The Identity of Indiscernibles," *Mind*, 1952.

Blakemore, Colin, and Susan Greenfield, eds. *Mindwaves*, Blackwell, 1987.

Bloom, Paul. *Descartes' Baby*, Basic Books, 2004.

Chalmers, David J. (1) *The Conscious Mind*, Oxford: Oxford University Press, 1995.

———. (2) "Consciousness and Its Place in Nature," in Stich and Warfield, *The Blackwell Guide to Philosophy of Mind*.

———. (3) "Perception and the Fall from Eden," in Gendler and Hawthorne, *Perceptual Experience*.

Chisholm, Roderick M. (1) *Person and Object*, Allen & Unwin, 1976.

———. (2) "Questions about the Unity of Consciousness," in Cramer, Fulda, Horstmann and Pothast, eds., *Theorie der Subjectivitat*, Surkamp, 1987.

623

————. (3) "Identity through Time," in H. Keifer and M. Munitz, eds., *Language, Belief and Metaphysics*, State University of New York Press, 1970, reprinted in van Inwagen and Zimmerman.

————. (4) "Is There a Mind-Body Problem?," *Philosophic Exchange*, 1978, sections reprinted as parts of "Which Physical Thing Am I?" in van Inwagen and Zimmerman.

————. (5) "Self-Profile," in Radu J. Bogdan, ed., *Roderick M. Chisholm*, Reidel, 1986, sections reprinted as parts of "Which Physical Thing Am I?" in van Inwagen and Zimmerman.

————. (6) "Which Physical Thing Am I?," in van Inwagen and Zimmerman.

Craig, E., ed. *Routledge Encyclopedia of Philosophy*, Routledge, 1998.

Crane, Tim, ed., D. M. Armstrong, C. B. Martin, and U. T. Place, *Dispositions: A Debate*, Routledge, 1996.

Cramer, Konrad, Hans Friedrich Fulda, Rolf-Peter Horstmann, and Ulrich Pothast, eds. *Theorie der Subjektivitat*, Surkamp, 1987.

Descartes, Rene. (1) *Author's Replies to the Fifth Set of Objections*, in *The Philosophical Writings of Descartes*, trans. J. Cottingham, R. Stoothoff, and D. Murdoch, Volume 2. Cambridge: Cambridge University Press, 1984.

————. (2) *Meditations*. In *The Philosophical Writings of Descartes*, trans. J. Cottingham, R. Stoothoff, and D. Murdoch, Volume II, Cambridge University Press, 1985.

————. (3) *The Philosophical Writings of Descartes*, trans. J. Cottingham, R. Stoothoff, and D. Murdoch, Cambridge University Press, 1985.

————. (4) *Principles of Philosophy*, Part 1, Paragraph 11, "How Our Mind Is Better Known Than Our Body," in *The Philosophical Writings of Descartes*, trans. J. Cottingham, R. Stoothoff, and D. Murdoch, Volume I, Cambridge University Press, 1985.

Fogelin, Robert. "Hume and Berkeley's Infinite Divisibility," *Philosophical Review*, 1988.

Foster, John. (1) *The Case for Idealism*, Routledge and Kegan Paul, 1982.

————. (2) *The Immaterial Self: A Defence of the Cartesian Dualist Conception of the Mind*, Routledge, 1991.

————. (3) "The Succinct Case for Idealism," in H. Robinson, ed., *Objections to Physicalism*, Oxford University Press, 1993.

Geach, P. T. *Reference and Generality*, 3rd edition, Cornell University Press, 1980.

Gendler, T., and J. Hawthorne, eds. *Perceptual Experience*, Oxford University Press, forthcoming.

Hasker, William. *The Emergent Self*, Cornell University Press, 1999.

Heil, John. "Properties and Powers," in *Oxford Studies in Metaphysics*, Volume 1, Dean W. Zimmerman, ed., Oxford University Press, 2004.

Hudson, Hud. *A Materialist Metaphysics of the Human Person*, Cornell University Press, 2001.

Hume, David. *A Treatise of Human Nature*, P. H. Nidditch, ed., (based on the 1888 edition of L. A. Selby-Bigge), Oxford University Press, 1978.

Jackson, Frank. (1) *Perception*, Cambridge University Press, 1977.

————. (2) "Mental Causation," *Mind*, 1996.

Keifer, H., and M. Munitz, eds. *Language, Belief and Metaphysics*, State University of New York Press, 1970.

Kripke, Saul A. *Naming and Necessity*, Harvard University Press, 1980.

Leslie, John. *Universes*, Routledge, 1989.

Lewis, David. (1) "Scorekeeping in a Language Game," *Journal of Philosophical Logic*, 1979, reprinted in Lewis, *Philosophical Papers*, Volume 1.

———. (2) *Philosophical Papers*, Volume 1, Oxford University Press, 1983.

———. (3) *On the Plurality of Worlds*, Blackwell, 1986.

———. (4) *Philosophical Papers*, Volume 2, Oxford University Press, 1986.

———. (5) "Humean Supervenience Debugged," *Mind*, 1994, reprinted in Lewis, *Papers in Metaphysics and Epistemology*.

———. (6) "Finkish Dispositions," *Philosophical Quarterly*, 1997.

———. (7) *Papers in Metaphysics and Epistemology*, Cambridge University Press, 1999.

Locke, John. *An Essay concerning Human Understanding*, P. H. Nidditch, ed., Oxford University Press, 1975.

Lockwood, Michael. *Mind, Brain & the Quantum*, Blackwell, 1989.

Martin, C. B. (1) "Dispositions and Conditionals," *Philosophical Quarterly* , 1994.

———. (2) Contributions in D. M. Armstrong, C. B. Martin, and U. T. Place, *Dispositions: A Debate*, Tim Crane, ed., Routledge, 1996.

Martin, C. B., and John Heil. "The Ontological Turn," *Midwest Studies in Philosophy*, 1999.

Mellor, D. H. "In Defense of Dispositions," *Philosophical Review*, 1974.

Molnar, George. "Are Dispositions Reducible?," *Philosophical Quarterly*, 1999.

———. *Powers*, Oxford University Press, 2003.

Nagel, Thomas. (1) "Brain Bisection and the Unity of Consciousness," *Synthese*, 1971, reprinted in Nagel, *Mortal Questions*.

———. (2) *Mortal Questions*, Cambridge University Press,1979.

O'Connor, Timothy. *Persons and Causes*, Oxford University Press, 2000.

Olson, Eric. *The Human Animal: Personal Identity without Psychology*, Oxford University Press, 1997.

Parfit, Derek. (1) *Reasons and Persons*, Oxford University Press, 1984.

———. (2) "Divided Minds and the Nature of Persons," in Blakemore and Greenfield, *Mindwaves*, reprinted in van Inwagen and Zimmerman, *Metaphysics: The Big Questions*.

———. (3) "The Puzzle of Reality: Why Does the Universe Exist?," *Times Literary Supplement*, 1992, reprinted in van Inwagen and Zimmerman, *Metaphysics: The Big Questions*.

Prinz, Jesse J. *Furnishing the Mind*, MIT Press, 2002.

Prior, E. W., R. Pargetter, and F. Jackson. "Three Theses about Dispositions," *American Philosophical Quarterly* 1982.

Raynor, David. "'Minimal Sensibilia' in Berkeley and Hume," *Canadian Journal of Philosophy*, 1980.

Robinson, Howard, ed. *Objections to Physicalism*, Oxford University Press, 1993.

Rosenthal, David M. "Dualism," in E. Craig, ed., *Routledge Encyclopedia of Philosophy*, Routledge, 1998.

Russell, Bertrand. (1) *The Analysis of Matter*, Kegan Paul, 1927; reprinted by Dover, 1954.

———. (2) *Human Knowledge: Its Scope and Limits*. New York: Simon and Schuster, 1948.

———. (3) "Mind and Matter," in *Portraits from Memory*, Spokesman, 1956.

Ryle, Gilbert. *The Concept of Mind*, Hutchinson of London, 1949.

Scala, Marc. "Homogeneous Simples," *Philosophy and Phenomenological Research*, 2002.

Shoemaker, Sydney. (1) "Time without Change," *Journal of Philosophy*, 1969, reprinted in Shoemaker, *Identity, Cause and Mind: Philosophical Essays*.

———. (2) "Causality and Properties," in van Inwagen, *Time and Cause*, reprinted in Shoemaker, *Identity, Cause and Mind: Philosophical Essays*.

———. (3) *Identity, Cause and Mind: Philosophical Essays*, expanded edition, Oxford University Press, 2003.

———. (4) "Microrealization and the Mental," Unpublished typescript.

Sosa, Ernest. (1) "Mind-Body Interaction and Supervenient Causation," *Midwest Studies in Philosophy*, 1984.

———. (2) "Subjects among Other Things," *Philosophical Perspectives*, 1987.

Sperry, R. W. (1) "Brain Bisection and Mechanisms of Consciousness," in J. Eccles, ed., *Brain and Conscious Experience*, Springer-Verlag, 1966.

———. (2) "Hemispheric Deconnection and Unity in Conscious Awareness," *American Psychologist*, 1968.

Stich, Stephen P., and Ted A. Warfield, eds. *The Blackwell Guide to Philosophy of Mind*, Blackwell, 2003.

Strawson, Peter F. *Individuals*, Routledge, 1959.

Swinburne, Richard. *The Evolution of the Soul*, Oxford University Press, 1986.

———. *The Evolution of the Soul*, revised edition, Oxford University Press, 1997.

Tye, Michael. *Ten Problems of Consciousness*, MIT Press, 1996.

Unger, Peter. (1) "An Analysis of Factual Knowledge," *Journal of Philosophy*, 1968, reprinted in Unger, *Philosophical Papers, Volume 1*.

———. (2) "A Defense of Skepticism," *Philosophical Review*, 1971, reprinted in Unger, *Philosophical Papers, Volume 1*.

———. (3) "An Argument for Skepticism," *Philosophic Exchange*, 1974, reprinted in Unger, *Philosophical Papers, Volume 1*.

———. (4) *Ignorance: A Case for Scepticism*, Clarendon Press, 1975, reprinted by the Oxford University Press, 2002.

———. (5) "Impotence and Causal Determinism," *Philosophical Studies*, 1977, reprinted in Unger, *Philosophical Papers, Volume 2*.

———. (6) "The Uniqueness in Causation," *American Philosophical Quarterly*, 1977, reprinted in Unger, *Philosophical Papers, Volume 2*.

———. (7) "I Do Not Exist," in G. F. MacDonald ed., *Perception and Identity*, Macmillan, 1979, reprinted in Unger, *Philosophical Papers, Volume 2*.

———. (8) "There Are No Ordinary Things," *Synthese*, 1979, reprinted in Unger, *Philosophical Papers, Volume 2*.

———. (9) "Why There Are No People," *Midwest Studies in Philosophy*, 1979, reprinted in Unger, *Philosophical Papers, Volume 2*.

———. (10) "Skepticism and Nihilism," *Nous*, 1980, reprinted in Unger, *Philosophical Papers, Volume 1*.

———. (11) "The Problem of the Many," *Midwest Studies in Philosophy*, 1980, reprinted in Unger, *Philosophical Papers, Volume 2*.

———. (12) "Toward A Psychology of Common Sense," *American Philosophical Quarterly*, 1982, reprinted in Unger, *Philosophical Papers, Volume 1*.

———. (13) "The Causal Theory of Reference," *Philosophical Studies*, 1983, reprinted in Unger, *Philosophical Papers, Volume 1*.

———. (14) "Minimizing Arbitrariness: Towards a Metaphysics of Infinitely Many Isolated Concrete Worlds," *Midwest Studies in Philosophy*, 1984, reprinted in Unger, *Philosophical Papers, Volume 1*.

———. (15) *Philosophical Relativity*, University of Minnesota and Press and Blackwell, 1984, reprinted by Oxford University Press, 2002.

———. (16) *Identity, Consciousness and Value*, Oxford University Press, 1990.

———. (17) *Living High and Letting Die*, Oxford University Press, 1996.

———. (18) "The Mystery of the Physical and the Matter of Qualities," *Midwest Studies in Philosophy*, 1999, reprinted in Unger, *Philosophical Papers, Volume 2*.

———. (19) "The Survival of the Sentient," *Philosophical Perspectives*, 2000, reprinted in Unger, *Philosophical Papers, Volume 2*.

———. (20) "Free Will and Scientiphicalism," *Philosophy and Phenomenological Research*, 2002, reprinted in Unger, *Philosophical Papers, Volume 2*.

———. (21) "The Mental Problems of the Many," *Oxford Studies in Metaphysics*, Volume 1, 2004, reprinted in Unger, *Philosophical Papers, Volume 2*.

———. (22) *Philosophical Papers, Volume 1*. Oxford University Press, 2006.

———. (23) *Philosophical Papers, Volume 2*. Oxford University Press, 2006.

van Inwagen, Peter. (1) ed. *Time and Cause*, Reidel, 1980.

———. (2) *Metaphysics*, Westview Press, 1993.

van Inwagen, Peter, and Dean Zimmerman, eds. *Metaphysics: The Big Questions*, Blackwell, 1998.

Weatherson, Brian. Encyclopedia entry on the Problem of the Many, in *The Stanford Encyclopedia of Philosophy*, Available online at: http://plato.stanford.edu/entries/problem-of-many/.

Williams, Neil. "Static and Dynamic Dispositions," *Synthese*, forthcoming.

Zimmerman, Dean W. (1) "Two Cartesian Arguments for the Simplicity of the Soul," *American Philosophical Quarterly*, 1991.

———. (2), ed. *Oxford Studies in Metaphysics*, Volume 1, Oxford University Press, 2004.

INDEX